The Diary Of Henry Machyn, Citizen And Merchant-Taylor Of London: From 1550 To 1563

Henry Machin

THE DIARY

OF

HENRY MACHYN,

CITIZEN AND MERCHANT-TAYLOR OF LONDON,

FROM A.D. 1550 TO A.D. 1563.

EDITED BY

JOHN GOUGH NICHOLS,

F.S.A. LOND. AND NEWC.

LONDON: PRINTED FOR THE CAMDEN SOCIETY,

BY J. B. NICHOLS AND SON, 25, PARLIAMENT STREET.

M.DCCC.XL.VIII.

PREFACE.

THE most remarkable passages of the Diary now printed have already attained their position in history from having been largely incorporated in the works of Strype, and quoted on his authority by subsequent writers.

It must not therefore be expected that the present publication will develope much new information of high historical importance: but it will have its value, like some former publications of the Camden Society, in ascertaining the real authority for certain statements of general history, the credit of which materially depends upon the quarter from whence they are derived.

The writer was a citizen of London, of no great scholarship or attainments, as his language and cacography plainly testify, sufficiently prejudiced no doubt, and not capable of any deep views either of religious doctrine or temporal policy; but the matters of fact which he records would be such as he either witnessed himself, or had learned immediately after their occurrence: and the opinions and sentiments which he expresses would be shared by a large proportion of his fellow-citizens.

For a great part of the period of his Diary, the times were very eventful. Important changes in the Church and in the State were attended by many extraordinary occurrences, particularly those deprivations, imprisonments, trials, and executions, the promotion of new ministers and prelates, and other incidents in the personal career of the great actors in the political drama which were most likely to attract the attention of a popular chronicler.*

Though the most important particulars which he affords on these subjects are known (as already remarked) from the extracts made by Strype, still their detail is occasionally more interesting, and not unfrequently more accurate,† in the language of the

* On one occasion of the deepest interest our citizen is wholly silent—very probably from fear. It is the execution of Lady Guilford Dudley, commonly called Lady Jane Grey. The Manuscript diary from which Stowe and the other chroniclers derived their most interesting details on this event, is also preserved in the British Museum, and the present Editor hopes to recommend it to the future attention of the Camden Society.

† Strype's extracts commence with a misapprehension as to the identity of the countess of Southampton, as pointed out in the note, p. 313. Some other instances of his errors are as follow: in his Ecclesiastical Memorials, vol. ii. p. 281, he mentions a "*walking* watch" instead of "*riding*;" in p. 285 "coats of *maile*" instead of "marble;" in p. 371 the 7th of October for the 17th. In p. 397, two passages which belong to the year 1553 are ascribed to the year 1552. In vol. iii. p. 59, he kills deer with *hands* and swords instead of hounds; in p. 301 he has the name of *Wray* for Verney; in p. 310 he says a *lord* bore queen Mary's train instead of lady Montagu; in p. 384 he records the funeral of Thomas Mildmay esquire instead of that of his wife; in p. 385 he names *lady* North and *lady* Sentleger instead of lord North and sir Anthony St. Leger; in p. 386 the name of *Dorel* instead of Tyrell; in p. 452 the corpse of queen Mary "was brought out of her chappel," instead of "brought out of her chamber into her chapel." In p. 298, besides the Diarist's error of the name of Dacre for Darcy, Strype has altered the town of "Roderam" into *Redegund;* and in p. 443 he changes the same into *Rothegam.* In Annals, vol. i. p. 169, he names St. Botolph's *Billingsgate* instead of Bishopsgate; in p. 192 *Chardin* for Carden, or Cawarden. In p. 196 he says, "The 20th, Bentham of London Bridge (so styled in my MS.) where at St. Magnus he seems to have been Preacher, now Bp. of Litchfield and Coventry, preached at St. Paul's:" but, by reference to p. 229, the reader will find that the MS. tells a very different story, viz. that bishop Bentham's wife was that day brought to bed, at a house on London bridge: and there is nothing to show he had any connection with St. Magnus. In p. 235 he introduces the *Earl of* Hunsdon instead of Lord Hunsdon. These are a few of the more glaring out of many minor errors which Strype committed in making his extracts, and in modernising at once their orthography and their language. In many other cases he has slightly altered the dates and numbers. The Editor has not thought it necessary to point all these out in the notes; for, wherever any doubt may arise from discrepancies between Strype and the present edition, it may be easily set at rest, as the original is perfectly accessible. It may be hoped, however, that in the next edition of Strype all his extracts from Machyn will be corrected from the Manuscript.

original writer, however colloquial and ungrammatical that language may be; and as even this rude London language has some philological interest, I have appended a brief glossarial index, at the suggestion of one whose judgment on the subject will not be disputed, and who has favoured me with his assistance in its compilation,—Mr. Albert Way.

After the times became less stirring, when Elizabeth was securely seated upon the throne, Strype has made but little use of this Diary, which in that part is now for the first time made public. There are also large portions throughout of matters which Strype deemed of minor importance, but which are not without their value, in illustration of the manners and customs of the age : these have been hitherto unpublished, except by occasional extracts.*

The Diarist takes a lively interest in the pageantry and holiday-making of the City, which were certainly esteemed by our ancestors as matters more important and indispensable than they are by their close-working posterity. He seldom fails to notice the shows of Lord Mayor's day, the gay doings in May, or the mummeries of Christmas ; and so deep was the impression which such performances made upon his mind that, on the death of a past Sheriff, in 1557,† he recurs to the magnificence with which that gentleman had maintained his "lord of misrule," when in office five years before.

Throughout the whole runs a pervading series of the Funerals

---

* In the Gentleman's Magazine for Oct. 1833, p. 315, I extracted several passages relative to the Lord Mayor's Shows (of which the Diary gives the earliest description); and in the Collectanea Topographica et Genealogica, vol. iv. I extracted the funerals which took place at St. Dunstan's in the West. It is this Diary also that Mr. Collier has repeatedly quoted in his History of the Stage.

† See p. 157.

of the nobility and principal citizens,* in respect to which the author was engaged in the way of his business. These records will afford valuable assistance to the family historian and genealogist; and more especially so because they are antecedent in date to the series of Funeral Certificates† recorded in the College of Arms.

In the Notes the Editor has furnished references to all the works he could consult, as containing the epitaphs or pedigrees of the same parties; and with regard to the civic senators, he has entered somewhat more fully into biographical and heraldic particulars, supposing such information may be especially looked for in a London chronicle. Among these are several names which not only London but their country is still proud to remember, as the founders of some of the most flourishing sources of public education—Sir Thomas White the founder of St. John's college at Oxford, Sir Andrew Judd of the grammar-school at Tunbridge, Sir William Harper of that at Bedford, Sir Rowland Hill of that at Drayton, and Sir William Laxton of that at Oundle.

It is a remarkable circumstance that in a diary extending over only thirteen years, occasion should be given to notice nearly forty contemporary aldermen—an evidence in part, perhaps, of the prevalent mortality of the times, and in part of the advanced age at which citizens were then raised to that honourable pre-eminence. In one period of ten months no fewer than seven Aldermen were removed from their mortal career.‡

* See a classified list of them in the Index, voce Funerals.

† These Certificates commence in 1567. There are, however, several Funerals of earlier date upon record in the College of Arms, to which the Editor has been permitted to make reference; and he has also availed himself of a very valuable MS. in the Harleian Collection (No. 897), which contains brief records of a large number of Funerals, principally in the 16th century.

‡ See the note in p. 353.

The Diary, in fact, originated from the nature of the writer's business as a furnisher of funeral trappings; and it is at first a mere record of the principal Funerals for which he was employed to provide. Commencing in August 1550, he describes two funerals in that and one in the following month, one in October, and several in November, the last of which belongs to Christopher Machyn, his own brother.

The first event of another kind commemorated is the committal of Bishop Gardiner to the Tower in Feb. 1550-1; after which he enters every occurrence that struck him as deserving of remembrance.

On religious matters his information is valuable, so far as it represents the sentiments and behaviour of the common people at this vacillating period of our ecclesiastical history. It is evident from numerous passages that his own sympathies were inclined to the old form of worship: which, indeed, in its pompous ceremonial, was the best encourager of the craft by which he gained his livelihood. He hailed with delight its re-establishment on the accession of Mary, and rejoices to chronicle all the ceremonies and processions which then enlivened the churches and streets of the city. From an extraordinary passage at p. 160, in which he mentions the uncompleted performance of the communion by the Gospellers at Islington, it is evident that, after having witnessed all the "gospel light" of king Edward's reign, master Machyn had still very confused ideas of the doctrines or objects of the Reformation. At that period, too, he gave credit to the charge made against Street the joiner for having drawn his dagger upon a priest that bore the sacrament in procession on Corpus Christi day; whilst the same occurrence is explained by Foxe as a casual and unpremeditated rencontre.*   It is instructive, however, to observe that, in common with the population at large, he afterwards took a great interest in the public sermons which were so zealously multiplied by the new preachers; at one of which it was his fate to perform penance, in consequence of having spread reports defamatory of master Veron, the French protestant minister.†

With this exception the Diary contains scarcely anything of personal adventure. It is as little egotistical as a private Diary could well be. With all the dignity of an old chronicler the writer even mentions himself in the third person, on the few occasions that he makes his appearance, and in the unfortunate penance affair he further disguises himself in French costume,—a whim which has amusingly misled our Ecclesiastical Historian.‡

Henry Machyn has twice noticed the occurrence of his birthday,§ from which we learn that he was more than fifty years of age at the time the Diary commences, and approaching seventy at the period of its close. In 1557 he records a birth in his family,‖ b¹ ;

* Strype has placed together both sides of the story, and in so doing regards our a:.hor as a prejudiced witness, speaking of him as "the writer of the Journal whence I ta¹-e this and divers other things, *otherwise a diligent man.*" Eccl. Memorials, vol. iii. p. 1²..

† See p. 272.

‡ "At Paul's Cross a certain *French* Gentleman, named *de Machin,* sat at the sermon-time [*i.e.* in the place of penance] for reporting," &c. (Annals, vol. i. p. 287.) Strype was, perhaps, misled the more readily because the person slandered was himself a Frenchman.

§ There seems to have been some little forgetfulness on this point about the old man, as the two entries do not perfectly agree. On the 16th May, 1554, he was fifty-six (p. 63); and on the 20th May, 1562, he was sixty-six (p. 283).

‖ P. 153.

so obscurely that it is uncertain whether the child was his own or no : possibly it was a grandchild. The " Harry Machyn merchant-taylor," mentioned shortly before,* seems to have been the Diarist himself. His brother Christopher, who died in 1550,† was of the same company.

Machyn himself has been taken by some for a herald, or at least a painter employed by the heralds.‡ In the absence of any direct proof of his occupation, I rather think that his business was in that department of the trade of a merchant-taylor which we now call an undertaker or furnisher of funerals. The banners, &c. which he provided were probably painted by men who worked as journeymen under his superintendence.

His parish, from several passages,§ is shown to have been that of Trinity the Little, by Queenhithe ; and in Trinity-lane adjoining was the Painter-Stainers' hall, in the vicinity of which would live many of the workmen with whom he had so much to do.

From the attention which he paid to events in the family of Hethe or Heath, it is highly probable that he was connected with it. Two married couple of this name are mentioned : John, serjeant of the King's bakehouse, who died and was buried at Linton in Cambridgeshire, the seat of Philip Paris esquire,‖ and whose widow Annes was remarried to James Sutton, clerk of the green cloth ;¶ and John, a painter-stainer, dwelling in Fenchurch-street, who died in 1552-3,** and his widow Annes in 1556. This

---

* P. 151. † P. 3.

‡ Some pages after he had begun to use the Diary, Strype speaks of it as a manuscript in the Cotton Library, " which formerly seems to have been a Journal of one who belonged to the Heralds' College."—Eccl. Memorials, vol. ii. p. 285.

§ See pp. 105, 132, 166, 205. ‖ Pp. 9, 168. ¶ P. 15. ** P. 32.

latter Annes I suspect, from the minuteness of our chronicler's entry * of the event, to have been his own sister or daughter.†.

I have traced nothing of the family of Machyn from any other quarter. The only possible connection that I am aware of is an alderman of Gloucester in the reign of James the First, to whom a handsome monument still stands in that cathedral.‡

The manuscript Diary (Vitellius F. v.) is one of those volumes which suffered severely in the fire of the Cottonian Library; but, though much was burnt away from the upper parts and edges of the pages, it does not appear that any leaves have been lost since the time when it was employed by Strype.§ Indeed, the way in which it commences, as already described, would show that little, if anything, can have disappeared from the beginning; and the circumstance of its closing at a time when the plague was prevalent in London, renders it not improbable that the author was a victim of that deadly scourge.

After the Cottonian fire the injured leaves of the Manuscript were kept loose in a case until the year 1829, when they were

---

* P. 105.

† In the MS. Harl. 1096, at f. 49, is a pedigree of Heath, which states that John Heath of Twickenham married Agnes Lee, and had issue 1. John and 2. Stephen. The latter married Agnes, daughter of Mildmay of Chelmsford, and had issue Thomas, William, Mary wife of Lawrence Lynnes grocer, Margaret, Elizabeth, and Agnes. There seems to have been a decided partiality in the Heaths to the name of Agnes or Annes; if this was the same family, the father and his two sons all selected wives of that name.

‡ Thomas Machen, esq. late alderman of the city of Gloucester and thrice maior of the same, died 1614. Christian his wife, with whom he lived in the state of marriage 50 years, died 1615. There is a plate of this monument, engraved by Bonner, in Fosbroke's History of the city of Gloucester, but in that engraving the arms of the city are erroneously repeated instead of those of the alderman, viz. Or, a chevron engrailed gules, between three . . . . leaves stalked vert; quartering, Azure, a branch of columbine? proper, flowered and tied with a ribbon or.

§ The interval deficient in the year 1558, (noticed in p. 169,) has *not* been lost since the fire, as is evident from Strype's extracts, Memorials, iii. 446, 449.

carefully arranged, and inlaid, under the superintendence of Sir Frederick Madden, who recorded the accomplishment of his useful labours by the following memorandum on a fly-leaf:

" The fragments forming the present Volume were formerly kept in a case, without any regard to order, and are thus described by Dr. Smith in his Catalogue:

" Cod. chartac. in fol. constans foliis solutis circiter 150. in pixide asservatis, *quæ ritè disponere frustra tentavimus.*'

" By the aid of Strype, who made use of the MS. when perfect, and who quotes largely from it, the leaves have been restored to their proper order; the chronology marked on each folio, and references given to the pages of Strype, who often supplies the *lacunæ* here visible. The curiosity and value of these fragments seemed a sufficient warrant for the labour and time consumed in arranging them in their present form.—F. M. 1829."

The first page of the MS. is shown to have been the original first page, by its soiled and worn appearance. It bears a memorandum, scarcely legible, connected with the author's accompts, " Remem' y^t my lade Masun('s) byll (for) armes and hers in m . . . . penter in . . . ."

It only remains to be added that the deficiencies, occasioned by the partial loss of the manuscript from fire, have been supplied in the present edition, either from Strype where he had quoted the injured passages, or in some other cases by conjecture from the context, such supplied readings being always distinguished by brackets [ ] and by modern orthography. Parentheses ( ) have sometimes been introduced to complete sentences left grammatically imperfect by the writer: and most of the obscurities of his spelling are made clear by the marginal notes.

OFFICERS OF STATE

DURING THE PERIOD OF THIS DIARY.

ACCORDING to the usage of the times many of the great nobility and courtiers are named by our Diarist under their titles of office. As there is no ready means of ascertaining their names (the best lists extant, those in Beatson's Political Index, being incorrect and very incomplete at this period of our history), it will be useful to consult the following lists, which have been compiled from authentic documents, and include references to certain passages of the Diary in which the parties are mentioned. They commence with the accession of Edward the Sixth. In the case of Bishops the same difficulty does not exist: and, indeed, the Editor has generally added their names in the marginal notes.

Governor of king Edward VI. and Protector of the realm.

1546-7.　Edward Seymour, earl of Hertford, declared Protector by the privy council 31 Jan. 1546-7 ; created duke of Somerset on the 16th of the following month; confirmed Protector by letters patent 12 March, 1546-7 (printed in Burnet's History of the Reformation), and by further letters patent 24 Dec. 1547 (printed in the Archæologia, vol. xxx. p. 478), revoked by letters patent 13 Oct. 1549 (printed ibid. p. 489).

Great Master of the Household (afterwards Lord Steward), and President of the Council.*

1544.　William Paulet, lord Seynt John of Basing ; created earl of Wiltshire 19 Jan. 1550-1.

---

* When the duke of Suffolk was Lord Steward of the Household, in 1531, the designation of the office was altered to Great Master, copying the French. The earl of Arundel, when made Great Master soon after the accession of Mary, procured the restoration of the former designation. The acts of parliament for both changes are printed in the Statutes of the Realm.

1549-50. John Dudley, earl of Warwick; patent 20 Feb. 4 Edw. VI. (printed in Rymer's Fœdera, xv. 208); created duke of Northumberland 11 Oct. 1551 [p. 19].

1553. Henry FitzAlan, earl of Arundel; re-appointed by queen Elizabeth in 1558 [pp. 46, 126, &c.]; resigned in 1564.

Lord Chancellor, or Lord Keeper.

1544. Sir Thomas Wriothesley, received the great seal as Lord Keeper 22 April, and as Lord Chancellor 3 May 1544; surrendered it 6 March 1546-7. (Close Roll, and Privy Council Book.)

1546-7. William Paulet, lord Seynt John, appointed Lord Keeper 7 March 1546-7, resigned 23 Oct. 1547.

1547. Richard lord Rich, received the seal 23 Oct. 1547; surrendered it 21 Dec. 1551.

1551. Thomas Goodrick, bishop of Ely; received the seal as Lord Keeper 22 Dec. 1551; as Lord Chancellor 19 Jan. 1551-2; surrendered it 20 July, 1553.

1553. Stephen Gardyner; bishop of Winchester; constituted Lord Chancellor 23 Aug. 1553, died 12 Nov. 1555.

1555-6. Nicholas Heath, archbishop of York; received the seal 1 Jan. 1555-6; surrendered it 18 Nov. 1558.

1558. Sir Nicholas Bacon, received the seal as Lord Keeper 22 Dec. 1558; died 20 Feb. 1578-9 [pp. 192, 197].

Lord Treasurer.

1546-7. Edward Seymour, earl of Hertford; patent 10 Feb. 1 Edw. VI. (printed in Rymer, xv. 124).

1549-50. William Paulet, earl of Wiltshire; patent 1 Feb. 4 Edw. VI. created marquess of Winchester 12 Oct. 1551 [pp. 12, 19, &c.]; patent of re-appointment by queen Mary in 1553 in Rymer, xv. 341; re-appointed by queen Elizabeth, and died in this office in 1571-2, æt. 97.

Lord Privy Seal.

1543. John lord Russell, appointed by pat. 3 Dec. 34 Hen. VIII. (printed in Rymer's Fœdera, xiv. 765); reappointed by patent 21 Aug. 1 Edw.

VI. (ibid. xv. 155); created earl of Bedford; died 14 March 1554-5 [pp. 19, 83].

1555.   Edward Stanley, earl of Derby. [Beatson : but of his appointment I have met with no proof.]

1555-6.   William lord Paget, pat. 29 Jan. 2 & 3 Phil. et Mar. [pp. 126, 168, 169].

Lord Great Chamberlain of England.

1546-7.   John Dudley, viscount Lisle; created earl of Warwick, and made Lord Great Chamberlain on king Edward's accession.

1549-50.   William Parr, marquess of Northampton by patent 4 Feb. 1549-50 (printed in Rymer, xv. 203). [See p. 19.]

Earl Marshal of England.

1546-7.   Edward Seymour, duke of Somerset; pat. 17 Feb. 1 Edw. VI.

1551.   John Dudley, duke of Northumberland; pat. 20 Apr. 5 Edw. VI.

1553.   Thomas Howard, duke of Norfolk; died 25 Aug. 1554.

1554.   Thomas Howard, duke of Norfolk (grandson of the preceding).

Lord Admiral.

1542.   John Dudley, viscount Lisle, pat. 27 June, 34 Hen. VIII.; he resigned this office for that of Lord Great Chamberlain, the latter being relinquished by the duke of Somerset when made Protector and Earl Marshal.

1547.   Thomas lord Seymour of Sudeley; patent 30 Aug. 1 Edw. VI. (printed in Rymer, xv. 157); attainted and beheaded 1548-9.

1548-9.   John Dudley, earl of Warwick, again; pat. 28 Oct. 3 Edw. VI. (printed in Rymer, xv. 194).

1550.   Edward lord Clinton and Say, by patent 14 May, 4 Edw. VI. [pp. 6, 20].

1553-4.   Lord William Howard, by patent 10 March, 1 Mary [pp. 52, 59]; created lord Howard of Effingham 11 March, 1553-4.

1557-8.   Edward lord Clinton and Say, again, by patent 13 Feb. 4 and 5 Ph. and M.; continued by queen Elizabeth, created earl of Lincoln in 1572, and died lord admiral in 1585.

Lord Warden of the Cinque Ports.

1540. Sir Thomas Cheney, K.G. pat. 32 Hen. VIII. [pp. 20, 37, 65]; died 20 Dec. 1558 [p. 184].

1558. William lord Cobham, "late made lord warden of the v. portes;" [p. 213] died Lord Warden in 1596.

Lord Chamberlain of the Household.

154—. Henry earl of Arundel.

15--. Thomas lord Wentworth; died 3 March 1550-1 [pp. 3, 314].

1551. Thomas lord Darcy of Chiche, K.G. [pp. 10, 13, 20]. " April 3, 1551, Thomas Darcy made lord Darcy of Chiche, and Lord Chamberlain, for maintenance whereof he had given 100 marks to his heirs general, and 300 to his heirs males." (King Edward's Diary.)

1553. Sir John Gage, K.G. (Stowe); died 18 April 1556 [p. 105].

1556. Sir Edward Hastings, appointed 25 Dec. 1557 [p. 162]; created lord Hastings of Loughborough, Jan. 19, 1557-8.

1558. William lord Howard of Effingham.

Treasurer of the Household.

1541. Sir Thomas Cheney, K.G. [pp. 13, 20]; died 20 Dec. 1558 [p. 184].

1560. Sir Thomas Parry.

Comptroller of the Household.

1542. Sir John Gage.

1547. Sir William Paget, K.G. resigned on being summoned to parliament as lord Paget of Beaudesert 3 Dec. 1550. (King Edward's Diary.)

1550. Sir Anthony Wingfield, K.G. (p. 5); died 15 Aug. 1552 (p. 23).

1552. Sir Richard Cotton; appointed Aug. 27, 1552 (p. 23, and King Edward's Diary).

1553. Sir Robert Rochester, appointed by queen Mary on her accession, Aug. 1553 (p. 39).

1557. Sir Thomas Cornwallis; appointed 25 Dec. 1557 [p. 162].

1558. Sir Thomas Parry; made Treasurer in 1560.

1560. Sir Edward Rogers; he died Comptroller in 1565.

Vice-Chamberlain and Captain of the Guard.

154–. Sir Anthony Wingfield, K.G.; made Comptroller Dec. 1550.

1550. Sir Thomas Darcy. Promoted to be Lord Chamberlain 1551.

1551. Sir John Gates "made Vice-Chamberlain and Captain of the Guard; and 120*l.* land, April 8, 1551." (King Edward's Diary.) Sent prisoner to the Tower 25 July 1553 [p. 37].

1553. Sir Thomas Jerningham, appointed 31 July, 1553 [p. 38]; promoted to be Master of the Horses 25 Dec. 1557 [p. 162].

1557. Sir Henry Bedingfeld, appointed 25 Dec. 1557 [p. 162].

1558. Sir Edward Rogers [?]; afterwards Comptroller in 1560.

1560? Sir Francis Knollys [p. 306]. (Q. Eliz. Progresses, i. 114.)

Cofferer of the Household.

In 1547 Sir Edmond Peckham—(among the council nominated in the patent of the protectorship). Still in office 1553, and probably to the death of king Edward.

In 1557 Sir Richard Freston [pp. 145, 148] died Jan. 1557-8 [p. 163].

1558. Michael Wentworth esquire died Oct. 1558 [p. 368].

Master of the Horses.

1539-40. Sir Anthony Browne, K.G.; appointed 12 March 1539-40; died 6 May, 1548.

1548. Sir William Herbert, created earl of Pembroke 10 Oct. 1551. "April 18, 1552. The earl of Pembroke resigned his Mastership of the Horses, which I bestowed on the earl of Warwick." (King Edward's Diary.)

1552. John Dudley, earl of Warwick [p. 19]; sent prisoner to the Tower 25 July 1553 [p. 37].

1553. Sir Edward Hastings, appointed July 1553 [p. 38]; promoted to be Lord Chamberlain [p. 162].

1557. Sir Henry Jerningham, appointed 25 Dec. 1557 [p. 161].

1558. Lord Robert Dudley, patent 1 Eliz. [pp. 214, 242].

Lord Chamberlain " to the Prince of Spain "—King Philip.

1554. Sir John Williams, lord Williams of Thame, 8 April, 1554 [p. 59].

Master of the Prince of Spain's Horses.

1554. Sir Anthony Browne 8 April 1554 [p. 59]; created Viscount Montagu 27 Sept. following. (In Collins's Peerage, &c. this appointment is erroneously stated as Master of the Horses to the Queen.)

Constable of the Tower of London.

1540. Sir John Gage, K.G. pat. 32 Hen. VIII. p. 3.

In p. 35 it will be found stated that sir James Crofts was discharged from the office of Constable of the Tower July 7, 1553, and the lord admiral put in his place: a statement which (through Strype) has found its way into Bayley's History of the Tower, p. 80. Sir James Crofts, however, was certainly not Constable: he may have been Lieutenant of the Tower.

Stowe incorrectly terms sir John Gage "lieutenant" at the time of the duke of Northumberland's execution in 1553.

On Sir John Gage's death, in 1556, the constableship is stated by Bayley, History of the Tower, p. 663, to have devolved, in pursuance of a reversionary grant, on sir Edmund Bray: but sir Edmund Bray had been long dead, in 1539. Indeed, that work affords scarcely any assistance to the present purpose.

Lieutenant of the Tower of London.

154-. Sir John Markham ; removed by the Council of Warwick's party in Oct. 1549. (Holinshed.)

1549. Sir Leonard Chamberlain. (Ibid.)

Sir John Markham, again.

1551. Sir Arthur Darcy. " Oct. 31. A letter directed to sir Arthur Darcy to take the charge of the Tower, and to discharge sir John Markham," &c. (King Edward's Diary.)

In 1553 Sir James Crofts ? (see note above).

In 1553 Sir John Brydges [pp. 41, 398].

In 1556 Sir Robert Oxenbridge [pp. 108, 127].

In 1559 and 1561-2 Sir Edward Warner [p. 203, and Queen Eliz. Prog. i. 114].

NOTE UPON FUNERALS.

As Funerals occupy so large a share of the ensuing pages, it may be acceptable to give references to some other accounts of a ceremonial on which so much time and expense was bestowed in former times.

Of Royal Funerals, that of Elizabeth queen of Henry VII. is printed in the Antiquarian Repertory; that of her son Arthur prince of Wales in Leland's Collectanea; that of king Henry the Eighth is inserted at length in the Appendix to Strype's Ecclesiastical Memorials; that of queen Mary is in Leland's Collectanea; and that of queen Elizabeth in the Vetusta Monumenta of the Society of Antiquaries, and Nichols's Progresses of queen Elizabeth. Those of Henry prince of Wales, queen Anne of Denmark, and king James the First, are also printed at length in the Progresses, &c. of king James I. and that of the Protector Oliver in Noble's House of Cromwell.

Of nobility, the funeral of Margaret duchess of Norfolk, 1563, is printed in Lord Braybrooke's History of Audley End; those of George earl of Shrewsbury, 1541, and Francis earl of Shrewsbury, 1560, in Hunter's History of Hallamshire; those of Robert earl of Sussex, 1542, and Henry earl of Sussex, 1556, in Wilson's History of the Parish of St. Lawrence Pountney; those of Muriel viscountess Lisle, 1505, Sir Thomas Lovell, K.G. 1524, and John lord Bray, 1557, in Lysons's Environs of London; that of John Islyppe abbat of Westminster, 1532, in the Vetusta Monumenta, vol. iv.; and that of sir Humphrey Stanley, 1505, in Malcolm's Londinium Redivivum. The dates of all these are antecedent to the regular Funeral Certificates. Of the latter, several have been published in Bigland's Observations on Parish Registers, 1764, in the Collectanea Topographica et Genealogica and its sequel the Topographer and Genealogist, and others interspersed in various topographical works.

The funeral of Edward Earl of Derby, in 1572, is described at great length in Collins's Peerage, edit. 1779, in Dallaway's Heraldry, 4to. 1793, and in Nichols's Illustrations of the Manners and Expenses of Ancient Times, 4to. 1797.

The general writers on Heraldry have of course something to say on

Funerals ; but it seems little and unsatisfactory when compared with the abundant materials which are stored in the MS. collections of their predecessors. The twenty folio pages devoted to this subject in Edmondson's " Complete Body of Heraldry," are very ill digested, and chiefly occupied with papers belonging to the more recent disputes between the College and the painters from the reigns of Charles II. to George II. when the ancient state and cost of these funeral pomps had nearly fallen into disuetude, and the interested parties were consequently quarrelling (as, indeed, they had often done before,) over the little that remained. In these pages of Edmondson, however, will be found three formularies,—for the funerals of a Countess, an Earl's daughter, and an Earl, all temp. Eliz.;* but he tells us nothing of the funerals of Citizens, upon which the Author of the present Diary details so much, though generally more in the way of eulogy than regular description, and consequently in a manner that seems to require the marshal's staff to restore the confused groups to their original order.

The Editor has consequently selected two or three documents of a more formal character, which will supply that arrangement in which master Machyn's descriptions are deficient, and will render intelligible some matters in which he is occasionally obscure.

The first is the *Funeral of an Alderman* before the Reformation (in the year 1523,) from the records of the Drapers' Company :

" The right worshipfull sir William Roche knight and alderman, decessyd betwene ix. and x. of the clock before none. On whose soule Jh'u have mercye. Amen. He was buryed the xv^th daye of this instant moneth of September at afternone, in this wyse. First, ij. branchys of whyte wax were borne before the priests and clerks in surplesys syngyng. Then a standard of his crest, which was the red roobuck's hedd, with gylt hornes, havyng also ij. wynges, the one of gold, the other verde. Thereafter certayne mourners ; then a pynion of his armys, and his cote armour, borne by the herald, which armys was a cheker of warren of sylver and azure, a bull passaunt goules, with hornes of sylver, and iij. roches, also sylver, being all sett in a felde of gold Then the corps borne next after the cote armure, by certayne clerks, and iiij. of the assystans of the Drapers, viz. Mr. Warner, Mr. Blower, Mr. Spencer, and Mr. Tull, who went in their livery and

---

* The " proceeding " (or order of procession) at the funerals of an Earl, a Countess, a Baron, a Baroness, a Knight, and a Citizen, follow the ceremonial of the Earl of Derby's funeral in the " Illustrations," &c. mentioned in the preceding page.

hodes about the said corps.   Ther followyd the corse Mr. John Roché his sone, as chief mourner, alone; and after hym ij. coples of mourners more.   Then the sword-berer and my lord maire in black.   Then the aldermen and sheriffs after theim, and the hole lyvory of this felowshippe, in order.   Then the ladys and gentylwomen, as the aldermen's wyfes and others, which, after dirige, cam home to his house and dranke, where they had spice-brede and comfetts, wyne, ale, and beere.

" On the morrow, the mourners went again in order to the church, where they had a collacion made by sir Stephen.   After which collacion the herald appointed the chief mourners, in order, to offer up the target, sword, and helmet, to the priest; and after they offered in order, and also my lord mayor, the aldermen, the livery, and others, which offering went to the poor.   Then the whole communion was ministered.   After which done, the herald again going before, there followed him the banner-bearers, and offered the banners also; and then, in order, again the mourners, my lord mayor, and others, returned to the house of the said Mr. Roche, where they dined all, save the livery of this fellowship, which dined in the Drapers' Hall, by reason he had given them towards the same vj*l.* xiij*s.* iiij*d.* which was bestowed by John Quarles and William Berwyck, stewards for the same, the xvj. day of September, in eight mess of meat, as follows : First, brawn and mustard, boiled capon, swan roast, capon and custard.   The second course, pidgeons and tarts, bread, wine, ale, and beer.   And my lady Roche, of her gentylnes, sent moreover four gallons of French wine, and also a box of wafers and a pottell of ipocras.

" For whose soul let us pray, and all Christian souls. Amen !"

(Herbert's History of the Twelve Companies, vol. i. p. 445.)

After the Reformation we have " The proceedinge to the funerall of a Knight in London," as follows :*

Fyrste, the children of the hospitall two and two.

Then two yeomen conductors, in blacke cotes, with blacke staves in their handes.

Then poor men in gownes two and two.

Then poor weomen in gownes two and two.

* MS. Harl. 1354, p. 37ᵇ.   In MS. Harl. 2129, p. 40, is " The order of the Obseque of sir William Garratt knight, late lord maior of London," who died temp. James I. which agrees in most particulars with this formulary.

Then the quyer.

Then the preacher.

Then the standard borne by a gentleman in gowne and hoode.

Then gentleweomen in gownes.

Then all the aldermen of the cytie that weare blackes.

Then the executors of the defunct.

Then the preacher, yf he be a deane.

Then the penon, borne by a gentleman in gowne and hoode.

Then the healme and creaste borne by a pursuevant.

Then the coate of armes borne by a herald.

Then Clarentius, kinge of armes of the province.

The corpes, covered with a pall of blacke velvett, borne by vj. yeomen in blacke cotes, assisted by iiij. gentlemen in gownes and hoodes, as also betweene iiij. penons of armes, videliz. one of the defuncts, one of the cities, one other of the companie wherof he was free, and the iiijth of the Marchante Venturers or of the Marchants of Muscovye, or such lyke.

Then next after the corpes followeth the chief mourner.

Then other two mourners.

Then other two mourners.

Then followeth the chamberlayne and towne clerke of London.

Then the swordbearer.

Then the lorde maior in blacke.

Then the aldermen havinge no blackes.

Then the estates of weomen havinge blackes.

Then aldermen's wyfes havinge no blackes.

Then the companyes.

Then the masters of the hospitalls, with grene staves.

Then the neyghbours and other parishoners.

The offeringe.

Firste the chief mourner to offer aloane, beinge attended
on by other iiij mourners.

Then the coate of armes by . . . .

Then the sworde by . . . .

Then the targe.

Then the heaulm and creste.

Then the pennon.

Then the standard.

Then the chief mourner to offer aloane for himselfe.

Then the lorde maior.

Then the other iiij. mourners.

Then the aldermen havinge blackes.

Then the aldermen havinge no blackes.

Then the executors.

Then the chamberlayne and towne clerke.

Then the gentlemen in blacke.

Then the maisters of the hospitalls.

Then the companies.

Then the weomen in blacke.

Then all the aldermen's wyfes and other gentleweomen

havinge no blackes.

In " The order observed by the Lord Maior, the Aldermen, and Sheriffes for their meetings and wearing of their apparell throughout the whole yeere," printed in Stowe's Survay, is the following : " For the buriall of Aldermen—the last love, duty, and ceremony one to another. The Aldermen are to weare their violet gownes, except such as have (of their friends' allowance) blacke gownes or mourning.* When an Alderman dieth, master Swordbearer is to have a blacke gowne, or three and thirty shillings and fourepence in money. And if the Alderman deceased doe give the Lord Maior mourning, then master Swordbearer is to have mourning also, or forty shillings in money as the value thereof, and so to carry the Sword in blacke before the Lord Maior. Master Chamberlain is not to weare his tippet but when the Lord Maior or Aldermen doe weare their scarlet or violet."

My friend John Nicholl, Esq. F.S.A. has kindly communicated to me the following entries regarding Funerals, which occur in the books of the Ironmongers' Company, with the contents of which he has made himself very conversant.

1531. Mr. John Guyva gave a herse-cloth richly imbroydered.

1570. It is agreyed at this court that Robart Goodyng and Giles Garton shalbe steuards for the buriall dynnar of the Lady Maris of London, which dynner to be kept at hir burriall daye, viz. the xvij of Julye, at oure hall; and the Lorde Mayor, sir Alexander Avenon, gave to the same

* Thus, in p. 218, " divers aldermen had black, and the residue in violet." See also pp. 112, 307.

dynner the somma of syxe pounds thirteen shyllings and foure pence. vj *li.* xiij*s.* iiij*d.*

1576. Yt is ordred that Robart Benne and Raphe Bright shalbe steuards for the dynner at the buryall of Mr. Alderman Hardyng, and whearas the same Mr. Hardyng dyd gyve to this company the some of tenne pownde, viz. v*li.* to the poorest of the company, and the other v*li.* to make the company a dynner; and for the better accomplyshment of the same dynner the steuardes shalbe allowyd them xxxiij*s.* iiij*d.*

1580. At this court wear apoynted to be stewards for Mr. Alderman Harvies wyff's burryall, which was appoynted to be the xxvij of June next comyng, beyng Monday, the persons underwrytten, John Masters (?), Harry Page, which persons had tenn pound delyvred unto them to make thear provission for a dynner for the holl lyverye and ther wyves, that had bynne wardens, &c.

1585. At this courte it is ordered that the auncyents, or eusignes, or anye other artilorye or furniture whatsoever pertayninge to the companie shall not be lent without the consent of a courte (the herse clothe appoynted for funeralls onelie excepte) uppon payne of fyve pounds.

1620. A court the 12th March, whereas the lady Harvey hath paid to the wardens xxi*lb.* for a dynner for the companye the 21st of this moneth, being the funerall day of Sir Sebastian Harvey deceased, it is ordered that Mr. Thomas Large and Mr John Wilson shall joine with the wardens for the provision of that dinner, to husband the same to the company's best profit.

1637. From the will of Thomas Willetts. Item, I give unto the master and wardens of the company of Ironmongers of London the sum of twenty pounds of like money to be by them bestowed on a dinner for themselves and such of the livery of the said company as shall go with my corps to the church at my funeral.

1657. Notice being given unto this court that the executors of the lady Cambell did desire the use of this hall upon Tuesday next for the said ladyes funerall, ansuare was returned by this court that they willingly assent thereunto.

1672. Notice being taken that since the rebuilding of severall halls in London there hath not been many funerialls out of this, by reason of the 30*s.* extraordinary charge layed thereon since the Fire, it is thereupon ordered that from this tyme each funerall shall only pay 50*s*. amongst the officers for their attendance, and the master and wardens to be invited to each funerall.

1678. It is ordered in the future that 40*s*. shalbe taken for all funeralls of strangers out of the hall, and of all freemen half that some that are members of this company, which is to be distributed amongst the company's officers, &c.

1719. The master acquainted the court that one John Turney, an undertaker for funeralls, had lately buried one Mrs. Mason from the hall, but had refused to give the master, wardens, and clerk each a ring &c. according to his agreement, the persons invited being served with gloves, hatbands, and rings. Ordered, the said undertaker be compelled to performe his agreement as the master and wardens shall direct.

———

A few observations may now be added on the various accessories employed at Funerals, and first of the several kinds of flags (to use that somewhat undignified word for want of a better generic term). The more ancient varieties of these insignia were Banners and Penons; the former of which answered to the "colours" of modern armies: the latter was the appendage of a weapon,—the lance.

The *Banner* was originally oblong in form, that is, about twice the depth of its width, thus corresponding to the early fashion of the shield; but latterly it grew to be nearly square. It displayed the armorial coat of its owner, spread entirely over its surface. The royal standard, as it is now called, is more properly a banner.

The *Standard* was originally an ensign too large to be borne by a man into battle: it was fixed on a carriage and placed in the centre of the host, where it remained stationary, as their rallying point; or, in the absence of alarm, it was posted at the entrance of the commander's tent. But afterwards standards were also made "to be borne." In the reign of Henry VIII. the King's standard for this purpose was of less dimensions than that set before his pavilion; and those of other persons were graduated according to their owner's rank, from the duke's standard of seven yards and a half in length, to the knight's of only four.* Standards differed from banners, not

* See Excerpta Historica, 1831, p. 50; where, in line 22, *for* " two yards" *read* ten.

only in form, but in not bearing the arms of their masters. Every standard
and guydon was " to have in the chief (that is, next the staff,) the cross of
Saint George; next, the beast (the modern supporter) or crest, with his
devise or word (his motto) ; and to be slit at the end." The standards borne
at funerals, as mentioned in the present volume, were made after this model.
Standards became more frequent in use than banners. They were borne
by knights ; but banners were confined to bannerets and persons of higher
rank.

The *Guydon* resembled the standard, but was only two and a half or
three yards in length ; and it was allowed to esquires,* or lieutenants. Its
derivation was the French Guide-homme; but the word was corrupted to
guydon, gytton, and geton.†

In the musters described in pp. 12, 19, the distinction of the Banner,
Standard, and Guydon may be observed. Only one great Banner appeared,
that of the king, carried by his pensioners ; the great lords each displayed
their Standards ; the earl of Warwick (the duke of Northumberland's son),
the lord admiral, and master treasurer Cheney had only Guydons.

At funerals banners and bannerolls seem to have been allowed to all
peers and their ladies ; standards, but not banners, to all knights and their
ladies ; penons, but not standards, to esquires. Mere gentlemen had no
penons, but only scocheons of arms.

In p. 6, therefore, where the word " banners " has been inadvertently
supplied to the funeral of a knight's widow, we should read only penons (as
before in the same page); and in p. 8 master Henry Williams would be
buried only with a penon of arms, like the esquire in the next paragraph.‡
Sir Anthony Wingfield had a banner at his funeral (p. 24), as had
other knights of the Garter ; and sir William Sydney (p. 31) had the same

---

* A docquet of a guydon allowed to Hugh Vaughan *esquire* in 1491 is recorded in the
College of Arms. Excerpta Historica, *ubi sup.*

† See pp. 18, 19. The word " costerells " in p. 13 remains unexplained.

‡ In p. 307 Machyn himself has committed the inadvertence of mentioning the
" *banner* of arms " of master Cholmley the recorder; but from the church notes of the
herald Nicholas Charles, we are assured it was only a penon, as he saw in Saint Dunstan's
church all the *three* penons which were carried at this funeral; one of the city of London,
one of the Mercers' company, and *the third of his own arms.* See the Collectanea Topographica et Genealogica, vol. iv. p. 102.

distinction, being a knight banneret (see the quotation from his epitaph in p. 329):

The *Penon* displayed at funerals (at which we do not meet with guydons) also resembled the standard in form, but was of a less size, and was rounded, instead of slit, at the end. It was also entirely different in its charges; as it bore the arms of the party, like the banner. This being the case, it was not superseded where a standard appeared, but always accompanied it, unless there were banners and bannerols.

The *Bannerolls* were banners of increased width, made to display impalements, representing the alliances of the ancestors of the deceased; as the duke of Norfolk (p. 70) had a dozen of banerolls of his " progeny " or pedigree; and at lady Cobham's funeral were nine banners of arms "of his and her pedigree " (p. 213); and they are sometimes mentioned as banners or bannerolls of marriages (pp. 244, 291, &c.).

But, if banners of arms were confined to persons of high rank, there was another kind of banner which was probably allowed to all who were inclined to pay for it. During the prevalence of the rites of the church of Rome, we meet with *Banners of Images*, (pp. 59, 61, 70, 81, 83, &c.) which were square, and represented either the personification of the Trinity or the figures of saints. Their number is almost uniformly four, and they were carried about the corpse, " at the four corners " (p. 155), but in two instances only two are mentioned.

The rich citizens of London * increased their funeral pomp with penons of the arms of the city and of the companies to which they belonged, in addition to one of their own arms. Thus, master Hussey (p. 237) had as many as five, which would be, 1. his own; 2. the city's; 3. the merchant-adventurers'; 4. the merchants' of Muscovy, and 5. the haberdashers'.

Pensels, the diminutive of penon, *penicillus*, were very small, like the vanes which sometimes terminate the pinnacles of pointed architecture, or the ironwork of the same period. They were supplied in large quantities, as at the funeral of sir William Goring there was a herse of wax, and eight dozen of pensels, and eight dozen of scocheons; the pensels and scocheons being chiefly, if not entirely, to deck out the herse. The queen of Spain's

---

* In the civic shows, particularly on the river, there was always abundance of banners and of streamers (pp. 38, &c.) In the Clerks' procession in 1555 there were a hundred streamers borne (p. 88). They were the peculiar flags of shipping.

herse (p. 90) took no less than thirty-six dozen of pensels; and so many as a thousand pensels, as well as flags and streamers, were used to adorn the two pinnaces in the lord mayor's water show in 1555 (p. 96).

A *Herse* is occasionally mentioned by our author; but the term was not then applied in its modern sense. With few exceptions the corpse was carried by men, whether on their shoulders or in a bier is not stated. The bodies of king Edward, queen Mary, the earl of Bedford, and the marchioness of Winchester (pp. 40, 83, 182, 187), were conveyed in "charetts;" that of bishop Gardiner in "a wagon with iiij. wheels all covered with black" (p. 101); that of sir John Haryngton "went into the country in a horse-litter" (p. 43), and in the same way that of lady Cawarden was conveyed to Blechingley (p. 225). But the Herse was, on grand occasions, ready to receive the corpse when it had arrived within the church: having been erected a day or two before (see pp. 155, 189, &c.) It was a frame "made of timber,* and covered with black, and armes upon the black," (pp. 44, 70). The grandest are often mentioned as being "of five principals," (pp. 111, 155, 173, 189, &c.) and that of lady Anna of Cleves was of seven (p. 145). Bishop Gardiner's was a herse of four branches (p. 97). The marchioness of Winchester's (p. 188) was "a herse of wax, adorned with eight dozen pensells, and arms and scocheons, and garnished with angels and arch-angels." The term "herse of wax" is one of continual recurrence (pp. 41, 71, 160, &c.), and is to be understood not of the material of the herse itself, but of the candles and tapers with which it was covered, and which, perhaps, in some cases, where economy was studied, were of tallow instead of wax. In the Vetusta Monumenta will be found an engraving of the herse of abbat Islyppe at Westminster, with all its lights burning. In some instances Machyn mentions, in further commendation of the herse, its "fair majesty, and valence gilded and fringed," (pp. 43, 160, 244), which may be supposed to have been a canopy or termination of the whole. The goodliest herse that he ever saw was that erected in Saint Paul's cathedral for the queen of Spain, which he has described in p. 90.

In the absence of a "herse of wax," there was an abundance of other lights; as, for instance, at the funeral of lady Bowes (p. 46), four great gilt

---

* The plan of the timber-work of a Herse is given in the Funeral Ceremonials in Nichols's Illustrations, &c. before cited; and Malcolm has engraved one of them with the mourners kneeling around it in his Londinium Redivivum, i. 414.

candlesticks, four great tapers, and two great white branches, besides twelve staff-torches borne by her servants.

The *Herse-cloth* was another sumptuous article of funereal pomp. That used at the funeral of the lady Anna of Cleves was " a herse-cloth of gold," (p. 146) ; and that at the king of Portugal's obsequies (misnamed Denmark's in p. 148), was " a goodly herse-cloth of tensell, the crosse of cloth of silver." Every parish kept a herse-cloth for the use of the inhabitants, for the loan of which at St. Margaret's Westminster the churchwardens received viij*d*. in the reign of queen Mary. The city companies had still more magnificent herse-cloths for their members, whose funerals they attended, and some of these are still preserved. That of the Fishmongers, which is beautifully embroidered with designs representing their patron Saint Peter, has been engraved in Miss Lambert's volume on Church Needlework. The Sadlers' company also preserve their herse-cloth,* and so do the Brewers.

The wardens of the Goldsmiths in 3 Hen. VIII. showed the company the goodly and rich herse-cloth which was made with the goods of sir Hugh Brice, dame Elizabeth his wife, and dame Elizabeth Terrell ; when it was agreed that the said cloth should not be lent to any other person than a goldsmith, or a goldsmith's wife ; that, whenever used, the company assembled should pray, as well for the said two donors' souls as for the soul of the said dame Elizabeth Terrell ; and that the beadle should have for his safeguard and attendance at least xij*d*.†

The Drapers had a burial-cloth given to them in 1518 by alderman John Milborne and his lady, " late the wife and executrix of John Chester, whilst he lived Draper of London." It is described as " a beryall-cloth of the value of j°. markes, for the wele of the soul of the said John Chester in especiall, and all other his good friends in generall."‡

Nor did the Reformation lead to the disuse of these public funerals, and the corporate provision made for them. In the middle of Elizabeth's reign, in the year 1572, John Cawoode (who had been printer to queen Mary) left to the Stationers' company " a herse-cloth of cloth of gold, pouderyd with blew velvet, and bordered abought with blacke velvet, embroidered and steyned with blew, yellow, red, and green."

* Described in the Gentleman's Magazine, vol. LXXXIII. i. 82.

† Herbert's History of the Twelve City Companies, i. 211.

‡ Ibid. p. 444.

There were also other insignia which were necessary adjuncts of the funeral furniture, as they were offered at the altar before the conclusion of the ceremonies (see pp. xxii. xxiii.), and afterwards suspended in the church. These were usually carried by the heralds. At the earl of Bedford's funeral (p. 83) there officiated (besides master Garter) five heralds, who bore, 1. his helmet, mantles, and crest; 2. his banner of arms; 3. his target with the garter; 4. his coat-armour; and 5. his sword. With the exception of the banner and the garter, those several articles will be found mentioned on every occasion; and, in place of the banner, the standard or the penon were substituted for inferior ranks, as already stated.

The *Helmet* is still seen lingering in some country churches: it is seldom found to be more than a fictitious helmet, made for the purpose to which it is applied. In early times a knight's real helmet was offered; but such have now almost entirely disappeared, having proved too tempting objects of antiquarian curiosity or cupidity.

The *Mantles*, which used to be made of black velvet (see pp. 126, 127), and the *Crest*, have now generally perished from decay; and the tattered fragments of the *banner* and *standard* have fallen from their poles.

The *Target* was a shield of the arms of the defunct, the successor of the knight's real shield, like that of Edward the Black Prince, which is still suspended over his tomb at Canterbury.*

The *Coat-Armour* was made like a herald's tabard, worked or painted before and behind with the same arms, and which were also repeated on its short sleeves.

The *Sword* was generally of the same description as the helmet, made rather for show than for use.

The lowest description of heraldic ensign allotted for Funerals was the *Scocheon*. Mere gentlemen had no penon; but as many scocheons as were desired. "Master Coldwell gentleman, and a lawyer" was buried "with half a dozen scocheons of buckeram" (p. 309). Mistress Draper (p. 144) had two dozen. A gentleman of Gray's Inn, who, perhaps, had no arms of his own, was buried with six "scocheons of arms of the house," i. e. the arms of his Hon. Society.

But the funerals of the higher ranks were also provided with scocheons,†

* See the interesting account of its recent examination by the Rev. C. H. Hartshorne.

† It was a practice (and which was kept up until recent times) for ambassadors to leave scocheons at the houses where they slept. An instance occurs in p. 248 of the earl of

in addition to their other insignia, and that sometimes profusely,—to the extent of four, six, or eight dozen; and at the funeral of sir Ralph Warren alderman there were no less than twelve dozen : together with his standard as a knight, and five penons, like master Hussey, already instanced. These scocheons were the prototypes of our modern hatchments. Originally made of some perishable material, and fastened up in the churches, they were required to be painted on panel, in order to last longer; and from these small atchievements on panel (still to be found in some country churches) they have grown into the large and unwielding frames of canvas now spread on the front of modern mansions, or stretched on the roof of the chancel or aisle, the walls of which scarcely offer sufficient space for their accommodation.

In p. 291 master Machyn is communicative as to the materials of which his articles were made. He there mentions scocheons of metal, of silk, of buckeram, of paper royal, and of pasted paper. In p. 290 he speaks of a herse of velvet and a pall of velvet; in p. 293 a black velvet pall with a white cross of satin and arms upon it; in p. 297 a pall of black velvet with arms upon buckeram scocheons. He elsewhere mentions a coat-armour as made of damask (p. 116). The royal mantles for the French king (p. 209) were of cloth of gold; but they were usually of black velvet, as is repeatedly mentioned.

The appearance of a set of funeral trophies, as left suspended in a church, is shown in the following engraving, from a sketch by Nicholas Charles in the MS. Lansdowne 874. They are those of sir John White, who was lord mayor of London in 1563, and was buried in 1573 in the church of Aldershot in Hampshire (see a note respecting him in p. 405). He had, it will be seen, a standard as a knight; four penons, of his own arms, the city of London, the merchant-adventurers, and the grocers ; a coat-armour ; a target ; helmet, crest, and mantles ; and sword. His armorial coat was, Per fess azure and or, a pale counterchanged, three fountains two and one, and three lion's heads one and two. The crest, a lion's head erased quarterly azure and or, guttée de sang in each quarter.

It will be observed that peculiar rests of iron were made for the reception of these trophies, which were inserted in the wall of the church. Suspended on these, they were left to testify to the worldly grandeur of the defunct so long as their fragile materials might endure.

Bedford, who was going ambassador to France, being provided with " three dozen of lodging scocheons " for this purpose.

STANDARD, FOUR PENONS, COAT ARMOUR, TARGET, SWORD, HELMET, CREST, AND MANTLES, OF SIR JOHN WHITE, IN ALDERSHOT CHURCH, HAMPSHIRE.

DIARY

OF A

RESIDENT IN LONDON.

THE *imperfect paragraph with which the Manuscript now begins relates to the funeral of Sir Thomas Wriothesley, Earl of Southampton, K.G. who died on the 31st July 1550, and was buried on the 4th of August at St. Andrew's, Holborn, Sir John Hoper, priest, preaching at his funeral.—Strype, Memorials, fol.* 1721, *ii.* (283).

. . . . and dyd there . . . . prest, and there was hys standard borne, and the . . . then came ys banurs of armes and the clarkes and pr[estes, and then] the haroldes a v, one carehyng ys elmet, anodur . . . with the garter, and anodur ys sword, and anodur ys crest, then came the cors with iiij baner of armes, then mo[urners] for hym a c powre men havyng gownes of manty[lle fryse] and ther was a grett dolle of monay and after a grett [dinner] and iiij banars rolles of armes borne a-bowt the body.

The xxvij day of August was bered sir Wylliam [Locke knight] and alderman and late shreyff of London, and bered [at St.] Thomas of Acurs, and a-ffor hym whent a lx pore men in mo[urning] gowns and whytt stayffes in ther handes ij and ij to-gether; [after] them the standard, and then mornars, and then came a . . with odur mornars, and then the clarkes and prestes, and then [a herald] with ys cott armor, target, elmet, sword, and then the corse [with] penons of armes borne a-bowt hym, and the stret [was] hangyd with blake and armes a-pone the cloth, and ther [was a] dolle of monay, and a grett denner as I have be hat.

The ffurst day of September was bered the good [lady] the contes of · Hamtun, sum tyme the wyff of sir Wylliam [Fitz] Wylliam, lord of the Preve-selle, and ded and bered att Farnham with mony mornars and harolds, and a-bowt the corse iiij banars of armes, and then the cheyff mornars sir Garves Clyfftun knyght and sir Antony Browne, with odur, and a gret dener.

The xviij day of October was bered Juge Hynde in sant Don-stones parryche in the whest, with standard, cot, elmet, sword, and penon, target, and a harold, and Juges ij and ij to-gether, and then serjantes of coyffe ij and ij together, and then clarkes syngyng, and my lade Hynde dyd make anodur standard, and a cote ar-mur, and a penon, and a elmet, and target, and sword, to be had at the moynthe myn[d] in the contrey for hym, and a grett dolle of monay and of mett and drynk, and gownes to the pore; for ther was [a] myche a doo ther for hym.

The next paragraph belongs to another funeral: the beginning of which is lost :—

· · · · · · gayffe unto xiij powre men xiij gowns · · ·
· · · yffe having a bage [b] of bokeram logent-fassyon [c] · · · ·
gold, with prestes and clarkes, with a pennon of ys armes · · ·
· · · tes of armes, and hangyd with blake and schochyons [d] of
the · · with a harold beyryng ys cott in ys armes.

The xvij day of November was bered the old contesse [of Derby], bered at Collam, sir Edward Hastyngs behyng her se— *unfinished.*

The xviij day of November was bered M. Heys, he · · · · of London, in the parryche of saynt Peter's, in Cornhylle · · · awllter with the feyleshyp of the Clarkes of London.

'The xix day of November was bured my lade Jude, ma[yress]

---

[a] *MS.* wache.   [b] badge.   [c] *i. e.* lozenge-fashion.
[d] *MS.* shokoyn'.

of London, and wyff of sir Androw Jude, mayr of London, and
bered in the parryche of saynt Ellen in Bysshope-gatt stret, for he
gayff mony, gownes, and to the powre men and women ij C·
gownes of mantyll . . . and the Clarkes of London had the
beryng of my lade, and then came . . . with ij harolds [e] a-for
with iiij baners a-bowt her borne, and after my [lord] mayre and
ys bredurne, and alle the stret and the chyrche wher hangyd with
blake and with schochyons of ther armes, and a gret dolle and a
grett [dinner.]

The xxiiij day of November was bered the nobulle ca[ptayn]
ser James Wylfford knyght, sum tyme captayn in Franse and
. . . . and ded at the Cruchydffrers, and was cared to beryng
from [thence] unto lytyll saynt Bathellmuw besyd sant Antonys, with a standard, a penon, and a harold carehyng the cott
armur, and mony m[ourners], and bered in the sam tombe that
ys grett unckulle M. James [Wylfford].   Ther was at ys bereyng
my lord Gray and the [f] Wylfford . . . captaynes, and the company of the Clarkes.   Mylles Coverdalle dyd [preach].

The xxx day of November was bered Crystoffer Machyn,
Marchand-tayllor, in the parryche of saynt James, and brodur
[of] Henry [g] Machyn : the compeny of Marchand-tayllers behyng
at ys berehyng, and the compeny of the Clarkes syngyng, and
. . . Maydwell dyd pryche for hym,—the iiij yer of K. E. vj[t].

The xiiij day of Feybruarii was dysposyd of ys bysshoppr[icke]
of Wynchestur, the old bysshope M. Stevyn [h] Gardener, and cared
in to the Towre—the v yer K. E. vj[th].

. . . . . and the compyny of the Clarkes . . . cheyffe
mornar was sir Garves Clyfftun and M. . . . . . dyd pryche
ther, and after they whent to dener unto the [earl of] Ruttland
plasse in Wyttyngton Colege parryche.

The vij day of Marche was bered my lord Wentworth, the lord
Chamburlayn of the kynges howse, in Westminster abbay, in

---

the sam chapell that the old abbatt was be[red ; there] was iiij of
the cheyffe harolds ther, M. Garter, M. Clar[enceux,] M. Yorke,
M. Chester, beyryng the cote armur, the elmett, t[arget], then
cam the standard, and then mornars alle in blake . . . and a
C. chylderyn and prestes and clarkes in ther surpl[ices ; then] the
cors with iiij baners rolles, and the qwyre was hangyd [with black]
and the raylles and armes. Mylles Coverdalle dyd pryche, and
ther [was a grett] dolle, and a grett compeny of lordes and knyghtes
and genty[lmen] mornars.

The ix day of Marche was a proclamasyon that no [man or]
woman shuld nott ett no flesse in lent, nor fryday, nor [wednes-
day] thrught the yere, nor ymberyng days, nor no days that ys
co[ndemned ?] by the chyrche apone payne of forfyte.

The xiiij day of Marche was hangyd, in Smyth-feld, on John
Mosbe and ys syster, for the death[i] of a gentyll man of Feyversham, one M. Arden the custemer, and ys owne wyff was decaul . .
. . . and she was burnyd at Canturbery and her sarvand hangyd
ther, and ij at Feyversham and on at Hospryng, and nodur in the
he way to Canturbery, for the death[k] of M. Arden of Feyversham.
[and at Flusshyng was bernyd Blake Tome[l] for the sam deth of
M. Arden.[m]]

The xiiij day of Marche wa(s) raynyd at the yeld-halle a C.
mareners for robyng on the see, and the captayne, behyng a
Skott,[n] was cared to Nugate the sam day, and serten cast.[o]

The sam day was cared in-to Norfoke on [p] Wyth, a grett ryche
man, and he was condemnyth to be drane and hangyd, for the
besenes that was done in Norffoke, at ys owne dore.

[The xv day the Lady Mary rode through London unto St.
John's, her place, with fifty knights and gentlemen in velvet coats
and chains of gold afore] her, and after her iiij [score gentlemen

---

[i] *MS.* derth.   [k] *MS.* derth.   [l] Black Will *in other accounts.*

[m] This last line was added to the entry some time after it was written.

[n] *MS.* shott.   [o] *i. e.* some were condemned.   [p] *one.*

and ladies, every] one havyng a peyre of bedes[o] [of black. She rode through] Chepe-syde and thrugh Smythfeld,—the v. K. E. vj.

The xvij day my lade Marie rod thrugh from Saynt [John's through] Flettstrett[p] unto the court to Westmynster [with many] nobull men of lordes and knyghtes and gentyllmen and ladies and gentyllwomen, and at the court gatte she a-lyttyd, and M. [Wingfield], the comtroller of the kynges howse, and mony lordes and [knights], and so she was browth thrught the halle unto the cham-[ber of] pressens; and so she tared there and ade a goodly ba[n-quet] ij owrs, and sone after she toke her horse and rod unto Sy[nt John's ;] and ther she laie alle nyght, and on the morowe her [Grace] rod to Nuw Hall in Exsex, and ther byd yn grasse[q] with honor, thanke be God and the kyng her brodur.

The iij day of May ther was a grett tryhumpe at Grenwyche. The Kyng and alle ys compeny wher alle blacke and whyt, fott men and trumpeters, hats, clokes, and baners blacke and whytt, and speres; and the thodur parte was the yerle of Harfford, and a grett compeny of lords and knyghts, alle yonge men, and trompeters, ther hats, baners, and fott men alle in yelow, and so they rayne [at the] rynge, and at tornay with swords—the v yer K. E. vjth.

The xiiij day of May, Chestur the reseyver[r] toke possessyon [of] the halle of the compeny of the Clarkes of London by fre . . the gentyllman, of wyche they have as sure a corporasyon [as] any haff in London, has I pray God gyff ym ylle sped, be[cause] of the pore men and women and other that yff they had falne to a [sudden] poverte ther they wher sure of a onest lyvyng as longe as [life did last.]

The xv day of May was bered my lade Hobullthorne, late

[o] Beads; "To make an open profession, no doubt," remarks Strype, "of their devotion for the Mass."

[p] *MS.* ffiettrett. [q] *i. e.* grace.

[r] *In the margin is written*, [I] pray God he be a good man.

[mayoress] of London, with ij harolds, iiij penons of armes, and
ther was [the] Clarkes of London, and ther had powre men and
women had many fryse gownes, and ther was iiij aldermen mornars, and ij of them knyghts, and ther a grett dolle ˢ was, and the
morow a grett dener.

> .   .   .   .

. . . . . for the spasse of xiiij days.

The xxij day of Maij was bered my lade Mores, wyff of sir
Crystoffer Mores knyght, and the M. of [the Ordnance] by kyng
Henry the viijᵗʰ, the wyche he ded of the h . . at Bullayn, and
she ded in saynt Peters in Cornhyll . . . in saynt Towlles ᵗ
in the Oll' Jury, and ther she . . . her first husband, with
ij harolds; and she gayff . . . men and women vijˣˣ mantylls,
fryse gownes, and o[ther] gownes and cotts a iiijˣˣ, and then cam
the corse [with banners] of armes borne abowt her, with iiij morners . . . . dyd pryche the Skott the curett, and a gret dolle
and a gret [dinner] as I have sene off fysse and odur thynges.

The xxv day of May was be syd Rygatt and Croydon, Suttun,
and Darkyng, a grett wondernus of herth ᵘ . . . and spess-
hall ᵛ at Darkyng, and in dyvers plasys . . . . pottes, panes,
and dyssys donst,ʷ and mett ˣ felle doune . . . abowt howse,
and with mony odur thyngs.

The xxxj day of May my lord the yerle of Darbe [came] to
Clessay ʸ owt of the North, with a goodly compeny of men and
horssys.

The v day of Juin cam to Clessay the yerle of Shrusbery with
vijˣˣ hors, and a-for hym xl welvet cotts and chynes,ᶻ and in ys
owne leveray, to hys plasse, and the resyduw of ys servandes.

The vj day of July the Kynges grace rod thrugh Grenwyche
parke unto Blake heth, and my lord of Darbe, and my lord of
Warwyke, and my lord admerall Clyntun, and sir Wylliam Harbard, and odur lordes and knyghts and gentyllmen, and trumpeters

---

ˢ dole.   ᵗ St. Olave's.   ᵘ earthquake.   ᵛ specially.   ʷ dishes danced?
ˣ meat.   ʸ Chelsea?   ᶻ chains.

playhyng, and alle the gardes in ther dobelets and ther hosse, with bowes and arowes and halbards ij and ij to-gether, and the Kynges grace in the myds on horsse-bake, and ther the Kynges grace ran at the ryng on Blake heth with lordes and knyghtes. [The earl of Warwick met the King there with a hundred men of arms, and great horses, and gentlemen] in clothe, and brodered the alffe, and the same night the Kyng suppyd at Depforth[a] in a shype with my lord Admyral, [and the lords] of the conselle, and with many gentylmen.

The vij day of July begane a nuw swet in London, and . . . ded my lord Crumwell in Leseter-shyre, and was bered [with a stand]ard, a baner of armes, and cote, elmett, sword, targett, and sc[ochyons, and] harold; and the sam tyme ded my lord Powes, and the x day [at W]ollwyche, sir John Lutterell, knyght, a nobull captayne.

The viij day of July was a plage, and a proclamasyon that [a testern shou]ld be but ix[d], and a grot iij[d]; and anodur proclamasyon cam [out the] xviij day of August, that testerns cryd at vj[d] a pese; a grot [at ij[d]]; ij[d] but j[d]; and a j[d] ob.; and a alpeny a fardyng.

The x day of July the Kynges grace removyd from Westmynster unto Hamtun courte, for ther ded[b] serten besyd the court, and [that] causyd the Kynges grase to be gone so sune, for ther ded in Lo[ndon] mony marchants and grett ryche men and women, and yonge men and [old], of the nuw swett,—the v of K. E. vj[th].

The xij day of July ded sir Thomas Speke knyght in Chanseler lane,[c] in saynt Donstonys parryche in the whest, at ys owne howsse; he fell [sick] in the court; and was bered with standard, penon, cote armur, elmet, sword, and target; and vj dosen of shokchyons of armes, and the compeny of the Clarkes; and the sam day ded on of the Gard, and bered ther by.

---

[a] Deptford.   [b] died, of the Plague.   [c] Chancery Lane.

The xiij day of July ded the old knyght and gentyll sir John [Wallop] and knyght of the nobull order of the garter, and captayn of the castyll [of Gynes], for he was a nobull captayne as ever was, the wyche I [pray] Jhesu have mercy on ys solle; and he was bered with standard and [banners] of ys armes, cote armur, elmet, target of the garter, sw[ord,] and viij dosen of skochyons; and a marmed d was ys crest; and [in his] stede ys chossen captayn sir Andrew Dudley knyght of the ga[rter.]

The xvj day of July ded of the swet the ij yonge dukes of Suffoke of the swet, boyth in one bed in Chambryge-shyre; and [buried] at *(blank in MS.)*; and ther ded from the viij day of July unto the xix ded of the swett in London of all dyssesus,e viijc. iijxx. and xij. and no more in alle, and so the chanseller is serteffyd.

The ensuing imperfect passage probably relates to the funeral of sir Peryn Negroo knt. (Strype, Mem. ii. 279.)

. . . . . targett, elmet, and sword . . . and apone the castyll a man with a shurt of . . . hand and with xij stayffes, torchys bornyng . . . flut playng, hoveles, and ys flag borne, and . . . . . in the grond, and the stret honge with blake with ys armes . . . ther dyd pryche the Doyttur Bartelet, and ther was the compeny [of Clarkes,] and a harold of armes, and mony morners of capt. . . .

The xxvij day of July was the nuw bisshope of W. . . was devorsyd from the bucher wyff with shame enog[h.]

The xx day of August was the berehyng of M. Har[ry Wylliam] sqwyre, sune and here unto sir John Wylliam knyght, with [banners of] armes and cote armur, and iiij dosen of schochyons,—the v. K. E. vj.

The xxj day of August bered yonge M. Sandes, sun unto the lord Sandes, sqwyre, with a penon and cote armur [and] iiij dosen of skochyons,—the v. K. E. vj.

The xxij day of August was bered sir Recherd Ly[ster], sune

---

d mermaid.   e *Sic in MS.* the sense appears to be, that during the prevalence of the sweat there died of all diseases 872.

and here to the lord cheyffe Justes, with standard, penon, and a baner rolle, target, elmet, and vj dosen of [skochyons].

The xxiij day of August ded the bysshope of Lynckolne,[c]—the v yer of Kyng Edward the vj[t].

The xxiij day [of] August the Kynges grace went from Amton courte unto Wyndsore, and ther was stallyd the Frenche Kyng of the nobull order of the garter, with a grett baner of armes inbrodered with flowrs delusys of gold bosted, the mantylls of tysshuw, and the elmett clene gylt and ys sword; and the goodly gere was.[d]

The iiij day of September ded my lade Admerell' wyffe[e] in Lynkolne-shyre, and ther bered.

The v day of September was bered serjant Heth, and of the Kynges bake howse, and was bered at Lyntun at M. Parryche sqwyre, in the conte of Cambrygshyre.

. . . .

chyke, and hard cheysse oꝺ fardyng . . .

The xxj day of September ded M. Roger [. . of] the Catre one to[f] owre soverayn lord kyng Edward the vj[th], and bered at (*blank*).

The xxij day of September was the monyth['s mind of the] ij dukkes of Suffoke in Chambryge-shyre, with [ij] standards, ij baners grett of armes and large, and banars rolles of dyver armes, with ij elmets, ij [swords, ij] targetts crownyd, ij cotes of armes, ij crests, and [ten dozen] of schochyons crounyd; and yt was grett pete of [their] dethe, and yt had plesyd God, of so nobull a stok they wher, for ther ys no more left of them.

The xxix day of September was Saynt Myghell, the Kyng grase dyd where[g] the robes of order of [Saint] Myghell with skalopshells of Franse; and the sam tyme was chossen of the order of the gar-

---

[c] Henry Holbech.   [d] *Sic in MS.*
[e] The wife of Edward Lord Clinton, Lord Admiral.   [f] *i. e.* unto.
[g] *i. e.* wear.

ter the lord chamburlayne Darcy, in the plasse of ser John Wallop knyght of the gartter and captayn of Gynes.

The ix day of October was stallyd at Wyndsore the lord chamburlayne Darcy knyght of the garter.

The same day was bered Gylles the kynges bere [-brewer] dwellyng at Sant Katheryns, and bered at Algate, with ys armes, and the craft of the Bruars; the wyche he ded with a chrache [h] of ys lege, and bled to deth.

The **xv** day of October was had to the Towre the duke of Somersett and the lord Gray.

The xvj day of October was had to the Towre the duches of Somersett and Sir Raff a Vane and Sir John Thyn, [as also Sir Thomas Holcroft, Sir Michael Stanhope, Mr. Hammond, Mr. John Seimour, Mr. Walley, Mr. Nudigate, Mr. Banister, Mr. Brayne, Mr. Crane and his wife, [i]] Sir Myles Parterege, and Sir Thomas Aru[ndell and Lady].

The xxj day of October was cared [to the Tower] my lord Pagett by the gard—the v yer K. [E. vjᵗ.]

The xj day of October wher creatyd [at Hampton] curtte my lord marqwes Dorsett duke of Suffolk; the yerle of Warwyke duke of Northumburland; [the earl] of Wyllshere created the marqwes of Wyncha[ster; sir] Wylliam Harbard made lord of Cardyff, and after the yerle of Penbroke; and knyghtes mad the sam [time, sir William] Syssyll, [k] secretery, knyght, and M. Hare[l] Nevylle knyght, [sir William] Sydney knyght, and M. Cheke, the kynges scollmaster.

The xxij day of October was alle the craftes [of London] commandyd to go to ther halles, and ther yt was [shewed] them that the duke of Somersett wold have taken the Towre, and to have taken the brod-selle, and to have [destroyed] the cete, [m] and

---

[h] *i. e.* scratch.

[l] Strype supplies these names, all apparently from our Diary, which is here burnt, the passage being at the top of a page.

[k] Cecil.   [l] Harry.   [m] city.

then to go to the ylle ˙of Whyth ; and so evere craft to ward at
evere gatt in London, and to have a rydyng wache thrugh the
cete,—the v K. E. the vj^th.

The ij day of November cam to Londun from Hamton courtte
and landyd at Benard castyll the old Qwyne of Schottes, and cam
rydyng to the bysshope('s) palles at Powlles with many lordes, the
duke of Suffoke, my lord marqwes of Northamptun, my lord of
Warwyke, the lord Welebe, my lord Haward, my lord Rosselle,
lord Bray, and dyvers mo lords and knyghtes and gentyllmen,
and then cam the Qwyne of Schottes and alle owre lades and her
gentyll women and owre gentyll women to ᵃ the nomber of a C.
and ther was sent her mony grett gyftes by the mayre and aldermen, as beyffes, mottuns, velles, swines, bred, wylld ffulle, wyne,
bere, spysys, and alle thyngs, and qwaylles, sturgeon, wod and
colles, and samons, by dyver men.

[The iiij day of November the Queen rode unto the court, attended with a great train of noblemen, gentlemen, and ladies.   At
the Court gate stood all the guards in their best coats.]   Ther the
yerle of Pe[mbroke saluted her and brought her] to the hall dore,
and ther mett her the duke [of Northumberland] and broyth her
into the hall, and ther mett the [King's grace, who salu]tyd her,
and dyd inbrasse her and kyssyd her, and [took her by] the hand,
and led her up in to the chambur of [presence ; and] so ther was
a bankett, and so when all was [done, the Queen] toke her horsse
and was browght unto the bysshopes palesse to soper, and ther she
laye ther tyll the *(blank)*

The vj day of November the Qwyne rod˙thrught [London] to
Bysshope-gatt, and the duke of Northumberland [and a hundred]
of grett horsys and cotes of welvet in-brodery, [with] hats of
velvet and whyt fethers and chynes ᵇ of gold ; [and the] yerle of
Penbroke with a C. gret horsses, cotes gardy[d with] velvet, and
chynes,ᵇ hats and whyt fethers, and every [man] havyng a new

ᵃ *MS.* tho.   ᵇ chains.

gayffelyns [o] in ther hands, and a bage [p]; and then cam the lord Tresorer with a C. gret horsse and ther cotes of marbull, with bage the facon [q] of gold and gayffelins; and with gret nombur of lords and knyghts, and gentyllmen and lades; and ther the Qwyne reseyvyd of the chamburlain of London at the gatt a C. marke owt of the chambur.

The viij day of November was cared to the Towre the good yerlle of Arundell and my lord Pagett.

The xxv day of November was cared to the Towre the lord Dacurs of the North,—the v yer kyng Edward the vj[t].

The xxx day of November ther was a grett skaffold mad in Westmynster halle agaynst the next day, that was [the] ffurst day of Desember, for the duke of Somersett, the [which] was raynyd of tresun and qwyt of ytt, and cast of fe[lony], and ther was shyth a shutt [r] of men and women, for they thowght that he had byne qwytt, for [they] thruw a C. caps on he [s] for gladnes, for ther was mony lost ther . . . . . .

. . . .

. . . and the stret hangyd with blake . . . mantyll frysse gowne boyth . . . meny blake gownes, and then cam the cors with . . . of armes borne a-bowt her, and a gret . . . and ther was the compeny of the Clarkes, and a gret . . .

The vij day of Desember at Hyd parke a gret muster of men of armes: the furst the kynges trumpeters; [then] my lord Bray, in gylt harnes, captayn of the pe[nsioners, and a] gret baner of the kynges armes; and then cam the pensyoners in caumplet [t] harnes, and gret hars [u], in [white and] blake, v and v a ranke, and after them cam the[ir servants, in number] a C. with grett harse [u], and harnes in whyt and blake, [and speres]. The secound my lord Tresorer, a C. men of [x] arms, broderyd cott, red and whyt, and ther spers, ys [standard] a faucon of gold. The iij was [the] duke of Northumberland, with [C. men] of armes in welvet in-brodery,

[o] javelin. [p] badge. [q] falcon. [r] such a shout.
[s] on high. [t] complete. [u] horse. [x] *MS.* or.

trumpeters, [his standard] a lyon crounyd gold. The iiij my lord marqws Northamtun a C. men of armes, in yelow and [black], spers and pensels and trumpeters. The yerlle of Bedford a C. men of armes and [in] red and whyt, ys standard a gott [x] whyt, and a trumpeter, and pensels and spers, cotes red and whyt and blake. The yerle of Rottland a C. men of armes in yelow and bluw ; ys standard a pekoke, and pensels. The yerle of Huntyntun men of armes l. in bluw, and speres, and standard, and pensels. The yerle of Penbroke C. men of armes. My lord Cobam l. men of armes, in blak and whyt. My lord Chamburlayne l. men of armes, cote(s) of whyt [and] red, and speres cotes in-brodere, and pensels. M. tresorer Cheyney a C. men of armes, all blake, and speres and pensells, by-syd costerells and geton.

. . . . . . and armes a-pone the blake at . . . pryche the Skott of saynt Peters in Cornhyll . . . the morow dyd pryche doythur [y] Bartelett a godly . . . at the berehyng was the masters and compeny of the . . .

The iiij day of Januarii was mad a grett skaffold [in Ch]epe hard by the crosse, agaynst the kynges lord of myss[rule] cumyng from Grenwyche ; and landyd at Towre warff, [and with] hym yonge knyghts and gentyllmen a gret nombur on [horseb]ake sum in gownes and cotes and chynes [z] abowt ther nekes, every man havyng a balderyke of yelow and grene abowt ther nekes, and on the Towre hyll ther they [went in] order, furst a standard of yelow and grene sylke with Sant Gorge, and then gonnes and skuybes,[a] and trompets and bagespypes, and drousselars and flutes, and then a gret compeny all in yelow and gren, and docturs declaryng my lord grett, and then the mores danse dansyng with a tabret, and afor xx of ys consell on horsbake in gownes of chanabulle lynyd with blue taffata and capes of the sam, lyke sage (men) ; then cam my lord with a gowne of gold furyd with fur of the goodlyest collers [b] as ever youe saw, and then ys . . . and after cam alff a hundred in red and wyht, tallmen [of] the

---

[x] goat.   [y] doctor.   [z] chains.   [a] squibs.   [b] colours.

gard, with hods of the sam coler, and cam in to the cete; and after
cam a carte, the whyche cared the pelere, the a . . , [the] jubett,[v]
the stokes, and at the crose in Chepe a gret brod s[kaffold] for to go
up; then cam up the trumpeter, the harold, [and the] doctur of
the law, and ther was a proclamasyon mad of my lord('s) progeny,[w] and of ys gret howshold that he [kept,] and of ys dyng-
nyte; and there was a hoghed of wyne [at] the skaffold, and
ther my lord dranke, and ys consell, and [had] the hed smyttyn
owt that every body mytht drynke, and [money?] cast abowt
them, and after my lord('s) grase rod unto my lord mer[x] and alle
ys men to dener, for ther was dener as youe have sene[y]; and
after he toke his hers[z], and rod to my lord Tresorer at Frer
Austens, and so to Bysshopgate, and so to Towre warff, and toke
barge to Grenwyche.

[The xxij of January, soon after eight of the clock in the morning, the duke of Somerset was beheaded on Tower hill. There was
as] grett compeny as have bene syne . . the kynges gard be-
hynge there with ther ha[lbards, and a] M[l]. mo with halbards of
the prevelege of the Towre, [Ratcliffe,] Lymhowsse, Whyt-chapell,
Sant Kateryn, and Strettford [Bow], as Hogston, Sordyche; and
ther the ij shreyfs behyng th[ere present] seyng the execusyon of my
lord, and ys hed to be [smitten] of, and after shortely ys body was
putt in to a coffin, [and carried] in to the Towre, and ther bered
in the chyrche, of [the north] syd of the qwyre of sant Peters,
the wyche I beseeche [God] have mercy on ys sowlle, amen!
And ther was [a sudden] rumbelyng a lytyll a-for he ded, as
yt had byn [guns] shuttyng[a] and grett horsys commyng, that a
M[l]. fell [to the] grond for fere, for thay that wher at the on syd
[thought] no nodur butt that one was kyllyng odur, that [they
fell] down to the grond on apon anodur with ther halb[ards],
they thought no nodur butt that thay shuld . . . . . sum
fell in to [the] dyche of the Towre and odur plasys, . . . and
a C. in to the Towre-dyche, and sum ran a way for [fear.]

[v] gibbet.   [w] i. e. genealogy.   [x] mayor.   [y] i. e. as great a dinner.
[z] horse.   [a] shooting.

The xxv day of Januarij begane the parlement [at] Westmynster agayne,—the v yer of K. E. vj[th].

The xxvij[th] day of January was reynyd at Westmynster Hall ser Raff a Vane knyght of tresun, and qwyt of hytt, and cast of felony to be hangyd,—the v yer K. E. vj[th].

The xxviij day of Januarij was reynyd sir Thomas Arundell knyght, and so the qwest cold nott fynd ym tyll the morow after, and so he whent to the Towre agayn, and then the qwest wher shutt up tyll the morow with-owt mett or drynke, or candylle or fyre, and on the morow he cam a-gayne, and the qwest qwytt ym of tresun, and cast hym of felony to be hangyd,—the v king Edward vj[th].

The v day of Feybruarii was reynyd sir Mylles Parterege knyght of tresun, and qwytt of yt, and cast of felony to be hangyd, the vj[th] yer of king Edward vj[th].

. . . . . . [sir Michael Stanhope was] cast of felony to be hangyd—the vj[[th] K. E. vj[th].]

The xxvj[th] day of Feybruarii, the wyche was [the morrow aft]er saynt Mathuwe day, was heddyd on the Tower [hill sir] Myghell Stanhope knyght, and ser Thomas Arundell; [and in]-contenent was hangyd the seylff sam tyme sir Raff [a Vane] knyght, and ser Mylles Parterege knyght, of the galowse besyd the . . . . and after ther bodys wher putt in to dyvers nuw coffens [to be be-] red and heds in to the Towre in cases and ther bered . . cent.

The xxviij[th] day of Feybruarii was mared M. James . . . . clarke of the gren cloth in (the) kyng('s) howsse, unto Annes . . late wyffe of John Heth, serjant of the kyng('s) bakhowsse, [at the] parryche of saynt Botoulffe with-owt Bysshopgate, and . .

The xxviij day of Feybruarii was bered the nobull [lady the] contes of Penbroke, and syster to the late qwyne and wyffe [to the] nobull Kyng Henry the viij. late kyng, and the good lade [the] contes of Penbroke the wyche she ded at Benard Castle, and so cared unto Powlls. Ther was a C. powre men and women had mantylle fryse gownes, then cam the haroldes, [then] the corse, and a-bowt her viij baners rolls of armes, and then cam the mornars boyth lordes and knyghts and gentyll men, and then cam the lades mornars and gentyll women mornars ij C. [then the] gentyll men and gentyll women, and after cam in cotts ij C. servandes and odur servandes, and she was bered by the tombe of [the duke] of Lankaster, and after her banars wher sett up over her [and her] armes sett on dyvers pelers,—the vj King Edward vj[th].

The xvij day of Marche rod thrugh London unto [St.] James in the feld, the kyng('s) plase, the kynges syster my [lady] Elsabeth, with a grett compeny of lordes and knyghtes and gentyll men, and after her a grett nombur of lades and gentyllwomen to the nombur of ij C. on horsse-bake, and yomen.

The xix day of Marche cam from Saynt James thrught the parke to the court, and from Parke gate unto the courtt was struys[a] with sand fyne, and afor her came dukes, lordes, and knyghtes, and after lades and gentyllwomen a gret compeny, and so she was reseyuyd in to the courte goodly.

.   .   .   .
. . . . . . cared thrugh Nuwgatt and Smyth . . . .
. . . s strett, and so a-ways,—the vj yer king Edward the vj[th].

The xxj day of Marche dyd ryd thrugh Lo[ndon on horseb]ake ij yonge feylles[b] boyth of on horse, and on [of them] carehyng a spytt up ryght and a duke[c] rostyd, and . . . Nugatt, and ther they alyth of ther horse and . .   and the duke at Nugatt, and so was led with the . . . begers thrugh Flett lane with many pepull won
. . . to the Rose at the Flet bryge, the taverne wher . . . to have hetten[d] yt there, and I left them ther, and [came to] the court to dener; one of them dweltt at the Sun . . .

The xxij of Marche was bered John Welle . . . myllner, dwellyng at the iiij mylls at Stratford, and . . .

The ix day of Aprell was bered M. Morgayne, gold-smyth, in the parryche of Saynt Foster, in Foster . . .

The xij day of Aprell was bered ser Umffrey . . knyght, with a standard and a penon, and a cott armur . . and sword, elmett, and mantylles, and vj dosen of skoychyons, meny gownes

---

[a] *Sic MS. for* strewn.   [b] fellows?   [c] duck.   [d] eaten.

gyffyn to the powre and the ryche, and a [great] dolle, and with a harold, and bered at the towne, and the [company] of the Clarkes wher ther syngyng, and ther was [a great] dener boyth to ryche and the powre.

The xvj day of Aprell rod thrugh London in a c[ar], a woman with a bannor pentyd with (a) yong damsell and a woman, with a carde in the woman('s) hand cardyng her mayd nakyd pentyd, the wyche she left butt lytyll skyn of her, and a-bowt her masters[a] neke a card hangyng downe; for thys ponyssment her masters[a] had for her; and she was cared unto her owne dore in a care, and the(re) was a proclamasyon by on of the bedylles of her shamful ded-dohyng, [of] the wyche the damsell ys lyke to dee.

The xxiij day of Aprell, the wyche was sant Jorge day, the Kyng('s) grace, behyng at Westmynster at ys plase, dyd where[b] ys robes of the garter, and the yong yerle of Warwyke beyryng of the kynges sword afor hym thrugh the halle unto the chapell; and ys grase dyd offer, and the resyduw . . . .

. . . .

evyngsong, and w . . . Kynges grace dyd chuysse in the sted of the [earl of Som]ersett the yerle of Westmorland, and sir Andrew [Dudley,] captayne of Gynes, was chosen of the garter the . .

The xxx day of Aprell was proclamyd un . . . parlementt that no man shuld nott in-gratt or in-g[ross] any maner of vetall commynge to the feyre after the furst day of May; and that no man shuld [put] ther money unto usery for gaynes nor pr[ivy] exchangyng of gold or sylver; and that no yn, [tavarn,] nor berehowse, but they must be bune in a coynys[ance[c] to] kepe good rulle and honeste; and the sam maner and that . . . ay that no man shuld feythe[d] in any chyrche or chyr[chyards] apon the payne ther-of; the acts be in fulle sthrenght—the morow after May-day, the vj king Edward vj[th].

The sam day the Kynges grase removyd from Westmynster unto Grenwyche at viij a-cloke in the mornyng.

[a] mistress.   [b] wear.   [c] bound in a recognisance.   [d] fight.

The sam day was sessyons at Nugatt for theyfes, and a cott-purs spessyally was for one James [Ellys] the grett pykpurs and cutt-purs that ever [was ar-]raynyd, for ther was never a presun and the Towr[a] but he had byne in them,—the vj king Edward vj[th].

The sam day was bornyd at the Towre-hylle at after[noon] vij mon and viij maymed and lyke to dee, and alle was by takyng [ill] heyde and by beytyng of gunpowder in a morter, and by stryk[ing] of fyre, that a sparke of fyre fell in-tho the powder, and so alle f[ired] . . .

The ij day of May was a proclamasyon for haledaye[s and] fastyng days to be observyd and kept, and alle othur fe[asts;] and for korears[b] and lethers sellers and tynkares, and pe[dlars.]

The sam day was hangyd at Tyborne ix fello[ns.]

The iij day of May was a proclamasyon how Gaskyn wyne shuld be sold at viij[d]. the galon; a barelle of alle at iij[s]. viij[d].: a barelle of dobulle bere at iij[s]. viij[d].; thre-holpeny bere the barelle iij[s].; syngyll bere the barelle ij[s].; and no no dobulle dobulle alle, nor dobulle dobulle no more be callyd no more dobulle dobulle.

.   .   .   .   tyme callyd Jehesus . . . a penon of armes and a cote . . . blake, and with ij dosen of skochyons . . .

The xij day of May the Kynges grace [rode through] Grenwyche Parke unto Blake-heth, with ys ga[rd with bows] and arowes, and in ther jerkenes and dobeletes. [The King's] grase ran at the ryng, and odur lordes and kn[yghts.]

The xiiij day of May my lord marqwes [of Northampton's] men of armes did muster in More felds . . . compeny and grett horssys, and a trompett blow . . . nombur of a C. men of armes and welle h[arnessed.]

The xvj day of May the Kyngs grace [rode into the said] parke for to se the goodly muster of ys [men] of armes, and every lord('s) men; severall [trumpets] bloghyng a-for ther men, and ther standards, and ther cottes in brodery of yche lords colers, and ther speyres coloryd lyke, and ther fott-men.

        [a] *i. e.* except the Tower of London.   [b] curriers.

The furst the kynges pensyonars, the lord Bray ther captayn, and the kyng's grett baner [of arms] borne of-fore of damaske, blue and red, and the trumpeters blohyng, and the pensyonars in goodly a[rray, and] in harnes from tope to the to, and goodly basses of cotes, and ther men in lyke colers of cloth.

The ij my lord Tresorer's men of armes, a whytt standard with faucon of gold, cotes whyt and red.

The iij my lord Grant Master, with men of armes, ys standard of red damaske, a whyt lyon sylver, crounyd gold, and with ragyd stayffes; cotes alle blake wellevet in-brodery the alff, and th'odur cloth blake in-brodery whyt and red.

The Duke of Soffoke, with ys men of armes, and ys standard a unycorne sylver armyn in a sune-beme gold, whyt and morrey, and ys penselles.

[The vth, the lord Privy Seal his men of arms; his standard of three colours, a whyt goat, the standard powdered with escallop shells; his coat white and red in-brodery, and pensils of the same.]

[The vj, the lord] Grett Chamburlayn, [marqwes of Northampton; his] standard yelow and blakke, a mayden hed [crowned gold; his coats] yelow welvet the alffe ys men, and th'odur [half cloth] and fott men in yelow welvet, and pensels.

The vii, Master of the Horse, Warwyke, ys men of [arms; his] gyttun a red damask, whyt lyon,[a] crounyd gold, [and pow]deryd with rag(ged) stayffes of sylver, and pensells.

The viij, the yerlle of Rottland with ys men of armes; [his] standard of yelow and bluw with pekoke in [pride] gold, and pensells with a pecoke; cottes bluw in-brod[ery].

The ix, the yerlle of Huntyngtun, with ys men; hys standard a babyon,[b] cottes bluw brodered [velvet;] the penselles with bulles hed, crone [c] a-bowt ys neke.

The x, the yerle of Penbroke ys men of armes; ys coler of hys standard of iij collers, red, whyt, and bluw, and a gren dragon with a arme in ys mowth; and penselles.

[a] *Read* his guidon of red damask bearing a white lion.   [b] baboon.   [c] crown.

· The xj, the lord Admerall with ys men of armes; hys gytton the crosse of sant Gorge blake, with a ankur of sylver, cottes blake, and brodered with whyt.

The xij, the lord chamburlayn Darcy ys men of armes; ys standard a mayden with a flowre in her hand; cotes red broderd with whytt; and penselles.

The xiij, the lord Cobham with ys men of armes, and ys stand-ard whyt and blake, and a Sarsunhed[a] in [it;] ys cotes blake gardyd with whytt; and penselles.

· [The xiiij, master treasurer Cheny, lord warden of the cinque ports; his guydon a red cross, and half a rose in a sun-beam black;] spers and pensells and alle companys.

The xxj day of May was a cart-lode [of befe] forfett be cause he wold nott selle ytt [according to the] proclamasyon was pro-clamyd,—the vj king [Edward the vj[th].]

The xxvj day of May came in to Fa[nchurch] parryche a goodly May-polle as youe h[ave seen. It was] pentyd whyt and gren, and ther the men and [women did] wher a-bowt ther neke bald-rykes [of white and] gren, the gyant, the mores-danse, and the . . . had a castylle in the myd with pensels, and . . plasys of sylke and gylded; and the sam [day the] lord mayre by conselle causyd yt to be [taken] done and broken, for I have not sene . . .

The vij day of Juin the duke of Northumberland and dyvers of the kynges consell sat at yeld-hall [to hear] serten causys, and toke up my lord mayre and [his] brodurne for vetell, because he lokyd not to yt, and for sellyng of the sam, and odur causys.

The xj day of Juin cam rydyng to London my lade Mare[b] grase through London unto Saynt Johns with a goodly compeny of gentyll men and gentyll women.

The xiij day of Juin rod thrugh London unto the Towre warffe my lade Mare grase, the kynges syster, and toke her barge to Grenwyche the kynges courte, and so cam agayn at vj a-cloke

---

[a] Saracen's head.   [b] Mary's.

at nyght, and so landyd at the Towre, and so unto Saynt Johns beyond Smyth-feld.

The **xv** day of Juin was bered Baptyst Borow the melener with-owt Crepull-gatte in saynt Gylles' parryche, with a penon, a cote armur, and a harold, and with xxiij stayffes-torches, and so xxiij pore men bere them, and many mornars in blake; and the compeny of the Clarkes wher ther, and ys plase was hangyd with blake, and armes vj dosen.

[The **xvj** of June the duke of Northumberland took horse at five of the clock in the morning, to look after the Marches towards Scotland, of which he was constituted lord Warden, with a] compeny of lords and knyghts [to bring him on his] way of his jornay,—the vj kyng Edward the vj[th].

The **xvij** of Juin ther wher sett on the pelore [a man and] a woman; the woman boythe [a] a pesse of mottun [and when she] had ytt, she toke a pesse of a tylle [b] and frust [c] yt [into the] myds of the mottun, and she sayd that she had ytt of b[utcher, and would ha]ve ym punnyssyd; for ytt was hangyd over [her head in ?] the pelore, and so there wher they sett boythe . . .

The **xxv** day of Juin was drownyd vj men from Grenwyche by a grett botte [d] of bere in the . . . of sayntt Kateryns, and thay wher take up on the . . after, and was cared by the serjant of the amr . . and bered in saynt Towllys [e] ender chyrche yerd in S[outhwark.]

The **xxvij** day of Juin the Kyng's mageste removed from Grenwyche by water unto Pottney, and ther [he] toke ys horsse unto Hamtun cowrte one ys progres, and ther lyvyng ther x days, and so to Ottland, and to Gy[lford.]

The furst day of July ther was a man and a woman on the pelere in Chepe-syd; the man sold potts of straberries, the whyche the pott was nott alff fulle, but fyllyd with forne; [f] the man nam ys Grege; sum-tyme he con[terfeited] ym selffe a profett, for he was taken for [it, and] sett by the pelere in Sowthwarke.

The **xj** day of July hangyd one James Ellys, the grett pykke-

---

[a] bought.   [b] tile.   [c] thrust.   [d] boat.   [e] St. Olave's.   [f] fern.

purs that ever was, and cutt-purs, and vij more for theyfft, at Tyburne.

The xij day of July was bered ser Robartt Do[rmer] knyght, a grett shepe-master in Oxford-shyre, with standard and a penon of armes, and ys cot and target, and crest, and elmett, and mantylls, and vj dossen of skochyons.

. . . .

. . . . . . the mornyng with-owt syngyng butt . . the clarke, and with-owtt any more serves done.

The xv day of July was wypyd [a] a yong man and ij women for vyssyones and synes; and the [woman] she was putt on the pelorie, for she wold [have] poysenyd her husband, for the same woman [permitted] her servand to com in to here.

The xvj day of July was bered master [Cowper's] wyff, behyng the shreyffe of London, with [as great funeral] as ever was on [b] a shreyff('s) wyff; doyctur Kyrkman dyd pryche there for her.

The xxij day of Julij was bered master . . porvear of wyne for the kyng, the wych was warden of the Fysmongers, and he fell in a . . at the berehyng of master Cowper('s) wyff, and cared unto hys brodur('s) howse hard by, and was cared [to the] paryche of saynt Marten organes, wher he . . .

The furst day of August was chossen the shreyffe of London, master *(blank)* Grymes, clothworker, dwellyng in saynt Laurans lane; and the vj day of August he was dysmyssyd of the shreyff-shyp; and in ys sted was chossen Thomas Clayton, baker, the wyche master Grymes gayff for ys fyne ij C lb.

The x day of August was bered masters Basseley [c] Cowper, late the wyff of master Hontley, haburdassher, late shreyff of London, and after the wyff of master Towllys, lat alderman and shreyffe of thys nobull cete of London,—the vj kyng Edward the vj[th].

[The same day were three dolphins taken up between Woolwich and Greenwich. One was sent] to the courte to the kynge, and the [others were sold in Fish] strette to them that wold by them.

[a] whipped.   [b] *i. e.* for.   [c] *i. e.* mistress Basilia.

The iij day of August was ther born [in Oxford]shyre, at a towne callyd Myddylltun Stonny [eleven miles] from Oxford, dwellynge at the syne of the Egyll, was the good wyff of the howsse deleverd of a chyld be-gotten of her late hosband of John [Kenner] of the towne of Myddylltun Stonny late dyssessed, . . . forme and shape as youe have sene and hard, and boyth the for parts and the hynder partes of the said . . . sam chylderyn havyng ij heds, ij bodys, iiij armes, [iiij] hands, with one bely, on navyll, one fondamentt at [which] they voyd both uryne and ordure; and then thay have [ij] leges with ij fett, one syd, and on the odur syd, on leg [with] ij fette havyng butt ix tooys—monstrus!

The xv day of August was dysmyssed of the shreyfshype master Thomas Clayton, baker, and for hym was chosen master John Browne, mercer, the wyche was the [son?] of sir Wylliam Browne, and late mere of London, the wych [sir] Wylliam Browne ded mer,[a] and for hym was chosen [to serve] owt ys tyme sir John Tate, behyng mayre by the tyme of kyng Henry the vij, and bered at saynt Antonys; he dyd byld be-syd Freres Augustynns; and for fyne master Clayton payd ij C lb.,—the vj king Edward vj[th].

The xv day of August ded the nobull knyght ser [Anthony] Wynckfeld, comtroller of the kynges honorabull howsse, [and of] ys preve consell, and knyght of the honorabull order of the garter; the wyche he ded at Bednoll Grene, at yong sir John G[ates] plasse,—the vj king Edward vj[th]. And (in) ys sted master Cottun comtroller.

The xvj day of August was taken up a' Broke Warff iij grett fysses, and in odur plasys ij more, and sold in Fysh [strete] to them that wold by them.

.   .   .   .   .   .

clothes or carsseys and wollencloythe   .   .   butt onlly Blakewell-hall, a-pon forffett of all ther cloyth, but only Blakewell. . . .

 * died mayor.

The xviij day of August ded the dobull chelderyn, one, and the th'odur ded the xix day; I pray God have mersy!

The xix day of August ther was a mon on the [pillory] in Chepe for spykyng ᵃ agaynst the mayre and ys br[ethren.] .

The sam day was dysmyssed of the shreyffe[ship] master Browne, and in ys sted was choyssen master . . Maynard, marser, the wyche master Browne payd for ys . . .

The xxj day of August was the monumentt of ser Anthony Wynckfeld knyght, and controller of the kynges h[owsse], bered at Stepnay with a grett compeny of mornars, [with] prestes and clarkes syngyng, and a harold ys ys ᵇ M. . . . and so cared from Bednoll Gren over Mylle End; with ys standdard and a grett baner of armes, and [his helmet] and ys targett of the garter, and ys sword, crest a [bull] gold and sabull; and at the communyon dyd pryche [the vicar] of Sordyche, a Skott; and after a grett dener for all that cam; and alle ys gayreᶜ was offered, the elmett, and then the targett,ᵈ and then the sword, and the standard, and then ys baner of armes; and after dener yt was sett up over hym, the wyche a goodly shyth to ᵉ, and alle was offered to the prest,—the vj king Edward the vjᵗʰ.

The xxvjᵗʰ day of August ded ser Clementt Smyth knyght, and unkull unto owre soverayn lord and kyng Edward the vjᵗʰ, the wyche ser Clement mared qwyne Jane('s) syster; and he ded in Essex, at a plasse callyd Badow.

The v day of September was a proclamasyon that the bochers of London shuld selle beyffe and motun and velle, the best for 1ᵈ. fardyng the lb., and nekes and legs at iij fardynges the lb., and the best lam the [quarter] viijᵈ. and yff thay wyll nott thay to loysse ther fredom for ever and ever.

The vij day of September ded ser John Jas . . . by-syd Hunsdon, in Essex, and bered (blank)

The viij day of Seytember was bered master Pagm . . of the

ᵃ speaking.   ᵇ Sic MS.   ᶜ gear—his insignia.   ᵈ MS. gargett.   ᵉ sight too.

grencloth onto owre soverayne lord kyng Edw[ard, the] wyche
he gayff to evere clarke of ys xl shepe and odur   . . .   ij lb.
and a good geldyng, and to ys maydes xx shepe a-pesse.

The x day of September ther wher iij grett [fishes] dryffyn
up to London bryge with a grett nom[ber of] botts,[a] sum
with netts, sum with bylls, and sum with m . . ; and then they
retornyd downe a-gayne, and botts [after] them, be-tweyn iiij
and v of the cloke at after-none; for that same day was thurn-
deryng, and after grett [rain?] and after that they wher sene.

Ther wher hangyd ix women and ij men for the . . .   the
xij day of September.

The xix day of September was had to the Towre master
Wallay, authetur[b] and reseyver of Yorke-shyre.

The xxij day of September was bered in saynt Dennys parryche
in Fanchyrche strett my lade Ley.

The xx day of September was browth to the Towre of London
one of the north contrey.

The xxvj day of September was the lyttyll barke ager[c] goyng in
too Spayne, and as sche was goyng ther mette with her ij great
schypes of the Frensche kynges, and bere her down sore, and
stroke her great mast a-sunder as sche was in fyght; the great
barke ager followed her and rescwed her, and so over-came them
bothe, and browght them in-too the havne of Portysmouthe, and
ther they doo lye.

The xxx day of September the mayre and the aldermen, and the
new shreyffes, took barges at iij Cranes in the Vyntre, and so to
Westmynster hall, and ther they toke [their] hoyth[d] in the
escheker, and then thay came to de[ner]. Ther was a grett dener
as youe have sene; for ther wher mony gentyll men and women.

The ij day of October cam to London owte of Skottland ij
(*blank*) sunnes, late of the kyng of [Scots?] and dyd lye at the iiij

<hr>

[a] boats.   [b] auditor.   [c] *in side note*, barke hager.   [d] oath.

Swanes with-in Bysshope-gate, and ther they have ther coke [a] and ther cater, and dress . . . seylff.

The iiij and v day of October was the good bysshope of Dorham [b] whent unto Towre-hylle [to the] late monestery of whyt monkes, the wyche place ys gyffyn [c] unto ser Arthur Darcy knyght, and a-ffor the chyff justes [d] of England, Chamley, and master Gudderyke, and master Gosnolle and odur, master Coke and master Chydley.

The viij day of October was a proclamasyon that no man shuld not selle ther grett horssys.

The ix day of October was taken and brought thrugh and undur London bryge and so to Parys garden, and the next day up to Westmynster thes ij grett fysshes, the one the malle and the feymalle.

The xiiij day of October was depossyd of ys bysshope-pryke the good bysshope of Duram, and whent unto the Towre agayn, and so remanyth stylle.

. . . .

. . . . hangman . . . styll and . . . . owtt the mydylle of them bowth with . . . from one syd to the th'odur syd of the . . .

The xvij day of October was made vii serjants of the coyffe; at ix of the cloke they whent to Westmynster halle in ther gownes and hodes of morrey and russet, and ther servants in the sam colers, and ther was gyffyn a charge and othe by the kynges juges, and the old serjants. This done, they retornyd with the juges and the old serjants, and men of law, unto Gray-yn to dener, and mony of the . . . for ther was a grett fest, and my lord mayre and the [aldermen], and many a nobull man; and the new serjants gayf to [the judges], and the old serjants and men of the law, rynges of gold, every serjant gayff lyke ryngs; and after dener they whent unto Powlls, and so whent up the stepes, and so round the qwere and ther dyd they ther homage, and so

[a] cook.   [b] Cuthbert Tonstall.   [c] given.   [d] justice.

[came unto] the north-syd of Powlles and stod a-pone the stepes ontil iiij old serjantes came to-gether and feythchyd iiij [new], and broght them unto serten pelers, and left them, and then dyd feyched [a] the resedue unto the pelers; and ther was an oration red unto them by the old sergants, and so done they whent unto Gray('s) in; and her be[b] ther names, master [Brook] recorder, master Gaude, master Stamford, master Dyer, master Carrell.

The xxj day of October was the feneralle of a gentyll knyght, ser Thomas Jarmyn, the best housekeper in the contey of Suffoke, with ys standard and ys penone of armes, cot-armur, target, and sword, and skochyons; and he kept a godly chapel of syngyng men, for the contray have a gret loss of ys deth, as any contrey in England.

.   .   .   .

. . . . . . a grett bage off . . . and so ys here [c] was naylyd to the pelory . . by-syd syd of ym hangyd a bage of contu . . ys neke hangyd a-pone strynges a gret nombur . .

The xvj day of Dessember was stallyd at Wy[ndsor] therle of Westmerland and ser Andrew Dodley off the nobull order of the garter.

The xv day of Desember was (buried) good master Deyffenett, marchand-tayller of London, and . . warden of the Marchand-tayllers, and he gayff . . . gowne for men and women of rat coller[d] of . . . yerde, and he gayffe as mony blake gownes . . . and he gayff iij prest[e] gownes of blake, master (blank), master Samsum, and ys curett; and ther was the master and ys compeny in ther leverer,[f] and the compeny of Clarkes a xxx, and Samsum dyd pryche at (the) berehyng . . on the morowe affter dyd (unfinished.)

The xix day of Desember was bered master John Semer, the eldest sune unto the duke of Somersett latt dyssesyd, and bered at the hospetall of Savoy, and ther was a dolle.

The xxj day of Desember rod to Tyborne to be hangyd for a robery done on Honsley heth, iij talmen and a lake.[g]

[a] Sic MS.   [b] MS. by.   [c] ear.   [d] colour.   [e] priests.   [f] livery.   [g] lacquey.

The xxiij day of Desember the Kynges grace removyd from Westmynster unto Grenwyche to kepe ys Crystymas, and so he begane to kepe Halle, and ys grasse had a lord of myss-rulle, keepyng goodly pastyme, for ys grace('s) plesur, and with alle passtyme as have bene sene.

.   .   .   .

.   .   .   . chylderyn of hospetalle to . . . chylderyn men-kyns and women in fry[se, and the] boysse red cape skotys,[a] and every boy a pe . . ; and master Maynard the shreyff had a lord of [misrule, and] the mores dansse, with a good compeny.

The iiij day of January was bered master Robyn, alderman of London, dwellyng in Marke lane, and [buried at] Barkyng chyrche, and the strett hangyd with blake [and the ch]erche and with armes, and ther was a harold beyryng [his cote] armur and with iij penons of armes; and ther were the lord mere and the althermen at ys beryng, and ther [did] pryche doctur Borne, and ther was the compeny of [the fe]lowshyp of the Clarkes, and ther was gret compeny of morners, and he gayff a grett meyne of gownes . . . . . . ley for men to the nombur, and affter they whent to d[ener, for] thys was a-ffor none.

The sam day a-ffor non landyd at the Towre w[harf] the Kynges lord of myssrulle, and ther mett with hym the [Shreyffes] lord of myssrulle with ys men, and every on havyng a reby[nd of blue] and whytt a-bowt ther nekes, and then ys trumpet, [druws,] mores dansse, and tabrett, and he toke a swaerd and bare yt a-fore the kynges lord of myssrulle, for the lord was gorgyusly a[rrayed in] purprelle welvet furyd with armyn, and ys robe braded with spangulls of selver full; and a-bowt ym syngers, and a-for hym on gret horses and in cottes and clokes of . . . in-brodered with gold and with balderykes a-bowt ther nekes, whytt and blue sarsenets, and chynes of gold, and the rest of ys servands in bluw gardyd with whytt, and next a-for ys consell in bluw taffata and ther capes of whytt . . . ys trumpeters, taburs, drumes, and flutes and fulles [b] and ys mores dansse, gunes, mores-pykes, bagpypes; and ys mass [c] . . and ys gayllers [d]

[a] Scotch caps ?   [b] fools.   [c] messengers ?   [d] jailers.

with pelere, stokes,[a] and ys axe, gyffes,[b] and boltes, sum fast by
the leges and sum by the nekes, and so rod thrugh Marke lane,
and so thrugh Grasyus strett and Cornhylle; and   .   .   .

.   .   .   .   .   .

trompet blohyng, makyng a proclamasyon   . . .   and so the
kyng('s) lord was cared from the   . . .   skaffold; and after
the shreyffes lord; and the kynges [lord gave] the shreyffes lord a
gowne with gold and sylver, and a[non] after he knelyd downe
and he toke a sword and gayff [him three?] strokes and mad ym
knyght, and after thay dran[k one to t]hodur a-pon the skaffold,
and ys cofferer castyng gold and sylver in every plase as they
rod, and [after his co]ffrer ys carege with hys cloth-saykes on
horsseback; [and so went] a-bowt Chepe, with ys gayllers and ys
presonars; and [afterwards] the ij lordes toke ther horssys and
rode unto my [lord] mare to dener; and after he came bake thrugh
[Chepe] to the crosse, and so done [c] Wodstrett unto the shreyffes
[house for] more (than) alff a nore,[d] and so forthe the Olde Jury
and Lo[ndon wall] unto my lord tresorer('s) plasse, and ther they
had a [great] banket the spasse of alff a nore; and so don to Bysshopgate and to Ledenhall and thrughe Fanchyrche strett, and so
to the Towre warffe; and the shreyff('s) lord gohyng with hym
with torche-lyght, and ther the kynges lord toke ys pynnes[e] with
a grett shott of gonnes, and so the shreyffes lord toke ys leyff of
ym and cam home merele [f] with ys mores dansse danssyng and so
forth.

The x day of January was the monyth myn[g] of ser (Thomas[h])
Wynsor knyght, in the contey of (Buckingham?), with a harold
and ys standard, ys penon of armes and ys cot armur, ys elmet,
target, and sword, mantylles, and the crest a whyt hartes ede,[i]
hornes gold; and he was elldest sune unto the lord Wynsor and
here,[k] and mared my lord Dakurs of the North doythur—the vj
king Edward vj.

The xiij day of January was put apon the pelore a woman for

she wold have poyssoned her husband dwellyng with-in the Powlles
bake-howsse, and the xiiij day she was wyped at a cart harsse,
and nakyd up-ward, and the xviij day folowhyng she was a-gayne
apone the pelere for slanderyng.

.   .   .   .

.   .   .   with the compeny of the   .   .

The xxj day of the sam monyth rod unto [Tyburn] ij felons, serten was for kyllyng of a gentylman [of] ser Edward North knyght, in
Charturhowsse cheyr[ch yard?]—the vij yere of kyng Edward the vj.

The iij day of January was cared from the Marshalleshe unto
saynt Thomas of Wateryng a talman, and whent thedur with
the rope a-bowt ys neke, and so he hangyd a whylle, and the
rope burst, and a whylle after and then th[ey went f]or a-nodur
rope, and so lyke-wyss he burst yt [and fell] to the grond, and so
he skapyd with ys lyffe.

The vj day of Feybruary cam to London and rod thrughe London my lade Mare('s) grasse, the kynges syster, with a grett nombur of lordes and knyghtes, and her grace a grett [number] of lades
and jentyll women and jentyll men to the [number] of ij honderd
horsse, and thrug Chepe unto Saynt J[ohn's].

The ix day of January a be-tweyn vij and viij of the cloke in the
evenyng felle downe the grett stepull [of] Waltham in Essex, and
the qwyre felle downe, and alle the gr[eat] belles to the grond, and
myche of the chyrche.

The x day of January a rod my lade Mare('s) grasse from Saynt
[John's] and thrugh Flettstrett unto the kyng at Westmynster,
with a grett nombur of lords and knyghtes, and alle the [great]
women lades, the duches of Suffoke and Northumberland, my lade
marqwes of Northamptun, and lade marqwes of Wynchester, and
the contes of Bedfford, and the contes of Shrowsbere, and the
contes of Arundelle, my lade Clynton, my lade Browne and
Browne, b and many mo lades and gentyllwomen; and at the
oter c gatt ther mett her my lord of Suffoke and my lord of

---

a These passages probably both belong to the month of February, to which Strype
has assigned them.   b Sic in MS.   c onter.

Northumberland, my lord of Wynchester, my lord of Bedfford, and therle of Shrusbery, the therle of Arundell, my lord Chamburlayn, my lord Admerolle, and a gret number of knyghtes and gentyllmen, and so up unto the chambur of pressens, and ther the Kynges grace mett her and salutyd her.

. . . owyn a-pon payne of presunmentt and a grett [penalty, as ye] shalle fynd in the actes in secund yere of kyng . . . the perlementt tyme of the sayd yere, and nott to be . . . plasse as taverns, alle-howses, ines, or wher . . . for cummers and gestes, and has commandyd unto alle shreyffes and baylles, constabulls, justes of pesse,[a] or any . . thay shall se truthe (and) justys as thay shalle [inform the] kyng and ys consell, and bryng them to pressun[b] of . . . sun or poyssuns as be the offenders ther off for . . . her of odur.

The sam day was sett on the pelere a man that dyd [set on a] man for to kylle a honest man that he myghtt have ys [wife,] and yett dyd he kepe her and spend ys goodes a-ffore, and [could not] be contentt with that, and so ys ere was nayled to the pelore.

The xvij day of February dyd ryd in a care th[rough London] Clarkes wyff a goldsmyth, at the syne of the Angell in Chepe, and . . . . . mayd and a-nodur, the ij wher[c] ray bodes on ther hedes, for . . .

The xxiiij day of Feybruarii was bered ser Wylliam Sydnay knyght, in the contey of Kentt, at ys plasse callyd Penthurst, with ij harolds of armes, with ys standard, and ys baner of armes, and ys cote armur, and iiij baner-rolles of armes, ys target, and mantyll, and helmett, and the crest a bluw porpyntyn,[d] and vij dosen and di. skochyons; and ther wher mony mornars, and ther wher a grett dolle of mony.

The xvij day of Feybruary th'erle of Penbroke cam rydyng in to London with iij C. horsse, and a-ffor hym a C. gentyllmen with

[a] justices of peace. [b] prison. [c] wore. [d] porcupine.

chenes of gold, alle in bluw cloth, playne, with a bage on ther slewe [a] a dragon,[b] and so to Benard Castyll, and ther he leyff. [c]

. . . .

The xxiiij day of the sam monyth . . . bowtt London.

The xxv day of Feybruary rod in a care . . . . ame a wyswer[d] and a prest [e] wyff and a-nodur bowdry; the ij women dyd wher [f] ray hods; the [priest's] wyff was persun Whyt here wyff of saynt Alphes.

The furst day of Marche be-gane the parlement [at] the kynges plasse within the courte, and the morowe [removed] to Westmynster.

The iiij day of Marche rod in a care on [g] of the bedylls of the begers,[h] for bowdry, dwellyn in saynt Bathellmuw lane be-syd my lord mayre.

The xxiiij day of February was bered in saynt Katheryns Colman master Hare [i] Webe sqwyre, and porter of the Towre, with a harold, and ys penon of armes, and ys cot armur, and with iiij dossen of skochyons.

The xxij day of Marche was bered master Syssylle sqwyr, and gentyllman of the kynges robes, and the father unto sir Hare [i] Sysselle knyght, and bered at saynt Margates at Westmynster, with cote armur and ys penon of armes; and he had a-nodur cote armur, and a penon, was mad and cared in-to the contrey wher he dwelt.

The sam day, wyche was the xxij day of Marche, was bered master John Heth, dwellyng in Fanchyrche strett, and ther whent a-ffor hym a C. chylderyn of Gray-freres boys [k] and gyrlles, ij and ij (to-)gether, and he gayff them shurts and smokes, and gyrdulls, and moketors; and after thay had wy.. and fygs and good alle, and ther wher a grett dener; and ther wher the cumpene of Panters, and the Clarkes, and ys cumpony had xx[s]. to make mere [l] with-alle at the tavarne.

---

[a] badge on their sleeve.   [b] wyver, *marginal note.*   [c] lives.
[d] wizard.   [e] priest's.   [f] wear.   [g] one.   [h] beggars.   [i] Harry.
[k] boyth *in MS.* The children of Christ's Hospital.   [l] merry.

.   .   .   .

The xvij day of Marche cam thrugh London,[from]Algatt, master
Maynard, the shreyff of London, wyth * a standard and dromes, and
after gyants bòyth [great and] smalle, and then hobe-horsses, and
- after them the g[. . .], and affter grett horsses and men in
cotes of velvet, [with chains] of gold a-bowt ther nekes, and men in
harnes; [and then] the mores dansse, and then mony mynsterels;
and af[ter came] the sergantes and yomen on horsse-bake with re-
byns [b] [of green] and whytt abowtt ther nekes, and then my lo[rd
justice ?] late behyng lord of myssrulle, rod gorgyusly [in cloth ?]
of gold, and with cheynes of gold abowt ys neke, with hand fulle of
rynges of grett waluw; the w . . . serjants rod in cotes of velvet
with cheynes of [gold;] and then cam the dullo [c] and a sawden, [d]
and then [a priest ?] shreyffyng [e] Jake-of-lent on horss-bake, and a
do[ctor] ys fezyssyoun, and then Jake-of-lent('s) wyff brow[ght him]
ys fessyssyons and bad save ys lyff, and he shuld [give him] a
thowsand li. for ys labur; and then cam the carte with the wyrth
hangyd with cloth of gold, and fulle of ban[ners] and mynsterels
plahyng and syngyng; and a-for rod master Coke, in a cot of
velvett with a cheyn off gold, and with flowres.

The iij day of Aprell whent unto saynt Mare spytyll, onto the
sermon, alle the masters and rulars, and skollmasturs and mastores, [f] and alle the chylderyn, boyth men and vomen chylderyn,
alle in blue [g] cotes, and wenssys [h] in blue frokes and with skoychyons in-brodered on ther slevys with the armes of London, and
red capes, [i] and so ij and ij (to-)geder, and evere man in ys plasse
and offes; [k] and so at the Spyttylle (a scaffold) was mad of tymbur,
and covered with canves, and setes on a-boyff a-nodur for alle the
chylderyn syttyn on a-boyff a-nodur lyke stepes, and after thrug
London . . .

[The xj day of April the King removed from Westminster by
water to Greenwich; and passed by the] Towre, and ther wher a
[great shot of guns and] chamburs, and all the shypes shott of

* wyrt *in MS*.   [b] ribands.   [c] devil.   [d] soudan, *i. e.* sultan, or Turk.
[e] shriving.   [f] mistresses.   [g] plue *in MS*.   [h] wenches.   [i] caps.   [k] office.
CAMD. SOC.   F+

gonnes [all the way to] Ratclyff, and ther the iij shypes that was
rygyng [a] [there, appointed to gó] to the Nuw-fouland,[b] and the ij
pennons [c] shott gunnes and chamburs a grett nombur.

The **xvij** day of Aprell cam a commondement [down] unto
London that alle the cherche-wardens of London [should go] unto
Gyldhall a-ffor the commyssyonars, the bysshope of London,
and my lord mare, and master Chamlay the kynges cheyff justes,
[and that] thay shuld bryng a truw sertycatt [d] of alle the chy[rch
goods,] juelles and monay, and belles, and alle copes and ornaments that [belong] to the chyrche.

The **xxv** day of Aprell wher hangyd at saynt T[homas] of
Wateryng, of saynt Marke day, vj feylons ; iiij [were] hangyd with
ij altars [e] a-pese,[f] and the ij wher pore (?) with one.

[*Having discontinued his diary during May, and left half a page blank, Machyn
subsequently inserted this memorandum:* " The stylle that ys sett forth by owre nuw
kyng Phelype and Mare by the grace of God kyng and quene of England, Franse,
Napuls, Jerusalem, and Ierland, deffenders of the fayth, and prynsses of Spayne and
Ses[ily,] archesdukes of Austherege, dukes of Melayn, Burgundye, and Brabantt,
contes of Haspurge, Flandurs, and Tyrole."

The **vj** day of Junii dyd falle downe a . . . a howsse in
saynt Clement lane be-syde . . . ther the good-man of the
howse was [killed,] and the good-wyff sore hurt, and the mayd.
The man's nam was (*blank*) Benbryke ; a sad [accident !]

The **xxx** day of Junii whas sett a post hard [by the] Standard in
Chep, and a yonge felowe ted [g] to the post, [with a collar] of yron
a-bowt ys neke, and a-nodur to the post with [a chain; and] ij men
with ij whypes wypyng [h] hym a-bowt the post, [for pretended]
vessyones,[i] and for obbrobyus and sedyssyus wordes—the vij
[king Edw. vj.]

The **ij** day of July was bond [k] unto the sam post . . man
for stryffyng at the condytt, with the sam coler [l] [about] ys neke,
al the day long, and ij rods ted [g] to the tope of . . for yt was
a-pon a Sonday,—the vij king Edward vj[t].

---

[a] rigging. *Strype has erroneously* riding.   [b] Newfoundland.   [c] pinnaces.
[d] certificate.   [e] halters.   [f] a piece.   [g] tied.   [h] whipping.   [i] visions.
[k] bound.   [l] collar.

The vj day of July, as they say, dessessyd the nobull Kyng Edward the vj. and the vij yere of ys rayne, and sune and here to the nobull kyng Henry the viij; and he was poyssoned, as evere body says, wher now, thanke be unto God, ther be mony of the false trayturs browt to ther end, and j trust in God that mor shall folow as thay may be spyd owt.

The vij day of July was a proclamasyon that all pentiss * shuld be no lower but x fott, and alle preve lyghts damnyd.

The sam day was a nold man sett on the pelere for conterffett falles wrytynges.

[The same day there came to the Tower the lord Treasurer, the earl of Shrewsbury, and the lord Admiral, with others; and there they discharged sir James Croft of the] constabullshype of the Towre, and ther thay put [in the said lord] Admerall, and toke ys othe and charge of the Towre, and [the morrow] after he convayd in-to all plasys of the Towre and . . . grett gunnes, as the Whyt Towre on hee.

The ix day of July was sworne unto the qwen Jane alle the hed offesers and the gard as qwen of England . . . doythur of the duke of Suffoke, and servyd as qwen of . . .

The x day of July was reseyvyd in to the Towre [the Queen Jane] with a grett compeny of lords and nobulls of . . . . . after the qwen, and the duches of Suffoke her mother, bering her trayn, with mony lades, and ther was a shot of gunnes and chamburs has nott be sene oft be-tweyn iiij and v of [the clock]; by vj of the cloke be-gane the proclamasyon the same [after-]non (of) qwen Jane with ij harold(s) and a trompet blohyng, [declaring] that my lade Mare was unlafully be-gotten, and so [went through] Chepe to Fletstrett, proclamyng qwen Jane; and ther was a yong man taken that tym for spykyng of serten wordes of qwen Mare, that she had the ryght tytle.

The xj day of July, at viij of the cloke in the mornyng, the

* pentices.

-yonge man for spykyng was sett on the pelere, and boyth ys heres[a] cutt off; for ther was a harold, and a trompeter blohyng; and [in-]contenent he was taken downe, and cared to the [Counter]; and the same day was the yong man('s) master dwellyng [at] saint John('s) hed, ys nam was Sandur Onyone, and a-nodur, master Owen a gone-maker at Lundun bryge, drounyd, dwellyng at Ludgatt.

The xij day [of] July by nyght, was cared to the Towre iij carts [full of all] maner of ordenans, as gret gune and smalle, bowes, bylls, speres, mores-pykes, arnes,[b] arowes, gunpowther, and wetelle,[c] monay, tentes, and all maner of ordenans, gunstones a gret nombur, and a grett nombur of men of armes; and yt had been for a gret army toward Cambryge; and ij days after the duke, and dyvers lordes and knyghts whent with him, and mony gentylmen and gonnars, and mony men of the gard and men of armes toward my lade Mare grace, to destroye here grace, and so to Bury,[d] and alle was agayns ym-seylff, for ys men forsok hym.

. . . . and of dyvers maters, and so in dyvers plases . . . . contres was her grace proclamyd quen of [England.]

The same day, wyche was the xvj day of July, was Raff Warren knyght, mercer and alderman, and twysse [lord mayor of] London, and marchand of the stapull and marchand ven[turer, buried] with standard and v pennons of armes, a cott armur, . . . a helmett, mantyll and crest, and sword, and a xij dosen of schochyons; and ther wher my lord mere morner . . . . . berer, the iiij sqyre mornars, and mony aldermen at ys beryng; [there] wher mony mornars in blake, and in blake cotes, and ther wher L. gownes gyffyn unto L. men, of rats coler, of a m . . . a yerd; and ther dynyd my lord mayre and mony aldermen, [and] ther wher a gret dener as I have sene.

---

[a] ears.　　　[b] harness (*i. e.* armour).　　　[c] victuals.　　　[d] bere *in MS.*

The xix day of July was qwene Mare proclamyd qwene of England, France, and Yrland, and alle domy(ni)ons, [as the] syster
of the late kyng Edward the vj. and doythur unto the nobull
kyng Henry the viij. be-twyn v and vj of the cloke at nyght, and
ther wher at proclamasyon iiij trumpeters and ij harold(s) of
armes, and the erle of Arundell, the erle of Shrossbery, th'erle
Penbroke, my lord Tressorer, my lord of Preveselle, my lord Cobham, my lord Warden, master Masun, and my lord Mare, and dyvers odur nobull men; and thys was done at the crosse in Chepe, and
from that plasse thay whent unto Powlls and ther was *Te Deum
Laudamus*, with song, and the organes playhyng, and all the belles
ryngyng thrugh London, and bone-fyres, and tabuls in evere
strett, and wyne and bere and alle, and evere strett full of bon-
fyres, and ther was money cast a-way.

The xxj day of July was taken in Cambryg the duke of North-
umberland, with dyvers lordes and knyghts; and that day qwen
Mare was proclamyd in Cambryg, and [in-]contenent thrugh
England.

.   .   .   .

The xxix day of July was a felow s[et in the pillory] for spykyng
agaynst the good qwen Mare.

The sam day cam rydyng thrugh London my lade Elssabeth
grace, and thrugh Fletstrett, and so to my [lord of] Somersett('s)
place that was, and yt ys my lade grasys [place; attended] with
ij M^l. horse, with speres and bowes and gunes, and odur . . .
. . . and spesyall sir John Wylliam, sir John Brygys, master
Chamb[urlain,] all in gren gardyd with whytt welvett saten taf-
faty . . .

The xxv day of July, the wyche was Saynt James, [there] cam
in-to London, and so to the Towre, serten traturs; the first was
doctur Sandes, a prest; and next hym ser Thomas Palmer, ser
Hare Gattes, ser John Gattes, ser Andrew Dudley, lord H[are
Dudley], lord Ambrose Dudlay, lord Hastynges, the erle of
Huntingdon, the erle of Warwyke, the duke of Northumber-

land [attended by] iiij M[l]. men be-syd the garde with gettenes [a] and trompeters, [and] with speres and gunnes to the Towre.

The xxvj day of July cam unto the Towre my lord marqwes of Northamton, by and my lord Robart Dudley, and the bysshop of London,[b] and ser Recherd Corbett; and after cam in to the Towre my lord cheyffe justes Chamley, the lord Montyguw, at v of the cloke at nyght.

The xxvij day of July the duke of Suffoke, maister [Cheke] the kynges scolmaster, maister Coke, (and) ser John Yorke, to the Towre.

The xxxj day of July was delevered owt of the Towre the duke of Suffoke; and the sam day rod thrugh London my lade Elssa-beth to Algatt, and so to the qwens grace her sester, with a M[l]. hors with a C. velvett cotes.

The sam tyme cam to the Flett the yerle of Ruttland and my lord Russell, in hold. The qwen('s) grace mad [sir Thomas [c]] Jar-nyngham vyce-chamburlayn and captayne of the garde, and ser Edward Hastyngs her grace mad ym the maister of the horsse the sam tym.

[The iij day of August the Queen came riding to London, and so to the Tower; making her entrance at Aldgate, which was hanged,] and a grett nombur of stremars ha[nging about the said gate;] and all the strett unto Ledynhalle and unto the [Tower were laid with] graffvell, and all the crafts of London stood [in a row, with] ther banars and stremars hangyd over ther heds. Her grace cam, and a-for her a M[l]. velvet cotes and [cloaks] in bro-dere, and the mar of London bare the mase, and the erle of Arundell bare the sworde, and all the trumpets [blowing]; and next her my lade Elssabeth, and next her the duches of Norffoke, and next her the marqwes [d] of Exseter, [and other] lades; and after her the aldermen, and then the gard with bowes and gaffy-lens, and all the reseduw departyd [at Aldgate] in gren and whyt,

---

[a] guidons.   [b] Nicholas Ridley.   [c] Thomas *erased in MS.*   [d] marchioness.

and red and whyt, and bluw and gren, to the nombur of iij M¹.
horse and speres and gaffelyns. ·

The fenerall, the iiij day of August, of my lade Browne, the
wyche she ded in chyld-bed; with a harold and iiij banars of
armes, and mony schochyons; and a gret dolle, and many mornars,
and a gret dener to the pore and ryche; the wyff of ser Antony Brown in Sussex.

The v day of August cam to the Towre doctur dene of Westmynster, master Cokes.

The sam day cam out of the Marsalsay the old bysshop of
London, Bonar, and dyvers bysshopes bryng hym home unto ys
plasse at Powlles; and doctur Cokes whent to the sam plasse in
the Marselsay that the bysshope was in.

The v day of August cam in to the Towre my lord Ferrys
by . . . . at ix of the cloke, and so whent he a-for the
consell, and so with-in a nowre he was delevered unto ser John
Gage, constabull of the Towre, and so he had the custody of my
lord for that tyme.

[The Queen released from prison the lord Courtenay, soon
after created earl] of Denshyre, and odur moo.

And the Qwene grace mad ser Edward Hastyngs master of
the horse, and ser Thomas Jernyngham vysse-chamburlayne
and captayn of the gard, and master Rochastur master controller; my lord marqwes of Wynchaster lord tresorer of England,
and dyvers odur offeserse, and dyvers odur.

The vj day of August cam in-to the Towre, from [Calais, ser]
Hare Dudley, that was gohyng in-to Franse.

The viij day of August was bered the nobull kyng Edward
the vj, and vij yere of ys rayne; and at ys bere[ing was] the
grettest mone mad for hym of ys deth [as ever] was hard or sene,
boyth of all sorts of pepull, wepyng and lamentyng; and furst
of alle whent a grett company of chylderyn in ther surples, and
clarkes syngyng, and then ys father('s) bedmen, and then ij harolds,
and then a standard with a dragon, and then a grett nombur of

ys servants in blake, and then anodur standard with a whyt grey-
hond, and then after a grett nombur of ys of[ficers,] and after
them comys mo harolds, and then a standard with the hed offesars
of ys howse; and then harolds, Norey bare the elmett and the
crest on horsbake, and then ys grett baner of armes in-brodery,
and with dyvers odur baners, and then cam rydyng maister Clarens-
sshuws with ys target, with ys garter, and ys sword, gorgyusly
and ryche, and after Garter with ys cotte armur in brodery, and
then mor [harolds] of armes; and then cam the charett with grett
horsses trapyd with velvet to the grond, and hevere[a] horse havyng
[a man] on ys bake in blake, and ever on[b] beyryng a banar-roll
[of] dyvers kynges armes, and with schochyon(s) on[c] ther horses,
and then the charett kovered with cloth of gold, and on the
[charett] lay on a pycture lyeng recheussly[d] with a crown of gold,
and a grett coler,[e] and ys septur in ys hand, lyheng in ys robes
[and the garter about his leg, and a coat in embroidery of gold;
about the corps were borne four banners, a banner of the order,
another of the red rose, another of queen Jane (Seymour), another of the queen's mother. After him went a goodly horse,
covered with cloth of gold unto the ground, and the master of the
horse, with a man of arms in armour, which] was offered, boyth
the man and the horsse. [There was set up a go]odly hersse in
Westmynster abbay with banar [-rolls] and pensells, and honge
with velvet a-bowt.

The sam day, the wyche was the viij day of August, cam to
London [the go]od yerle of Darbe, with iiij[xx] in cottes of velvet
and oder ij C. xviij yomen in a leveray, and so to Westmynster.

The ix day of August cam the bysshope of Wyncheaster[f] owt
of the Towre (conducted) by the yerle of Arundell to ys owen
parish of sant Mare Overeys, and from thens with my lord of
Arundell to dener to Bayth plasse.

The x day of Augùst was drounyd vij men at L[ondon] bryge by folij[a]; on was master Thomas of Brygys the leyff-[tenants] sune and heire, and iij gentyllmen more, be-syd odur; and one . . .

The xiij day (of) August dyd pryche at Powlles crosse doctur [Bourn] parsun of hehnger,[b] in Essex, the qwen('s) chaplen, and ther [was a] gret up-rore and showtyng at ys sermon, as yt [were] lyke madpepull, watt yonge pepell and woman [as] ever was hard, as herle-borle, and castyng up of capes[c]; [if] my lord mer and my lord Cortenay ad not ben ther, ther had bene grett myscheyff done.

The xvj day of August was a man sett on the pelere[d] for forgeng of falss letters in odur mens name.

The xvij day of August was mad a grett skaffold in Westmynster hall agaynst the morow, for the duke of Northumberland commyng to be raynyd,[e] with odur, as the marqwes of Northamton and the yerle of Warwyke.

The xviij day of August was reynyd[e] at Westmynster hall the marqwes of Northamton, and the duke, and th'erle of Warwyke, and so they wher condemnyd to be had to the place that thay cam fro, and from thens to be drane thrugh London onto Tyburne, and ther to be hangyd, and then to be cott[f] downe, and ther bowells to be brentt, and ther heds to be sett on London bryge and odur [places.]

[The xix day were arraigned at Westminster hall sir Andrew Dudley, sir John Gates, sir Harry] Gattes, ser Thomas Palmer, and cast [to be hanged and] quartered.

The sam day was a gret feyre[g] at Chelsay [beyond] Westmynster, and ther was dyvers howsses brent, [and] dyvers barnes with corne brent, to the nombur . . .

The xx day of August dyd pryche at Powlles crosse master Wattsun, chaplayn unto *(blank)*, and ther wher [present all the] craftes of London in ther best leveray, syttyng on formes, [every] craft by them-seylff, and my lord mere and the aldermen, and ij C. of [the guard,] to se no dysquyet done.

[a] folly.   [b] High Ongar.   [c] caps.   [d] pillory.   [e] arraigned.   [f] cut.   [g] fire.

CAMD. SOC.   G

The sam day was bered master Kyrtun, alderman and marchand tailler, and marchand of the stapull of Cales, a-for non.

The xxj of August was, by viij of the cloke in the mornyng, on the Towre hylle a-boythe[a] x M[l]. men and women for to have [seen] the execussyon of the duke of Northumberland, for the skaffold was mad rede,[b] and sand and straw was browth, and all the men [that] longest[c] to the Towre, as Hogston, Shordyche, Bow, Rat-clyff, Lymhouse, Sant Kateryns, and the waters[d] of the Towre, and the gard, and shyreyffs offesers, and evere man stand in order with ther holbardes, and lanes made, and the hangman was ther, and sodenly they wher commondyd to [depart].

And the sam tym after was send for my lord mer and the alder-men and cheyffest of the craftes in London, and dyvers of the con-sell, and ther was sed mas[e] a-for the Duke [and the rest] of the presonars.[f]

The xxj day of August was sett on the pelere[g] ij men, on a prest and a-nodur a barbur, and boyth ther herers[h] nayllyd to the pelere, the parsun of sant Alberowgh[i] with-in Bysshope-gate for hannus[k] wordes and sedyssus wordes aganst the qwen('s) magesty hygnes at the sermon at Powlles crosse, that was the Sonday the xiij day of August, and for the up-rore that was ther don. The prest . . . twys.

The xxj day of August was a proclamasyon, that no man shuld reson aganst her grases magesty and her conselle, dohyng the wyche she wyll doe to the honor of God and ys mother.

The xxiij day of August was the sam prest sett on the pelere agayne for mo w[ordes.]

The sam day be-gane the masse at sant Nicolas Colabay, goodly song in Laten, and tapurs, and [set on] the owtter,[l] and a crosse, in old Fysstrett.

Item, the next day a goodly masse songe [at] sant Necolas Wyllyms, in Laten, in Bredstrett.

[a] about.   [b] made ready.   [c] belong.   [d] waiters.   [e] mass was said.

[f] *Here follow some words erased, which appear to have been,* and a-for the consellors and the mare and alle odur cr.... and dyvers wher howslyng after the old fasyon, and kept the pa..   [g] pillory.   [h] ears.   [i] St. Ethelburga.   [k] heinous.   [l] altar.

The xxv day of August was bornyd the [Great] Hare,[a] the grettest shype in the world, and yt was pete and yff yt had plesyd God, at Wolwych, [by] neckclygens and for lake of over-syth; the furst y[ere of queen Mary.]

The xxviij day of August ded ser John [Haryngton] knyght, of Rottland-shyre, with-in Saynt Ellens, Bysshopgatt stret, and from that day that he ded tyll he was cared in-to ys contray, was mas and dirige evere day songe; and Monday the iiij day of September, [he] whent in-to the contray in a horse lytter, with ys stand-ard and ys penon of armes, and after ys horsse . . . . . with iiij pennons of armes borne a-bowt hym, and with a goodly helmet gylt, with targett, sword, and crest, and a x dosen of schochyons, and x dosen of pensells for a herse, and staff torchys, and a herse of wax, and a fere[b] mageste, and the walans[c] gylded and frynged, and so to Ware, and so (forwards.)

The vj day of September cam owt of the Towre my lord Fer-rys, my lord cheyff justys Chamlay,[d] and my lord Montyguw, unto the denes place, for ther satt the consell, and ther thay wher delevered and dyscharged of the Towre with a grett fyne.

The iij day of August, at Rychemond, was my lord Cortnay created the yerle of Denshyre of owre nobulle qwene Mare.

[The xij day of September the citizens began to adorn the city against the Queen's coronation; to hang the streets, and prepare pageants at] Fanchyrche and Grasse-chyrche and Leaden-hall, in Gracyus strett, and at condutt in Cornhyll, and [the great con-duit in] Chepe, at standard in Chepe, the crosse reparyd, [at] the lytyll coundytt, a pagantt in Powlles chyrche[-yard], a-nodur pagant and mony spechys, and Ludgat nuly reparyd, and mony chylderyn; [at the condy]tt in Flettstrett a pagantt, and nuwe trymmyd [very gorg]yously, and the strett hangyd, and plases for every cr[aft to stan]d seve(ral)ly, mad with tymber from evere cr[aft] ther standyng, and so to remane unto evere halle [for ev]er when they shall have nede for shyche dohyng.

[a] The Great Harry.   [b] fair.   [c] vallance.   [d] Sir Roger Cholmley.

The xxj day of September was the obseqwe of the baron of
Dudley ser John Dudley at Westmynster, the bake-syd of Sant
Margatts; and ther was at ys beryng prestes and clarkes syngyng
in Laten, the prest havyng a cope and the clarke havyng the hale-
water sprynkull in ys hand, and after a mornar baryng ys standard,
and after a-nodur beyryng ys gret baner of armes gold and sylver,
and a-nodur beyryng ys elmett, mantyll, and the crest a bluw lyon('s)
hed standyng a-pon a crowne of gold, and after a-nodur mornar
bayryng [his] targett, and a-nodur ys sword, and after cam master Somersett the harold bayryng ys cott armur of gold and selver,
and then the corse covered with cloth of gold to the grond, and iiij
of ys men beyryng hym, and ys armes hangyd a-pone the cloth of
gold, and xij men of ys servands bayryng xij stayffs torchys bornyng to the chyrche; and in the qwer was a hersse mad of tymbur
and covered with blake, and armes apon the blake, and after the
mornars a grett compene; and a-for the durge began, the harold
cam to the qwer dore and prayd for ys soll by ys stylle,[a] and so
began the durge song in Laten, all the lessons, and then the
harold prayd for a for masse, and so the masse songe in Laten;
and after ys helmet ofered, and cott and targatt, and after all
was endyd offered the standard and the baner of armes; and so
hom to dener, and ther was goodly ryngyng and a gret doll.

. . . .

The xxj day of September was a grett wache in . . . . . .
. . ser Edward Hastynges, the master of the horse, in sant
G[eorge's] on the banke a-bowt my lord of Wynchester('s); for
ther wher serten taken, and Sowthwarke w . . .

The xxiiij day of September dyd pryche master doctur Fecknam
at Powlles crosse, the Sonday a-for the qwuen('s) crounasyon; he
mad a godly sermon as was hard in that place. [b]

The xxviij day of September the Qwen('s) grace removed from
Sant James, and so to Whyt Hall, and ther her grace took her
barge unto the Towre, and ther all the craftes and the mare and
the aldermen in bargurs[c] with stremars and mynstrells, as trum-

[a] his style.   [b] i. e. as goodly as ever was heard.   [c] barges.

pets, wettes,ᵃ shames, and regalls, and with a gret [shooting] of gunes tyll her grace cam in-to the Towr, and   .   .   .

The xxix day of September the Qwuen('s) grace mad knyghts of the Bathe xv; the furst was the yerle of Devonshyre, the yonge yerle of Surray, the iijᵈᵉ lord of Borgane, and lord Barkley, the lord Monjoye, lord Sowche, ser Wylliam Pallet, my lord Cardyff, the lord Wyndsore('s) sune, sir   Ryche('s) sune, sir Clynton, ser   Pagett, ser Robart Rochaster, ser Hare Jernyngham, ser Edward Dormer.

The xxx day of September the Qwuyen('s) grace cam from the Towre thrugh London, rydyng in a charett gorgusly be-sene unto Westmynster; by the way at Fanche-chyrche a goodly pagant, with iiij grett gyants, and with goodly speches, the geneways ᵇ mad yt; at Grache-chyrche a-nodur goodly pajant of esterlyngs ᶜ makyng; and at Ledyne-hall was nodur pagant hangyd with cloth of gold, and the goodlyst playng with all maner of musyssoners, and ther was on ᵈ blohyng of a trumpet all the day longe; at the conduyt in Cornhyll a-nodur of the sete ᵉ; and (at) the grett condutt a-nodur goodly on,ᵈ and the standard pentyd and gyldyd, and the crosse pentyd; and (at) the lytyll conduyt a goodly pagant; in Powlles chyrche-yerde ij pagants; and ij scaffolds on Powlles stepull with stremars; and ᶠ Ludgat pentyd; at the conduyd in Flett-stret a goodly pajant and pentyd   .   .   .   .   .   .

.   .   .   .

holy] water-stokes and sensers and copes   .   .   .   Westmynster chyrche, and ther her grace hard masse, and was crounyd a-pon a he ᵍ stage, and after [she was] a-nontyd Qwene, the forst day of October.   [When all] was don, her grace cam to Westmynster hall   .   .   .   .   .   yt was iiij of the cloke or she whent to dener [or pa]st; and ther the duke of Norffoke rod up and done the hall, my lord the yerle of Darbe he ᵍ constabull, the yerle of Arundell he ᵍ boteler, and my lord of Borgane cheyff larderer, master Dymmoke the qwyen('s) champyon; and ther was [great me]lode;

ᵃ waits.   ᵇ Genoese merchants.   ᶜ Easterling merchants.   ᵈ one.   ᵉ City.
ᶠ at in MS.   ᵍ high.

and the erle of Devonshyre bare the sword, and the yerle of Westmorland bare the cape of mantenans, and the erle of Shrowsbery
bare the crowne, and the duke of Norffoke [was earl] marshall, and
the yerle of Arundell lord stuard, and the erle of Surray was doer
under the duke ys grandshyr, and the erle of Woseter was
her grace('s) carver that day at dener, my lord Wyndsore was
(blank); and at the end of the tabull dynyd my lade Elisabeth and
my lade Anne of Cleyff; and so yt was candyll-lyght or her grace
or she had dynyd, and so [anon] her grace toke barge.

The ij day her grace mayd lxxiiij knyghts, the morowe after her
crownnasyon, the wyche her be ther names folowyng: *(not inserted by the Diarist; but see the Illustrative Notes.)*

The iiij day of October was cared to the Towre the archebysshope of Yorke, [a] and dyvers odur to *(blank)*

The v day of October the Qwuen('s) grace rod unto Westmynster
chyrche, and ther her grace hard masse of the Holy-gost, and ther
wher ij bysshopes; on [b] delevered her the shepter [c] and odur thyng.
Her grace rod in her parlement robes, and all the trumpeters
blohyng a-for them all; and so, after her grace had hard masse,
they whent to the Parlement howsse all to-geyther, and the yerle
of Devonshyre bare the sworde, and the yerle of Westmorland
bare the cape [d] of mayntenans.

The xxij of October dyd pryche at Powlles doctur Westun, dene
of Westmynster, and [there at] evere gatt in Powlles cherche
yerd wher mad, [to prevent the breaking in of] horses, and for
grett throng of pepull, grett bars.

The xxij day of October was bered the good [lady] Bowes, the
wyff of ser Marten Bowesse late alderman and goldsmyth of London, with harolds, and with a C. men and women in gownes and
cotes of . . and xxiiij gownes of mantyll frys, alff men and the
[half] women, and ys howse and the strett and the chyrche hangyd
with blake clothe, and with ther armes a-pon the blake . . . .
hangyd with blake and armes, and ther wher iiij grett candyll-

<hr>

[a] Robert Holgate.   [b] one.   [c] sceptre.   [d] cap.

stykes gyldyd, with iiij grett tapurs of . . . and ij grett whytt branchys bornyng gyldyd, and the compeny of Clarkes, and prestes; and then cam the corpse with iiij penons of arms borne a-bowt her . . . stayffes torchys bornyng a-bowt her with xij of ys servands beyryng of them; and then cam the cheyffe mornars; and then my lord mare and the swordbeyrer, and ser Hare Hubbellthorne and ser Rowland Hyll knyghtes, and mornars many, and ij knyght(s) more, and dyvers gentyllmen, and after the craft of Goldsmyth(s); and when all was done they whent, and the durge, so home to ys placsse; and the marow after a goodly masse song in Laten, and a sermon, and when all was done they whent to dener ther.

The xxix day of October dyd pryche *(unfinished.)*

[The same day the new Lord Mayor[a] went] toward Westmynter [attended by the] craftes of London in ther best leveray . . . . . . with trumpets blohyng and the whets[b] playng . . . . a goodly fuyst[c] trymmed with banars and guns . . . waytyng of my lord mayre('s) barge unto Westmynster [and] all the craftes bargers with stremars and banars [of every] craft, and so to the Cheker, and so hom-wards; my lord mayre landyd at Banard Castyll and [in St. Paul's] chyrche-yerd dyd hevere[d] craft wher set in [array]: furst wher ij tallmen bayreng ij gret stremars [of] the Marchand-tayllers armes, then cam on[e] [with a] drume and a flutt playng, and a-nodur with a gret f[ife ?] all they in blue sylke, and then cam ij grett wodyn[f] [armed] with ij grett clubes all in grene, and with skwybes bornyng . . . with gret berds and syd here,[g] and ij targets a-pon ther bake . . . and then cam xvj trumpeters blohyng, and then cam in [blue] gownes, and capes and hosse[h] and blue sylke slevys, and evere man havyng a target and a gayffelyn[i] to the nombur of lxx . . and then cam a duyllyll,[k] and after cam the bachelars all in a leveray, and skar-

---

[a] Sir Thomas White.   [b] waits.   [c] a foist, or pinnace.   [d] every.   [e] one.
[f] wood-men, or savage men of the wood. *Next year written* wodys.
[g] beards and side (*i. e.* long) hair.   [h] caps and hose.   [i] javelin.   [k] devil.

lett hods; and then cam the pagant of sant John Baptyst gorgyusly, with goodly speches; and then cam all the kynges trumpeters blowhyng, and evere trumpeter havyng skarlet capes,[a] and
the wetes[b] capes[a] and godly banars, and then the craftes, and then
the wettes playhyng, and then my lord mayre('s) offesers, and
then my lord mayre and ij good henchmen, and then all the
aldermen and the shreyffes, and so to dener; and after dener to
Powlles, and all them that bare targets dyd [bare] after stayff-
torches, with all the trumpets and wettes blowhyng thrugh Powlles,
thrugh rondabowt the qwer and the body of the chyrche blowhyng, and so home to my lord mere('s) howsse.

The v day of November dyd pryche master Feknam at sant
Mare Overays a-for non, and ther wher at ys sermon the yerle
of Devonshyre, ser Antony Browne, and juge Morgayn, and dyvers odur nobull men.

The sam day at after-non dyd prych master Feknam at sant
Sthevyns in Walbroke, and ther wher serten pepull mad besenes[c]
for the sermon, and ther wher juge Browne, ser Rownland Hyll,
ser Rechard Dobes, ser John Yorke; and sum wher sent to the
mare,[d] and to the Conter.

[The 13th of November were arraigned at Guildhall. doctor
Cranmer, archbishop of Canterbury, the lord] Gylfford Dudlay,
the sune of the duke of Northumberland, and my lade Jane ys wyff,
the doythur of the duke of Suffoke-Dassett, and the lord Ham-
brosse Dudlay, [and the] lord Hare Dudlay, the wyche lade Jane
was proclamyd [Queen]: they all v wher cast for to dee.

The xix day of November dyd pryche master Feknam at sant
Stheyns in Walbroke, and ther he mad the goodliest sermon that
ever was hard of the blessed sacrament of the body and blud for
to be after the consecracion.

The xxiiij day of November dyd ryd in a c[art] Cheken, parsun
of sant Necolas Coldabbay, [round] a-bowt London, for he sold
ys wyff to a bowcher.

[a] caps.   [b] waits.   [c] *i. e.* made a disturbance.   [d] mayor

The **xxv** day of November was sa[nt Katharine's] day, and at nyght they of Powlles whent a prossessyon abowt Powlles stepull with gret lyghtes, and [before them] sant Kateryn, and syngyng, with a v^c. lyghtes allmost halffe a noure, and when all was don thay rong all the belles of Powlles at vj of the cloke.

The **xv** day of November wher creatyd serten harolds, as Ruge-dragan creatyd Yorke, and Ruge-crosse creatyd Lankastur, and Huw master Garter('s) servand created Ruge-crosse, and Wyllyam my lord Cobham('s) servand [created Rouge-dragon^a], and Kokes the duke of Northumberland('s) servand creatyd Parkolles.

The **xxvj** day of November dyd pryche master Whyt, warden at Powlles, mad a goodly sermon that we shuld have prossessyon.

[On the same day was a goodly herse for the late King Edward, hung with cloth of tissue, and a cross and a pax, silver] candyll-stykes, and xiij bedmen holdyng of tapurs, and the durge song in Laten, and the masse on the morowe.

The **xxx** day of November was a godly sermon [at St. Paul's,] the wyche was sant Andrew's day, the wyche dyd pryche [master] doctur Borne; and after a generall prossessyon abowt [the church] in Laten with *ora pro nobis,* and the morow after a-nodur [sermon preached by Dr.] Harfeld, and prossessyon with the old Latene; and so [the Wednesday after a] prossessyon, and so thrugh England to be had.

The **vj** day of Desember was bered my old lade . . . . wedew at Lambeth at my lord of Canturberes plasge . . . . whytt branchys and tapurs and torchys and armes ha . . . . . on blake cloth.

The **ix** day of Desember was a man sett on the pelere^b for sedyssyous wordes agaynst the quen('s) grace and her consell, in Chepe.

The **viij** day of Desember was prossessyon at Powlles. When

---

^a Edit. See the Illustrative Notes.   ^b pillory.

all was don, my lord of London commondyd that every parryche chyrche shuld provyd for a crosse and a staffe and cope for to go of prossessyon evere Sonday and Wedynsday and Fryday, and pray unto God for fayre wether thrug London.

The   day of Desember was bered in Essex my lord Morley with iiij penons of armes and with schochyons and with torchys and mony mornars in blake.

The   day of Desember endyd the parlement at Westmynster, and regornyd^a unto the *(blank)*

The .   day was a proclamasyon thrugh London and all England that noman shuld syng no Englys serves nor communion after the xx day of Desember, nor no prest that has a wyff shall not menyster nor say masse, and that evere parryche to make a auter and to have a crosse and staff, and all othur thinges in all parryches all in Laten, as hale-bred,^b hale-water, as palme and assesse.^c

[The ij day of January the king of Spain's ambassadors landed at Tower wharf. During whose landing there was great shooting of the guns. The lord] Wylliam Haward dyd saff-gard them ; and so rod to-gether, and in Fanchyrche stret my lord of Devonshire and dyvers odur mett them, and rod with them unto Durram Plasse, and ther they dyd a-lyght.

The iij day of January my lord mayre and the chamburlayn of London dyd present unto the enbasadurs gyfts of dyvers thyngs, as *(blank)*

The ix day of January dynyd the enbasadurs of [Spain] and all the quen('s) consell at my lord chansselers the bysshope of Wynchester, for ther was a grett dener as [could] be had.

The x day of January the enbasadurs rod unto Hamtun Courtt, and ther they had grett chere [as] cold be had, and huntyd, and kyllyd tage and rage with honds and swords.

The xiij day of January ther was a man drane from the Towre

---

^a re-journed, *for* adjourned.   ^b holy bread.   ^c ashes.

thrugh London a-pone a sled unto Tyborne, and ther hangyd, dran, and quartered, for conterffeytyng the quen('s) senett. [a]

The sam day was had to the Flett doctur Crom, persun of Aldermare, for [preaching on Christmas-day without licence.[b]]

The xiiij day of January was had to the Towre master Hadyntun, dwellyng in Bouge-rowe, and all ys goods seysenyd for the quen and in the contrey for proffessyng of serten [beretical doctrines.][b]

[The xv day of January, the lord mayor, and the] aldermen whent to Westmynster [to the court, and] my lord chanseler mad a protestacyon [to them, and to]othur pepyll, that the quen('s) grace ys myndyd [to marry] with the prynche of Spayne, and the reme [c] for to have [great] benefett commyng in to the rayme; [c] and that he not . . . . . thyngs, [d] butt her consell of thys reame sh . . . . .

The xvj day of January was bered master Wylliam, marchand of the stapull of Callys, with mony mornars [at] sant Androus ondershaft, as ser Rowland Hyll, ser Hare[e] Hubbellthorne, ser Androu Jude, and dyvers aldermen, with . . . . . stayffes torchys, and ij whyt branchys, and a good sermon ; . . . . . powre men and women had good gownes.

The xxij day of January was reynyd at yeld hall the lord Robart Dudlay for tresun, the duke of Northumberland('s) sune, and cast the sam day.

The xxv day of January was bered master Sturley sqwyre, at Rychemond, with cot armur and penon and skochyons of armes, stayffe torchys and ij whyt branchys, and mony mornars.

The xxv day of January was a goodly prosessyon at Powlles with a l. copes of cloth of gold, with *Salve festa dies;* yt was sant Powlles day, and ther was a godly masse ; and the sam day master Feknam was mad a prebendary at evyngsonge.

<hr>

[a] Queen's signet.   [b] Strype : blank in the original.   [c] realm.

[d] " that the said Prince was not to meddle with the public affairs of the State, but the Queen's great Council of the Realm, as before was accustomed." Strype.

[e] Harry.

The xxvj day of January began wachyng at evere gatt in arness,[a] for tydyngs cam the sam tym to the quen and her consell that ser Thomas Wyatt, ser George Harper, ser Hare Ysseley, master Cobam, and master Rudston, and master Knevetts, and dyvers odur gentyllmen and commons, wher up, and tha say because the prynche of Spayne commyng in to have owre quen, for they kepe Rochaster castell and the bryge and odur plases.

[The xxvij day of January the city sent into Kent a great number of men in white coats. The captains to command them, and the rest of their forces, were the duke of Norfolk, earl of Ormond, sir George Howard,[b] and divers others. But many of the guards, and of the white-coats, deserted[c]] them, and captaynes cam hom a-gayn. [Wyatt had gotten some of the late king's] ordenanse; and so, after their removyng, cam towards Dartford with ys army towards London.

The xxviij day of January the Quen('s) grace dyd send to master Wyatt [and his company the] master of the horsse and master Cornwales, to know their intentt; and thay send word that they wold have the Quen and the Towre in kepyng, and odur thynges.

The xxix day of January master Wyatt, master Harper, master Rudston, master Knevett, and the commons, commyng [marched to] Blake-heth, and so forward toward London with [a great] army commyng.

The furst day of Feybruary cam nuw tydyngs that all craftes shuld fynd the dobull [number of men]; non butt hossholders unto the bryge and the gattes, and the drae-bryge, and ther lay grett gones; and the bryge was broken done after; and that evere man to make whyt cotes for evere howsse.

The sam day at after-non was a proclamasyon in Chepesyde, Ledyn-hall, and at sant Magnus corner, with harold of armes and on of the quen['s] trumpeters blohyng, and my lord mare, and my lord admerall Haward, and the ij shreyffs, that ser

---

[a] harness (*i. e.* armour).

[b] Hayward *in Strype, but no doubt* Haward *in orig.*   [c] Strype.

Thomas Wyatt was proclamyd traytur and rebellyous, and all ys fellowes, agaynst the Quen('s) mageste and her consell, and that he wold have the Quen in costody, and the Towre of London in kepyng ; and thay convayd unto evere gatt gonnes and the bryge ; and so evere gatt with men in harnes nyght and days. And a-bowt iij of the cloke at after-non the Quen('s) grace cam rydyng from Westmynster unto yeld-hall with mony lordes, knyghts and lades, and bysshopes and haroldes of armes, and trompeturs blohynge and all the gard in harnes. [Then she declared, in an oration to the mayor and the city, and to her council, her mind concerning her marriage, that she never intended to marry out of her realm but by her council's consent and advice ; and that she would never marry but all her true] sogettes* shall be content, [or else she would live] as her grace has don hederto. [But that her gr]ace wyll call a parlement [as] shortely as [may be, and] as thay shall fynd, and that [the earl of] Penbroke shall be cheyffe capten and generall agaynst ser Thomas Wyatt and ys felous in the [field,] that my lord admerall for to be sosyatt with the [lord mayor] to kepe the cete from all commars therto. [After this] the Quen('s) grace came from yeld-hall and rod to the iij cranes in the vyntre, and toke her barge [to] Westmynster to her own place the sam day.

The iij day of Feybruarii was a proclamacyon that who so ever do take ser Thomas Wyatt, exsept Harper, Ys[seley, and] Rudston, shuld have C. lb. land to ym and ys heirs for ever.

The iij day of Feybruary cam in to Sowthwarke ser Thomas Wyatt and odur captaynes at after-none with ys army ; and the morow after thay mayd trenchys in dyvers parts and dyvers placys, with ordenanse.

The vj day of Feybruary was Shroyff-tuwysday in the mornyng master Wyatt and ys compeny retorned bake towhard Kyngton

marginal note: Wyat's speed

---

* subjects. The preceding passage supplied by Strype.

apon Temes, and ther the bridge was pluckyd up, and he causyd on
of ys men to swym over for to feytche a bott, [a] and so whent at
nyght toward Kensyngtun, and so forward.

The sam day was ij hangyd apon a jebett in Powles churche yerd;
the on a spy of Wyatt, the thodur was under-shreyff of Leseter,
for carryng letturs of the duke of Suffoke and odur thinges.

The sam day cam rydyng to the Towre the duke of Soffoke and
ys brodur by the yerle of Huntyngton [b] with iij C. horse.

[The vij day of February, in the forenoon, Wyatt, with his
army and ordnance, were at Hyde Park Corner. There the
Queen's host met with, with a great number of men at arms on
horseback, beside foot. By one of the clock [c]] the Quen['s men
and Wyatt's had a skirmish;] ther wher mony slayn: butt master
Wyatt toke the way don by Sant James with a grett company
and so to Charyngcrosse, and so forth, crying 'God save quen
Mare!' tyll he cam to Ludgatt and [knocked there; thinking to
have entered; but the gate being kept fast against him, he retired,] and bake agayne unto Tempull Bare, and folouyd hym
mony man, and ther he yelded unto master Norray the harold of
armes in ys cote of armes, and ther he lycted [d] be-hynd a gentleman
unto the cowrte; but by the way mony of them wher slayne by the
way or thay cam to Charyng-crosse, what with mores pykes and
bylls; and mony of Wyatt('s) men, as they whent, wher the quens
fryndes and Englys-men under a fallss pretens that he whent
a-bowtt to . . . . . . way as thay whent, and cam for to
make men beleyff that the quen('s) grace had gyffvyn them pardon;
and dyvers of ys men toke the quen('s) men by the hand as thay
whent toward Ludgatt. Thys was done on As-Wedynsday the
furst yere of quen Mare of England; and the sam nyght to the
Towre ser Thomas Wyatt, master Cobham, and master Vane, and
ij Knewetes and odur captaynes.

[a] boat.   [b] i. e. conducted by the Earl.   [c] Strype.
[d] He mounted on horseback: see the Illustrative Notes.

The viij day of Feybruarij was commondyd by the quene and the bysshope of London that Powlles and evere parryche that thay shuld syng *Te Deum Laudamus*, and ryngyng for the good vyetory that the quen('s) grace had aganst Wyatt and the rebellyous of Kent, the wyche wher over-come, thankes be unto God, with lytyll blud-shed, and the reseduw taken and had to presun, and after wher dyvers of them putt to deth in dyvers places in Londun and Kent, and prossessyon evere wher that day for joy.

The xij day of February was mad at evere gate in Lundun a newe payre of galaus and set up, ij payre in Chepesyde, ij payr in Fletstrett, one in Smythfyld, one payre in Holborne, on at Ledyn-hall, one at sant Magnus London [-bridge], on at Peper allay gatt, one at sant Gorgeus, on in Barunsay [a] strett, on on Towr hylle, one payre at Charyngcrosse, on payre besyd Hyd parke corner.

The xiiij day of Feybruary wher hangyd at evere gatt and plasse: in Chepe-syd vj; Algatt j, quartered; at Leydynhall iij; at Bysshope-gatt on, and quartered; Morgatt one; Crepullgatt one; Aldersgatt on, quartered; Nuwgat on, quartered; Ludgatt on; Belyngat iij hangyd; Sant Magnus iij hangyd; Towre hyll ij hangyd; Holborne iij hangyd; Flettstret iij hangyd; at Peper alley gat iij; Barunsaystret iij; Sant Gorgus iij; Charyng crosse iiij, on Boyth the fottman, and Vekars of the gard, and ij moo; at Hydparke corner iij, on Polard a waterbeyrar; theys iij hanges in chynes; [b] and but vij quartered, and ther bodys and heds set a-pon the gattes of London.

The xvj day of Feybruary was mad a grett skaffold in Westmynster hall for the duke of Suffoke.

The xvij day of Feybruary was the duke of Suffoke rayned [c] at Westmynster halle, and cast for he tresun, and cast to suffer deth.

The xviij day of Feybruary was had in-to Kent serteyn captens, as Bart and xxij mor of the rebellyous, to suffer deth.

The sam day was a proclamasyon in London that all the pre-

[a] Bermondsey.   [b] chains.   [c] arraigned.

sonars in alle the presuns of the rebellyous of Kent that thai shuld go in-to Sowthwarke, and thay that wher seke [a] that ther names shuld be browth theder.

[The xxth day of February was arraigned] . . . . lord John Gray, the duke of Suffoke('s) brodur . . . .

The sam day was bered master Gorge Pargeter, Thomas Pargeter('s) sune late mare of London, with mony mornars, and with armes, and mony gownes gyffyn to pore men and vomen, and with stayff [b] torchus [and] whyt branchys; and in the chyrche wher iiij gylt candellstyks with iiij grett tapurs bornyng and ys armes, and the compeny of the Clarkes.

The sam day was Mans gohyng in-to Kent, to Canboroke, [c] and fochyd [d] a-gayn, and browth to sant Gorgeus cyrche, and ther he was hangyd by iiij of the cloke at nyght, for he was a ryche man.

The xxj day of Feybruary ther was a man rydying a-bowt London, ys ffasse [e] toward the horsse taylles, a quarter of velle on a-for and a-nodur behynd hym, and a pyge borne be-for hym skaldyd a-pone a . . .

The sam day cam rydyng to the Towre the lord Thomas Gray, the duke of Suffoke('s) brodur, and ser James a Croft knyght, sum tyme depute of Yrland.

The xxij day of Feybruary was reynyd [f] at Westmynster one *(blank)* Bowthe, sum tyme of Calles, and cast for tresun.

The sam day alle the Kent men whent to the cowrt with halters a-bowt ther nekes, and bone [g] with cordes, ij and ij to-gether, through London to Westmynster, and be-twyn the ij tyltes [h] the powr presonars knelyd downe in the myre, and ther the Quen('s) grace lokyd owt over the gatt and gayff them all pardon, and thay cryd owt 'God save quen Mare!' and so to Westmynster hall, and ther thay cast ther alters a-bowt the hall, and capes, [i] and in the stretes, and cryd owt 'God save quen Mare!' as thay whent.

---

[a] sick, *i. e.* wounded.   [b] staff: *in MS.* tayff.   [c] Cranbrook.   [d] fetched.
[e] face.   [f] arraigned.   [g] bound.   [h] The Tilt-yard.   [i] caps.

. . . .
of the qwen('s) garde att . . . . the man that was
kyld was sir John Pr. . . . .

The same tyme and day be-twyne iiij [and v of the] cloke at nyght
my lade Elssabeth('s) grase c[ame riding]to London thrught Smyth-
feld unto West[minster] with a C. welvett cottes a-for her grace.
A[nd her] grace rod in a charett opyn of boyth sydes. [And with]
her grace rydyng after her a C. in cotes of [scarlet and] fyne red
gardyd with velvett, and so thrught Fletstret unto the cowrt
thrught the qu[een's] garden, her grace behyng syke.[a]

The xxiiij day of Marche [*read* xxiij of February] was heddyd
the duke of Suffoke-Dassett[b] on the Towre hylle, be-twyn ix and
x of the cloke a-for none.

The sam day the qwyn('s) grace gaff pardon unto serten of mo[c]
men of Kentt, in Sowthwarke; ther they cryd " God save quen
Mare ! ". and cast ther alters on hed in the stretes and a-bowt, that
sum had[d] iiij or v halters.

The vij day of Marche rod a bocher[e] rond a-bowt London, ys face
toward the horsse taylle, with ha[lf of] a lame[f] be-fore and a-nodur
behynd, and vell and a calff borne a-for hym, a-pon a polle, rawe.

The viij day of Marche cam owt of the Towre of London the
archbysshope of Canturbere Crenmer, and bysshope of London
was Rydley, and master Lathemer condam,[g] and so to Brenfford
and ther ser John Wylliam reseyvyd them, and so to Oxfford.

The ix day of Marche was reynyd[h] at Westmynster my lord
Thomas Gray, the duke of Suffoke('s) brodur, and cast   .   .
.   .   .   .   .   [to lose h]ys hed.

The xj day of Marche was bered ser Wylliam [Goring] knyght in
Sussex, with a standard, a penon of armes, [with coat] armur, target,
sward, and a helmet; and ther was a h[erse of] wax and viij dosen of
penselles and viij dosen of sh[ocheons], ij whyt and branchys of
wax, and iiij dosen of stay[ff] torchys, and a harold of armes

---

master Chastur; and he ded^a . . . . owe, and cared in-to the
contrey by water to Kyngstun, [and] after by land to ys on ^b contrey.

The xiiij day of Marche was in Aldergat-stret a woy[ce heard] in
a walle that dyd spyke unto serten pepull, the wyche . . . .
was complenyd unto my lord mayre, and so after yt was [made]
knowen by dyvers what ther wher, and after cared unto [prison,]
as Nugatt contur^c and the Towre.

The xv day of Marche was raynyd at Westmynster ser Thomas
Wyatt knyght, the captayn cheyffe [of] Kent, and cast to be
hedyd and after quartered and sett up.

The xviij day of Marche was kared^d to the Towre of London
my lade Elsabeth('s) grace, the quen('s) syster, a-for none.

The xxiiij day of Marche was delevered owt of the Towre and
had the quen('s) pardon the lord marques of Northamtun, my lord
Cobham, and ij of ys sunes,^e and dyvers odur mo.

The xvj day of Marche was deprevyd the archebysshope of
Yorke,^f and the bysshope of Lynkolne doctur Tayller, and the
bysshope of Chester,^g the bysshope of sant Davys. ^h

The xvij day of Marche was deprevyd the bysshope of Harfford ⁱ
and the bysshope of Glosetur; ^k commyssyonars that dyd depreyffe
them my lord chansseler and my lord of Durram, my lord of
Londun, my lord of Chechastur, and my lord of sant Asse.

[The first day of April my lord chancellor did consecrate six new
bishops at St. Mary Overy's, before the high altar; and a goodly
mass was said. And when all] was done thay yede unto my lord
ch[ancellor's,] for ther was as grett a dener as youe ha[ve seen.]
Thes be the bysshopes names that wher consecrated, [doctor]
Whyt, warden of Wynchastur, the bysshope of Ly[ncoln]; doctur
Borne, bysshope of Bathe; doctur Morg[an, bishop] of sant
Davys; doctur Brokes, bysshope of Gloss[ter]; doctur Cottes,
bysshope of Westtchastur; bysshope of sant Asse^l changyd to
be bysshope of Arfford ^m; master [Griffith] parsun of sant Magnus
bysshope of Rochastur.

The sam day at after-non was bered my lade [Ascough] the wyff

---

^a died.   ^b his own.   ^c counter.   ^d carried.   ^e sons.   ^f Robert Holgate.
^g John Bird.   ^h Robert Ferrar.   ⁱ John Harley.   ^k John Hooper.
^l Robert Warton, *alias* Parfew.   ^m Hereford.

of Sir Crystofer Askuw, lat mare of London : [she was] bered in sant
John the evangelett paryche, in Watlyngstrett, and the stret and
chyrche hangyd with blake and armes, and iiij gylt candyllstykes
and iiij grett tapurs and armes, and ij goodly whyt branchys, and
xx men in frysse gownes bayring of stayf-torchys, and mony vomen,
and then the compeny of the Clarkes; and mony mornars, and
then came a herald of armes a-for the corsse in ys cot armur ;
and then the corsse, with iiij banars of hemages [a] borne [about]
her, and the mornars ; and then the craft of the Drapers ; and the
parrysonars ; and so to the durge and the morowe masse. [Master]
doctur Smyth dyd pryche ; and when all was done, to [dinner.]

The ij day of Aprell began the parlemente, and the Quen('s) grace
rod thedur in her robes, and bysshopes and lordes in parlement
robes, and ther was a goody [b] masse of the Holy-gost ; and [so] to
the parlement howsse.

The viij day of Aprell wher creatyd lordes sir John of Brygys
creatyd lord Shandoys ; sir John Wyllyams baron of Tame, and
lord chamburlayne to the prynche of Spayne ; and ser Antony
Browne, master of the prynsse of Spayne('s) horsses. And the sam
day my lord Wylliam [c], admerall, and ys captayns, wherin [d] whyt
and gren velvet and saten and taffata and sarsenett, and trumpeters all in gren and whyt, and all the marenars in whyt and gren
cloth for shypes.   [On the same day somebody unknown hanged
a cat on the gallows beside the cross in Cheap, habited in a garment like to that the priest wore that said mass ; she had a shaven
crown, and in her fore feet held a piece of paper made round, representing the wafer. [e]]

The xj day of Aprell was heddyd ser Thomas [Wyatt of Kentt,]
the cheyffe captayn of the rebellyous of [Kent, be-] twyn ix and
x of the cloke a-for none, on Towre hyll, . . . after and by xj of the
cloke was he quartered on the skaffold, and hys bowelles and ys

---

[a] images.   [b] *Sic. MS. for* goodly.   [c] Howard.
[d] wearing.   [e] Strype ; see afterwards under the 13th April.

members burnt be-syd the skaffold; . . . . and so ther
was a care [a] and a baskett, and the iiij quarters and hed was putt
in-to a baskett to nuwgat to be parboyled.

The xij day of Aprell was ser Thomas Wyatt sett a-pon the
gallaus on Hay-hyll be-syd Hyd Parke; wher dyd hang iij men
in chynes a-pon a stake wh . . . . cam to cum to London,
and ther the qweyns men and [Wyatt's] men dyd skryssmys,[b] wher
he and ys captayns wher over-cum, thanke be unto God; and on[c]
quarter of ys sett a-pon a jubett on Mylle-end gren, and a-nodur
at Nuwyngton be-yonde sant Gorges in Sowthwarke, and [the iij]
be-syd sant Thomas of Waterynges, and the iiij quarter at *(blank)*

The xiij day of Aprell was a proclamasyon was made that what
so mever [d] he wher that cold bryng forth hym that dyd hang the
catt on the galaus, he shuld have xx marke for ys labur.

The xvj day of Aprell was sett up in sant Androwes Undershafft
for master Kyrtun, alderman of London and marchand tayller of
London, and marchand of the stapull of Calles, with a cote armur,
iij penons of armes, goodly ons, and sett up over ys tombe.

The xvij day of Aprell was had to Yeld-hall ser Necolaus Frogmortun, ser James a Croft, master Wynter, master Vaghan; and
ther Waghan gaff evedens agaynst ser Necolas Frogmortun of tresun, but the qwest dyd qwytt hym.

[The xxj day of April were two men set on the pillory in Cheap,
for speaking seditious words and false lies against the queen and
her council: And one of] them had hys here[e] naylyd to the
pelory.

The xxiij day of Aprell, was sant Gorge day, her grace whent
unto the chapell and whent a prossessyon with all the kynghtes
of the garter that was ther pressent [to St.] James in the Feld;
ther wher creatyd the sam day knights of the garter, the prynsse
of Spayne one, and the yerle of Sussex.

[a] car.   [b] skirmish.   [c] onc.   [d] *Sic MS.*   [e] ear.

The xxviij day of Aprell was heddyd on^a Towre hyll, betwyn ix and x of the cloke a-for none, my lord Thomas Gray, the duke of Suffoke-Dassett ^b brodur, and bered at Allalow's Barkyng, and the hed (*unfinished*)

The xxix day of Aprell was raynyd ^c at Yeldhall ser James a Croft, late depute of Yrland, and cast; and master Wynter whent ther too.

The sam day was bered my lade Dudley lat wyff of barne ^d of Dudley, in sant Margarett in Westmynster, with iiij baners of emages, and mony gowens, and hon[g with] blake and armes, for my lade was ontt ^e unto the [duke] of Suffoke-Dassett, the wyche was hedyd latt.

The xxx day of Aprell began the postyll-mas^f at Powles at the v of the cloke in the mornyng evere day.

The iij day of May, at the cowrt of sant James, the quen('s) grace whent a prossessyon within sant James with harolds and serjants of armes, and iiij bysshopes mytred, and all iij days thay whent her chapell a-bowt the feldes, first day to sant Gylles and ther song masse; the next day tuwyse-day to sant Martens in the feldes, [and there] a sermon and song masse, and so thay dronke ther; and the iij day to Westmynster, and ther a sermon and then masse, and mad good chere; and after a-bowt the Parke, and so to sant James cowrt ther.

[The same Rogation Week went out of the Tower, on procession, priests and clerks, and the lieutenant with all his waiters; and the ax of the Tower borne in procession: the waits attended. There joined in this procession the inhabitants of] sant Katheryns, Radclyff, Limehouse, Popular, Sthracfford, Sordyche, with all them [that belonged to] the Towre, with ther halbards, a-bowt the feldes of sant Katheryns and the prevelegys.

The day of May was raynyd ^c at Yeld-hall master Wylliam

---

^a *MS. of.*   ^b *See before, p.* 57.   ^c arraigned.   ^d baron.
^e aunt.   ^f apostle-mass.   ^c arraigned.

Thomas, clarke to the consell, and cast to suffer deth, to be dran and quartered.

The *(blank)* day of May was a proclamasyon that no man shuld not talke of no thynges of the qwen.

The viij day of May war all the craftes warnyd to cum . . . . . . in ther leveray, and they wher commondyd that they shuld *(unfinished)*

The x day of May was durge at Westmynster and at Powles, with torche lyght; and the morow after and at Westmynster was masse, and ther they dyd offer, mony of the quen('s) consell and dyvers lordes, for the solles of kyng Henry the vij[th]. and quen Elsabeth, and for kyng Henry the viij[th]. and qwene Katheryne, and kyng Edward the vj[th].

The xiij day of May was the Fyssmongers and sant Peters in Cornhylle prossessyon, with a goodly qwyre of clarkes syngyng, and a iiij[xx] of prestes wayryng copes of cloth of guld, and so folohyng my lord mayre and the althemen in skarlet; and then the compeny of Fyssmongers in ther leveray, and they and the offesers beyryng whyt rods in ther handes, and so to Powlles, and ther they dyd the oblassyon after old fassyon.

The vj day of May was a goodly evyngsong at Yeldhall colege, by the masters of the Clarkes and ther felowshype of Clarkes, with syngyng and playng as youe have hard.

[The morrow after was a great mass at the same place, by the same fraternity, when every clerk offered a halfpenny. The mass was sung by divers of the queen's chapel and children. And, after mass done, every clerk went their procession two and two together, each having] a surples and a ryche cope, and a garland; [after them] iiij[xx] standards, stremars, and baners; and evere on [a] that bare them had a nobe [b] or elles a surples; and ij and ij together; [then came] the waytes playng, and then be-twyn xxx clarkes, a qwre syngyng *Salve fasta dyes;* so ther wher iiij qweres.

[a] every one.   [b] an albe.

[Then cam] a canepe borne by iiij of the masters of the Clarkes [over the] sacrament, with a xij stayff-torchys bornyng; [up sa]nt Laurans lane, and so to the farther end of Chep, then back a-gayn up Cornhylle, and so to Ledynhalle; and so down to Byshopegatt unto sant Albrowsse[a] chyrche; and ther they dyd put off ther copes and so to dener evere man, and ther evere on[b] that bare a stremar had monay, as they wher of bygnes ther.

The xiiij day of May was creatyd my lord Garrett the yerle of Kyldare.

The xv day of May cam Haknay prossessyon to Powlles; and after cam sant Clement('s) prossessyon and the mayre and althermen; and ther wher goodly quersse[c] syngyng.

The xvj day of May cam to Powlles Eslyngton prossessyon.

The xviij day of May was drane a-pone a sled a proper man namyd Wylliam Thomas from the Towre unto Tyborne; the . . he was clarke to the consell; and he was hangyd, and after ys hed stryken of, and then quartered; and the morow after ys hed was sett on London bryge, and iij quarters set over Crepull-gate.

The xx day of May my lade Elsabeth the quen('s) syster cam owt of the Towre, and toke her barge at Towre warfe, and so to Rychemond, and from thens unto Wyndsor, and so to Wodstoke.

The xvj day of May, and the furst yere of quen Mare, was Henry Machun lvj yere old, Anno Domini M. v[c] liiij.

[The xxiij day of May a certain woman was set on the pillory in Cheapside for speaking lies and seditious words against the queen's majesty.]

The xxiiij day of May was Corpus Christi day, and . . . . . ther wher mony goodly pr[oss]essyons in mony parryches . . was yll, for mony had long torchys garnyshyd [in the] old fassyouns, and stayffe torchys bornyng, and mony [canopies] borne

---

[a] Ethelburga.　　　　　[b] every one.　　　　　[c] quires.

a-bowt the strett; and sant Pulcurs parryche went a-bowt ther owne parryche, and in Smythfeld; as they wher goohyng, ther cam a man unto the prest [that bare] the sacrament, and began to pluke ytt owt of ys hand, and contenent a he druw ys dager *(blank)*, and contenent a he was taken and cared to Nuwgate.

The xxv day of May was ij men set on the pelere in Chepe; one ys ere was naylyd for horabull lyes and sedyssyous wordes aganst the quen('s) mageste and her consell; and th'odur was sedyssyous slanderous wordes gaynst the quen('s) mageste and her consell and the mages . . . . .

The xxv day of May, wyche was the sam day, whent owt of the Towre northwarde the yerle of Devonshyre, and cared into North-hamtunshyre to a castyll called (Fotheringay b) with serten of the gard, and dyvers knyghtes, by iij and iiij of the cloke in the mornyng.

The xxvj day of May was the sam man that had ys her c naylyd a-for, was ys thuder her d naylyd; and a woman sett on the pelere for spykyng of serten words thuchynge the quens prosedynges and the consell.

The xxvij day of May whent owt of the Towre unto West-mynster hall by land, and cam my lord John Gray, the duke of Suffoke['s] brodur latt beheddyd.

[The xxix day of May the Queen removed from St. James's, passing through the park, and took her barge at Whitehall, and so to] Rychmond, on her progress.

The xxx day of May was ij sett on the pelere, a [man and a woman]; but the woman had here ere nayled to the pelere for spykyng of falles lyes and rumors; the man was for sedyssyous wordes and slanderous wordes.

The xxxj day of May was a marchand-man of   .   .   :
slayne by a servyng-man with-in Sant Marten .   .   .   .

---

a incontinently.   b *Blank in MS.*   c ear.   d other ear.   e touching.

The furst day of Junii was the sam woman set on the [pillory, that] her ere was nayled a-ffor, was her thuder ᵃ nayled thys sam day for the sam offense.

The iiij day of Junii wasse all the galus ᵇ in London plokyd done in all plases.

The sam day the mayre of London and the althermen commanded that a skaffold shuld be mad abowt the crosse, for to be gyldyd agaynst the prynse of Spayne commyng in.

The sam tyme wher granted by the lord mayre and the aldermen and the common consell a xv and a d. for the commonse, payd forth-with-all toward the commyng of the prynsse of Spayne.

The sam tym wher commondyd that ij althermen to wache evere nyght, and j or ij constabulls to wache evere nyght, tyll iij or iiij of the cloke in the mornyng.

The ix day of Juin was the crosse in Chepe covered with canves from the fott to the tope, and endyd, for the pry [nce's coming,] and gyldyd.

The x day of Juin dyd pryche at Powlles crosse master (doctor Pendleton ᶜ); and be-twyn x and a xj of the cloke ther was a gunne shott over the prycher, and yt ᵈ the wall, and yt was a pellett of tyne.

.   .   .   .

The xij day of Juin was a gret fray be-twyn the lord Warden('s) servands of Kent and the Ines of   .   .   .   Gray('s) inn, Lynkolne('s) inn, and sum slayn and hurt.

The xxiiij day of Juin was a goodly masse kept at sant Edmond in Lumbard-strett for the strangers, and the chyrche hangyd with ryche cloth.

The xxv day of Juin anodur masse kept at the Gray-frers for the sextons of London, and after pressessyons with the whetes ᵉ plahyng, and clarkes syngyng, thrug Chepe-syd unto Soper lane, and agayn thrug Powlles chyrche yerd by master denes [place,]

ᵃ other.   ᵇ gallows.   ᶜ Strype; blent in MS.   ᵈ hit.   ᵉ waits.

and thrug Warwyke lane unto the Gray-frers, and so to dener unto the Kukes [a]-hall.

The sam day cam to Londun by water the prynche of Pymon[b] with a grett compeny of Spaneards; sum had crosses, sum red, and sum gren, and sum whyt, and so to *(unfinished.*[1]

The xxix day of Juin, the wyche was sant Peter and Powlles day, was a fayre at Westmynster abbay; and ther was a goodly pressessyon, and after masse; and ther the prynse of Pymon and dyvers Spaneards, and hard messe in kyng Henry the vij chapelle.

The vj day of Julij was a goodly sermon [by] on of the preben-dares of Powlles; and ther was a nuw skaffold mayd ther for the mayd that spake in the wall and wystelyd in Althergat stret; and she sayd openly that yt was on John Drakes ser Antony Knevett servand; and she whept petefully, and she knelyd and askyd God mercy, and the quen; and bad all pepull be ware of false thechyng[c], for she sayd that she shuld have many goodly thynges gyffyn her[d] . . . . .

The xxj day of July by x of the cloke [was proclaimed] thrug London that the prynche of Spayne was [arrived at Southampton] and that evere pere and lord and lade shuld [resort] unto her grace['s] cete of Wynchester with all spede to her graceus wed-dyng.

The sam after non commondyd by my lord mayre that hevere man shuld make bone-fyres in evere strett, so ther was mony plases had tabuls and [. . . [e]] tyll x at nyght, and ryngyng and plahyng.

The xxiij day of July wher commondyd that evere . . shuld goo a prossessyon and to syng *Te Deum laudamus* in evere parryche in London, and ryngyng of the belles.

The xxix day of July dyd pryche at Powlles crosse master

[a] Cooks'   [b] Piedmont.   [c] teaching.   [d] *i. e.* had been promised.
[e] Plenty of good liquor for all comers. *Strype.*

Harpfeld and he dyd pray in ys bedes for the kyng and the quen Phelipe and Mare by the grace of God kyng and quene of England, Franse, Napuls, Jerusalem, Ierland, deffendors of the fayth, prynces of Spayne and Sycylye, archedukes of Austryche, dukes of Mylayne, Burgundye, and Brabant; contes of Haspurge, Flandurs, and Tyrole ; whyt thes stylle a as ys a-ffor.

The xxx day of July was bered at Grenwyche ser Robart Whentworth knyght, with armes and dyvers mornares.

The vj day of September wher creatyd ser Antony Browne creatyd vyconte lord Montyguw.

[The j day of August the King and Queen were proclaimed in London, by the titles as above,] dukes of Melayne, Burgundye and Brabant, contes of Haspurge, Flandurs and Tyrole.

The . . . day of August b was bered master Lambard, altheman and draper, with mony mornars, and they bare stayff torchys, had mantyll fryresse c gownes, and the armes of ys craft and the armes (of) the marchant adventorers. d

The vij day of August was bered the wyff of master Lambard alderman and draper, with-in the monyth of the sam, with torchys and tapurs.

The viij day of August was bered the jen[tle] master Austyne Hynd altherman, the wych hyt [had] plesyd Almyghty God that he had levyd tyll myghe[lmas,] he shuld had byne the nuw mayre of thys no[ble] cete of London; with a standard and a cote of armur and iiij penons of armes and a C. iiij xx. of mantyll frysse gownes for men and women, and the women havyng raylles, with xxiiij torchys, and ij fayre whyt branchys, and mony mornares, and the compenye of the Clarkes, and with vj dosen of schochyons of ys armes, and a C. of blake gownes, and a-boyffe e the nombur, and after a gret dener.

The vij day of September was bered in sant Bothulff with-owt Bysshope-gate chyrche, good master James Suttun sqwyre, and

---

a with this style.   b This apparently, from the next paragraph, should be July.
c friese.   d MS. the ventorers.   e above.

clarke of the gren cloth unto kyng Henry the viijth. and unto kyng Edward the vjth. and unto quen Mare, and so buried^a with a cot armur, and a penon of armes, and ij dosen of schochyons, and ij whyt branchys and xij stayff torchys, and mony mornars, and the compene of the Clarkes; and vj of ys servantes bare hym in blake cotes, and ther dyd pryche master doctur Smyth at ys masse.

[The same day was the funeral of sir Harry Huncotes knight, alderman, and fishmonger.^b] . . . .

. . . . pore men and women of . . . . mantyll frysse . . . . . Fyssmongers halle hangyd with blake and with armes; [then] came the standard and then mornares; and then [came] ys armes, and then a harold bayryng ys cot armur . . . master Clarenshws the kyng at armes in ys ryche cote; then cam the corsse, and a-bowtt the corsse iiij mo penons, and a-bott xxiiij torchys bornyng, and ij goodly whytt branchys, ... and cam mornars the sward-berrer, my lord mayre, and [the alder]men mornars, and the resedue of them in vyolett, and then . . . . . boyth men and women; and so to the chyrche, and then on ha . . . . prahynge for ys solle, and then began the durge and . . pepull whent to the halle to drynke boyth spysse^c and wyn; and the morow mass of *requiem;* and after they offered furst ys cot armur, and after cam the harold and . . . offered ys target; and after ij offered ys sword; and after ij morn[ers] ys elmet with the crest; and then the mayre offered, and the altherman, and the mornars, and the craft; and, all done, master doctur Smyth dyd pryche; and when masse was don then offered the standard and the v penonsse of armes; and after to the Fyssmongars hall to dener; and my lord mayre and the althermen and all the mornars; [and] ther was a grett dener as youe have sene now a [days].

The xiiij day of September was iij sett in the pelere for play-hyng with falsse dysse and deseyffeng honest men in playng; and the same day was ij wypyd a-bowt London, [after] a care-hars,[a] for lotheryng,[b] and as wacabondes wher they taken.

The xvij day of September was a proclamasyon that all vacabonds and lotherus,[c] boyth Englys men and all maner of strangers, that have no master, shuld avoyd the cete and the subarbes a-pon gret payn.

The xx day of September was ij men dran of ij hyrdles unto Tyburne and un-to hangyng, the ij for qwynnyng[d] of noythy[e] money, and deseyvyng of the quen('s) subjects; the one dwelt in London sum tym.

Item the *(blank)* day of October was a woman sett on the pelere for sedyssyous wordes.

. . . . . and alle to evere body that wold oum . . . . . money a-way for lake of pepull.

The xxiij day of September dyd pryche doctur Rud at Powlles crosse, and he recantyd' and repentyd that he ever was mared,[f] and sayd openly that he cold not mare by God's law.

The xxvj day of September wher ij yonge men sett on the pelere, and ther ere nayled for spykyng sedyssyous wordes and malessyous wordes aganst the commonwelth.

The xxvij day of September wher iiij hangyd, on was a Spaneard, at Tyburne: ij wher goodly felows.

The xxviij day of September the Kyng and the Quen removyd from Hamtun court unto Westmynster tho her grace('s) plasse.

The xxx day of September dyd pryche at Powlles crosse my lord Chansseler the bysshope of Wynchester, and he mad a goodly sermon; and ther wher as grett a audyensse as ever I saw in my lyff.

The ij day October whent from Westmynster xx carres with veges[g] of gold and sylver to the Towre to be quennyd.[h]

The iiij day of October was the monyth myn[i] at Waltham

---

[a] cart-horse.   [b] loitering.   [c] loiterers.   [d] coining.   [e] naughty.
[f] married.   [g] wedges.   [h] coined.   [i] month's mind.

Abbay of master James Suttun sqwyre, and clarke of the gren-cloth; and ther was a sarmon, and a dolle of money unto evere howsse that ned the charete, and after a grett dener.

The ij day of October was bered the nobull duke of Norffok at a plasse callyd Fremyngham [a] chyrche; and ther was a goodly hersse of wax as I have sene in thes days, with a dosen of baner-rolles of ys progene,[b] and xij dosen penselles, xij dosen of kochyons, and with standard, and iij cotes of armes, and a baner of damaske, and iiij banars of emages, and mony mornars, and a gret dolle, and after gret dener. [For the furnishing of which dinner were killed forty great oxen and a hundred sheep, and sixty calves, besides venison, swans, and cranes, capons, rabbits, pigeons, pikes, and other provisions both flesh and fish. There was also great plenty of wine; and of bread and beer as great plenty as ever had been known, both for] ryche and pore: all the co[untry came thither; and] a grett dolle of money ther wher [bestowed upon the poorer sort;] for he was cared from *(unfinished).*

The v day of October was the obsequy of the duke of Northfoke at sant Mare Overes; a hers mad with tymber, and hangyd with blake, and with ys armes, and iiij goodly candlestyks gyldyd, and iiij grett tapurs, and with ys armes, and alle the qwyre hangyd with blake and armes; and durge and masse on the morowe. And my lord chanseler cheffe morner, and next master [controller,] and master Gorge Haward; at the durge my lord Montyguw, my lord admerell, and my lord Brugys, and divers others; and a xl in gownes and cotes in blake; and after to my lord['s place], and gret ryngyng ij days.

The vij day of October was the monyth myn[d of] ser Hare Huncotes knyght, late mayre and altherman, and Fyssmonger of London, and ther ys hersse bornyd . . . . . durge, and the morow-mas the furst[c] masse of the tr[inity], and with a harold, and after the masse of requiem; and doctur Smyth dyd

---

Framlingham.   [b] *i. e.* ancestral descent.   [c] *MS.* ffurt.

pryche, the reder of Oxford, and after [a great] dener; and he gayff muche money to evere w[ard] in London and he has fondyd ij prestes to syng, on in London and th'odur in Lynckolneshyre, wher he was borne: thys shall be for ever.

The vi day of October was bered at Westmynster a grett man a Spaneard, with syngyng, boyth Englys and Spaneards, with a hand-belle, a-for ryngyng, and ever[y] Spaneard havyng gren torchys, and gren tapurs to the nombur of a C. bornyng, and ther bered in the Abbay.

The ix of October was bered master Gorge Medley merser, and lat Chamburlayn of this cete of London, with ij whyt branchys and xij pore men with xij stayffes torchys, and xij gomes,[a] and dyvers men and women in blake gownes; and ys armes a-pone ys body, and the compene of the Clarkes, and of the Marsars; and when alle was don, they whent hom to drynke; and the morow after the masse of *requiem;* and ther dyd pryche doctur Smyth; and after hom to dener.

The x day of October was bered the good lord De la Warr in Sussex, with standard, banar of armes, banar-roll, [coat] armur, targat, sword, elmet, with harolds of armes; then cam the corsse with iiij baners borne abowt hym. [He] was the best howsse-keper in Sussex in thes days, and the mone [b] (was greater) for ym, for he ded withowt essue; and ther wher mony morners in blake; and ther wher a goodly hersse of wax and pensels, and viij dosen skochyons; and ther was a grett dolle of money, and met [c] and drynke as was (ever known in) that contrey.

The xij day of October ther was on of the pelere for spykyng of sedyssyous wordes, a colyar,[d] iij tymes.

The xiiij day of October dyd pryche in the shruds [e] the good bysshope of Durram, Donstall, that was Sonday.

The xj day of October was the obsequy of (*blank*) a Spaneard at

---

[a] *Sic MS. qu.* gownes.   [b] moan.   [c] meat   [d] collier, *i. e.* a seller of charcoal.
[e] The shrouds, or triforium, of St. Paul's cathedral.

Westmynster; ther wase a praty herse after the fassyon of Spayn, with blake, and a goodly masse of *requiem;* and the chapell that he was bered in was hong with blake; and ys harmes [a] mony, with a baner of armes and cote of armes, alle in gold, and target and elmett and mony skochyon, and a fere [b] hers-clothe of blake, and a crosse of cremesun velvet, done [c] to the ground—the ij yer of quen Mare.

The xv day of October was kyllyd with-owt Tempall bare almost at stren [d] a servand of ser Gorge Gyfford, shamfully slayne by a Spaneard, a-bowt iiij of the (clock) at after-non.

The xvj day of October cam rydyng owt of Northfoke on John Day prynter and ys servand, and a prest, and an-odur prynter, for pryntyng of noythy [e] bokes, to the Towre.

[The xviij day of October king Philip came down on horseback from Westminster unto Paul's, with many lords, being received under a canopy, at the west end: and the lord Montagu bare the sword afore the king. There he heard mass, and] Spaneards song mase; and after masse [he went back to] Westmynster to dener.

The xxj day of October ded [f] the yerle of Warwyke, the eldest sune of the duke of Northumberland that was heddyd,[g] at ser [Henry] Sydnay plasse at Penthurst at mydnyght he ded.

The xxiiij day of October was bered . . . Rechard Townlay in sant Austyn parryche syd Powlles with xvj torchys and iiij grett [tapers], and ij whyt branchys, with a harold of armes, with a standard, a penons of armes, cote, helmet, target, sword, the crest a hauke w . . . , and vj dosen of skochyons, and prestes and clarkes; a C. of the in(ns) of the cort cam to the berehyng, and the morow masse, and a sermon.

The xxvj day of October was hangyd at Charynge-crosse a Spaneard that kyld a servant of ser Gorge Gefford, the wyche was slayne with-owt Tempull-bare.

The xxix day of October the nuw lord mayre of London, mas-

---

[a] arms.   [b] fair.   [c] down.   [d] Strand.
[e] naughty.   [f] died.   [g] beheaded.

ter Lyons groser, toke ys hoathe at Westmynster; and alle the craftes of London in ther barges, and with stremars; and ther was a grett penoys decked with ij topes and stremars and . . . . gones and drumes and trumpetes, rohyng to Westmynster up and don; and when thay cam hom thay landyd at Powlles warff, and ther mett the mayr lx in rosett gownes and with targetts and gyffelyns* and blue hattes; and then a goodly pagant, a gryffen with a chyld lyung in harnes, and sant John Baptyst with a lyon, and ij vodys b and a dulle c with squybes bornyng, and trumpetes blohyng, and drum(s) and flute(s), and then the bachelers with cremesun damaske hedes, d and then trumpeters, and the wettes e of the cete; and so to yeld-hall to dener, for ther dynyd my lord chanseler and all the nobuls, and the Spaneardes, and the juges and lernyd men.

[The same day sir Thomas Audley, a famous captain, was buried in saint Mary Overy's. There attended his funeral the lord Gray, lord Fitzwalter, and divers other] captaynes and knyghtes and gentyllmen [to the number of] lx. be-syd odur.

The furst day of Novembar was [carried] by the gard into Nuw-gatt serten men.

The ij day of November was bered at sant Peters in chepe on master Pekeryng with ij fayre whyt branchys and viij torchys, iiij grett tapurs, and he gayffe unto xij [pore men] xij gownes that dyd bere them, and eldyd th . . . . dyvers mornars, and the felowshype of the . . . . and the morow the masse of *requiem.*

The iiij day of November dyd pryche at Powlles crosse master Harpfeld; and ther wher v dyd penance with shetts f a-bowt them, and tapurs and rods in ther handes, and the prycher dyd stryke them with a rod, and ther dyd they stand tyll the sermon was all done; and then the sumner toke the shets and the rods, and they whent into Powlles a-gayn, and so up the syd of the quer;

---

* javelins.   b woods, i. e. wild men.   c devil.   d hoods.
                    e waists.   f sheets.

on prest,[a] ys nam ys ser Thomas Lawes, odur wysse callyd ser Thomas Gryffyn, sum tyme a chanon at Eyssyng spyttyll; iiij of them wher relegyous men, and the feyth[b] was a temporall man that had ij wyeffes.

The iiij day of November be-gane a grett fray at Charyng crosse at viij of the cloke at nyght be-twyn the Spaneardes and Englysmen, the wyche thrugh wysdom ther wher but a fuwe hort, and after the next day thay wher serten taken that be-gane yt; on was a blake-mor, and was brought a-for the hed offesers by the knyght-marshall('s) servandes.

[The vj day of November the earl of Shrewsbury came riding to London with vj[xx] horse, and of gentlemen in velvet caps thirty, to his place in Coleherber in Thames-street.]

The vij day of November was ij men sett in the pelere in ther fordgownes;[c] on had the wry[ting over] ys hed for falshood[d] and wylfull perjury; and th'odur for subtyll falshod[d] and crafty desseytt.

The ix day of November cam rydyng to London the yerle of Penbroke with ij C. horsse, and in velvet cottes and cheynes, the cotes with iij lasses of gold, and lx reseduw in bluw cotes gardyd with velvet, and badge a gren dragon, to the parlement.

The xj day of November dyd pryche master Pendylltun at Powlles crosse and mad a good sermon.

The xij day of November the Kyng and the Quen rod unto Westmynster chyrche to the masse of the Holy-gost, and after masse to the parlement-howsse; and all the bysshopes and the lordes in ther parlement robes, with trompeters blohyng, and all the harolds in ther cote armurs, and the juges in ther robes; the yerle of Penbroke bare the kyng('s) sword, and the yerle of Comberland bare the quen('s) sword, and the yerle of Shrowsbery bare the kyng('s) cape[e] of mantenance, and the yerle of Arundell bare the quen('s) cape of mantenance; and a-for them rod to-gether my lord chansheler and my lord tressorer in ther parlement robes.

---

[a] one a priest.   [b] fifth.   [c] furred gowns.   [d] *MS*. falhod.   [e] cap.

The xiij day of November was commondyd by the bysshope of London to all clarkes in the dyoses of London for to have sant Necolas and to go a-brod, as mony as wold have ytt.

[The xiiij day of November, saint Erconwald's day, it was commanded that every priest in the diocess . . . .]

The *(blank)* day of November cam to the Fleet [Barlow a] sumtyme bysshope of (Bath and Wells), and master Kardmaker parsun of sant Brydes in Fletstret was the. . . . . . thay wher gohyng over see lyke marchands.

The xviij day of November dyd pryche at Powlles crosse the nuw bysshope of Lynckolne, doctur White, late the warden of Wynchaster,

The sam day was consecratyd nuw [bishops], on b bysshope of Brystow, and a-nodur c byshope of Lycheffeld and Coventre.

The xix day of November was bered at sant Martens at Charyng-crosse with ij crosses a gentyllman a Spaneard, and a iiij^{xx} torchys and tapurs in ther handes, and with syngyng to the cherche, and the morowe-masse boythe Spaneards and Englysmen syngyng.

The sam day whent to met my lord cardenall Polle in Kent my lord of Elly, with odur—doctur Thurlbe bysshope of Elly.

The xxiij day of November was a man and a woman stode on the pelere for tellyng of falsse lyes thatt kyng Edward the vj^{th} was a-lyffe.

The xxiiij day the sam man (and) woman was sett on the pelere a-gayne that dyd say that kyng Edward was a-lyffe, and for odur thynges.

[The same day cardinal Pole came from Gravesend by water, with the earl of Shrewsbury, the lord Montagu, the bishops of Durham and Ely, the lord Paget, sir Edward Hastings, the lord Cobham, and diverse] knyghts and gentyllmen, in barges, and thay all [did shoot the] bryge be-twyn xij and on of the cloke, and a-g[ainst] the steleard d of Temes my lord chanseler mett [them

---

a Strype.   b John Holyman.   c Ralph Bayne.   d steel-yard.

in his] barge, and my lord of Shrousbury [had his] barge with
the [talbot, all] ys men in bluw cotes, red-hosse, skarlett capes,
[and white] fethers; and so to the cort gatt, and ther the Kyng('s)
grace [met him] and inbrasyd hym, and so lad ym thrughe the
kyng('s) hall;] and he had borne a-for hym a sylver crosse, and [he
was arrayed in] a skarlet gowne and a sqware skarlett cape; and
my lord [North] bare the swarde a-for the Kyng; and so they
whent up unto the Quens chambur, and ther her grace salutyd
hym; and after he toke ys leyffe, and toke ys barge to ys plase at
Lambeth, that was the bysshope of Cantorberys, Crenmer, and
so to dener.

The xxv day of November dyd pryche at Powlles crosse master
Fecknam, den of Powlles, and a godly sermon.

The sam day, the wyche was Sonday, at after-non, the Kyngs
grace and my lord Fuwater[a] and dyvers Spaneards dyd ryd in
dyvers colars, the Kyng in red, and som [in] yellow, sum in gren,
sum in whyt, sum in bluw, and with targets and canes in ther
hand, herlyng of rods on at a-nodur,[b] and thrumpets in the sam
colars, and drumes mad of ketylles, and banars in the sam colars.

The xxvij day of November was the obsequy of sir Hugh Ryche
knyght, the sune and here to the lord Ryche, and knyght of the
Bathe mad by quen Mare the Furst, in Essex, with a standard, a
penon of armes, and a cot armur, elmet, targat, sword, skochyons,
and torchys.

The xxvij of November the Kynge and the lordes of the parlement satt with-in the court, and ther my lord cardenall dyd make
a orayson to the Kyng and the lords of the parlement what . .

.   .   .   .

. . . thankes unto God of the Quen('s) grace qwyckenyng.

The xxix day of November was commondyd by the byshope of
London, thrughe ys dyosesse, that thay shuld say the masse of
the Holy-gost (with) prossessyon, and to syng *Te Deum*, and ryng-

---

[a] Fitswater.   [b] *Here is this side-note,* The Kynges rydyng at Jube de Cane.

yng, [and to] pray to God to gyffe hym thankes of owr [gracious] quen of her qwyckenyng with chyld, and to pray.

The xxx day of November the Kyng('s) grace and ys [lords] rod to Westmynster abbay to masse, for the Spaneards [sung], and ther mett ym at the cort gate a C. He-Alman [a] in hosse and dobeletes of whyt and red, and yelow welvet cotes [trimmed], with yelow sarsenet, and yelow velvet capes and fethers . . . coler, and drumes and flutes in the sam coler, and with gylt [halbards], and C. in yolow hosse, dobelets of welvett, and jerkens of [leather] gardyd with cremesun velvett and whyt, fether yelow and red; and thos be Spaneards; and a C. in yelow gownes of velvett with (*blank*) And the sam nyght my lord cardenall cam to the courte, and whent to the chapell with the Kyng, and ther *Te Deum* songe.

The furst day of Desember was bered in Powlles chyrche-yerd Recherd Wethers penter,[b] the wyche he ded with-in Ludgat as a presoner, and he was a proper man and a conyng man as any ys now.

The ij day of Desember dyd com to Powlles all prestes and clarkes with ther copes and crosses, and all the craftes in ther leverey, and my lorde mayre and the althermen, agaynst my lord cardenall('s) commyng; and at the bysshopes of London plase my lord chansseler and alle the bysshopes tarehyng for my lord cardenall commyng, that was at ix of the cloke, for he landyd at Beynard Castell; and ther my lord mayre reseyvyd hym, and browgth ym to the Powllse, and so my lord chanseler and my lord cardenall and all the byshopes whent up in-to the quer with ther meyturs;[c] and at x of the cloke the Kyng('s) grace cam to Powlles to her mase with iiij C. of gaard, on C. Englys, on C. He-Almen, on C. Spaneards, on C. of Swechenars,[d] and mony lords and knyghtes, and hard masse. Boyth the quen('s) chapell and the kynges and Powlles qwer song.

[The v day of December, the which was saint Nicholas' eve, at

---

[a] High Almaines.　　　[b] painter.　　　[c] mitres.　　　[d] Switzers.

evensong time, came a commandment that saint Nicholas should
not go abroad, nor about.   But, notwithstanding, there went
about these saint Nicholases in divers parishes, as st. Andrew's,
Holborn, and st.] Nicolas Olyffe in Bredstret.

The viij day of Desember, the wyche was the Conceptyon of
owre blessed lady the Vyrgyn, was a goodly prossessyon at the
Save^a be the Spaneards, the prest carehyng the sacrement ryally
be-twyne ys hands, and on deacon carehyng a senser sensyng, and
anodur the ale-water stoke,^b and a nombur of frers and prestes
syngyng, [and every] man and woman, and knyghts and gentylmen, bayryng a gren tapur^c bornyng, and viij trumpeters blohyng;
and when they had don plahyng, and then begane the sagbottes
plahyng; and when they had don theyr was on that cared ij drumes
on ys bake, and on cam after playng; and, so don, they whent
a-bowt the Sawve^d with-in; and a wyll^e after playing a-gayn, and
so cam in syngyng, and so after they whent to masse, wher the
bedes w . . (unfinished).

The ix day of Desember dyd pryche at Powlles crosse doctur
Borne, bysshope of Bathe, and prayd for the pope of Rome
(Julius) the thurde, and for alle the solles of purgatory.

The sam day at after-non was a bere-beytyn^f on the Banke
syde, and ther the grett blynd bere broke losse, and in ronnyng
away he chakt^g a servyng man by the calff of the lege, and bytt
a gret pesse away, and after by the hokyll-bone, that with-in iij
days after he ded.

The xij day of Desember dyd ryd in a car a-bowt London for baldre
one Kay wyffe dwellyng be-syd sant Mare Spytyll at the corner.

The xiiij day of Desember was sant Donstones in (the) est
chyrche and chyrche-yerde halowyd by a sofferacan,^h the wyche
was sospendyd one owr Lade day, the Consepsyon, by a man of
the parryche.

^a Savoy.   ^b holy-water stock.   ^c MS. tapurs.   ^d Savoy.
^e while.   ^f bear-baiting.   ^g caught.   ^h suffragan bishop.

The xvj day of Desember dyd pryche at Powlles crosse doctur Cottes the bysshope of West Chastur, and h[is] sermon of the blessyd sacrement of the auter . . . . owt dyvers actours [a] of the sacrement of dyvers . . . .

The xviij day of Desember was a grett tryhumph at the court gatte, by the Kyng and dyvers lordes boyth English-men and Spaneards, the wyche the Kyng and his compene [were] in goodly harnes, and a-pon ther armes goodly jerkyns of bluw velvett, and hosse in-brodered with sylver and bluw sarsenett; and so thay rane on fott with spayrers [b] and swerds at the tornay, and with dromes and flutes in whyt velvet [drawn] owt with blu sarsenett, and ther wher x aganst [the King] and ys compene, the wher xviij in odur colers.

The xxvj day of Desember cam by water from . . . the prynche of Pymon [c] with my lord of preve-sale and my lord Monty-cute, and shut the bryge,[d] and cam unto (*unfinished*).

The last day of Desember was bered at Margatt [e] at West-mynster a Spaneard, a lord, and bered with baner, cott, targett, and skochyons, and with grett lyght, and elmet, and the mantyll, and mony torche lyght.

The furst day of January where asymbulle [f] of men and vomen in Bowe chyrche-yerde at nyght of a xxx and a-boyffh,[g] and ther thay had the Englys serves and prayers and a lectorne, and thay wher taken by the shreyffes, and Thomas Rosse the menyster, and thay wher cared to the contors and odur plases, and ser Thomas Rosse to the Towre.

The viij day of January the prynsse of Pyemon [i] whent by water to the Towre with my lord Admerall and my lord Clynton, and dyvers odur, and he was shud [k] evere plasse ther, and ther wher grett shutyng of gones.

[The ix day of January certain Spaniards killed an Englishman basely: two held him while one thrust him through, and so he died.]

---

[a] authors.　　[b] spears.　　[c] Piedmont.　　[d] shot the bridge.　　[e] St. Margaret's.　　[f] assembly.　　[g] above.　　[h] So in *MS*.　　[i] Piedmont.　　[k] shown.

The xiiij day of Januarij ther preched [at Paul's cross] doctur Chadsay persun of Allalowes in Bred-strett.

The xvj day of January was bered the lade Fuwater,ᵃ the wyff of the lord Fuwater, in [Essex] at Odam Water,ᵇ with iiij baners of armes, [a standard ?] of armes, and ij emages, with a hers, and vij dosen penselles, and viij dosen of skochyons, and a mantyll, and whyt branchys, and iiij dosen stayff-torchys.

The xviij day of January wher hangyd at Tyborne ij men and iiij women.

The sam day whent to the Towre my lord chansseler, and dyvers odur lordes and of the conselle, and delyvered a nomber presonars, as ther names folowes—ser James a Croft, ser Gorge Harper, ser Gawynn Carow, ser Necolas Frogmortun, master Vaghan, ser Edward Varner, Gybbs, the bysshope of Yorke, master Rogers, and dyvers odur presonars, and after ther was a gret shottyng of gones.

The xxij day of Januarij was raynydᶜ at my lord chansseler plasse by-syd sant Mare Overes ser John Hoper latt bysshope of Glosetur, doctur C[rome], as the parsun of Wyttyngtun colege, harold Tomson, Rogars parsun or veker of sant Pulkers, and dyvers odur.

The xxiiij day of January ther wher grett ronnyng at the tylt at Westmynster with spayrers,ᵈ boyth Englys men and Spaneards.

[The xxv day of January, being saint Paul's day, was a general procession of saint Paul by every parish, both priests and clarkes, in copes to the number of a hundred and sixty, singing *Salve festa dies*, with ninety crosses borne. The procession was through Cheap into Leadenhall. And before went the] chyldryn of the Gray-frers and Powlles skolle. [There were eight bishops, and the] bysshope of London myteryd, bayryng the sacre[ment, with . . eym] of torchys bornyng, and a canepe borne [over]; so a-bowtt the chyrch-yerde, and in at the west dore, [with the] lord mayre

---

ᵃ Fitzwater.   ᵇ Woodham Walter.   ᶜ arraigned.
ᵈ spears. *As a side-note to this paragraph is this word*, Jostyng.

and the althermen, and all the craftes in ther best leverays.   And with-in a wylle after the Kyng cam, and my lord cardenall, and the prynsse of Pyamon,[a] and dyvers lordes and knyghtes; thay hard masse, and after to the court to dener, and at nyght bone-fyres and grett ryngyng in evere [church].

The xxvij day of January ther was a goodly prossessyon cam from Westmynster unto Tempull bar with crosses and a C. chylderyn in surples and a C. clarkes and prestes in copes syngyng, the wyche the copes wher very ryche of tyssuw and cloth of gold; [and after] that master dene Weston carehyng the blessyd sacrement, and a canepe borne over yt, and a-bowt yt a xx torchys bornyng, and after yt a ij C. men and women.

The xxviij day of January was examynyd at sant Mare Overes bysshope Hoper, doctur Crom, and Cardmaker, and odur, and Cardmaker recantyd.

The xxix day of January wher raynyd[b] at sant Mare Overes for herese Hoper and Rogers, and cast to be brentt, and from thens cared to Nugatt.

The xxx day of January was raynyd in the sam plasse Bradford, Tayller, and Sandur, and cast to be brentt in dyvers places.

[The j day of February was buried the duchess of Northumberland at Chelsea where she lived, with a goodly herse of wax and pensils, and escocheons, two baners] of armes, and iiij [banners of images, and] mony mornars, and with ij haroldes of armes. Ther was a mageste and the valans, and vj dosen of torchys and ij whyt branchys, and alle the chyrche hangyd with blake and armes, and a canepe borne over her to the chyrche.

The iiij day (of) Feybruary the bysshope of London went into Nugatt, and odur docturs, to dysgratt[c] Hoper, and Rogers sumtyme vycker of sant Polkers.

The sam day was Rogers cared be-twyn x and xj of the cloke in-to Smyth-feld, and bornyd, for aronyus[d] apinions, with a grett compene of the gard.

[a] Piedmont.   [b] were arraigned.   [c] degrade.   [d] erroneous.

CAMD. SOC.   M

The v day of Feybruarij be-twyn v and vj in the mornyng, (departed) master Hoper to Gloceter, and Sandurs to Coventre, boyth [to be] bornd.

The vj day of Feybruary doctur Tayller was sent in-to Suffoke, and to be brentt.

The xij day of Feybruary was my lord Strange mared to the lade of Cumberland the yerle of Cumberland doyctur ; and after a grett dener, and justes, and after tornay on horsbake with swordes, and after soper *Jube the cane*, a play,[a] with torch-lyght and cressett-lyghtes, lx cressets and C. of torchys, and a maske, and a bankett.

The ix day of Feybruary was raynyd at Powlles, a-for my lord mayre and the shreyffes and the bysshope of London and dyvers docturs and of the conselle, vj heretykes [of] Essex and Suffoke, to be brent in dyvers places.

The xvij day of Feybruary at bowt mydnyght ther wher serten lude feylous cam unto sant Thomas of Acurs, and over the dore ther was set the ymage of sant Thomas, and ther thay brake ys neke and the tope of ys crosier, the wyche was mad of fre-ston ; with grett sham yt was done.

.   .   .   .   .   .

The v day of Marche was playd a-fo[r the king and] the conselle Whyt the master of fensse[b] and ys [fellows, and] all odur that wold come at the court at Vest[mynster.]

The viij day of Marche ther was a general prossessyon from Powlles and thrugh Chepe and Bucklers[bery] and thrug Walbroke and up Boge-row and Watling stret, and so to Powlles ; and all the chylderyn of Powlles and of the hospetall, and the bysshope and my lord mare and aldermen, and all the crafts, and all clarkes and prestes syngyng.

The sam day was a man sett on the pelere [for hurting] of one of the vj men that was sworne, and lyke [to have] bene slayne, and dyd suspend the chyrche of [saint] Donestones in the est.

The xiiij day of Marche in the nyght ther serten velyns[c] dyd

---

[a] *Juego de Canas*, or tilting with canes, a sport introduced by the Spaniards.
[b] master of fence.   [c] villains.

breke the neke of the ymage of sant Thomas of Canturbere,ᵃ and on of ys arms broke.

The xv day of Marche ther was a proclamassyon the morowe after that wo so ever dyd know or cold bryng word to the mayre who dyd breke ys neke, shuld have a C. crones of gold for ys labur.

The xvj day of Marche was a veyverᵇ bornyd in Smyth-feld, dwellyng in Sordyche, for herese, by viij of the cloke in the morn-yng, ys nam was (Tomkins ᶜ).

The xviij day of Marche was browth to the Towre owt of Cambryge-shyre master Bowes, master Cutt, and master Hynd, and dyvers odur, for a nuw conspyrase, the wyche shuld have byne don in Suffoke and odur plases.

The xix day of Marche in the mornyng the Kyng('s) grace rune at the tylt a-gaynst odur Spaneards, and brake iiij stayffes by viij of the cloke in the mornyng.

[The xx day of March the earl of Bedford, lord privy-seal, who died at his house beside the Savoy, was carried to his burying-place in the country, called Chenies, with three hundred horse all in black.   He was carried with three crosses,] with mony clerkes and prestes, [till they came to the hill] a-boyffe sant James, and ther returnyd [certain of them] home; and thay had torchys and almes ᵈ and money gyven them.   And after evere man sett in aray on horssebake.   First on red ᵉ in blake bayryng a crosse of sylver, and serten prestes on horsebake wayryng ther surples; then cam the standard, and then all the gentyllmen and hed officers; and then cam haroldes, on beyryng ys elmet, and the mantylls, and the crest, and anodur ys baner of armes, and anodur ys target with the garter, and anodur ys cott armur; and anodur ys sword: and then master Garter in ys ryche cott armur and then cam the charett with vj banars rolles of armes, and a-bowt the charett iiij banars of ymages, and after the charet a gret horsse trapyd in cloth of gold with the sadyll of the sam; and then cam mornars, the

---

ᵃ *In a side note,* sant Thomas of Acurs.   ᵇ weaver.
ᶜ *blank in MS.*   ᵈ *in MS.* armes.   ᵉ one rode.

cheyffe (of whom) my lord Russell ys sune,[a] and after my lord trayssorer, and the master of the horse, and dyver odur nobull men all in blake; and evere[b] towne that he whent thrughe the clarkes and prestes mett ym with crosses; and thay had in evere parryche iiij nobuls to gyffe to the pore, and the prest and clarke of evere parryche x[s]., tyll he cam to ys plasse at Cheynes; and the morowe after was he bered, and a grett doll of money; and ther the deyn of Powlles mad a godly sermon; and after a grett dener, and gret plenty to all the contrey a-bowt that wold com thether.

The xxv day of Marche, the wyche was owre lade [day,] ther was as gret justes as youe have sene at the tylt at Vestmynster; the chalyngers was a Spaneard and ser Gorge Haward; and all ther men, and ther horsses trymmyd in whyt, and then cam the Kyng and a gret mene[c] all in bluw, and trymmyd with yelow, and ther elmets with gret tuyffes[d] of blue and yelow fether, and all ther veffelers[e] and ther fotemen, and ther armorers, and a compene lyke Turkes red[f] in cremesun saten gownes and capes, and with fachyons,[g] and gret targets; and sum in gren, and mony of dyvers colers; and ther was broken ij hondred stayffes and a-boyff.[h]

The iiij day of Aprell the Kyng('s) grace and the Quen removyd unto Hamtun cowrte to kepe Ester ther, and so her grace to her chambur ther.

.   .   .   .

The xvij day of Aprell was a commandment [from the bishop of London that every] parryche in London shuld have the sam day, and the morowe, durge and masse and ryngyng for pope Jully [the third] of that name, and for all crystyn solles.

The xiiij day of Aprell, the wyche was [Ester day,] at sant Margatt parryche at Westmynster, af[ter masse] was done, one of the menysters a prest of the ab[bay] dyd helpe hym that was the menyster [to] the pepull who wher reseyvyng of the blessyd sacrement of [the lord] Jhesus Cryst, ther cam in-to the chyrche a man

---

[a] son.   [b] every.   [c] menée, *i. e.* retinue.   [d] tufts, *or* plumes.
[e] whifflers, *or* forerunners.   [f] rode.   [g] falchions.   [h] above.

that was a monke of Elly, the wyche was marryed to a wyff; the sam day ther that sam man sayd to the menyster, What doyst thow gyff them ? and as sone as he had spokyn he druw his wod-knyffe, and hyt the prest on the hed and struck hym a grett blowe, and after ran after hym and struck hym on the hand, and cloyffe ys hand a grett way, and after on the harme ˣ a grett wond ᵇ; and ther was syche a cry and showtt as has not byne; and after he was taken and cared to presun, and after examynyd wher-for he dyd ytt.

The xx day of Aprell was raynyd ᶜ at Powlles a-for the bysshope of London and many odur and my lord cheyffe justys and my lord mayre and the shreyffes; ys name was (master Fowler, alias Branchᵈ); he was a monke of Ely; and ther was a goodly sermon, and after he was cast and condemnyd to have ys hand that hurt the prest cut off or he shuld suffer,ᵉ and after dysgracyd, and after cared to Nuwgatt.

The xxj day of Aprell ther was wypyd at a cart-hors iij, j man and ij women, and anodur man a-lone, ij old men with whyt berdes, and on was for carehyng . . . . . .

[The xxiijd day of April, being saint George's day, at Hampton Court, the King, with other lords and knights of the garter, went in their robes on procession, with three] crosses, and clarkes and prestes, and my lord chancellor, the cheyff menyster, metered, ᶠ and all thay in copes of cloth of tyssue and gold, syngyng *Salva fasta dyes* as thay whent a-bowt; the Quen('s) grace lokyd owt of a cassement, that hundereds dyd se her grace after she had taken her chambur ; and arolds ᵍ gohyng a-bowt the Kyng('s) grace.

The xxiiij day of Aprell was the sam man cared to Westmynster that dyd hurt the prest, and had ys hand stryken of at the post, and after he was bornyd aganst sant Margett chyrche with-owt the cherche-yerde.

ˣ arm.   ᵇ wound.   ᶜ arraigned.   ᵈ *Blank in MS.*
ᵉ *i. e.* before he should suffer death ; *see under the* xxiiijth.
ᶠ heralds.   ᵍ wearing his mitre.

The **xxvj** day of Aprell was cared from the Marselsee in a care thrugh London unto Charyng-crosse to the galows, and ther hangyd, iij men for robyng of serten Spaneardes of tresur of gold owt of the abbay of Vestmynster. ·

The sam day was a yonge man wypytt at a post with a coler of yron to the post, by the standard in the Chepe, that ys callyd the post of reformassyon, for brybyng and pyky . .

The **xxix** day of Aprell was cutte downe of the galows a man that was hangyd the **xxvj** day of Aprell,· a pulter('s) servant that was one of them that dyd robed ᵃ the Spaneard with-in Westmynster Abbay, and he hangyd in a gowne of towny ᵇ fryse and a dobelet of townny taffata and a payre of fyne hose lynyd with sarsenet, and after bered undur the galaus, rayllyng a-ganst the pope and the masse, and hangyd iiij days.

The **xxx** day of Aprell and the last day of Aprell thydynges cam to London that the Quen('s) grace was delevered of a prynce, and so ther was grett ryngyng thrugh London, and dyvers plases *Te Deum laudamus* songe; and the morow after yt was tornyd odurways to the plesur of God ! But yt shall be when yt plesse God, for I trust God that he wyll remembur ys tru servands that putt ther trust in hym, when that they calle on hym.

[The **ij** day of May three persons for their abominable living were carted through the city, from Guildhall to Cheapside, and so through Newgate, and through Smithfield, and back again to the Standard in Cheap, where the proclamation of their unclean living was made, viz. master] Manwaryng a gentyllman, and ij women, on . . . . . Waren dwellyng at the Hare in Chepe, and the odur a gold-smyth('s) wyff, for baudry and hordom, and dyvers [times taken] with-all; and so cared owt of Algatt.

The **vij** day of May was taken owt of ys grave the sam man that was bered be-syd the galaus at Charynge crosse, a pulter, and bornyd be-syd the galaus.

The **x** day of May was browth ᶜ unto [the court at] Hamtun to

ᵃ *Sic MS.*   ᵇ tawny.   ᶜ brought.

the consell a yonge man the wyche sayd he was kyng Edward the
vj[th], and was [examined] a-for the conselle, and so examynyd how
he [dared be] so bold, and after delevered unto the marshall and
conveyed to the marshellsay, and ther he bydyth the conselles
pleasure.

The xv day of May was a generall prossessyon from Powlles
and unto Leydynhall and downe Gracious-strett, and tornyd done
Estchepe, and so to Powlles a-gayn; for [there] whent ij C. pore
men with bedes in ther handes, and iiij C. powre women of evere
parryche, ij men and ij vomen, ij and ij to-gether, and after all the
men-chylderyn of the hospetall, and after the chylderne of sant
Antonys, and then all the chyltheryn of Powlles and all ther
masters and husshers, and then all the prestes and clerkes, and
the bysshope, and my lord mare and the althermen, and all
the crafftes of London in ther leveray. The sam tym as thay wher
a-gohyng a-prossessyon in Chepe ther cam a frantyke man and
hangyd a-bowt a prest ij podynges, and after he was browth [a] to
the bysshope, and after to my lord mayre, and after to the contur
for ys folyssnes.[b]

. . . .

. . . . . wypyd at a care-hars [c] a-bowt the . . .

The xvij day of May was bone [d] to a post in [Cheap and] wyped
for *(blank in the MS.)* as they wher gohyng a-prossessyon the
Wednysday a-for, a-for non,[e] a man dwellyng at Belyngatt [f] in
Bore['s head]-alley; ys nam ys *(blank)* Halle a leyterman.

The xviij day of May was nodur lad wypyd at the same post
in Chepe for loytryng and ronnyng a-bowt master-les as a vaca-
bond.

The sam day of May was (arraigned) iiij men at Powlles, a-for
none and after-non, of Essex, and thay wher cast for heresse, [g]
all iiij cast to be bornyd, and so cared unto Nugatt.

---

[a] brought.   [b] foolishness.   [c] cart-tail.   [d] bound.
[e] noon.   [f] Billingsgate.   [g] heresy.

The xix day of May dyd pryche at Powlles crosse master Hapffeld; and ther wher ij women stode ther a-fore the precher, and ther the ij women declaryd that yt was falsse that they sayd a-fore, that the chyld dyd nott spyke, and bad all men take hed [a] how eny man or voman shuld beleyffe any shuche person the wyche shuld spyke a chyld be-syd Powlles, the wyche the chyld shuld spyke and shuld bed [b] men pray, and sayd that the kyngdom of God ys at hand.

The xvij day of May was bered the contesse of Vestmerland at Sordyche, for ther was a goodly hersse with iiij banars of emages, and iiij banars-rolles, and mony mornars, and ther was master Garter and Ruge-crosse, and after all done a gret dener.

The xxij day of May one Wylliam *(blank)*, sum tyme a lake, [c] rod in a care from the Marsalsey thrugh London unto Westmynster and in-to the Hall, and ther he had ys jugement to be wypyd be-caws he sayd that he cam as a messynger from kyng Edward the vj[th].

[The xxv day of May were arraigned at St. Paul's for heresy, before the bishop, master Cardmaker sometime vicar of St. Bride's in Fleet-street, and one] John Warren a cloth[worker in Walbrook] and a-nodur of *(blank)*, and cast to be brent; and [carried back to] Nugatt.

The xxix day of May was a goodly prossessyon of the chylderyn of the hospetall and all the skolles in [London].

The xxx day of May was burnt in Smythfeld master Cardmaker sum-tyme veker of sant Bryd and master Varren clothworker dwellyng aganst sant Johns in Walbroke, an hupholster, and ys wyff behyng in [Newgate].

The xxvij day of May was the Clarkes' prossessyon from Yerdhall [d] college, and ther was a goodly masse be hard, [e] and evere clarke havyng a cope and garland, with C. stremers borne, and the

---

[a] heed. [b] bid. [c] lacquey. [d] *Sic in MS. for* Yeldhall, *i. e.* Guildhall.
    [e] as goodly a mass as has been heard.

whettes [a] playng round Chepe, and so to Ledynhall unto sant Albro [b] chyrche, [and ther] thay putt off ther gayre, [c] and ther was the blessyd sacrament borne with torche-lyght a-bowt, and from thens unto the Barbur-hall to dener.

The xxvj day of May was a goodly May-gam at sant Martens in the feld, with gyant and hobehorsses, with drumes and gonnes and mores danse and with othur mynsterelles.

The iij day of Junij cam a godly prossessyon from sant Peters in Cornhylle with the Fyssmongers, and my lorde mayre, with a C. copes, unto Powlles, and ther thay offered; with the whettes [d] playhyng and syngyng.

The sam day was a goodly May-gam at Westmynster as has ben synes, [e] with gyantes, mores-pykes, gunes and drumes, and duwylles, [f] and iij mores-dansses, and bag-pypes and wyolles, [g] and mony dysgyssyd, and the lord and the lade of the May rod gorgyously, with mynsterelles dyver playng.

[The same day was the procession of saint Clement's parish without Temple bar, set forth with a great many streamers] and baners, and the whetes of London [with crosses.] In the myds of the crosses was the Spaneards crosse of the Savoy, and yt was rond lyke to that hangys over [the sacrament,] of cremesun welvett inbrodere ryche, and after clarkes and prestes in ryche copes syngyng *Salve fasta dies*; [and] folowyng all the ines of the cowrt ther; and after all the parryche with whyt rods in ther handes a gret nombur.

The sam day cam Eslyngtun prosessyon, with standard and baners, with clarkes and prestes in copes syngyng *Salve fasta dies*, and after all the parryche boyth men and women.

The x day of Juin was delevered owt of Nuwgatt vij men to be cared in-to Essex and Suffoke to borne. [h]

The sam day was Grossers' fest, and ther was my lord mayre

| [a] waits. | [c] Ethelburga. | [e] gear. | [d] waits. | [e] *Sic MS. lege* seen. |
| | [f] devils. | [g] viols. | [h] to be burned. | |

and dyvers althermen, and ther my lord mayre dyd chuysse master Lee altherman shreyffe for the kyng, and master Whytt grocer
and altherman the master of the Grosers, and master Graftun warden and master Grenway warden for that yere.

The xj day of Juin be-gane they to sett up the frame for the
hersse at Powlles for the quen of Spayn, the wyche was the goodlest that ever was sene in England; the bare frame cost xv^l. the
carpynter('s) dute.

The xvij day of Juin was the hersse fenyssyd at Powlles a-boyffe
the qwyer with ix prensepalles garnyshyd, (the) goodlest that ever
was sene, and all the prensepalles covered with blake velvett, and
the mageste of taffata and the frynge [gold]; and all the qwyre
and a-boyffe the qwyre and the sydes and ondur [foot] and
the body of the chyrche one he ᵃ hangyd with blake and armes,
and with xxxvj dosen of pensells of sylke welvett with gold and
selver, and xvj baners-rolles of armes, and iiij baners of whyt
emages wroght with fyne gold; over-nyght durge, and the morow
masse; and mony mornars, the forst a stranger and the yerle of
Shrusbere, and yerle of Penbroke, my lord treysorer, ser Recherd
Sowthwell, and mony mo as Englys as Spaneards; and a vij skore
powre men havyng nuwe blake gownes, and evere man holdyng
torchys; and after messe a grett dener at the bysshope of Lon-
don('s) plasse, and gret plente.

The xiiij day (of) Juin was a proclamassyon [that all] bokes
shuld be broyth ᵇ in of Luter, Tendalles, ... and Cover-
dals and bysshope Cremer,ᶜ and all shyche as . . . . shuys
and all hereses bokes, and he that dyd nott [bring them] in with-in
the xv days after shuld go to presun with-owt prysse, of what
degre they be of.

The furst day of July whent in-to Smythfeld to borne ᵈ master
Bradford, a grett precher by kyng Edwards days, and a talow-

ᵃ on high.   ᵇ brought.   ᶜ Cranmer.   ᵈ burn, i. e. to be burnt.

chandler('s) prentes ª dwellyng by Nugatt, by viij of the cloke in the mornyng, with a grett compene of pepull.

The sam day was bered good master Thomas . . . . . . altherman, sum tyme shreyff of London, and [a hearse] with ij whyt branchys and xij longe torchys [a hearse] stayffe torchys and iiij grett tapurs, and xij gownes gyffen unto xij pore men of blake peneston, and the compene of the Clarkes and mony prestes and . . . armes of the body and the tapurs, and ther wher . . . blake gownes, and after durge speysse-bred and wine; and the morow masse of requeem, and ther dyd pryche a frere of Grenwyche, and a grett dolle.

The ij day of July was the Marchand-tayllers' fest, and ther dynyd my lord mayre and dyvers of the conselle and juges and the shreyffes and mony althermen and ʼgentyllmen, and thay had agaynst ther dener lviij bokes and ij stages ᵇ; the master of the compene master Jeye Wade sqwyre, (and the wardens) master Eton, master Rowe, and master Hylle, and master God, and all v borne in London and tayller(s') sunnes alle.

The vj day of July rod to Tyburne to be hangyd iij men, and on drane ᶜ upon a hyrdyll unto Tyburne for qwynnyng ᵈ of money.

[The viij day of July were three more delivered out of Nugate, and sent into the country to be burned for heretics.]

The xij day of July was bornyd at Canturbery iiij men for herese, ij prestes and ij laye men.

The xx day of July was cared to the Towre, [in the] morning erlee,ᵉ iiij men; on was the good-man of [the] Volsake ᶠ with-owt Algatt.

The xxj day of July dyd pryche at Althermare [church] Recherdson the Skott, that was the reder at Wyttyngton college, from on ᵍ tyll iij of the cloke, and ther was the grettest audyense that has ben sen in a parryche; and he came thedur to have recantyd, butt he wold nott.

ª apprentice.   ᵇ bucks and stags.   ᶜ one drawn.   ᵈ coining.
      ᵉ early.   ᶠ Woolsack.   ᵍ one.

The ij day of August was a shumaker bornyd at sant Edmunde-bere in Suffoke for herese.

The viij day of August, between iiij and v in the mornyng, was a presoner delevered unto the shreyff of Medyllsex to be cared unto Uxbryge to be bornyd; yt was the markett day—owt of Nuwgatt delevered.

The ix day of August was a generall prossessyon at London with all the chylderyn of skolles[a] in London; and all sextens, and all clarkes, and all prestes; and the bysshope of London, and my lord mayre, in ther leveray, from Powlles done[b] Chepesyd, and thrugh Bokelars-bere and Walbroke, and up Watlyng-stret to Powlles.

The iij day of August the Quen and Kynges grace removyd from Hamtun Court unto Hotland,[c] a iiij mylles of: has her grace whent thrugh the parke for to take her barge, ther mett her grace by the way a powre man with ij chruches, and when that he saw[d] her grace, for joy he thruw hys stayffes a-way, and rane after her grace, and sche commondyd that one shuld gyff ym a reward.

.   .   .   .
.   .   .   .

Ox]fordshyre.

The xv day of August was a grett ffett on the see[e] be-twyn the Frencmen and the Flemmyng, and ther wher dyvers of boyth partes slene, and boyth men and shypes and dyvers taken, and the goodes.

The xxiij day of August was bornyd at [Stratford]-of-bowe, in the conte of Mydyllsex, a woman, [wife] of John Waren, clothworker, a huphulster [over] agaynst sant Johns in Walbroke; the wyche . . . . John her hosband was bornyd with on Cardmaker in Smythfeld,[f] for herese boyth; and the sam woman had a sune[g]

[a] schools.   [b] down.   [c] Oatlands.   [d] MS. say.
          [e] fight on the sea.   [f] See before, p. 88.   [g] son.

taken at her bornyng and cared to Nuwgatt [to his] syster, for they will borne boyth.

The xxiiij day of August cam from Rome at afternone the bysshope of Ely,[a] the bysshope of Banger,[b] the lord Montycutt vycontt, ser Hare Husse, and dyvers odur.

The xxvj day of August cam from Westmynster, rydyng thrugh London unto Towrs-warff, the Kyng and the Quen, and ther thay toke ther barge unto Grenwyche, and landyd at the long bryge, and reseyvyd by my lord chanseler, and my lord of Ely, and my lord vycont Montyguw, master comtroller, master Sowthwell, and dyvers mo, and the gard, and dyvers holdyn torchys bornynge, and up to the Frers, and ther thare graces mad ther praers, and at her grace('s) landyng received ix or x suplycasyon(s), and so bake agayn to the court with a c. torchys bornyng.

[The xxviii day of August went out of Newgate certain] here-tykes to borne in the contrey.

The xxix day of August, (which) was the day of Decolacyon of sant John Baptyst, the Marchand-tayllers kept masse at Sant Johnes be-yond Smyt-feld, and my lord of Sant Johnes dyd offer at masse, and ser Hare Hubylthorne, ser Thomas Whytt and master Harper, althermen, and all the clothyng. And after the iiij wardens of the yeomanry, and all the compene of the tayllers, a 1d. a pesse; and the qwyre honge with cloth of arres, and after masse to the Tayllers' halle to dener.

The same day the Kyng('s) grace toke ys jorney toward Dover, and with a grett compeny, and ther tared for the wynd, and ther the shypes lying rede[c] for ys grace gohyng over see.

The xxx day of August was cast at yeld-hall, for robyng[d] of the quen('s) warderobe, one John Boneard, a servantt of hers, dwellyng be-syd the Warderobe at the Blake Frers, and cast. The sam day were cast, for robyng of ther masturs, ij. wher prentes,[e] and the thurd was a servyngman, the prentes dwellyng in Boke-

---

[a] Thomas Thirlby.   [b] William Glynn.   [c] ready.   [d] robbing.   [e] apprentices.

larbere, for kepyng of herers,[a] and after send[b] unto the bysshop('s) presun at Startford in Essex.

The xxxj day of August whent out of Nugatt a man of Essex unto Barnett for herese, by the shreyff of Medyllsex, to borne ther.

The iiij day of September the Quen('s) grace and my lady Elsabeth, and all the court, dyd fast from flessh, and toke the Popes jubele and pardon grantyd to alle men.

[The same day were certain bishops, viz. doctor Corwyn archbishop of] Duvylyne, [doctor William] Glyne bysshoppe of Bangor, (and) doctur (James Turberville) bysshope of Exsseter, alle consecratyd at Powlles.

The x day of September was bered my lade Lyons, the mares[c] of London, with a goodly [herse] mad in sant Benet-sherog parryche, with ij branchys, and xxiiij gownes of blake for pore men; and thay had xxiiij torchys, with v banars, one of armes, and iiij of emages, and vj dosen pensells, and vij dosen of skochyons, and ij harold(s) of armes, and c. mornars in blake, and the althermen folohyng the corsse, and after the [company of] the Grosers, and the morow the masse, and master H . . dyd pryche, and after a grett dener.

The xv day of September dyd pryche at Powlles (*blank*), and he declaryd (the) Pope('s) jubele and pardon from Rome, and as mony as wyll reseyffe ys pardon so to be shryff,[d] and fast iij days in on[e] wyke, and to reseyffe the blessed sacrement the next Sonday affter, clen remyssyon of all ther synes *tossyens quossyens*[f] of all that ever they dyd.

The xx day of September was cared from Nugatt unto the lolrar stowre[g] serten men.

The xxix day of September was the grettest rayn and fludes that ever was sene in England, tbat all low contreys was drounyd, and in dyver plasses boyth men and catell drounyd, and all the

---

[a] whores?   [b] sent.   [c] mayoress.   [d] shrived.   [e] one.
[f] *toties quoties.*   [g] *So in MS.* The Lollards' tower at Lambeth palace *is meant.*

marssys,[a] and sellers[b] boyth of wyne and bere and alle[c] and odur marchandysse, in London and odur plassys, drounyd; and the rayne begane after Bathellmuw-tyd telle sant Edwardes tyde, after not x days fayre.

. . . .

. . . . . . ij goodly whytt branchys and xij longe torchys . . . . . stayffes torchys grett, and a c. mornars in blake, [xij poor] men and xij women, and all xxiiij in rosett gownes [and the] vomen raylles apon ther heds, and iiij gylt candyll-stykes, with iiij grett tapurs and xx prestes and xx clarkes.

The sam day at after-none was bered master Barthelett sqwyre and prynter unto Kyng Henry; and was bered with pennon and cote-armur, and iiij dosen of skochyons and ij whytt branchys and iiij gylt candyllstykes, and mony prestes and clarkes, and mony mornars, and all the craftes of prynters, boke-sellers, and all stas-syoners a . . .

The vij day of October was a robere be-syd . . . . parke of clothears, so they foyth[d] long, at last the th[ieves] over-cam them, and toke alle the goodes, and cot ther hors leges off and kyllyd sum.

The ix day of October was a servyngman, [the] penter('s) broder that war bornyd at Staynes, was bered in Morefeld be-syd the doge-howsse, be-caus he was not resseff[e] the ryctes of the chyrche, and thys lawe.

The (blank) day of October was bered doctor Wottun, phes-syssyon, in Woodstrett, with ij whyt branchys and xij longe torchys and vj stayff torchys and mony (mourners).

The xvj day of October was the Sargent(s') of the law fest,[f] and vij mad the sam day, and a grett dener after, and kept at the (blank).

[The same day were burnt at Oxford for heresy doctor Latimer,

---

[a] marshes.   [b] cellars.   [c] ale.   [d] fought.
[e] was not to receive.   [f] feast.

late bishop of Worcester, and doctor Ridley,] late bysshope of London; [they were some] tyme grett prychers as ever was; and at ther bornyng dyd pryche doctur Smyth, sum-tyme the master of Vetyngtun[a] colege (*blank*).

The xxvj day of October was sett on the pelere [one] for spyk-yng of sedyssyous wordes, and had

The xxviij day of October in the mornyng was set up in Flet-strett, be-syd the well,[b] a payre of galaus, and ij men hangyd, for the robere of a Spaneard, (and they were) hangyng aganst the Spaneardes gate be-tyme in the mornyng, and so hangyng alle the day in the rayne.

The xxix day of October ther wher ij goodly pennes[c] deckyd with gones and flages and stremars, and a m. penselles, the penes pentyd, on whyt and bluw, and the thodur yelow and red, and the oars and gowne[d] lyke coler; and with trumpets and drumes, and alle the craftes in barges and stremars; and at the ix of the cloke my nuw lord mayre and the shreyffes and the althermen toke barge at the iij Cranes with trumpets and shalmes, and the whetes playhyng; and so rod to Westmynster, and toke ys othe in the cheyker,[e] and all the way the penoys[f] shutyng of gones and play-hyng up and done; and so after cam backe to Powlles warffe, and landyd with gret shutyng of gownes and playng; and so in Powlles cherche-yerde ther mett the bachelars and a goody pagyant, and a lxvi. men in blue gownes, and with goodly targates and gaffelynes[g] and a duwlle,[h] and iiij talle men lyke wodys alle in gren, and trumpets playing a-for the mare—the iij yere of Quen Mare.

[The xiij day of November doctor Gardiner, bishop of Win-chester, and lord chancellor of England, died in the morning, between twelve and one of the clock, at the King's] plasse, the wyche ys callyd Whyt-hall; [and by] iij of the cloke he was browt by water [to his own] plasse by sant Mary Overes; and by

---

[a] Whittington.   [b] St. Bride's well.   [c] pinnaces.   [d] guns.   [e] Exchequer.
[f] pinnace.   [g] javelins.   [h] *See pp.* 47, 73.

v of the [clock his bow]elles was taken owt, and bered a-fore the he ª [altar; and] at vj the knyll begane ther, and at durge and masse contenuyd ryngyng alle the belles till vij at nyght.

The xiiij day of November be-gane the knyll for the most ryght reverent father in God my lord chaunseler of England, doctur Sthevyn Gardener, byshope of Wynchastur, and of the preve consell with kyng Henry the viij.th and unto quen Mare quen of England; and with a hersse of iiij branchys, with gylt candyll-stykes, and ij whytt branchys and iij dosen of stayffes-torchys, and all the qwyre hangyd with blake and armes, and a durge songe; and the morow masse of *requiem*, and alle bysshoppes and lordes and knyghtes and gentyllmen; and my lord bysshope Bonar of London did syng masse of *requiem*, and doctur Whyt bysshope of Lynkolne dyd pryche at the sam masse; and after all they whent to his plasse to dener.

The sam day at after-none was durge in evere parryche in London, and a hersse and ryngyng, and the morow masse of *requiem*, and so prayd for after the old custom.

The xxj day of November at none be-gane the knyll for my lord chanseler, for then was the body browt to the chyrche of sant Mare Overes, with grett compene of prestes and clarkes, and alle the bysshopes; and my lord of London dyd exsecute the offes, and ware ys myter; and ther wher ij goodly whyt branchys bornyng, and the harsse with armes and (tapers) bornyng, and iiij dosen of stayffes; and all the qwyre with blake, and ys armes; and afor the corse the kyng of haroldes with ys cot, and with v baners of ys armes, and iiij of emages wrothe ᵇ with fyne gold and inowlle ᶜ; and the morowe-masse iij masse, one of the Trenete, on of owre Lade, and (the) iij of *requiem* for ys solle; and after to dener; and so he was put in a hersse tyll a day that he shall be taken up and cared unto Wynchaster to be bered ther.

[The xxvj of November a stripling was whipt about London,

ª high.   ᵇ wrought.   ᶜ enamel.

and about Paul's cross, for speaking against the bishop] that dyd pryche the Sonday a-for.

The iiij day of Desember was a voman [set in the] pelere [a] for beytyng of her chyld with rodes and . . . . . to peteusly; and the sam day was a man and a voman cared a-bowt London at a care-arse [b] for baudry and . . .

The furst day of December was reseyvyd with pressessyon my lord cardenall Pole into Westmynster abbay; and ther mett hym x[viij bishops,] and the bysshope of Yorke dyd menyster with ys myter; [and they] whent a pressessyon a-bowt the chyrche and the cloyster.

The ix day of Desember was the parlement [adjourned] at the Whyt Hall, her grace('s) place—the iij yere; and so to Sant James thrughe the parke.

The x day of Desember was had to the Towre ser Anthony Kyngston knyght, and to the Flett, and cam owt a-gayn shortely after.

The xiij day of Desember was bered at sant Androwes in the Warderobe master Recherd Stokdun, gentyllman of the warderobe, with ij goodly whyt branchys and xiij stayffes-torchys, and xiij pore men, and thay had gownes of mantell frysse, and iiij grett tapurs, and money mornars; and the strett hangyd with blake and armes; and money prestes syngyng; and the morowe masse and alffe a trentall of masses, and after the offeryng a sermon (by) a doctur callyd master Sydnam, a gray frere of Grenwyche.

[The xv day of December, before the sermon at Paul's cross began, an old man, a shepherd,] be-gane to spyke serten thynges and rayllyng, [whereupon he was] taken and carett [c] to the conter for a tyme.

The xviij day of Dessember be-twyn [8 and 9] of the cloke in the mornyng, was cared in-to Smythfeld to be bornyd on master (Philpot, archdeacon of Winchester,[d]) gentyllman, for herese.

---

[a] pillory.   [b] cart's tail.   [c] carried.   [d] *This name is supplied by Strype.*

The xx day of Dessember was bered at sant Donstones in the Est master Hare Herdsun, altherman of London and skynner, and on of the masturs of the hospetall of the gray frers in London, with men and xxiiij women in mantyll fresse gownes, a hersse of wax, and hong with blake; and ther was my lord mare and the swordberer in blake, and dyvers odur althermen in blake, and the resedew of the aldermen, at ys beryng; and all the masters, boyth althermen and odur, with ther gren stayffes in ther handes, and all the chylderyn of the gray frersse, and iiij men in blake gownes bayryng iiij gret stayffes-torchys bornyng, and then xxiiij men with torchys bornyng; and the morowe iij masses songe; and after to ys plasse to dener; and ther was ij goodly whyt branchys, and mony prestes and clarkes syngyng.

The xij even was at Henley [a] a-pon Temes a mastores Lentall wedow mad a soper for master John Venor and ys wyff, and I and dyver odur neybors; and as we wher at soper, and or whe had supt, ther cam a xij wessells,[b] with maydens syngyng with ther wessells, and after cam the cheyff wyffes syngyng with ther wessells; and the gentyll-woman had hordenyd [c] a grett tabull of bankett, dyssys [d] of spyssys and frut, as marmelad, gynbred, gele, [e] comfett, suger plat, and dyver odur.

.   .   .   .

. . . dwellyng in Ive-lane, stuard unto master G . . . ser Rechard Recherdsun, prest, with ij whytt . . . . , xij stayfftorchys, and iiij grett tapurs, a dolle, and a knell at Powlles, and a-nodur at sant Feyths.

The xxij day of January whent in-to Smythfeld to berne [f] betwyn vij and viij in the mornyng v men and ij women; on of the men was a gentyllman of the ender tempull, ys nam master Gren; and they wer all bornyd by ix at iij postes; and ther wher a commonment thrughe London over nyght that no yong folke

---

[a] *MS.* enley.   [b] visors, or masques.   [c] ordained.
[d] dishes.   [e] jelly.   [f] to be burnt.

shuld come ther, for ther the grettest [number] was as has byne sene at shyche ª a tyme.

The v day of Feybruary was bered master Cry[stopher] Allen, sum-tyme altherman of London, in sant . . . in London, with iiij dosen torchys, on dosen of [staff]-torchys, ij whyt branchys, and iiij grett tapurs, and pore men and women had gownes, and ther wher mony mornars in blake, a lx; and the xxviij was the monyth['s mind ?]

The viij day of Feybruary dyd pryche at Powlles crosse master Peryn, a blake frere, and at the sam sermon was a prest, on ser Thomas Samsun, dyd penanse for he had ij wyffes, and a shett abowt hym, and a tapur in ys hand bornyng a-for the precher, and the mayre of London and the althermen and worshephull men, and mony odur.

The xij day of January was bered in Essex master Leygett, justes of pesse,ᵇ with ij whyt branchys and a v dosen of torchys, and iiij gret tapurs and a gret dolle, and mony mornars, and a gret dener; and shroyff sonday was ys monyth myne,ᶜ and ij dosen stayffes more, and a grett dolle to the pore and a ij dosen skochyons.

. . . . Grenwyche, and to the courtt gatt for the Spaneardes and odur, one master Kayes kepyng [there] tavarne and vetell.

The xxiiij day of Feybruary was the obsequies of the most reverentt father in God, Sthevyn Gardener, docthur and bysshope of Wynchastur, prelett of the gartter, and latte chansseler of England, and on of the preve consell unto Kyng Henry the viij and unto quen Mare, tyll he ded; and so the after-none be-gane the knyll at sant Mare Overes with ryngyng, and after be-gane the durge; with a palle of cloth of gold, and with ij whytt branchys, and ij dosen of stayffe-torchys bornyng, and iiij grett tapurs; and

---

ª such.   ᵇ justice of the peace.   ᶜ month's mind.

my lord Montyguw the cheyffe mornar, and my lord bysshope of
Lynkolne and ser Robart Rochaster, comtroller, and with dyvers
odur in blake, and mony blake gownes and cotes; and the morow
masse of requeem and offeryng done, be-gane the sarmon; and so
masse done, and so to dener to my lord Montyguw('s); and at ys
gatt the corse was putt in-to a wagon with iiij welles, ^a all covered
with blake, and ower the corsse ys pyctur mad with ys myter on
ys hed, with ys and ys^b armes, and v gentyll men bayryng ys v
banars in gownes and hods, then ij harolds in ther cote armur,
master Garter and Ruge-crosse; then cam the men rydyng, carehyng of torchys a lx bornyng, at bowt the corsse all the way; and
then cam the mornars in gownes and cotes, to the nombur unto
ij C. a-for and be-hynd, and so at sant Gorges cam prestes and
clarkes with crosse and sensyng, and ther thay had a grett torche
gyffyn them, and so to ever^c parryche tyll they cam to Wynchaster,
and had money as money ^d as cam to mett them, and durge and
masse at evere^c logyng.

[The iiij of March a young man named Fetherstone, who gave
himself out to be King Edward the Sixth, and whose sayings and
pretences had occasioned many men and women to be punished,
was hanged, drawn, and quartered;] and ys hed was sett up
the v day upon London bryge, and ys quarters was bered.

The vij day of Marche was hangyd at Tyborne x theyffes for
robere^e and odur thynges.

The vij day of Marche be-gane the blassyng [star] at nyght, and
yt dyd shutt^f owt fyre to grett [wonder] and marvell to the pepull,
and contynud serten [nights].

The viij day of Marche dyd pryche at Powlles crosse doctur
(*blank*), and ther was a man dyd penanse with ij pyges rede dythe,^g
on apon ys hed sowd, the [which] he browth ^h them to selle.

The v day of Marche was the obseques of the bysshope of
Peterborowthⁱ in Lynkolne shyre, [and] bered with a goodly

---

^a wheels.   ^b *so the MS.*   ^c every.   ^d many.   ^e robbery.
^f shoot.   ^g pigs ready dight, *i. e.* dressed.   ^h brought.   ⁱ John Chambers.

hersse and armes and pensells; and with ij whyt branchys and viij dosen of stayffes, and with an harold of armes and v baners and a C. in blake gownes and cotes, and a gret meyne of pore men in gownes, and the morow masse, and after a grett dener der.[a]

The Fryday the vij day of Marche was hangyd in chaynes be-syd Huntyntun on *(blank)* Conears, and Spenser after-ward, for the kyllyng of a gentyllman that kept them bowth lyke gentyll-men; and ther be-syd wher thay hange, the wyche on Benett Smyth ded promessyd and hyred them, and promesed them xl[l]. to do that dede.

The xiiij day of Marche was on [b] sett on the pelere[c] for sedys-syous wordes and rumors and conseles agaynst the quen('s) ma-geste—the iij yer of her grace.

[The xviij day of March were divers gentlemen carried to the Tower by certain of the guard, viz. John Throgmorton,] Hare Peckam, master Bethell, master Tornur, master [Hygins, master] Daneell, master Smyth marchand, master Heneage of the chapel, [George the] sherche of Graffend,[d] master Hogys, master Spenser, and ij Rawlins, and Rosey keper of the Star-chambur, and master Dethyke, and [divers] odur gentyllmen that I have not ther names.

The ix day of Marche was hangyd at Brykhyll Benett Smyth, in Bokyngham-shyre, for the deyth of master Rufford, gentyllman, the wyche Conears and Spenser sluw—the iij yer of quen Mare.

The Sonday xxij day of Marche was at the Gray-ffrers at Gren-wyche was my lord cardenall Polle was consecratyd, with x byshopes mytyred—the iij yer of the quen Mare.

The xxv day of Marche was owre Lady day, the Annunsyasyon, at Bow chyrche in London was hangyd with cloth of gold, and with ryche hares[e] and cossens[f] for the commyng of my lord cardenall Polle; ther dyd the bysshope of Vosseter[g] dyd synge he[h] masse mytyred; and ther wher dyver bysshopes, as the bysshope

---

[a] there.   [b] one.   [c] pillory.   [d] search of Gravesend.
          [e] arras.   [f] cushions.   [g] Worcester.   [h] high.

of Ely, bysshope of London, and bysshope of Lynkkolne, and the
yerle of Penbroke, and ser Edward Hastynges, the master of
horsse, and dyvers odur nobuls, and after masse done to my lord
(unfinished).

The xxvij day of Marche was hangyd be-yonde Huntyngtun in
cheynes on Spenser, for the deth of master Rufford of Bokyngham-shyre, by ys fellow Conears hangys.

The xxj day of Marche was bornyd at Oxford doctur Cranmer,
late archebysshope of Canturbere.

.   .   .   .

The iiij day of Aprell was in London [a proclamation] thrugh
London of serten gentyllmen, the wyche [fled] over the see, as
trayturs; the furst was Hare Dudley, Crystoffer Aston the elther,
and Crystoffer the yonger, and [Francis] Horssey and Edward
Horssey, and Edward Cornwell *alias* [Corewel], and Recherd Tre-
mayn and Necolas Tremayn, and [Richard] Ryth and Roger
Renold, and John Dalle and John [Caltham], and Hamond, and
Meverell, and dyver odur.

The xvj day of Aprell, erly in the mornyng, dyd *(blank)* Vyntoner, servand at the syne of the Swane, with owt . . . . dyd
hange hym(selff[a]) in a gutter on he.[b]

The xiij day of Aprell was mared[c] in sant Gylles' with-owt
Crepull-gatte Thomas Gre . . wax-chandeler unto Jone Wakffeld,
wedow.

The xv day of Aprell was electyd at Grenwyche bysshope of
Wynchastur master doctur Whyt, byshope of Lynckolne; and
doctur Westun, dene of Westmynster, to be bysshope of Lynckolne; and the dene of Durram[d] to be bysshope of Karlelle.

The xvij day of Aprelle was on[e] on the pelere[f] for fasshele[g]
deseyvyng of the quen('s) subgettes sellyng of ryngs for gold, and
was nodur seylver nor gold but couper, the wyche he has
deseyved money : thys was done in Chepe.

---

[a] *marginal note.*   [b] bigh.   [c] married.
[d] *Read*, Owen Oglethorpe, Dean of Windsor; *not* Thomas Watson, Dean of Durham.
          [e] one.   [f] pillory.   [g] falsely.

The xxj day of Aprell cam from the Towre over London bryge
unto the ssessyonsse house in Sowth-warke, and ther raynyd[a] and
cast to be drane and quartered, for a consperacy agaynst the quen,
and odur maturs, master John Frogmorton, and master Wodall,
captayn of the ylle of Whyth; the accusars master Rossey, master
Bedyll, and master Dethyke.

. . . .
. . . grett stayffe torchys and they had gownes .
. . a nobull a yerde, and xij women in cassokes of rosett
. . .. iiij men holdyng iiij grett tapurs, and iiij dosen of
skochyons.

The xxiiij day of Aprell, in the mornyng be-tyme, was cared
to Smyth-ffeld to be bornyd vj men, [and] more was cared in-to
the contrey to be bornyd.

The sam day was sett on the pelere[b] in Chepe iij [men; two]
was for the prevermentt of wyllfull perjure, the iij was for
wylfull pergure,[c] with paper sett over their hedes.

The xxviij day of Aprell was drane from the Towre to Tyborne
ij gentyll-men; on ys name was master Waddall captayn of the
yle of Wyth, and the odur master John Frogmorton; and so
hangyd, and aftar cut downe and quartered, and the morowe after
ther hedes sett on London bryge—the iij of quen Mare.

The xxix day of Aprell was a man baude sett up one the pelere[d]
for bryngyng unto men prentes[e] harlots, the wyche they gayff
hym and them serten of ther masturs goodes and wastyd.

The sam day was cared unto the Towre ser Wylliam Cortenay,
ser John Paratt, ser John Pallard, ser Necolas Arnold, ser John
Chechastur, and with dyvers odur.

The ij day of May was a man and a woman (placed in the
pillory) for falshod and perjure, the man had ys here[f] naylled—
the iij of quene Mare.

The iij day of May dyd ryd in a care a-bowt London a woman
that dwelt at Quen-heyffe at the hott howsse, for a bawde.

---

[a] arraigned.   [b] pillory.   [c] perjury.   [d] pillory.   [e] men's prentices.   [f] ear.

The v day of May at after-none the sufferacan of Norwyche dyd consecratyd and halohyd iij auters in Trenete parryche—the iij yere of quen Mare.

. . . .

The xxv of Aprell was bered lord chamberlayne Gage to the quen, with ij haroldes, with a standard, . . [banners of] armes and iiij of emages, and with a hersse and ij [white branches,] ij dossen of stayffes, and viij dosen of skochyons; bered at (*blank*)

The ix day of May was a audetur dyd [wear a paper] round a-bowtt Westmynster Hall, and after he [was placed] apon the pelere,[a] for deseyvyng the quen of her rents, and dyd reseyff of her tenantes money and after dyd [avow he] reseyvyd non; ys nam ys master Leyke; the wyche [queen's] tenantes had ther qwyttans of hym of [his hand].

The x day of May was bered Annes [Heth], the wyff of John Heth, penter stayner, Anno M.v^c.lvj. the iij yere of quen Mare, ser Wylliam Garr[ard being] mayre of London, and master John Machyll and master Thomas [Leigh] shreyffes of London, and bered at Allalowes-staynyng Fanchurche-strett.

The xij day of May was raynyd[b] at Yeld-hall Wylliam Stantun, sum-tyme captayn, and cast to be drane from the Towre unto Tyburne, and hangyd and quartered, for a consperacy against the kyng and the quen and odur maters.

The xiij day of May ded[c] ser Rechard Dobes late mayre of London, and skynner, and altherman, betwyn iiij and v in the mornyng.

The xv day of May was cared in a care from Nuwgatt thrug London unto Strettford-a-bow to borne[d] ij men; the on blyne,[e] the thodur lame; and ij tall men, the (one) was a penter, the thodur a clothworker; the penter ys nam was Huw Loveroke, dwellyng in Seythin lane; the blynd man dwellyng in sant Thomas apostylles.

---

[a] pillory.   [b] arraigned.   [c] died.   [d] to be burned.   [e] one blind.

CAMD. SOC.   P

. . . .

The xviij day of May at after-non was bered ser Recherd Dobes
latt mayre of London and altherman; ther wher at ys berehyng
mony worshefull men; . . . my lord mare and the swordbeyrer
in blake, and the recorder cheyff morner, and master Eggyllfield
and master (*blank*) and master . . . . [ov]ersear, and a lx mornars,
and ij haroldes of armes, and the althermen and the shreyffes,
and master Chestur bare ys cott armur, [with] helmett and
targatt, sword, a standard, and penone, and iiij baneres [of]
images, and a xxx pore men in rosett gownes holdyng . .
torches, and iiij gylt chandyllstykes with iiij grett tapurs [with]
armes on them; and all the cherche and the stret hangyd with
blake and the qwyre, and armes, and ij grett whyt branchys; and
alle the masturs of the hospetalle boyth althermen and the
commenas ª with ther gren stayffes in ther handes; and the chyeff
of the hospetalle, and prestes and clarkes; and after *dirige* to the
place to drynke; and the morow masse of *requiem* ij masses, on
of the Trenete in pryke songe, and a-nodur of our Lade; and after
a sermon, and after to dener: and ther wher x dosen of skochyons.

The xix day of May was dran ᵇ from the Towre unto Tyborne
captain Wylliam Stantun, and ther hangyd and quartered, and ys
hed sett on London bryge the morow after.

The xviij day of May was the Clarkes' pressessyon, with a C
stremers, with the weyttes, and the sacrementt, and viij stayffes
torchys bornyng, and a goodly canepe borne over the sacrementt.

The ij day of June was bered at sant Magnus at London bryge
ser Recherd Morgayn knyght, a juge and on of the preve consell
unto the nobull quen Mare, with a harold of armes bayryng ys
cott armur, and with a standard and a penon of armes and elmett,
sword, and targatt; and iiij dosen of skochyons, and ij whytt
branchys and xij torchys and iiij gret tapurs, and xxiiij pore men
in mantyll ffrysse gownes, and mony in blake; and master
chansseler of London ᶜ dyd pryche.

ª commoners?   ᵇ drawn.   ᶜ Dr. Darbishire.

[The same day were arraigned at Westminster hall three gentlemen, master Rosey, master Bedyll, and master Dethick, for] the
the experyng ª the kyng and quen majeste deth.

The viij day of June was a goodly pressessyon at Whyt-hall by
the Spaneards; the hall hangyd with ryche cloth, and at the
[screen] in the halle was a auter mad, and hangyd rychely with
[a canopy], and with grett baseins clen gylt and candyll-stykes;
and in the [court] at iiij corners was mad iiij godly auters hangyd
with clothe of gold, and evere auter with canepes in brodere; and
[in the] court mad a pressession way with a C. yonge okes sett
in the grond and of evere syd sett ard ᵇ to the wall with gren
boughs; and then cam the pressessyon out of the chapell syngyng
and playing of the regalles; and after the sacrement borne, and
over ytt the rychest canepe that the Quen had, with vj stayffes
borne by vj goodly men, and a-bowt the sacrement a C. torchys
burnyng, and sum of whytt wax; and at ever auter [was ringing]
and senst ᶜ with swett odurs, and all the kyng['s] garde ᵈ with
[partizans] gyltt, and after to messe in the chapell, and song by
the Spaneardes.

The xxv day of May was slayne by my lord Dacre's son master
West sqwyre; ther wher xl men a-ganst master West and ys viij
men, be-syd Roderam in Yorke-shyre. The lord Dacre dwellys
at Aston in the sam contrey.

The ix day of June was drane from the Towre unto Tyborne iij
gentyllmen for a consperace, master Rosey, master Bedylle, and
master Dethyke, and ther hangyd and quartered, and ther quarters bered, master Rosey('s) hed on London bryge, and Bedylle('s)
hed over Ludgatt, and master Dethyke('s) over Althergatt.

The sam day was a woman sett on the pelere ᵉ in Chepe, a baude,
for conveyhyng of harlottes unto men('s) prentes ᶠ and servandes.

The xj day of June was a man sett on the pelere ᵍ, a gold-smyth

---

ª conspiring.   ᵇ hard, *i. e.* close.   ᶜ censed.   ᵈ garge *in MS.*
ᵉ pillory.   ᶠ prentices.   ᵍ pillory.

in Lumbarstrett, for raysyng of an oblygasyon, and mad ytt a syn-
gull oblygassyon falsely and deseytt for money.

[The xiv day of June father Sydnam, a grey friar of Greenwich, preached at Trinity church, and after dined with Sir Robert
Oxenbridge knight. [a]]

The xv day of June was raynyd[b] at Yeld-hall [master] Lecknolle,[c] grome porter unto kyng Edward the vj and quen Mare,
the iij yere of quen Mare, and cast to suffer deth.

The sam (day) was the Grosers' fest; and ther dynyd [the
lord] mayre and xiiij althermen, and my lord cheyff justice, master
Chamley the recorder, and mony worshefull men, and my lade
mares[d] and mony lade[e] and althermen wyffes and gentyll-women,
and then was the master of the compene master Whyt grocer and
altherman, and master Grafton and master Grenway wardens that
tyme, and master Harper altherman marchand-tayller was chosyn
shreyff for the kyng.

The xviij day of June was hangyd at sant Thomas of Wather-
ing for robyng of a cartt with grett reches that came from a fayre
(at) Beverlay my lord Sandes sune.

The sam day was raynyd[f] at Yeld-halle for a consperace master
Frances Varney and captayn Tornar, and thay cast to be drane,[g]
hangyd, and quartered.

The xxvij day of June rod from Nuwgatt unto Stretford-a-bow
in iij cares xiij, xj men and ij women, and ther bornyd[h] to iiij postes,
and ther wher a xx m. pepull.

The x day of Juin was bered ser Gylles Capell knyght, sune and
here unto ser Wylliam Capell late mayre of London and draper,
the wyche he ded[i] in Essex, with standard and penon and iiij
baners of emages and ij dosen of torchys and ij whyt branchys,
and iiij dosen of penselles and vj dosen of skochyons, and mony

---

[a] *Strype, who adds*, now, or soon after, Lieutenant of the Tower. *These words,
apparently, were not in the Diary, but Trinity church was near the Tower.*

[b] arraigned.   [c] Lewkner?   [d] mayoress.   [e] ladies.
[f] arraigned.   [g] drawn.   [h] burnt.   [i] died.

mornars; and the morow masse, and after to dener, and after a grett dolle, and ther was a harold of armes.

.   .   .   .

.   .   . sant John and dyver.   .   .   .   .   .

.   .   . juges and sergantes of coyffe and dyver knight and gentyllmen and mony lades and gentyllwomen, and mony strangers; ther wher l. bokes [a] and iiij stages [b] that wher b. . . . the dener and the morow after.

The last day of Juin was led from the Towre unto Yeld-halle Wylliam West sqwyre odur-wyse callyd lord La Ware, and cast of he [c] treson, to be drane and quartered.

The ij day of July rod in a care v. unto Tyborne; on was the hangman with the stump-lege for stheft, [d] [the] wyche he had hangyd mony a man and quartered mony, and hed [e] mony a nobull man and odur.

The iij day of July was a man wypyd a-bowtt the post of reformacyon be [f] the standard in Chepsyd for sellyng of false rynges.

The vij day of July was hangyd on the galaus on Towre-hylle for tresun a-gaynst the quen, on [g] master Hare Peckham, and the thodur master John Daneell, and after cutt downe and heded, and ther hedes cared unto Londune bryge and ther sett up, and ther bodys bered at Allalows-barkyng.

The viij day of Julii was on [h] of the laborars of Bryd-welle for brykyng upon [i] of a chest was hangyd in the mydes of the furst courtt apon a jubett.

[The . . . day of July was buried the lady Seymer, wife of sir Thomas Seymer knight, late lord mayor; with . . . .] armes; with ij whyt branches, xx torchys, and xx men [had] xx gowne of sad mantyll fryse, and xx women [xx gowns] of the sam frysse, and iiij baners of emages, and iiij grett [tapers] apon

---

    [a] bucks.   [b] stags.   [c] high.   [d] theft.

  [e] beheaded.   [f] by.   [g] one.   [h] one.   [i] open.

iiij grett candyll-stykes gylted, and a vj dosen skochyons; and
the strett hangyd with fyn brod clothes, and the chyrch [hung
with] armes; and after durge they whent home to her plasse.
[On the] morow iij masses songe, on of the Trenete, and on of
owr Lade, the thurd of *requiem,* and a sermon; and after masse
hard [to] her plasse to dener, for ther was mony mornars, and a
grett mone mad for her for her deyth, and gyffen money . . .
wardes in London.

The xvj day of July was the obseque of my lade Norwyche,
the wyff of the lord Norwyche juge, cheyf baron, at *(blank)* in
Essex, with baners and armes and dyver mo[urners.]

The xxj day of July the Quen('s) grace removyd from sant
James in the ffelds unto Heltem[a] thrugh the parke and thrugh
Whyt-alle, and toke her barge, and so to Lambeth unto my lord
cardenoll('s) place; and there here grace toke here charett, and so
thrugh sant Gorge('s) ffeld unto Nuhyngton, so over the feldes
to-wherd Eltem at v of the cloke at after-none; and ther wher of
pepull a-boyff x M. pepull to se her grace; and my lord cardi-
noll rod with her, and my lord of Penbroke and my lord Mon-
tyguu and dyvers lordes and knyghtes and mony lades and gentyll
women a grett nombur rod with her grace.

The xxvj day of July was bered at the Sayvoy a whyt monke
of the Charterhowsse, and bered in ys monke('s) wede with grett
lyght.

The xxvij day of July was bered Thomas Lune grocer in sant
Mare Mawdlyn in Mylke-strett, with ij whytt branchys and xviij
stayffes torchys and iiij grett tapurs; and alle thay[b] had mantyll
fryse gownes, and dyvers women had lyke gownes, pore men and
women; and mony morners in blake, and dyver althermen with
gren stayffes; and the masturs of the hospetalle with gren
stayffes;   .   .   .   .
and vj long torchys and vj tapurs of iij[li] a [peice] and iiij grett

---

[a] Eltham.   [b] The 24 bearers of the lights.

tapurs with armes, and the cherche hangyd with blake a-for-none;
and mony mornars and mony prestes and clarkes, [and so] home
to dener; and a vj dosen of skochyons, and the powre.   .   .   .
The sam day was bered at saynt Katheryn .   .   . cherche master
Thomas Henege, with a penon and a harold bayring his cott armur,
and ij whyt branchys, and a dosen stayffes [torches, . .] tapurs
and a v. dosen of skochyons; and the cherche hangyd with blake;
and after to the hosse a to dener.

The same day at nyght be-tweyn viij and ix ded d ser W[illiam
Laxton] knyght and late mayre of London, and grocer, in Alther-
mary.

The xxxj day of July was raynyd b at the Yeld-halle .   .   .   .
robars of the see a vj, and the morow after thay wher hangyd at
Wapyng at the low-water marke.

The sam day stod on the pelere c in Chepe a man and a woman,
the wyche wher offesers of Brydwelle, [the which] favered them
and convayd from thens sondry harlottes, the wyche dyver of them
wher taken a-gayn and browth a-gayn.

The (blank) day of August was bered the bysshope of Chechastur doctur Day, with armes, in the contrey.

The v day of August dyd drowne here-seylff in More-ffeldes, in
corner by the tre, a woman dwellyng besyde the Swane with the
ij nekes at Mylke-street end.

The (blank) day of August ded d ij bysshops, the bysshope of
Chechastur Day, and the bysshope of Wosseter doctur Belle sum-
tyme bysshope.

[The ixth day of August was buried sir William Laxton, late
lord mayor, in the church of saint Mary Aldermary; with] a
goodly hers with v prynsepalles, [and the majesty] and the valans
gyltyd, and viij dosen of penselles [and] xiij dosen of skochyons
and a half of bokeram; and a standard and iiij penons, and ij baners
of [images]; and the howsse, chyrche, and the stret hangyd with

---
a house.   b arraigned.   c pillory.   d died.

blake [and] armes; and a cott armur and helmett, target, and swyard, mantylles and crest a teyger-hed with a colynbyn and the slype.[a] [There were two] grett and goodly whyt branchys, and xxxiiij stayffes torchys, and xxxiiij mantyll frysse gownes to powre men, and a c blacke gownes; morners master Loges altherman cheyff mornar and master Machyl secund morner and master Wanton iij morner, and dyver odur, the lord mare and master Whytt and dyvers odur, and alle the thodur althermen in vyolett; and then cam the women morners, lades and mony althermens wyffes and gentyll-women; and after durge to the plasse to drynke and the compene of the Grocers, and after prestes and clarkes, to the place to drynke, and the harolds, and the Wax-chandlers and the Penters, to drynke, with mony odur. And the morow iij masses song, ij pryke songe and (the) iij(d) *requiem;* at masse dyd pryche doctur Harpsfelle archeydekyn; and after to dener, for ther was a grett dener as I have sene at any berehyng, for ther dynyd mony worshepfull men and women.

The xiij day of August was bered at Clarkynwell doctur Belle sum-tyme bysshope of (Worcester), and wher that he was put in ys coffen lyke a bysshope, with myter and odur thynges that longyst to a bysshope; with ij whyt branchys and ij dosen of stayffes torchys and iiij grett tapurs, and a surmon; doctur Harpfelle dyd make yt.

The sam day a woman for baldry and procuryng a chyld, she and the chyld beyng on the pelere;[b] the wyche she was her chyld browth[c] to hordome.

The xxiiij day of August was bered at *(blank)* beyonde Hamtun cowrt master *(blank)* Banester sqwyre, with cott armur and penone of armes and iiij dosen of skochyons of armes, and xij stayffe torchys, and iiij grett tapurs   .   .   .   .   .
.   .   .   .   cott-armur, helmett, targatt, and swerd   .   .   .   of skochyons of armes and iiij baners of emages

---

[a] a columbine slipped.   [b] pillory.   [c] brought.

and iiij dosen of penselles and ij whyt branchys . . . and tapurs; and master Norrey the harold.

The xxviij day of August was bered at Wa[ltham?] abay master *(blank)* Jakes dwellyng in Cornehylle, sum-tyme the master of the Marchand-tayllers of [London]; with ij whytt branchys and ij dosen torchys . . . . grett tapurs and iij dosen skochyons of armes.

The xxxj day of August was bered masteres . . . Sawde sumtyme weyff unto John Sawde su . . . . quen Katheryn['s ex-] chekare, and here sune ᵃ p . . . . unto queu Mare her dowther; with ij grett branchys and xij torchys and iiij grett tapurs, and bered in sant Dunstones parryche in the est, with many morners; and to master Grenway('s) to drynke [ale?] and spyssebred; and the morow masse and a sermon, and after a grett dener; and the morowe after ther was gyffyn for her boyth wod and colles to the powre pepulle.

The xxx day of August was the monyth mynᵇ of ser Wylliam Laxtun knyght and grocer, and the hersse bornyng with wax; and the morowe masse and a sarmon, and after a grett dener; and after dener the hersse taken downe.

The furst day of September was sant Gylles day, and ther was a goodly prossessyon abowt the parryche with the whettes, and the canepe borne, and the sacrement, and ther was a godly masse songe as bene hardᶜ; and master Thomas Grenelle,ᵈ waxchandler, mad a grett dener for master Garter and my lade, and master Machylle the shreyffe and ys wyff, and boyth the chamburlayns, and mony worshefull men and women at dener, and the whettes playng and dyver odur mynsterelles, for ther was a grett dener.

.　.　.　.　.　.　.　.　.　.

The vj day of September was bered at Barking church in London master Phelype Dennys sqwyre, with cote [armour, . . .] of armes, and ij whytt branchys and xij torchys, [iiij] grett tapurs,

---

ᵃ her son.　　ᵇ month's mind.　　ᶜ as has been heard.　　ᵈ Greenhill.

a ij dosen of skchochyons of armes; the wyche he was a goodly man of armes and [a great] juster, kyng Henry the viij[th] behyng at Tornay beyond see in Franse, the wyche was englang t . . . .

The vij day of September was bered within the Towre of London, the wyche was the evyn of the natevete of owre Lade, on master *(blank)* Lecknolle, sum-tyme grome porter onto quen Mare, the wyche was kast to suffer deth for the conspderacy agaynst the kynge and the quen.

The xv day of September was bered at sant Peter the Powr hard by Frer Austyne, with a harold kareyng his cott armur and a penon of armes, and ij fayre whyt-branches and xij stayffe torchys and . . . . tapurs and a dosen and d. of skochyons, and the powre men had mantyll frys gownes; and mony mornars; on master *(blank)* Lucas sqwyre, sum-tyme on of the masters of the request unto kyng Henry the viij[th].

The xix day of September dyd the Quene('s) grace remove from Croydun the bysshope of Canthurbere('s) plasse unto sant James in the feld be-yond[a] Charyng-crosse, her own plasse, with my lord cardenall and *(unfinished)*.

The xix day of September was proclamyd in London by a xij of the cloke, the crear havyng the quen('s) selle,[b] that rosse pense[c] shullde nott be taken after the cry was mad, butt in Yrland to be taken for pense.

The xxj day of September was a grett rumor in London a-bowtte stesturns[d] in Chepe, Belynggatt, Leydynhalle, Nuwgatt markett, amonge markett folke and meyllmen, by noythe[e] par-suns, and that my lord mayre and the ij shreyffes was fayne to go in-to the marketts for (to) sett pepull in a stay, and so to Nuwgatt markett, and ther sold melle for . . . . .

[The . . . day of September was buried at saint] Martens be-syd Charyng-crosse ser [Humphrey Forster] knyghtt of *(blank)* shyre, with ij goodly whytt branchys, xxiiij stayffe torchys, and iiij

---

[a] be long *in MS.*   [b] seal.   [c] rose pence.
[d] testerns.   [e] naughty.

tapurs . . . a pesse, and with a harold of armes with hy[s coat
armour,] and ys pennon of armes and ys cott armur, [targatt,] and
sword and elmett, and crest, and vj dosen of [scocheons] ; and
the chyrche hangyd with blake and armes ; [and many] morners.

The xxvj day of September was bered in Essex at South-
mynster, on master William Har[ris,] sheriff of Essex, notabulle
ryche both in landes and fermes; with a pennon . . . . . and
cott armur, and iiij baners of emages of armes, and a vj dosen of
skoychyons ; and mony morners, and a grett dolle.

The iij day of October was the sessyon at Oxford, and ther wher
condemnyd lx to [die.]

The viij day of October was bered in Kentt at a towne callyd
(blank, sir John) Champney knyght late mare of London and
altherman and skynner, with ij whytt branchys, ij dosen torchys,
and iiij grett tapurs; and with a harold of armes beyryng ys
cote-armur, hys standard, and pennon of armes, with elmett, targatt, and sword, and vj dosen of skochyons and mony gounes and
cottes ; and after a grett dener to alle the contrey.

[The . . day of October was buried the lo]rd Waus* of
Northamptonshyre, wyth baner of armes, elmett, targett, and
sword, [and with a v]j dosen of skochyons, and a dosen of penselles.

The xviij day of October was bered ser Recherd Cottun knyght,
and comtroller unto the kyng Edward the vj[th] of ys honorabull
howssehold, with a harold of armes, and a standard, penone, and
cote of armes, and a vj dosen of skochyons, and bered at Warl-
bryltun[b] in (Hampshire).

The xviij day of October, was sant Luke day, was bered at
sant Peter in Cornehyll ser Henry Hobulthurne knyght and late
mayre of London, the wyche he was mare at the crownenasyon of
kyng Edward the vj[th]; and marchand-tayller of London, and marchand of the stapull of Calys; and he had [ij] fayre whytt

* Vaux.   b Warblington.

branchys, and xx grett staffe torchys, and iiij grett tapurs a-pon iiij gylt candyll-stykes; and a standard and a penon of armes, and a harold of armes bayreng ys cott armur, and a helmet, target, and sword; and a vj dosen of skochyons; and the chyrche and the strett hangyd with blake and armes; and mony mornars; and pore men had new gownes.

The xx of October was bered ser John Olyff knyght and altherman, and sum-tym he was surgantt[a] unto kyng Henry the viij[th], and after he was shreyff of London; and [b] he had levyd tylle the next yere he had beyn mayre, for he tornyd from the Surgens unto the Grosers; and bered at sant Myghelles in Bassynghall, with a harold of armes bayryng ys cott armur, and with a standard and a pennon of armes, and iiij baners of emages, and ij grett whytt branchys, and iiij grett tapurs and (blank) dosen of torchys; and mony powre men had gownes; and with a elmett, targat, and sword; and the crest a crowne and a holyff-tre[c] standyng with-in the crowne.

.   .   .   .

.   . hytt and mad a nobull haration.

The xxij day of October was bered doctur [Man], sumtime the pryor of Shen the charterhowse, and after mad bysshope of Man by kyng Edward the vj[th]; [and] was mared[d]; and bered at sant Andrews hundershaft, London, and ded[e] at master Whetheley('s) marchand tayller.

The xxx day of October was bered ser [John] Gressem,[f] knyght and merser, and marchand of tbe [staple] of Callys, and marchand venterer,[g] and late mere [and alderman] of London; with a standard and a penon of armes, [cote-]armur of damask, and iiij pennons of armes .   .   . a elmett, a targett and a sword, mantylles, and ys .   .   .   . and a goodly hersse of wax and x dosen of [pensels] and xij dosen of skochyons; and he gayff a c blake g[owns] unto pore men and powre women of fyne blake [cloth]; iiij dosen

[a] surgeon.   [b] if.   [c] olive-tree.   [d] married.   [e] died.   [f] Gresham.   [g] adventurer.

of grett stayffe torchys, and a dosen of . . longe torches; and
he gayff a C. d.[a] of fyne blake . . . . ij unto the mare and the
old mare, and to ser Rowland Hylle and to ser Andrew Jude and
to boyth the chamburlayns, and to master of Blakwelle, and to
master the common huntt and ys man, and to the porters that
longes to the stapull, and to all ys farmers and ys tenantts; and all
the chyrche hangyd and the strett with blake and armes grett store;
and morow iij goodly masses song, on of the Trenete, and a-nodur
of owre Lade, and the iij of *requiem*, and a goodly sermon; master Harpfeld dyd pryche; and after as grett a dener as has bene
sene for a fysse-day,[b] for alle that cam to dener, for ther laket
nothyng dere.[c]

The xxx day, a' for-none, was bered at sant Thomas of Acurs,
by ys father, master Loke the sune of ser Wylliam Loke, the wyche
he ded[d] at ys plasse in Walbroke, and bered at sant Thomas of
Acurs; and alle the qwyre hangyd with blake, and armes, and
iiij grett tapurs, and ij whyt branchys and xij torchys; and master doctur Pendyltun dyd pryche.

. . . .

. . . torchys and iiij grett tapurs and [there were at his]
. . . bereng the felowshype of the Drapers, master Cha[ster
herald and] odur, and greet mon[e] mad for hym at ys berehying.

The xxx day of October was hanged at the [palace gate] at
sant James iiij men for robyng [at the] courte of one of the
quen('s) maydes, and ij for robyng [of the] knyght marshall('s)
servandes.

The xxviij day of October the new mare toke ys oythe, and so
whent by water to Westmynster [with] trumpettes and the
whettes[f] ryalle,[g] and a galant [pinnace] deckyd with stremars and
gonnes and dromes; [the new] mayre master Hoffeley, marchand-
tayller, and marchand of the stapull of Calles, and the ij heynch-
men in cremesun velvett in-brodered with gold an ell brod; and
iiij[xx] [poor] bachelers, and they dyd gyff iiij[xx] blue gownes, cape,

---

[a] a hundred and fifty?	[b] fish-day.	[c] there.	[d] died.
	[e] moan.	[f] waits.	[g] royally.

dobelet, and hose to the iiijˣˣ poure men; and there was a godly pageant; and the trumpets had skarlett capes, ᵃ and the whetes. ᵇ.

The xx day of October was delivered out of the Lowlar towre ᶜ alle the heretykes that cam out of Essex, and odur plassys, and so to kepe ·them ᵈ good and truw to God and to the king and quen.

The iij day of November was bered in the parryche of sant Towlys ᵉ in Sowthwarke master *(blank)* Goodyere, sum-tyme altherman of London and letherseller, marchand of the stapull of Callys, with ij whytt branchys, xij stayffes torchys, and iiij grett tapurs, and mony mornars in blake, boythe men and vomen, and the compene of the Lethersellers, in ther levere.ᶠ

The iiij day of November was bered my lade Wylliams of Tame, with iiij baners of emages and vi dosen of skoychyons of armes, &c.

.   .   .   .

other]wys called the kynges henchmen.

The xvj day of November cam out of the Towre [to be arraigned] at Westmynster on *(blank)* Walker servant [to my] lord of Densher,ᵍ for carehyng of letters, and cond[emned to] perpetuall presun, and for kepyng consell with the[m that had died] affor.

The xxj day of November was raynyd ʰ [at Guild?] halle on ⁱ master Smyth a marchand, for kepying [the counsel] of them that wher put to deth, and condemnyd to perpetual presun.

The xxj day of November a-fforen[oon was taken] ronde a-bowtt Westmynster halle a servand of master . . . the master of the rolles, with a paper on ys hed, and so to the . . . in Chepe, and ther he was sett apone the pelere ᵏ with [the paper] on ys hede that every man shuld know what he [had done], the wyche was thes wordes *(not added).*

The sam day was the new abbott of Westmynster putt in,

ᵃ caps.   ᵇ waits.   ᶜ the Lollards' tower at Lambeth Palace.
ᵈ *i. e.* charged to keep themselves.   ᵉ Olave's.   ᶠ livery.
ᵍ Devonshire.   ʰ arraigned.   ⁱ one.   ᵏ pillory.

docthur Fecknam, late dene of Powlles, and xiiij moo monkes shorne in; and the morow after the lord abott with ys coventt whentt a prossessyon after the old fassyon in ther monkes' wede, in collys [a] of blake say, with ij vargers carehyng ij sylver rodes in ther handes, and at evyngsong tyme the vergers whent thrugh the clostur to the abbott; and so whentt in-to the churche affor the he auter,[b] and ther my lord knellyd downe and ys coventt, and after ys praer mad was browtt in-to the qwyre with the vergers and so in-to ys plasse, and contenentt [c] he be-gane evyngsong—xxij day of the sam monyth, that was santt Clementt evyn last.

[The xxiv day of November, being the eve of saint Katharine, at six of the clock at night,] sant Katheryn('s) lyght [went about the battlements of Saint Paul's with singing,] and sant Katheryn gohying a prossessyon.

The xxv day of November my lord of Pembroke toke ys barge toward Cales, and *(unfinished)*.

The xxvj day of the sam monnth was bered masteres H[eys] a mersere('s) wyff in Althermanbere, with ij whyt branchys [and] ten stayffe torchys, and iiij grett tapurs, and xvj women bayreng them and holdeng them, and they had nuw gownes and raylles, and a iiij dochen of skochyons, and mony morners; and alle ys howsse and ys gatt hangyd with blake and [with ar]mes, with hers and Mersers' and Stapull and Venterers' armes: and doctur Perryn dyd pryche at her masse, and after a grett dener.

The xxvij day of November was a proclamassyon in London thatt ever [d] man to loke that no enfanttes shuld be layd in the streetes nor men('s) dores, and that ther shuld be a day watche, and a nyghtes, that ther shuld be non led [e] in no plase in London by nyght nor day, and he that do take ane shytt [f] person shall hayffe xxs. for ys payne.

The xxix day of November was my lord abbott consecratyd at Westmynster abbay; and ther was grett compene, and he was

---

[a] cowls.   [b] high altar.   [c] incontinently.   [d] every.   [e] laid.   [f] any such.

mad abbott, and dyd wher[a] a myter; and my lord cardenall was ther, and mony byshopes, and my lord chanseler dyd syng masse, and the abbott mad the sermon, and my lord tressore[b] was [there].

The xxviij day of November came rydyng thrugh Smythfeld and Old Balee and thrugh Fletstrett unto Somesset place my good lade Elisabeth('s) grace the quen('s) syster, with a grett compene of velvett cottes and cheynes, her graces gentyllmen, and after a grett compene of her men all in red cottes gardyd with a brod gard of blake velvett, and cuttes; and ther her grace dyd loge at her place; ther her grace tared *(blank)* days till the iij day of Dessember or her grace dyd remowyffe.

The iij day of Desember was bered in Essex my lord Morley, with iij harolds, master Garter and odur [heralds, a] standard and a banur of ys armes, and iiij baners [rolls], and iiij baners of emages, and elmett, and cott[-armour,] targett and sword, and viij dosen of skochyons . . . dosen of torchys, and ij whytt branchys, and [many] mornars, and after the masse a grett dener.

The sam day at after-non in London [at saint] Mare Colchyrche in Chepe, on master Robart Downes the master of the Yrmongers with xij torchys, [ij white] branchys, and iiij grett tapurs; and vj pore men [did bear] hym to the chyrche, and all theys pore men had gownes, xxij gowns[d]; and he had [a] tombe m[ade, in the] tombe a caffen[e] of led, and when that he cam to the grayff[f] he was taken out of one of wood, and putt in-to that of lede; and the morow ij (masses) song, and a godly sermon, and after a grett dener; and ther wher mony blake gownes gyffyn to men and women.

The iij day of Desember cam rydyng from her plasse my lade Elizabeth('s) grace, from Somersett place downe Fletstreet, and thrugh Old Bayle, and thrugh Smyth-field, with a grett compene; and her servandes alle in red gardyd with velvett; and so her grace toke her way toward Bysshope Atfeld[g] plasse.

[a] wear.   [b] treasurer.   [c] remove.
[d] The men who bore the lights and the corpse amounted in all to twenty two.
[e] coffin.   [f] grave.   [g] Bishop's Hatfield.

The v day of Desember was Sant Necolas evyn, and Sant Necolas whentt a-brod in most partt in London syngyng after the old fassyon, and was reseyvyd with mony good pepulle in-to ther howses, and had myche good chere as ever they had, in mony plasses.

[The vj day of December the abbot of Westminster went a procession with his convent; before him went all the] santuary men with crosse keys apon [their garments, and] after whent iij for murder; on [a] was the lord Dacres sone of the Northe was wypyd [b] with a shett [c] a-bowt [him, for] kyllyng of on master West sqwyre dwellyng be-syd . . . . ; and anodur theyff that dyd long to one of master comtroller . . . . . dyd kylle Recherd Eggyllston the comtroller('s) tayller, and k[illed him in] the Long Acurs, the bak-syd Charyng-crosse; and a boy [that] kyld a byge boye that sold papers and pryntyd bokes [with] horlyng of a stone and yt [d] hym under the ere in Westmynster Hall; the boy was one of the chylderyn that was [at the] sckoll ther in the abbey; the boy ys a hossear [e] sune a-boyff London-stone.

The ix day of Desember was berd [f] at Hyslyngton [g] ser Recherd Brutun knyght, with a dosen torchys, and ij whytt branchys, sum tyme of the preve chambur unto kyng Henry the viij[th].

The x day of Desember was bered at the Sawvoy master Clarenshus' syster, with a herse mayd with ij stores,[h] and a c. whytt candyllstykes, and in evere candyllstyke a grett qwarell of alff a lb. of wax, and her armes apon the herse, and a dosen of torchys and her armes apon.

The xvj day of Desember, was the sessyons at Nuwgatt, and ther was John Boneard,[i] and on Gregory a Spaniard, a smyth, raynyd for a robere that thay wold have done to Halesandur [k] the keper of Nuwgatt; and ther was one that gayff evydens aganst them that Gregore had a knyff, and he dyd ffrust[l] in-to the man

---

[a] one.   [b] whipt.   [c] sheet.   [d] hit.   [e] hosier's.   [f] buried.
[g] Islington.   [h] stories.   [i] *See before*, p. 93.   [k] Alexander.   [l] thrust.

CAMD. SOC.   R

a-for the juges, and after he was cast ; and contenent ᵃ ther was a
gebett sett up at the sessyons gatt, and ther ys ryght hand strykyn
of, and nayllyd apone the jubett, and contenent he was hangyd up,
and Boneard was bornyd in the hand, and Gregore hangyd all
nyght nakyd.

[The xx day of December the Queen rode in her chariot through
the park from] Santt James unto the galere, and so [took] her
barge unto Westmynster, and landyd [at the palace,] and so in-to
the abbay, and ther her grace hard [even song], and my lord
cardenalle and my lord Montyguw, [and my] lord Darse of Essex
dyd bere the sword a-for [her grace], and my lade Montyguw
bare up the quen[’s train].

The xxij day of Desember the Quen(’s) grace [removed] from
Sant James thrugh the parke, and toke [her barge] unto Lambyth
unto my lord cardenalles place, [where] her grace dynyd with
hym and dyvers of the [council] ; and after dener her grace toke
her gornay ᵇ to Grenwyche, to kepe her Cryustynmus ther.

The xxiij day of Desember was a proclamasyon thrugh London,
and shall be thrugh the quen(’s) reuym, that watt man somover
thay be that doysse forsake testorns and do not take them for vjd.
a pesse ᶜ for corne or vetelles or any odur thynges or ware, that
they to be taken and browth a-for the mayre or shreyff, baylle,
justus a pesse, or constabulle, or odur offesers, and thay to ley
them in presun tyll the quen and her consell, and thay to remayn
ther plesur, and to stand boyth body and goodes at her grace(’s)
plesur.

The xx of Desember was bered at Westmynster master Brysse
the sergantt of the quen(’s) wod-yarde, with *(unfinished)*

.   .   .   .
.   .   .   .   strett ma .   .   .

The xxix day of Dessember was bered [at] Barkyng towne
yonge masteres Bowes, the [daughter] of my lord Skrope, with

ij whytt branchys and　.　. dossen torchys and iiij grett tapurs, and a iij dosen of skochyons of armes, and after a grett dener.

The xxxj day of Desember was maltt sold in Gracyous strett markett for xliiij s. a quarter, melle ᵃ sold for vj s. a bussell; of whett melle after at xlvj s. a quarter.

The iiij day of January at nyght was serten feyres ᵇ [seen] in Fynsbere feyld and in More-feld at the wynd-mylle, and at the Doge-howse, and in gardens by mony men, and yt was sene at Damanes cler,ᶜ and mo plases.

The viij day of January dyd ryd in a care at Westmynster the wyff of the Grayhond, and the Abbott['s] servand was wypyd becaus that he toke her owt of the care, at the care-harse.

The x day of January was bered at sant Botullf without Althergatt on master Tayller a gold-fyner,ᵈ with ij fayre whytt branchys and a xij stayffes torchys, and iiij grett tapurs, and mony morners, and the compene of the Goldsmyth(s) in ther levery.

The xj day of January was bered my lade Challenger,ᵉ the wyff of ser Thomas Challenger, and was the wyff of ser Thomas Lee of Hogston, and bered at Shordyche chyrche, with ij whyt branchys, and ij dosen stayffes torchys and iiij grett tapurs, and a harold of armes, and iiij baners of emages and a viij dosen of skochyons of armes, and the strett hangyd with blake boythe the strett and the chyrche and armes.

[The xiij day of January, in alderman Draper's ward, called] Chordwenerstrett ward, a belle-man [went about] with a belle at evere lane end and at the ward [end, to] gyff warnyng of ffyre and candyll lyght, [and to help the] powre, and pray for the ded.

The xv day of January was bered at A[llhallows-] stannyng in Fanchyrche-strett on master Croker, w[ith a herse] and a dossen stayffes torchys and iiij grett tapers, and [arms] a-pone them, and

ᵃ meal.　　ᵇ fires.　　ᶜ Dame Agnes Clare.
　　ᵈ refiner.　　ᵉ Chaloner

armes a-bowt ys body and se . . . . . mornars and mony prestes and clarkes syngyng.

The xx day of January at Grenwyche parke the quen grace('s) pensyonars dyd mustur in bryth ᵃ [harness] and mony barbe horsses; and evere pensyonar had iij men in grene cottes gardyd with whytt; so thay rod a-bowt [the park,] iij in ranke apone grett horssys with spers in ther handes pentyd whyt and grene, and a-for rod trumpeters blohyng; and next a man of armes bayryng a standard of red and yelowe, in the standard a whytt hart, and on the thodur syd a blake eygyll with goldyd leges; and be-twyn ij and iij of the cloke thay cam downe and mustered a-for the Quen('s) grace a-for the parke gatt, for ther stod the Quen('s) grace on he,ᵇ and my lord cardenall, and my lord admerall, and my lord Montyguw, and dyvers odur lordes and lades; and so a-for the pensyoners rod many gentyll-men on genetes and lyght horsses, butt spesyalle ᶜ ther rod on ᵈ gentyll-man, ys nam ys master *(blank)*, apon the lest mulle thatt evere I say; ᵉ and so thay rod to and fro a-for the Quyne; and ther cam a tumbeler, and playd mony prate fettes ᶠ a-for the Quen and my lord cardenalle, that her grace dyd layke ᵍ hartely; and so her grace dyd thanke them alle for ther peyne; and so after they partyd, for ther wher ʰ of the pensyonars l. and mo, besyd ther men of armes; and ther wher ʰ of pepulle of men and vomen a-boyff x m. pepulle and mo.

[The xxvj day of January went to Cambridge, Watson bishop elect of Lincoln, Scot bishop of Chester, and Christopherson bishop elect of Chichester,] comyssyoners to the [lord cardinal, to the] chyrche of sant Mares,ᶦ and thay toke up on ᵏ Martin [Bucer] that was bered ther, and Paulus Phagius [was] taken up at Sant Myghelle cherche that was [buried there,] and after brentt boyth.

The xxv day of January was bered master[ess] Ogull, the wyff of master Ogull, in the parryche [church of] sant Gylles with-out

---

ᵃ bright.   ᵇ high.   ᶜ especially.   ᵈ one.   ᵉ ever I saw.
ᶠ pretty feats.   ᵍ laugh.   ʰ were.   ᶦ Mary's.   ᵏ one.

Crepulgatt, with ij whytt branchys, and a dosen stayffe torchys, and iiij grett gylt candylstykes, and with iiij grett tapurs and armes apone them, and a ij dosen of skochyons of armes; and a blake frere dyd pryche at masse for here.

The xxviij day of January was bered at Powlles ser . . . Trekett, on of the keeper(s) of the westre,[a] the wyche he was worth a grett sum of money and gold.

The sam day cam thrugh London to (blank) a fayre (blank) cowe and a grett hynd and fat that ever that I have sene, to goo to-gether to (unfinished)

The xxviij day of January was had to the Towre my lorde Sturton for murder of ij gentyllmen, the father and the sune and ere,[b] master Argylles[c] and ys sune, the wyche was shamfully murdered in ys own plasse.

The xxxj day of January my lord tresorer('s) lord of mysrulle cam to my lord mare, and bad my lord to dener, and ther cam a grett cumpene of my lord tresorer('s) men with portesans,[d] and a grett mene[e] of musysyonars and dyssegyssyd, and with trumpets and drumes, and with ys consellers and dyver odur offesers, and ther was a dullvyll[f] shuting of fyre, and won was lyke Deth with a dart in hand.

[The vijth day of February master Offley, the lord mayor, and divers aldermen, taking their barge, went to Greenwich to the Queen's] grace, and ther she mad ym [knight, he] behyng mayre, and master William Chester, altherman, mayd hym knyght the sam tyme and day.

The sam day was a santhuary man of W[estminster] wypyd a-for the crosse for murder.

The x day of Feybruary was bered at sant Dunstones in the West ser Wylliam Portman, cheyffe justice of Englande, with a harold of armes, and a standard of armes, and pennon, and a cott armur, and a targett, a helmett, and the crest a leberd-hed gold,

<hr>

[a] vestry.   [b] heir.   [c] *The name was* Hartgill.   [d] partisans.
[e] meyne, *i. e.* company.   [f] devil.

with ij snakes [coming] out of ys mowthe, with a crosse peyche [a]
gulles; a [herse], and sword, and the mantylles of blake velvett,
and ij grett wytt branchys fayre with shochyons of armes, and ij
dosen of torchys, and the powre men had go . . . gownes, and
iiij grett gylt candylstykes, with iiij p . . . garnyshed with
angelles, and armes, and penselles, and mo[ny] morners; and after
came vj juges and vij sergantes of [the coif], and after all the ynes
of the cowrte, ij and ij together; and the morow iij goodly masses
songe, and a sermon mad.

The x day of Feybruary was slayne in Nugatt market, on
Robartt Lentall, odur-wyse callyd Robart (blank), servant unto
my lord tresorer the marques of Wynchester, by a servand unto
the duke of Norffoke, and ys fottman, the wyche was ys on
sekyng.[b]

. . . .

. . . and iij women.

The xvij day of Feybruary was my lord Sturton cam from the
Towre, and one of ys men, unto Westmynster a-for the consell
and juges, and ther the evydens was declared a-for ys owne face
that he cold nott deny ytt.

The xvij day of Feybruary ded [c] in Chanell-rowe the good yerle
of Sussex at Westmynster.

The xviij day of Feybruary cam from the Towre unto my lord
of Preve-selle a-for serten of the consell, iiij of my lord Sturtun('s)
servandes, and ther thay where examynyd of the deth of master
Argyll and ys sune; and after they wher cared bake a-gayne by
iiij of the gard unto the (Tower).

The xxvj day of Feybruary was rayned at Westmynster halle
my lord Sturton, and for [d] the juges and dyvers of the consell, as
lord justes Broke, and the lord stuard, and my lord tresorer, and
dyvers odur lordes and knyghtes; and longe yt wher [e] or he wold
answer, and so at last my lord justes stod up and declaryd to my

---

[a] fitchy.   [b] his own seeking.   [c] died.   [d] before.   [e] were.

lord and [a] he wold nott answer to the artyculles that was led [b] to
hym, that he shuld be prast [c] to deth by the law of the rayme [d]; and
after he dyd answer, and so he was cast by ys owne wordes to be
hangyd, and ys iiij men, and so to be cared to the Towre a-gayne
tyll thay have a furder commondement from the consell.

[The same day was buried the earl of Sussex . . . . .
of] England at sant Lauruns [Pountney . . . .], and the
chyrche hangyd with blake, and ys armes . . borne, and ij
goodly whytt branchys, and ij . . ; and ij haroldes of armes,
and a baner of ys armes, [and iiij] banars of emages, and a x
dosen of skochyons . . . . dosen of penselles, and a cote
armur, target, [sword,] the elmett, crest, and mantylles of blake
velvett.

The xxvij day of Feybruary cam toward London out of Skottland a duke of Muskovea, as [ambassador,] and dyvers of the marchandes of England, as we[ll as others] of all nassyons, and so they
mett him be[yond] Sordyche in cottes of velvett and cottes of fyne
cloth gardyd with velvett, and with frynge of sylke [and] chenys [e]
of gold; and after comys my lord Montycutte and dyvers lordes and
knyghtes and [gentlemen, in] gorgyus aparelle; and after comys
my lord mayre and althermen in skarlett, and the enbassedur ys
garment of tyssuw brodered with perlles and stones; and ys
[men in] corsse cloth of gold downe to the calffe of the leg, lyke
gownes, and he copyng capes, [f] and so to master Dymmokes plasse
in Fanchyrche street, the marchand; and ys cape and ys nyght
cape sett with perles and stones.

The ij day of Marche rod from the Towre my lord Sturtun with
ser Robart Oxinbryge the leyff-tenantt, and iiij of my lordes
servandes, and with serten of the gard, thrugh London, and so to
Honsley, [g] and ther thay lay alle nyght at the seyne [h] of the Angell,
and the morow after to Staynes, and so to Bassyng-stoke, and so
to Sturtun, to sufer deth, and ys iiij men; and to [i] more men for

[a] if.   [b] laid.   [c] pressed.   [d] realm.   [e] chains.
    [f] high coping caps.   [g] Hounslow.   [h] sign.   [i] two.

robyng of a ryche farmer in that contrey, to be hangyd, for ther
was layd by the sam farmer a-for the consell that a knyght and
ys men dyd rob him, and the knyght was layd in the Flett tylle yt
plessyd God that the theyff was taken; the knyght ys nam ys
callyd ser [*blank*] Wrothun knyght.

[The v day of March was buried in Northamptonshire sir
Edward Montagu, late lord chief justice of England; with] cott
armur, and targett, and sword, helmett, and man[tylls of] velvett, and iiij dosen of stayffes, ij whyt branchys . . . . dosen
of skochyons, and iiij dosen of penselles, and with . . . .
harold of armes and a hersse of wax.

The vj day of Marche was bered in Huntyngtun[shire sir]
Olever Leyder knyght, with a harold of armes, a standard and
penon of armes, a cott armur, a targett, and sword, elmett,
. . . . mantylles of velvett, and vj dosen of skochyons, and
iiij dosen of torchys, and a hersse of wax.

The sam day was hangyd at Salysbere in the markett plasse the
lord Sturtun for the deth of old master Argylle and yong Argyll
ys sune; the wyche they wher shamfully murdered by the lord,
and dyvers of ys servandes; the wyche he mad grett lamentasyon
at ys deth for that wyllfull ded that was done, and sayd as he was
on the ladder (*unfinished*).

The viij day of Marche was bered master (*blank*) with armes
and ij whyt branchys and viij storchys and iiij gret tapurs, in sant
Androws in Holborne, with prestes and clarkes.

The xvij day of Marche cam rydyng from kyng Phelype from
be-yond the see unto the court at Grenwyche, to owre quen, with
letters in post, my lord Robart Dudley, and after master Kemp
of the preve chambur, that the kyng wold com to Cales the xvij
day of Marche; and the sam day dyd pryche a-for the quen the
nuwe bysshope of Lynckolne doctur Watsun.

The xviij day of Marche was the monyth myn * of the yerle

* month's mind.

of Sussex, and the hersse bornyng and standyng tyll durge, and
masse done on the morow after yt was taken downe; and master
Garter was ther to se ys standard and ys elmet, targat, cott, and
banars sett up over hym, with alle thyng longyng therto.

.   .   .   .

.   .   . man shuld where no   .   .   .

The **xx** day of Marche the Kyng cam from be-yond the see, and
cam at **v** to Grenwyche; at the sam tyme ther cam a shype
up by the tyde, [and as] he cam agaynst the courte gatt, he shott
a **xvj** [pieces] of twys,[a] the wyche wher vere [b] grett pesses, and
[cried,] *God save the Kyng and the Quen.*

The **xxj** day of Marche the Kyng and the Quen [went] thrugh
the galere unto ther closett, and ther thay [heard mass] ; and ther
was ij swordes borne a-for them, on by lord Cobham, and the
thodur (by) my lord admerall; [and from] ther closett bake to
dener, boyth the Kyng and the Quen together, and ther my lord
chanseler was ther and dyvers [other lords.]

The sam day at after-non cam downe that evere[c] chyrche shuld
in London syng *Te Deum laudamus* by the commondement of my
lord bysshope of London, and rynggyng alle that whylle, to ryng
with grett presse[d] to God; and ther cam iij huwysse[e] of Spaneards
the sam day to London.

The **xxiij** day of Marche was a commondement cam that the
Kyng and the Quen wold ryd from the Towre-warff thrugh London with the nobuls of the rayme,[f] boyth lordes and lades; and
at the Towre-warff my lord mayre mett ther gracys boyth, and
thrugh London my masters the althermen and the shreyffes and
alle the crafftes of London in ther leveres, and ther standynges
set up of evere craft of tymbur, and the strett and the trumpettes
blohyng with odur enstrementtes with grett joye and plesur, and
grett shutyng of gones at the Towre, and the waytes plahyng on

---

[a] off twice.   [b] very.   [c] every.   [d] praise.   [e] hoys.   [f] realm

sant Peter's ledes [a] in Chepe ; and my lord mayre bare the septer a-for the Kyng and the Quen.

[The **xxv** of March] the duke of Muskovea whent to [court, with] a **x** althermen and a grett compene of [merchants, which] be fre of Muskovea; [b] and the lord toke ys ba[rge at the] iij Cranes in the Vyntre; and ys garment was of cloth of tyssuw, and ys hatt and ys nyght-cape was sett with grett perlles and ryche stones, as evere I say, [c] and ys men in cloth of gold and red damaske in syd gownes ; and so he dy. *(unfinished.)*

The **xx** day of Marche was taken up at Westmynster agayn with a hondered lyghtes kyng Edward the confessor in the sam plasse wher ys shryne was, and ytt shalle be sett up agayne as fast as my lord abbott can have ytt don, for yt was a godly shyte [d] to have seen yt, how reverently he was cared from the plasse that he was taken up wher he was led [e] when that the abbay was spowlyd and robyd [f]; and so he was cared, and goodly syngyng and senssyng as has bene sene, and masse song.

The **xxxj** day of Marche the duke of Muskovea rod to dener unto my lord mayre, and **v** knyghtes althermen and **v** other althermen, and mony notabull marchandes men, all they fre of Muskovea. The duke rod in a gowne of tyssuw rychĕ, and ys under garmentt in purpull velvett in brodere, the gard and ys hatt and the border of ys nyght-cape sett with owtchys of perlles and stones, and ys horse trapyd in cremesun velvett in-brodere of gold, and the brydylle gorgyusly be-senne; and a vii of ys men in gownes of cremesun damaske and cloth of gold; and after dener to ys logyng to master Demmoke('s) plasse, with the althermen and marchandes.

[The **iij** day of April five persons, out of Essex, were condemned for] herese, iij men and ij women, [one woman with a staff in her hand,] to be bornyd in Smyth-feld.

---

[a] leads, *i. e.* roof.   [b] *i. e.* members of the Muscovy company.
[c] ever I saw.   [d] sight.   [e] laid.   [f] spoiled and robbed.

The iij day of Aprell dyd pryche doctur Wattsun bysshope of
Lynckolne at Allallows the Mor[a] in   .   .   . at after-non, wher
was grett audyens of pepull.

The sam day dyd pryche docthur Perryn the master of the
blake frers in sant Bartholomuw in Smyth-feld, at Bowe in Chepe-
syd dyd pryche .   .   .   .

The v day of Aprell, the wyche was Passon [Sunday,] at Westmynster my lord abbott dyd pryche, and mad [a goodly] ser
mon as has bene hard in owre tyme.

The vj day of Aprell hangyd at Tyborne viij f   .   .   .   .

The vj day of Aprell was bornyd in Smythfeld v, iij men and ij
women, for herese; on was a barber dwellyng in Lym-strett; and
on woman was the wyff of the Crane at the Crussyd-frers be-syd
the Towre-hylle, kepyng of a in[b] ther.

The vj day of Aprell was hangyd at the low-water marke at
Wapyng be-yond santt Katheryns vij for robyng on the see.

The   .   . day of Aprell was slayn in Flestrete a man *(blank)*
.   .   .   .

The xvj day of Aprell dyd pryche at Powlles Crosse *(blank)*
Murryn,[c] that was Good Fryday, and mad a godly sermon, and
ther was grett audyens.

The xix day of Aprell dyd pryche a' sant Mare spyttell docthur
Pendyltun, and mad a goodly sermon; ther was my lord mare
and xxiij althermen besyd my lord mayre, and iij juges, and alle
the masters of the hospetall with grenstayffes in ther handes,
and alle the chylderyn of the hospetall in bluw garmenttes boyth
men chylderyn and women chylderyn, that be kept with serten
landes and the cherete of the nobull cette of London, and aboyff
xx M. pepull of old and yonge, to her the sermon of old custom,
and my lade mares and the *(unfinished)*.

The xx day of Aprell dyd pryche docthur Yonge at santt Mare
spyttylle; and ther was my lord mare and xxv althermen, none
lackyng butt master Wodderoff, the wyche makyth the full nom-

---

[a] *i. e.* the Great.   [b] an inn (the Crane).   [c] Morwen.

bur of xxvj; and my lord Broke the cheff justes, and my lord
justes Browne, and my ser John Baker, and ser Roger Chamley,
and mony nobull gentyllmen, with the holl cete* boythe old and
yonge, boythe men and women.

The xix day of Aprell was a wager shott in Fynsbere feld of
the parryche of the Trenete the lytyll, of vj men agaynst vj men,
and one parte had xv for iij and lost the game; and after shott
and lost a-nodur game.

The sam owre master parsun and entryd in-to helle and ther ded
at the barle breyke with alle the wyffe of the sam parryche; and
ever was master parsun in the fyre, ser Thomas Chambur; and
after they whent and dronke at Hogston vij* in bred and bere,
butt ij quarttes of claret, alle, and after they cam to the Swane in
Wyttyngtun college to on master Fulmer a vetelar, ther they mad
good chere, and payd for yt. b

[The same day went to Westminster to hear mass, and to the lord
abbot's to dinner, the] duke of Muskovea, and after dener [came
into the monastery, and went] up to se sant Edward shryue nuw
set up, [and there saw] alle the plasse thrugh; and after toke ys
leyff of [my lord abbot], and ther mett hym dyvers althermen and
mony [merchants]; and so rod in-to the parke, and so to London.

The xxij of Aprell dyd pryche at sant Mare speytyll [doctor]
Watsun nuw-choyssen bysshope of Lynckolne a godly sermon.

The sam day the Kyng and the Quen removyd from Grenwyche
unto Westmynster, a-ganst sant [George's day.]

The xxiij day of Aprell was sant Gorge('s) day [the King's]
grace whent a pressessyon in ys robes of the garter; lord Talbott
bare the sword a-for the Kyng, and master (blank) bare the rod;
and doctur (blank) bare the boke of the record; and the bysshope
of Wynchaster ware ys myter, and song masse that day; and x
knyghtes of the Garter be-syd the Kyng; and secretere Peter

* whole city.

b *This paragraph, which is clearly written as here printed, seems to commemorate
some wild merry-making of the diarist's parish.*

ware a robe of cremesun velvett with the Garter; and after the
Kyng and odur lordes and knyghtes of the garter whent to evyngsong; and ther was the duke of Muskovea was in chapell at evyngsong, and after he whent and toke ys barge and whent to London,
and after wher iij knyghtes of the garter chossen, furst my lord
F(itz)uater, my lord Gray of Wylton, and ser Robart Rochaster;
thes iij wher mad of the order.

The xxiij day of Aprell cam rydyng from the Towre the kynges
kynswoman the duches of *(blank)*

. . . .

. . ., armes and a cott armur, targett, sword, helmett.

The xxx day of Aprell was bered at sant Mare Overes master
Frances Browne('s) wyff with iiij branchys [and iiij] tapurs apon
iiij gylt candyllstykes and with armes and penons; [the church
hung a]bowt with blake cloth and armes, and ij whyt branchys
and xx . . . . . stayffe torchys; and the powre men had blake
gownes; and mony mornars; and a iij dosen of skochyons, and a
grett dolle of money.

The iij day of May was bered my lord Shandowes,[a] odur-wys
callyd ser John of Bryges, with ij haroldes of armes, and a herse
of wax, and ij whyt branchys, and a iiij dosen of torchys, and a
standard and a baner of armes and a targett, and iiij baners of
emages, and elmett, mantylles, and viij dosen of skochyons and
iiij baner-rolles of [arms], and viij dosen of penselles mad in the
contrey; and money mornars; and ther was a grett dolle of money,
and mett[b] and drynke grett plente as has bene sene of shyche[c] a
man in the contrey.

The xxx day of Aprell was master Perse[d] was mad knyght and
baroun.

The furst day of May was creatyd at Whytt-halle master Perse
the yerle of Northumberland, with viij haroldes and a dosen of
trumpeters thrugh the quen('s) chambur, and thrugh the hall, and

[a] Chandos.   [b] meat.   [c] such.   [d] Percy.

a-for hym my lord of Penbroke and my lord Montyguw and then my lord of Arundell and my lord of Rutland, and hym-self whent in the myddes, alle in cremesun welvett in ther parlement robes, and whyt[a] a hatt of velvett and cronet of gold on ys hed.

Item the sam day a-bowt non ther wher sarten Spaneardes fowyth[b] at the cowrt-gate a-gaynst one Spaneard, and one of them frust[c] hym thrugh with ys raper, and ded contenent[d]; and ij of the Spaneardes that kyld hym was browt in-to the cowrt by on of the gard, and he delevered them to the knyght marshall('s) servandes to have them (to) the Marshellsay.

.   .   .   .

.   .   .   serten skochyons.

The xxiij day of Aprell was sant George('s) day [the King's] grace whent a pressessyon at Whyt-halle [through the hall] and rond abowt the court hard by the halle; and so [certain of] the knyghts of the garter as they whent in ther [robes] of the garter; the bysshope of Wynchaster dyd exsecute the masse with ys myter; the furst as they whe[nt the lord] Montyguw, my lord admerall, ser Antony Sely[ger, the] lord Cobham, the lord Darce, ser Thomas Chenne, [the lord] Pagett, the lord of Penbroke, the lord of Arundel, [the] lord tressorer, and secretore Peter in a robe of cremesun velvett with the garter brodered on ys shuder,[e] and [one bare] a rod of blake, and a docthur bare a boke; and [then went all] the harodes, and then my lord Talbott bare the sword, then sergant(s) of armes, and the Kyng('s) grace [came next], and Quen('s) grace lokyng owt of a wyndow [beside] the cowrt on the garden syde.

The sam after-non was chossen iiij knyghtes of the garter, my lord Fuwwater depute of Yrland, my lord Gray depute of Gynes, and ser Robart Rochaster comtroller of the quen('s) howsse the iij. And after cam the duwcke of Muskovea cam thrugh the halle, and

[a] with.   [b] fought.   [c] thrust.
[d] he died incontinently (immediately).   [e] shoulder.

the gard stod in a-ray in ther ryche cottes with halbardes, and so up to the quen('s) chambur, and dyvers althermen and marchandes; and after cam downe a-gayne to the chapell to evyngsong, and contenent[a] cam the Kyng and the knyghtes of the garter to evyngsong; and when that evyngsong was down[b] cam the Kyng and the knyghtes up to the chambur of presens; and after cam the duke of Muskovea, and toke ys barge to London, and that tyme my lord Strange bare the sword to evyngsong.

The ij day of May dyd pryche at Powlles crosse dyd pryche docthur Chadsay, and mad a godly sermon, and ther he declaryd that serten trayturs that was taken at Skarborow castyll, the wyche they fled over the see a-for .   .   .   .   .

.   .   .   .

[The iij day of May came five persons to the Tower, the chief of those that had taken the] castylle of Skarborow in Yorke-shyre, [viz. Stafford, Saund]urs, Seywelle, and Prowtter, and a Frenche man.

The iiij day of May dyd ryd a-for the Kyng and Quen in her grace('s) preve garden ser James Garnado, and so the bridle bytt dyd breke, and so the horsse rane aganst the wall, and so he brake ys neke, for ys horsse thruw ym agane the wall and hys brauns[c] rane owtt.

The v day of May a-for non was bered my lade Chamburlayne, the wyff of ser Lenard Chamburlayne of Oxffordshyre, with ij whyt branchys and a fayr [herse] of wax, and v dosen penselles and skochyons and ij dosen of [staff-torches]; xxiiij powre men and women dyd bere them, and they [had] gownes of fyne brode cottun of blake; and iiij baners borne abowte her; and with prestes and clarkes, a grett compene of mornars; and ther dyd pryche att the masse docthur Chadsay, and he mad a godly sermon; and after a grett dener; and master Longkaster was the harold; and ther was a grett dolle of money at the cherche.

---

[a] incontinently.   [b] done.   [c] brains.

The vj day of May was bered in sant Donstones in the est ser James Garnado knyght, with ij whytt branchys and xij stayffe torchys and iiij grett tapurs and a ij dosen of skochyons.

Item, the xij day was bered master Tadeley haburdassher at sant Mangnus parryche, with ij whytt branchys and xij stayff torchys, and iiij grett tapurs, and xvj pore men bare them, and they had xvj blake cassokes and nuw capes,[a] and xvj payre of blake stokes;[b] and he was one of the masturs of the hospetall; with a dosen of skcohyons and d.[c]

The xiiij day of May was bornyd in Chepe-syd and odur places in Lundon serten melle[d] that was nott swett; and thay sayd that hey[e] had putt in lyme and sand to deseyffe the pepull, and he was had to the conter.

The xxvij day of May at after-none was a woman grett with chyld was slayne gohyng in Fynsbere feld with her hosband with a narow[f] shott in the neke, the wyche she was a puterer('s) wyff.

.   .   .   .

.   .   .   . masteres sumtyme the wyff of .   .   .   . kynges bakehowsse and after the wyff of master .   .   .   . clarke of the grencloth boyth sqwyrers,[g] and d

The xxij day of May cam owt of the Towre .   .   .   . vj pre-sonars, on Thomas Stafford, and captayn Sanders, Seywell and Prowther, and a Frencheman, and one othur; wher cast v, and so cared to the Towre agayn [through] London by land, the wyche thay cam from .   .   .   .

The xxij day of May was bered master Doge .   .   .   . gren cloth at sant Martens in the feld be-syd Charyng-crose, with ij whytt branchys and .   .   .   . and ij dosen of skochyons and dyver mornars.

The xxiij day of May dyd pryche the bysshope of Wynchaster doctur Whytt at sant Mare Overes in Sowthwarke, and ther was a heretyke ther for to here the sermon.

[a] caps.   [b] stockings.   [c] a half.   [d] meal.
[e] he, *i. e.* the seller.   [f] an arrow.   [g] esquires.

The xxv day of May was raynyd at Westmynster one, a Frenche man, that was taken at Skarborow when that Thomas Stafford was taken with ys adherentes, and cast to dee, and so cared to the Towre agayn.

The sam day was hangyd at Tyburne xvij; on was a nold[a] voman of lx yere, the trongyest[b] cut-purs a voman that has ben herd off; and a lad a cut-purs, for ys tyme he be-gane welle.

The xxvij day of May, the wyche was the Assensyon day, the Kynges and the Quen('s) grace rod unto Westmynster with all the lords and knyghtes and gentyllmen, and ther ther graces whent a prossessyon abowt the clowster, and so thay hard masse.

[The xxviij day of May Thomas Stafford was beheaded on Tower hill, by nine of the clock, master Wode being his] gostly father; and after ther wher iij more [drawn from the To]wre, and thrugh London unto Tyburne, and ther [they were] hangyd and quartered; and the morow after was master [Stafford] quartered, and hangyd on a care, and so to Nuwgatt to [boil.]

The sam mornyng was bornyd be-yond sant George's parryche iij men for heresee, a dyssyd[c] Nuwhyngtun.

The sam for-non was bered masteres Gattes wedow, and she [gave] vij fyne blake gowens, and xiiij for pore men of bro . . , with ij whytt branchys and x stayffes torchys and iiij grett tapurs, and after masse a grett dener.

The xxix day of May was the iiij heds sett upon London bryge, and ther xvj quarters sett up, iij and ij, on evere gatt of London; the sam mornyng was Thomas Stafford('s) body quartered.

The xxx day of May was a goly[d] May-gam in Fanch-chyrche-strett with drumes and gunes and pykes, and ix wordes[e] dyd ryd; and thay had speches evere man, and the morris dansse and the sauden,[f] and a elevant with the castyll, and the sauden and yonge morens[g] with targattes and darttes, and the lord and the lade of the Maye.

---

[a] an old.   [b] strongest?   [c] at this side.   [d] go[od]ly, *or* jolly.
[e] The Nine Worthies.   [f] sowdan, *or* sultan.   [g] moors.

The v day of Junj was bered in sant Peters in Chepe master
Tylworth goldsmyth, with mony mornars, and with ij whytt branchys
and xij stayffes torchys, and the xij pore men had gownes of mantyll frysse, and iiij grett tapurs; and ys mas was kefth.[a] . . .
on Wyssunmonday, and after ther was a grett deener.

The vij day of Juin was a proclamassyon in London by the
quen('s) grace, of the latt duke of Northumberland was supported
and furdered by Henry the Frenche kyng and ys menysters, and
by the heddes of Dudley, Asheton, and by the consperacy of
Wyatt and ys trayturs[b] band; and the sayd kynges mynysters dyd
secretly practysse and gyff, and they favorabulle; with trumpeters
blohyng, and a x harroldes of armes, and with my lord mayre and
the althermen; and by the lat Stafford and with odur rebelles
whom he had interteynyd in ys rayme,[c] and dyver odur mo, the
wyche be ther yett on-taken.

[The same day was the Fishmongers' procession. The mass
kept at saint Peter's, in Cornhill; three] crosses borne and a C.
prestes in [copes; and clerks] syngyng *Salve festa dies;* and then
cam the [parish with] whyt rodes, and then the craft of Fysmongers; [and after] my lord mayre and the althermen, and alle the
offesers with whyt rodes in ther handes; and so to Polles, and
ther offered at the he[d] auter, and after to dener to the Fysmongers hall to dener.

The sam day be-gane a stage play at the Grey freers of the
Passyon of Cryst.

The viij day of Juinj cam a goodly prossessyon unto Powlles,
and dyd oblassyon at the he[e] auter, sant Clementes parryche
with-out Tempylle-bare, with [iiij^xx] baners and stremars, and the
whettes[f] of the cete[g] playing; and a iij^xx copes, and prestes and
clarkes, and dyver of the ennes[h] of the cowrt whent next the
prestes; and then cam the parryche with whytt rodes in ther

---

[a] kept.   [b] traiterous.   [c] his realm.   [d] high.
[e] high.   [f] waits.   [g] city.   [h] inns.

handes, and so bake agayne with the whettes playing, and prestes and clarkes syngyng, home-warde.

The x day of Junij the Kyng and the Quen toke ther jorney toward Hamtun courte for to hunt and to kyll a grett hartt, with serten of the consell; and so the howswold tared at the Whytt-halle, tylle the Saterday folowhyng they cam a-gayne to Whytt-halle.

The xvj day of June my yong duke of Norfoke rod abrod, and at Stamford-hylle my lord havying a dage hangyng on ys sadylle bow, and by mysse-fortune dyd shutt [a] yt, and yt on [b] of ys men that ryd a-for, and so by mysse-forten ys horse dyd flyng, and so he hangyd by on of ys sterope(s), and so thatt the horse knokyd ys brayns owt with flyngyng owt with ys leges.

[The xvij day of June, being Corpus Christi day, the King and Queen went in procession at Whitehall] thrughe the halle and the grett cowrtt-gate; [attended with as goodly] synging as ever was hard; and my (*unfinished*)

The xviij day of Junj was ij cared to be bornyd beyonde sant Gorgeus, almost at Nuwhyngtun, for herese and odur matters.

The xix day of June was bered in the parryche of sant Benett-sheyroge old masteres Halle, the mother of master Edward Halle, of Gray('s) in, the wyche he sett forthe the cronnacle the wyche hes [c] callyd master Halle('s) cronnaculle; and she dyd give serten good gownes boyth for men and vomen a xx; and ij feyre whytt branchys and x stayffes torches; and master Garrett and my lade behyng secturs [d], and my lade War . . and master Mossear and ys wyff and dyver odur had blake gownes.

The x day of June dyd on of the chantere prest,[e] dyd hang hym-selff with ys gyrdylle in ys chambur; ys name was ser John.

The xiiij day of June was cared to the Towre serten gentyllmen, blyndfeld and muffelyd.

The xx day of Junj dyd pryche my lord abbott of Westmyn-

---

[a] shoot. [b] hit one. [c] is. [d] executors. [e] one of the chantry priests.

ster at Powlles Crosse, and mad a godly sermon of Dyves and Lazarus, and the crossear holdyng the stayffe at ys prechyng; and ther wher grett audyense, boyth the mayre and juges and althermen, and mony worshepfulle.

The **xxi** day of Junj was the Sextens' prossessyon, with standards and stremars a xxx and ode, with good syngyng and the westes[a] playing, and the canepe borne, with iij qwerers[b] songe, thrughe Nuwgatt and Old-bayle, and thrugh Ludgatt, and so to Powlles chyrche-yerde and in-to Chepe a-longe to the Cowper(s') halle to dener.

. . . .

. .   Westmynster abbay, at afternone, and the . . xij of the cloke.

The **x[vij]** day of Junj was the store-howsse at Port[smouth] bornyd, and a gentyll-mansse howsse next unto hytt, and [both were] borntt, and all maner of thynges for war and vetelle.[c]

The **xxiij** day of Junj was bered master Byrd, cow[per, at] sant Martens in the vyntere, with ij whytt branchys and viij grett stayffe torchys; and he gayff vare[d] good gownes to the pore men and women; and money mornares gownes, and the powre had blake gownes; and iiij grett tapurs . . . clarkes, and after to drynke spysse-bred and wyne; and the morowe masse and a sarman, and after a grett dener and a dolle, for he dyd gyffe (*unfinished*)

The sam day at sant Martens, the santuare lane e[nd, was a] pelere[e] sett ther, and ther was a gold-smyth sett on for [making] conterfett rynges, and causyd them for to be sold for g[old, and] bolles[f] lyke sylver and gold; and a woman sett up, for she was the broker, and theseller of the rynges.

The **xxiiij** day of June was goodly serves[g] kept at the Frere Austens by the marchandes strangers as has bene sene.

The **xxix** day of June, was sent Peters day, was a smalle fare[h]

---

[a] waits.   [b] quires?   [c] victual.   [d] very.   [e] pillory.
[f] bowls.   [g] service.   [h] fair.

keft[a] in sant Margatt cherche-yerde, as wolle[b] and odur smalle thynges, as tornars and odur: and the sam day was a godly prossessyon, the wyche my lord abbott whent with ys myter and ys crosse and a grett nomber of copes of cloth of gold, and the wergers[c], and mony worshephull gentyll-men and women at Westmynster, went a prossessyon.

The sam day at after-non was the ij-yere myne[d] of good master Lewyn, yrmonger, and at ys durge was alle the leverey; the furst master altherman Draper; and after to her plasse,[e] and they had a kake and a bone a pesse,[f] be-syd the parryche and all comers, and wyne he-nowgh for all comers.

[The last day of June, saint Paul's day, was a goodly procession at saint Paul's. There was a priest of every] parryche of the dyosses of Londun, [with a cope, and the bishop] of Londun wayreng ys myter; and after cam [a fat buck,] and ys hed with the hornes borne a-pone a baner[-pole, and] xl hornes blohyng a-for the boke and be-hynd.

The sam day was the Marchandes-tayllers' fest, [where] was master of the compene master George Eytune; and thay [had] lx bokes[g] at the fest, and he gayffe to ys one[h] parryche [two] bokes to make mere[i]; and ther dynyd at the fest [the lord] mayre and the shreyffes, and dyver worshephulle men, and my lord mayre dyd chusse master Malere altherman shreyff for the kyng for thys yere folohyng.

The sam day the Kyng('s) grace rod on untyng[k] in-to the forest, and kyllyd a grett stage[l] with gones.

The ij day of July the duke of Norfoke('s) sun was crystened at Whytt-hall at after-non, and the kyng and my lord chanseler was the godfathers, and my old lade the duches of North-foke was the god-mother, and ther wher iiij[xx] storchys bornyng.

---

[a] kept.	[b] wool.	[c] virgers.	[d] two years' mind.
[e] their place—the Drapers' hall.		[f] a cake and a bun apiece.	[g] bucks.
[h] his own.	[i] merry.	[k] hunting.	[l] stag.

The iij day of July the Kyng and the Quen toke ther gornay[a] toward Dover, and lay all nyghtt at Syttyngborne.

The vi day of July was bered at sant Pulkers with-owtt Nuwgatt, master Stukley; with ij whytt branchys and (*blank*) stayffes torchys, and with armes.

The x day of July was bered at Peterborow my lade Tressam, with iiij baners, and a herse of wax, (*blank*) torchys, and a iiij dossen of skochyons.

[The v day of July the King took shipping at Dover] towarde Callys, on hys jornay [toward Flanders].

The (*blank*) day of Aprell suffered dethe in [several] plases in the Northe for entryng in-to Sk[arborough] castyll, (for) the wyche at London master Thomas [Stafford] was heddyd on Towre hylle; and at Tyborne John Procter aleas Wylliamsun, Wyllyam Stowe, John Bradford, and more in dyvers plases; [in York]shyre, John Wylborne, Clement Tyllyd, John Cawsewelle, and Robart Hunter, at York, [by the] dethe of hangyng, drahyns,[b] and quarter[ing].

Item, at Skarborow suffered dethe master Thomas Sp . . , John Adames, John Wattsun, skott, John . . a frencheman.

At Hulle, John Browne, Owyn Jones, suffered.

At Beverley, Hary Gardener and John Thomas suffered.

At Whyttby, Thomas Warden and John Deyctam, skott.

Att Malton, Wyllyam Palmer, John Mortfurth, scott.

Att Flamborow, at Assyley, Thomas Wylkynsun.

At Byrlyngton, John Wallys.

At Awdborowre, Antony Persevall.

At Hornesey, Wylliam Wyllamsun.

At Pawlle in Holdernes, Roger Thomas.

At Hassylle, Roger Raynoldes.

At Alefax,[c] Lawransse Alssope.

At Donkester, in Yorkeshyre, Thomas Jordayn.

At Howden, John Grey, skotte.

---

[a] journey.   [b] *So in MS.*; *read* drawing.   [c] Halifax.

At Wakefeld, Robert Hawgatt, skott; and all thes for enteryng in Skarborow castylle.

. . . .

.   . es Stanley, of Le, in Essex.

Thomas Thorley, of Prykkyllwell, in Essex.

Hare Ramsey, of Amwell, in conte of Harford.

The xiiij day of July was bered at [saint] Bowtolfe in Temes strett master Tornburn, fysmonger, with ij whytt branchys, and xii torchys, and iiij grett tapurs, and mony morners.

The same day was bered good master Worley in the parryche of sant Mare-bowe, in Chepe, with ij whytt branchys, and xij torchys, and iiij gret tapurs, and a xviij morners, and a ij dosen of skochyons.

The xv day of July the Quen('s) grace dynyd at Lambeth with my lord cardenall Polle, and after dener removyd to Rychmond, and ther (her) grace tares ther her plesur.

The xv day of July was nuw coffend again and le[aded] master Wyttyngtun and my lade ys wyff, at Wyttyngtun college, and had durge over nyght, and the morow masse; the wyche was the fonder of the same colege, and beldyd Nugatt and other places, and was mere of London.

The moneth of July whent a grett army after that the kyng was gone over; my lord of Pembroke, cheyff capten of the feld, and my lord Montyguw whent, and my lord Clyntun, and dyvers lordes and knyghtes and gentyllmen by water and land, and goodly aparelle; they wher sent to Dover. London fond v c. men all in bluw cassokes, sum by shypes and sum to Dover by land, the goodlyst men that ever whent, and best be-sene in change (of) aparelle.

The xxx day of July master Dave [a] Gyttons, master Meynard, and master Draper, and master Smyth, master Coldwelle, and master Asse and Gybes, and master Packyngtun, and monser the Machyn de Henry,[b] and mony mo, ded ett alff a busshell of

---

[a] David.   [b] A playful designation of the writer's own person.

owsturs [a] in Anckur lane at master Smyth and master Gytton's seller [b] a-pone hoghedes, and candyll lyght, and onyons and red alle [c] and clarett alle, [c] and muskadylle and malmesey alle, fre cope, [d] at viij in the mornyng.

[The xvi day of July died the lady Anna of Cleves, at Chelsea, sometime wife and queen to king Henry the] viij [th], but she was never crounyd, butt [remained in England,] and she was seyryd [e] the nyght folohyng.

The xv day of July was bered master Reche('s) wyff, [who] was mere of London and knyght and altherman of London, with ij wyth [f] branchys, and xij torchys, iiij tapurs, and ij dosen of armes.

The xxij day of July was bered in Essex master Latham, with ij whytt branchys, and xij stayff-torchys, and iiij grett tapurs.

The sam day cam from my lord Dacurs of the North, beyond Carlylle, (blank) lyght hors-men to go [beyond] see.

The xxiij day of July sir Gorge Pallett and ser Wyllyam Cortnay toke ther barge at Towre warff, at . . . of the cloke at after-non, toward Dover, and dyvers captaynes.

The xvij day of July was a scresmys [g] at Margyson be-twyn the Englysmen and Frenchemen, and ther owre men had the beter and had good bote [i] of cattell; and ther wher slayne ix men of armes and xviij taken presoners of Frenche-men, and of owrs iij taken presoners and v hurtt, by the helpe of men of Gynes and Calles horse-men.

The xxvj day of July was bered masteres Draper of Camurell, [k] with ij whytt branchys and xii stayff torchys, and iiij grett tapurs, and ij dosen of skochyons of armes.

The xxix day of July was fechyd out of Westmynster [l] by the constabyll of the Towre of London, the wyche ys constabull, and browth [m] on (blank) Waxham, the wyche he brake out of the Towre, and was browth thrugh London.

[a] oysters.   [b] cellar.   [c] ale.   [d] all free cups ?
[e] cered, i. e. inclosed in waxed cloths.   [f] white.   [g] skirmish.
[i] booty.   [k] Camberwell.   [l] i. e. out of the sanctuary.   [m] brought.

[The same day, being saint Olave's day, was the church holiday in Silver street; and at eight of the clock at night began] a stage play of [a goodly matter, that continued until] xij at mydnyght, and then they mad an end with a g[ood song.]

The sam day began the herse at Westmynster for my lade Anne of Cleyff, with carpynters worke of vij prensepalles, as goodly a hers as　.　.　.　.

The first day of August was the nones[a] of Syon was closyd in by my lorde bysshope of London and my lord abbott of Westmynster, and serten of the consell, and serten frers of that order, of shepe coler as the shepe bereth; and thay had as grett a charge of ther leyfvyng,[b] and never to goo forth as longe as they do lyffe, but ever　.　.

The iij day of August my lade Anne of Cleyff, sumtyme wyff unto kyng Henry the viij[th] cam from Chelsey to be [buried] unto Westmynster, with all the chylderyn of Westmynster and [many] prest[c] and clarkes, and then the gray ames[d] of Powlles and iij crosses, and the monkes of Westmynster, and my lord bysshope of Lo[ndon] and my lord abbott of Westmynster rod together next the monkes, and then the ij sekturs[e] ser Edmond Peckham and ser (Robert) Freston, cofferer to the quen of England; and then my lord admerall, my (lord) Darce of Essex, and mony knyghts and gentyllmen; and a-for her servandes, and after her baner of armes; and then her gentyllmen and here hed offesers; and then here charett with viij baners of armes of dyvers armes, and iiij baners of emages of whytt taffata, wroght with fyne gold and her armes; and so by sant James, and so to Charying-crosse, with a C. torchys bornyng, her servandes beyrying them, and the xij bed-men of Westmynster had new blake gownes; and they had xij torchys bornyng, and iiij whyt branchys with armes; and then ladies and gentyll-women all in blake, and horsses; and a viij haroldes of armes in blake, and ther horses; and armes sad[f] a-bowt the herse behynd and

[a] nuns.　　[b] living.　　[c] priests.　　[d] amice.　　[e] executors.　　[f] set.

be-for; and iiij haroldes barying the iiij whyt baners; and at (the) chyrche dore all dyd a-lyght and ther dyd reseyvyd the good lade my lord of London and my lord abbott in ther myteres and copes, sensyng her, and ther men dyd bere her with a canepe of blake welvett, with iiij blake stayffes, and so browth in-to the herse and ther tared durge, and so ther all nyght with lyght bornyng.

[The iij day of August, in the afternoon, came from the Exchequer about seventeen horses laden with money towards Berwick, and divers men riding with it with javelins and pole-axes, on horseback, and] bowes and sheyffes of arowes, be-twyn viij and [ix of the clock.]

The iiij day of August was the masse of *requiem* for my lade prenses [a] of Cleyff, and dowther to [William] duke of Cleyff; and ther my lord abbott of Westmynster mad a godly sermon as ever was mad, and [then] . . . the byshope of London song masse in ys myter; [and after] masse my lord byshope and my lord abbott mytered dyd [cense] the corsse; and afterward she was caried to her tomb, [where] she leys with a herse-cloth of gold, the wyche lyys [over her]; and ther alle her hed offesers brake ther stayffes, [and all] her hussears [b] brake ther rodes, and all they cast them in-to her tombe; the wyche was covered her co[rps] with blake, and all the lordes and lades and knyghtes and gentyllmen and gentell-women dyd offer, and after masse agrett [dinner] at my lord (abbat's); and my lade of Wynchester was the cheyff [mourner,] and my lord admeroll and my lord Darce whent of ether syde of my lade of Wynchester, and so they whent in order to dinner.

The vj day of August cam anuw commondement that the cette [c] shuld fynd a M. men with all maner of wepons, cottes and harnes, gones and mores-pykes, and horse-men.

The x day of August was bered master Dause, gentyllman to

---

[a] princess.   [b] ushers.   [c] city.

the quen, at sant Botulff with-owt Altergatt, with armes and ij branchys, xij stayffes, and iiij tapurs.

The xj day of August was bered at Clrakenwell my lade Page, with (*unfinished*).

The xiij day of Angust was a proclamasyon of alle [a] and bere, and whatt men shall pay for barelles of alle and bere and kylderkyns.

The xiiij day of August cam tydynges from beyond the see that the Kyng our master had taken mony nobull men of France gohyng to vetell [b] Sant Qwynten, the constabull of Fransse and a vj m. presonares taken, and vj . . cartes and wagens laden with tresur and vetell, at a plasse callyd Sant Qwynten, and ther my lord Hare Dudley was slayn at the wynnyng of ytt.

. . . .

The xv day of August cam a commondement to [all the churches] of London to go to Powlles, all prestes in copes a prosses[sion. Before] they whentt, they of Powlles songe *Te Deum laudamus;* [and after that] down [c] they whent a prossessyon into Chepe, round [about] the crosse syngyng *Salve festa dies,* and my lord mayre [and aldermen in] skarlett round a-bowtt Powlles with-owtt; and after [to Paul's] crosse to sermon; and ther prychyd the archedeken of London, [doctor] Harpfeld, and mad a godly sermon; the wyche day was the [day of the] Assumsyon of owre blessyd Lade the Vyrgyn, and in ys sermon [he] declared how many wher taken, and what nobull men they were.

The sam day at after [d] evyngsong all chyrchys in London was *Te Deum laudamus* songe, and ryngyng solemn[ly;] at nyght bone-fyres and drynkynge in evere strett in Lo[ndon,] thankyng be to God Almyghty that gyffes the vyctore.

The xvj day of August be-gane to sett up the herse for the kyng of Denmarke, a frame of iiij-sqware.

The xvij day of August was the obseque of master (*blank*) Heyron, the sune of the basterd Heyron of the North, with cot armur, and pennon of armes, with torches and lyght.

---

[a] ale.   [b] victual.   [c] done.   [d] *So in MS.*

The xviiij day of August was the hers for the kyng of Denmarke
fenysshed, with wax, the wyche was never sen shyche on [a] in
England of that fassyon, of sqware tapurs, and xxj baners and
baners rolles of all ther leneges and mareges in baner-rolles.   The
sam nyght was the durge, my lord tresorer cheyff morner; and
after that my lord Darcy, ser Robart Uxinbryge, ser Edmond
Peckam, ser [Robert] Freston, cofferer to the quen, and ser
Recherd Sowthwell, ser Arthur Darcy, and mony nobull men and
gentyllmen alle in blake; and my lord of London begane the durge,
with ys myter [on] alle the durge wylle [b]; and after the durge alle
the haroldes and the lordes whent to the bysshope of London('s)
plasse and dronke; and iiij goodly whytt branchys, and vj dosen
torchys, and the qwer hangyd with blake and armes; and vj
pilers [c] covered with velvet, and a goodly hers-cloth of tensell, the
crosse of cloth of selver; and the morow masse, and a goodly
sermon, and after to my lord('s) of London to dener for the kyng
of Denmarke('s) obseque and fenerall, and a mageste and valans
fryng of gold, and x dosen pensels, and x dosen skochyns of
armes.

.   .   .   .

The xxij day of August was the herse [of my lade Anne of
Cleves] taken downe at Westmynster, the wyche the monkes [by
night had spoiled of] all welvett cloth, armes, baners, penselles, of
all the [majesty and] valans, the wyche was never sene a-fore so
done.

The xxv day of August was bered at (*blank*) ser John Pollard
knyght, with standard, pennon, cott-armur, sword, and a herse;
and iiij dosen of torchys and vj dosen of skochyons, ...
dosen pensells.

The xxiij day of August was the hers of the kyng [of Denmark]
at Powlles taken downe by master Garter, and serten of the lord
tressorer('s) servandes, and the waxchandlers and carpynters.

---

[a] seen such an one.   [b] while, *i. e.* duration.   [c] pillars.

The xxiiij day of August was bered master Thomas [Halley, Clarenceux] kyng at armes, and on of cheyff of the haroldes [by ?] ys servand in sant Gylles parryche with-owt Crepullgate, with cote-armur and penon of armes, and skochyons of ys armes, and ij whyt branchys, and xij stayffes torchys, and iiij grett tapurs; and a crowne; and after durge, and [then] whent the haroldes unto master Grenell('s) [a] the waxchandeler, [and there] thay had spysse-bred and cheysse,[b] and wyne grett plente. [On the] morow masse, and a sermon; and after a grett dener, with all the haroldes at dener, and the parryche dynyd ther; and soper [c] ther.

The xxvj day of August was bered master *(blank)* Barenteyn sqwyre, with cott armur, and penon of armes, and ij dosen of sko-chyons, ij whyt branchys, and xij stayffes torchys, iiij grett tapurs; bered in sant Mare Somersett at Broken-warff; and he had a godly masse of owre Lade in pryke songe; and after a masse of *requiem* songe, and so ys cote offered; and after a grett dener.

The xxviij day of August begane to sett up the herse at sant Clementes with-owt Tempull-bare for my yonge duches of North-foke, the wyffe to the yonge duke of Northfoke.

The xxix day of August was the Marchand-tayllers' fest on the decolassyon of sant John babtyst, and my lorde mayre and ser Thomas Whytt and master Harper shreyff, and master Row, and all the cloythyng, and the iiij wardens of the yomenre, and the com-pene, hard messe at sant Johns in Smyth-feld; and offered evere man a pene;[d] and from thens to the halle to dener, ij and ij together. The sam day a grett shoutyng; and the cheyff warden master Horne marchand-tayller.

The furst day of September at after-none be[ried the] yonge duches of Northfoke, and the chyrche and the plasse and the strett [hangyd with black] and armes; and be iij of the cloke she was

---

[a] Greenhill ?   [b] cheese.   [c] supper.   [d] penny.

browth ^a to [the church with] a c morners; and her grasse ^b had a canepe ^c of blake [velvet, with] iiij stayffes, borne ower her; and many baners, and baner[-rolls borne ab]owt here; and the byshope of London in ys cope and ys myter [on his head,] and all the qwyre of Powlles; and with ij grett whytt branchys, and xij dosen stayffes torchys; and viij haroldes of armes; and my [lady Lumley] the cheyff morner, and mony lordes and knyghtes, and gentyll lades and gentyll-women.

The x . . . day of August was bered master . . . . in the contrey of *(blank)* sqwyre with cote-armur and . . . . and ij dosen of skochyons and ij dosen of torchys.

The *(blank)* day of August brake owt of the Towre master Wa[. . .] ^d the ij tyme, and toke santtuary at Westmynster agayn.

The iij day of September was bered ser Hare Husse knyght, in the towne callyd Slynford in Sussex.

The sam day at nyght cam commondement that evere chyrche in London, and oder contrey and shyre, to syng and make bonfeyrs for the wynnynge of Sant Qwynten; and ther was slayn my lord Hare Dudley the yonger sone of the duke of Northumberland that was he[aded,] with mony mo, at the wynnyng of yt.

The x day of September was bered in Hardford-shyre master Coke, master of reqwest(s).

The x day of September was browth ^e to the Towre agayne master Wathan by the consell from Westmynster.

.   .   .   .
.   . iiij grett tapurs . . . . . torchys and a grett dener.

The xj day of September was a man set in the pelere ^f for spykyng sedyssus wordes.

The xij day of September was a commondement that matens and masse to be done by ix of the cloke, [and every] parsun or

---

^a brought.   ^b grace.   ^c canopy.
^d *Before* Waxham, *and afterwards* Wathan *and* Wakham.
                ^e brought.   ^f pillory.

curett to go to Powlles with surples and copes [and to] go a' pressessyon ther thrugh and a-bowt [Paul's] and *Te Deum laudamus*
song; and my lord mayre and the althermen in skarlett; and after
they whent into the shroudes [and] docthur Standyche dyd pryche
ther; and at after [even-]song *Te Deum laudamus* and ryngyng
thrugh [London] for the good nuwes that cam from owre. cap-
teynes beyond the see, the wynnyng of *(unfinished)*.

The xiij day of September ded[a] ser John Cheyke, sumtyme
skollmaster unto kyng Edward the vj[th] tyll he [died].

The xv day of September Raff Qwalett payd unto master
Ley, clarke of the paper, x[li]. for the wyche was payd for master
was secondare of the conter by a oblygassyon bond for Thomas
Browne. Wytnes at the pament of thys money Hare Machyn
marchand-tayller, and Dave Edward, servant unto my lord bysshope of Wynchester, and with dyvers odur gentyllmen; the
wyche sum full payd xij[li] and I to have a qwyttans as sone as the
wylle of master Gy Wade, sqwyre, and secondare of the kontur[b]
in Wodstrett.

The xvj day of September was bered master Heyns, stuard
unto my lord cardenall, at Hamsted heth, with ij dosen skochyons, xij torchys, ij whyt branchys, and iiij grett tapurs; and a
grett dener.

.   .   .   .

The xv day of September was restoryd unto Westmynster santuary agayn master Wakham that brake owt of the [Tower].

The xvj day of September cam owt of Spayn [to the] quen('s)
cowrt in post monser Regamus, gorgys[ly apparelled,] with dyvers Spaneardes, and with grett cheynes, and ther hats sett with
stones and perlles, and sopyd[c]; and by vij of the cloke [were
again on] horse-bake, and so thrugh Fletstrett and at the Horne
[they] dronke, and at the Gray-honde, and so thrugh Chepe-syde
and so over the bryge, and so rod all nyght toward Dover.

[a] died.   [b] counter.   [c] supped.

The xvij day of September whent owt of Nuwgatt unto Yslyng-
ton beyonde the buthes [a] towardes the chyrche in a valley to be
bornyd iiij; iij men, on women, for herese duly [proved;] ij of
them was man and wyff dwellyng in sant Donstans in the Est, of
the est syd of sant Donstons cherche-yerd with master [Waters,]
sargant of armes, and att ther bornyng was *(unfinished)*.

The xix day of September cam a commondement downe to all
parryche(s) in London that they shuld go in prossessyon at
Powlles, and *Te Deum laudamus* songe; all the chyrches in London to synge, and rynge for wynnynge of Perro ·in Franse and
odur plasses.

The xx day of September was bered mastores Fynche with ij
whyt branchys, xij torchys, and iiij gylt candyllstykes and ij grett
tapurs, and ij dosen of skochyns, att the Sayvoy; on [b] of the
preve chambur to the quen.

The xxj day of September was the monyth myn [c] and obseque
of ser Hare Husse, knyght, with a standerd and pennon of armes,
cott-armur, targett, elmett, and sword; and vj dosen of skochyons;
with a harold of armes.

The xxj day of September was bered doctur Pendyltun, in sant
Stheyn [d] in Walbroke, wher he was parsun, and browth [e] with all
Powlles qwyre to berehyng ther.

[The iij day of August the good ship called the Mary-Rose]
of London, acompanyd [with the Maudlyn Dryvers, and a] smalle
crayer of the Whest-contrey, commyng [by south] chansyd [f] to
mette with a Frencheman of war [of the burden] of x skore or
ther bowth [g]; the wyche Frenche shyp [had to] the nomber of ij C.
men; and in the Mare-Rows xxii [men and . . .] bowys, [h] the
Maudelyn xviij, the barke of the West-contr[ey xij]. The Mare-
Rows saylyng faster then the French [man,] and so in-continent
the Frenche shype sett upon the [other] ij shyps, whom seyng

---

    [a] butts (for archery).   [b] one.   [c] month's mind.   [d] Stephen.
    [e] brought.   [f] chanced.   [g] there-about.   [h] boys?

the master of the Mare-Rowse cast a-bowtt, and [set upon] the Frence shype, and borded her; and slew to the number of C men with the captayn or ever thatt the other came to the fyght; ther wher slayne in Mare-Rowse ij men, and one ded a senett[a] after, and vj hurte wythe [the master,] whos name was John Couper. Then cam the men of the Mare-Rosse, and shott on pesse[b] of ordenanse in[to the] Frenche shype('s) starne, and gahyng by here[c] shott arow[s at the] Frenche-men; the Maudelyn dyd no more hurtt; [the] barke nothyng at all. Thus thay fought ij owrs[d]; [but at] the lengh the Frenche-men wher were[e] of the[ir parts] and for-soke them, nott haveng men to gyde ther sayls; butt yff the Mare-Rosse had had men to enter the Frenche shype, and a setter on, they had browght her a-way [ere] the othur shypes had helpyd her. After-ward nuws was browght owt of Depe[f] by a presoner that had payd hys ransom that l. men was cared owt of the Frenche shype on barows to the surgayns, and the shype sore spoyllyd and hurtt.

The xxv day of September was browth a' bed[g] with a whenche, be-twyn xij and on at mydnyght, wher-of my gossep Harper, servand unto the quen('s) grace, was dyssesed of rest of ys nest,[h] and after he whent to ys nest a-gayn—the iiij and v of k. q.[i]

The xxvij day of September was crystened Katheryn Machyn, the doythur of Hare[j] Machyn; the godmothers' names masteres Grenway, master altherman('s) wyff, and masteres Blakwelle, and master Grennelle,[k] godfather; and at byshopyng[l] the godmother's nam masteres Johnsun in Ive[m] lane.

.   .   .   .

.   .   .   . whytt branchys, xij stayffes torchys and . . . .
The v day October was bered master Sakefeld,[n] squwyre, [the

---

[a] sevennight.   [b] one piece.   [c] going by her.   [d] hours.   [e] were weary.   [f] Dieppe.
[g] *The Diarist's wife, apparently.* wench, *i. e.* a daughter.
[h] *Harper seems to have been the surgeon-accoucheur summoned to attend on Mrs. Machyn.*   [i] king and queen (Philip and Mary).   [j] Harry.
[k] Greenhill.   [l] *In MS.* byshopopyng.   [m] Ivy.   [n] Sackville.

father] unto ser (Richard) Sakefeld, knyght, late chanseler of the [Court of Augmentations], with a penon of armes and cott armur, and iiij baners of armes, ... ij fayre whytt branchys, and iiij branchys tapurs, ... dosen of penselles, and iiij dosen of stayffes torchys, and . . . . harold of armes, and viij dosen of skochyons of armes.

The v day of October was bered at Chemford[a] in Essex the wyff of master Thomas Myldmay, sqwyre, and audetor, with ij whytt branchys, and ij dosen of grett stayffe torchys, and iiij dosen of skochyons, and mony mornars in blake.

The *(blank)* day of October was bered my [lade] Husse in Sussex, at Slynkford,[b] by ser Hare Husse[c] her husband.

The vj day of October cam a comondement in-to London that evere parryche shuld make bon-fyers and ryngyng that the pope and the emperowr be fryndes and lovers, and the ware[d] endyd be-twyn them.

The Thursday the last day of September ded[e] master Recherd Docket, grocer of London, and marchand of Flanders and *(blank)* of Flanders of the Englysmen howse.[f]

. . . . was bered with a penon of armes . . . . . baner of emages, and iij dosen of penselles, and . . . . . skochyons, and ij whytt branchys, and . . . . stayffs torchys, ... iij grett tapurs; at the monyth myn[g] was as . . . . . and a gret dener after masse.

The xiij day of October was a man sett a-pon the pelere[h] for heynous wordes and sedyssyus wordes and [opprobrious] wordes aganst my lord mayre and the althermen, [and a common] slander(er) of pepull and ys neyburs; ys nam was Davesun, tayller.

The sam day was a proclamasyon *(unfinished)*

---

[a] Chelmsford.   [b] Slinford.   [c] Harry Hussey.   [d] war.   [e] died.
[f] *A few lines above the same entry was written, and erased, thus:* The last day of September was bered beyond see master Recherd Dokett, grocer, and marchand, and comtro[ller] of the Englysse marchandes.   [g] month's mind.   [h] pillory.

The **xxj** day of October was cared thrugh Smyth-feld and Nuw-gatt and thrugh Chepe-syde to the Towre l. grett gones that wher nu mad,[a] and ij C. men with gones, bowes, and pykes, in harnes and shurtes of maylle.

The **xxj** day of October ded[b] my lade the contes of Arundell at Bathe plase in sant Clement parryche with-owt Tempylle-bare.

The **xxvj** day of October was a goodly hers sett up in sant Clementes parryche with-owt Tempylle-bare, of v pryncepalles, and with viij baner-rolles, and a x dosen penselles, and iiij grett skochyons of armes at the iiij corners.

The **xxvij** day of October my lade was browth[c] to the chyrche, with the byshope of London and Powlles qwyre and the master and clarkes of London, and then cam the corse with v baners[d] of armes borne; then cam iiij harolds in ther cotes of armes, and bare iiij banars of emages at the iiij corners; and then cam the chyff mornars, my lade of Wossetur, and my lade Lumley, and my lord North, and ser Antony Selenger. [Then came a hundred mourners of men, and after as many ladies and gentlemen, all in black; and a great many poor women in black and rails, and] xxiiij pore men in blake beyryng of torchys, and mony of her servandes in blake cotes beyryng of torchys.

The **xxviij** day of October was the masse of *requiem* song, and a goodly sermon; and after masse her grasse[e] was bered; and all her hed offesers with whytt stayffes in ther handes, and all the haroldes waytyng abowt her in ther cott armurs, and my lord abbott of Westmynster [was the] precher, a godly sarman; and my lord of London song the masse, and the byshope of *(blank)* song the masse of the *(blank)*, and ther was a *(blank)* masse sayd; and after to my lordes plase to dener, for ther was a gret dener.

The **xxix** day of October dyd my nuw lorde mayre [take] ys owth[f] at Westmynster; and all the craftes of London [in their] bargys, and the althermen; and after-ward landyd at Powlles warf; and at the Powlles cheyrche-yerd ther the pagantt stod;

---

[a] new made.   [b] died.   [c] brought.   [d] *paners in MS.*   [e] grace.   [f] his oath.

and the bachelers with ther saten hodes and a lx pore men in
gownes, and targets and gayffelyns in ther handes, and the
trumpetes and the whettes playhyng, unto Yeld-halle; and ther
dynyd, and after to Powlles, and after to my lord mayre('s)
howse, and ther the althermen, and the craftes, and the bachelers,
and the pagantt browth [a] hym home.

The xxx day of October was bered ser Wylliam Cand . . .
knight, with ij whytt branchys, and xij stayff torchys, iij grett
tapurs, and *(blank)* skochyons, at sant Botulff with-owt Althergatt.

The iij day of November was bered in the parryche of sant
Donstones in the West, sargant Wallpoll, a Northfoke man, with
a pennon and a cott of armes borne with a harold of armes; and
ther was all the juges, and sergantes of the coyffe, and men of
the law a ij C. with ij whytt branchys, xij stayff torchys, and iiij
grett tapurs, and prestes, and clarkes; and the morow the masse
of *requiem*.

. . . .
. . . my lade W. . . . . wher her
husband and she had a harold . . . . mony morners, as ser
Recherd Southwell . . . and dyvers odur, with ij goodly whyte
branchys . . . grett stayffe torchys, and xij pore men that
bare . . . and xij powre women xij gret tapurs of ij . . .
and the men had gownes of mantyll frysse and . . . and the
women gownes and raylles; and the morow m[ass, and] after a
grett dener and a sermon.

The v day of November rod thrugh [the city] a man on horse-
bake, ys fase toward the horses tail, and a wrytyng on ys hed;
and he had a fryse gown, [and] ys wyff leydyng the horse, and a
paper on her h[ead, for] horwdom [b] the wyche he lett ys wyff to
ho . . . to dyvers men.

The viij day of November was bered [c] with-in the Tempull ser
Necolas Hare, knyght, and master of the rolles, with ij whytt

[a] brought.   [b] whoredom.   [c] buried.

branchys and *(blank)* torches, and a herse garnyshed with wax and penselles and armes; and with a harold of armes; and with a standard, and a penon, and cote of armes, elmett, targatt, and sword; and a viij dosen of skochyons.

The ix day of November was bered at Stonesthett ford [a] master *(blank)* Langfold, with pennon and cote armour, a sqwyre.

The xj day of November was bered besyd Cambryge ser John Hodyllstone knyght, with standard and pennon, cote armur, elmett, targat, sword, and penselles, and a vj dosen of skochyons and of torchys.

[The xij day of November was buried at Stepney master Maynard, merchant, and sheriff of London in the sixth] yere of kyng Edward the vj[th], the wyche kept a grett howse, and in the time of Cryustymas he had a lord of mysrulle, and after the kynges lord of mysse-rulle cam and dynyd with hym; and at the crosse of Chepe he mad a grett skaffold, and mad a proclamasyon. [b] [He was buried] with ij whytt branchys, and xij torchys, and iiij grett [tapers]; and after to Popeler to dener,[c] and that was grett.

The sam day was bered at sant Augustyne master . . . anell with ij whytt branchys, and xii stayff torchys, and iiij grett tapurs, and after masse to . . . . . and mony morners, and a ij dosen skochyons of armes.

The xij day of November ther was a post sett up in Smythfeld for iij that shuld have beyn bornyd, butt[d] boyth wod and colles; and my lord abbott of Westminster cam to Newgatt and talked with them, and so they wher stayd for that day of bornyng.

The xiij day of November was sant Erkenwald eve, the iiij and v yere of king and quen, whent owt of Newgatt unto Smyth-feld to be bornyd iij men; on was [*blank*] Gybsun, the sun of sergantt Gybsun, sergantt of armes, and of the reywelles,[e] and of the

---

[a] Stony Stratford.   [b] See before, p. 28.   [c] dinner.
[d] *So in MS.*   [e] revels.

kynges tenstes[a]; and ij more, the whyche here be ther names—
Gybsun, Hali[day,] and Sparow, thes iij men.

The xv day of November was bered ser (*blank*) Arundell
knyght, with iiij branche tapers of wax, and penselles ij dosen, and
vj dosen skochyons, and a standard, pennon, and cott armur,
elmett, targatt, sword; and ij whyt branchys, and ij dosen torchys,
and mony morners, and a grett dener. [b]

The xvj day of the sam monyth was bered at sant Martens at
Ludgatt, master (*blank*) Terrell, captayn of the galee,[c] and knyght
of the Rodes [d] sum-tyme was; with a cote, penon, and ij baners of
emages, and iij haroldes of armes, and ij whyt branchys, and xij
torchys, and iiij gret tapurs.

[The xviij day of November died the lord Bray, within the
Black-friars, near Ludgate]; the wyche he gatt ys deth [at St.
Quintin's.]

The xviij day of November cam tydynges from the yerle of
Northumberland owt of Skottland that the [Scots] and our men
mett and ther fowth,[e] and ther was taken and . . . of the Skotts,
att a place callyd (*blank*).

The xxj day of November dyd pryche my lord [abbat of] Westmynster, and ther he mad a godly sermon, at Powlles crosse.

The Sonday, the xxj day at November, the quen('s) grase [did]
sett a crowne of master Norrey('s) hed kyng at armes, [and] created hym Clarenshus,[f] with a cup of [wine], at Sant James, her
grace('s) place.

The xxiij day of November was cared from Blake-freres to Temes
syd, and ther wher rede to[g] grett barges covered with blake and
armes hangyng for my lord Bray, and so by water to Chelsey, to
be bereyd by ys father, with iiij haroldes of armes, and a standard
and a baner of armes, and ij baners of emages borne by ij haroldes
of armes in ther cott armurs, and so mony nobull men morners in

---

[a] tents.   [b] dinner.   [c] galley.   [d] Rhodes.
[e] fought.   [f] William Harvey.   [g] were ready two.

blake, and xvj porre men had new gownes, and a xvj grett torchys, ij whytt branchys, and iiij grett tapurs, and a cott armur, elmett, target, sword, and mantylles, and a viij dosen of skochyons; and after messe, and ther wher mony prestes and clarkes, and the dener at ys plase at Blake-frers, and so they cam bake from Cheshey* to dener.

[The xxv day of November died the lady Hare, late wife] unto ser Necolaus Hare, knyght, and [master of the rolls, the] wyche she ded at (*blank*).

The xxvj day of November was bered my lade [Clifford] the wyff of ser Thomas Clyfford knyght, the wyche [was] bered in Westmynster abbay, the wyche lade was bered in the [cou]ntie of (*blank*), with a harold of armes, and a ij dosen torchys, and iij dosen of skochyons, and iiij baners of armes, [and] a herse-cloth of blake saten, the crosse whyt saten.

The xxx day of November was sant Andrewes day, a prossessyon at Powlles, and a preste of evere parryche in [London,] and ther wher a goodly sermon, and after the processyon was *Salve festa dyes*.

The sam day the Quen('s) grace and my lord cardenell cam from Sant James unto Whytt-halle, and ther they hard masse; and after masse done, and ther wher all the byshopes and the juges and sergantes of the lawe, and ther wer creatyd ser Thomas Tressam lord of sant John's of England, and iiij knyghtes of the Rodes[b] made; and the sam tyme my lord abbot whent a prossessyon in ys myter, and all the monkes and clarkes syngyng *Salve festa dies;* and rond abowt the abbay, and my lord abbott sange the masse.

The sam day at after dener my lord cardenall mad a godly sermon in the chapell, and ther wher all juges and bysshopes, and my lord mayre and all the althermen, and mony lordes and knyghtes, and lades and gentyllmen.

---

* Chelsea.   b Rhodes.

.   .   .   .

.   .   . assyon by the mare.

The iiij day of Desember was bered at S[heen at the] the charter-howse ser Robart Rochester knyght, the wyche he was chossen knyght of the garter, but he was never stallyd at Wyndsore, so [he] was not bered with the garter, butt after [the manner of another] knyght, for ther was a goodly herse of wax, v prensypalles, with viij dosen penselles, and viij dosen skochyons, and vj dosen torchys, and ij whyt [branches] ; and a standard, and a penon of armes, and cot armur, elmett, targett, sword, mantylles, and iiij baners of emages, and a majeste and valanse, and master Claren[ceux] and master Lankester aroldes,[a] and mony morners in [black] ; and the masse and a sermon, and after a grett dener.

The vij day of Desember ther was a woman [rode] in a care for horedume and bawdre.

The viij day of Desember was bered my lade Rowlett, the wyff of ser Raff Rowllett knyght, in the parryche of santt Mare Stannyng, with ij haroldes of armes and iiij baners of emages and iiij dosen skochyons, and ij whyt branchys, and ij dosen torchys and iiij gylt candyll-stykes, and iiij gret tapurs ; and mony morners, and the clothyng of the Gold-smythes ; and ys servandes bare torchys in blake cotes.

The v day of Desember was sant Necolas evyn, and sant Necolas whent a-brod in most plases, and all Godys pepull received ym to ther howses and had good chere, after the old custum.

[The xij day of December, being Sunday, there met certain persons that were Gospellers, and some pretended players, at] Yslyngtun, takyng serten men, [and one Ruffe,] a Skott and a frere, for the redyng of [a lecture, and] odur matters ; and the communyon was play[ed, and should] have byne butt the gard cam to sune,[b] or ever [the chief] matter was begone.

The xiij day of Desember was bered in the parryche of sant

---

[a] heralds.   [b] too soon.

Pulkurs with-owt Newgatt ser Wylliam West knyght, with iij haroldes of armes, with a standard, penon of armes, cott-armur, elmett, targatt, sword, and ij baners of emages, ij whytt branchys, xij torchys, and the xij powre men had nuw gownes; and iiij gylt candyll-stykes, and iiij grett tapurs; and mony morners, boyth men and women; and iiij dossen of skochyons of armes; and the morowe iij masses songe, on of the Trenete, a-nodur of owre Lade, and the iij of *requiem;* and a trentalle of masses songe; and ther was ys standard and cott and elmet and the sword and the baners offered; and a sermon; and after to dener, for ther was a grett dener.

The xvij day of Desember dyd ryd in a care a yonge man and a woman the wyff of John a badoo the bowd, and she was the bowd, and she was wypyd at the care-ar[se], and the harlott dyd bett[a] her: and nold[b] harlott of iij skore and more led the hors, lyke a nold hore.

The xx day of Desember was condemnyd for herese ser John Ruffe prest, a Skotte, and a woman, for to be bornyd in Smyth-feld for *(unfinished)*

The Fryday x day of Desember was at Wyndsore deposyd of ys denry of Wyndsor doctur Weston.

. . . .

[The xxij day of December were burned in] Smyth feld ij, one ser John Ruffe [the] frere and a Skott, and a woman, for herese.

The xxv day of Desember was bered [the lady] Freston, the wyff of ser Recherd Freston knyght, and cofferer unto quen Mare—the iiij and v of the [king and queen's reign] of England, —in Suffoke.

The x day of Desember ther ryd a man thrugh London, ys fase toward the horse tayle.

The xxv day of Desember wher dyvers [courtiers] was removyd unto he-her[c] rommys; as ser Edward Hastynges, master of the

---

[a] beat.   [b] an old.   [c] higher.

quen's hors, was mad lord chamburlayn; and ser Thomas Cornwalles comptroller; ser Hare Jarnyngham the master of the hors; and ser Hare Benefeld fee ᵃ-chamburlayn and captayn of the gard.

The furst day of January, was nuwyerevyn,ᵇ ther cam a lord of mysrulle from Westmynster with ys harold and ys trumpettes and ys drumys, and mony dysgyssyd in whytt; and so he cam in to London, and so he was browth ᶜ in-to the contur ᵈ in the Pultre; and dyver of ys men lay all nyght ther, and ys men whent a-stray hom agayn by iiij and vj to-geder to Westmynster on hors-bake and of fott.

[The iij day of January came tidings to the Queen] that the Frenche kyng was [come to] Nuwnam bryge with a grett host of men [of war], and layd batheryng pessys unto ytt, and unto Rysse-banke by water, and to Cales, [and] led grett batheryng peses to hytt, for ther wher [great shooting].

The iiij day of January the cete of London toke a vᶜ. men to go to Calles,ᵉ of evere [craft,] to fynd boyth harnes, bowes, morespykes and [guns,] and men of ther charge and cost, and prest money, they cam to the quen('s) naveᶠ of shypes.

The vj day of January thes men wher browght unto Leydenhalle, and mustered afor my lord mayre and the althermen; and at after-none by iiij of the cloke they toke ther way to the Towrewarff, and ther thay toke shypyng toward Callys.

The viij day of January the marchandes of the stapull of Calles toke up c. and odeᵍ men to go toward Calles of ther cost.

The viij day of January thay toke shypyng at the Towre-warfe toward Calles, and odur men of ware, and from odur plases to the see-ward, betwyn v and vj of the cloke at nyght.

The viij day of January was sett up at Wyndsore the yerle of Sussex the depute of Yrland ys baner of armes, and ys elmett, crest, mantylle, and ys sword for ys stallasyon of the garter.

[The x day of January heavy news came to En]gland, and to

ᵃ vice.   ᵇ new year's eve.   ᶜ brought.   ᵈ Compter.

ᵉ Calais.   ᶠ navy.   ᵍ odd.

London, thatt the Fre[nch had won] Cales, the wyche was the
hevest tydy[ngs to London] and to England that ever was hard
of, for lyke a trayter yt was sold and d[elivered unto] them the
(blank) day of January; the duke of [Guise was] cheyff capten,
and evere man dyschargyd the town.

The xj day of January the cete of London [took up] a m. men
mo, and mad them whytt cottes of . . . . and red crosses,
and evere ward of London fund *(blank)* men.

The xiij day of January was bered at [Westminster] in sant
Margerett parryche my lade Powes, [daughter] to the duke of
Suffoke, Charles Brandon, [with two] whytt branchys, xij torchys,
and iiij grett [tapers,] with xij skochyons of armes.

The xvj day of January was bered in Suffoke ser Recherd
Freston knyght, and cofferer unto the quen Mare—the iiij and v
of King Philip and Quen Mare—with a standard, a penon of
armes, cote-armur, elmet, target, and the sword and mantyll, and
iiij dosen of skochyons.

The xvij day of January was the monyth myn* of ser Gorge
Gyfford knyght, with a standard, a penon of armes, cott-armur,
elmett, targett, and sword, mantylles, and ij baners (of) emages,
and vj dosen skochyons, and iiij dosen torchys; thy(s) was don in
Bukyngham shyre.

[The *(blank)* day of January was buried master Alsop apot]he-
kare unto kyng Henry [the viij^{th} and to] kyng Edward the vj^{th} and
sergant [of the confectionary] unto quen Mare; with ij gret whytt
[branches, and] xij torchys; and the xij pore men had nuw [gowns
of] mantyll frys; and iiij grett tapurs; and mony morners in
blake; and the morow masse, and after a grett dener; and a ij
dosen skochyons.

The xx day of January begane the parlement at Westmynster
—the v yere of quen Mare. Her grace toke her charett at the
Whytt-halle, and her lordes of the parlement, and the bysshopes

---

* month's mind.

and prestes, and so to the abbay to the masse, and after to the parlement-howse, and so the trumpetes.

The xxj day of January cam a nuw commondement tho ª my lord mayre, that he shuld make *(blank)* men rede ᵇ in harnes, with whyt cotes weltyd with gren, and red crosses, by the xxiij day of the sam monythe [to be at] Leydenhalle to go toward *(un-finished)*

The xxij day of January ther was a nold ᶜ man sett up of the pelere for sedyssyous words and rumors.

The sam day was a boy wypyd at the post callyd the Refor-massyon, for sayhyng that Lon . . . .

The sam day was bered docthur Bartelett, fessyssyon at Blake-frers, at sant Barthellmuw in Smythfeld, with a dosen of sko-chyons of armes, and ij whyt branchys and ij torchys, and iiij gret tapurs.

[The xxiv day of January the soldiers appeared before the lord mayor in Leadenhall, where he took a view of all] the men that the compene(s had furnished), and deleverd (them) unto the cap-taynes at v at nyght, and thay toke shypyng [at eight].

The sam day ther whent unto Westmynster *(blank)* men that wher qwynners,ᵈ the wyche wher taken at Cambryge.

The Sonday the xxx day of January dyd pryche at Powlles Crosse the byshope of Wynchester, and mad a goodly sermon.

The iij day of Feybruary was browth ᵉ unto sant Bathelmuw be-syd sant Antonys to be bered [by his] granser ᶠ ser Wylliam Capell knyght, and mare of London, ser Hare Capell knyght sune and here to ser Gylles Capell, the wyche ser Gylles was bered in Essex. [Sir Harry was] bered by ys granser with iij haroldes of armes, and a standard, and a penon of armes; and cott-armur, targett, sword, and elmett and crest; and all the cheyrche hangyd with blake and armes; and a ij dosen of torchys, and iiij grett tapurs, and iiij gylt candyllstykes, and ij grett whytt branchys;

ª to.   ᵇ ready.   ᶜ an old.   ᵈ coiners.   ᵉ brought.   ᶠ grandsire.

and xij pore men had blake gowns; and after to the howse to dener; and doctur Brekett mad the sermon at the masse.

The v day of Feybruarij cam from Westmynster iiij, iij men and on woman, and cared to the Towre for kuynnyng [a] and they wher *(unfinished)*

The vj day of Feybruarij dyd pryche at Powlles Crosse the byshope of Westchaster; and ther wher at ys sermon xvj bys-shopes, and my lord mayre and the althermen, and mony juges, and ther he declaryd that of Wedynsday next to go on generall prossessyon and pray to God.

[The ix day of February a commandment came that all bishops, priests, and clerks, should go a procession about London, and] my lord mare and the althermen, [and all the crafts] in London in ther leverey, to pray [unto God; and all] the chylderyn of all skolles, and of the hos[pitals, in] ordur, a-bowt London,—callyd the general prossessyon.

The x day of Feybruary was reynyd [b] at Westmynster [at the] kyng('s) benche my lord Darce('s) sune of the North, for [the death] of master Whest, sune and here of ser Wylliam West knyght, [the] wyche West was slayne commyng from Roth[erham] feyre, [c] the wyche ther wher (forty men) apon hym [and his six] men, and shamfulle he was murdered, for . . . wher in harnes and ther wher a-for the kyng('s) by[nch] [d] certen men dyd wag [e] batelle with ym, to feythe [f] with combat at a day sett.

The xj day of Feybruary was bered at sent Marten's-in-the-feyld master Arthur Sturtun sqwyre, the keper of the [White] halle, and brodur to the lord Sturtun, and he was the reyseyver of all copes of cloth of gold that was taken owt of all chyrches, and he dyd delevered them unto serten parryches agayne to them that cowld know them, the wyche wher taken away by kyng Edward the vj[th] tym by the dewyse of the duke of Northumberland [and] serten of bysshopes of nuw doctryne that was then; and now,

---

[a] coining.   [b] arraigned.   [c] *See p.* 107.   [d] bench.   [e] wage.   [f] fight.

when that good qwyne Mare cam to the crown, she lett evere parryche for to have them agayne by her commyng to the crowne, yf they wher nott gyffyn to odur places in the reyme of England; but Trenete parryche had nott ther cope of cloth of gold agayne.

The xvj day of Feybruary was bered master Pynoke fysmonger, marchand of Muskovea, and brodur of Jhesus, with ij goodly whytt branchys, and xij grett stayffes torchys; and xij pore men had good blake gownes; and iiij grett tapurs, and a the compene of the clarkes and mony prestes, and then cam the mornars, and after the bredurud of Jhesus, a xxiiij of them, with blake saten hodes with 𝕴𝕳𝕾 on them, and after the compene of the Fysmongers in ther leverey, and after to the howse to drynke.

[The xviij day of February died sir George Barnes knight and haberdasher, late mayor of London, at the] crownenassyon of qwyn Mare.

The xx day of Feybruary dyd pryche [at Paul's] crosse docthur Watsun bysshope of Lyncoln, and mad a godly sermon, for ther wer [present ten] bysshopes, be-syd my lord mare and the althermen and juges, and men of the law, and gret [audience] ther was.

The xxiiij day of Feybruary was [buried] ser Gorge Barnes knyght, late ma[yor] and haberdasser, and the cheyff marchand of Muskovea, and had the penon of Mu[scovy] armes borne at ys berehyng; and the [mayor] and the swerdberar had blake gownes and a . . . . . in blake, and a iij^xx pore men in blake [gowns;] and had a standard and v penons of armes, and cote and elmett, sword, targett, and a goodly hers of wax and ij grett branchys of whytt wax, iiij dosen torchys, and viij dosen pensels, and ix dosen skochyons; and doctur Chadsay mad the sermon on the morow, and after a grett dener. Master Clarenshus and Lanckostur the haroldes (conducted the ceremony.)

The xxv day of Feybruary cam rydyng to London my lade Elsabeth the quen('s) syster, with a gret compene of lordes and nobull men and nobull women, to here plasse calyd the Somersett-plasse beyond Stron-bryge.

The **xxvj** day of Feybruary ded[a] my lade Whyt, the wyff of ser Thomas Whyt late mare of London, and marchand tayller, and marchand of the Muskovea, and altherman of London.

. . . . W]hyut-halle with many lordes and lades.

The *(blank)* day of Marche the qwyn('s) grace['s pensioners] mustered in Hyd-parke, and all ther men in gren [cloth and] whytt; and ther my lord of Rutland toke the [muster of] them.

The **ij** day of Marche my lade Whyt was bered in Althermare parryche, and ther was a goodly herse of wax, and ther was viij dosen pensels, and viij dosen skochyons and d',[b] and iiij dosen torchys; and the harolde was master Clarenshus; the cheyff morner my lade Laxtun, and master Roper led her; and mony morners; and after cam my lord mayre, and **xx** althermen folod the corsse, and iiij baners of emages, and ij grett whytt branchys; and the morow masse and a godly sermon, and all the craft in ther leverey; *(blank)* pore men had gownes, and powre women had gownes, and after to ys plasse to dener, and my lord mayre and the althermen, and mony gentyllmen, for ther was a grett dener as [has] bene sene; and ther was iij masses songe, on of the Trenete, and on of owre Lade, the iij of *requiem.*

The **iiij** day of Marche a' for-non my lade Elsabeth('s) grace toke her horss and red[c] to her plasse at   ,[d] with mony lordes, knyghtes, and lades, and gentyllwomen, with a goodly com-pene of horsse.

. The sam day at after-non the pensyoners mustered in sant James parke in harnes, and ther men with spers, and the trum-petes blohyng, and se them in a-ray rydyng.

The *(blank)* day of Marche ther was never so low a nebe,[e] that

---

[a] died   [b] eight and a half dozen.   [c] rode.

[d] *Originally blank in MS. and apparently incorrectly filled with the word* Strone, *meaning* the Strand, *from which she was returning to the country.*   [e] an ebb.

men myght stand in the mydes of Tames, and myght a' gone from the brygys to Belynggatt, for the tyd kept not ys course; the wyche was never sene a-fore that tyme.

[The vj day of March, being the second Sunday in Lent, preached before the lord mayor and the bishops] at [Paul's cross] my lord abbott of Westmynster docthur [Feckenham]; ther he mad a godly sermon as as bene [heard].

The vj day (of) Marche was cared in a hersse [to] be bered in Cambrygshyre ser Phylype Pares knyght, at a [place] callyd Lyntun, wher sergant Heth ded, and was . . . .

The vij day of Marche was the parlement holden at the Whytt-halle the quen('s) plasse, and endyd at vij of [the clock at night], and watt[a] actes mad at the end of the parlement.

The ix day of Marche was a yonge man namyd *(blank)* dyd ryd in a care, ys fasse toward the hors tayle, [with] ij grett pesses of beyff of . [b] clodes poudered.

The x day of Marche the Quen('s) grace removyd unto Gren-wyche, in lentt, for to kepe ester.

The xiiij day of Marche ded[c] and bered at the Munyrys,[d] at vj of the cloke at nyght, my lade Jennynges, doythur to ser John Gage knyght.

The xvj day of Marche my lord mare and the althermen wher commondyd unto Yeld-halle, for thay had a commondement by the qwyen that thay shuld lend the quen a *(blank)* of ħ.; for ther sat my lord stresorer, my lord preve-saylle, and the bysshope of Elly as commyssyonars, and my lord chanseler, with odur of the conselle.

.   .   .   .

.   .   . with ij whyt branchys and xij torchys . . . . great tapurs, and after a grett dener within the . . . .

The xix day of Marche my lord mayre and the althermen

---

[a] *So in MS. but this word was at first, apparently, left blank for the number of the Acts passed.*   [b] x? *(erased.)*   [c] died.   [d] Minories.

whent unto Yeld-halle, and ther all the craftes in London browth[a] in the bylles what ther compene[b] wold lend unto the quen('s) grace for to helpe her in her fa . . .[c] toward the wars.

The xxj day of Marche was the Paskalle for the abbay of West-mynster mad ther, the wheyth[d] of iij C. of wax ; and ther was the master and the wardens of the Waxchandlers [with] xx more at the makyng, and after a grett dener.

The sam day at after-none the yerle of Sussex toke gorney[e] in post toward Yrland.

The sam day of Marche wher browth[f] in-to the *(blank)* afor the bysshope of London and odur lernyd men of the temporolte iij men, the wyche ther openions wher shyche[g] that they wher juged and condemnyd to suffer deth by fyre ; one man was a hos-sear[h] dwellyng in Wodstret, ys nam ys *(blank).*

The xxij day of Marche my lord mayre and the althermen whent unto Yeld-Halle, and ther the quen('s) consell cam theder, furst my lord chanseler, my lord treysorer, my lord of preve-selle, the bysshope of Ele, and ser John Baker, secretore Peter, and mony more, and after whent to my lord mare to dener.

The xxiij day of Marche was a proclamasyon of serten actes that was sett forth by the last parlement, that was endyd the vij day of Marche the iiij and v of kyng (Philip) and quen Mare.

[*Here two or three leaves of the Diary appear to be lost, involving the space of nearly four months*].

[The iij day of August was buried the lady Rowlett], wyff of ser Raffe Rowlett knyght, in [saint] Mare Staynnynges, with ij goodly whyt branchys, *(blank)* stayff torchys, and iiij gylt candyllstykes, and iiij grett tapurs, with ij haroldes of armes, and iiij baners of saints; *(blank)* was cheyffe morner, and mony . . . . . . The cherche and the raylles hangyd with blake, and the street and the plasse hangyd with armes and blake, and ij

---

[a] brought.   [b] companies.   [c] affairs?
[d] weight.   [e] journey.   [f] brought.   [g] such.   [h] hosier.

song masses and a sermon, and after masse to the [place] to dener, for ther was a grett dener for vene[son, fresh] solmon, and fres sturgean, and with mony dysse ª (of) fy[sh.] . . .

The furst day of August was chossen shreyff [for the] kyng at Yeld-halle master Hawes clothworker, [and] after was chosen shreyff of London master Cha[mpion] draper by the come(n)s ᵇ of the cete.

The vj day of August was bered at Tempull . . . . . master Thornhylle, with ij whyt branchys, x torchys, and iiij grett tapurs, and xviij skochyons of armes, and mony in blake.

The vij day of August was bered in Powlles cheyrchyerd on Archer, the wyche was slayn at sant James feyre in the feld by on *(blank)* shamfully, for he was panchyd with ys owne sword.

The viij day of August was bered master Dodmer sqwyre at Putteney, with ij dosen skochyons, and ij whyt branchys, and xij torchys, and iiij grett tapurs, the wyche was ser Raffe Dodmer('s) sune, late mayre of London.

The viij day of August was bered master docthur Huwys, the quen('s) fesyssyon, with ij grett whyt branchys, and xij grett stayffes torchys, and iiij grett tapurs, and iij dosen of skochyons, and mony morners boyth men and women, at after-non.

.   .   shyre, with cote armur and penon of arms . . . . . of skochyons and d' of bokeram.

The xij day of August at mydnyght ded ᶜ good master Machyll, altherman of London, clothworker, and marchand of Muskovea, the wyche was a worshephulle man, and a godys ᵈ man to the pore, and to all men in the parryche of Maremaudlyn in Mylkestrett, (where he lived in) the sam howse that master Hynd ded, and was ys plasse. [If] he had levyd, he had byn mayre next yer folohyng.

The xvij day of August whent from the Jorge ᵉ in Lumbard

ª dishes ?   ᵇ commons.   ᶜ died.   ᵈ *So in MS.*   ᵉ George.

strett the bysshope of Yrland,* [and was] cared by water unto
(*blank*), to be bered ther.

The xx day of August whent from London unto Fullam to be
bered my lord of London('s) crossear, master Mortun, on of the
gray ames [b] of Powlles, with *(unfinished)*

The xxj day of August was bered at sant Donstones parryche
in the est mastores Chalenger wedow, mother unto master Wylliam Allen, lether-seller, a' for-non, bered with money morners in
blake.

The xxj day of August at after-non was bered in the parryche of
sant Mare Maudelyn, in Mylke strett, master Machyll, altherman
and sqwyre and clothworker, with v pennons of armes and cott
armur, and iiij dosen torchys, and iiij branche tapurs, dobyll store,
with armes and penselles apon wax, and all the chyrche hangyd
with blake and armes, and the strett with blake and armes, and
the plase; and ther was my lord mayre and the althermen, and a
C. in blake; and a viij dosen skoohyons, and iiij dosen penselles;
and a C. pore men in mantylle fryse gownes; and the morow iij
masses song, ij of pryksong, and the iij of *requiem*, and a sarmon,
a good man a grayfrer; [c] and there my lord mare and the althermen
whent to dener, and all the mornars and lades, the wyche was a
nobull dener as has bene sene, for ther lakt no good mett boyth
flesse and fysse, and a xx marche-paynes.

.   .   .   .

. . durge, and after cared thrugh Bathelmu [to the] Blake
freres, and at the gat all the freres mett . . . thay had durge,
and they bered ym ther ys m. *(unfinished)*

The xxiiij day at after-non was [buried] ser Gorge Pallett
knyght, and brodur [to the lord] tressorer the marques of Wynchester, and with standard of armes, cott, elmett, targett, sword,
and a vj dosen [of pensils] and iiij dosen of skochyons.

The xxij of August was bered docthur [Peryn,] master of frers
blake in Smythfeld, the wyche was the [first] howsse that was sett

---

* George Dowdall, archbishop of Armagh.   [b] amices.   [c] Grey friar.

up by quen Mare('s) tyme, [buried] at the he[a] auter syd afor sant Bathelmue.

The xxviij day of August was bered master [Cooke,] docthur, dene of the Arches, and he[b] juge of the Amralte; the chyrche hangyd with blake, and armes; and he had ij whyt branchys and xij stayff torchys, and iiij grett tapurs; and with armes and a iij dosen skochyons of armes; and alle the bredurne of Jhesus in saten hodes, and Jhs apone them, and all the prestes of Powlles.

The xxix day of August was the berehyng of my lord Wyndsor at ys (blank) with a hersse of wax, and vj dosen penselles, and ij dosen longe torchys and iiij dosen of gret stayffe torchys, with iiij haroldes of armes and a standard, a baner of ys armes, and viij baners rolles of ys armes, and iiij baners of emages, and xij dosen of skochyons; and putt in ij coffens; and mony morners, and a grett compene of pepull; and the morow masse, and after a gret dener.

.   .   .   .

.   .   .   wyffe of master Rayff Grenway, altherman [c] .   .   .   .

.   Sonday after he kept a gret fest, and alle the .   .   .   .   .   .

Sonday was after soper ther was a goodly ma[ske .   .   .   .   .   .

cloth of gold, and grett dansyng in the maske.

The sam day was bered be-yond Barnet (blank) [ju]ge Stamford knyght,[d] with standard, cotte armur, penon of armes, elmett, targett, sword, and the mantylles; and iiij dosen of skochyons, and ij dosen torchys, and tapurs; and master Somerset the harold of armes.

The vj day of September was bered juge Morgan in Northamtunshyre, with cotte armur, penon of armes, and a hersse of iiij branchys, and iiij dosen pensels, and vij dosen skochyons, and iiij dosen torchys, and iiij baners of emages; and mony mornars; and a grett dolle of money, and mett [e]; and master Lanckostur the harold.

---

[a] high.   [b] high.

[c] This passage, when perfect, probably recorded the marriage of alderman John White with the widow of alderman Ralph Greenway: the christening of whose son occurs on the 25th May following (p. 198).

[d] Sir William Stamford, judge of the common pleas.   [e] meat.

The iiij day of September was bered in Althermare parryche in London master Dalbeney, marchand-tayller, with ij grett branchys whyt, and xvj grett stayffe torchys; and theys xvj men had xvj good blake gownes; and iiij grett tapurs with gylt candyllstykes, and with armes, ij dosun and d'ᵃ; and mony morners in blake, and mony clarkes and prestes; and all the compene of the clothyng of the marchand-tayllers, and after home to drynke as the compene, with spycyse bred;ᵇ and the morow masse, and after to dener.

The vj day of September whent in-to the contrey to be bered master Ryges audetur, with ij dosen skochyons, and cared by nyght with-owt any cost more her done butt (*unfinished.*)

The viij day of September was bered at Stamford beyond Northamtun-shyre, ser Thomas Cayffe,ᶜ knyght, with iiij branchys, tapurs of wax, and penselles, with ij whyt branchys, and iiij dosen torchys and vj dosen of skochyons; with a standard and a cott-armur, and pennon of armes, and iiij baners of santes in owlle,ᵈ wroth with fyne gold, and many morners, and master Lankoster the harold.

The ix day of September was bered ser Recherd Brygys in the conte of (*blank*).

[The xiv day of September was buried sir Andrew Jud, skinner, merchant of Muscovy, and late mayor of London; with a] . . .
. . . pennon of armes, and a x dosen penselles . . .
skochyons, and a herse of wax of v prynse[pals, garnished with] angelles, and a (*blank*) pormenᵉ in nuw gownes, and master Clarenshus kyng of armes, and master Somersett harold, [and the morrow] masse and a sermon, and after my lord mare and the althermen had (*unfinished*)

The xxij day of September was bered master Anth[ony . . . . . sqwyre, with a pennon of armes and cott of armes, and . . . dosen skochyons.

ᵃ half.　　ᵇ spice-bread.　　ᶜ Cave.　　ᵈ oil, wrought.　　ᵉ poor men.

The xxvij day of September was the obsequies of ser Thomas Essex, knyght, of Barkshyre, with standard and . . . . and cott-armur, targett, sword, elmet, mantylles, ... dosen penselles, and iiij dosen skochyons, and iiij baners [of saints,] and a harold of armes, Ruge-crosse the harold, and iiij . . . .

The xx day of September was bered my lade [Southwell] at Sordyche, with prestes and clarkes syngyng, with ij whyt [branches] and ij dosen torchys, and iiij gret tapurs, and iiij dosen . . . and the chyrche hanged with blake and armes and mony morners; and he gayff xxiiij gownes to xxiiij women, and xxiiij ij ℔ tapurs.

The xx day of September was bered my lade Cisele Mansfield at Clerkenwell, with a harold of armes, and browth [a] unto the blake frers in Smyth-feld, the wyche was sant Bathelmuw, with iiij baners of santes and a ij dosen torchys, and ij grett whytt branchys, and iiij gylt candylstykes and armes on them, and many clarkes syngyng, and mony morners: and my lade Peter cheyff morner, and odur lades and gentyll-women and knyghtes and gentyllmen; and her servandes bare my lade, and bare the torchys all in blake cottes; and bered a-for the he [b] auter at the hed of the old pryar Boltun; and the chyrche and the qwer and the raylles hangyd with blake and armes; and the frers song durge after ther songe, and bered her after ther fasyon, with-owt clarkes or prestes; and after to the plasse to drynke; and the morow iij masses songe, ij pryke-songe masses; and after to Clerkenwell to dener to her plasse; and ther was a godly sermon as ever was hard to lyf welle of; the father of the howsse dyd pryche, master (blank).

. . . .

. . . . harold of armes master Somersett . . . . . . that he has beldyd, the nam ys callyd (blank).

The xx day of September was bered at Gret All[hallows] in Temstrett [c] the altherman of the Steleard, with ij whyt branchys and xij torchys, and iiij gret tapurs with . . . .

---

[a] brought.   [b] high.   [c] Thames street.

The xxvj day of September ded [a] good lade Pecsalle in (*blank*),
the wyff of ser Recherd Pecshall knyght, and the dowther of my
lord maurqwes of Wynchester, and lord tressorer of England, and
bered the last day of September.

The xxvj day of September was the monyth myn [b] of master
Barnes, sqwyre, and ys wyffes, at a towne called (*blank*), and ther
was grett chere ther, and venysun plente, and wyne; and he had
cott and penon of armes—in Essex.

The xxv day ded [c] my lord Cobbam in Kentt, knyght of the
garter.

The iiij day of October was bered at sant Faythe at Powlles,
master Kalkarne, procter of the archys, with ij whytt branchys
and xij torchys, and iiij tapurs, and ij dosen skochyons of
armes.

The sam day a'for-non was bered at Barmes . . . [d] in Suthwarke
master Whettley, justes of pesse, [e] with ij whyt branchys and xij
torchys, and iiij grett tapurs and ij dosen skochyons, and dyvers
morners.

The sam day at after-non was bered in sant Martens with the
well and ij bokettes, mastores Altham, the wyff of master Altham
altherman, the wych ded in chyld-bed; he gayff mony gownes to
pore women of roset cloth brod, and ij grett whyt branches, and
iiij men held iiij gret tapurs, and had gownes; and many morners,
and no harold of armes.

. . . torchys . . . . of fyne mantylle fryse, and
mony morners . . . . . men and women, and a xvj clarkes
of . . . . . whent to the plasse to drynke, and wyne and
spyse [bread; and the] morow masse.

The (*blank*) day of October was bered ser Robart . . . .
knyght, with a harold of armes, master Somersett.

The x day of October was bered in sant Faythe mastores Alene,

---

[a] died.   [b] month's mind.   [c] died.   [d] Bermondsey.   [e] justice of peace.

the wyff of master (*blank*) Allen, with ij [white] branchys, and xviij
torchys, and iiij gret tapurs, and [many] morners in blake, and all
the belles of Powlles, and . . . .

The xij day of October was bered at [saint] Mangnus a prest, [a]
the wyche ded [b] at sant M[ichael's in] Cornhyll, and gayff unto the
poure men of the Salters . . . . ther lyffwyng, [c] and gayff to
the Salters alle.

The (*blank*) day of October was the obseque of master Thomas
Fawkener, sqwyre, with cote armur and pennon of armes, and a ij
dosen of skochyons of armes.

The xij day of October was bered in Althermare parryche Raff
Prestun, skynner, with ij whyt branchys and vj staffe torchys;
and they had vj gownes of mantyl frys; and the masters of the
cloythyng of the Skynners was ther; and after they whent to the
Skynners' hall to dener, for master Percy and master Bankes was
morners ther, and vj women in blake; and ther was the compene
of the Clarkes at ys berehyng.

. . . .

. . haroldes of armes with standard and a gret . . . armes,
and vj baners-rolles and iiij baners of [saints, and] x dosen of penselles, and a herse of v prynse[pals . . .] wax and ij gret whyt
branchys and a viij dosen of skochyons and a cote-armur, elmett,
targett, mantylles, and xj dosen of torchys, and mony mornars;
[and the] morow masse and a sermon, and grett chere and . . .
dere for hym.

The xviij day of October was the obseque of . . . . . (*blank*)
sqwyre, with cote armur and pennon of armes, and iiij dosen of
skochyons of armes and iiij branche tapurs.

The xxiij day of October was bered at Westmynster master
Wentworth, sqwyre, and cofferer unto quen Mare, with ij whyt
branchys and ij dosen torchys, and a cot-armur and a pennon of
of armes, with a harold of armes, and a iiij dosen of skochyons of

[a] priest.   [b] died.   [c] living.

armes and serten morners, and mony of the quen Mare['s] servandes at ys berehyng at sant Marg(ar)et there.

The sam day was bered in the abbay master Gennyngs, with ij
whyt branchys and a ij dosen skochyons of armes, and xvj torchys
and iiij gret tapurs, and mony morners in blake, and pore men
had gownes.

The xxiiij day of October was bered at sant Stevyn in Walbroke master doctur Owyn, phesyssyon, with a ij haroldes of
armes and a cote armur and penon of armes, and iiij dosen of
armes, and ij whyt branchys, and xx torchys ; and xx pore men
had gownes, and ther dener ; and iiij gret tapurs ; and the morow
masse, and master Harpfheld dyd pryche ; and after a gret dener.

.   .   .   .

master Ambros Wylliams sqwyre, and grocer .   .   .   .
hersse of wax, and v dosen penselles and vj .   .   .   .   .   . and
ij gret whyt branchys and ij dosen torchys .   .   .   .   . of armes
and a cotte armur and a pennon of armes, and mony morners in
blake ; and hegayff the sam[e church a] goodly crosse of sylver
and the stayff to the chyrche ; [and] a grett dolle of money, a
iiij^d. a pesse, and aft[er a] dener.

The xxvj day of October was bered [at Saint Giles's] withowt
Crepullgatt master Cottun, a grett rich man of law, with ij grett
whytt branchys and xij [torches] and iiij gret tapurs, and mony
morners ; and after a gret dener.

The xxvij day of October was bered in Al. .   . parryche master Perce('s) wyff the quen('s) skynner .   .   . branchys and xij
torchys and iiij grett tapurs .   .   . morners in blake ; and after
masse a grett dener ; [and he] gayff to ys compene serten money
to dyne [at] ther hall the sam day.

The vj day of November was bered at sent Benettes at Powlles
Warff master John Stokes (the) quen('s) servand and bruar,[a] with
ij whytt branchys and x gret stayffes-torchys and iiij gret tapurs ;

---

[a] brewer.

and x pore men had rosett gownes of iiij⁸. the yerd, and xvj gownes, and cottes of xij⁸. the yerd.

The xij day of November was Saterday ther was a woman sett on the pelere ᵃ for sayhyng that the quen was ded, and her grace was not ded then.

The xvij day of November be-twyn v and vj in the mornyng ded ᵇ quen Mare, the vj yere of here grace('s) rayne, the wyche Jhesu have mercy on her solle! Amen.

. . . .

[The same] day, be-twyne a xj and xij a' for[noon, the lady Eliza]beth was proclamyd quen Elsabeth, quen of England, France and Yrland, and deffender of the feyth, by dyvers haroldes of armes and trumpetors, and dukes, lordes [and knights,] the wyche was ther present, the duke of Norfoke, [the] lord tresorer, the yerle of Shrousbere, and the yerele of Bedford, and the lord mayre and the althermen, and dyver odur lordes and knyghtes.'

The sam day, at after-non, all the chyrches in London dyd ryng, and at nyght dyd make bonefyres and set tabulls in the strett, and ded ett and drynke and mad mere ᶜ for the newe quen Elsabeth, quen Mare('s) syster.

The xix day of November ded ᵈ be-twyn v and vj in the morning my lord cardenall Polle at Lambeth, and he was byshope of Canturbere; and ther he lay tyll the consell sett the tyme he shuld be bered, and when, and wher.

The sam day all London song and sayd *Te Deum laudamus* in evere chyrche in London.

The xx day of November dyd pryche at Powlles crosse doctur Bylle, quen Elsabeth('s) chaplen, and mad a godly sermon.

The xx day of November ded ᵉ the bysshope of Rochestur ᶠ and parsun of sant Mangnus on London bryge.

The xxij day of November was bered in Jhesus chapell master

ᵃ pillory.   ᵇ died.   ᶜ made merry.
ᵈ died.   ᵉ died.   ᶠ Maurice Griffith.   ᵍ In St. Paul's.

Robertt Jonsun gentyllman, and *(blank)* to the byshope (of) Lundon, Boner; with ij whyt branchys and xiiij grett stayff-torchys, and iiij grett tapurs, and ii dosen and d'[a] of skochyons of armes; and mony morners in blake, and all the masters of Jhesus with ther blake saten hodes, and a xxx morners; and the morow masse and a sermon, and after a grett dener, and a dolle of money.

The xxiij day of November the quen Elsabeth('s) grace toke here gorney from Hadley be-yond Barnett toward London, unto my lord North('s) plase,[b] with a M. and mor of lordes, knyghtes, and gentyllmen, lades and gentyllwomen; and ther lay v days.

. . . .

cote armur and pennon of armes and . . . . . with ij whytt branchys and xij torchys and iiij gret tapurs.

The xxv day of November was bered in sant . . . Flettstrett master Skynner sqwyre, on of the vj clarkes of the Chansere, with a harold of armes beyryng ys cote armur, and ys pennon of armes, and ij dosen skochyons of armes, and ij grett whyt branchys and xvj torchys and iiij g[reat tapers;] and mony morners, and all they of the Chanserey.

The xxvj day of November was bered in [Kent] my lord Cobham here husband[c] with iij haroldes . . . . with a gret baner of armes and iiij baners of [images], and a iiij dosen of armes— my lade Cobbam.

The xxvj day of November was bered at the Blake Frers in Smythfeld master Bassett sqwyre, on of the [privy] chambur with quen Mare; and he had ij whyt branchys, and xij torchys, and iiij gret tapurs, and a harold . . . a cote armur, a penon of armes, and ij dosen of [shocheons.]

The xxv day of November was mared ser Thomas W[hite] knyght, late mare,[d] unto my lade Warren, the wyff of ser Raff Warren, knyght, twys mare of London.

<hr>

[a] a half.   [b] The Charter-house.   [c] Lady Cobham, *as explained by the postscript.*
[d] mayor.

The xxx day of November, was saut Andrewes day, the bysshope
of Rochestur was cared from the plasse in Sowthwarke unto sant
Mangnus in London; for he was parsun ther; and he had a herse
of wax, and a v dosen pensels, and the qwyre hangyd with blake
and armes; and he had ij whyt branchys and ij dosen torchys;
and he had ij haroldes of armes, ser Wylliam Peter cheyff morner,
and ser Wylliam Garrett, master Low, master Catter, and dyvers
odur, and mony morners; and xij pore men had blake gownes,
and xij of ys men bare torchys; and after my lord of Wynchester
dyd pryche; and after he was bered they whent to ys plasse to
dener, for ther was a grett dener, and he had a gret baner of armes
and iiij baners of santes and viij dosen of skochyons.

[The xxviijth day of November the Queen removed to the Tower
from the lord North's] plasse, (which) was the Charter Howsse.
[All] the stretes unto the towre of London was newe gravelled.
Her grace rod thrugh Barbecan and Crepulgat, by [London-wall]
unto Bysshope-gate, and up to Leden-halle and thrugh Gracyus
strett and Fanchyrchestrett; and a-for rod gentyllmen and [many]
knyghtes and lordes, and after cam all the trumpetes blohyng, and
then cam all the haroldes in a-ray; and my lord of Penbroke [bare
the] the quen('s) sword; then cam here Grace on horsbake, [appa-
relled] in purpull welvett with a skarpe * abowt her neke, and [the
serg]anttes of armes abowt here grace; and next after rod [sir]
Robart Dudley the master of her horse; and so the gard with halbards. [And] ther was shyche shutyng of gunes as never was
hard a-for; so to the towre, with all the nobulles. And so here
Grace lay in the towre unto the v day of Dessember, that was sant
Necolas evyn. And ther was in serten plasses chylderyn with
speches and odur places, syngyng and playing with regalles.

The v day here Grace removyd by water undur the bryge unto
Somersett plase, with trumpetes playng, and melody and joye and
comfortt to all truw Englys-men and women, and to all pepulle.

* a scarf. *Fr.* éscharpe.

The vij day of Desember was bered my lade Chamley, the wyff of ser Roger Chamley knyght and late lord cheyffe barne,[a] in the parryche of sant Marten's at Ludgate; and ther was iiij branche tapers, garnyshed with iiij dosen pensels; and the howse hangyd with blake and armes, and the strett and the chyrche with blake and armes; and ther was a harold of armes; and ij whyt branchys, and xxiiij torchys, and mony morners; and the morow masse and a sermon, and after a grett dener; and she had iiij baners of santtes.[b]

The viij day of Desember was bered at the Sayvoy doctur Westun sum-tyme dene of Westmynster, with ij dosen torchys.

The vj day of (December) was bered in the west contray ser Antony Hongerford knight, with standard, penon, cot, elmett, target, sword, and iiij dosen skochyons of armes, and no harold of armes.

[The ix day of December was buried at St. Paul's doctor Gabriel Dune] prest, with ij whyt [branches . . . . tapurs, and the pore men had gownes.

The x day of Desember was browth do[wn from] her chambur in-to her chapel quen Mare, [with all the heralds,] and lordes and lades and gentyllmen and gentyllwomen, [hir] offesers and servands, all in blake, with (*unfinished*)

The sam mornyng my lord cardenall was [removed from] Lambeth, and cared toward Canturbery with grett [company in] blake; and he was cared in a charett with [banner-]rolles wroth[c] with fyne gold and grett baners [of arms,] and iiij baners of santes in owllo.[d]

The ix day of Desember was creatyd at Somersett plasse, wher the quen('s) grace lys, master Rychmond[e] Norroy, and Rysbanke[f] creatyd Bluw-mantyll.

The xij of Desember was bered at sant Martens at Ludgat ser Gorge Harper knyght, with ij haroldes of armes, with ij whyt branchys, xij torchys, and iiij gret tapurs; and a standard, a pennon, and cote armur, target, sword, mantyll, and crest a gylt bore,[g] and v

---

[a] baron.   [b] saints.   [c] wrought.   [d] oil.   [e] Laurence Dalton.
[f] John Hollingworth.   [g] boar.

dosen of skochyons of armes, and mony morners, and ther had xvj pore men had gownes.

The xj day of Desember was bered with-in the Towre master Verney, the master of the Juell-howse; and he gayff to xij pore men good gownes.

The (*blank*) day of Desember was bered in sant Edmonds in Lumbarstret my lade Wynddebanke, late of Cales,[a] with ij dosen of skochyons of armes.

[The xiij day of December, the corpse of the late Queen was brought from St. James's, in a cha]rett, with the pyctur of emages [b] lyke [her person], adorned with cremesun velvett and her crowne on her hed, her septer on her hand, and mony goodly rynges on her fyngers; up the he-way [went] formett [c] [the] standard with the Faucon and [the Hart]; then cam a grett compene of morners; and after anodur godly standard of the Lyon and the Faucon; and then her houshold servandes, ij and ij together, in blake gownes, [the] haroldes rydyng to and fro to se them go in order; and after cam the iij standard with the Whyt Grahond and the Faucon; and then cam gentyllmen in gownes, morners; and then cam rydyng sqwyrs, bayryng of baners of armes; and then cam my lord marques of Wynchester on hors-bake, bayryng the baner of the armes of England in-brodered with gold; and then cam after Chester the harold, baryng the helm and the crest and mantyll; then cam master Norroy, bayryng the targett with the garter and the crowne; and then cam master Clarenshus bayreng the sword; and after cam Garter, bayryng her cot-armur, on hors-bake they all; and baners borne abowt her, with knyghts, lords, and baners a-bowt the corse; with iiij harolds bayryng on horss-bake iiij whyt baners of santes wroth [d] with fyne gold, master Samersett, master Lanckostur, master Wyndsor, and master Yorke; and then cam the corse, with her pyctur lyung over her, and the corse covered with cloth of gold, the crosse

---

[a] Calais.   [b] A painted effigy.   [c] foremost.   [d] wrought.

sylver, and then cam iij *(blank)* with the cheyff morners ; and then lades rydyn, alle in blake, trapyd to the grond ; and the charett that the quen was in rode the pages of honor with baners in ther handes ; and a-for the corse her chapell, and after all the monkes, and after the bysshopes in order ; and so by Charyng-crosse to Westmynster abay ; and at the grett dore of the chyrche evere[a] body dyd a-lykt[b] of ther horse ; and then was gentyll-men rede[c] to take the quen owt of her charett, and so erles and lordes whent a-for her grace to the herse ward, with her pyctur borne betwyn men of worshype ; and at the cherche dore met her iiij byshopes, and the abbott, mytered, in copes, and sensyng[d] the body ; and so she lay all nyght under the herse, and her grace was wachyd. [And there were an hundred poor men in good black gowns] bayryng longe torchys, with [hoods on their heads, and arms] on them ; and a-bowt her the gard bayryng [staff-torches] in blake cottes ; and all the way chandlers [having] torchys, to gyffe them that had ther torchys [burnt out].

The xiiij day of Desember [was] the quen('s) masse ; and [all the lords] and lades, knyghtes and gentyll women, dyd offer. [And there was] a man of armes and horse offered ; and her cot-armur, and sword, and targett, and baner of armes, and iij [stan-dards] ; and all the haroldes abowt her ; and ther my lord bys-shope of Wynchester mad the sermon ; and ther was offered cloth of gold and welvet, holle pesses,[e] and odur thynges. [After the] masse all done, her grace was cared up [to the chapel] the kyng Henry the vij byldyd, with bysshopes [mitred ;] and all the offesers whent to the grayffe,[f] and after [they] brake ther stayffes, and cast them in-to the grayffe ; in the mayn tyme the pepull pluckt [down] the cloth, evere[a] man a pesse[g] that cold caycth[h] [it,] rond a-bowt the cherche, and the armes. And after[wards,] my lord bysshope of Yorke, after her grace was [buried,] he declaryd

---

[a] every.   [b] alight.   [c] ready.   [d] incensing.   [e] whole pieces.
      [f] grave.   [g] piece.   [h] catch.

an colasyon,[a] and as sone as he had made an end, all the trumpetes bluw a blast, and so the cheyff morners and the lords and knyghtes, and the bysshopes, with [the] abbott, whent in-to the abbay to dener, and all the offesers of the quen('s) cott.[b]

The xvj day of December was cared in a charett from sant Baythelmuw the grett unto Essex to be bered, with baners and banerrolles abowt her, my lade Ryche, and so to the plasse wher she dwelyd.

The xviij day of Desember was [buried] my lade Ryche, the wyff of the lord Ryche, with a herse of v prynsepalles and a viij dosen penselles and a viij dosen skochyons and a grett baner of my lordes and my lades armes and iiij baner rolles, and iiij baner(s) of santtes;[c] and grett whytt branchys and vj dosen of torchys; and xxiiij pore men had gownes; and the morow masse and a grett dener, and ij haroldes and mony morners.

[The xxviij day of December the late bishop of Chichester[d] was buried at Christchurch, London,] . . . . skochyons, and torchys, and xviij stayffe . . . . . branche tapers, with iiij dosen penselles and iiij . . . . . . and a d'[e] of bokeram, and a grett baner of armes [of the see] of Chechastur, and ys own armes, and iiij baners of [saints]; master Clarenshus was the harold; and v bysshopes dyd offer [at] the masse, and iij songe masses that day, and after a grett [dinner,] and xviij pore men had rosett gownes of frys.

The xxiij day of Desember was the obseque at Westmynster [with the] sam herse that was for quen Mare, was for Charles the V., Emporowre of Rome, was durge, and the morow masse with . . mornars[e] and (blank) was the cheyff morner.

The (blank) day of January was bered in the ylle of Shepay my lord warden of the v porttes,[f] and master tresorer to the quen('s) howsse, and knyght of the garter, with standard and a grett baner of armes, and v baner-rolles of armes, and iiij baners of emages, and a iii haroldes of armes, and a herse of v prynsepelles of wax,

---

[a] qu?   [b] court.   [c] saints.   [d] John Christopherson.
[e] a half.   [f] Sir Thomas Cheney, K. C.

v dosen of penselles and a x dosen of skochyons of armes, and iiij whyt branchys and a dosen of torchys, and l. pore men had gownes, and a c. and a d'ᵃ in blake gownes and cottes.

The ij day of January was bered mastores Matsun, the wyff of capteyne Mattsun, the wyche she mared with master Shelley of Sussex was her furst husbond; with ij whyt branchys and xij torchys, and iiij grett tapurs, and ij baners of santtes, and ij dosen of skochyons of armes, and a harold of armes.

The *(blank)* day of January was bered in Kent ser John Baker knyght, and master of *(blank)*; with a standard and a cotte armur, pennon of armes, and iiij baners of santes and a herse of wax, and vii dosen penselles, and x dosen skochyons and a *(blank)* dosen of torchys, and mony morners in blake gownes, and ij gret whytt branches, and a harold of armes, and a grett dolle, and after a grett dener, and pore men had gownes and ther dener.

. . . . Whyt-hall ser . . . . . Lee . . . . and the althermen all in skarlett.

The viij day of January was bered Edmund . . . . penterᵇ in sant Botulf with-owt Althergatt, and ther the masters of the Penters in ther leveray, with . . . . and vj sthayffe torchys; for he was a good wor[kman] as any ys, the wyche he retayned toᶜ master Ga[rter] . . .

The sam day was creatyd of my lorde of [Norfolk a] pursewantt, Bluwe mantyll, and creatyd Rychemund,ᵈ [who] cam latt over the see owt of Franche.

The *(blank)* day in Crystynmas weyke they begane [to build] skayffold(s) in dyvers plasses in London for pa[geants] agaynst the crounassyon of quen Elesabetth, that [is to be the] xv day of January, and the condut nuw paynted.

The viij of January dedᵉ at the Grayffes-endᶠ Lankoster the harold of armes,ᵍ the wyche ded comm home from the berehyng of

---

ᵃ a half.　　ᵇ painter.　　ᶜ was retained by.　　ᵈ Nicholas Narboone.
　　ᵉ died.　　ᶠ Gravesend.　　ᵍ Nicholas Tubman.

ser John Baker knyght, and bered the ix day of January at Grayffes-end.

The xij of January ded ª master Grennell,ᵇ my lord cardenall's waxchandler, at sant Gylles.

The xij day the Qwen('s) grace toke her barge at Whytt-halle toward the Towre, and shott the bryge, and my lord mare and the althermen, and all the craftes, in barges with stremars and baners of ther armes.

The xiij day of January with-in the Towre the Quen mad Knyghtes of the Baythe x.

The sam day was creatyd at Crechyrche at my lord of Norffoke('s) plasse Cokes,ᶜ Perkollys, mad Lanckostur the harold.

[The xiv day of January the Queen came in a chariot from] the Towre, with all the lordes and ladies [in crimson] velvet, and and ther horses trapyd with the sam, and [trumpeters in] red gownes blohyng, and all the haroldes in ther cottes armur, and all. the strettes stroyd ᵈ with gravell; and at Grasyus strett a goodly pagantt of kyng [Henry] the viij and quen Ane ys wyff and of ther lenege, and in Cornelle ᵉ a-nodur goodly pagantt of kyng Henry and kyng Edward the vjᵗʰ.; and be-syd Soper lane in [Cheap a]nodur goodly pagantt, and the condyth pentyd; [and] at the lytylle condutt a-nodur goodly pagant of a qwyke tre and a ded, and the quen had a boke gyffyn her ther; and ther the recorder of London and the chamburlayn delevered unto the quen a purse of gold fulle to the waluw of (*blank*); and so to the Flett strett to the condyt, and ther was a-nodur goodly pagantt of the ij chyrchys; and at Tempylle bare was ij grett gyanttes, the one name was Goott-magottᶠ a Albaoṅ and the thodur Co(rineus.)

The xv day was the crounasyon of quen Elsabeth at Westmynster abbay, and theyr all the trumpettes, and knyghtes, and lordes, and haroldes of armes in ther cotte armurs; and after all theyᵍ in ther

---

ª died.   ᵇ Greenhill.   ᶜ John Cooke, or Cox.
ᵈ strewed.   ᵉ Cornhill.   ᶠ Gogmagog.   ᵍ *So in MS.*

skarlett, and all the bysshopes in skarlett, and the Quen, and all
the fottmen waytyng a-pone the quene, to Westmynster hall;
ther mett all the byshoppes, and all the chapell with iij crosses, and
in ther copes, the byshops mytered, and syngyng *Salve festa dyes;*
and all the strett led with gravell, and bluw cloth unto the abbay,
and raylled on evere syd, and so to the abbay to masse, and ther
her grasse was crounyd; and evere offeser rede ᵃ against she shuld
go to dener to Westmynster hall, and evere offeser to take ys offes
at serves a-pone ther landes; and my lord mare and the althermen.

[The   day of January was buried at saint Giles's with-]
owt Crepull-gatt master Thomas Grennell, ... with iiij
gylt candyllstykes and iiij grett tapurs, ... whyt branchys
and xvj stayffe torchys, and the [company of] the Wax-chandlers;
and he gayff to the ys compene [for to] make mere ᵇ *(blank)*; and
ther was the compene of Flechers at ys berehyng, and all they dyd
offer . . . they had iiij nobuls to make mere ᶜ at the S[un ? in]
Crepullgatt; and, after mase done, ther was a grett dener and soper
at ys owne howsse.

The xvj day of [January] was gret justes at the tylt-[yard], iiij
chalengers, the duke of Northfoke and *(unfinished)*

The xvij day of January was tornayhyng at the barears ᵈ at Whyt-
halle.

The xviij day of January whent to berehyng ser Olever Laurans
knyght, with standard, cote armur, and penon of armes, elmett,
target, sword, and mantylle; and v dosen of skochyons.

The xx day of January was set up for doctur Koke of the Arches,
in the parryche of sant Gregores be-syd Powlles, a cott-armur
and a pennon of armes, and ij baners of santtes.

The iiij day of Feybruary was cared in a charett with vj baner-
rolles, and a-for a grett baner of armes, and iiij baners of santtes,
alle in owlle, ᵉ and thos iiij borne by iiij haroldes of armes in ther

ᵃ ready.   ᵇ merry.   ᶜ merry.   ᵈ barriers.   ᵉ oil.

cott armurs, with a vij^{xx} horsse, toward Bassyng to be bered ther;
and ther was a goodly herse of wax; my lade marques of Wynchester was the lade; and at evere towne had money and torchys,
master Garter, master Somersett, master Rychmond, master
Lanckoster, and Bluwmantyll, and viij dosen penselles and viij
dosen of skochyons.

. . . . . of armes and iij dosen of skochyons.

The vj day of Feybruary went to the chyrche to be bered at
Clarkenwell ser Thomas Pope knyght, with a standard and cott,
pennon of armes, a targett, elmett and sword, and a ij dosen of
armes, and xij for the branchys and vj for the . . . . of bokeram; and ij haroldes of armes, master Clarenshus and master
Yorke; master Clarenshus bare the cott, and master Yorke bare
the helmett and crest.   And he gayff xl mantyll frys gownes, xx
men and xx women; and xx men bare torchys; and the vomen ij
and ij to-gether, with torchys; and ij grett whyt branchys, and
iiij branchys tapurs of wax garnysshed with armes, and with iiij
dosen pensels.   And ser Recherd Sowthwell knyght and ser Thomas Stradlyng, and dyver odur morners in blake, to the nomber
of lx and mo in blake, and all the howsse and the chyrche with
blake and armes; and after to the plasse to drynke, with spysse-
bred and wyne; and the morow masse, iij songe, ... with
ij pryke songe, and the iij of requiem, with the clarkes of London;
and after he was bered; and, that done, to the plasse to dener,
for ther was a grett dener, and plente of all thynges, and a grett
dolle of money.

The vij day of Feybruary was bered my lade marques of Wynchester at Bassyng; and ther was a herse of wax, and viij dosen
penselles, and armes, and skochyons, and garnyshed with angelles
and archangells and with baner-rolles, and a x dosen skochyons;
and ther was grett cher mad, [*] and a grett dolle, boyth money and
mett and drynke, and a grett dener, fysshe and flesse, and venesun.

[*] cheer made.

The viij day (of) Feybruary dyd pryche a-for the quen, wyche was Aswedynsday, doctur Kokes sumtyme dene of Westmynster.

The Fryday dyd pryche after master Parker a-for the quen.

The Sunday after dyd pryche master Skore.[a]

The Wedynsday after dyd pryche Whythede.

The Fryday after dyd pryche a-for the quen *(blank)*

The Sunday after dyd pryche a-for the quen *(blank)*

.   .   .   .

The xviij of Feybruary and the xx [a man stood in the] pelere[b] with a coler[c] of smeltes a-bowtt ys neke [who had bought the] smeltes of the quen('s) prysse[d] in Chepe, and sold them at ys vantege a-monge the fys-wyffes, and ther the pelere sett aganst cherche.

The xxij day of Feybruary was the obseque of . . . Pottnam sqwyre, with cote armur and pennon of armes and a iiij dosen of skochyons.

The xvij day of Feybruary was a herse of wax [erected] gorgyously, with armes, a ix dosen penselles and armes, [for the] old lade contes of Oxford, the syster to the old Thomas [duke of] Norffoke, at Lambeth.

The xx day of Feybruary was the sam herse wa[s taken] done, the wyche was v prynsepalles, and was never . . .

The xxj day of Feybruary my lade[e] was browth[f] in-to Lambethe chyrche for[g] the qwer and dobull reylyd, and hangyd with blake and armes; and she had iiij goodly whyt branchys and ij dosen of grett stayffes torchys, and ij haroldes of armes, master Garter and master Clarenshus, in ther cotte armurs; a-for a grett baner of armes, and iiij baners rolles, and iiij baners of santtes; and then cam the corsse, and after morners; the chyff morner was my lade chamberlen Haward, and dyvers odur of men (and) women; and

---

[a] Scory.   [b] pillory.   [c] collar.
[d] prise, *i. e.* as taken for the royal household by pre-emption.   [e] lady.
[f] brought.   [g] before?

after durge done to the dukes plasse; and the morow, masse of requiem done, my lade was bered a-for the he awtter.^a

The xxiij day dyd pryche afor the quen Gryndalle.

The xxv day of Feybruary dyd pryche Sandes.

The *(blank)* dyd pryche doctur Kokes.

.   .   .   .

[The . . day] of Feybruary was bered . . . . hylle master Elthestun sqwyre, with ij whyt branchys and . . . stayffe torchys and iiij grett tapurs, and ij dosen skochyons.

The xxiij day of Feybruary was bered at Alder . . . . . my lady Roche, the wyff of ser Wylliam Roche draper, latte mare of London; and he was bered at santt Peters Powre be-syd frere Augustynes.

The *x* day *Marche** was a goodly herse of wax set up for my old lade of Oxford at Lambeth.

The *xij* day of *Marche** was the sam hers was taken downe the day a-for she was browth^b to the chyrche, the wyche was as goodly hers of v prynsepalles as has bene sene, with armes and penselles.

The *xv* day of *March** was my lade the contes of Oxford was browthe^c to the cherche at Lambeth, with ij harordes of armes, master Garter and master Clarenshux, in ther cot armurs, a-for the cors a grett baner of armes, and iiij baners of santtes, and iiij baner-rolles of armes borne a-bowtt her and iiij grett whyt branchys and ij dosen grett long stayffes torchys borne by her sar-vandes in; and my lade Haward cheyffe morner, and money in blake, and the quwere was hangyd with lx . . . with armes and raylles a-bowt with blake and armes; and the morow masse with small chere after-ward, butt evere man a . . .

.   .   .   .

<hr/>

      ^a high altar.   ^b brought.   ^c brought.

  * *It will be observed these paragraphs are repetitions of those in the preceding page: and, as the dates (printed in italics) were filled in subsequently to their being written, the former dates are probably to be preferred.*

The xxj day of Marche was bered at [Chenies, in] Bukyng-
hamshyre my old contes of Bedford . . . . . of armes and a
grett baner of armes and a v [banner-] rolles of her progene ᵃ and
vii dosen of skochyons . . . . vj of sarsenett, and iiij dosen of
grett stayffe torchys.

The xxj of Marche the quen('s) master cokes and odur her
offesers, and at Mylle-end ther they dynyd, [with] all maner of
mett and drynke; and ther was all maner of artelere, as drumes,
flutes, trumpetes, gones, mores pykes, halbardes, to the nomber of
v C.; the gonners in shurtes of maylle and . . . . pykes in
bryght harnes, and mony swardes and v grett pesses of gones and
shot in . . . the wyche dyd myche hurt unto glass wy[ndows;]
and cam a grett gyant danssyng, and after [that a] mores dansse
dansyng, and gones and mor[es pikes]; and after cam a cart with
a grett wyth ᵇ and ij [bears?] with-in the cartt, and be-syd whent
a gret . . . . of grett mastes; ᶜ and then cam the master cokes
rydyng in cottes in brodere, and chynes of gold, and mony of the
quen('s) servandes in ther levery, to the cowrt, and ther they shott
ther pesses, ᵈ and with-in the parke was ij C. chamburs gret and
smalle shot, and the Quen('s) grace standyn in the galere; and so
evere man whent in-to the parke, showhyng them in batell ray,
shutyng and playhyng at bowt the parke; and a-for the quen was
on of bayres ᵉ was bated, and after the mores dansers whent in-to
the cowrt, dansyng in mony offeses.ᶠ

The xxiij day of Marche was bered at sant tellens ᵍ ser John
Sentlow knyght, with ij haroldes of armes, master Clarenshux
and master Somerset, with standard and penon, and cott and elmet, target and sword, but nodur crosse nor prest, nor clarkes, but
a sermon and after a salme of Davyd; and ij dosen of skochyons of
armes.

* * * * * * * * * *

ᵃ *i. e.* ancestors.   ᵇ whip ?   ᶜ mastiffs ?   ᵈ pieces.
ᵉ one of the bears.   ᶠ *i. e.* many of the offices of the house, as the kitchen,
ewery, &c.   ᵍ St. Helen's.

The *(blank)* day of Marche ser Antony [Saint Leger, knight of the] garter, latte deputte of Yrland, was bered in Kentt, with a standard, a grett baner of armes, [helmet,] crest, target, and sword, and vj dosen of skochyons; [and two] harold(s) of armes, master Garter and master Lankestur, and *(unfinished)*

The viij day (of) Marche ded [a] my lade ys wyffe, and was bered at *(blank)*.

The xvj day of Marche was bered in Northamt[onshire] ser Thomas Tressam, lord of sant Jones,[b] with iiij baner rolles and a grett baner of armes, and a standard, elmett, targett and sword, and cott armur; and a viij dosen of [scocheons], and a iiij dosen of torchys and iiij dosen penselles, and [ij] whyt branchys, and mony morners in blake, and ij haroldes of armes, master Clarenshux and master Somersett.

The xxvij day of Marche dyd pryche at sant Mare Spyttyl doctur Bylle the quen('s) amner.[c]

The xxviij day of Marche, the wyche was Ester-tuwysday, doctur Cokes sum-tyme dene of Westmynster dyd pryche.

The xxix day of Marche dyd pryche at sant Mare Spyttyll master Horne, parsun sum-tyme at Allalows in Bredstrett.

The ij day of Aprell dyd pryche at Powlles crosse master Samsun.

The furst day of Aprell ther was at Westmynster a desputyng shuld a bene be the bysshopes and the nuw prychers, and ther they pute in a *(blank)* agaynst Monday, after that the bysshopes shuld gyff a an(s)wer of the sam.

The iij day of Aprell the bysshopes and the nuw prychers mett at the abbay a-for my lord keper of the brod seylle, and dyvers of the consell, and ther to gyff a answer of the matter; the sam nyght, my lord bysshope of Wynchester and my lord of Lynkolne was send [d] to the towre of London by the gard by water, to the Old Swane, and to Belynsgatt after.

· · · · · · · · · ·

[a] died.   [b] John's.   [c] almoner.   [d] sent.   ·

The vj day of Aprell was bered at [saint Clement's] withowt
Tempyll-bare my lade Gray,[a] the [wife of sir John] Gray, and the
wyff was of master Walsyngham, ... with ij whyt
branchys and iiij grett tapurs, and fo[ur] staff-]torchys, and ij
dosen and d'[b] of skochyons of armes . . . masse and or[c] communyon.

The vij day of Aprell was browth[d] unto [saint Thomas] of Acurs
in Chepe from lytyll sant Barthellmuw [in] Lothbere masteres
. . . . , and ther was a gret compene of pepull, ij and ij to-
gether, and nodur[e] prest nor clarke, the nuw prychers in ther gowne
lyke ley[-men,] nodur[e] syngyng nor sayhyng tyll they cam [to the
grave,] and a-for she was pute into the grayff a [collect] in
Englys, and then put in-to the grayff, and after [took some]
heythe[f] and caste yt on the corse, and red a thynge . . . for
the sam, and contenent[g] cast the heth[f] in-to the [grave], and contenent[g] red the pystyll of sant Poll to the Stesselonyans[h] the (blank[i]
chapter,[h] and after thay song *pater-noster* in Englys, boyth prychers
and odur, and [women,] of a nuw fassyon, and after on of them
whent in-to the pulpytt and mad a sermon.

The viij day of Aprell ther was a proclamasion of pesse[i] be-
twyne the Quene('s) grace and Hare[k] the French kyng, and Dol-
phyn the kyng of Skottes, for ever, boyth by water and land ; and
ther was vj trumpeters and v haroldes of armes, master Garter
and master Clarenshux, proclamyd yt, and Lankoster, Ruge Crosse,
and Bluwmantyll, and my lord mayre and all the althermen in
skarlett ; and Bluw-mantyll dyd proclaymyd that no players shuld
play no more tyll a serten tyme of no mans players ; but the mare
or shreyff, balle,[l] constabull, or odur offesers take them, lay them
in presun, and the quen('s) commondement layd on them.

---

[a] *This name should be* Carey : *the mother of the great Walsingham.*

[b] half.　[c] *So in MS.*　[d] brought.　[e] neither.　[f] earth.　[g] incontinently.

[h] Strype supposes the 1 Thessalonians, iv. 13 : unless Thessalonians be an error for
Corinthians, as now in the Common Prayer Book.　　　　[i] peace.

　　　　　[k] Harry.　　　　　　　　　　　　[l] bailiff.

The ix day of Aprell dyd pryche at Powlles crosse doctur Bylle the quen('s) awmer,[a] and declaryd warfor[b] the byshopes whent to the Towre.

[The xij day of April was brought from Clerkenwell unto] Blake-frers in Smyth-feld with ij haroldes of armes, master Clarenshux and master Somersett, ser Richard[c] Monsfeld knyght, with ij gret whyt branchys, . . . ij dosen torchys and iiij gylt candyll-stykes and iiij grett tapurs, and the plasse and the frers hunge with blake and armes; and xxiiij prestes and clarkes [prayers] all Laten, and durge wher he ded,[d] and wher he was bered; and ther was a standard and a penon of armes, and a cott armur, and elmett, target and sword, and the[re were] iiij baners of santtes. and a xviij men morners in blake gownes and xx in blake cottes; and after to the plasse to drynke, and the morow masses in all the chyrches, and then after ys standard, cotte, elmet, target, [and sword] offered up; and after all done to the plasse to dener; and a vij dosen skochyons of armes to be bere[d].

The xiij day whent to the Towere master Adelston, captain of Rysse-banke, a hold of Cales.

The vij day was chosen at Yeld-halle a-for my lord mayre and the masters the althermen, and all the comm(on)ers of the cete,[e] and the craftes of London, the masters of the bryghows, master Wylliam Draper, yrmonger, and master Assyngton, lether-seller.

The (blank) day cam from Franse my lord chamburlayn Haward and my lord bysshope of Elly and master doctur Wotton, and (unfinished)

The xiij day of Aprell ther cam unto Brydewell dyvers gentyll-men, and ruffelars, and servyngmen, and ther they begane a tymult and or[f] fray, that the constabulles and altherman deputte cam to se the pesse[g] kepte, but thay wold have serten women owt of the bryd-welle, and ther thay druw ther swordes and be-gane myche besenes.

[a] almoner.   [b] wherefore.   [c] Rice   [d] died.   [e] city.
[f] So in MS.   [g] peace.

. . . .

. . . ye Tempull, and ix . . . . .

dener, and ther dynyd the consell and dyvers notabyll . . . .

and juges, and my lord mayre and the althermen, and the [officers
of the] Chansseres [a] and the Flett, and the Kyngesbynshe, and the
Marshalsea ; [and they] gayff gownes of ij collers, morreys and
mustars, and . . . ij collers . . . hondered; and at v
of cloke at after-non [the new] serganttes[b] whent unto sant Thomas
of Acurs in a . . . gowne and skarlette hodes a-bowt ther
nekes, and whyt [hoods on] ther hedes, and no capes ;[c] and after
they whent unto Pow[les with] typstayffes and offesers of the
Kyngbynche, and odur plasses, and [they were] browth [d] be ij old
serganttes, one after a-nodur in skarlett . . . of north syd,
and ther thay stod tyll thay had brou[th them] unto ix sondre
pellers [e] of the north syd, and after the . . . cam unto the
furst, and after to the reseduu; and thay whe[nt back] unto the
Tempull on a-lone,[f] and a-for whent the . . . and the rulers
and the Chansere and of the Kyngbynche [ij and ij to]gether, and
after cam a hondered in parte [g] cottes of . . .

The xx day of Aprell ther was a grett fray in . . . be-twyn
v and vj at nyght, betwyn servyng men and . . Flett-strett;
ther was one ix bones taken out of ys . . . and a-nodur had
ys nosse cutt off.

The (*blank*) day of Aprell was browth [h] from the Towre unto
Westmynster Hall to be reynyd,[i] my lord Wentworth, last depute
of Calles, for the lossyng of Calles ; and ther wher serten of ys
a-cussars ; but he quytt hym-seylff, thanke be God, and clen delevered, and whent in-to Wytyngtun colege, and ther he lys.

[The xxiij day of April, being saint George's day, the Queen
went about the hall, and all the knights of the] Garter that [went
singing in proces]syon, and a-bowt the cowrt ; the sam day at after

---

[a] Chancery.   [b] Compare these ceremonies with those on a like occasion in 1552,
at p. 26.   [c] caps.   [d] brought.   [e] pillars.   [f] *i. e.* one by one.
   [g] parti-.   [h] brought.   [i] arraigned.

[noon were] knyghtes electyd of the Garter the duke of Norfok, the marques of Northamtun, the erle of Rutland, and my lord Robard Dudley, the master of the quen('s) horse.

The xxv day of Aprell was prossessyon, the wyche was [saint Mark's] day, in dyvers parryche in London, whent with ther baners a[broad in] ther parryche, syngynge in Laten *Kerelyson* after the old fassyon.

The xxviij day of Aprell ther was a man sett on the pelere[a] [for] lewd wordes and slanderers wordes.

The xxv day of April,[b] was sant Markes day, the Quen('s) grace supt at Beynard castyll at my lord of Penproke('s) p[lace,] and after supper the Quen('s) grace rowed up and downe Temes, and [a] C. bottes[c] at bowte here grace, with trumpettes and drumes and flutes and gones, and sqwybes horlyng on he [d] to and fro, tyll x at nyght, or her grace depertyd, and all the water-syd st . . . with a M. pepull lokyng one here grace.

The furst day of May ther was ij pennys[e] was dekyd with stremars, baners, and flages, and trumpetes and drumes and gones, gahyng a Mayng,[f] and a-ganst the Quen('s) plasse at Westmynster, and ther they shott and thruw eges[g] and oregns[h] on a-gaynst a-nodur, and with sqwybes, and by chanse on fell on a bage of gune-powdur and sett dyvers men a'fyre, and so the men drue to on syd of the penus,[c] and yt dyd over-swelmed the pennus, and mony fell in the Temes, butt, thanke be God, ther was but on man drownyd, and a C. bottes[i] abowtt here, and the Quen('s) grace and her lordes and lades lokyng out of wyndows; thys was done by ix of the cloke on May evyn last.

The xxix day of Aprell at Dowgatt in London ther was a mayd dwelling with master Cotyngham, on of the quen('s) pulters ;[k] the mayd putt in-to a pott of (*blank*) serten powyssun[l] and browth[m] them unto her mastores, and to iiij of her servandes, and they dyd

[a] pillory.	[b] Marche *in MS.*	[c] boats.	[d] high.
[e] pinnaces.	[f] going a Maying.	[g] eggs.	[h] oranges.
[i] boats.	[k] poulterers.	[l] poison.	[m] brought.

ett them ; and as sone as they had ett them thay be-gane to swell and to vomett peteusle ; and ther cam a good woman causyd to be feychyd serten dolle of salett owylle [a] to drynke, and thanke be to God they be-gayne to mend and never one ded [b] of ytt.

. . . .

and servandes, and ther herers [c] nayled to the pe[llory,] . . was thes ij persunes have dullysly [d] gyffen poyssun [to their] mastores and ther howshold, and ether of them ij handes cute off.

The x day of May the parlement was endyd, [and the] Quen('s) grace whent to the parliament howsse.

The xj day of May the sam fellow and the [maid] was sett on the pelere a-gayne, and ther thodur [e] handes cut off for the sam offens.

The xij day of May be-gane the Englys [service] in the quen('s) chapell.

The xv day of May dyd pryche at Powlles [cross] master Gryndalle, and ther was the quens consell, the duke of Norfoke, my lord keper of the seylle, and my lord of Arundell, my lord treysorer, my lord marques of Northamtun, my lord admerall, my lord of Sussex, my lord of Westmorland, my lord of Rutland, and mony mo lordes and knyghtes, my lord mare and the althermen; and after sermon done they whent to my lord mayre to dener, and my lord Russell.

The xxj day of May dyd pryche at Powlles crosse master Horne, and ther was my lord mayre and the althermen and mony juges and sergantes of the law, and a grett nombur of pepull to the nombur (*blank*)

The xxiij day of May cam from be-yonde the see out of France and landyd at Towr-warff, and cam thrugh London, and unto my lord bysshope of London docthur Benard,[f] monser Memeranse [g] ij sunes,[h] and . . . unto ys palles [i] to ly ; and mony lord(s) and nobull men browth [k] them to their logying.

[a] oil.	[b] died.	[c] ears.	[d] devilishly.	[e] other.
[f] Bonner.	[g] Montmorenci.	[h] sons.	[i] palace.	[k] brought.

.　.　.　.　.　.　.　.　.　.　.

.　.　attes and mony mo for serten Frenche-men.

The xxiiij day of May the inbassadurs the Frenche [were] browth [a] from the byshope('s) palles [b] by land thrugh Flet-street [unto] the quen's pales [b] to soper, by the most nobull men ther was a-bowt the cowrt, and ther was the hall and the [privy] chambur and the grett chambur of pressens [c] hangyd with ryche clothes of arres, as ever was sene, and the cloth [of] state boyth hall and grett chamburs, and they had as [great] chere at soper, and after a bankett as goodly as has be[en seen,] with all maner musyke tyll mydnyght, for they wher (*unfinished*)

The xxv day they wher browt to the cowrt with musyke to dener, for ther was gret cher ; and after dener to b[ear] and bull baytyng, and the Quen('s) grace and the embassadurs stod in the galere lokyng of the pastym tyll vj at nyght ; and after they whent by water unto Powll wharff, and landyd, and contenent [d] unto ther logyng to the byshope of London('s) to soper, for ther wher gorgyus aparell as has bene sen in thes days.

The xxvj day of May they whent from the byshope('s) howsse to Powlles warff, and toke barge, and so to Parys garden, for ther was boyth [e] bare and bull baytyng, and the capten with a C. of the gard to kepe rowm for them to see [f] the baytyng.

The sam day was a proclamassyon of v of the actes ; on was for (*unfinished*)

The thursday the xxv day of May master John Whyt alther-man and grocer ys chyld was cristened in lytyll sant Barthelmuw be-syd sant Antonys ; thes wher the god-fathers' names, my lord marques of Wynchester now lord tresorer of England, and my lord byshope of Wynchester docthur Whytt, and the god-moder my lade Laxtun, lat the wyffe of ser Wylliam Laxtun latt mare of London and grocer ; and after ther was waferers [g] and epocras grett plente ; and after they whent home to the plasse, with the

---

[a] brought.　　　[b] palace.　　　[c] presence.　　　[d] incontinently.

[e] both.　　　[f] *MS.* sed.　　　[g] wafers.

chyld nam(ed) John Whytt; the wyche wyff was master Raff
Grenway altherman and grocer of London wyff.

[The xxviij day of May . . . .
bisho]pryke of yt by quen Mare, [for that he had] a wyff, and
odur maters that he was fayn to . . .

The sam day the inbassadurs of France whent [away,] and
toke barge toward Grayffhend ᵃ and they had . . . . gyftes
gyffyne them, and they cared money mastiffs [with] them for the
wolf, and (*unfinished*)

The xxj day of May was bered at sant [Andrew's] in the
Warderobe mastores Boswell, the wyff [of . . .] Boswell
clarke of the wardes, with ij whytt branchys . . , the wyche she
ded ᵇ with chyld, and a dosen and (*unfinished*)

The xxx day of May was mared ᶜ in the parryche of sant Andrews in the Warderobe, master Mathuw, draper, unto the dowther of master Wylliam Blakwell, towne-clarke of [London?] the
mornyng; and they wher mared in Laten, and masse, and after
masse they had a bryd cupe and waffers and epocras and muskadyll plente to hevere ᵈ body; and after unto master Blakwell('s)
plasse to bryke-fast, and after a grett dener.

The ij day of Juin was bered at lytyll sant Baythelmuwes my
lade Barnes, the wyff of ser George Barnes, knyght, and late
mare of London; and she gayff to pore men and powre women
good rosett gownes a (*blank*), and she gayffe to the powre men
and women of Calles (*blank*) a-pesse,ᵉ and she gayff a C. blake
gownes and cottes; and ther she had penon of armes, and master
Clarenshux kyng of armes, and ther was a xx clarkes syngyng
afor her to the chyrche with blake and armes; and after master
Horne mad a sermon, and after the clarkes song *Te Deum
laudamus* in Englys, and after bered with a songe, and a-for songe
the Englys pressessyon, and after to the place to dener; ser
Wylliam Garrett cheyff morner, and master Altham and master

ᵃ Gravesend.   ᵇ died.   ᶜ married.
          ᵈ every.   ᵉ a piece.

Chamburlayn, and her sunes and doythurs; ther was a nobull dener.

[The vj day of June saint George's feast was kept at Windsor;] the yerle of Pembroke was the [Queen's substitute,] lord Monty-cutt and my lord of . . . . ; ther was stallyd at that tyme the duke of [Norfolk], my lord marques of Northamtun, and the yerle of [Rutland], and my lord Robart Dudley the master of the quen('s) horse, nuw mad knyghtes of the Garter, and ther was gret [feasting] ther, and ther be-gane the comunion that day and Englys.

The xxix day of May was depreved of ys byshopepryke of London doctur Boner, and in ys plasse master Gryndall; and [Nowell] electyd dene of Powlles, and the old dene depreved, mas-ter [Cole].

The xj day of June dyd pryche at Powlles master [Sandys], and ther was my lorde mayre and the althermen, and my lord of Bedford, and with dyvers odur nobull men; and postulles ᵃ masse mad an end that day, and masse a' Powlles was non that day, and the new dene toke possessyon that was afore, by my lord of Bed-ford, and thys was on sant Barnabe day; and the sam nyght thay had no evyng-song at Powlles.

The sam nyght abowtt viij of the cloke at nyght the Quen('s) grace toke her barge at Whyt hall, and mony mo barges, and rod a-longe by the banke-syd by my lord of Wynchaster('s) place, and so to Peper alley, and so crost over to London syd with drumes and trumpetes playhyng ard ᵇ be-syd, and so to Whyt hall agayne to her palles.ᶜ

The xviij day of June dyd pryche at Powlles crosse docthur Juell, and ther was my lord mare and the althermen and master comtroller of the quens howse ser Edward Rogers, and mony mo, boyth men and women.

The xxj day of June was v bysshopes deprevyd, the bysshope of Lychfeld and Coventre,ᵈ and the bysshope of Carley,ᵉ the

ᵃ Apostles.　ᵇ hard.　ᶜ palace.　ᵈ Ralph Bayne.　ᵉ Carlisle, Owen Oglethorpe.

bysshope of Westchester,[a] the bysshope of Landaffh,[b] and the bysshope of (   ).

The xxiij day of June was electyd vj nuw byshopes, com from beyond the see, master Parker bysshope of Canturbere, master Gryndall bysshope of London, docthur Score bysshope of Harfford, Barlow Chechastur, doctur Bylle of Salysbere, doctur Cokes (of) Norwyche.

The xxiiij day of June ther was a May-game,   .   and sant John Sacerys,[c] with a gyant, and drumes and gunes [and the] ix wordes[d], with spechys, and a goodly pagant with a quen c . . and dyvers odur, with spechys; and then sant Gorge and the dragon, the mores dansse, and after Robyn Hode and lytyll John, and M[aid Marian] and frere Tuke, and thay had spechys rond a-bowt London.

The xxv day of June the sam May-gam whent unto [the palace?] at Grenwyche, playng a-for the Quen and the consell, and the   . . . thay whent by land, and cam (back by water?)

The sam day at afternone was bered, at sant Fayth, Dokeray,[e] docthur of the law, with ij grett whyt branchys, . . . grett stayff torchys, and iiij grett tapurs, and a dosen and d'[f] [of scocheons,] and mony morners; and the morow a grett dener.

The xxvj day of June was bered in the sam parryche [mistress] Gybbons a doctur of the law('s) wyff, the wyche she ded in . . and she had ij grett whyt branchys and xij torchys and iiij . . tapurs and ij lb. tapurs, and viij women bare here all in . . . and the branchys and the torchys, and ther was a sarmon, and mony morners, and a dosen of armes, and a grett dener.

The sam day was deprevyd of ther bysshoprykes the bysshope of Wynchestur[g] and the bysshope of Lynckolne[h] at master Hawse the kyng('s) shreyff in Mynsyon lane, and the bysshope of Wynchester[g] to the Towre agayne, and the bysshope of Lynckolne[h] delevered a-way.

[a] Cuthbert Scot.   [b] Anthony Kitchin.   [c] Zachary's.   [d] the Nine Worthies.
[e] Docwra.   [f] an half.   [g] John White.   [h] Thomas Watson.

CAMD. SOC.   2 D

The furst day of July all the craftes of London send[a] owt a (*blank*) men of armes, as well be-sene as ever was when owt of London, boyth waffelers[b] in cott of velvet and cheynes, with gunes, mores-pykes, and halbardes, and flages, and in-to the duke of Suffoke('s) parke in Sowthwarke, and ther they mustered a-for my lord mayre; and ther was a howsse for bred and dryng,[c] to gyffe the sawgyars[d] to ett and drynke, and they then after thay lay and mustered in sant Gorges ffeld tyll x of the cloke. [The next morning they removed towards Greenwich to the court there, and thence into Greenwich park, where they tarried] tyll viij of the cloke, and then thay [marched] to the lawne, and ther thay mustered in harnes, [and the gunners] in shurttes of maylle, and at v of the cloke at nyght the Quen [came] in to the galere of the parke gatt, and the inbassadurs and lordes [and ladies, to a] grett nombur, and my lord marques, and my lord admerall, and my [lord Robert Dudley, and] dyvers mo lordes and knyghtes, and they rod to and fro [to view them, and] to sett the ij batelles in a-ray; and after cam trumpeters bluwing [on] boyth partes, and the drumes and fluttes; and iij ansettes[e] in evere bat[elle]; so thay marchyd forward, and so the gunes shott and the mores-pykes [en]contered to-gether with gratt larum, and after reculyd bake [again]; after the towne army lost ther pykes and ther gunes and bylle . . rely, and contenent[f] they wher sturyd with a-larum; and so evere man toke to ther weypons agayne; by and by the trumpetes and the drumes and gones playd, and shott, and so they whent to-gether as fast as they could. Al thys wyll the Quen('s) grace and the inbasadurs and the lordes and lades be-held the skymychsyng;[g] and after they reculyd bake agayn; and after master chamburlayn and dyvers of the commenars[h] and the wyffelers cam to the Quen, and ther the Quen('s) grace thankyd them hartely, and all the cette;[i] and contenent[k] ther was the grettest

---

[a] sent.   [b] whifflers.   [c] drink.   [d] soldiers.
[e] onsets.   [f] incontinently.   [g] skirmishing.   [h] commons (of the city).
                   [i] city.   [k] incontinently.

showtt that ever was hard, and hurlyng up of capes,[a] that her grace was so mere,[b] for ther was a-buyff[c] lyk M pepull besyd the men that mustered; and after ther was runyng at the tyltt, and after evere [man] home to London and odur plasses.

The iij day of July was cared to be bered unto (*blank*) on master Sadler, latt altherman and draper, and the chyrche hangyd with blake, and with ys armes, and a sarmon, and a iij dosen of skochyons.

The iij day of July (the) Quene('s) grace toke her barge at Grenwyche unto Wolwyche to her nuw shype, and ther yt was namyd Elesabeth Jon[as,] and after here grace had a goodly bankett, and ther was grett shutyng[d] of gunes and castyng of fyre a-bowt mad[e] for plesur.

The v day of July was deposyd of ther byshopeprykes the archebyshope of Yorke doctur Heth, and the bysshope of Ely docthur Thurlbe, at my lord treysorer('s) plasse at Frers Augustyne.

The vij day of July, was sant Thomas of Cantebere day, my good lord of Wynchastur doctur Whytt came owt of the Towre, with the leyftenantt ser Edward Warner, by vj in mornyng, and so to my lord keper of the brod selle, and from thens unto master Whyt, John,[f] altherman, and ther he lys.

[The x day of July was set up in Greenwich park a goodly] bankett[ing-house made with fir] powlles, and deckyd with byrche and all maner [of flowers] of the feld and gardennes, as roses, gelevors,[g] [lavender, marygolds,] and all maner of strowhyng erbes[h] and flowrs. [There were also] tentes for kechens and for all offesers agaynst [the morrow,] with wyne, alle, and bere.

The xj day of July ther was mad a plasse [for the queen's] pensyoners to rune with-owt[i] a tyltt with spayrers.[k] [There were three] chalengers, my lord of Urmon,[l] and ser John Paratt, and master [North], and ther wher (*blank*) deffenders boyth with spares[m] and sw[ords.] Abowt v of the cloke at after-non the Quen('s) grace

---

[a] caps.　　[b] merry.　　[c] above.　　[d] shooting.　　[e] made.　　[f] Thomas?
[g] gilliflowers.　　[h] herbs used for strewing chambers.　　[i] *So in MS.*
[k] spears.　　[l] Ormond.　　[m] spears.

[came,] and the inbassadurs, and dyver lordes and lades stode [over the] gatt for to se; and after thay rane one chassy[ng the other], and after the Quen('s) grace cam down in-to the parke [and] toke her horse, and rod up to the bankett howse, [with] the inbassadurs and the lordes and lades, and so to soper [and] a maske, and after a grett bankett, and after grett castyng [of fire] and shutyng of gunes tyll xij at nyght.

The xij day of June *(sic)* the frers of Grenwyche whent away.

The xiij [a] day of July whent the frers blake in Smythfeld went a-way.

The iiij day of July, the Thursday, the presters and nuns of Syon whent a-way, and the Charter-howsse.

The abbott of Westmynster and the monkes was reprevyd. [b]

The xx day of July kyng Phelype was mared [c] unto the Frenche kyng('s) dowthur, and grett justes mad ther, and the Frenche kyng dyd just, and ther he had on of ys ees stryken owtt with a spyld [d] of a spayre, that he ded of the stroke, by one *(blank)*.

.   .   .   .   .   .

The xvj day dyd pryche at Powlles crosse *(blank)*

The xviij day of July the vesetars [e] satt at the [bishop] of London palles.

The xvij day of July the Quen('s) grace removyd from Grenwyche of her prograsse unto Darford in Kent; so the next day removyd unto Cobham, my lord Cobham('s) plasse, and ther her grace had grett chere.

The xx day of July the good old the bysshope of D[urham [f]] cam rydyng to London with iij[xx] hors, and so to Sowth[wark] unto master Dolman('s) howsse, a talowchandler, and ther he lys aganst the chene gatte. [g]

The *(blank)* day of July a haburdassher, dwellyng a-ganst sant John('s) hed at Ludgatt, dyd kyll hym-seylff.

The sam day a mayd dwellyng in Colmanstrett dyd cutt her

---

[a] *The MS. indistinct; perhaps* xvj.   [b] *The writer probably meant* deprived.
[c] married.   [d] splinter.   [e] visitors.   [f] Cuthbert Tunstall.   [g] chain gate.

thrott a-pesse,[a] and after she lepyd in-to a welle and drownyd yr seyllff.

The xxv day of July, was sant James day, the warden of Wynchaster and odur docturs and prestes wher delevered owt of the towre, and masselsay,[b] and odur.

The sam nyght was the Mersers' super, and ther supyd my lord mare and my lord treysorer and dyvers of the consell and dyvers althermen, and ther was chossen the shreyff for the quen master Logee,[c] altherman and groser, for the yere to cume and nowe.

The xxvj day of July cam tydynges in-to London the yonge Frenche kyng has proclamyd ym-seyllff kyng of Skottland and England and Franse and (*unfinished*)   .   .   .   .

.   .   .   .

and the morow a grett dener   .   .   .   chylderyn of the hospetalle, and a-for and after   .   .   unyalles, and ther was a goodly compene of .   .   .   .   .

The xxviij day of July cam home [sir Thomas Chamber] from Whytchyrche and be-syd Wynchaster at nyght [parson of the Trinity at] Quen-heyff,[d] and agaynst the Blake Bull [he met] a yonge man servand unto the woman that owr [parson] delt nowghtly[e] with ys masteres the Fryday a[fore, and the] sayd yonge man haskyd ym[f] why that he dyd or .   .   .   .   . so evyll, and so thay changyd a blow or ij, [and by] chanse ser Thomas Chambur hyt ym on .   . with a botell that he browth[g] from Wy[nchester,] and the sam nyght the parsun was had to the [counter,] and ther lay fryday at nyght, saterday, so[nday, and] monday tyll iiij at after-none, and ther wher serten of the offesers of Brydwell feychyd [him] from the conter in Wodstrett, and so cared hym [to Bride]well a-for master Grafton, master Hakworth, and master Sy[monds, and] mony mo masturs of Brydwell, and ther was .   .   . and dyvers men of Trenete parryche and women; and he sayd that he wold not tare[h] longe, and desyred them to gett

---

[a] *i. e.* slightly.   [b] Marshalsea.   [c] Lodge.   [d] Queenhithe.
[e] naughtily.   [f] asked him.   [g] brought.   [h] tarry.

a-nodur prest to serff ys turne, for he wold nott tarre, for he wold gett a-nodur serves as sune as he cold gette, but or he whent h .   .

The v day of August the Quen('s) grace removyd from Eltham unto Non-shyche, my lord of Arundell('s), and ther her grace had as gret cher evere [a] nyght, and bankettes ; but the sonday at nyght my lord of Arundell('s) howse [b] mad her a grett bankett at ys cost, the wyche kyng Henry the viij byldyd, [c] as ever was sene, for soper, bankett, and maske, with drumes and flutes, and all the mysyke that cold be, tyll mydnyght ; and as for chere has nott bene sene nor hard.   [On monday] the Quen('s) grace stod at her standyng [in the further park,] and ther was corse [d] after ; and at nyght the Quen .   .   .   . and a play of the chylderyn of Powlles and ther master Se[bastian], master Phelypes, and master Haywod, and after a grett bankett as [ever was s[ene, with drumes and flutes, and the goodly banketts [of dishes] costely as ever was sene and gyldyd, tyll iij in mornyng ; and ther was skallyng [e] of yonge lordes and knyghtes of the .   .   .   .   .

My lord of Arundell gayffe to the Quen('s) grace a cubard of platt.

The x day of August, the wyche was sant Laurans day, the Quen('s) grace removyd from Non-shyche unto Hamtun cowrte.

The sam day was browth [f] to the Towre Sthrangwys, the rover of the see, and serten odur.

The xj day of August the vesetars [g] satt at Powlles, master docthur Horne, and master (blank) and master (blank), apon master Harpfeld, and master Harpfeld [h] and dyvers odur.

The xiij day of August dyd pryche at Powlles crosse the bysshope of Harford, Skore. [i]

The xiiij day of August landyd at the Bryghowsse a iiij[xx] rovers and mareners that was taken with Strangwys, and send [k] unto the masselsay [l] and to the kynges bynche, and ther trumpeter, and as sone as thay cold make hast put on fetters on ther leges for ther offensys.

[a] every.	[b] i. e. the officers of his household.	[c] i. e. the house.
[d] a course.	[e] qu ?	[f] brought.	[g] visitors.
[h] So in MS.	[i] John Scory.	[k] sent.	[l] Marshalsea.

pesse over chargyd at master Hyksun . . . . . and one of
ys servand dyd fyre yt that was . . . and yt hytt brust in
pesses, and on pesse yt . . . and smott on of ys leg a-way
by the . . . smott a pesse of the calff of ys lege a-way . . .
of the pesse fluw over Temes a-pon the . . and in dyvers
plases.

The xv day of August the Quen('s) grace returned from Hamtun cowrte unto (. . .) my lord [admiral's] place; and ther
her[a] had grett cher, for my lord [admiral] byldyd a goodly bankett-
howsse for her grace; [it was] gyldyd rychely and pentyd, for he
kept a gret [many] of penters[b] a grett wylle in the contrey.

The xx day of August, was sonday, ther was sarmon at Powlles
crosse; ys name was (blank); and ther was a menester dyd pe-
nans for the marehyng[c] of a sertenn cupulle that was mared a-fore
tyme.

The xxj day of August dyd the veseturs[d] sat at sant Brydes,
doctur Horne and ij more, for ij churche-wardens and ij more
wher sworne to bryng a truw envetore[e] of the chyrche.

The xxij day of August the vesaturs sat at sant Larens in the
Jure, docthur Horne and mo veseturs.

The xxiij day of August the veseturs sat at santt Myghell in
Cornell[f] lyke-wysse for the chyrche gudes.[g]

[The xxiiij day of August, the lord] mare and the althermen
and the [sheriffs? w]her at the wrastelyng at Clarke-in-w[ell,
and it was the] fayre day of thynges kept in Smyth-feld, [being]
sant Bathellmuw (day), and the same day my lord [mayor]
came home thrugh Chepe, and a-gaynst Yrmonger [lane] and
a-gaynst sant Thomas of Acurs ij gret [bonfires] of rodes[h] and of
Mares and Johns and odur emages, ther thay wher bornyd with
gret wondur.

The xxvij day of August ther was a tentt sett up at Fynsbere

<hr>

[a] So in MS.   [b] painters.   [c] marrying.   [d] visitors.   [e] inventory.
[f] Cornhill.   [g] goods.   [h] roods.

for my lord mare and the enbassadurs and the masters the althermen, and mony commenars, and ther was the shutyng of the standard for the best gune, and dyvers odur dyd shut [a] for odur games, after the wyche was . . to be wrastelyng—Bathellmuw day and iij sondays after.

The xxix day of August was the Marchand-tayller(s') fest, for thay had a xxx bukes,[b] be-syd al odur mettes.[c]

The xxx day of August was bered, in sant Thomas apostylle, captayn Matsun, with xx clarkes syngyng, and armes a-bowtt hym, and bered in the qwyre.

The sam tym afterward was bered in the body of the chyrche master Allen, nuw electyd bysshope of Rochaster, with a fuw clarkes syngyng, and ther dyd pryche for hym master Huntyngtun the prycher—the wyche he had a wyf and viij chylderyn.

The xx .. day of August ded at Non-shyche ser Thomas Carden knyght, devyser of all bankettes and bankett-howses, and the master of reyvelles [d] and serjant of the tenttes.

The tyme afor Bathellmuwtyd and after was all the rodes [e] and Mares (and) John, and mony odur of the chyrche gudes,[f] bowth[g] copes, crosses, sensors,[h] alter-clothes, rod clothes, bokes,[i] baners, bokes, and baner-stays, waynskott, with myche odur gayre,[j] abowt, London   .   .   .   .

.   .   .   . [and the xxv day of August, at saint Botulph's] with-owt Bysshyope-gatt the rod, Mare and John [patron of that] chyrche, and bokes [k]; and ther was a felow within the chyrche [wall] mad a sermon at the bornyng of the chyrche goodes . . . thruw in serten bokes in-to the fyre, and ther thay [took away the] crosse of wod that stod in the chyrche-yerde, of master . . . cost, a tawhear [l] of skynnes.

The iij day of September dyd pryche at Powlles on Makebray, a Skott.

The v day of September was bered at [Bletchingley] ser Thomas

[a] shoot.	[b] bucks.	[c] meats.	[d] revels.	[e] roods.	[f] goods.
[g] both.	[h] censers.	[i] books.	[j] gear.	[k] books.	[l] tawer.

Karden knyght, with a standard and . . . . of armes and a cot of armes, a helmet, targat, ... with the mantylls and crest, and a iij dosen of skochyons of armes, the wyche he had mony goodly offeses in . . . . .

The sam day at non [a] was shytt a thornderyng [b] [as] was never hard a-for the tyme, for with a clap at Alalowes in Bred strett yt kyld a water span[iel] at the chyrche syde, and fellyd a man on of the bedman[c] of the Salters, ys nam ys Hare[d] *(blank)*, and sexten of the sam chyrche, and more-over yt crakyd the stepull a-boyfe the batelment all of stone, that sum of (it) fluw owtt in pesses, that mony pepull resortyd theder to se that marvels thrugh-owt London. I pray God help! Thys was done be(tween) xij and on[e] the v day of September. At myd-day at non at Tottenam-he[f]-crosse was ij

. . . .

The vj day of September the nuwe bysshope of London and dyver odur *(unfinished)*

The xvj day of September was (the) rod[g] and Mare and John and sant Mangnus bornyd at the corner of Fystreet, and other thynges.

[The v day of September was a frame set up for the French king deceased, in] Powlles qwyre, of ix storys, and [with a] valens of sarsenetes and blake fyne fryng, [and pensils, and] rond a-bowt the hers a pesse of welvett; [all the] viij pellers and all the quer hangyd with blake and [arms; and] the herse garnyshed with xxx dosen penselles and xv dosen [of arms].

The viij day of September at after-none [was] the obseque of Henry the Frenche kyng, the herse garnyshed with grett skochyons of armes bosted [h] with grett crownes, and all under ther fett [i] with blake, and a grett palle of cloth of gold, and ys helmett and mantyll of cloth of gold and cott armur, targett and sworde, and crest, and angy[d[k] all] the quer with blake and armes, and my lord tresorer the cheyff [mourner], and next my lord chamburlen,

---

[a] noon. [b] such a thundering. [c] beadmen. [d] Harry. [e] one.
[f] high. [g] rood. [h] *Probably* embossed *with needlework, the scocheons usually being painted only.* [i] Under the mourners' feet. [k] hanged.

my lord of Burgany, my lord of Hunsdon, and my lord Cobam, my lord Dacurs of the Sowth, and my lord Pallett, ser Recherd Sakefeld,[a] and ser Edward Warner, and mony mo morners all in blake; and contenent [b] songe durge, and a xiiij haroldes of armes in ther cott armur afor the lordes, and after to the bysshope('s) palles to drynke.

The ix day (of September) a-fore none thay cam to the chyrche from the byshope palles, the haroldes a-for them, master Garter, master Clarenshux, master Norrey, master Somersett, master Chaster, master Rechmond, master Yorke, master Wyndsor, master Lanckostur, and Ruge-crosse, Ruge-dragon, Bluw-mantyll, Perkullys, and ther thay had serves; my lord of Canturbere the meny[ster?], the bysshope Harford, Skore,[c] dyd pryche, and the bysshope Barlow, thes iij had blake gownes and grett hodes lynyd with sylke, and drestes' capes; [d] and after all done to (the bishop's) plasse to dener, for ther was offesers of the quen('s) howsse, of evere offes[e] sum, for ther was grett chere.

The vj day of September was bered in sant Edmondes in Lumberdstrett on master Day, the cheyffe chaffer of wax unto my lord chanseler of England.

. . . .

. . . master . . . . a xxiiij clarkes syngyng to the chyrche; [the mourners] ser Wylliam Chastur, draper and altherman, and master *(blank)* and master *(blank)* serjant of the coyffe, and master Berre draper [with] odur in blake to the nomber of xl gownes . . . he gayffe to xij men and xij women xxiiij gownes . . . dyd pryche bysshop Barlow; all the chyrche and the [street] was hangyd with blake with armes; and master Clarenshux sett them in order, and the morrow after a grett . . . with iij dosen of skochyons and d' [f] of bokeram.

The x day of September dyd pryche at Powlles [cross] Torner, and ther was my lord mayre and the [aldermen], and grett audyens of pepull boyth of the cowrt, [city, and country.]

[a] Sackville.   [b] incontinently.   [c] Scory.   [d] caps.   [e] office.   [f] a half.

The xij day of September was bered at sant Martens [at] the welles with ij bokettes* *(blank)* a barber-surgan, with clarkes syngyng and a lx chylderyn, xxx boys and xxx wemen[-children], and evere chyld had ij d. a pesse.

The xv day of September ther was a car-man that cared wod unto serten men, and he sold sum by the way, and when that he cam to tell the bellets he told them that he wold a savyd[b] the nombur of the belettes, but he was spyed, and so the bellets was told over agane, and so he was cared to the contur tyll fryday the market day, and then he was fechyd owt and sett on hors-bake, ys fasse to the hors taylle, with ij belettes a-for hym and ij behynd ys (back) rond abowtt London (to) ys dwellyng.

The sam day was the Frenche kyng('s) herse taken downe at Powlles by the haroldes, and so they had al thyng that was a-bowt yt, boyth cloth, velvet, banars, skochyons of armes, and penselles, and sarsenet, and tymber that mad the raylles of viij-sqware, and the baner stayffes.

The *(blank)* day of September was a fyre in Holborn by neclygens, and bornyd *(unfinished)*

[The xvij day of September did preach at Paul's cross master Veron a new] prycher, and ther was my lord mare and . . grett audyense, and ther he sayd, Wher ar the bysshopes [and] old prechers? now they hyd ther hedes.

The xix day of September was bered in . . Laurans lane one mastores Longe wedow, with . . dosen of skochyons, and prestes and clarkes, and mony [mourners] in blake, and a sermon.

The sam day was bered in sant Fosters on Oswold See, goldsmyth, with a dosen of skochyons of armes, and prestes and clarkes syngyng.

The xx day of September was bered at sant Katheryn crechyrche ser John Raynford knyght, of Essex, with ij haroldes of armes, and a standard, pennon of armes, and a cott armur, targett, sword,

---

* St. Martin Outwich was formerly thus distinguished : see again, p. 215.

[b] that he would have saved, *i. e.* so that he might save.

helmet, mantylls, and the crest; and a v dosen of skochyons of armes; and all the cowrt hangyd with blake and armes; and the qwer hangyd and the raylles with blake and armes; and parson Veron dyd pryche, and after the haroldes tok the mornars, and thay whent and offered ys helmet, and after the cot, and odur morners offered the targett, and after the sword, and after the standard and the pennon of armes; all that wyll[a] the clarkes sang *Te Deum* in Englys, and contenent[b] vj of ys men putt ym in-to the graff; and when all was done all the mornars whent to the plasse to dener, for ther was boyth fles and fysse[c] at the dener, but my lade[d] was shott[e] up all the dener wylle, tyll all was done and the pepull gone; then my lade cam, and she had iiij eges[f] and a dysse[g] of butter to her dener.

The *(blank)* day of September be-gane the nuw mornyng prayer at sant Antholyns in Boge-row, after Geneve fassyon, —be-gyne to rynge at v in the mornyng; men and women all do syng, and boys.

. . . clothworker of London . . master . . . . Harstrang, cloth-worker.

The xxij day of September was raynyd[h] [at Southwark] master Strangwys, the grett roffer[i] of the see, and a . . . marenars and odur men, and cast all to suffer.

The xxx day of September be-gane the mornyng [service] at Powlles at that owr[k] as the postylles masse.

The xxiiij day of September dyd pryche at Powlles crosse *(blank)* Huntyngtun the prycher, and ther was my lord mare and my masters the althermen, and grett [audience] of pepull.

The xxv day of September ded my yonge lade Cobham in Kent, the wyff of lord Cobham, and the [lord] warden of the Synke Porttes in Kentt.

---

[a] while.   [b] incontinently.   [c] flesh and fish.   [d] lady.   [e] shut.   [f] dish.
[g] eggs.   [h] arraigned.   [i] rover.   [k] the same hour.

The xxvij day of September tydynges cam to London that the prynche of Swaythen he was landyd at Harwyche in (Essex).

The xxviij day of September ther was preparyd for the berehyng of yonge lade Cobham, ix baners of sondre armes, and a viij dosen of skochyons of armes, and a x dosen penselles for her herse at Cobham, the wyche was never shyche ᵃ sene with lyke fassyon.

The xxxj day of September the nuw shreyffes of London toke ther barge to Westmynster to take ther howth,ᵇ master Loge and master Marten, althermen, in the cheker, and after home to dener with ther craftes.

.   .   .   .

The ij day of October master Strangwys and v [of his men were] lad from the Towre unto the Masselsay.

The xxx day of September, was Myghelmas day, the [lord] mare was chosen at the yeld-hall, good master Huett, clo[thworker,] the wyche was ther never mare of that ocquwpassyon a-for; ther wher iij (aldermen), but when that ther turne [came] they ded,ᶜ master Towllys and master Hynd and master Machyll, clothworker.

The iij day of October was sett up ij nuw payre of galows, one at sant Thomas of wattrynges, and the thodur at the low-water marke at Wapyng.

The iiij day of October master Strangwys and all ys men shuld have suffered dethe, but ther came tydynges that they shuld stay tyll yt plessed the quen('s) grace and her consell.

The iiij day of October whent to bere ᵈ from Cobbam hall my yonge lade Cobbam, the wyff of my lord Cobbam, latte mad lord Warden of the v portes, with prestes and clarkes syngyng, and ij· haroldes of armes, master Clarenshux and Ruges-Dragon, with ix baners of armes of hys and hers petegree ᵉ; one was a grett baner of ys harmesᶠ and hers ; and mony morners in blake a C., and a lx women in rosett cassokes of brod cloth, be-syd men in mantyll frys-gownes, and the women had nuw raylles; and ther was a

---

ᵃ such.   ᵇ oath.   ᶜ died.   ᵈ to be buried.   ᵉ pedigree.   ᶠ arms.

goodly hers[a] with-owtt wax, and garnyshed with grett baners and
velvett, and xx dosen penselles, and vij dosen skochyons of armes;
and the chyrche and the plasse hangyd with blake and armes,
and a bony . . the velvett a goodly bordur mad and gyldyd,
and with ther armes ; and so the dene of Rochastur and all the
colege both prest and clarke dyd syng, and the qweresters ;
and Torner the precher dyd pryche ; and after all done, they
whent to the plasse to dener, for ther was a gret dener, and ther
was a ij M. pepull that had ij d. apesse, and after dener pore
pepull had boyth mett and drynke ; all thys done in Kent.

The xxviij day of September, was Myghellmas-evyn, was the
old bysshope of Durram doctur Dunstall[b] was deposyd of hys
bysshope-pryke of Durram, be-cause he shuld not reseyff the
rentes for that quarter.

.   .   .   .

[The] v day of October cam to [London by Ald]gatt the
prynse of Sweythen,[c] and [so to Leadenhall], and done[d] Gracyous-strett corner in a howse stod [the lord] marques of
Northamtun and my lord Ambros Dudley [and other gentlemen
and] lades ; and my lord of Oxford browth[e] (him) from Col-
[chester] and my lord Robart Dudley, the master of the quen('s)
horse ; and trumpettes bloyng in dyvers places ; and thay had [a
great] nombur of gentyllmen ryd with cheynes a-for them, and after
them a ij C. of yomen rydyng, and so rydyng over the bryge unto
the bysshope of Wynchastur('s) plasse, for [it] was rychely hangyd
with ryche cloth of arres,[f] wrought with gold and sylver and sylke,
and ther he remanyth.

The viij day of October dyd pryche with-in the [queen's]
chapell at Whyt-hall parson Veron, the Frenche[-man], and he
leyd thynges that the nuw bysshopes electyd [should] have landes
as the old byshopes had, or elles [they] wher not abull[g] to mantayne
and kepe good howse.

[a] hearse.   [b] Cuthbert Tunstall.   [c] Sweden.   [d] down.   [e] brought.   [f] arras.
[g] able.

The x day of October was bered Bluw-mantyll the harold,[a] the wyche latt was Rysbanke, in sant Brydes in Fletstrett, with *(unfinished)*

The ix day of October was master Row altherman('s) dowthur mared in santt Martens with well with ij bokettes,[b] to a marchand, and ther wher mony worshype-full men and women ther; and ther was a sermon, and after to ys plasse to dener; and he gayff ij C. payre of glovys, and at nyght ther cam ij goodly maskes as has bene.

The xij day of October whent by water unto the court the kyng of Sweythen('s) sune, and ys gard, and ther he was honorabull[c] reseyvyd with mony honorabull men at the hall-dore, wher the gard stod in ther ryche cottes, unto the quen('s) chambur, and ther he was reseyvyd of the Quen('s) grace, and after he had grett chere as cold be had.

The xiij day of October at nyght ded [d] the good lade the contes of Ruttland at Halewell,[e] sum-tyme yt was a nunre,[f] that ser Thomas Lovell dyd beld [g] yt for hym.

The xv day of October did pryche [at Paul's] crosse Crolley sum-tyme a prynter.

The xij day of October they be-gane to [erect a] skaffold, to take downe the tope of the stepull, that was brosyd [h] with a thondurbolt with that tem[pest].

The xvj day of October was bered at Wy . . ser Wylliam Fuw-Wylliam [i] knyght, with a standard and pennon of armes, cott armur, targett, sword, helmett and a iiij dosen of skochyons, with a harold of armes, that was master Clareshux, kyng of armes; [and] grett mon mad [k] for ym, for he kept a [good] howse for the pore.

The xix day of October the prynche of Swaythen whent to the court agayn, for my lord Robart [Dudley gave] ym a grett bankett.

The xx day of October they begane to make a herse for my lade

---

[a] John Hollingworth.   [b] *See before, p.* 211.   [c] honourably.   [d] died.
[e] Halywell, near Shoreditch.   [f] nunnery.   [g] build.   [h] bruised.
[i] Fitz-William.   [k] moan made.

the contes of Rutland at Sordyche; yt was garnysshed with armes and penselles, and all the chyrche hangyd with blake and armes.

The xxj day of October was cared from Halewell unto Sordyche chyrche my lade the contes of Rutland, with xxx clarkes and prestes syngyng, and mony pore men and powre women in blake gownes a lx and mo, morners to the nomber of a C. and ij haroldes of armes, master Garter and master Yorke; then cam the corsse; a-for a grett baner of armes, and a-bowt her iiij goodly baner-rolles of dyvers armes; and master Beycon mad the sermon; and after a grett dolle of money, ij d. a-pesse[a]; and so to dener, and yt was wryten a-bowt the valans *Sic transit gloria mundi*, and ther was vj dosen penselles and vj dosen skochyons.

. . . .

The xxiij day of October [the visitors sat at saint Paul's, when] master Harpfeld the archedecon of London . . . . was deposyd, and dyvers prebendarys and vecurs.

The xxv day of October was proclamyd in the . . . and Westmynster of aperell of all kyndes, and the morow in London.

The xxvij day of October was cristened at sant Benettes at Powlles warff ser Thomas Chamburlayn['s son]; and the chyrche hangyd with cloth of arres, the godfathers names the prynche of Swaynthen one and my lord Robart Dudley, and the godmoder was my lade of Northamtun; after the cristenyng waffers, spys-bred, comfettes, and dyver odur bankettes, dysses[b], and epocras and muskadyll [in great] plente; the lade was the wyff of master Machyll, altherman and clothworker.

The iiij day of November was a prest mared[c] with a prest('s) wedow of Ware in Hardforshyre at sant Botulfe with-owt Bys-shopegatt; and ther was one West, a nuw doctur, and he raylyd of the rod-loft, and that whe owght to helpe them that fled for the word of God, and to gyff them a lyffyng.

The v day of November ther was grett justes at the quen('s) palles[d], and ther was my lord Robartt Dudley and my lord of

[a] apiece.   [b] dishes.   [c] married.   [d] palace.

Hunsdon wher [a] the chalengers, and all they wher [a] (in) skarffes of whyt and blake, boyth haroldes and trumpeters; and deffenders my lord Ambros [b] with odur; and the haroldes and trumpeters and the fotmen with skarffes of red and yelow sarsenett.

The vj day was bered in sant Androsse in Holborn master Mortun sqwyre, with a harold of armes, a penon of armes, and a cott armur, with a dosen of skochyons.

The vij day of November was bered in Westmynster abbay master Recherd Knevett sqwyre, with a dosen skochyons.

[The viij day of November was buried in Kent] ser Robartt Sowthwell knyght, sum-tyme master of the rolles, with a harold of armes, and a standard, a penon of armes, a cot armur, a target, a elmett, and a viij dosen skochyons of armes.

The ix day of November was a hers mad for my lord Wylliam of Tame, and the chyrche and the [place] hangyd with blake and armes and a x dosen penselles.

The xv day of November was bered at Tame my lord Wylliam of Tame, with a iij harold of armes, master Clarenshux, master Chester, and Ruge-dragon, with a standard, a grett baner of armes, and viij baner-rolles of armes, and a xij dosen skochyons, and a C. morners, and a lx gownes for pore men, and grett dolle of money, and after a grett dener.

The v day (of) Dessember was bered in Westmynster abbay my lade Frances the wyff of Hare [c] duke of Suffolke, with a gret baner of armes and viij banar-rolles, and a hersse and a viij dosen penselles, and a viij dosen skockyons, and ij haroldes of armes, master Garter and master Clarenshux, and mony morners.

The vj day of Dessember was bered in sant Dennys parryche in Fanchyrche stret, the chyrche and the qwyre hangyd with blake and armes, and the plasse and the strett, ser Thomas Cortes [d] knyght and latt mare of London, and Fysmonger and Puterer; ther was iij haroldes of armes, and ther had my lord

---

[a] were.   [b] Lord Ambrose Dudley.   [c] Harry.   [d] Curteis.

mare and the sword-bayrer and dyvers althermen had blake, and
the residuw in vyolett; and ther was a C. in blake gownes and
cottes; and he had a standard and a v penon of armes, and a x
dosen skochyons; and ther dyd pryche master Recherdson the
Skott; and after to the plasse, and the mare and the althermen to
dener, for ther was a grett dener, and pore men in gownes and the
clarkes of London syngyng; a grett denner for all men that wold
come.

[The xij day of November preached at Paul's cross] Coverdall
the (*unfinished*)

The xix day of November dyd pryche at P[aul's cross] master
Bentun.[a]

The xix day of November was bered at Lambeth the old byshope of Durram doctur Donstalle,[b] sum-tyme byshope of London,
with *(unfinished)*

The xxiij day of November was bered in sant [Olave's] in
Hart strett master Watsun the quen('s) marchand.

The sam day was bered in sant Sythe parryche John Lyons'
sune and here, with armes, and xij pore [men] had xij nuw gownes,
and they bare xij gret stayffe torchys bornyng, and ther was a
sarmon.

The xxvj day of November dyd pryche at Pow[l's cross] master
Juell, byshope of Salysbere, and ther was my lord mare and the
althermen and mony of the courte, and ther was grett audyense
as (has ever) bene at Powlles crosse.

The xx day of November was bered master (*blank*) sqwyre
with a penon and a cott armur and a dosen of skochyons.

The furst day of Desember was raynyd at the Yeld-hall master
Grymston captayn.

The sam day was ij men of the contre was sett on the pelere for
pergure,[c] a-for non.

The sam day was a woman ryd a-bowt London on horse-bake
a-bowt London with a paper on her hed for (*blank*)

[a] Bentham.   [b] Cuthbert Tunstall.   [c] perjury.

The ij day of Desember was a penon and a cot-armur ᵃ for master Brune sqwyre in the contre.

. . . .

. . mared . . . . Holle marchand unto . . . the dowthur of master James Suttun sqwyre (who) ded ᵇ [clerk of the] grencloth by keng Henre the viij. and kyng Edward the vj. [and] quen Mare('s) days; and they gayff a C. payre of glovys, and ther was a grett dener and soper, and next day went h[ome.]

The viij day of Desember, was the day of the Conseption of owre Lade, was a grett fyre at the Gorge in Bredstret; yt begane at vj of the cloke at nyght, and dyd grett h[arm] to dyvers howses.

The xj day of Desember was bered in Warwyke-shyre ser Foke Gryffylle ᶜ knyght; and he had a herse of wax and penselles, and with armes; and he had a harold of armes, and a standard and a pennon of armes, and a cott armur, and a helmett, targett, and sword, mantylles of velvett, and a vj dosen skochyons; and mony morners; and pore men had gownes; and a grette dolle; and after a grett dener, for the ryche and pore; and the best howse-keper in that contre.

The ix day of Desember was a proclamassyon mad for folles ᶜ and capuns and conys and gesse and all maner (of) fulles ᵈ and the pryse; and eges, with odur thynges.

The xiij day of Desember in the mornyng was by mysefortune in sant Dunstones in est a nold ᵉ man on ᶠ master Cottelle a talow-chandler, he fell downe in a trape dore and pechyd hys hed a-pone a pesse of tymbur, and brust owtt ys braynes, for he was beldyng, so the trape dore was left opyn.

The sam day cam serten fellous unto the Gorge in Bredstret, wher the fyre was, and gatt in-to the howse, and brake up a chest of a clothear, and toke owtt xl lb. and after cryd *fyre, fyre,* so that ther cam ij C. pepull; and so they toke one.

The xvj day of Desember was the sam man bered in sant Don-

ᵃ *Side note* mad(e).   ᵇ died.   ᶜ Fulke Greville.   ᵈ fowls.   ᵉ an old.   ᶠ one.

stones in the est, master Cottell, that was slayne with (the) falle, and he had a sarmon, and all ys compene in ther clothyng, and a grett dener, for ther was mad mon[a] for hym, and a dolle.

. . . .

Park]er electyd byshope of Canturbere.

The xvij day of Desember was the nuw byshope of [Canterbury,] doctur Parker, was mad[b] ther at Lambeth.

The xviij day of Desember dyd a woman ryd a-pone [horseback] with a paper on her hed, for bawdere, with a basen ryngyng.

The xij day tydans cam to London that ther was marchandes and shypes lost, boyth Englys and Frenche, and many good masters of shypes, and mony good marenars, and odur shypes in dyvers plasses that wher lost.

The xix day of Desember was slayne with-owt the weste dore of Powlles on master Wynborne gentyllman (of) Suffoke, by Wylliam North and ys man, he dwellyng at sant Ane chyrche-yerd, with a foyne slayne.

The xx day of Desember a-for non, was sant Thomas evyn, my lord of Canturbere whent to Bow chyrche and ther wher v nuw byshopes mad.[b]

The sam day was raynyd at the Yeld-hall master Hodylston and master Chamburlayn, captayn of the castyll in Calles, and cast boyth to suffer deth.

The sam day dyd ryd in a cart a-bowt Lundun the wyff of Hare Glyn,[c] gold-smyth, for behyng bowd to her owne dowther.

The xxix day of December was bered at sant Martens at Ludgatt Luste Strange[d] sqwyre, with the clarkes syngyng, and he had a harod of armes, master Somerset, with a pennon and a cott armur, and a vj skochyons, and a sermon.

The xxxj in the mornyng and the last ded[e] my lade Darce the wyff of ser Arthur Darce knyght, dwellyng in the nwe abbay on the Towre-hylle.

[a] made moan.   [b] made.   [c] Harry.   [d] Le Strange.   [e] died.

. . in Sowth-warke unto sant Towlys[a] in Sowthw[ark to be] bered my lade Copley wedow, with **xx** grett stayffe torchys bornyng, with prestes and clarkes syngyng, with a harold of armes, and a pennon of armes, and mony morners; and the chyrche hangyd with blake, and the quer; and ther was a sermon, and communyon; and after to her plasse to dener and a dolle . . . of skochyons.

The sam day at nyght at the quen('s) court ther was a play a-for her grace, the wyche the plaers plad shuche matter that they wher commondyd to leyff off, and contenent[b] the maske cam in dansyng.

The furst day of January the prynche of Swaythen rod to the cowrt gorgyusle and rychele, and in gard in velvet jerkyns and holbardes in ther handes, and mony gentyll-men gorgyosly with chenes of gold.

The iij day of January was cared from Knyghtryder-stret unto Jhesus chapell under Powlles with prestes and clarkes syngyng my good lade Shandos wedow, with ij harolds of armes, with v baners of armes of her hosbandes and hers and of her petegre, and iiij dosen skochyons, and the chyrche wher hangyd with blake and armes; and a sermon; and after to her plasse to dener.

The iiij day of January was bered in sant Donstons in the west latt byshope of Carlell doctur Hobbellthorpe,[c] with alff a dosen skochyons of armes.

The *(blank)* day was bered doctur (Bayne),[d] late byshope of Lychfeld and Coventre, in sant Donstons in the west.

The v day of January ryd a-bowt London iiij women for baudere, dwellyng (*unfinished*)

The sam day was a gentyll-man a-restyd for dett, and ther was dyvers gentyll-men and servyng-men, master Cobam and odur, and toke ym from the offesers, and cared im to the Rose taverne;

---

[a] St. Olave's.   [b] incontinently.   [c] Owen Oglethorpe.   [d] Ralph Bayne.

and ther was a grett fray, that boyth the shreyffes wher fayne to cum, and so they cam to the Rose taverne, and toke all the gentyll-men and ther servandes, and cared them to the conture.[a]

[The vj day of January, being Twelfth day, in the afternoon] my lord mare and the althermen, and all the [crafts,] and the bachelers of the mare('s) cumpene, whent to [saint Paul's] after the old custum, and dyd pryche *(blank)*

The sam nyght was sett up a skaffold for the play [in the] halle,[b] and after play was done ther was a goodly maske, and after a grett bankett that last tyll mydnyght.

The viij day of January was bered at sant Botulf with-owt Algatt my lade Darce, the wyff of ser Arthur Darce knyght; and so the chyrche and the quer wher hangyd with blake and armes, and so browth[c] to the chyrche with xxx [priests] and clarkes syngyng, and ther was ij haroldes of armes, master Clarenshux and master Somersett in ther ryche cottes; [then] cam the mornars, in gownes and cottes; then came . . . that bare a pennon of armes, and the corse, with a ryche palle; there was a C. in blake, and xxiiij men and women pore had gownes; and master Juell byshope of Salysbere dyd pryche; and the(re) was a communyon; and all the morners offered; and after a grett dolle of money; and, all done, to the plasse to dener, for ther was a grett dener, and there were[d] vij dosen of skochyons of armes.

The sam day of January dyd pryche at Powlles crosse the nuw byshope of London, master Gryndalle.

The ix day of January was sessyons in the Old Bayle, keft[e] for one Wylliam North and ys man for the kyllyng of on master Wynborne with-owt the west dore of Powlles, be-syd master Harpfeld('s) howse, and ther they wher cast by the xij men to be hangyd in Powlles chyrche-yerd by that plasse wher he was kyllyd.

The x day of January in the mornyng was a nuwe payre of galows sett up with-owtt the west dore of Powlles, and be-twyne

---

[a] Counter.   [b] *Probably the* hall of the lord mayor's company.   [c] brought.
    [d] *In MS.* way.   [e] kept.

ix and x of the cloke a-for none wher Wylliam North and ys man browth ^a thether by the ij shreyffes, and ther hangyd boyth tyll iiij at after-non; and so the hangman cutt them downe, and cared (them) in-to sant Gregore chyrche-yerd, and ther was a grayff ^b mad, and so they wher strypyd of all, and tumbelyd nakyd in-to the grayff, in the corner of the est syd of the chyrche-yerde.

. . . .
. . . . . abowt a xij of the [clock] . . . . gentyll-man with-in the Whyt frers . . .

The xij day of January was cared from the Whyt frers master Recherd Chetwod sqwyre, with prest and clarkes, and with a penon of armes and a cott armur, and master Somersett, harold of armes, bare ys cot-armur; and a xx morners in gownes and cottes; and a ij dosen skochyons of armes. Master Benton mad the sermon; and after to ys plasse to dener; ther was a grett dener; and vj pore men had good blake [gowns]; and a dolle.

The sam day was sessyons at Nuwgatt, and ther . . . wher cast xij, and vj was bornyd in ther hand, and the . . . . was iij cared to Tyburne, and ther hangyd, and on rep[rieved].

The sam nyght was a fray be-twyn ij of the Swaythen^c; on kyllyd, a gentyll-man of ys owne contrey.

The xij day of January ded ^d good master docthur Whyt, latt byshope of Wynchestur, in Hamshyre, at ser Thomas Whytes plasse, the wyche ded of a aguw; and he gayff myche to ys servandes.

The xix day of January dyd ryd in a care on Laugh, a brown baker, for fornycasyon, dyver tymes provyd.

The sam day was a man sett on the pelere ^e in Sowthwarke, for he toke cartes for the quen, and was no taker, but toke a pesse of money, and lett them goo to dyvers men, sum ij s., xx d., xij d., and vj d., so yt was knowne.

The xx day of January the sam man was set on the pelere in Chepe-syde for the sam offens.

^a brought.   ^b grave.   ^c Swedes.   ^d died.   ^e pillory.

The xv day of January was cared to be bered [a] master doctor Whyt, late byshope of Wynchester, unto Wynchester, and bered ther.

The xxj day of January by ix of the cloke my lord mare [b] and the althermen whent by water to the cowrt in skarlett, and ther he was mad knyght by the quen.

. . . .

The xxiij day of January . . . . unto Westmynster, and ther they wher cast . . .

The xxvij day of January was cared from [Black] frers unto sant Martens at Ludgatt to be bered my lade Harper, by her furst hosband ser Gorge H[arper knyght,] and the wyff of master Carlton, with a pennon of armes, and ij dosen and a d' [c] of of skochyons of armes, and re . . mad in the chyrche and hangyd with blake and armes; and haroldes of armes, master Clarenshux and master Somersett, [and] mony morners in blake; the cheyff morner was . . .

The sam day cam rydyng to London, and so [entered] at Ludgatt, the good yerle of Shreusbery, with a C. [men] rydyng, and so to Cold Harber to ys owne plasse.

The xxv day of January wher mad at Powlles by the nuw byshope of London lx prestes, menysters, and decons, and more.

The xxx day of January was bered in sant Margettes-moyses master Busse skynner, on of the masturs of the hospetall, [d] and ther was all the masturs of the hospetall with gren stayffes in ther handes, and all the masters of ys compene in ther leverey, and a xx clarkes syngyng; and he gayff a xij mantyll frys gownes, vj men and vj women; and ther dyd pryche master Juell the nuw byshope of Salysbere, and ther he sayd playnly that ther was no purgatore; and after to ys howse to dener, and ther was a xvj morners in blake gownes and cottes.

. . . .

[a] buried.   [b] William Hewit.   [c] half.   [d] i. e. Christ's Hospital.

The xxx day of January the vecontt Montacute and ser Thomas Chamburlayn knyght toke theyr journey toward the kyng of Spayne.

The ij day of Feybruary ther was taken [at the] Frenche inbasadur's plasse, the dene of Powlles,[a] was candyllmas day, ther was a masse sayd, and ther was dyvers men and women taken [up,] and browth [b] to my lord mayre, and sum to the conter.

The sam day at after-non my lord mare and the althermen, and all the craftes, whent to Powlles after old maner, and ther was a sermon by the (*blank*).

The iiij day of Feybruary was bered in sant Mare Wolnars [c] in Lumbard-strett master (*blank*) with ij dosen skochyons of armes.

The sam tyme besyd Pye corner a man dyd hang ym-seylff.

The ix day of Feybruary at after-none, a-bowtt iij of the cloke, wher v men wher hangyd at sant Thomas of watherynges; one was captayn Jenkes and (*blank*) Ward and (*blank*) Walles and (*blank*) Beymont and a-nodur man, and they wher browth [d] up in ware [e] all ther lyffes,—for a grett roberre done.

The xv day of Feybruary was cared from Flett-strett unto sant Alphes at Crepull-gatt to be bered master Francis Wyllyams, the brodur sune [f] to my lord of Tame.

.   .   .   .

cheyffe ere to my lord of Tame, with . . . . armes and a cott armur and a harold master Rychmond, and mony morners in blake, and a xij gentyllmen . . . . and a xx clarkes syngyng, and master Veron dyd pryche a sermon.

The xxiij day of Feybruary was cared from (Black) frers over the water to Parys garden, and ther was a hors-lytter rede to care [g] her to Blechyng-led [h], [my] lade Carden, the wyff of ser Thomas Carden, to be bered.

The xxviij day of Feybruary, was Aswedensday, at . . . in Turnagayn-lane in sant Pulkers paryche a lame [woman] with a kneyff kyllyd a proper man.

---

[a] *i. e.* the ambassador was lodged at the Deanery.   [b] brought.   [c] Woolnoth.
[d] brought.   [e] war.   [f] brother's son.   [g] ready to carry.   [h] Blechingley.

The **xxix** of Feybruary was bered in sant Martens parryche the wyff of master (*blank*) Cage sarter,[a] and he gayff **xx** . . . gownes and **xij** mantyll frys gownes unto **xij** pore women, and **xij** clarkes syngyng; and master Pylkyngton dyd pryche, the nuw byshope of Wynchastur,[b] and after a dolle of money, a j d. a-pesse.

The **xx** day of Feybruary dyd pryche at Powlles crosse master Nowell; and ther was a man dyd pennans for he would have a-nodur wyffe, the wyche he had on afore.

The furst day of Marche was a proclamasyon by the quen('s) grace and the consell that no man nor woman, nor they that kepys tabulles, shuld ett no flese in lentt nor odur tyme in the yere that ys commondyd[c] by the chyrche, nor no bucher kyll no flese, but that they should pay a grett fyne, or elles vj ours[d] on the pelere,[e] and in-presoment **x** days.

. . . .

. . and after taken downe and cared . . . . knyght marshall('s) servandes unto the nuw pet . . . . . Cornhylle and ther a serten tyme. . .

The **iij** day of Marche, abowtt vij of the [clock] in the mornyng, cam in a servyngman with a [horse-load] of flesse of dyver kyndes, and ther yt was st[ayed] and after cared[f] the horse and yt to my lord mare (by) the porter of Byshope-gatt, and lett hym goo.

The sam day dyd pryche at Powlles crosse the nuwe byshope of London master Gryndall, in ys rochet and chyminer; and after sermon done the pepull dyd syng; and ther was my lord mayre and the althermen, and ther was grett audyence.

The sam day at after-non dyd pryche at the curte[g] the byshope Skore,[h] in ys rochett and chyminer, and ther was grett audyens, and after (*unfinished*)

The **vj** of Marche dyd pryche at the court doctur Byll dene of Westmynster that day in the quen('s) chapell, the crosse and ij candylles bornyng and the tabulles standyng auter-wyse.

[a] salter?   [b] *Read* Durham.   [c] *i. e.* forbidden.   [d] hours.
[e] pillory.   [f] carried.   [g] court.   [h] Scory.

The sam day at after-none was sessyons at Nuwgatt, and ther was raynyd [a] the lame woman that kyllyd the yonge man in Turn-agayne lane and a dosen more, and the lame woman cast.

The viij day of Marche dyd ryd in a cart abowtt Londun a bocher and a bocher('s) wyff, that [b] was here servand, and the wyche was her hosband('s) brodur.

The sam day of Marche [rode to hanging] xj; vij wer men, and iiij women; on woman the sam woman that kyllyd the man in Turnagayne lane; and on man was a gentyllman; and a-nodur [a priest,] for cuttyng of a purse of iij s. but he was [burnt] in the hand afore, or elles ys boke [c] would have [saved] hym,—a man of liiij yere old.

The viij day of Marche dyd pryche at the cowrt, afor non, master Pylkyngtun the nuw byshope of Wynchaster, [d] and ys matter whent myche to ma[intaining] Oxford and Cam-bryge skullors, [e] and the byshopes and [clergy] to have better levyng. [f]

The x day of Marche dyd pryche at Powlles the byshope Skorre, [g] and ther was my lord mare and the althermen, and grett audyence, and he prechyd in ys rochett and ys chymber.

The xj day of Marche dyd pryche at the court doctur Sandes byshope of Wosseter.

The xij day of Marche was bered at Dyttun my lade Barkeley, the wyff of ser Mores Barthelay knyght, with a penon of armes and a iiij dosen of skochyons, and a harold of armes, master Rychemond.

The tuwsday the xij day of Marche was slayne in Powlles chyrche-yerd on master Bodeley a gentyll-man of the Tempull by on of master Alcokes servands, wher he supyd the sam nyght, at the constabulle('s) howse of sant Martens the Sanctuarij.

The xiij day of Marche dyd pryche at the cowrt master (*blank*)

---

[a] arraigned.   [b] *i. e.* the man.   [c] *i. e.* the benefit of clergy. See Mr. Thoms's Anecdotes and Traditions, pp. 1, 119.   [d] *Read* Durham.   [e] scholars.   [f] living, *i. e.* income.   [g] Scory.

[The xv day preached at court] master (*blank*) the wyche he mad a nottabull sermon that the quen('s) grace gayff hym th[anks] for hys payne, butt sum men wher offendyd.

The xvj day of Marche whentt to berehyng [from the] Bell in Cartter lane on master Bodeley, a gentylman of the Tempull that was slane in Powlles cherche-yerd by on of Alkokes servands, and ther fechyd hym a C. ge[ntlemen] and odur to bryng hym to the Tempull, and xx clarkes syngyng, and after bered.

The xvij day of Marche dyd pryche at Powlles cross Veron, parsun of sant Marttens att Ludgatt, and ther was my lord mare and the masters the althermen, with mony more pepull; and after the sermon done they songe all, old and yong, a salme in myter,[a] the tune of Genevay ways.

The sam day at after-non dyd pryche at the cowrt [at] the prychyng plasse master Juell the nuw byshope of Salysbere, in ys rochett and chymmer.

The xix day of Marche at santt Martens at Ludgatt all the belles of the chyrch dyd ryng a grett pelle,[b] and after done all the pepull dyd syng the tune of Geneway, and with the base of the organes, for ther he[c] was myttyd parsun, and he mad a sermon that tyme.

The xiiij day (of) Marche was cared from London, when they were examynyd be-for the consell, for a grett robere by one Duncombe gentyllman and ys companyons by them commytted; and (received by) master Autre shreyff of Bedford-shyre; and then he and ys sayd fellous wher hangyd, wher the sad[d] master Duncombe myght se thow[e] or iij lordshyps whyche shuld have bene his yf his behavyor had bene good; and ther they were hangyd all.

The xxij day of Marche dyd ryd in a care, with a basen tynglyng a-for, ij that rode a-bowt London that cam owtt of Sowthwarke, for the woman was bowd to a gyrle of xj yere olde, and browth[f] her to a stranger.

---

[a] metre.   [b] peal.   [c] Apparently Veron.   [d] said.   [e] two.   [f] brought.

The xx day of Marche was the nuw byshope of Lychfeld and Coventre ys wyff was a broght to bed, ys nam master Bentun,[a] on London bryges at the sygne of (*blank*)

[The xxij day of March preached at court the same master Bentham,] byshope of Lychfeld and Coventre.

The xxiiij day of Marche, was mydlentt sonday, dyd pryche at Powlles [doctor] Sandes the nuw byshope of Wosseter, and ther was m[y lord mayor] and the althermen, and he prychyd in ys rochett [and chiminer,] and ther was my lord the erle of Bedford, and dyvers g[entlemen] and grett audyens of pepull.

The xxiiij day of Marche, was mydlent sonday, master Barlow byshope of sant Davys dyd pryche at the cowrtt, but the quen was not at yt; butt ther was mony pepull; and he was in ys rochett and ys chymmer, and at v of the cloke yt ended; and contenentt[b] her chapell whent to evy[ning song,] and ther the crosse stood on the auter, and ij candylstykes and ij tapurs bornyng, and after done a goodly anteme song.

The xxvij day of Marche was proclamasyon [at the] cowrt and at the crosse in Chepe and at the strett tyme . . Lumbard street in dyvers plasses, of the Frenche [king] and the Skottys quen, boyth in Englyus and Frenche, with [a] trumpett blohyng, and a harold of armes, master Clarenshux, in ryche cotte, with a serjant of armes with a grett masse,[c] and the ij shreyffe(s) all on hors-bake.

The sam day dyd pryche at the cowrt master Wysdom.

The xxviiij day Marche cam by water at afternone unto Somersett plasse the duke of Vanholtt.[d]

The xxix day of Marche dyd ryd in a cartt ij women.

The xxxj day of Marche dyd pryche at Polles crosse Crolley, the wyche was Passyon sonday, sum tyme a [exile, and a learned writer, afterwards minister of St. Giles, Cripplegate.[e]]

---

[a] Bentham,   [b] incontinently.   [c] mace.
        [d] Holstein.   [e] *Strype.*

[The ij day of April, Alley, bishop elect of Exeter, preached at court,] aganst blasfemy, dysse,[a] and women, and drunkenes.

The (v) day of Aprell dyd pryche at the courtt master Chenney, that was Fryday afor Palm sonday.

The vij day of Aprell, the wyche was Palm sonday, dyd pryche at Powlles crosse master Wysdom.

The sam day dyd pryche at the court my lord the byshope of Canturbere,[b] and made a nobull sermon.

The x day of Aprell cam from sant Mare spytyll the Quen (of the May ?) wyth a (*blank*) M. men in harnes, boyth queners [c] in shurth [d] of malle and cosselet and mores pykes and a x gret pesses, cared thrugh London unto the court, with drumes and fluttes and trumpetes, and ij mores dansyng, in the cartt wher ij quyke bers,[e] and London fond a *(unfinished)*

The xj day of Aprell toke ys jorney from the byshope of Wyn-chastur('s) plasse the duke of Swaynland,[f] the wyche he kept the nobulle howse that ever dyd stranger in England for cher, for he spent more and gayff grett gyftes and reywardes as a . . .

The xj day of Aprell the Quen('s) grace kept her monde [g] in her halle at the cowrt at afternon, and her grace gayff unto xx women so many gownes, and on woman had her best gowne, and ther her grace dyd wosse ther fett, [h] and with a nuw whyt cupe her grace dronke unto evere woman, and they had the cupe, and so her grace dyd leyke-wyse unto all, and evere woman had in money (*blank*). [The same afternoon she gave unto pore men, wo]men, and chylderyn, both holle [i] and lame, in sant James('s) parke ij d. a-pese, a [thousand people and upwards.]

The xiij day my lord mare mad a proclamassyon that all maner of wyld fulle [k] and capons and conys and odur thynges and set a pryse of all kyndes of pultere [l] ware, and a penalte for the bryk-yng.

---

[a] dice.   [b] Matthew Parker.   [c] queeners, *attendants on the* queen.
[d] shirts.   [e] live bears.   [f] Swedeland, or Sweden.   [g] Maundy.
[h] wash their feet.   [i] whole.   [k] fowl.   [l] poultry.

The xv day of Aprell dyd pryche at sant Mare spyttyl with-owt Byshope-gatt master Bentun.[a]

The xvj day of Aprell was bered in the parryche of sant Myghell in Quen-heyff master John Bedy . . sqwyre latt clarke of the gren cloth unto quen [Mary ?] with the compene of the Clarkes of London, and then cam the morners, and then the corse, with vj skochyons with ys armes a-pone hym, and master Beycun [b] mad the sermon, and after to ys plasse to dener, for ther was a grett [dinner].

The sam day dyd pryche at sant Mare spyttyll master Colle.

The sam nyght be-twyn vij and viij of the cloke yt lythenyd and thundered and after raynyd vare[c] sore as has bene.

The xvij day of Aprell dyd pryche at sant Mare spytyll master Juelle.

The xvj day of Aprell at viij of the cloke at nyght ther was a kyng cam from the dene of Rochester from super, and gohyng to ys logyng, and he had ij knyghtes that dyd wheyt[d] on ym, and ther was shyche lythnenyng and thunderyng that yt thruw down on of ys knyghtes to the grond, and lykyd a bornyd the dodur,[e] and on of (his) servand(s) was so freyd[f] that ys here[g] stod up, and yt wyll never come downe synes.

.   .   .   .

bishop of Lond]un docthur Boner, with *(unfinished)*

The xxj day of Aprell dyd pryche at the Powlles [cross] master Samsun, and ther was my lord mare and all the althermen, and ther he concludyd[h] the iij sermons that was at the [cross] ; ther was grett audyense as has bene sene ther.

The sam day at after-non was grett justes at the curtt, and at the tylt, and ther rod the trumpeters blohyng (in) skraff(s)[i] of whyt and blake sarsanett, and master Clarenshus, Norrey, Somer-sett, and Lankaster, and Rychemond, and Yorke, and Ruge-

---

[a] Bentham.   [b] Becon.   [c] very.   [d] wait.   [e] other.
[f] affrayed, i. e. frightened.   [g] hair.   [h] i. e. recapitulated. This was termed the Rehearsal Sermon.   [i] scarfs.

dragon, and evere of them havyng a skarff a-bowt ther ne[cks, of] whyt and blake sarsenett, and ther rane of the *(unfinished)*

The xxiij day of Aprell, was sant Gorge day, the Quen('s) grace and the knyghtes of the Garter whent a prossessyon with all her chapell in copes of cloth of gold, a xxviij copes, and the Quen and all the knyghtes wore ther robes, rownd a-bowt the hall to the cowrt-y[ard,] and all the haroldes of armes in ther cottes of armes.

The xxiiij day of Aprell was bered good mastores Malere,[a] the wyffe of master Malore altherman and latt shreyff of London, the wyche she ded in chyld-bed of xvij chyldern, and bered with-in sant Thomas of Acurs; the wyche she gayff [to the] pore *(blank)* gownes, and ther was the clarkes syngyng; master *(blank)* dyd pryche; and mony mornars, and gret mone mad[b] for her.

The xxiv day of Aprell was bered at sant Magd[alene's] master Hansley a grocer, and he had a dossen of skochyons of armes, and ther was the masturs of the compene of the Grocers, and prestes and clarkes syngyng, and master Juelle the byshope of Saylbere[c] dyd pryche, and he gayff *(blank)* gownes unto pore men; and ther was at ys berehyng all the masters of (the) hospetalle with ther gren stayffes in ther handes.

. . . . [the Queen with the lord R]usselle whent downe unto Depford . . . . . . shype and her nuw galley, and dynyd in the s[hip] and ther my lord admerall mad her grett ch[eer, and] after wher serten brygendar[d] wher red[e] with [furniture of] ware;[f] and ther wher iiij lytyll pennys[g] de . . . . . . hordenanse, and gayff grett sawtt[h] unto the breg[antine] and shott grett ordenanse and fowth[i] were ser . . . . . . all maner of artelere, and ther youe shuld [have] sene men sthrone[k] in-to the water, and horlyng stones and mores pykes; and ther was grett fythe[l] be-twyne the bryg-

---

[a] Mallory.   [b] moan made.   [c] Salisbury.   [d] brigantine.   [e] ready.
[f] war.   [g] pinnace.   [h] assault.   [i] fought.   [k] thrown.   [l] fight.

dendar [and the] pennys, and as grett shutyng as cold be; ther wher a-boyff iiij thowsand of pepull [on the water] and the land.

The xxviij day of (April) dyd pryche at the [Paul's] crosse master Coverdalle, and ther was my lord mare and the althermen, and ther was grett audyense.

The sam day at after-none att the court was grett justes, my lord of Sussex and my lord Robartt Dudley and ij more a-gaynst the yerle of Northumberland and my lord Ambrose Dudley and my lord of Hunsdon and master Cornewalles and (*blank*): and ther was mony stayffes broken; and ther stod in the standyng as juges my lord markes of Northamtun, my lord of Ruttland, and my lord of Penbroke, and my lord admerall and the Frenche in-bassadur, and master Garter and master Norey dyd wrytt wome [a] dyd rune; and by chanse of the brykyng of a stayff a pesse fluw up wher the juges sitt and hyt my lord of Penbroke (*blank*) and ther rod the trumpeters and the haroldes of armes.

The xxix day of Aprell whent to hangyng ix men and one woman to Tyburne.

The xxx day of Aprell was bered in sant Gregore chyrche in Powlles chyrche-yerd master Payne skynner, and gayff armes, and ther was the masturs of compene of the Skynners in ther (livery,) he had a sermon, and the clarkes . . . .

. . . .

The . . . day of May was a . . . . . knyghtes of the Garter for soper, and the next . . . . and soper with all maner kyndes of fysse [and flesh,] boyth venesun and all maner of folle [b] [of all] kyndes and by (*blank*) cloke [c] was send [d] a com[mand] that they shuld come away, boyth . . . knyghtes and all here servandes of all offeses, [and] brynge as myche as cold be savyd; the [same] nyght was browth [e] unto Westmynster, the quen . . . for sant Gorge('s) fest that shuld have bene at W[indsor] as the old costume has bene.

[a] who.   [b] fowl.   [c] clock.   [d] sent.   [e] brought.

The sam nyght cam the Quen('s) grace came from Westmynster in her barge, and dyvers odur barges, with drumes and fluttes
and trumpettes blohyng, and odur musyke, downe on London
syd, and over the water to the thodur syd, and so up and downe
to the cowrt with *(unfinished)*

The v day of May dyd pryche at Powlles crosse master Mollens
archedeyken of London, and he mad a goodly sermon, and ther
was my lord mare and the althermen, and grett audyense was ther.

The xij day of May was kept the fest of sant Gorge at Wyndsore, with serten knyghtes of the Garter a-poyntted ther for the
fest.

The xiij day of May was bered mastores Palmer, the wyff of
(*blank*) Palmer vyntoner dwellyng at the sant . . . hed at Ludgatt, and he gayff in gownes and cottes a x . . . and at her
berehyng was the cumpene of the Vyntoners in ther leverey, and
Veron dyd pryche at her berehyng.

The sam day was serten qwynners[a] taken and browht[b] a-for the
consell, and from thens cared to the Towre.

The xiiij day of May was the sam men cared to Westmynster
hall how they shuld do theyre, and ther they wher cast and cared
to the masselsay.

The xiiij day of May ded   .   .   .   .   .   .

The xiij day of May ded ser Marmeduke Constabull . . . .
in the contey of . . . .

The xiiij day of May the Quen('s) grace removyd from Westmynster by water unto Grenwyche, and as her grace was gohyng
by water not so farre as . . . , cam by water to her grace
master Henry Perse[c] owt of F[rance,] with serten tydynges.

The xviij day of May ther was sent to the shypes men from
evere hall in whyt cottes and red crosses, and gones[d] to the quen('s)
shypes.

The xix day of May dyd pryche at Powlles [cross] my lord

<hr />

   [a] coiners.   [b] brought.   [c] Percy.   [d] guns.

byshope of Ele, docthur Kókes,[a] sum-tyme dene of Westmynster, and ther was browth[b] hym word that one had fond a (blank) of money, and any man cold or cane tell what money yt was, lett cum, and they shall have yt.

The xx day of May was send to the Towre master Fecknam, docthur Wattsun latt byshope of Lynkolne, and docthur Colle latt dene of Powlles, and docthur Chadsay; and at nyght abowtt viij of the cloke was send to the Flett docthur Score, and master Fecknam the last abbot of Westmynster, to Towre.

The sam day was bered mastores Russell wedow in sant Mathuw parryche, and she gayff a xx gownes and cottes of blake, and a xij gownes to xij women, and they gayff unto master Parre a blake gowne and a tepytt[c] that mad the sermon; and ther was the compene of the Clarkes syngyng, and after a grett dener.

The xxij day of May was a mayd sett on the pelere[d] for gyffyn[e] her mastores and her howse-hold poysun, and her ere cutt, and bornyd in the brow.

The xxiiij day of May the sam mayd was set on the pelere[f] the sam mayd, and after had her thodur ere[g] cut for the sam offens.

.   .   .   .

The   .   .   day of May [was buried mistress Allen the] wyff of master Wylliam Allen altherman and lethers[eller; and] she ded in chyld-bed, and ther wher mony morners in blake, and the masters of the hospetalle with ther gren stayffes; and he gayff to pore women (blank) gownes   .   .   .   when the compeny of ys craftes and the compene of [the Clerks,] and after to ys plase, and ther spyse-bred and wyne.

The xxvj day of May dyd pryche at Powlles crosse [master] Skambeler, my lord of Canturbere('s) chapelen, and ther was my lord mayre and my masters the althermen, and a grett audyense.

The xxvij day of May was the obseque and fen[eral] of master docthur Wende, fessyssyon[h] at Cambryge, a penon of armes and a

[a] Cox.   [b] brought.   [c] tippet.   [d] pillory.   [e] giving.   [f] pillory.
[g] other ear.   [h] physician.

cott armur, and vj dosen and d'[a] of skochyons of armes, and a
harold of armes master Somersett, and . . morners in blake,
and he gayff mony gownes to pore men, and ther was a grett dolle,
and thether resortyd xx m[iles] off vC. pepull and had grett plente
of mett and drynke, boyth hosses[b] and barnes and feldes, grett store
as has bene [seen] for a men[c] gentyllman, and gret mone mad.[d]

The sam day was the Clarkes' dener, and they had evynsong
over-nyght at Yeld-hall colege, and the morow a communion, and
after to the Carpynters' hall to dener.

The sam day was bered mastores Grafton at Criste-chyche, the
wyff of master Grafton the cheyff master of the hospetall, and of
Brydwell; and sche had a ij dosen and a half skochyons of armes,
and ys plase and all the cowrt to the grett gatt next the strett was
hangyd with blake and armes, and mony morners in blake, and he
gayff unto powre (unfinished)

Item in gaune[e] wyke callyd Rogasyon weke they whent a prosessyon with baners in dyvers plases, boyth in Bockynghamshyre
and in Cornwall in dyvers plases, and in dyvers plases they had
good chere after.

.   .   .   .

The xxviij day of May ther was a m[aid] sett on the pelere[f]
for the sam of-fense [of poisoning,] and bornyd in the brow.

The xxix day of May toke ther gorney[g] into Skotteland master
Syssell[h] secretore and master docthur Wattun[i] my (unfinished).

The xxx day of May was the ij maydes [set] on the pelere,[j] one
for the ruwmor rane that she was ded because she fell in a swone
the iij .   .   .

The furst day in mornyng of June ded master [Hussey] sqwyre,
and a grett marchand of the Muskovea and odur plases, and a-ganst
ys bereall was mad pennons of armes and a cott armur, and a vj
dosen of skochyons of armes.

---

[a] half.   [b] houses.   [c] mean, *i. e.* of the middle rank.   [d] moan made.
[e] gang, *i. e.* perambulation.   [f] pillory.   [g] journey.   [h] Cecill.
[i] Wotton.   [j] pillory.

The ij day of June my lord the byshope of London mad a goodly sermon a-boyff in Powlles.[a]

The iij day of June at nyght whent to the Towre my old lord the byshope of Ely, doctur Thurlbe.

The v day of June was bered master Husse sqwyre, and a grett marchand-ventorer and of Muskovea and haburdassher, and with a C. mornars of men and vomen; hand[b] he had v pennons of armes, and a cotte armur, and ij haroldes of armes master Clarenshux and master Somersett; and ther was Powlles qwyre and the clarkes of London, and bered at sant Martens at Ludgatt by ys sun[c]; and all the cherche hangyd and ys plasse with blake and armes, and a vj dosen and d'[d] of skochyons of armes; and master Alley the reder[e] of Powlles prychyd boyth days; ser Wylliam Garrett, ser Wylliam Chester, master Loge the shreyf, master Argalle, master Bulle, and master Husse (his) sune, and dyver odur mornars, and after to the plasse to dener, a godly plasse.

.   .   .   .
.   .   .   . Barwyke by captayn .   .   .   . mantyll frys jerkens all gunners.

The x day of June was the master of the compene of Skyners fest, and ther mony worshepfull men wher [at] dener, for ther was a worshepfull dener, and ther was chosen the master of felowshipe master Flecher, and master warden[s chosen] master Clarenshux[f] and iij mo, and afterward they wher [brought] home by the leverey; and master Clarenshux mad a grett bankett for the masters and ys compene, furst spyse-bred, cheres[g], straberes, pepyns, and marmelade, and sukett, comfets, and portynggalles[h] and dyvers odur dyssys[i], epocras, rennys[k] [wyn], clarett wyn, and bere and alle grett plente; and all was welcome.

The sam day was the masters the Grosers, and ther dynyd my

---

lord mare and dyvers althermen and the shreyffes and [many] worshepfull men and dades[a] and gentyllmen and gentyll-women; ther was a nobull dener as has bene ther.

The sam day was had to the Towre the (arch-)byshope of (York) docthur Heth, latt chanseler of Engeland by quen Mare('s) days, and part by quen Elesabeth('s) days.

The sam (day) was cared to the Flett docthur Colle[b] latt dene of Powlles.

The xij day of June dyd ryd in (a) care[c] a-bowtt London ij men and iij women; one man was for he was the bowd, and to brynge women unto strangers, and on woman was the wyff of the Bell in Gracyous-strett, and a-nodur the wyff of the Bull-hed be-syd London stone, and boyth wher bawdes and hores, and the thodur man and the woman wher brodur and syster, and wher taken nakyd together.

The sam day at after-non toke hys horse toward Walles,[d] with a vij-skore horse, ser Henry Sydney to be the lord presidentt ther of Walles, as my lord of Tame was; the quen and the consell gayff yt hym to be governer ther.

. . . .

The . . day of . . . . browth women unto strangers.

The xviij day of June was sent to the Towre secr[etary] Boxhalle unto quen Mare, and doctur Borne latt byshope of Bayth, and docthur Trobullfeld[e] latt byshope of Excetur.

The xxiij day of June was had to the contur docthur Frere, and the next day was delevered hom.

The xx day of June was the fenerall of ser Marmaduke Constabull knyght, with ys standard and ys cott armur and ys pennon of armes, and with skochyons [of] ys armes and hers.[f]

The xxiiij day of June, was Mydsomer day, sant John the baptyste, was Marchand-tayllers' fest, and ther was grett chere, and the

---

[a] *Read* ladies.   [b] Cole.   [c] car.   [d] Wales.   [e] Turberville.
[f] *i. e.* his wife's.

nuw master was chosen master Manearlin, and master warden master Rosse, and the ij. warden master Meryk; and ij renters master Duckyngtun and master Sparke.

The xxviij day of June dyd ryd in a care[a] abowt London mastores Warner, sum-tyme the wyff of master Warner sum-tyme serjantt of the ammerallte, for baudre to her doythur and mayd, and both the doythur and the mayd with chyld, and she a hore.

The sam day was bered[b] at Maydston in Kentt master Hearenden **qwyre, with xij skochyons of armes.

The xxvij day of June the penters[c] whent in hand with the yerle of Huntyngtun('s) berehyng.

.   .   .   .

The . . day of July be-twyn . . . in the mornyng with-in Crokyd lane ther . . by a gone[d] or ij, an(d) ther they shott a pese [which burst] in pesys by mysfortune yt thruw that ho . . . a v howses and a goodly chyrche goyn . . . . . yt laft never a glasse wyndow holle and . . . . goodly chyrche as any chyrche in London, ... a grett pesse of the on syd downe and t . . viij men and on mayd slayne and hurtt dyvers . . and a-nodur dede[e] with-in a senett[f] after.

The xiiij day of July was bered the nob[le] erle of Hunting(don) knyght of the garter, with a st[andard] and mony morners, and then cam ys grett baner of [arms], and then cam mo morners, and then cam iij har[olds of arms] in ther cott armurs, on bare the helme and the [crest] and the mantylles, and a-nodur cared the targett with the g[arter] and the sword, and a-nodur ys cott armur, and then [came] the cors with viij goodly grett banar-rolles a-b[out] hym; and then mony mornars; and the chyrche and the [place] and the strett hangyd with blake and armes; and ther was a goodly hers,[g] and garnyshed with grett skochyons of armes, and a grett mageste[h] of taffata and the valans gyldyd, and a-pone hym a nuw pall of blake velvett, and iij haroldes, master Garter, master Clarenshux, and (*blank*)

[a] car. [b] buried. [c] painters. [d] gun. [e] died. [f] seven-night. [g] hearse. [h] majesty.

The xiiij day of July was mared[a] in sant Ma[ry] Wolnars in Lumbard strett iij dowthers of master Atkynson the skrevener in ther here[b] and goodly pastes[c] with chenes and perle and stones; and they whent to the chyrche all iij on after a-nodur with iij goodly cupes garnysshes with lases gilt and goodly flowrs and rosmare,[d] commyng home after to hys howse, for ther was a grett denner, for all the iij dowthers dynyd in ys howse to-gether.

.   .   .   .

The . . day of July . . . . master Loves mercer; he gayff to . . . . ther was the clothyng of ys compene . . . . blake gownes and the compene of the Clarkes sy[ngi]ng, [and there preached] master Alley the byshope of Exseter, and a goodly sermon.

The xxij day of July was a proclamacion by the mare[e] that no man shuld have no gone-powder in ther howses nor sellers,[f] and that men shuld take hed[g] for pyche and tere[h] and flax and wax, or elles hyre sum plase nere the townes endes.

The xxiij day of July was bered my good lade [Chester,] the wyff of ser Wylliam Chester knyght and draper and altherman and marchand of the stapull, and the howse and the cherche and the strette hangyd with blake and armes, and she gayff to xx pore women good rossett gownes, and he gayff unto iiij althermen blake gownes and odur men gownes and cottes to the nombur of a C. and to women gownes . . . and ther was ij harold(s) of armes; and then cam the corse and iiij morners beyryng of iiij pennon of armes abowtt, and cam morners a-for and after, and the clarkes syngyng; and master Beycon dyd pryche over nyght; and the morow after to the howse to dener; vj dosen of skochyons and a d'[i] of bokeram.

The xxv day of July saint James fayer by Westminster was so great that a man could not have a pygg for mony; and the beare[j] wiffes hadd nother meate nor drinck before iiij of cloke in the same

---

[a] married.   [b] hair.   [c] i. e. head-dresses.   [d] rosemary.   [e] mayor.
[f] cellars.   [g] heed.   [h] tar.   [i] half.   [j] beer.

day. And the chese went very well away for 1*d. q.* the pounde. Besides the great and mighti armie of beggares and bandes that ther were.[a]

The ij yere of the quen Elesabeth was alle the rod-loftes taken done in London, and wrytynges wrytyne in the sam plase.

. . . .

. . . byshope of London at Powlles crosse by the . . sonday. ·

The xxix day of July the Quen('s) grace removyd from Grenwyche on her grace('s) progresse, and at Lambeth she dynyd with my lord of Canturbere and her consell; and after [took her] gorney [b] towhard Rychmond, and her grace lay ther v days; and after to Ottland, and ther So[nday and] Monday dener, and to Suttun to soper.

The furst day of August was Lammas day, and the lord mare and the masters the althermen and the commenars and all the craftes in ther leverey for to chus the shreyff, and ther serten althermen and serten commenars in the elecsyon to be shreyff for London, butt serten men callyd mygg . master Blakwell skrevener to be shreyff, butt after-ward [the more] vowys whent a-pon master Fokes clothworker and altherman was electyd shreyff, for at the mare('s) fest was chosen master altherman Draper and yrmonger was chosen the quen('s) shreyff.

The vij day of August was Suttun bornyd, wher the Quen('s) grase dyd ly iij nyghtes a-for, that was master Westun's plase.

The x day of August was bered within the Towre withowt a offeser of armes, and (with) master Alley the nuw byshope of Excetur, and the chyrch hangyd with blake and armes, my lade Warner, the wyff of ser Edward Warner.

The xij day of August was bered [c] at Powlles master May the nuw dene of Powlles, and my lord of Londun mad the sermon in ys rochett, bered hym.

The xiij day of August was a grett robere [d] done with-in Cle-

---

[a] This entry is in a different hand to the rest of the Diary.

[b] journey.   [c] buried.   [d] robbery.

mentt('s) inn with-owt Tempulle bare, by on master Cutt and iij
mo, and iij of them was taken, on [a] led into Nuwgatt and a-nodur
in Wostrett contur,[b] and a-nodur in the contur in the Pultre.

The . . day [of August] . . . . lygthenyng and
rayn vj owre[s] . . .

The xix day of August my lade Northe [was carried] from
Charter howse toward Cambregshyre . . . with a C. men in
blake rydyng, and master Clarenshus sett them in ordur, and a
grett denur with venesun, wyne, and stronge bere.

The xxj day of August ryd a-bowt London in a care iij for
baudre, a man and ys wyff and a woman the wyff of (*blank*) Brown
dwellyng with-owtt Nuwgatt a talowchandeler.

The xxij day of August was bered in Cambregshyre my lade
North, the wyff of my lord North, with ij haroldes of armes, master
Clarenshus and master Somersett, and mony mornars in blake
gownes; then cam a grett baner of armes borne; and then cam the
corse kevered [c] with a pall of blake welvett and armes, and banars.
borne abowtt the corse; and then cam mony women mornars in
blake; and the plase and the chyrche hangyd with blake and armes,
and after to the plase to dener, for ther was myche a-doo; and
thys was at Cateleg my lord('s) place; and (*blank*) dyd pryche at
the bereall, and was mony pore men and women that had gownes
and met [d] and drynke.

The xxviiij day of August at sant Towlys [e] in Sowthwarke the
menyster (*blank*) Harold dyd cristenyd a chyld with-owtt a godfather, and the mydwyff haskyd hym how he cold do yt, and he
hanswered her and sayd yt was butt a seremony.

The (*blank*) day of August was bered my lade Dudley the wyff of
my lord Robart Dudley the master of the quen('s) horse, with a
grett baner of armes and a vj baners-rolles of armes, and a viij
dosen penselles and viij dosen skochyons, and iiij grett skochyons

---

[a] one.　　[b] Wood-street counter.　　[c] covered.　　[d] meat.　　[e] St. Olave's.

of armes, and iiij haroldes, master Garter, master Clarenshux, master Lanckostur, and *(blank).*

. . . . with ij harolds, master Clarenshux and Ruge-crosse, and a standard and a pennon of armes, a cot armur, helmett, and crest, and mantylles, and sword, and a viij dosen of skochyons of armes and vj of bokeram, and [many] mornars in blake, and ther was grett [dinner and] a dolle of mones [a] as many as cam.

The xx day of September was bered in (Kent) master Recherd Howllett of Sydnam sqwyre, in the parryche of Lussam, [b] with a pennon of armes and a cott armur and a ij dosen of skochyons of armes and a d' [c] of [buckram,] and master West dyd pryche, and after to Sydnam to dener, the wyche was a fyse [d] dener and the godlest dener that has bene in Kentt for all kyndes of fysse [both] fresse and salt, and ther was *(unfinished)*

The xxiij day of September was bered in Sussex ser John Pellam knyght, with a standard and a pennon of armes and a cott armur, elmett, crest, targett, mantylls, and sword, a iiij dosen of skochyons and d' [e], and master Somersett was the harold.

The xxv day of September was bered [f] my lord Montegul, with a herse and a mageste [g] and valans of sarsenett, and iiij grett skochyons of armes, and a vj dosen of skochyons and vj of bokeram, and a standard and a grett baner of armes, and iiij baner-rolles of dyvers armes, and a cott armur, targett and sword, elmett, mantylles, and [crest;] and master Norrey and Ruge-dragon the haroldes, and iiij dosen of . . .

The xxvij day of September was a proclamassyon that the best testons should goo for no more but iiijd. [a piece]; and the testons of the lyone, the flowre de lusse, and the harpe [but] for ij pens *q.*; and a penny iij fardynges; and ob hopene [h] and a fardyng.

The x day of October was mared [i] in the parryche of sant Alphes

---

[a] money. [b] Lewisham. [c] half. [d] fish. [e] half.
[f] buried. [g] majesty. [h] *So in MS.* [i] married.

at Crepullgatt master Wylliam Drure unto lade Wylliams of
Tame, and mared by master Frence on of the masters of Wyndsore, and after gohyng home to dener. the trumpettes blohyng,
and after the flutt and drum, and at the furst corse [a] servyng the
trumpettes blohyng, for ther was a gret dener and gret museke
ther.

> .   .   .   .

The xv day of October was bered [the countess] of Shrowsbere, Frances, in Halumshyre, with [iij heralds] of armes, master
Garter, master Chester, master Lankostur ; .   .   .   . with a standard, a grett baner of armes, [and baner-]rolles of mareges,[b] and
a x dosen penselles, ... skochyons of armes, and a mageste[c]
and valans .   .   . dosen of bokeram skochyons, and a thousand
in .   .   .   .   . and cottes with the pore men and women, and a
grett dolle of money, and of mett and drynke, for all that cam,
and all the prestes and clarkes of .   .   .   . cam, and had boyth
money and mett and drynke.

The xiiij day of November was kyllyd in Powlles chyrche-yerde
a hossear [d] by on Necolles a tayller.

The xxij day of November was bered in sant .   .   .   .   . on
master Bulthered [e] with a pennon of armes and cote [armur, and]
vj skochyons of armes.

The xxiij day of November was bered in s[aint Stephen's] in
Colmanstrett ser John Jermy knyght of Suff[olke be]yonde Ep-
wyche [f] iiij mylles, the wyche was a goo[d man] of the age of
iiij[xx] and ode,[g] the wyche he left iiij sunes [h] and iij dowthers, and
he had a standard and a pennon of armes, and cott armur, elmett,
targett, and sword, and mantyll, and a iij dosen of skochyons and
alff a dosen of bokeram ; and the chyrche was hangyd with blake,
and with armes ; and ther was mony morners ; and gohyng to the
chyrche a mornar beyryng the standard in blake, and anodur a
pennon of armes, and then serten mornars ; then cam master So-

---

[a] course.   [b] marriages, i. e. alliances.   [c] majesty.   [d] hosier.
     [e] Bulstrode?   [f] Ipswich.   [g] odd.   [h] sons.

mersett the harold bere the elme [a] and crest, and after cam master Clarenshux beyryng ys cote armur and the clarke(s) syngyng; and (then) cam the corse with a palle of blake velvett with skochyons on yt, and (then) cam the cheyff morners, and after ys servandes in blake; and master Mollens the archdeacon dyd pryche; and after all done hom to a fleccher('s) howse to dener.

The xxiiij day cam downe from my lord mare that sertten of craftes shuld walke in evere markett, with a whyt rod in ther handes, to loke that men shuld take testons of the ratt [b] as the quen has proclamyd in all markettes thrughe all London, that the markett folke take the money, be-cause the rumore rane that they shuld falle.[c]

. . . master Nuwwell, and *Te Deum* sung . . . .
. . . . . with all the quer.

The xxix day of November ther was a man ryd [in a cart?] for bryngyng of messelle porke to selle.

The xxx day of November ther was iiij men sett on the pelere [d] for purjure, and a-for they wher sett on the pelere at Westmynster.

The last day of November, that was sant Andrews day, was a grett fray at the cowrt be-twyn my lord Robart [Dudley's] men and (*blank*) Harbard('s) [e] men; and that day was no water in [any] condyth[f] in London but in Lothbere.

The xix day of November was electyd the byshope of Wynchester at the cowrt, master Horne late dene of Durram.

The ix day of Desember was bered in sant Andrews undershaft mastores Lusun wedow, the wyff of master Lusun merser and stapoler and late shreyff of London, with a lx in blake gownes, and her plase and the chyrche hangyd with blake and armes, and a xxiiij clarkes syngyng; and she gayff xl gownes to men and women of brod cloth, and evere woman had nuw raylles, and ther

---

[a] helmet.   [b] rate.   [c] fail?
[d] pillory.   [e] Herbert.   [f] conduit.

was a sermon, and a iiij dosen of skochyons of armes; and after a gret dole, and after a grett dener.

The xiiij day (of) Desember was ij men wypyd for cuttyng of pypes of lede, the wyche lettyd[a] that w[e] had no water on sant Androwes day last.

The xv day of Desember was a proclamasyon that no fremen shuld were[b] no clokes in London.

The xxiij day of Desember was bered in sant Lenardes in Foster lane master Trapes gold-smyth; the howse, the stret, and the chyrche hangyd with blake and armes, and gayff mony gownes boyth to men and women. Master Beycun dyd pryche, and powre men had gownes, and a iij dosen skochyons; and after a grett dener.

The xvij day of Desember after mydnyth[c] wher sene in the element open, and as red and flames of fyre over London, and odur plases in reme,[d] and sene of M. men.[e]

.   .   .   .

Elesabeth in the mydes .   .   .   . and armes, and the over hend[f] was .   .   .   ., and he had a standard and a pennon of armes, elmett, targett, and sword, mantylles and crest, and a vj [dozen scocheons] and alffe a dosen of bokeram; and ther was iij haroldes in ther cottes armurs, master Clarenshus, master Somersett .   .   .   .   . and mony mornars in blake, a iiij[xx], and master Skam[bler the] byshope electyd of Peterborow mad the serm[on, and so] in-to the abbey ys plase to dener.

The xx day of Desember was a man .   .   .   . was slayne and browth[g] in-to sant Margaret's Westmynster chyrche-yerde, and ther he was .   .   .   .   . brod, and he was repyd, and ys bowhelles taken owtt, and .   .   .   . the wyche after-ward was knowne that he was slayne in .   .   .   .   .

The x day of Desember cam tydans to the quen('s) grace and to the consell that the Frenche kyng was ded—the yonge kyng.[h]

The **xxix** day of Desember at nyght be-twyn vj and vij of the cloke was slayn on [a] Wylliam Bettes, a master of fense, by one (*blank*) at Warwyke lane corner, and was frust [b] throwth-owt the body.

The **xiij** of Desember was stallyd at Wyndsor the duke of Wanholt,[c] knyght of the nobull order of the gartter, and the good erle of Ruttland was the quen('s) depute at that tyme.

The **xij** day, the wyche was the vj day of January, was bered in sant Benettes at Powlles warff master Antony Hyll, on of the quen('s) gentyllman of (*blank*), and a xvj clarkes syngyng to the chyrche, and to the berehyng.

. . . .
.   .   .   . a]boyffe iiij[xx] of gentyll-women [to . . . . whe]re they had as grett chere as have bene sene, behyng a fysse [d] day; and after ther w . . . . . the cheff men of the parryche and odur, and [they had] a grett dener and grett chere for fysse.

The **xvj** day of January was bered at sant Aus[tin's] Jakobe the husser [e] of Powlles skolle; at ys berehyng wher a xx clarkes syngyng ym to the chyrche, and [there] was a sermon.

The **x** day of January was bered at Cam[berwell] master Skott, justes a pese,[f] a vere good man; and he had [a] ij dosen of sko-chyons of armes.

The **xvij** day of January was bered in sant Peters in Corne-hylle master Flammoke grocer, and he gayff mony gownes of blake, and he gayff to pore men (*blank*); and he was cared to the chyrche with-owt syngyng or clarkes, and at the chyrche a sphalme [g] songe after Genevay, and a sermon, and bered con-tenentt.[h]

The **xxvij** day of January was mared [i] in sant Pancras par-ryche Wylliam Belleffe vyntoner unto with master Malore('s) dougthere, arderman; and ther was a sermon, and after goodly syngyng and playhyng; and ther was dyver althermen at the vedyng [k] in skarlett; and they gayff a C. payre of glovys; and after

---

[a] one.   [b] thrust.   [c] van Holstein.   [d] fish.   [e] usher.
[f] justice of the peace.   [g] psalm.   [h] incontinently.   [i] married.   [k] wedding.

a grett dener, and at nyght soper, and after a maske and mummeres.

The sam day dynyd at master Clarenshux my lord Pagett and ser John Masun and my lade Masun and ser Crystefer Allen and ser Hare[a] Pagett and dyvers gentyllmen.

The xxv day of January toke ys gorney in-to Franse inbassadur to the Frenche kyng the yerle of Bedford, and he had iij dosen of logyng skochyons.[b]

.   .   .   .

The xxvij day of January . . . . a man ys nam . . . . . a puterer . . . . by on (*unfinished*)

The xxix day of January dyd ryd a[bout] London, ys fase toward the horse taylle, ... and sellyng of messelle bacun.

The xxxj day of January the sam man was sett on the pelere[c] and ij grett peses of the m[easly] bacun hangyng over ys hed, and a wrytyng [put] up that a ij yere a-goo he was ponyssed for [the] sam offense for the lyke thyng.

The iij day of Feybruary was master John Whytt altherman('s) sune Thomas was cristened in Lytyll sant Bathelmuw parryche; and ser Thomas Offiley knyght latt mare of London and master Altham altherman late shreyffe of London godfathers, and mastores Champyon (the) altherman('s) wyff godmother; and after to ys plase, and mad good chere.

The ix day of Feybruary dyd pryche at Powlles crosse master Pylkyngtun, electyd byshope of Durram, and ther was my lord mare and the althermen and my lord Robart Dudley and master secretore Sysselle,[d] and dyvers odur of the quen('s) consell; and after to my lord mare to dener.

The xj day of Feybruary was bered in sant Martens at Ludgatt master Daltun of the North sqwyre, and ther was mony mornera in blake gownes, and parson Veron the Frenche man dyd pryche

[a] Harry.
[b] scocheons to leave at the houses in which he lodged by the way.
[c] pillory.   [d] Cecill.

ther, for he was parson ther, and ys menyster; and after was ys cott and pennon of armes and ij dosen of skochyons of armes.

[The   day of February was excommunicated Hethe,] latt chanseler of England and [arch]byshope of Yorke, he lyung in the Towre.

The **xxv** day of Feybruary was excom[municated] at Bowe chyrche doctur Thurlbe late byshope of Ely, and on of the consell unto quen Mare, he lyeng with-in the Towre.

The **xxvij** day of Feybruary mastores Whyt the wyff of master John Whyt altherman and grocer was chyrched, but the menyster wold nott, owt-sept she wold com at vj in the mornyng, and so her mastores fayne to take a menyster to do yt at her plase; and after a grett dener was ther, and mony worshephull lades and althermen wyffes and gentyll women and odur.

The furste day of Marche was bered in sant Fosters parryche on master Bumsted gentyllman, with vj skochyons of armes.

The begynnyng of Lent there was on[a] master Adams dwellyng in Lytyll Estchepe, and ther was a proclamasyon mad that yff any bocher dyd kyll any flesse for [Lent, he should] pey xx*l.* at evere tyme so dohyng; and this man kyllyd iij oxen, and ther was a quest whent on hym, and they cast ym in the fyne to paye the money.

.   .   .   .

The **x** day of Feybruary [was buried?] in Garlykeheyffe master Gybes, on[a] of the mar[shal men?] of London.

The **vij** day of Marche was bered in sant Stephens Colmanstrett master Patensun bruar, and on[a] of the cu[ncil,] and a gentyllman, and with the clothyng of the bruars and of the clarkes, and he had *(unfinished)*

The **xij** day of Feybruary was a chyld [christened] in the parryche of owre Lade[b] of Bowe in Chepe, [the son of] Hare Loke[c] mercer, the sune of ser Wylliam Loke, the wyche had nodur godfather nor godmother hym-seylff.

---

[a] one.   [b] Lady.   [c] Harry Locke.

The iij yere of quen Elezabeth the xviij day of [February] was sant Gorge fest; how all the knyghtes of the garter stod that day in order, the furst

<table>
<tr><td>On the Quen['s side.]</td><td>On the Emperowre('s) syd.</td></tr>
</table>

On the Quen['s side.]	*On the Emperowre('s) syd.*
The Quen('s) grace.	The emperowre Ferna[ndo.]
The kyng Phelype.	The prynse of Pyamont.
The constabulle of France.	The duke Vanholtt.
The yerle of Arundell.	+
The yerle of Darbe.	The markes of Wynchester,
+	tresorer.
The duke of Northfoke.	The yerle of Penbroke.
The lord Pagett.	The lord admerall Clynton.
The yerle of Westmerland.	The maques of Northamtun—
The lord chamburlayn, Haward.	Pare.
The yerle of Shrowsbere	The yerle of Rutland—Rosse.
The lord Montyguw—Browne.	The yerle of Sussex.
The lord Gray of Wyltun.	The lord of Lugborow.
	The lord Robart Dudley.
	The lord of Hunsdon—Care.

. . . . cause he dyd nott justely exp . . . slanderyng of the consell.

The sam day at after-none was a great . . . . playd a-for the Quen('s) grace with all the masters [of fence;] and serten chalengers dyd chalenge all men, whatsumever they be, with mores pyke, longe sword, and . . . . and basterd sword, and sword and bokeler, and sword and dager, [and] crosse staffe, and stayffes, and odur wepons; and the next [day] they playd agayne, and the quen('s) grace gayf serten . . .

The xij day of Feybruary xj men of the north was of a quest; because they gayff a wrong evyde[nce, and] thay ware paper a-pon ther hedes for pergure.

The same day was reynyd[a] in Westmynster hall v men, iij was for buglare,[b] and ij were cuttpurses; and cast to be hangyd at sant Thomas of Wateryng; on was a gentyllman.

The xiij day of Feybruary was a man sett on the pelere,[c] a skryvynor dwellyng in Sowthwarke, and ther was a paper sett over ys hed wrytten for sondrys and practyses of grett falsode and muche on-trowthe, and sett forthe under coller of sowth-sayng, and ys nam was (blank)

The xvij day of Feybruary was wrastelyng at the cowrte in the prychyng-plase a-for the quen.

The xvj day of Feybruary at after-none was bered at Allalowes in Wall master Standley, prest and sthuard[d] unto my lord treyssorer, with xij clarkes syngyng, at after-none; and he gayff myche money to evere on[e] of my lordes servandes; and iiij of my lordes men bare hym; and he had iij dosen skochyons of ys armes.

The sam day at Lambeth was consecratyd nuwe byshopes, master Horne of Wynchastur, and master Skamler byshope of Peterborowe.

.   .   .   .

The xix day of Feybruary dyd pryche a-for the quen master Nevell,[f] the [dean of Saint Paul's,] and he mad a godly sermon, and gret [audience].

The xxj day of Feybruary dyd pryche a-for the quen and the consell master Skamler, the n[ew bishop] of Peterborow, in ys chymner and ys whyt r[ochet.]

The sam day sessyons at Nuwgatt, and [there] was cast xvij men and ij women for to [be hanged.]   .   .   .

The xxij day of Feybruary cam the sum[mons] for to have ther jugement, and so (blank) [were] bornyd in ther hand at the place of jugement.

The xxiiij day of Feybruary whent to hang xviij men and ij

* arraigned.   b burglary.   c pillory.   d priest and steward.   e every one.
f Nowell.

women, and serten ware browth* to be bered in serten parryches in London; the barbur-surgens had on of them to be a notheme᷎ at ther halle in *(blank)*.

The sam day was bered in sant Peters parryche in Cornehyll mastores Gowth,ᶜ latt the wyffe of master Laycroft, armorer, dwel-lyng in the sam parryche, the wyche he gayff for her in gownes to men and women that wher poreᵈ *(unfinished)*

The **xxvj** day of Feybruary dyd pryche at the cowrt master Samsun a-for the quen.

The **xxviij** day of Feybruary dyd pryche at the cowrt master Pylkyngtun electyd pyshope of Durram a-for the quen('s) grace, and made a godly sermon, and grett audyens.

. . . .

. . the Marsalsay to be caredᵉ into the co[untry . . .] men that was cast in Westmynster hall for robere done the last day of terme.

The **iiij** day of Marche was a tall man wypyd a-bowtt West-mynster and throwge London and over London bryge and Sowth-warke for conter-feythyng the master of the quen('s) horse hand.

The **ij** day of Marche was consecratyd at the byshope of Lon-don('s) pallesᶠ master Yonge byshope of Yorke, was byshope of (Saint David's).

The **vj** day of Marche was beredᵍ in sant Gorge parryche in Sowthwarke, the wyche he cam owtt of the kynges bynche, master Seth Holand, latt dene of Vossetur,ʰ and the master of All Solles colege in Oxford, and a **lx** men of gentyllmen of the inⁱ of the corttes, and of Oxford, browthᵏ ym to the chyrche, for he was a grett lernydman.

The **ix** day of Marche dyd pryche at the cowrt the byshope of London master Gryndall.

The sam day cam owt of Franse the yerle of Bedford.

ᵃ brought.   ᵇ *probably* Gough.   ᶜ anatomy.   ᵈ were poor.   ᵉ carried.
ᶠ palace.   ᵍ buried.   ʰ Worcester.   ⁱ inns.   ᵏ brought.

The sam day dyd pryche in the shroudes at Powlles master Gresshope of Oxford.

The vii day of Marche at nyght cam a servyngman in Towre stret, and toke from a cyld[a] neke (a . . .) of sylver, and the pepull bad stope the theyffe, and he rane in-to Marke lane, and stopyd and gayff ym a blowe that he never went farther, and ded.[b]

.   .   .   .

The xvj day of Ma. . .

The xvij day dyd pryche at the cowrt the [bishop] of Durram, that was Mydlent sonday.

The xx day dyd pryche at the courtt the [dean] of Powlles, master Nowell.

The xx day of Marche ded[b] at the cowrt the yonge lade Jane Semer, the duke of Somerset('s) dowther, on of the quen('s) mayds.

The xxiij day of Marche dyd pryche at [Newington] be-yonde sant Gorgus the byshope of Canturbere, docthur Parker, and mad a goodly sermon.

The sam day dyd pryche at the cowrte the byshope of Ely, docthur Cokes, and he w[ould that none] shuld pryche of he[c] matters butt they that were well le[arned.]

The xxij day of Marche dyd a woman ryd a-bowt Chepesyd and Londun for bryngyng yonge frye of dyvers kynd of fysse un-lafull, with a garland a-pone her hed hangyng with strynges of the small fysse, and on the horse a-for and be-hynd here, led by on of the bedylls of Brydwell.

The xxiij day of Marche dyd pryche at Powlles crosse a by-shope.

The xxij day of Marche ther was a wyff dwellyng in sant Martens in the vyntre, within the clostur dwellyng, of the age of lii. toke a woman into her howse at the done-lyhyng,[d] and the sam nyght she was delevered with chyld, and the sam woman of the howse led[e] her-seyff in bed, and mad pepull beleyff that yt was her owne chyld.

 <a> child's ?   <b> died.   <c> high.   <d> down-lying.   <e> laid.

[The xxvj day of March master Sampson preached at the court.]

The sam day of Marche at after-none at Westmynster [was brought] from the quen('s) armere [a] my lade Jane Semer, with [all the quire] of the abbay, with ijC. of (the) quen('s) cowrt, the wyche she was [one] of the quen('s) mayd(s) and in grett faver, and a iiij[xx] morners of [men and] women, of lordes and lades, and gentylmen and gentyllwomen, all in blake, be-syd odur [b] of the quen('s) preve chambur, and she [had] a grett baner of armes bornne, and master Clarenshux was the harold, and master Skameler the nuw byshope of Peterborow dyd pryche. [She was] bered in the sam chapell wher my lade of Suffoke was.

The iij day of Aprell ded ser Arthur Darce knyght at Bedyngtun besyd Crowdun, the [which] was my lord Darce('s) [son] the wyche was heded on the Towre hyll for the surpryse in the Northe.

The iiij day of Aprell dyd pryche at the Powlles crosse the archdeken of London master Mollens.

The vij day of Aprell dyd pryche at sant Mare spytyll the nuwe byshope of Wynchester master Horne, and ther was all the masters of the hospetall,[c] and the chylderyn in bluw cotes, and my lord mayre and the althermen, and mony worshephull men.

The viij day of Aprell dyd pryche at sant Mare spytyll the byshope of Durham master Pylkyngtun, and ther was gret audyense, and my lord mare and my masters the althermen, with the masters of the hospetall.

The sam day of Aprell ded the good lade Huett, late mayres of London, in the parryche of sant Dennys.

The ix day of Aprell dyd pryche at sant Mare spyttell master Colle the parsun of Hehonger [d] in Essex.

The sam day was bered in Mylkstrett mastores Dock[wra?], with the clarkes of London, and she had vj skochyons of armes, and ther was geyffen for gownes to the pore men and women, and the byshope of Duram dyd pryche ther.

[a] almonry.   [b] other.   [c] Christ's Hospital.   [d] High Ongar.

The x day of Aprell was wyped on that cam owt of Bedlem for he sayd he was Cryst, and on Peter that cam owt of the Masselsay, boyth wyped, for he sayd that he was the sam Peter that dyd folow Crist.

. . . .

. . toward Chelsey unto my lo . . . . . a man fond slayne by the way, and so . . . . that fonde hym, the wyche man dwelt in sant . . . with-owt Alther-gatt in More lane.

The xij day of Aprell was sett in the stokes . . . markett a stranger, the wyche he goys ᵃ all in red, and [says] that he (is) lord of alle lordes and kynge of alle kynges.

The xiij day dyd pryche at the Powlles master Juell byshope of Salysbere.

The xiiij day of Aprell a-for non was cared from sant Ellens in London, owt of a howse [where once] lyved old Clarenshus master Benolt the kyng at a[rms in the] tyme of kyng Henre viijᵗ. ser Arthur Darce, and cared [to saint] Botolffe with-owt Algatt to (be) bered by my lade ys [wife, with] a xx clarkes syngynge, and then cam the standard . . . of armes and ys cott armur, ys target and sword and helmet, . . . and ij haroldes of armes, on beyryng the elmett and nodur ᵇ [the coat armour;] and the chyrche hangyd with blake and armes and raylles, [and the place] with blake and armes, and then cam the corse and vj of ys [servants] that bare hym, and mony mornars in blake ; and he had a pall of blake velvett, and with armes of bokeram ; and master Beycun dyd pryche ther.

The sam day was bered in Cornyll mastores Hunt wedow, and the chylderyn of the hopetall and the masters wher at her bere-hyng with ther gren stayffes, and the xxx chylderyn syngyng the Pater-noster in Englys, and a xl pore women in gownes ; and after the clarkes syngyng, and after the corse, and then mornars, and after the craftes of the worshephull compene of the Skynners ; and ther dyd pryche the byshope of Durram master Pylkyngtun ; and after to the Skynners halle to dener.

ᵃ goes.   ᵇ another.

The xvj day of Aprell wher all the alters in Westmynster taken downe, [in] the chapell wher the kyng Henry the vijth was bered, and wher kyng Edward the vjth, and the stones cared wher quen Mare was bered.

[The . . day of April was the funeral of Lady Hewett, formerly] mayres of London, and xxiiij pore women in nuw gownes and xij pore men, and after a xl in blake . . . . viij althermen in blake gownes, and my lord mare and [the rest] of the althermen, and xx clarkes syngyng, and then cam a penon of armes, and cam Ruge-crosse, and after master Clarenshus kyng at armes, and after the corse and iiij pennon of armes, and the pall of blake velvett and with armes, and then the cheyffe morners, a xl women mornars, and after the Cloth[workers] in the leveray, and after ij C. folohyng, and master (*blank*) dyd pryche; and the cherche hangyd with blake and armes; and after to ys plase to dener in Phylpot lane, and the plase hangyd with blake and armes.

The xviij day of Aprell was raynyd at Nuwgat master Putnam gentylman for a rape, and cast, and dyvers odur.

The xix day of Aprell wher cast iij, ij men and a woman, for kyllyng of a man besyd sant James, and odur.

The xxj day of Aprell wher hangyd ix, at Hyd parke korner iij, and vj at Tyborne.

The xxij day of Aprell was had to the Towre ser Edward Walgraff and my lade ys wyff, as good almes-foke as be in thes days, and odur cared thethur.

The xxiij day of Aprell was browth * unto my lord of Penbroke my lord of Lughborow, ser Edward Hastynges.

The xx day of Aprell be-gane at xij of the cloke at none the grettest thondur, lyghtenyng and gretest rayne, and the grett halle-stones as has bene sene.

The sam day wher ij hangyd at Wapyng, ij for robyng of the see.

.   .   .   .

* brought.

[The xxiij of April, saint George's day, was kept] holy at the quen['s court   .   .] her halle in copes to the nombur of xxx, with [O God,] *the father of Hevyn, have merce on* . . . . and the owtter cowrt to the gatt, and rond abowt st[rewed with rushes;] and after cam master Garter, and master Norres, and master dene of the ch[apel, in copes] of cremesun saten, with a crosse of sant Gorge red, and [eleven knights] of the garter in ther robes, and after the Quen('s) grace in [her robes, and] all the garde in ther ryche cottes; and so bake to the [Chapel,] after serves done, bake thruge the hall to her graces chambur, and that done her grace and the lord(s) wh[ent to din-ner,] and her grace wher [a] goodly servyd; and after the lordes [sit-ting on one] syd, and servyd in gold and sylver; and after dener [there were] knyghtes of the Garter electyd ij, my lord of Shrews-bere [and my] lord of Hunsdon; and ther wher [b] all the haroldes in ther cote armurs a-for the quen('s) grace, master Clarenshux, Lanckostur, Rychemond, Wyndsor, Yorke, Chastur, Blumantyl, Ruge-dragon.

The xxvj day of May [c] was bered in Oxfordshyre . . . . . Dalamore, with a cott armur and a pennon of armes and a iij [dozen scocheons] of armes.

The furst day of May was cared to Powlles to be bered [one] Bathellmuw Comopane, a marchand stranger dwelling [by saint] Cristoffer at the stokes, and throughe Chepe, and vj men in blake gownes and hodes, and a xxx gownes for pore men and women of mantyll frys, a liiij in blake gownes; and with-in the gatt of Powlles cherche-yerd mett all the quer of Powlles, and the clarkes of Lon-don whent a-for the corse with ther surples onder ther gownes, tyll they cam in-to the Powlles cherche-yerd, and then they be-gane to syng: and the quer wher hangyd with blake and armes, a iij dosen of skochyons of armes; and Veron dyd pryche, the Frenche-man, and after browth [d] ym to the neder end of the stepes under the belles, and bered hym, and after home to dener.

----

[a] were, *for* was.   [b] were.   [c] *Probably* April.   [d] brought.

The sam day at after-none dyd master Godderyke('s) sune, the gold-smyth, go hup in-to hys father('s) gylddyng house, toke a bowe strynge and hangyd ym-seylff, at the syne of the Unycorne in Chepe-syd.

.   .   .   .

The x day of May dyd ryd in a care a-bowt [London] mastores Whytt shepster, dwelling in Fletstreet.

The xj day of May cam rydyng thrugh London, with a ix^{xx} horse and with men in ys leverey with a iij^{xx} in . . and with bages [a] a talbott of the gold-smyth('s) makyng, my yonge yerle of Shrowsbere to ys plase at Cold[-harbour,] all in bluw clothe, and on sant Gorge day was electyd knyght of the garter in ys father('s) stede.

The xiiij day of May, was Assensyon evyn, was bered in sant Pulkers parryche my lade Esley the wyff of ser Henre Hesley [b] knyght, of Kentt, the wyche he cam in with sir Thomas Wyett knyght by quen Mare('s) days, and he was hangyd and drane and quartered, and ys hed sent unto Maydston, and set a-pone *(blank)* and she had nothyng done for here, butt master Skammeler mad a sermon for here—the byshope of Peterborow.

The xviij day of May was sant Gorge fest keptt at Wyndsor, and ther was stallyd ther the yerle of Shrowsbere and my lord of Hunsdon, and the yerle of Arundell was the quens depptte, and the way [c] my lord Monteguw and my lord Pagett, and so they came to cherche; and after matens done, they whent a prosessyon rond about the cherche, so done the mydes and so rond a-bowt, and a x almes-knyghtes in red kyrtylles, and a-loft a robe of purpull cloth syd with a crosse of sant Gorge, and after the verger, and then the clarkes and prestes a xxiiij syngyng the Englys prossessyon in chopes [d] xxxiiij, and sum of them in gray ames [e] and in calabur, and then cam my lord of Hunsdun, and after my lord Montyguw, and after the yerle of Shrowsbere, and after my lord Pagett, and after the yerle of Arundell, all they in their robes, and master Garter and master Norres and master dene in cremesun saten robes, with

[a] badges.   [b] Isley.   [c] *So in MS.*   [d] copes.   [e] amices.

red crosses on ther shuldurs, and after rod up to the castylle to dener.

. . . .

[The iiij day of June, being Corpus] Christi evyn, be-twyn xj and xij of the cloke, [there was] thonderying and lythenyng, and at sant Martens [by Ludgate came a] boltt and smytt downes serten grett stones of the [battlement of] the stepull, and the stones fell downe a-pone the [leads], and brake the ledes and bordes, and a grett gest* in ij peses.

The sam day be-twyn iiij and v of the cloke at after-[non the] lythenyng toke and entered in-to one of the olles[b] that was [in the outward] parte of the stepull[c] a ij yerdes under the bolle, and sett [the steeple] on fyre and never left tyll the stepull and belles and [all the] chyrche bowth north, est, south, and west, tyll yt

. . . . archys, and consumyd boythe wod and led, and the belles [fell] be-low wher the grett organes stod be-ne[ath the] chapelle wher the old byshope was bered ondur . . . and in in dyvers plases of England grett hurtt done.

The iij day of June the Sessyons keptt at . . . wher serten knyghtes and lade,[d] and gentyllmen and [gentlewomen] and serten prestes with odur, wher endytyd for (*unfinished*)

The xvj day of June my lord mare and the althermen [were] sent for unto the cowrte at Grenwyche.

The v day of June dyd hange ym-seylff be-syd London stone (*blank*) . . lle a harper, the servand of the yerle of Darbe.

The xiiij day of June was bered in Essex my lade Wartun, the wyff of ser Thomas Wartun, behyng presoner in the towre of London at here deth and berehyng, and master Somersett the harold of armes, a gret baner of armes, and iiij dosen of skochyons of armes, the wyche the good lade ded of a thowgh,[e] and she was as fayre a lade as be, and mony mornars in blake, and grett mone mad for her in the contrey.

The xv day dyd pryche at Powlles crosse master Nowell the dene of Powlles, and mad a goodly sermon, and my lord mayre

---

* chest.   [b] holes.   [c] Of St. Paul's cathedral.
                  [d] ladies.   [e] cough.

and the althermen and the most of the worshephull craftes wher commondyd to be ther, and ther wher grett audyense.

.   .   .   .

[The   day of June was the Skinners' feast; and there was chosen the master of fellowship master . . . . . , and for wardens] master Clarenshux, [a] kyng at armes, [the ij master . . . ,] the iij master Dennam, the fort master Starke; [and] for denner iij stages [b] (and) viij bokes,[c] a gret . . .

The xvj day of June was the masters the Grossers fest; ther dynyd my lord mare, ser Roger Chamley, ser John Ly[ons, sir] Marten Bowse, ser Wylliam Huett, and ser Wylliam Garrett, [master] Loge, master John Whytt, master Cryster [d] Draper, master Rowe, and master Cha[mley? master] Marten, master Baskerfeld, and master chamburlayn of London, and mony worshephull men and mony lades and gentyllwomen; and grett chere; boyth the whettes [e] and clarkes syngyng, and a nombur of vyolles playhyng, and syngyng, and they had xxx bokes [c] [and] (*blank*) stages.[b]

The xvij day of June was a proclamassyon for slypes [f] and alffe slypes, that they should be corrant tyll the xx of July, tyll then they shuld have iij*d.* in the pound and no lenger.

The xviij day of June was a woman sett in the stokes in New-gatt markett with serten fylles [g] and odur instrumentes, the wyche she browth to Newgatt to here hosband for to fylle the yrons of ys leges, and odur thynges.

The x day of June was grantyd at Yeld-halle by my lord mare and my masters the althermen and the commen consell iij xv [h] toward the beldyng of Powlles chyrche and the stepulle, with as grett sped as they may gett tymbur rede,[i] and odur thynges, and worke-men.

The xvij day of June my lord mare and the althermen and the commen conselle how that and watt men shuld loke and over-se the workemen, and what men shuld take hed too in alle placys for the beldyng of Powlles, and to chose men of knolleg to loke and over-se the worke and the workmen.

[a] William Harvey.   [b] stags.   [c] bucks.   [d] Christopher.
[e] waits.   [f] *See Appendix of Notes.*   [g] files.   [h] three fifteens.   [i] ready.

The xix day of June was a grett wager shott in Fynsbere feld be-twyn my lord Robartt Dudley and my *(unfinished)*

The xx day of June was reynyd[a] at Westmynster serten men for kungeryng[b] and odur maters.

. . . .

. . . of the offesers of Brydwelle and in serten [places] procla-massyon made of ther dohyng and . . .

The xxij day of June dyd pryche at Powlles [cross master] Skynner, dene of Durram, and mad a godly sermon, [giving] men warnyng of a notheboke[c] that ys pryntyd, and [bade every] man be ware of yt, for yt ys vere herese.[d]

The xxiij day of June was sett on the pelere for kungeryng[b] on prest,[e] ys name ys master Belissun [of] Westmynster.

The xxiiij day of June, was Mydsomer-day, at Grenwyche was grett tryum(ph) of the rever, a-gaynst the cou[rt; there] was a goodly castylle mad a-pone Temes, and men of armes with-in ytt, with gones and spers, for to deffend [the same,] and a-bowt ytt wher serten small pynnes[f] with . . . and grett shottyng of gonnes and horlyng of ba[lls of] wyld fyre, and ther was a barke with ij tope [castles ?] for the Quen('s) grace to be in for to se the passe-tyme, the wyche was vere latt or yt was done.

The xxv day of June was sett in Chepesyde ij peleres[g] for vij men that was sett on the pelere at Westmynster on Mydsomer evyn for kungeryng, and odur matters.

The xxiij day of June, was Mydsomer evyn, the serves at sant Gregore chyrche be-syd Powlles (by) the Powlles quer tyll Powlles be rede mad.[h]

The xxx day of June was the Goldsmyth(s') fest, and ther was ser Mertens Bowsses,[i] knyght, and dyvers worshephull gentyllmen and gentyllwomen.

[The　　　day of June was the Merchant-Taylors' feast. . . . . . Thomas Hoffeley, master John Whyt, master Ma . . .

---

[a] arraigned.　　　[b] conjuring.　　　[c] naughty book.　　　[d] very heresy.
[e] one priest.　[f] pinnaces.　[g] pillories.　[h] ready made.　[i] Martin Bowes.

master Bas]kerfeld, and ser Wylliam Garrett, and mony worshephull, [and] mony lades and gentyll women, and they had (*blank*)
b[ucks and] (*blank*) stages, and ther was the wettes [a] plahyng,
and gret plente.

The furst day of July be-gane workemen and la[bourers] at
Powlles for the reparyng of the chyrche and the stepull, and the
oversers and the doars of the sam here be ther namys, master
Graftun grocer, and master Haresun [b] goldsmyth, and master
(*blank*) grocer.

The iiij day of July dynyd at the in-bassadurs of Sweythen in
Lymsthrett all the quen('s) consell, furst (*unfinished*)

.The v and vj day of July was grett rayne and thonderyng in
London boyth the days.

The vij day of July dyd pryche at the Gray Frers, because yt
reynyd that they cold not pryche at Powlles crosse.

The viij day of July was bered in sant Clement parryche with-
owt Tempull bare mastores (*blank*) the wyff of master (*blank*) comtroller unto the nobull yerle of Arundelle, the wyche she ded in
chyld-bede, and she had a xiiij in blake gownes and cottes, and
iiij women dyd bere her, and they had cassokes nuw and raylles,
and on the body wher vj skochyons of armes, and master Recherdsun the parsun of sant Mathuw mad the sermon.

The ix day of July was the pelere [c] set up in Chepe for a
prentes [d] that had conveyed from ys master the sum of a (*blank*)
l., and had bowth [e] hym nuw aparell, nuw shurtt, dobelet and
hose, hat, purse, gyrdyll, dager, and butes,[f] spurs, butt-hose, and
a skarffe, and thys nuw all, and thys dyd hang up on the pelere,
and goodly geldyng and sadyll, cot, cloke, sadyll   .   .   .

.   .   .   .

[The x day of July the Queen came by water] unto the Towre
of London by x [of the clock, until] v at nyght, and whent and sa(w)
all her my[nts; and they gave the] Quen serten pesses of gold,
and gayff the [lord] of Hunsdon had on, and my lord marques of

[a] waits.   [b] Harrison.   [c] pillory.   [d] prentice.   [e] bought.   [f] boots.

[Northampton,] and her grace whent owt of the yron gatt [over] Towre hyll unto Algatt chyrche, and so down Hondyche [to the] Spyttyll, and so downe Hoge lane, and so over the feldes to the Charter howse my lord North('s) plase, with trumpetes and the penssyonars and the haroldes of armes and the servantes, and then cam gentyllmen rydyng, and after lordes, and then [the] lord of Hunsdon and bare the sword a-for the quen, and then cam [ladies] rydyng; and the feldes full of pepull, gret nombur [as ever was] sene; and ther tared tylle Monday.

The xiij day of July was bered in sant Andrewes in Holborne master Phassett, gentyll-man, on of the (*unfinished*)

The sam day was bered in sant Pulkurs parryche master (*blank*) alle-bruar,[a] and ther was all the compene of the Bruars in ther levere, and Veron the Frenche-man dyd pryche for hym.

The sam nyght the Quen('s) grace whent from the Charter-howse by Clarkyne-welle over the feldes unto the Sayvoy unto master secretore Sysselle to soper, and ther was the consell and mony lordes and knyghtes and lades and gentyll-women, and ther was grett chere tyll mydnyght, and after here grace ryd to my lord North('s) to bed at the Charter-howse.

The xiiij day of July was nuw graveled with sand from the Charterhowse through Smyth feld, and under Nuwgate, and through sant Nycolas shambull, Chepe-syd, and Cornhyll, unto Algatt and to Whyt-chapell, and all thes plases where hangyd with cloth of arres and carpetes and with sylke, and Chepe-syd hangyd with cloth of gold and cloth of sylver and velvett of all colurs and taffatas in all plases, and all the craftes of Londun standyng in ther leverey from sant Myghell unto Algatt, and then cam mony servyng-men rydyng, and then the pensyonars and gentyll men, and then knyghtes, and after lordes, and then the althermen in skarlett, and the serjant(s) of armes, and then the haroldes of armes in ther cottes armurs, and then my lord mare bayryng here septer;[b] [then the lord Hunsdon bearing the

---

[a] ale-brewer.   [b] the queen's sceptre.

sword; and then came the Queen's grace, and her footmen richly habited; and ladies and gentlemen; then] all lordes' men and knyghtes' [men in their masters' liveries; and at] Whytt-chapell my lord mare and the althermen [took their leave of] here grace, and so she toke her way to-ward [her pro]gresse.

The **xv** day of July was bered in sant Laurence in the Jure mastores the wyff of master (*blank*), with the compene of the Clarkes, and she had ij dosen of skochyons, on of bokeram, and a-nodur of paper in metalle.

The **xx** day of July was bered in Westmynster abbay master Bylle dene of Westmynster abbay and master of Etton and master (of sant John's) college in Cambryge, and cheyffe amner [a] to the quen('s) grace.

The sam day, behyng sant Margat [b] evyn, master Clarenshus rod and toke ys jorney in-to Essex and Suffoke on ys vese[tation], and parte of Northfoke, and Ruge-crosse rod with hym, and a v [of his] servantes in ys leverey and bage.

The **xx** day of July dyd pryche at Powlles crosse *(blank)*

The **xxj** day of July yt dyd rayne sore, and yt be-gane on son-day at nyght and last tyll monday at nyght.

The **xviij** day of July was the obseque of my lade Hamptun the wyff of ser *(blank)*, with a pennon of armes and a iiij dosen and a d' [c] of bokeram.

The **xvj** day of July was cristened Robard Dethyke the sune of ser Gylbartt Dethyke, Garter, in the parryche of sant Gylles with-owt Crepull-gatte, and the chyrche hangyd with clothes of arrys and the cloth of state, and strode with gren rysses [d] and strode with orbese, [e] and ser Wylliam Huett depute for my lord of Shrowsbere and master Care [f] depute for my lord Honsdon, and my lade Sakefeld the quen('s) depute; and after wafurs and epo-crasse grett plente, and myche pepull ther, and my lade Yorke bare my lade depute's trayne; and so hom to here plase, and had a bankett.

---

[a] almoner.   [b] Margaret's.   [c] half.   [d] rushes.   [e] herbs.   [f] Carey.

a bankett .   .   .   .   .   .   [master Alexander Ave-non was] chosen the shreyff for the quen('s) grace.

The xxx day of July at bowt viij and ix at nyght [there was] lythenyng and thonderyng as any man has sene [until] x, and after a grett rayne tyll mydnyght, that we [supposed] that the world where at a nend,ᵃ that evere one [thought] that the day of dome wher come at hand, yt . . . .

The furst day of August, was lammas day, my [lord mayor] and the althermen and all the craftes in London in ther [liveries, met] to chuse the shreyff of London, that was master Bas[kerville] altherman;ᵇ and the sam day was chosen master Gyl[bert,] nuw altherman in the stede of master Altham lat[e alderman] and clothworker of London, the wyche he was dysmy[ssed].

The iiij day of August was Clothworkers' fest, and ther was a worshepulle dener ther.

The x day of August, was sant Laurens day, Veron the Frenche-man prychyd at Powlles crosse.

The xxj day of August dyd pryche at Powlles crosse master Molens the archedecon of London.

The xij day of August cam tydynges that ther was a ix trybes that have bene in a contrey ever synes they wher dryven owt of Egype, and they be redeᶜ to sett on the Grett Turke with grett armesᵈ of men.

The xix day of August at xij of the cloke at mydnight was a fyre at the corner be-yonde Smytfeld pond, and a one howse bornyd, the wyche was a cutteller('s) howse, and perechestᵉ ij howses junnyngᶠ to hytt.

The ix day of August the quen('s) grace has commondyd that all chathredalles and coleges and studyans places that they shuld putt ther wyffes from them owt of the serkuttᵍ of evereʰ colege.

.   .   .   .

The xxx day of August tydans cam that the kyng of [Sweden was] sendyng (*blank)* of waganns laden with massé bol[lion.]

ᵃ an end.   ᵇ alderman.   ᶜ ready.   ᵈ armies.   ᵉ purchased? *in the sense of* took hold on.   ᶠ joining.   ᵍ circuit.   ʰ every.

The furst day of September ded [a] the good and gentylle knyght
ser Edward Walgraff whyle in the Towre, the wyche he was put
for herryng of masse and kepyng a prest in ys howse that dyd
say masse, and was putt to hys fyne.

The iij day of September was a yonge stryplyng whypyd at a
post in Chepe-syd for *(blank)*; and the sam day was bered with-
owt Althergate old master Swyft, aude[tor,] with grett ryngyng
and syngyng and much money delt.

The sam day was bered with-in the Towre, with[-in] the quer
be-syd the he [b] auter, by torche lyght, the wyche (confinement)
kyld hym, for he was swone [c] vere grett, ser Edward [Walgrave].

The v day of September was browth [d] to the Towre the yonge
yerle of Harford from the cowrte, a-bowtt ij of the cloke at after-
none he cam in-to the Towre.

The vj day of September was serten gayre [made] for on master
Swyft, sqwyre, cott-armur, pennon of armes, and a ij skochyons,
at Roderam, in Yorke-shyre.

The ij day of September was bered at sant Andrews parryche in
the Warderob, master Wast, bere-bruar, with a iij dosen of
skochyons of armes, and the howse and the chyrche hangyd with
blake and armes, and ther was the compene of the Clarkes syngyng,
and *(unfinished)*

The viij day of September cam owt of the Towre my good lade
Walgraff, and in Red-cross stret she lys.

.   .   .   .

The vj of September [was the funeral] of ser James Bullen,
and standard, [coat armour,] and elmett, targett, and sword,
and a vj dos[en of scocheons of] armes, and master Chester was
harold.

The Fryday, the v day of September, was bornyd at Oxford, by
the master of the colege of *(blank)* [f] grett reches that myght have
bene sene, and gyffyne to . . . .

---

[a] died.   [b] high.   [c] swoln.   [d] brought.   [e] year.
[f] Sampson, dean of Christ's church. *Strype.*

The viij day of September, the wyche was the day of the nativity of owre Lade, they begane to sett up the raylles of Powlles apone the battellmentt on he.[a]

The xiij day of September was bered at sant [Dunstan's] Fletstrett, master Cottgrave, the wyffes brodur of master Grysse, lat . . . . master Tott, sergent penter unto kyng Henry the viij[th], with . . . . skochyons of armes.

The xv day of September tydynges cam to London [that] the kynge of Sweythland was landyd in the North at . . . ., and [b] yt be truw as the sayng was then.

The sam day the Quen('s) grace removyd from Hatford [c] castyll in Hatford-shyre unto Enfeld within x mylle of London.

The xvij day of September was a wodmonger sett in the pelere [d] for false markyng of belletes, dwellying in Temstret be-syd the Red Bull beyond Coldharber, with belletes hangyng abowt hym.

The xxij day of September the Quen('s) grace cam from Enfeld unto Sant James beyond Charyng crosse, and from Ellyngtun [e] unto Sant James was heges and dyches was cutt done the next way, and ther was a-boyff x M. pepull for to se her grace, butt yt was nyght or her grace cam over beyond Sent Gylles in the feld by Colman('s?) hege.

The xxj day of September dyd pryche at the Powlles crosse, master Huttun, master of Trenete colege, and mad a godly sermon — of Cambridge.

[The xx day of September came a commandment from the queen unto the college of Windsor, that the priests belonging thereunto that had wives, should put them out] of the colege, nott for to cum to lye [any more within that] plase, or any colege or cathedrall [church, or] any universete of Oxford or Cambryge.

The xxj day of September was browth [f] [to bed of] a sune my lade Katheryn Gray, the dowther of the duke [of Suffolk] that

---

[a] high.   [b] *i. e.* if.   [c] Hertford.   [d] pillory.   [e] Islington.   [f] brought.

was heded on the Towre hylle, and ys brodur lord Thomas Gray the sam tyme.

The xxiij day was mad dene of Westmynster master Goodman.

The xxv day of September was cristened with-in the Towre my lorde Harford('s) sune by my lade Katheryn Gray, late dowther of the duke of Suffoke — Gray.

The xxix day of September, was Myghellmas evyn, the old shreyffes master Cristofer Draper and master Thomas Rowe unto the nuw shreyffes master (Alexander) Avenon, and master (Humphrey) Baskerfeld, was delevered Nugatt and Ludgatt, and the ij conters, and the presonars.

The xxx day of September my lord mayre and the althermen and the new shreyffes toke ther barges at the iij cranes in the Vintre and so to Westmynster, and so into the Cheker, and ther toke ther hoythe;[a] and ser Rowland Hyll whent up, and master Hogys toke ser Rowland Hyll a choppyng kneyff, and one dyd hold a whyt rod, and he with the kneyff cute the rod in sunder a-for all the pepull; and after to London to ther plases to dener, my lord mayre and all the althermen and mony worshephulle men.

The furst day of October was a fyre whet-in[b] the Towre of London be-yond the Whyt Towre.

The xxix day of September was nuw mayre electyd master Harper, marchand-tayller, on Myghellmas day.

[The iij day of October came to London to Gracechurch] strett, to the Cross-keys, xviij grett horses [all pyed-coloured] from the kyng of Swaythland.

The iiij day of October cam to Wolwyche from Swathland ij shypes laden with *(unfinished)*

The vj day of October was unladen a[t the water] syd serten vesselles with *(blank)* and cared to the [Tower].

The ix day of October at iiij of the cloke in the mornyng ded[c] the old lade Dobes in sant M[argaret's]-mosses in Frydey strett.

---

[a] oath. [b] within. [c] died.

The sam day of October at nyght ded good Alesandar Carlylle, the master of the Vyntonars, of *(unfinished)*

The x day of October was sett on the pelere[a] the gatherer of the kyng('s) bynche, ys name ys *(blank)*, for he cam untowe dyvers gentyllmen and gentyllwomen and gayff them fayre nose-gaysse, and told them that he shuld be mared,[b] and to dyvers odur onest pepull gayff nose-gaysse, and that *(unfinished)*

The x day of October [the] quen('s) grace dyd gret cost at Westmynster boyth with-in here plase, and pavyng from the end of the Tyltt rond abowt the sydes, and closyd in the tylt.

The xij day of October dyd pryche at Powlles crosse (master) Crolley, sum-tyme a boke-prynter dwelling in Holborne, in the byshope of Ely('s) renttes.

The xviij day, was bant Lukes day, dyd pryche for[c] the master of the Penters on *(blank)* Gowth,[d] the sune of on Gowth boke-prynter, the wyche ded[e] in kyng Henre the viijth, the wyche he dwelt in Lumbarstrett.

[The . . . day was the funeral of lady Dobbes, late the] wyff of ser Recherd Dobes knyght and skynner late mayre, with a harold of armes, and she had a pennon of armes and iiij dosen and d'[f] skochyons; [she was buried] in the parryche of sant Margat Moyses in Fryday stret; [she] gayff xx good blake gownes to xx powre women; she gayffe xl blake gownes to men and women; [master] Recherdsun mad the sermon, and the clarkes syngyng, [and] a dolle of money of xx nobulles, and a grett dener after, and the compene of the Skynners in ther leverey.

The sam day of October was bered in Whytyngtun colege master Alesandur Karlelle the master of the Vyntoners, the wyche he mared the dowther of ser George Barnes knyght, [late] mare of the nobull cete of London and haburdassher; and he gayff a xx blake gownes, and he gayff *(blank)* mantyll [frieze] gowne(s) unto *(blank)* pore men; and ther wher the Clarkes of London syngyng, and [master] Crolley dyd pryche, and then to the plase to denner,

[a] pillory.   [b] married.   [c] before.   [d] Gough.   [e] died.   [f] half.

and a dolle, and a ij dozen of kochyons of armes, and the leverey of the Vyntonars.

The xviij day of October ther was (a) fray be-twyn my lord Montyguw('s) men and my lord Delaware('s) men, and after the ij lordes wher sent to the Flett, and the men to the Masselsay.

The xxij day of October my lord Montyguw and my lord Delaware wher delevered owtt of the Flett home.

The xiiij day they wher a-for the consell at Westmynster hall the ij lordes.

The xxv day of October cam rydyng from Skotland serten Frenche-men thrugh London, my lord of Bedford and my lord Monge and my lord Strange was ther gyd ᵃ with a M. horse thrugh Fletstreet, and so to my lord of Bedford('s.)

The sam tyme was delt thrugh alle the wardes of London xij*d.* a howse for ser Rowland Hylle, late mayre of London, behyng vere syke that time.

.   .   .   .

master Nowelle, the dene of Powlles.

The sam day a-bowtt iij at after-non cam [my lord] of Beydford and my lorde Monge and my lord Strange and mony odur gentyllmen, and mony of the pensyonars to my lord of Bedforth('s) plase, and browt the inbassadurs of France to the cowrt that lye there at my lordes plase.

The xxviij day of October, the wyche was sant Symon and Jude day, was at Whyt-hall grett baytyng of the bull and bere for the in-bassadurs of Franse that cam owtt of Scottland, the wyche the Quen('s) grace was ther, and her consell and mony nobull men.

The xxix day of October the nuw mare toke ys barge towhard Westmynster my nuw lorde mare master Harper, with the althermen in ther skarlett, and all the craftes of London in ther leverey, and ther barges with ther baners and streamers of evere occupasyon('s) armes ; and ther was a goodly foist mad with stremars, targatts, and banars, and [arms], and grett shutyng of gunes and trum-

ᵃ guide.

pettes blohyng; and at xij of the cloke my lord mare and the althermen landyd at Powlles warffe, and so to Powlles chyrche-yarde, and ther met ym a pagantt gorgyously mad,[a] with chylderyn, with dyvers instrumentes playng and syngyng; and after-non to Powlles with trumpetes, and ther wher[b] a (*blank*) men in bluw gownes and capes [c] and hose and bluw saten slevys, and with targetts and shyldes of armes.

The xxviij day of October at xij of the cloke at mydnyght ded [d] good ser Rowland Hylle knyght and late mayre of this nobull cette of London, and merser, the wyche he ded of the strang-wyllyon.

The xxx day of October was mad for the berehyng of ser Reynold Chamburlayn knyght and capten of Garnsey a standard and a pennon and a cote armur and a target, sword, and mantyll, helmet and crest, and a (*blank*) dosen of skochyons of armes, the wyche he had iiij wyffes and (*unfinished*)

The (*blank*) day of (*blank*) was be-gone the serves at Powlles to synge, and ther was a grett comunion ther be-gane, the byshope and odur.

[The j day of November went to saint Paul's the lord mayor] and the althermen at afternon [and all the crafts of] London in ther leverey, and with iiij[xx] men all carehyng of torchys, and my lord mare [tarried until] nyght, and so whent home with all torches [lighted,] for my lord mare tared the sermon; my lord of London mad the sermon; but yt was latt, [and so] there torchys was lyght to bryng my lord home.

The ij day of November was a yonge [man] stod at Powlles crosse in the sermon tyme with a [sheet] a-bowtt hym for spyk-yng of serten wordes agaynst Veron the precher.

The v day of November was bered in sant Stephen's in Walbroke ser Rowland Hylle, latt mare and altherman and mercer and knyght, with a standard and v pennons of armes, and a cott

---

[a] made.   [b] were.   [c] caps.   [d] died.

armur and a helmet, a crest, sword, and mantyll, and xj dosen of
skochyons of armes; and he gayff a c. gownes and cottes to men
and women; and ther wher ij haroldes of armes, master Clarenshux and master Somersett, and my lord mayre morner, the cheyff
morner; ser Recherd Lee, master Corbett, with dyvers odur
morners, ser Wylliam Cordell, ser Thomas Offeley, ser Martens
Bowes and master Chamburlan althermen, and the ij shreyffes,
and master Chambur . . and master Blakewell, with mony mo
morners, and a l. pore men in good blake gownes, besyd
women; and the dene of Powlles mad the sermon; and after
all done my lord mayre and mony and althermen whent to the
Mercers'[a] hall and the craft to dener, and the resedu to ys plase
to dener, and grett mon mad[b] for ys deth, and he gayff myche to
the pore.

The sam day was wypyd at Quen-heyff at a post a waterman for
opprobryus wordes and sedyssyous wordes agaynst the magystrates.

The sam day of November dyd pryche at Westmynster abbay
master Alway, one of the plasse, and mad a godly sermon ther,
and grett audyense.

The (*blank*) day of November   .   .   .   had master
Walkenden a servand that   .   .   . of the age of xv .
and ther dyd. . .

The xiiij day of November ther was a procla[mation] of gold and
sylver that none shuld be take[n be]twyn man and man butt the
Frenche crowne and the Borgo[ndian] crowne and the Flemyche,
and that phystelars[c] and Spa[nish] ryalles shuld not goo, butt to
cum to the Towre ther to have wheth for wheth,[d] gold and sylver.

The xxiij day of November, the iiij yere [of] quen Elesabeth,
dyd pryche at Powlles crosse Renagir, yt was sant Clement day,
dyd sy[t e] alle the sermon tyme monser Henry de Machyn,[f] for

---

[a] masers *in MS.*   [b] moan made.   [c] pistoles.   [d] weight for weight.
[e] *i. e.* in the place of penance.   *Strype.*
[f] The Diarist: see some remarks on this passage in the introductory memoir of him.

ij [words ?] the wyche was told hym, that Veron the French[man] the precher was taken with a wenche, by the rep[orting] by on Wylliam Laurans clarke of sant Mare Maudle[n's] in Mylke strett, the wyche the sam Hare [a] knellyd down [be-]for master Veron and the byshope, and yett (they) would nott for[give] hym, for alle ys fryndes that he had worshephulle.

The xiij day of Desember was bered at sant Katheryns-chryst [b] chyrche my lade Lyster, sum-tyme the wyff of master Shelley of Sussex, and the dowther of the erle of Sowthamtun late lord chanseler of Engeland —Wresseley, with a harord of armes and a ij dosen of skochyons of armes.

The xv day of Desember was bered in sant Donstons in the whest master Norrey, *alleas* Dalton, kynge of armes of the North from Trent unto Barwyke.

.   .   .   .

were hanged at Tyb]orne, and on [c] off them the sur[geons took] for a notyme [d] in-to ther halle.

The sam day was a man wypyd at [a cart's] arse for *(unfinished)*

The sam day was a pelere [e] sett up in Powlles chyrche-yerd agaynst the byshope('s) plase for a man that mayd a fray in Powlles chyrche, and ys ere [f] nayllyd to the post, and after cutt off, for a fray in Powlles chyrche.

The xx day of Desember my lade the contes of Bayth ded [g] at here plase at Nuwhyngtun, late the wyff of ser Thomas Kyttsun and to ser Recherd Longe and wyff to the yerle of Bayth latt dissessyd, and she had a vj baners-rolles and a gret baner of armes and a x dosen of skochyons and vj of sylke.

The xxvj day of Desember, was sant Stheyn [h] day, was creatyd at the cowrte my lord Ambros Dudley lord Lylle and after the yerle of Warwyke, with haroldes of armes.

The xxvij day of Desember cam rydyng thrugh London a lord

---

[a] Harry.   [b] St. Katharine Cree.   [c] one.   [d] anatomy.   [e] pillory.
[f] ear.   [g] countess of Bath died.   [h] Stephen's.

of mysrull, in clene complett harnes, gylt, with a hondered grett
horse and gentyll-men rydyng gorgyously with chenes of gold, and
there horses godly trapytt, unto the Tempull, for ther was grett
cher all Cryustynmas tyll *(blank)*, and grett revels as ever was
for the gentyllmen of the Tempull evere[a] day, for mony of the
conselle was there.

.   .   .   of myssrule   .   .
playhyng and syngyng unto the [court with my] lord, ther was grett
chere at the . . . . gorgyusly aparrell(ed) with grett cheynes.

The iiij day of January cam to the c[ourt the] yerle of Kyldare,
and browth[b] the grett O'Nelle of Yrland, for he had the charge of
hym [to bring] hym to the quen.

The iiij day dyd pryche at Powlles crosse [the] dene of Powlles,
and ther dyd a man pennans; he was dume, but the masters of
Brydwell mad ym [speak], and for that cause he was there.

The xij day the lord mayre and the althermen whent to Powlles,
and all the craftes in London in ther leverey, and the bachelars,
and after cam into Chepe-syd a lord of mysrulle from Whytt-
chapell with a grett compene with many gones[c] and halbardes,
and trumpettes blohyng; and ys men well be-sene; and thrugh
Nuwgatt and in at Ludgatt and so abowtt Powlles, and so into
Chepe-syde, and so hom to Algatt.

The x day of January was cared in-to the contrey, to be bered
by her hosband the yerle and her hosband ser Thomas Kyttsun,
the contes of Bathe.

The *(blank)* day of *(blank)* master Recherd Alyngtun, the sune
of ser Gylles Alyngtun knyght of Cambryge-shyre, the wyche he
ded[d] of the smalle pokes.[e]

[The . . day of January Thomas Howard duke of Norfolk was
conducted by] the master and the ward[ens of the Fishmon]gers and
all the clothyng in-to the [guild-hall in] London, and ther he was
mad fre of [the company]; ys grane-father was Thomas Haward

---

[a] every.   [b] brought.   [c] guns.   [d] died.   [e] spokes *in MS.*

[duke of] Northfoke the last, and fre of the worshephull c[ompany of] the Fyssmongers ; and after to my lord mare to dener. The compene of the Fyssmongers dynyd at the Kyng('s) -hed in . . . . Fysstrett.

The xiiij day of January cam rydyng in-to [Cheap-] syd *(blank)* John Onelle, the wyld Yrys-man,[a] and [went] and dynyd at the sant John('s) hed at master Daneell['s the] goldsmyth ; the wyche was the sune of the erle of (Tyrone).

The xj day of January was bered in Suffoke my lade contes of Bayth wedow, and the last wyff to the sed erle, and late the wyff of ser Thomas Cutsun,[b] and late to ser Recherd Longe knyght ; with a grett banar of armes and vj banar-rolles of all mareges,[c] and a x dosen skochyons of armes, and vj of sylke wrought with fyne gold.

The xv day of January the Quen('s) grace cam to Beynard Castyll to the yerle of Penbroke to dener, and mony of here consell, and tared soper, and at nyght there was grett chere and a grett bankett, and after a maske, and here grace tared all nyght.

The xviij day of January was a play in the quen('s) hall at Westmynster by the gentyll-men of the Tempull, and after a grett maske, for ther was a grett skaffold in the hall, with grett tryhumpe as has bene sene ; and the morow after the skaffold was taken done.

. . .   women for . . . .

The sam day was ij sett on the [pillory] for conterfetyng a wrytyng that serten . . . . had sett ther hand too a lysens for to [beg ?,[d] in] dyvers sheyrs and contreys, the wyche was fa[lse.]

The 25[e] day of January was created master [Robert Cooke, Blanch-]Rosse pursewant at armes, my lord Robart [Dudley's servant,] the wyche he never servyd in no plase a-for.

The xxvij day of January was bered master Charlys Wrys[seley] *alyas* Wyndsore, with all the haroldes of armes, master [Garter,]

---

[a] Irishman.   [b] Kytson.
[c] marriages, *i. e.* impalements of the alliances of the family.
[d] *See again in p. 292.*   [e] *In MS. 27 altered to 25.*

master Clarenshux, master Chaster *alleas* Norrey, master Somersett,[a] [master York,] master Rychmond, master Lankester, Ruge-
crosse, Ruge-dragon, [Portcullis,] and Blumantylle, with vj
skochyons of armes, in sant P[ulcher's] parryche, bered in the
body of the chyrche; and they[b] payd the ch[arges].

The xxxj day of January was a proclamasyon thrughe London
that the quen('s) qwyne[c] shuld go styll from man to man; and that
Lent to be fastyd,[d] with grett charge, penalte, and sumes, and the
next tyme be punyssed.[e]

The sam day at after-none was bered in sant Necolas Oleffe
parryche good masteres Fanshawe, the good gentyll-woman, and
wyff unto master Phanthawe, on of the cheycker,[f] with no armes.

The furst day of Feybruary at nyght was the goodlyest masket
cam owt of London that ever was seen, of a C. and d's gorgyously
be-sene, and a C. cheynes of gold, and as for trumpettes and
drumes, and as for torche-lyght a ij hundered, and so to the cowrt,
and dyvers goodly men of armes in gylt harnes, and Julyus Sesar
played.[h]

[The viij day of February William Flower, Chester herald, was
created Norroy king of arms from the] Trentt north-ward; and
pursewant [Blanch-Rose,] the servand unto my lord Robart
Dudley, [was created Chester herald].

The x day of February, was Shrowse tuwsday, [was a just] at
Westmynster agaynst the qwyne('s) grase plase; the chalengers
the duke of Northfoke and the yerle of W[estmorela]nd.

The xj day of February, was Aswednysday, dyd pryche a-for the
quen master Nowelle the dene of [saint Paul's.]

The fryday after dyd pryche a-for the quen at the cowrt the
dene of Westmynster master Goodman.

The furst sunday prychyd a-for the quen master [Sandys,] the
bysshope of Wossetur.

---

[a] *Another hand has interlined* the chefe mo[urner].   [b] *i. e.* the heralds.
[c] coin.   [d] *i. e.* kept with fasting.   [e] punished.   [f] one of the Exchequer.   [g] *i. e.* 150.
   [h] *The word* played *has been added in another hand, and, though resembling the old,
may be an imitation and not contemporary.*

The xviij day of Feybruary dyd pryche at the cowrt master Nowell, the deue of Powlles, Wednysday the furst.ᵃ

The xv day of February ded ᵇ with-in the kynge('s) bynche on Hareᶜ Saxsay merser, for he was browthᵈ into the star-chambur a-for my lord keper and dyvers of the consell, and he was juged to stand on the pelereᵉ ij tyme in the weke for the spase of (*blank*) and he was condemnyd the last day of the terme, and a-pone that he toke a purgasyon that he d . . .

The xx day of Feybruary dyd pryche at the cowrt a-for the quen's grace *(blank)*

The xiiij day of Feybruary dyd rune at the rynge John Onelleᶠ be-yond sant James in the feld.

The viij day of Feybruary was crystened the dowther of master *(blank)* Crumwelle, and she the dowther of ser Raff Warren knyght,ᵍ gohyng to the chyrche a fayre mayd carehyng the chyld in a whyt saten gowne, and a-bowt and the mantylle of cremesune satyn fryngyd with gold of iiij ynchys brod, and the master of the rolles was the godfather and my lade Whytt godmother and *(blank)*, and after a grett bankett at home.

.   .   .   .

The xxiij day of Feybruary ryd in v cares [.   .   men] and iiij women for dyvers fellonsᵇ done.

The xxvij day of Feybruary was a no[ldⁱ man set] on the pelere for falsely conterfeytyng in oder men['s hands ?]

The sam day of Feybruary ryd in ij cares . . . ys wyff the master(es ?) of ser Recherd Shakfeldᵏ the master . . . for baldre, Logentt and ys wyff, and all viij for baldre.

The xvij day of Feybruary was bered in sant [Andrew's] in Holborne master Culpapare, on of the gentyll[men of] Gray('s) in, with vj skochyons of armes of the ho[use].

ᵃ *i. e.* in Lent.   ᵇ died.   ᶜ Harry.   ᵈ brought.   ᵉ pillory.   ᶠ O'Neill.

ᵍ The diarist probably means the child's mother; or else the fair maid who carried the child to the church.   ʰ felonies.

ⁱ an old man; *see* xxviij Feb.   ᵏ Sackville.

The xxviij day of Feybruary the sam old man was [set in the] pelere [a] agayne, the last day of Feybruary, for the sam offense.

The furst day of Marche, the wyche was the iij sonday (in Lent,) dyd pryche at after-none at the cowrte a-for the quen master Allen the byshope of Exsetur.

The sam day dyd pryche at Powlles the byshope of Bayth and Welles, master Bartelett.

The iiij day of Marche dyd pryche at the cowrte a-for the quen's grace (blank)

The vj day of Marche dyd pryche at the cowrt a-fore the quen('s) grase (blank)

The viij day of Marche dyd pryche a-for the quen('s) grace, the iiij sonday in Lentt, called Mydlent sonday, master Horne, the byshope of Wynchaster.

The ix day of Marche, behyng monday, one Trestram a coke with-in Westmorland plase with-in Selver strette, rode a-pone a colle-stayffe with a baskett of graynes be-for hym, bycause that on of ys neybur wyff brake her husband hed, and cast graynes on the pepull.

. . . .

. . . . . gownes and cottes and with a xx clarkes [singing; and he gave] mantyll fryse gownes to xij pore men, [and the church] hangyd with blake and armes and a iiij dosen of [sco-cheons; . . . . and strod with rysses [b] for the cheyff mornars; [master Crol]ley dyd pryche, and ther was grett audyens, and [there was] all the clothyng of the masters of the Skynners, [and a] grett dolle of money, and after hom to dener, and [went to] ther hall to dener, and a-for all the mornars offered . . . the compene of the Skynars offered ther.

The xj day dyd pryche at the cowrt the dene of Powlles master Nowell, that was wedynsday.

The sam day in the mornyng be-twyn iij and iiij begane a grett

---

[a] pillory.   [b] strewed with rushes.

tempest of wynd, that dyd grett hurt of howses and bottes,[a] and the quen-yffe[b] stayres borne a-way.

The xiij day of Marche was a proclamassyon that no man shuld [dare to] spyke[c] of fallyng of money, butt they shuld be taken and putt in pressun iij monyth, and after had to the pelere.[d]

The sam day dyd pryche at the cowrte, that was fryday a-for Passyon sonday, master Nowell the dene of Powlles.

The xij day of Marche at after-none at iij yt flod, and at v yt flod agayne the sam day.

The xv day of Marche dyd pryche at the cowrt, the wyche was the v sonday and Passyon sonday, master Nowell the dene of Powlles, for the byshope of London master Gryndall; he dyd pryche be-cause the byshope was syke[e] that day.

The xviij day of Marche dyd pryche at the cowrt master (*blank*)

The sam day was mad for a sqwyre, master (*blank*), a cott and pennon of armes and a ij dosen of skochyons of armes in metall.

The xx day of Marche dyd pryche at the cowrt, that was Palm-sonday, master Juell, the byshope of (Salisbury.)

The xxvij day of Marche dyd pryche at after-non a-for the quen, that was Good-fryday, the byshope of London.

The sam day prychyd at Powlles crosse the parson of sant Mangnus.[f]

. . . .

The xxxj day of Marche dyd pryche at the [court], that was Ester tuwysday, master Nowelle the dene of Powlles.

The furst day of Aprell master Torner of Cantur[bury preached,] the wedynsday in Ester wekke, at sant Mare spytty[l, and the] pepull kept haleday thrughe London do[g] yt was n[ight.]

The ij day of Aprell was bered in the parryche [of Allhallows] in Bredstrett master Robart Melys,[h] latt master of the Marchand [taylors,] and he gayff in gownes and cottes to the number of iij[xx]

---

[a] boats.   [b] Queen-hythe.   [c] speak.   [d] pillory.   [e] sick.
[f] Miles Coverdale, formerly bishop of Exeter.   [g] to.   [h] Mellishe. *Epitaph*.

[coats of] rattes coller [a] of vij*s*. the yerd to the pore men, and the chylderyn of the hospetall ij and ij together, and [masters] of the hospetall with ther gren stayffes in ther [hands; and master] Nowelle the dene of Powlles dyd pryche; and after to dener at ys sune [b] howse.

The v day of Aprell, behyng Low-sonday, [did preach] at Powlles master Samsun, the wyche he declaryd [c] [the sermons] thatt was mad the iij days at the spyttyll in [Lent.]

The xij day of Aprell dyd pryche at Powlles crosse (*blank*)

In Aprell was browth [d] to London a pyde calff with a grett ruffe [about] ys neke, a token of grett ruff that bowth men and women.

The xiij day of Aprell was cared unto Tyburne ix, vij men and and a boy and on woman, to be hangyd ther.

The xiiij day of Aprell was bered at sant Botulffe with-owtt Althergate mastores Hunderell,[e] with a dosen of skochyons of armes, and ther dyd pryche for here (*blank*)

The xix day of Aprell dyd pryche at Powlles crosse master Nowelle the dene of Powlles.

The xx day of Aprell was mared in the parryche of sant Don-stones in the est master Bacun('s) dowther, the salter, and brodur unto my lord keper of the selle of England; and ther was a grett wedyng; and after the marege done home to dener, for ther dynyd my lord keper and most of the conselle, and mony lades and mony of the quen's maydes gorgyowsly aparrell(ed), and grett chere; and master Valuntyne Browne dyd mare [f] here, the audetour of Bar-wyke; ther was as gret chere as has byne sene in thes days.

. . . .

The xxiij day of Aprell was sant Gorge's day, a[nd at White-h]alle the Quen('s) grase whent from her chapell with xij . knyghtes of the Garter in robes with colars of gold with garters, [and] xx of here chapelle, in copes of cloth of gold, to the of[fering, s]yngyne

---

[a] colour.   [b] son's.   [c] *i. e.* rehearsed or recapitulated: *as before in p.* 231.
       [d] brought.   [e] Underhill.   [f] marry.

the Englys presessyon from the chapell rond [about the] halle and bake agayne to the chapelle syngyng; and master [dean of] her chapell bare a boke and a robe, and master Norres [bare the] blake rod in a robe, and master Garter, all iij in cremesun saten; [and] the byshope of Wynchester warre ys robe of red (*blank*); and ser William Peter, master Clarenshux, Somersett, Yorke, Lanckaster, Rychemond, and Chaster, Ruge-dragon, and R[ouge-croix, Port-] colles, Blumantyll, Wyndsor.

The xxv day of Aprell where hangyd at Wapyng at the low-water marke v for robere on the se, and ther was one that had hys alter abowt ys neke and yett a pardon cam be tyme.

The xxx day of Aprell was mad for master Strange knyght a standard, a cott, and pennon of armes, helmett, targett and sword, and crest and mantyll, and a vj dosen of skochyons of armes, and was bered at (*blank*)

The xx day of Aprell was reynyd[a] at Yeld-hall a grett compene of marenars for robyng on the see, and a (*blank*) wher cast to be hangyd at a low-water mark.

The viij day of May was a proclamacion of the aht[b] of a-ray, and grett ruffes and grett brechys, and that no man to have butt a yerd and a halff of kersey; that no swerd to be butt a yerd and a quarter of lenth the blad, and dagars butt xij ynche the blad, and that buckelles shall not have longe pykes, but of a sysse.[c]

The ix day of May was ij prentes[d] was wypyd[e] a-bowt London for (*blank*)

Item, ther was (a) pyge brothe[f] to London in May with ij alff bodys, behyng with viij fette, that mony pepull dyd se ytt; and after cam a syne and token of a monstorous chyld that was borne be-syd Colchester at a town callyd (*blank*)

. . . .

The xj day of May was bered at (*blank*) master Swallow sqwyre,

[a] arraigned.   [b] act.   [c] of assize—or fixed form.   [d] prentices.
[e] whipt.   [f] brought.

of the chycker,[a] with a .   .   of armes, and a iij dosen skochyons
[of arms, and] ther was grett dole of money and mett.[b]

The sam day of May was the Clarkes of [London] ther communion at the Gyldhalle chapell, and ther .   .   .   .   persuns,
and after to ther halle to dener, and after a good[ly concert of]
chylderyn of Westmynster with wyballes[c] and regalles.

The ix day of May was a lade[d] and here ij systers browth[e] to
Yeld-hall, for ther was a quest that shuld .   .   .   .   .   of them
for ther nostylevyng[f] of baldre done.

The xij day of May was a goodly wedyng [at master] Whytt('s)
howse altherman be-twyne master (*blank*) unto ser Thomas Whytt('s)
dowther of the contey of (Southampton ?)

The sam day at nyght ther was a grett frey, [and my] lord mare
and the ij shreyffes was send fore,[g] and they had a do to pasefy the
pepull, and dyvers wher hurtt, and s[ertain] cared to Nuwgatt
and to the conturs, and ther was .   .   .   . .. the best archers
of London with the flethe,[h] and master Underelle hu. .   the
master of the comen-huntt.

The next nyght after my lord mare commondyd that serten constabulles shuld kepe all Smyth-feld to stand in a-ray in harnes to
see wo[i] wold be so bold to com and make any besenes,[j] and my
lord mare and the shreyffes dyd walke abowt Smyth-feld to se
wether any wold make any salt[k] as they dyd over nyght.

The xv and vj[l] day of May was sessyons at Nuwgatt, and so
many wher cast doys[m] ij days; and the sam monyth were[n] dyvers
token sene in dyvers placys in England, a calffe and *(unfinished)*

.   .   .   .

[The xvj day of May died] my [lady] Chenne, latt wyff of ser
Th[omas Cheyne, the] warden of v porttes, and ded at Todyngton.

The xx day of May they begane to make [for my lady] Chenne,

[a] Exchequer.   [b] meat.   [c] viols.   [d] lady.   [e] brought.   [f] naughty living.
[g] were sent for.   [h] Fleet ?   [i] who.   [j] business.   [k] assault.
[l] *So in MS*. 15th and 16th.   [m] those.   [n] water *in MS*.

for here buryall, a grett baner of armes [of] nuw damaske and
wroth ᵃ with fyne gold, and a xij dosen of skochyons of bokeram,
ij dosen and vj of taffata [wrought with] fyne gold; and the sam
day was Hare Machynᵇ iijˣˣ and vj yere, [the which] was Wedynsday in Wytsonwyke.

The xxj day of May was a man was cared . . . grett stayff
from Belyngattᶜ abowt London for takyng of money of pepull
for fysse,ᵈ and whent away [with] ytt.

The xxv day of May was bered master Godderyke sqwyer, the
wyche he ded at ys place with-in Whyt-freres, and cared unto
sant Andrew's in Holborne to be bered; and ther was the compene of the Clarkes syngyng pryke-song, and then cam a morner
careng ys pennon of armes, and then cam master Yorke beyryng
ys cott armur, and after master Clarenshus; and then cam the
corse with a ryche palle of tynsell and ryche cloth of sylver with
armes of bokeram; and then the morners, and after the byshope
of Canturbere and the byshope of Ely and the byshope of London,
and next my lord keper and my lord cheyffe justus of England and
mony worshephull men, and after ij C. of the ines of the cowrt fo-
lowd; and the dene of Powlles dyd pryche for hym.

The sam day was sett up at the cukold haven a grett May-polle
by bochers and fysher-men, fulle of hornes; and they mad grett
chere, for ther was ij fyrkens of fresse sturgeans, and grett konger,
and grett burttes,ᵉ and grett plente of wyne, that yt cam to viij*l.*

The sam day was a yonge man dyd hang ym-seylff at the
Polles hed, the in in Carter lane.

The sam day was the masturs the Skynners' fest, and the master
was chosen, master Gunter master, and master (*blank*) master
warden.

[The . . day of May was the funeral of lady Cheyne, late wife
of ser Thomas Cheyne councillor to] kyng Edward the vj and unto
quen [Mary and queen] Elesabett tyll he ded, and she was be[ried

---

ᵃ wrought.   ᵇ Harry Machyn, *the writer of this Diary.*
ᶜ Billingsgate.   ᵈ fish.   ᵉ butts, flounders.

at Toddington] with mony mornars; master Garter and master Norrey [were] the haroldes, and (the) dene of Powlles dyd pryc[h the sermon,] for ther was grett chere, and a grett dole [as ever] in that contrey sene—iij mylles from Donstabull.

The sam day was on [a] sett to a p[ost at the] grett gatt to Westmynster-ward, hys . . . . . for stellyng [b] of the quene('s) dyssys [c] . . . . . in Chancheler lane.[d]

The xxx day of May was a boye wypyd [e] . . . . the standard in Chepe for (*blank*)

The furst day of June was the Yrmongers' fest keptt in Fanchyrche strett be-syd . . . . time, and ther dynyd the ij shreyffes and (*blank*) althermen.

The iiij day of June ther was a chyld browth [f] to the cowrte in a boxe, of a strange fegur,[g] with a longe strynge commyng from the navyll,—browth [f] from Chechester.

The v day of June the Quen('s) grace removyd from Westmynster unto Grenwyche by water, and ther was grett shutyng of gones at the Tower as her grace whentt, and in odur places.

The vj day of June was ther on [a] Crane wyff, dwellyng in Basyng lane, toke a kneyff and frust [h] here-seylff be-tweyn the small rybes, and she ded the morowe after, and the vij day at after-none was the sam woman was bered, and serten clarkes was at her berehyng, and Veron the Frenchman dyd pryche for here, and more-overe he wold not the clarkes to brynge here to the chyrche.

. . . .

The xiij day of June was a man sett on the pelere [i] at Westmynster, for he toke money and was hyryd for [to] kylle on man, and ys here was cutt off.

The xiiij day of June whent unto the quen at Gr[eenwich] the sam prophett that men calle hym Helyas Ha[ll;] and master (*blank*) dyd pryche—master Pylkyntun, and declared of hym and off ys levyng.

---

[a] one.   [b] stealing.   [c] dishes.   [d] Chancellor or Chancery Lane.   [e] whipt.   [f] brought.   [g] figure.   [h] thrust.   [i] pillory.

The xv day of June was the Grocers' fest, and ther mony althermen and worshephull men, and ther dyd pryche master (*blank*)

The sam day was the Goldsmyth(s') fest, and at sant Foster's ther prechyd master Gowth [a] the parsune of sant Peter's in Cornhyll, and dynyd my lord mare and the ij shreyffes, ser Marten Bowse, and master Gylbart, with dyvers odur althermen.

The sam day a-for none was the pelere [b] sett up in Chepe for a man that was sett up on the pelere for the takyng of money to (*blank*)

The sam day was raynyd [c] at Westmynster hall on master Brutun gentyllman for (*blank*)

The xvj day of June was the tombe of ser Wyllyam Walw[orth] knyght and fysmonger of London and mare, and mad knyght by kynge Recherd the ij for kyllyng of Jake Kade and Wyll Walle that cam owt of Kent, yt ys nuwe frest and gyld, [d] and ys armes gyltt, with the pyctur all in aleblaster lyung in ys armur gyltt, at the cost of Wylliam Parys fysmonger, dwellyng at the Castyll in nuw Fystrette, the wyche hys a goodly rememborans for alle men of honor and worshype; he was twys mare, and when he was mare he kyld Jake Cade in Smythfeld a-for the kynge; he lyeng in sant Myghell in Crokyd lane; and he mared ys master('s) wyff that was iiij tymes mare of London, master (Lovekyn).

.   .   .   .

The xvij day of June on [e] Joh[n] Bullok [ordered?] for to make for ser Thomas Skneworth [f] knyght and late mare of London by kyng Henry the vij, and bered [in Guildhall] chapell, furst a standard and v pennons of armes, . . targett and sword and crest and mantylles of welvett, . . and at the cost of the masturs the Fyshmongers, for he [was one of the] benefacturs to the howse, and he mad a conduitt at . . . ., and at that time was nuw gare [g] mad for hym, [and the old] taken away, and the (*blank*) day of (*unfinished*)

---

[a] Gough.   [b] pillory.   [c] arraigned.   [d] freshed and gilt.
[e] one.   [f] Kneesworth.   [g] gear.

The xviij day of June was bered master Fuw[illiam][a] in the parryche of sant Johns Sacres,[b] the wyche [died] at master Kyndylmarche('s) howse of the sam parryche, wyche he kepyth a tabull for gentyllmen, [and] he had vj skochyons of armes, the wyche w[as son?] of the lord Feywylliam late lord of the preveshalle[c] and (who died) be[fore New]castyll, the wyche (*unfinished*)

The xix day of June was the sam man was [set] the pelere [d] for the sam offensys that he had at Westmynster, and the sam day was ys here [e] cut of at the standard in Chepe.

The xxj day of June dyd pryche at Powlles crosse master dene of Ettun colege be-syd Wyndsor.

The xxij day of June was the masters the Salters' fest, and ther dynyd my lord keper of the selle [f] and my lord of Bedfoord and my lord cheyff justes.

The xx day of June was a gret shutyng [g] of the compene of the Barbur-surgeantes for a gret soper at ther owne hall for a xxx mess of mett of, for they dyd make ij godley [h] stremars agaynst that day of ther harmes,[i] the wyche they wher agmentyd by the most valeant kyng at armes master *(blank)*, and they had vj drumes plahyng and a flutt; and ij grett ansutts,[k] and as a shot was wone, downe whent that and up the thodur,[l] and as they whan the shut; [m] and master Gall and ys syd wan the soper—the master of the compene.

.   .   .   .

The sam day was a man be-syd Broken-warffe frust [n] throwgh with a sword, he dwellyng at Bra   .   .   .

The sam day ded [o] docthur Crom, a grett p[reacher;] he was parsune of Aldermare.

The xxvij day of June whent to Tyburne v men and iiij women for to hange for thefte.

The xxix day of June was bered docthur Crom, parsun of Althere-Mare, with prestes and clarkes syngyng [unto] the chyrche, and bered.

[a] Fitzwilliam.   [b] Zachary's.   [c] privy seal.   [d] pillory.   [e] ear.   [f] seal.
[g] shooting—archery.   [h] goodly.   [i] arms.   [k] ancients ?—flags.   [l] other.
[m] won the shot.   [n] thrust.   [o] died.

The furst day of July was the Marchand-tayllers' fest, and dynyd my lord mare, the yerle of Sussex, the yerle of Kyldare, ser (*blank*) Stanley, and ser Thomas Whytt, ser Thomas Offeley and master Ro . ., ser Wyllyam Huett, ser Marten Bowes, master Cowper, master Allen, master Gyl[bert,] master Chamburlayn altherman, master Champyon, master Avenon, master Malere, and master Baskerfeld, and the master and the iiij wardens and the clarkes and the bedyll of the Skynnars, and mony worshephull men, and mony lades and gentyllwomen, and they had agaynst the dynner iij^{xx} and (*blank*) bukes [a] and iiij stages; [b] and master Wylliam Allen electyd shreyff for the quen, and master Whettelle the master, and master Raff Whytt hed warden and master Mar . . and master serjant Halle and master Browne wardens ; and master Garter and master Clarenshux dynyd there.

The xxviij day of June grett wache [c] at the Towre and at Towrehylle and sant Katharyn's, a C. hagabuttes and a C. in cossellettes, vj drumes and iiij flages, on sant Peter's evyn last past, and a castylle and sqwybys.

The v day of July ther wher at Westmynster ij chylderyn plahyng to-gether, behyng sonday (*unfinished*)

The vij day of July, Symon Smyth browth [d] to the gyld-halle Kynlure Machen for to have lyssens [e] to have here to have a hosband Edward Gardener cowper, and they wher browth in-to the consell chamber a-for my lord mayre and the althermen and master recorder and master Surcott and master Marche, and they wher examynyd whether they where sure or not, but at the last yee sayd . . . .

.   .   .   .

do]wther of Cristofer Machyn.

The xiiij day of July was a grett sh[ooting of the] parryche of sant Gregores in Powlles chyrche-yerd, [the one] halff agaynst the thodur; [f] on [g] syd had yelow [scarfs, and] thodur red skarffes,

---

[a] bucks.   [b] stags.   [c] watch.   [d] brought.
[e] licence.   [f] other.   [g] one.

and a vj drumes and iiij fluttes; [and so] to my lord of London('s) plase to soper, a c. mes[ses.]

The xx day of July was goodly weddyng in (*blank*) parryche, of master Coke and master Nycolles dowther; for ther w[ere the lord] mare and alle the althermen, and mony lades * and mony w[orship-ful] men and women, and after the wedyng was done [they went] home to the Bryghowse to dener, for ther w[as a great dinner] as ever was sene, and all maner musyke, and d[ancing all the] day longe, and at nyght goodly soper; and after a goodly [masque? at] mydnyght; at the wedyng master Becon dyd pryche; for [there were] no maner mettes * nor drynges * that cold be had for m[oney that were wanting].

The sam day was bered mastores Wast in sant [Andrew's] in the Warderobe, with alff a dosen skochyons of armes, now the wyff of (*blank*)

The sam nyght was the Mercers' soper, and ther sopy[d my] lord of Penbroke and (*unfinished*)

The xxj day of July was grett cher at the Bryghowse, at the sam wedyng at master Necolles, and after soper cam iij maskes; on was in cloth of gold, and the next maske was frers, and the iij was nunes; and after they dansyd be-tymes, and after frers and nunes dansyd to-gether.

The xxij day of July was a grett shutyng * of the paryche of (*blank*)

The xxiij day of July was my lord Gylles * dowther cristened at sant Botulf with-owtt Byshope-gatt, Mare, the dowther of my lade Powlett; the godfather master Smyth of the custum-howse, and master John Whyt('s) wyff altherman and mastores (*blank*)

.   .   .   .

[The . . day of July was christened the do]wther of Wylliam Harve *aleas* Cla[renceux king of] armes, in the parryche of sant Brydes, th[e godfather] Cordall master of the rolles knyght, and

---

* ladies.   * meats.   * drinks.   * shooting, i. e. archery.
                    * lord Giles Powlett.

the godmothers my lade Bacon my lord keper('s) wyff, and my lade Sysselle [wife of] ser Wylliam Sysselle;[a] and after unto master Clarenshux('s), and ther was a grett bankett as I have sene, and wass[ail, of] epocras, Frenche wyne, Gaskyn wyne, and Reynys [wine,] with grett plente, and all ther servandes had a banekett in the hall with dyvers dyssys.[b]

The sam day a commondementt cam downe to my lord mare that evere craft in London shuld resortt to theyre [halls] to make owt a vj C. men well be-sene in cosseletts, gones and bowes and pykes, with all sped, and to take clen . . . up and comely.

The xxx day of July was bered in sant Talphes[c] in Crepullgatt mastores Parston, late the wyff of master Howelle doctur of phe-syke, with a xij clarkes syngyng; and then cam the corse with vj skochyons of bokeram, and a xij mornars, and xvj pore women in blake gownes; and master Coverdalle mad the sermon; and after to the plase to dener.

The furst day of August was bered mastores Starke the wyff of master Starke skynner, and the docthur[d] of master Avenon shreyff of London, with a xvj clarkes syngyng and a x pore women in mantyll fryse gownes, master shreyff the cheyffe morner, and after a xx mornars in blake, boyth men and women, and master Busken mad the sermon.

The sam day was bered a mayd, and the docthur of Thomas Grenway, brodur unto master altherman Grenway, dwellyng in Northfoke at a towne (*blank*)

The sam day my lord mare and the althermen and all craftes of London whent to Yeld-hall to chuse a nuw shreyff, and thay dyd chuse master Chamburlayn altherman, yrmonger, shreyff for the nex(t) yere.

.   .   .   .

The iiij day of August the menysters wyff [of . . .] parryche fell done a stayre and brake here neke.

The vj day of August was reynyd[a] at Yeld-hall vij, vj for qwynnyng[b]; iiij was cast for deth, Thomas Wylford, Thomas Borow, . . . Maltby, Phelipe Furney gold-smyth, and ij fr[eely] qwytt; and ther satt a-pone them my lord [justice] Chamley, ser Recherd Sakefeld, the master of the rolles, [sir Martin] Bowes, ser Wylliam Garett, ser William Huett, master re[corder], master Surcott, and master Chydley and master Eldertun.

The x day of August was drane from . . . . unto Tyborne Phelype Furney gold-smyth d[welling in] sant Barthelmuwe in Smythfeld for cowyning,[c] and hangyd after, and (blank) Walker was cared in a care to Tyburne, and hangyd for robere.

The x day of August was Barbur-surgyons' fest, and they capt[d] ther communion at sant Alphes at Crepull-gatt, and master Recherdsun dyd pryche, the Skott; ther was good syngyng; and after to ther halle to dener, and after dener a play.

The xvij day of August was the Waxchandler(s') fest, for ther was good chere.

The xviij day of August was a commondementt to my lord mare and to my masters the althermen that all the compene of all craftes that dyd dyscharge[e] alle the men that where prest and taken up to go of the qwene('s) afarerse[f] where her grace wold, that shuld goo to grett charge to the cette of London and here grace, boyth corselettes and clokes of brod bluw gardyd with red, and gones, and bowes, and mores pykes.

. . . .

. . . . . ther hall; and ther dynyd ser Thomas Whytt, ser Tho . . . . .

The xxxj day of August was bered in Essex the good erle [of Oxford, with] iij haroldes of armes, master Garter, master Lancostur, master Rych[mond, with a st]andard and a grett baner of armes, and viij baner-rolles, [helmet,] crest, targett, and sword, and cott armur, and a herse with velvett [and a] palle of velvett, and

[a] arraigned.　　　[b] coining.　　　[c] coining.　　　[d] kept.
[e] *Apparently*, that they should despatch.　　　[f] affairs.

a x dosen of skochyons, [and with] mony mornars in blake, and grett mone mad for hym.

The furst day of September was bered in the parryche [of saint B]rydes in Fletstrett master Hulsun skrevener of London and master Heyword('s) depute,[a] and on of the masturs of Brydwell; and ther wher all the masturs of Brydwell with gren stayffes in ther handes, [and] the chylderyn of the hospetall, at ys berehyng; and ther was mony mornars in blake, and [master] Crowley dyd pryche; [and there] was grett ryngyng as ever was hard,[b] and the godely ry . . ; and he had a dosen of skochyons of armes in metalle.

The iij day of September cam rydyng owt of Essex from [the funeral] of the yerle of Oxford ys father the yonge yerle of Oxford, with vij-skore horse all in blake throughe London and Chepe and Ludgatt, and so to Tempulle bare, and so to *(blank)*, be-twyn v and vj of the cloke at after-none.

The sam day be-gane to make rede[c] for the good lade contes[d] of Bedford a grett baner of armes and vj grett baner-rolles and . . skochyons of armes of sylke, and of paper-ryalle vij doshen skochyons of armes.

The sam tyme they be-gane to make for my lord Mordant in Bedfordshyre furst a standard and a gret baner of armes, and *(blank)* banar-rolles and vj skochyons of armes of [silk,] and of bokeram *(blank)* dosen, and of paper *(blank)* dosen skochyons, and a targett, sword, helme, and crest, mantylls and *(blank)* dosen of sylke, and a cott armur, and grett skochyons of armes for the herse [of] past[e] papur, and goodly bordurs rond abowt the herse.

The ix day of September was bered the contes of Be[dford] at Chennys with iij haroldes of armes, with a[f] grett baners of mareges,[g] and vj banar-rolles, and viij dosen of skochyons, and mony mornars in blake.

The viij day of September whent thrughe London a prest,[h] with

---

[a] Deputy to Rowland Heyward, alderman ?   [b] heard.
[c] ready.   [d] lady countess.   [e] pasted.   [f] *So in MS.*   [g] marriages.   [h] priest.

a cope, taken sayhyng of masse in Feyter lane at my lade (*blank*), and so to my lord mare, and after to the contur in . . . ; and the thursday after he was cared to the Masselsay.

. . . .

. . . an for kyllyng of her . . . .

The xj day of September was a man sett on [the pillory] for conterfeytyng a false wrytyng to bege in dyvers places in London, and puttyng in mony honest men('s) ha[nds [a] to] gyff ym lysens to bege, butt yt was false, the w . . .

The xiij day of September cam tydynges to [London that] *(blank)* was delevered unto the *(blank)*

The xv day of September cam from Mylle[-end saint] Antony('s) skoll[b] done Cornnyll[c] and so to the Stokes, and so to . . ., with stremars and flages and a viij drumes plahy[ng, with] C. chylderyn of the skolle well be-sene; and after [they went] home to ther fathers and fryndes.

The xvj day of September was bered my [lady] Mordantt in the conte of (Bedford).

The xviij day of September my lord mare and my masters the althermen, and mony worshephull men, and dyvers of the masturs and wardens of the xij compenys, red[d] [to the] condutth hedes for to se them, after the old coustum; and a-[fore] dener they hundyd the hare and kyllyd, and so to dener to the hed of the condyth, for ther was a nombur, and had good chere of the chamburlayn; and after dener to hontyng of the fox, and ther was a goodly cry for a mylle, and after the hondys kyllyd the fox at the end of sant Gylles, and theyr was a grett cry at the deth, and blohyng of hornes; and so rod thrugh London, my lord mare Harper with all ys compene home to ys owne plase in Lumberd strett.

The xviij day of September was my lord mare dyd warne all the craftes to bryng in ther men in harnes[e] to Leydynhall with pykes

---

[a] *i. e. forging their signatures.*   [b] school.   [c] down Cornhill.   [d] rode.   [e] harness.

and gones and bowes and bylles, in bluw clokes gardyd with red, and ther to take a wue [a] of them tyll nyght, and they wernyd [b] to muster in Morefeld the morowe after, and ther captaynes' names master Wakham and master (blank)

. . . .

. . . . . ard Brandford, and at vj captayn (blank) . . . . ther jorney to Byshope-gatt, and so to Sowthwarke, [and so to Por]thmowth, and ther harnes [c] cared in dry fastes.[d]

The xxx day of September was raylles mad at sant [Giles's with]wtt Crepull-gatte, and hangyd with blake and armes, [for the] gentyll knyght ser Hare Gray, and was brodur unto the [earl of Ke]nt, with ij haroldes of armes, master Clarenshux kynge, and Ruge-crosse pursewantt of armes, and he bare the helme and [crest, master] Clarenshux the cott of armes, and then the standard and [banners of] armes; and the clarkes syngyng; and then the corse covered [with a bla]ke velvett pall with a whyt crosse of saten and armes a-p[on it,] and many mornars in blake; and ther dyd pryche master (Nowell) the [dean of] Powlles; and after he was bered home to the plase to d[inner, where] ther was good chere, dener after dener tyll iiij of the [clock.]

The sam day the nuw shreyffes of London toke ther barges, and yed to Westmynster halle, and toke ther othe in the checker, master Allen and master Chamburlayn shreyffes.

The sam day at nyght be-twyn viij and ix was a grett fray in Redcrosse stret betwyn ij gentyllmen and ther men, for they dyd mare [e] one woman, and dyvers wher hurtt; thes wher ther names, master Boysse [f] and master Gaskyn gentyllmen.

The ij day of October was bered in sant Austen's parryche master Robartt Duckyngtun marchand-tayller, and latt warden of the Marchand-tayllers' compene; and ther wher all the masters of the compene in ther leverey, and he gayff mony gownes bowth to pore and ryche, and he was the best howse-kepar of a comm[oner] in London, and the feynest mett drest and plente.

---

[a] view.   [b] were warned.   [c] harness.   [d] So MS. for fattes (vats).
       [e] marry.   [f] Bowes?

The viij day of October my lord the duke of Northfoke and the duches my good lade ys wyff cam rydyng thrughe London and thrughe Byshope-gatt to Leydyn-hall, and so to Chrychyre [a] to ys own plase, with a C. horse in ys leverey was ys men gentyll-men a-fore cottes gardyd with velvett, and with iiij haroldes a-for hym, master Clarenshux kyng at armes, master Somersett and master Ruge-crosse and master Blumantylle ryd a-fore.

.   .   .   .

.   .   .   .   .   . to be bered at sant [Dunstan's in the west?] mastores Chamley the wyff of master Ch[amley recorder? of Lo]ndon, with a palle of blake velvett and with .   .   .   .   .   . ther dyd pryche at her berehyng master (blank) .   .   . mornars, and she had a harold of arm .   .   .   . dosen of skochyons of armes; and after home t[o dinner.]

The xxix day of October the nuw mare [b] [went by] water unto Westmynster, and all the althermen and the craftes of London in barges deckyd with stremars, [and there] was a goodly fuste [c] decked with stremars and banars, with drumes, trumpetes, and gones to Westmynster playce,[d] [where] he toke ys oythe,[e] and so home to Beynard castylle, [and] with all the artheralthmen; [f] and in Powlles chyrcheyerd ther mett (him) all the bachelars in cremesun damaske hodes, with drumes and flutes and trumpettes blohyng, and a lx powre men in bluw gownes and red capes,[g] and with targettes and jaffelyns [and] grett standardes, and iiij grett banars of armes and .   .   . and after a goodly pagantt with goodly musyke plahyng; and to Yeld-halle to dener, for ther dynyd mony of the consell and all the juges and mony nobull men and women; and after dener the mare and all the althermen yede to Powlles with all musyke.

The xxxj day of October was bered good mastores Luwen, wedowe, latte the wyff of master Thomas Luwen yrmonger and altherman, and she gayff a xxiiij gownes to powre women, and she

---

gayff mony blake gownes; and ther was the compene of the Clarkes; and a ij dosen of skochyons of armes; and master Chamburlayn the shreyff and John Dune here servand was here sekturs,[a] and master Wylliam Draper oversear; and dyre[b] dyd pryche for here master Goodman the dene of Westmynster; and all the crafte of the Yrmongers ther; and after to here plase, for ther was a grett dener for as mony as wold cum, and after was sent spyse bred to evere howse and about the cette[c] unto worshephulle men and women.

The iiij day of November dyd ryd a woman thrugh London, she dwellyng in sant Necolas shambulles, for baldre, or okuwpyng of here owne gayre.

. . . . forth and shuld have bene . . . . as Blakewelle the sune of master Blakwell . . . . was cheyfe mornar there.

The viij day of November the Quen('s) grace removyd from Hamtun cowrt toward London, and be-twyn iij and [iiij o'clock] cam by Charyng-crosse, and so rod unto Some[rset plac]e with mony nobull men and women, and with har[olds of a]rmes in ther cotte armurs; and my lord Thomas [Howard bare] the sword a-for the quen to Somersett plase, and the [Queen will abide] ther tyll Criustynmas, and then to Whyt-halle.

The xiiij day of November dyd ryde in a care a w[ife] dwellyng in the longe entre at the Stokes at the syne of *(blank)* kepyng a taverne, for okuwpy here own . . . . .

The sam day at nyght cam a commondement [to] the masturs of every parryche and mastores shuld pray to [God] thys iij days for to helpe them that be send[d] [be-]yond the see agaynst the Duke of Gwys, the wyche the prynce of Co[ndé] doys in-tentt[e] for to mett in the feld on Tuwsday.

The monday the xvj day of November was mar[ed at Bow] parryche master Allen the shreyff('s) dowthur unto master Star[ke] marchand and skynner, and ther was mony worshep-

---

[a] her executors.   [b] there.   [c] city.   [d] sent.   [e] does intend.

[ful] men and women, and dyd pryche master Crolley, and after a gre[at dinner.]

The xix day of November at after-non was [a] fray with-owtt Tempull-bare agaynst master Huntun *['s house ?] that mared my lady of Warwyke, and ther was sl[ain] master Banaster, servand unto master Huntun, by *(blank)*

The xviij day of November was bered at Hakenay master Dedycott sqwyre and draper of London, and ther he gayff to *(blank)* pore men xxiiij gownes of rattes coler of vij*s.* the yerd, and had a penon of armes and cott armur, and master Rychemond was the harold; and he gayff mony blake gownes a xx . . . and ij dosen of skochyons of armes, and ther was a xx [of the] clarkes of London syngyng, and ther dyd pryche master *(blank)*; and ther was the masters of the hospetall with gren stayffes; master Avenon and master Mynors cheyff mornars; and after to ys plase to dener.

　　　．　　．　　．　　．　　．　　．　　．　　．　　．

． . . . Dormer] sqwyre, [the son] of ser Myghell Dormer, late mare [of London].

The xxj day of November was bered in Colm[an street ?] . .
． . . . . om the phesyssion, with a dosen of skockyons [of arms, and] all the clothyng of the Penters in ther leveray, and . . . . . there at ys berehyng.

The xxij day of November was bered at Why[techapel ?] mastores Typkyn wedow, latt the wyff of master Typkyn, bered . . . dosen of skochyons of armes; and she gayff a xij gownes [of frie]sse unto xij pore women, and she gayff a xl blake [gowns and] cassokes and blake cottes; and ther was a xvj clarkes, and master Phylpott dyd pryche; and after to sant Katheryn's [to her] howse to dener, for ther was good chere.

The xxvj day of November at nyght was slayne a carter by a Frenche-man, because that the carter cold [not give] hym rome for presse of cartes that was ther that tyme.

　　　　　* Unton.

The ij day of Desember was bered mastores Welles the . . .
of master Clarenshux kyng of armes,[a] with a palle of blake v[elvet,
and] with a dosen of skochyons of armes, and master Clarenshux
and the . . . . wher the mornars, and browtt to the chyrche
of sant Brydes; and master Phylpott made the sermon; and after
hom unto master Clarenshux ['s place, and] a grett dener as cold
be had for the tyme.

The v day of Desember ded ser Homfrey Browne knyght in the
mornyng and juge of *(blank)* and lord justes Browne.

The xv day of Desember was cared by the Clarkes of London
from Seypulkurs unto sant Martens orgaynes in Kanwykstrett[b] to
be bered be on of ys wyffes the lord justes Browne and knyght,
with ij haroldes of armes, master Clarenshux and master Somersett; furst whent a-for xxiiij pore men in mantyll fryse gownes,
and after a xx clarkes carehyng ther surples on ther armes, and
next the standard borne by a mornar, and then cam the ij
chaplens and dyvers mornars, and then cam a harold bayryng
the helme and crest, and next cam master Clarenshux beyryng
the cott of armes, and then cam the pennone of armes, and then
cam the corse with a palle of blake velvett with armes on yt, and
then the cheyff mornars and my lord Mordantt with odur, and
then came the juges and sergant(s) of the coyffe, and next all the
ynes of the cowrt in a-ray, a gret nombur, and thruge Chepesyd;
and master Renakur mad the sermon, and after home to a grett
dener.

. . . .
. . . . . , and armes and after ys helmet . . . . . .
. . . . . targett and after ys sword, and after ys cott [armour]
. . . . . . offered, and ys pennon offered, and after alle . .
. . . . . serjantes of the law and servandes offered.

The xx day of Desember was bered my lord Gr[ey of Wilton]
knyght of the Garter, sum-tyme capten of Gynes, and bered [at]

---

[a] William Harvey.   [b] Candlewick-street, *now* Cannon-street.

(blank) with a herse garnyssed with velvett and blake and armes,
[with four] haroldes of armes, master Garter prensepalle, and master
Norrey kyng at armes, [Chest]ur harold and Ruge-dragon, and ther
was a xx clark[es syng]yng all the way, furst ij porters in blake with
blake sta[ffs and] in gownes, and then the standard borne, and then
mo . . . . the grett baner of ys armes, and then the harold
[bearing the] helmett and crest, and a-nodur the targett and the
sword, and a-nodur [the coat armour;] then master Garter, and
then the corse, with a ryche palle; and . . . . of ys men
bayryng ytt; and iiij grett banar-rolles of m[arriages;] after the
cheyffe mornars and after mony mornars, and th[ere did prea]che
master *(blank)*; and ther was iij dosen of bokeram skochyons of
armes, and viij dosen of penselles to garnys [a] the herse, and . . .
grett skochyons of pastyd paper, and the chyrche hangyd with blake
and armes, and a viij dosen of skochyons of armes; and after a[ll
done at] the berehyng all they when(t) bake agayne unto master
de[an's] plase to dener, for ther was a nobull dener as [has] bene
sene for venesun and wyld fulle.[b]

The xxvj day of Desember cam tydynges unto the cowrt thatt
the prynse of Condutt [c] and the duke of Gwys mett in the [field,]
and that the prynse was taken, and mony taken and slayne, [and
many] taken pressonars.

The xxx day of Desember was slayne in John's strett . Gylbard
gold-smyth dwellyng at the sene [d] of the Blake Boy in the Ch[eap,]
by ys wyff('s) sun callyd *(blank)*

The *(blank)* day of January ther was a Frenche mayd dwellyng
in the Whytt frerers in Fletstrett she was delevered of a pratte [e]
gyrlle, and after she brake the neke of the chyld, and cared yt in-to
Holborn feld, and bered (it) undur a turffe; and ther was a man and
a woman dyd folowe her, and saw wher she layd yt, and toke her,
and browth [f] her thedur, and mad her take yt up, and browth
here to the altherman's depute, and he send [g] her to the conter.

---

[a] garnish.   [b] fowl.   [c] Condé.   [d] sign.   [e] pretty.
          [f] brought.   [g] sent.

[The xij day of January the Queen's second Parliament began to sit at Westminster, and the] lordes and byshopes rod in ther [parliament robes, and] the Quen('s) grase in cremesun welvett, [and the earl of] Northumburland [a] bare the sword a-for the quen; [all the] haroldes of armes in ther cotte armurs, and all the trumpettes [blowing], and lythe [b] at owre lade of Grace chapell, and they [went in]to the abbay, and ther was a sermon (by Nowell, dean of Saint Paul's.[c])

The xxix day of January was bered in sant [Olave's?] in the Jury my lade Dormer, late the wyff of ser Myghell Dormer [knyght], latt mare of London and merser and stapuller, ... and master doctur Dalle and ser Thomas her chaplen her sekturs,[d] and ther [were four] haroldes of armes, master Somersett, master Clarenshux, Marshalle and Ry[chmond,] and the qwyre hangyd with blake and armes, and ther was . . . . the corse and hangyd with blake and armes, and then cam the corse [covered with a] palle of blake velvett with armes a-pon bokeram skochyons; [and there were] iij pennons of armes borne a-boutt the corse; and xxvj roset gownes for so many pore women, and a lx blake gownes and cottes; [and there] dyd pryche the vekar, callyd Busken, of the parryche; and a v dosen of skochyons of armes, and after to here plase to dener.

The xxx day of January dyd ij women ryd a-bowtt London in a care; on for a common skold, with a dystaffe in her hand; the thodur with a whyt rod in here hand, with bluw hodes on ther hedes, for okuw-pye her owne gayre.

The ij day of Feybruary callyd Candyllmasse day ther was serten men whent to Duram plase and to sant Mare spyttyll to here masse, and ther was serten of them cared by the gard and othur men to the contur and odur plases.

The vij day of Feybruary dyd pryche at Powlles crosse the byshope of Durram, the sonday callyd Septuagesyma.

---

[a] *D'Ewes says* the Earl of Worcester. *Strype.*   [b] alighted.
[c] *D'Ewes.*   [d] executors.

The x day of Feybruary was browth a-bed within [the] Towre with a sune my lade Katheryn Harfford,[a] wyff to the yerle of Harfford, and the god-fathers wher ij warders of the Towre, and ys name was callyd Thomas.

The (blank) day of Feybruary was crystened at sant Androwes in the warderobe Gorge Bacun the sune of master Bacun sqwyre, sum-tyme serjant of the catre[b] by quen Mare days; ys god-fathers wher yonge master Gorge Blakewelle and master Walpolle; god-modur mastores Sens Draper of Cammerell[c] be-yond Nuw-hyngtun; and after grett chere.

.   .   .   .

The .   . day of Feybruary was mared[d] at Allalows .   .   . Davenett marchand-tayller unto master Sparke('s) dowther; .   . .   . of Wynchester mad the sermon at the marege, and after a grett dener, and at nyght a maske.

The xv day of Feybruary cam rydyng to London [through Ch]epe unto Cold Harbard my yonge lord Talbott with iij skore [horse].

The xvj day of Feybruary were ij men sett on the pelere[e] at Westmynster, one master Thymbulbere and on (blank) Charnok for .   .   .

The xvij day of Feybruary was a dobull marege at [Baynard's] Castyll at the yerle of Pembroke('s) plase, my lord Talbot unto my lade (Anne) Harbard, and my lord Harbard of Cardyff unto my lade the [eldest] syster unto my lord Talbot; and after was a grett denner as [has] bene sene, for iiij days, and evere nyght gret mum-meres[f] and m[asks.]

The xx day of Feybruary was bered at sant Brydes in Flett-strett master Denham sqwyre, and the chyrche ther was mad[g] ray[led] and hangyd with blake and armes, and he was cared to the chyrche, a-for him a mornar bayryng a pennon of armes, and after cam a harold of armes bayryng ys cott armur, and then cam the corse with a palle of blake velvett with armes

[a] Hertford.   [b] Acatry.   [c] Camberwell.   [d] married.   [e] pillory.
[f] mummeries.   [g] made.

on yt, and iiij of ys men bare hym; and then the mornars, the cheyffe was ser Recherd Sakfeld, and a xx mo mornars; and the dene of Westmynster mad the sermon; and after ther was a grett dener of all maner of fysse; and a ij dosen of skochyons.

The sam day was bered at my lord of Bedford('s) one master Sant John, with vj skochyons of armes of bokeram.

The xxij day of Feybruary, was Shroyff-monday, at Charyng-crosse ther was a man cared of iiij men, and a-for hym a bagpype playng, a shame [a] and a drum playhyng, and a xx lynkes bornyng a-bowtt hym, because ys next neybor('s) wyff ded bett [b] here hosband; ther-for yt (is) ordered that ys next naybor shall ryd a-bowtt the plase.

. . . . . gayff xxiiij good gownes . . . . . gayff a lx gowne and cottes of blake and . . . . . worshephull men and women to bryng her; [and the] cheyrche was hangyd with blake and armes, . . . skochyons of armes; and master Beycun mad the sermon; [and so] home to ys plase to dener.

The . . day of Feybruary was cared by water unto [the . . . . vj on master Foskue [c] . . . of the Poolles.

The iiij day (of) Marche ther was a man's dowther dwellyng in sant James in Garlyke heyff,[d] in the plase that w[as the] yerle of Wosetur('s) plase, she was delevered with a chyld, and after caste yt owt of a wyndow in-to Temes, and after Daker co . . .

The viij day of Marche wher hangyd at Tyburne x men; [one] was Brutun, and (blank) after browth [e] bake to sant Pulkurs ther to be bered, and ther master Veron the vecar mad a sermon for them.

The sam (day) mastores Bacun was chyrched at sant Androw's in warderobe, the wyff of master Bacun sergantt of the catre unto quen Mare, and after she whent home unto here father's howse master Blakwelle, and so she and a grett compene of gentyll women had a grett dener as cold be had as for lentt, as for fysse.

The xvij day of Marche dyd on master Lynsey armorer dwellyng

[a] shawm.   [b] beat.   [c] Fortescue?   [d] hithe.   [e] brought.

in Byshope-gatt strett dyd hang hym-seylff in a preve howse with-in ys hone howse,[a] for he had ys offes taken away from hym by on that he had browth [b] up.

The sam day ther was a mad [c] dwellyng in Hay lane with master Campyon berbruar [d] in grett Allalowes in Temes-strett dyd falle owt of a wyndow and brake her neke.

The sam day at the Well with ij bokettes in sant Martens ther was (a) woman dwellyng ther toke a pere of sherers [e] for to have cutt here throwtt, butt she myssyd the pype in here syknes and madnes, and with a day after she ded [f] and was bered ther in the parryche.

. . . . . . and to the Masselsay to the . . . . that he had a lysens for to kyll fl[esh.]

[The . .] day of Marche ther stod a man at Powlles [with a white] shett [g] a-bowtt hym for gettyng ys owne dowther . . , that after she ded.

The xxj day of Marche dyd pryche at Powlles crosse the by-shope of Wynchastur, and mad a godly sermon.

The xxij day of Marche was mad [h] for ser Wylliam Fuw[illiam [i]] that ded [j] in the tym of kyng Henre the viij[th] and was bered [in the county] of Northamtun, furst a nuw standard and a penon and armes, [coat] armur, elmett and mantyll, crest, targett, and sword; and the old tak[en away; the] crest a busse of fethers standyng with-in a crown of gold.

The xxj day of Marche tydynges cam to the cowrt that on off the quen's shypes callyd the Grahond was lost gohyng to Nuw-havyn; the captayn was ser Thomas Fynche knyghtt of Kent, and ys brodur and on of my lord Cobbam('s) brodur and ij of my lord Whentforth[k]('s) bredurne and mony gentyll men and mynstorels; [one] of my lord of Warwyke('s) newys, [l] and a good mastur; and mony [good] marenars and sawgears [m] to the nombur of (*blank*)

---

[a] own house.   [b] brought.   [c] maid.   [d] beer brewer.   [e] pair of shears.
[f] died.   [g] sheet.   [h] made.   [i] FitzWilliam.   [j] died.
[k] Wentworth.   [l] nephews.   [m] soldiers.

The xxvj day Marche was bered the good lade Chastur [at] Rayston, the wyff of ser Robartt Chastur knyght, with a pennon of armes and a iiij dosen of skochyons and a vj of bokeram, and the chyrche hangyd with blake and armes, and master Somersett was the harold; and ther was mony mornars in blake, and grett mon[a] mad for her, and a sarmon, and a grett dolle of money, and mett[b] and drynke, and after a grett dener.

The xxix day of Marche was browthe[c] from sant Savyour's late abbay in Barmsey-strett[d] to be bered my good lade Lane the wyff of ser Robart Lane of Northamtunshyre, and was bered in sant Towllys[e] in Sowthwarke, and ded[f] in chyld-bede; and with xx clarkes, and a-for the corse a xij of her servandes in blake cottes a-for here, and then cam serten gentyll-men mornars, and then cam the penon of armes borne by a gentyll-man, and then cam master Clarenshux, and next the corse borne by vj women, and iiij gentyll-men mornars beyryng the iiij corners of the palle of blake velvett, and with armes, and after to the chyrche, and syngyng the clarkes; andt her dyd pryche master Coverdalle.

[The . . day of March was buried master David Woodroffe, alderman and haberd]asher [of London,] . . . . and l blake gownes and cottes and . . . . . whent a-for hym and after a xx clarkes [with their surplices] a-pon ther armes, and next iiij althermen in [violet]; then cam a morner, beyryng hys pennon of ys [arms], a harold beyryng ys cotte armur, and next master Clarenshux [in his] cott armur kyng of armes, and next cam the corse covered with a pall of blake velvett and with armes hangyng of ytt, and vj [mourners] beyreng the corse, and next ij pennons borne on evere syd; [the chief] mornar master Voderoff ys eldest (son), and next master Stonhowse ys sune [in law, and a]nodur sune and a-nodur sune-elaw[g], and mony odur mornars, [to the] chyrche, and then mony women mornars; the iiij althermen [sir William] Garrett, ser Thomas Offe-

[a] moan.   [b] meat.   [c] brought.   [d] Bermondsey-street.
    [e] St. Olave's.   [f] died.   [g] son-in-law.

ley, ser Wyllam Chastur and master Cristoffer D[raper]; and
(the) chyrche hangyd with blake and armes rond a-bowtt, andin
. . . . the chyrche was raylles mad[a] and hangyd with blake,
[and] the strett hangyd with blake and armes, and the howse;
and . . . . dyd pryche; and after they offered ys cott and
pennon of armes, and all the mornars and the craft offered, and
after [to his place] to dener.

The xxx day of Marche in Kent master Marlow, a marchand
[living] at Crayford, dyd ryd to ys farme a mylle off to loke [over
it], and after ryd in-to the marche[b] a-pon the walle, and by mys-
f[ortune] fell of on ys horse, and ded[c] for lake of help, for ther
[was no]body with hym to help ym.

The furst day of Aprell ther was a man dwellyng at the Bryg-
howse, on Chalenger a baker of the Bryg-howse; he was send for
to the yeld-hall a-for my lord mayre and the althermen, and he
was juged to go be-twyne ij of the off-ffesars of the hospetall to
the bryg-howse, and a-for him was cared a fyne pelere[d] by on of
the hospetalle.

The vii day of Aprell at sant Katheryns be-yond the Towre the
wyff of the syne of the Rose a tavarne was set on the pelere[e] for
ettyng of rowe flesse[f] and rostyd boyth,[g] and iiij women was sett
in the stokes all nyght tyll ther hosbandes dyd feyche them hom.

The (blank) day of Aprell cam serten of the consell to the By-
shope('s) hed in Lumbardstrett.

. . . .

. . . . . . ys fase toward the hors taylle . . . . . .
. . . . . hym and that he was taken for tellyng . . . .
honest men of talle pellettes.[h]

The xij day of Aprell, was Ester monday, dyd pryche at sant
Mare spyttyll master Horne the byshope of Wynchastur, and
ther was my lord mare and the althermen in skarlett, and certen
juges and serjantes of the law, and mony worshephulle men and

---

[a] made.   marsh.   [c] died.   [d] pillory.   [e] pillory.
          [f] raw flesh.   [g] both, i. e. also.   [h] billets?

women, and the masturs of the hospetall with ther gren stayffes in ther handes, [and the] chylderyne of the hospetall boyth boysse and wenchys in bluw [coats and] red capes[a] to the nombur of a *(blank)*, and ther was geydered at the sermon for the Frenche men [refugees] in-to England women and chylderyn the sum of xlv *li*.

The xiij day of Aprell dyd pryche at sant Mare spyttyll tuwysday in Ester weeke master Colle parsun of Hehenger[b] in Essex and (dean elect) of Norwyche, and my lord mare and ij juges and the althermen and byshopes, with all the masturs of the hospetall and the chylderyn.

The xiiij day of Aprell dyd pryche at the spyttylle the wedynsday the dene of Powlles in Ester wyke.

The xviij day of Aprell dyd pryche at Powlles crosse master Bradley, and he declaryd[c] the iij sermons that was prychyd at the spyttylle.

The sam day at after-none was cristenyd my lord mayre['s son;] the godfathers wher, on[d] the yerle of Penbroke, and (*unfinished*)

The sam day in Sowthwarke was cristenyd the dowther of master Necolles, the god-father master Spryngham, the godmodurs my [lady] Garrett and my lade Bowyes, and after to the bryghe-howse to her father('s), and ther was a grett bankett at master Necolles plase.

The xxij day of Aprell, was sant Gorge's evyn, at v of the cloke the knyghtes of the Garter cam downe from the quen('s) chambur thrugh the halle to here[e] chapell, and yt was strod with gren ryssys,[f] [and all] the haroldes in ther cott armurs, master Perkullys, master Ruges-dragon, master Lanckaster, master Rychmond, and master Somersett, and master Norray and master Clarenshux, master Garter, and master dene, my lord of Hunsdon, my lord Montyguw, my lord Robartt, my lord of Lughborow, the yerle of Shrowsbere, my lord admeralle, my lord chamburlayn, the yerle

---

[a] caps. [b] High Ongar. [c] *i. e.* recapitulated; *see before, pp.* 231, 280.
[d] one. [e] her, *i. e.* the Queen's. [f] rushes.

of Ruttland, the yerle of Darbe, the marques of Northamtun, the duke of Northfoke, (the) yerle of Arundell, and the yerle of Penbroke, and so evere man to ys own plase in the chapell of ther owne sett.[a]

.   .   .   .

.   .   .   .   cam a prosessyon up thrugh the halle to .   .   .   .   . furst the serjant of the vestre with a sylver rod, [then the] chylderyn in ther surples, and then the qwyre sy[nging the English] prosessyon in copes of cloth of gold to the nombur of .   .   .   . haroldes of armes and sergantes of armes, furst Ruges[croix and] Ruge-dragon, and then cam master Lonkastur and master Rychmond and master [Somerset;] furst[b] my lord of Hunsdon, my lord Montyguw, my lord Robartt,[c] my lord of Lowthborow, my lord admeralle, my lord chamburlayn, the yerle of Rutland, the yerle of [Shrewsbury,] the yerle of Darbe, the yerle of Penbroke, the marques of [Northampton,] the yerle of Arundell, the duke of Northfoke; and then [master Garter,] master Norres, the dene of the chapell, they iij in cremesun saten v[elvet;] and next the byshope of Wynchestur and ser Wylliam Peter in [robes of] cremesun velvett with red crosses on ther robes, and ser .   .   .   . and the yerle of Northumberland bare the sword, and the(n) the [Queen] in her robe, and master Knolles bare the quen('s) trayn, and after .   .   .   .

The xxiiij day of Aprell was a proclamasyon by my [lord mayor] that no mylle-man shuld bryng nodur melle[d] nor whet [from] May-day unto Myghellmas next, a-pon pene[e] of *(blank)*, tyll they had spentt the whett and rye that the cete[f] [had made] provessyon for.

The sam day was elected knyghtes of the Garter the yerle of Northumberland and the yerle of Warwyke.

The xxv day of Aprell ded[g] master Chamley the recorder of Lo[ndon.]

---

[a] seat, *or* stall.   [b] *Two lines of repetition in the MS. are here omitted.*
[c] Lord Robert Dudley.   [d] meal.   [e] pain, *or* penalty.   [f] city.   [g] died.

The **xxx** day of Aprelle was cared to berehyng from sant Margett in Lothbere unto sant Donstones in Whest master Chamley the recorder, and ther was a C. mornars in blake, and the sward-bayrer, and my lord mare and dyvers althermen and the reseduw vyolett, and a lx gowne to pore men; and sant Donstones cherche hangyd with blake and armes, and raylles mad for the body; and so they whentt throughe Chep-syd, and so to Nuwgat, and so up Flett strett to sant Donstones, furst ij porters in blake, and then the pore men, and then serten mornars, and on bayryng ys baner of armes, and then ij haroldes of armes, and on ys cot beyryng, and then cam the corse with a pall of blake velvett and with armes, and then cam ij mornars baryng ij pennons of armes, and then the mornars cam, ser Thomas Lee, ser Wylliam Garrett, ser Thomas Offeley, master John Whytt, and after my lord mayre; and after ij C. of the yn of the cortes[a] to the chyrche, and a xx of clarkes syngyng; and master Goodman mad the sermon; and after to the plase to dener, for ther was the grettyst dener that ever I sawe.

. . . . strett, and he gayff for ys . . . . . of rattes coller unto xxx pore men, and . . . . chyrche was hangyd with blake and armes . . . the mornars and the corse hangyd with blake and armes . . . furst whent the pore men, then cam a mornar beyryng a pennon of armes, and next a harold beyryng ys cote armur, and then cam the corse with a pall of blake velvett and with [arms, and] then the clarkes metyng the corse, and then cam master . . . cheyff mornar, and dyvers odur mornars; and the dene of Westmynster mad the sermon.

The **v** day of May was bered at Powlles ser Peter . . . . sum-tym Popes collectur and prebendare of Powlles; master Ser-cotte was ys sectur;[b] with a ij dosen of skochyons, . .

---

[a] inns of court.   [b] executor.

master (*blank*) mad the sermon, and bered a-for wher that the postulles mas [a] was keptt and songe.

The x day of May was cared to be bered from Chanell row unto sant Margattes at Westmynster ser James Stumpe knyght, with ij haroldes of armes, one beyryng ys helmet and crest, and master Somersett beyryng ys cote armur; furst pore men whent a-for a mornars, and then a clarke syngyng, and next a mornar beyryng ys standard and anodur ys pennon of armes, and then the haroldes, and then cam the corse with a pall of blake velvett a-pon hym, and with armes, and a herse for the body hangyd with blake and armes, and the chyrche hangyd.

The *(blank)* day of May was mad for on master Gyfford of Northamtunshyre sqwyre a pennon and a cote of armur and a ij dosen of armes.

The *(blank)* day of May was mayd for a gentyllman of Dovre ys nam *(blank)* the wyche he was drownyd at Rye [going] with ser Thomas Fynche;[b] he had a pennon of armes and a cote armur and a dosen of skochyons.

The xj day of May was a fyre in Barbykan at my lade Suffoke's plase be-syd the Red-crosse strett, by a Frenche man that kept the plase—a part bornyd.

The xxiij day of May . . . . lord the duke of Northfoke was . . . . . . vycont Montyguw and my lord of Luthborow . . . . . . and the yerle of Northumberland and the yerle of [Warwick] stallyd knyghtes of the Garter; and ser Henry Sy[dney was] depute for the yerle of Warwyke, and he bare ys hode and ys coller of the garter a-pone ys arme.

The xxix day of May be-twyn iij and iiij a[fter noon] came a grett clape of thondur and after a grett [rain] that yt rane in-to many men's howses, [and lasted] tylle nyght.

---

[a] apostles' mass.   [b] In the Greyhound: *see p.* 302.

The iij day of June was bered in sant James [Garlick-hithe?] master Coldwell gentyllman and a laer[a] with halff a [dozen] skochyons of bokeram, and ther was a x mornars . . . . . and women, and ther was a xij clarkes syngyng . . . . . ded of a laske[b]; and master Beycon mad the sermon.

The x day of June was a degre[c] mayd a-for my lord [the duke] of Northfoke, and master Garter and master Clarenshux and master Norrey, that master Garter have the berehyng[d] of all knyghtes of the Garter and all yerles and ther [wives] and all lordes and ther wyffes and vyconttes.

- The sam day ded my lord Pagett at Draytun.

The xiij day of June by a stylle the fyre had taken hold of a pese of tymber; yf that ther had not bene good helpe yt had done myche hurt, for yt was a-monge the drapers in Watlyngstrett be-syd Bowe lane.

The xiiij day of June the Quen('s) grace removyd from Whythall by water toward Grenwyche, and a-bowt Ratclyff and Lymhowse capten Stukely dyd shuwe here grace the pleysur that cold be on the water with shuttyng of gones after lyke warle[e] with plahhyng of drumes and trum[pets.]

. . . .

[The . day of June was the funeral of the lord Paget] . . . . with a standard and a grett banar . . . . banar-rolles of armes and a cott armur . . . . garter, helme, and crest, and mantylles and sword . . . . dosen of skochyons, and a iiij dosen of penselles [about the] herse.

The xvj day of June dyd ryd in a care [to the] yeld-hall docthur Langton the phesyssyon in a g[own] of damaske lynyd with velvett and a cott of velvett . . . . and a cape[f] of velvett, and he had pynd a bluw ho[od on] ys cape, and so cam thrugh Chepe-syd on the market [day,] and so a-bowtt London, for was taken with ij wenchys yonge a-tones.[g]

[a] lawyer.　[b] died of a . . . ?　[c] decree.　[d] burying.　[e] war?　[f] cap.　[g] at once.

The xix day of June yt raynyd swett showrs tyll x of the cloke.

The sam day in the mornyng ther was sett on dyvers chyrche dorres, be-cause that he [*] sayd that they dyd not ryng when that the quen whent to Grenwyche, and that they shuld not open the chyrche dors tyll that he had a nobull on evere chyrche by the water syde from Tempull bare unto the Towre, but he cold gett no thyng yett.

The sam day was browth [b] to the Towre serten . . . . . for ther was capten callyd . . . . conveyed them away for they [were gone to] Grayff-ende [c] and browth bake to the Towre agayne.   .

The xxvj day of June ther was taken in Dystaffe lane the persun of Abchyrche be-syd London stone . . . . . . he havyng a wyff, and wher that he la a-bowtt . . . . have hys pleasur on her, and offered her serten money, and the plase [ap-] ponted, and she mad her fryndes [aware] of yt, and so they stod in a plases tyll he had mad . . . . . off with gowne and jakett, and downe with hosse . . . .

  . . . .
. . . . . . whether that any . . . . . that the curett and the chyrche wardens . . . . howse wher the plage [d] shall hapen . . . . . . they . . . . that they shall not come to the chyrche for the spase . . . . . . next folohyng after that the plage has bene, and so [a cross was] sett at evere dore of bluw and a wrytyng un[der] . . . .

The v day of July ded master Ellys Oggraffe of Lan .. .. Harfordshyre sqwyre, and bered the x day of July.

The ix day of July cam a commondementt . . . . that evere man in evere strett and lane for to ma[ke fires] iij tymes in the weke for to have the ere [e] opon .. . . . . sese the plage in the cete, and yff ytt plese God so . . . . . so to contenew the fyre in evere strett and lane [every] Wedynsday and Fryday.

---

[*] *So in MS.*   [b] brought.   [c] Gravesend.   [d] plague.   [e] air?

The viij day of July cam a commondementt that [all] halles of craftes in London shuld fynd to the iiij . . . . in alle the hast that may be, for to goo to Porthm[outh] in all the sped that may.

The xiij day of July master Clarenshux rod toward Suffoke a-pon ys vesytassyon of ys offes.

The xvj day of July was bered in the parryche of saynt Step[hen's by] London stone master Berre sqwyre and draper and marchand of the stapull, [with a] harold of armes, and he had a cott armur and a penon . . . . of skochyons of armes, and ys plase was hangyd with blake . . . . . . the cherche hangyd with blake and armes, and [there were] all the craft in ther leverey; ser Wylliam Ch[ester] cheyff mornar, and master Argall next, and master John Bere, [and then the] corse with a pall of blake velvett and mony . . . . . . mad the sermon, and all dune to the plase [to dinner, for there was a] grett dener.   .

. . . . bered in lytyl Allalows
. . , ... master Crolley mad the [sermon]
. . , ...

. . . .

. The . . day of July was on (blank) Penred [that had a] chyld to lerne, and for a sm[all fault did] hett ᵃ hym so [severely] with a leden ᵇ gyrdyll with bu[ckles, that he left] no skyne [on his] body and . . . . . almost pu . . . . ys master was sett on the pelere ᶜ and wypyd ᵈ with [. . . that his] blude ran downe, and with that my lord mare [passed] thrughe Chepe-syd the boye was sett on the pelere,ᵉ [and his c]oatt was taken of ys body that my lord and all the [people] myght see how that he was beyten, the petest ᶠ [sight to] se at any tyme.

The sam tym was a proclamassyon mad that [no] Englys man so-mever he was had lyberte to take [no] Frenche man by water and by lande, and to take shyp[s, mon]aye and goodes, and the men to ransum; and at after-none wen . . . e that cold take one, they that wold myght have hym.

ᵃ beat.   ᵇ leathern.   ᶜ pillory.   ᵈ whipt.   ᵉ pillory.   ᶠ most piteous.

The xxxj day of July was a-nodur proclamassyon that no man shuldmedyll with no Frenchman, nodur with no in-bas [sador] nor ys servandes, nor fre-denesun.[a]

The iij day of August was a-nodur proclamassyon . . . . who shuld not medyll with no Frenche man.

The iiij day of August was a-nodur proclamassyon [from] my lord mare that ther ys on [b] man hyred [to kill] doges as many as he cane fynd in the stretts, and has a fee for loke [c] every day and nyght.

The xxviij day of July was the gr[eat news that New]haveyn by owr men and the F[renchmen . . . . . . mony a man slayne ther.

The iij day of August owr . . . . Porthmowth and so evere da . . . .

The viij day . . . . mares [d] of London . . . . late shreyff . . . . Palmer la . . . . late . . . .

. . . .
. . . .

___

[a] free denizen.   [b] one.   [c] *So in MS. read* looking.   [d] mayoress.

NOTES.

Page 1. *Thomas Wriothesley, earl of Southampton.* The first person noticed by our funereal chronicler was one of the most remarkable men of his age: one who had attained the summit of the law, and who was aspiring to the summit of the state. The historian Carte attributes his death to mortified ambition, and so does Lord Campbell in his recent Lives of the Chancellors: on this part of his history see the Archæologia, vol. xxx. p. 468.

It should be remarked that, though the body of the earl of Southampton was at first buried in Saint Andrew's Holborn, it was afterwards removed to Tichfield in Hampshire, where a sumptuous monument with his effigy still exists. There is a fine portrait of him in Chamberlain's Holbein Heads.

Ibid. Funeral of alderman sir William Locke. He was a member of the Mercers' company, and sheriff of London in 1548. Not living to be lord mayor, he died "in his howse in Bow lane the xxiiijth of August in the 4. of Edward the 6, and buryed 27. day of the same mounth in the Mercers' cherche St. Thomas of Acres." MS. Harl. 897, f. 15. Stowe notes "Locke his armes in the windowes" of that church. Lady Locke died on the 5th Dec. 1551 ; and the imperfect funeral in p. 12 perhaps belongs to her. See an historical account of the Locke family in the Gentleman's Magazine for 1792, vol. LX. p. 799 ; also Lord King's Life of Locke, and the Autobiography of sir John Bramston, where at p. 9 are some traditional anecdotes of sir William Locke (but for 1530 read 1533).

P. 2. *Funeral of the countess of Hampton.* Mabel daughter of Henry lord Clifford, and sister to Henry first earl of Cumberland. Her husband William FitzWilliam, earl of Southampton, K.G. died without issue in 1543, and was buried at Midhurst in Sussex. Strype, Mem. vol. ii. p. 283, has appended this lady's funeral to the particulars he had taken from our Diary of the funeral of the first earl of Southampton of the Wriothesleys (as mentioned in p. 1). "And *Sept.* 1," he says, "his Lady and Widow was buried at Farnham: Who had sometime been the wife of sir William Fitz-Williams, Lord Privy Seal to King Henry VIII."—evidently unaware that sir William FitzWilliam had also been earl of Southampton, and that it was from the lady's union with him that she acquired the title of countess, and not from sir Thomas Wriothesley, to whom she was not related.

P. 2. *Funeral of judge Hynde.* Sir John Hynde, made a serjeant at law 1535, a judge of the Common Pleas 1546. When Nicholas Charles surveyed the church of St. Dunstan's in the West, the armorial insignia of sir John Hynde (made by our diarist) were remaining over his tomb: see them described in Collectanea Topogr. et Geneal. 1837, vol. iv. p. 100. Nicholas Charles was wrong in styling him "*Chief* Justice of the Common Pleas."

Ibid. *Funeral of the countess of Derby.* Anne, daughter of Edward lord Hastings and Hungerford, and sister to George first earl of Huntingdon of that name, was married (before 1503, when her eldest son John was buried, at St. James's, Garlick Hill) to Thomas Stanley, second earl of Derby, who died at his house at Colham in the parish of Hillingdon, Middlesex, May 23, 1521, and was buried in the neighbouring monastery of Syon. She was the mother of Edward third earl of Derby. It is stated in Collins's Peerage (edit. 1812, iii. 69) that she was married secondly to John Ratcliffe, lord Fitzwalter, but that is impossible, for he died in 1495. Sir Edward Hastings, who attended her funeral, afterwards lord Hastings of Loughborough and K.G., was her nephew. The The word *se*—— left imperfect (p. 2) was probably *sectur* (executor).

P. 3. *Funeral of sir James Wylford.* The blank in this passage may be filled up with "Scotland." See the Memoirs of Lord Grey of Wilton, by Sir Philip Egerton, p. 47. Sir James Wilford was knighted by the duke of Somerset after the taking of Leith, Sept. 28, 1547. Holinshed also mentions the circumstance of his being taken prisoner at Dunbar in 1549, by a Gascoigne of the country of Basque called Pellicque, "that won no smal commendation for that his good happe, in taking such a prisoner, whose name for his often approved prowes was so famous among the enimies." This noble captain was of a city family, which had buried for some generations at St. Bartholomew the Little. James Wilford, taylor, one of the sheriffs 1499, founded by will a sermon there on Good Friday for ever. John Wilford, merchant-taylor, alderman, was buried there 1544. (Stowe.)

Ibid. *Funeral of sir Richard Manners.* The paragraph of the diary partly defaced belongs to the funeral of an uncle of the earl of Rutland, whom we find thus noticed in another place: "Sir Rychard Manners knight dyed the ix[th] of February a°. r. E. vj. v[to]. and was beryed at Kateren Cryst churche the 14. of the same mounth; and the right honorable Henry erl of Rutland was his hole executer and over-syer of his last wyll, to whom he gave all his goodes and landes." (MS. Harl. 897, f. 14.) Sir Richard Manners was twice married, as may be seen in the peerages.

Ibid. *Funeral of lord Wentworth.* "March 3. The lord Wentworth lord chambarlaine died about tenne of the cloke at night, leaving behind him 16 children." (King Edward's Diary.) "Thomas lord Wentworth, lord chamberlan of the kinges majesties most honorable houshold, dyed in the kinges majesties paleys at Westmynster on tewsday the 3. of Marche in the 5 yere of E. the 6. and from thence broughte to his house at Westmynster and was buryed in the mynster there on Saterday the 7. of Marche folowing." (MS. Harl. 897, f. 78ᵇ.) A longer account of his funeral is preserved in the College of Arms, I. 11, f. 115. He was buried in the chapel of St. John the Evangelist (Dart ii. 60), but has no monument. There is a portrait of him among Chamberlain's Holbein Heads.

P. 4. *Proclamation for keeping Lent.* A printed copy of this proclamation is preserved in the valuable collection of proclamations, &c. in the library of the Society of Antiquaries. The word printed " co[ndemned ?]" in the text of our Diary should be altered to " commonly accepted or reputed as a fishe day."

Ibid. *The murder of master Arden of Feversham.* The particulars of this memorable domestic tragedy will be found very fully narrated in Holinshed's Chronicle ; and from the Wardmote Book of Feversham in Jacob's History of that town, 8vo. 1774, p. 197. See also a long narrative among Stowe's transcripts, MS. Harl. 542, ff. 34-37. It created so great a public interest that it became the subject not only of a Ballad which will be found in Evans's collection, 1810, vol. iii. pp. 217-225 ; but also of a Play published in 4to. 1592, again in 1599 and 1633, and lastly in 1770, when the editor, Edward Jacob, esq. who afterwards published the History of Feversham above mentioned, in his preface offered " some reasons in favour of its being the earliest dramatic work of Shakspeare now remaining." Mr. Collier's remarks on this subject will be found in his History of the Stage and of Dramatic Poetry, iii. 52. Lillo also began a tragedy founded on the same story, which was finished by Dr. John Hoadly, and printed in 12mo. 1762.

The concern taken by the government in the prosecution of the parties guilty of this murder, is shown by the following extracts from the Privy Council book :—

" 1551, 5ᵗʰ Marche. A Lettere to the Justyces of Peace in Kente, advertesinge them the order taken for the punishmente of those that murdered Mr. Ardeyrn ; Videliset, Sicely Pounder, widowe, and Thomas Mosbye, to be hanged in Smithfield, in London ; Alice Ardeyrn, to be burned at Canterburye, and Bradshawe, to be hanged there in cheanes ; Michaell Saunderson, to be hanged, drawne, and quartered, at Feversham, and Elizabeth Stafford to be burned there." (MS. Harl. 352, fol. 156ᵇ.) On the same day, "A Letter to the Sherifes of London, to receave of the Sherife of Kent, Cicelye Poundere, widowe, and Thomas Mosbye, to be hanged in Smithfield, for the Murder of Thomas Ardeine of Fevershame ; and a Letter to the Maiore of Canterburye, to receave of the Sherife of Kente Alice Ardeine, to be burned at Canterburye, and Bradshawe, to be hanged there, for the Murder of Mr. Ardeine." (Ib. fol. 157.)

The actual murderer, and also one Greene, a confederate, had escaped. The following entries will be found to correct and explain Holinshed's account of their capture.

" 1551, 28ᵗʰ May. A Lettere to Mr. North, to enlarge one Bate out of the countere, who convayed away one Greene, of Fevershame, after the Murdere of Mr. Ardeine was ther don, and undertaketh to brynge forthe Greene again, yf he may have libertie ; providinge that he take sufficient sureties, either to become prisonere againe, or else to bringe forthe the said Greene." (Ib. fol. 174.)

" 1551, 15ᵗʰ June. A Letter to Sʳ. William Godolphine knighte, of thankes for his dilligence in the apprehencione of Blacke Will, that killed Mr. Arderne of Feversham, and to send him in saufe garde, with promise of paymente for the charges of the bringeres." It appears from Holinshed and from our Diary (in which this person is called Black Tom,) that he was not sent home, according to this request, but was "burnt on a scaffold, at Flushing, in Zealand."

"1551, 20th June. A Lettere to the Lord Chancellor, to directe out a Comission for gaoll delivery unto the Maiore of Feversham and otheres, for the attaynder of Greene, alredie indicted for the Murder of Mr. Ardeine." (Ib. fol. 180.)

"A Warrante to the receiver of the Wardes, to pay unto them that apprehended Greene of Feversham, xx markes, for their costes in bringing him hether, and conveying him to Feversham, to be hanged.

"A Lettere to the Maiore of Feversham, and certain otheres, upon the attainder of Greene, to see him hanged in chaynes." (Ib. fol. 180b.) This direction was complied with, Greene being hanged in chaines, according to Holinshed, "in the high waie betwixt Ospring and Boughton against Feversham." (Holinshed, iii. 1030. edit. 1808.)

P. 4. *The lady Mary rode to St. John's, her place.* That is, to the house of the late knights hospitallers at Clerkenwell. On the circumstances of the princess's visit to court at this time see her brother's diary in Burnet.

P. 5. *A great triumph at Greenwich.* Thus noticed in the King's diary:
"March 31. A chaleng made by me that I, with 16 of my chaumbre, shuld runne at base, shote, and rune at ring, with any 17 of my servauntes, gentlemen in the court."—

"May 3. The chaleng at running at ringe performed, at the wich first came the kinge, 16 footmen, and 10 hor[se]men, in blake silk cootes pulled out with wight tafeta; then al lordes, having three [*sic. qu.* their] men likewise appareled, and al gentlemen, ther footmen in whit fustian pulled out with blake taveta. The tother side came al in yelow tafta. At lenght the yelow band toke it thrise in 120 courses, and my band tainted often, wich was counted as nothing, and toke never, wich seemed very straunge, and so the price was of my side lost. After that turnay folowed, betwen 6 of my band and sixe ofthers."

Ibid. *Chester the receiver took possession of the hall of the company of Clerks of London.* Sir Robert Chester was receiver of the court of augmentations. This proceeding is notified a few months before in the minutes of the Privy Council: "16 March, 1550. A lettere to the Chauncelor of the augmentacion to put the kinges majestie in possession agayne of the Clerkes hall in London, if the law will suffer it; yf not, to repaire to the Lordes to shewe cause of the impedimente therof." The company of Clerks seems to have been more liable to this attack than the other city companies, from being regarded as a *religious* foundation. Their hall stood in Bishopsgate street, and Stowe has related the story of its subsequent fate, sir Robert Chester pulling it down, when the fraternity had commenced a suit for its recovery in the reign of queen Mary.

P. 6. *Funeral of lady Morice.* Stowe mentions the interment at St. Peter's Cornhill of sir Christopher Morice, master gunner of England, temp. Henry VIII. His lady appears to have had a previous husband, and, though she lived and died in that parish, was removed to the church of St. Olave's to be laid by his side. There was a family connection between sir Christopher Morice and Arthur Plantagenet, viscount Lisle: see Miss Wood's Letters of Royal and Illustrious Ladies, ii. 76, iii. 35. "*The Skott the curate*" was of St. Peter's in Cornhill; see p. 13, and note hereafter.

P. 6. *Earthquake.* "The 25. daye of May, beyng Monday, betwene the howers of eleven and one of the clock at afternoone, was an earthquake of halfe a quarter of a howre long at Blechynglye, at Godstone, at Croydon, at Albery, and at divers other places in Southery and Myddlesexe." Stowe's Summarie.

P. 7. *The king supped at Deptford.* Machyn has dated this event two days too late. It is thus recorded in the king's own diary: "4. I was banketted by the lord Clinton at Detford, where I saw the Primrose and the Marie Willoughby launched."

Ibid. *Death of lord Cromwell.* Gregory lord Cromwell died on the 4th of July 1551, and was buried at Laund in Leicestershire: his mural monument there is engraved in Nichols's History of that County, vol. iii. pl. xlv.

Ibid. *Death of lord Powis.* Edward third lord Grey of Powis. The funeral of his widow, a daughter of Charles Brandon, duke of Suffolk, occurs in p. 163.

Ibid. *Sir John Luttrell*, of Dunster castle, co. Somerset, knighted at the taking of Leith in 1547, and made a knight banneret soon after, at the taking of Yester. Just before his death he had been divorced from his wife, for Strype notices "A Commission to sir William Petre, secretary, sir Richard Read, &c. upon due proof of the manifest adultery of the lady Mary Luttrel, to separate and divorce her from sir John Luttrel her husband. Dated in June, 1551." (Memorials, Book ii. chap. 29.) She was the daughter of sir John Griffith, K.B. and was remarried to James Godolphin, of Cornwall.

Ibid. *Proclamations for depreciation of the coinage.* Printed copies of these proclamations are in the collection in the library of the Society of Antiquaries, and their substance is stated in Ruding's Annals of the Coinage, 4to. 1817, ii. 107. Mr. Ruding, in a note in that page, throws some discredit on king Edward's accuracy as to dates in his Diary; but on that point it may be remarked that the proclamations were clearly prepared by the privy council some days before it was thought proper to make them public. The proclamation which according to the present diary was made known in London on the 8th of July, is printed with a blank date, "the   of June."

A remarkable example of the effect produced by this depreciation of the currency is given in the account of Arden's murder in the Wardmote book of Feversham. The proceeds of the murderers' effects, after the payment of expenses, amounted "after the old rate," to 120*l*. " whereof there was lost by abasing or fall of the said money 60*l*." In consequence of this act of government rumours were current that further abasements were contemplated ; and " By the letteres from London " it was reported " that on the 25. daye of July, or on St. James' daye, was a proclamation declaringe it was not the kinge nor his counseles intente to altere or abase any more his coynes yet ; for heare wee greate rumors that in all haste, and that prively, the kinge and counsell was busye aboute the alteringe thearof, to be done out of hand, whearuppon many men wane their debts, which else would not have byn payde this vij. yeares." (MS. Harl. 353, f. 107.)

In the journals of the Privy Council are frequent entries relative to the prosecution of persons guilty of predicting further depreciations.

Ibid. Funeral of sir Thomas Speke. Sir Thomas Speke was an eminent lawyer : he was steward of the royal manors of Greenwich, &c. and keeper of Eltham palace. His funeral achievements were remaining in St. Dunstan's church in the time of Nicholas Charles, as described in the Collectanea Topogr. et Genealog. iv. 98 ; and from them it appears that he married a Berkeley.

P. 8. Death of sir John Wallop, K.G. He died and was buried at Guisnes. Full particulars of him will be found in Collins's Peerage, edit. 1779, v. 64, with an abstract of his will, dated May 22, 1551, in which he styled himself " lievtenant of the castill and countye of Guysnes." See " The Chronicle of Calais," p. 203.

Ibid. Death of the two young dukes of Suffolk. Henry and Charles Brandon, the only sons of Charles Brandon, duke of Suffolk. Their mother was his second wife, Katharine, daughter and sole heir of William lord Willoughby de Eresby. (See some excellent letters of hers in Miss Wood's collection, vol. iii.) The report which reached our diarist is incorrect in two respects: the noble youths did not die " in one bed " nor " in Cambridgeshire." Their deaths took place at the bishop of Lincoln's palace at Bugden, in the county of Huntingdon. A narrative, entitled " Epistola de vita et obitu duorum fratrum Suffolciensium, Henrici et Caroli Brandon," written by sir Thomas Wilson, was shortly after printed. Two interesting extracts from this rare volume will be found in the Gentleman's Magazine for Sept. 1825, vol. xcv. ii. 206. The young men, accompanied by their mother, had just arrived at Bugden, when the duke was suddenly taken ill of the fatal sweat, which in five hours deprived him of life. The younger brother Charles, though placed in a distant chamber, immediately learned what had happened, and being asked by the physician upon what he was meditating, replied, " I am thinking how hard it is to be deprived of one's dearest friend." " Why do you say so ? " said he. He answered, " How can you ask me ? My brother is dead. However, it is of little matter, I shall soon follow him." And so he did, in half an hour. Sir Thomas Wilson admits the title of duke to the younger brother immediately on the elder's demise, and so we find from our Diary " the ij. dukes " were so called in London. The other extract given in the Gentleman's Magazine is a very high character (in Latin) of the young duke Henry, written by Dr. Walter Haddon, regius professor of civil law in the university of Cambridge : of this

Strype (Memorials, Book ii. c. 4,) has given the substance in a translated form. Sir Thomas Wilson, in his Arte of Rhetorique, has also an interesting passage describing the characters of these young noblemen; and some Latin verses on their death, " Carmina in Mortem," &c. were written by Michael Reniger, and printed in 1552, 4to. The circumstance that their mother the duchess was the great patroness of the reforming divines accounts for the extraordinary interest excited by their death. An engraving in Chamberlain's Holbein Heads is taken from two miniatures, supposed to represent these brothers: but if the dates given in the inscriptions are compared, they will be found both to belong to the elder boy.

Ibid. *Mortality from the sweating sickness.* Two other reports of this have come down to us, and, though the figures do not exactly correspond, yet they seem all to have been derived from official returns, and there is also some difference in the periods of time. " Letteres from London reporte there died in London of the sweatynge sicknes from the 7. of July till the 20. of the same 938 persons, but howe many have died since to this daye, beinge the 23., I knowe not. I truste it is nowe cleane gone." (MS. Harl. 353, f. 107.) Shortly after the disease had terminated, the celebrated Dr. Caius wrote a treatise upon it, which was printed in the following year, under the title of " A boke or counseill against the disease commonly called the sweate, or sweatyng sicknesse. Made by John Caius, doctour in physicke. 1552." Printed by Richard Grafton in black letter, 40 leaves, 12mo. The Dedication to the earl of Pembroke is dated 1st April, 1552. (Caius also wrote a Latin treatise on the same subject, of which a late edition, entitled " Johannis Caii de Ephemera Britannica liber unus," was printed in London, 8vo. 1721.) From this curious volume we learn that the disease first appeared with the army of Henry the Seventh, which arrived at Milford, out of France, the 7 Aug. 1485; next in 1506; again in 1517; a fourth time in 1528; and a fifth in 1551, shortly before the composition of his treatise. On this occasion, " Beginning at Shrewesbury in the middest of April, proceadinge with greate mortalitie to Ludlowe, Prestene, and other places in Wales, then to Westchestre, Coventre, Oxenfoorde, and other tounes in the Southe, and suche as were in and aboute the way to London, whether it came notablie the seventh of July, and there continuing sore, with the loss of vijC.lxi. from the ix. day until the xvi. daye, besides those that died in the vii. and viii. dayes, of whom no registre was kept, from that it abated until the xxx. day of the same, with the loss of C.xlii. more. Then ceasing there, it wente from thence throughe al the east partes of England into the northe, untill the ende of Auguste, at which tyme it diminished, and in the ende of Septembre fully ceassed." The following singular passage relating to this disease occurs in a report of the preaching of Thomas Hancocke, minister of Poole in Dorsetshire. " ———— in his doctrine he taught them that God had plagued this Realme most justly for their sins with three notable plagues. The first plague was a warning to England, which was the Posting Sweat, that posted from town to town thorow England, and was named *Stop-Gallant:* for it spared none. For there were some dauncing in the Court at nine a'clock that were dead at eleven. In the same sweat also at Cambridge dyed two worthy imps, the duke of Suffolk his sons, Charles and his brother." (Strype, Memor. iii. chap. vii.) The singular name here noticed occurs also in the register of Uffculme, Devonshire, where the disease prevailed in the month following its devastation in London. "Out of 38 burials entered in that year, 27 were in the first 11 days of August, and 16 of them in three days. The disease of which these persons died is called, in the parish-register, *the hote sickness or stup-gallant.*" Magna Britannia, by Lysons, who adds that he had not been able to find the term elsewhere.

P. 8. *Funeral of sir Peter Negro.* "Sir Pyter Negro knight dysceased the xiiijth day of July in the yere of our Lord 1551, in the vth yere of the raigne of our soveraigne lord kyng Edward the 6. His crest is a castell broken, and upon the castell a man with a shert of male and a sword in his hand." (MS. Harl. 897, f. 14^b.) He was one of the knights made by the duke of Somerset after the taking of Leith, Sept. 28, 1547.

Ibid. *The xxvij of July was the new bishop of W——— divorced from the butcher wife with shame enough.* Though the name is burnt, this appears to belong to John Ponet, bishop of Winchester, who had been translated to that see on the 23^d March preceding. He had published " A Defence of the Marriage of Priests " in 1549, which is noticed in Strype, Memorials, Book ii. chap. 18. And it seems that he married again very shortly after this divorce, the following entry occurring in the register of Croydon : " 1551, Oct. 25.   Reverendus pater Johannes episcopus Wynton' duxit Mariam Haymond generosam in ista ecclesia coram multitudine parochianorum, presente reverendissimo patre Thoma Cantuar' archiepiscopo cum multis." (Collectanea Topogr. et Geneal.iv. 91.)

Ibid. *Funeral of master Harry Williams.* Sir John Williams, his father, was master of the jewel-house ; and by queen Mary was created lord Williams of Thame, and made lord chamberlain of the household. The son had married Anne, daughter of Henry lord Stafford, but died childless, leaving his father without male heirs.

Ibid. *Funeral of master Sandys.* Henry Sandys esquire, eldest son of Thomas second lord Sandys, and father of William third lord Sandys : see Dugdale's Baronage, ii. 303. There is a portrait of a master Sands in Chamberlain's Holbein Heads which perhaps represents this person.

P. 9. *The French king installed at Windsor.* This was of course by deputy. He had been elected of the Garter on the St. George's day preceding, and the marquess of Northampton had conveyed the insignia to France. See various documents relating to his election described by Strype, Memorials, 1721, ii. 512.

Ibid. *Death of the lord admiral's wife.* This lady was the mother of the duke of Richmond, the natural son of king Henry the Eighth : to whom she gave birth at Jericho, a manor near the priory of Blackmore in Essex, in the year 1519. She was married shortly after to sir Gilbert Talboys, who was summoned to Parliament as lord Talboys in 1529, died 15 April, 1530, and was buried at Kyme in Lincolnshire. She became secondly the wife of Edward lord Clinton, lord admiral of England, who after her death was in 1572 created earl of Lincoln. She had issue by her first husband two sons, Robert and George, who both died without issue, and one daughter, Elizabeth, who became his heir, and was, first, the wife of Thomas Wymbish (who claimed the barony of Talboys *jure uxoris*), and, secondly, of Ambrose Dudley, earl of Warwick. By lord Clinton she had issue three daughters : viz. Bridget wife of Robert Dymoke of Scrivelsby co. Linc. esquire, Katharine wife of William lord Burgh of Gainsborough, and Margaret wife of lord Willoughby of Parham. Her royal offspring the duke of Richmond died on the 24th July, 1536, at the age of seventeen years.

P. 9. *Price of provisions.* The imperfect lines in this page refer to this subject, thus noticed by the king under " Sept. 9. A proclamation set furth touching the prises of cattel, of hogges, pegges, befs, oxen, muttons, buttyr and chese, after a reasonable price, not fully so good-cheap as it was when the coyne was at the perfeictest, but within a fift part of it, or ther abouts."

Ibid. *The king wearing the order of St. Michael.* "The fest of Michelmas was kept by me in the robes of th'ordre." (King Edward's Diary.) The following minutes are from the register of the privy council :

" 14 June, 1551. This daye the French ambassador had accesse to the lordes, to whom he declared that the kinge his master and the company of the ordere of Saint Michael had appointed the kinges majestie to be of the same order, for which purpose the marshall St. Androwe was enjoyned to bringe the same order to his majestie, prainge his majestie that he would accepte the same accordinglye." (MS. Harl. 352, f. 160ᵇ.)

"June 22, 1551. A Letter of apparance to the deane of Windsore, that for asmuch as there shall arive here shortely a nobleman sente from the French kinge wᵗʰ the order of St. Michalle to bee presented to the kinges Maᵗⁱᵉ, and to bringe wᵗʰ him such recordes as remayne in his custodie, as well for the acceptacion of the said order by his majesties behalfe, or for any other thinge by ceremony concerning the said order ; and that all thinges there may be put in good order for the celebracione of St. George's feaste, and to bringe wᵗʰ him also a note of so muche money of the poore knights as he hathe in his custodie." (Ibid. f. 161ᵇ.) King Edward was invested by the ambassador at Hampton Court on the 16th of July, as detailed by himself in his diary, and more fully in Ashmole's History of the Garter, pp. 368, 369. The documentary instruments brought to England on this occasion are still preserved in the Chapter House at Westminster.

P. 10. *Creation of new peerages.* The intended creation of the dukes of Northumberland and Suffolk, the marquess of Winchester, and the earl of Pembroke, was made known to the Privy Council on the 4th Oct. 1551, as thus recorded in their minutes : " This daye the lord chamberlen together wᵗʰ the lord chamberlen *(sic)*, beinge sente from the kinge to the lordes, declared on his majesties behalfe, that, for asmuch as the lord marques of

Dorset hath lately opened to his highness the occasyones of his inhabilletie to serve in the place of generall warden of the marches towardes Scotlande, and therefore besought his majestie to call him from that place ; his majestie, thinkinge the same lord marques' suite reasonable, and mindinge not to leave such a rowme of importance unfurneshed of an able personage, hath resolved both to revoke the said marques from that offyce, and to appointe the earle of Warwicke in his steed, who for his greate experience, and namly in those partes, his highnes taketh to be moste meeteste for that rowme. And hath further determyned, as well to th'ende that the said earle of Warwicke may the rather be had in the estymacione he deserveth for his digneties sake, as for that also his majestie thinketh necessarye, the noble houses of this his realme being of late much decayed, to erect other in their stead by rewardinge such as have alredye well served, and maye be therby the rather encowraged to contynewe the same, to call both his lordship and other noble personages to hier estates and digneties ; and therfore hath appointed to advaunce firste the said earle of Warwicke to the degree of a duke ; the lorde marques Dorsett, as well for his service sacke as for that he is lyke by waye of maryage to have claime to the tytle of duke of Suffolke, his highnes is pleased to call to that degree ; the lord treasuror nowe earl of Wiltesheir to the degree of a marques ; the master of the horse [sir William Herbert] to the degree of an earle ; which his majesties mynd and determenacion his highnes pleasure is shalbe gon through with all, and these personages to be created on Sondaye nexte ; to the assistance whereof his majestie willeth that such of the lordes and nobles as shalbe thought needfull, to be presente," &c. (MS. Harl. 352, f. 188ᵇ.)

P. 10. *The three new knights.* Mr. Sidney and Mr. Neville had been made gentlemen of the privy chamber on the 18th April 1550, and Mr. Cheke held the same appointment. (King Edward's Diary.) Sir Henry Neville was the first settler at Billingbere of his name and family. He married Frances, only daughter and heir of sir John Gresham, and died July 13, 1593.

Ibid. *The duke of Somerset, &c. sent to the Tower.* On the particulars of these state trials it is only necessary to refer to several passages in the King's diary, and to Strype and our general historians.

P. 11. *Visit of the old queen of Scots.* The queen dowager of Scotland (Mary of Guise) embarked at Edinburgh to visit her daughter in France, Sept. 7, 1550. On her return she landed at Portsmouth on the 2d Nov. 1551. (Lettres de Marie Stuart, edited by the Prince Alexandre Labanoff, 8vo. 1844, vol. i. 5.) The privy council addressed, " 25 Sept. 1551. A Letter to the lord chauncelor requiring him to passe under the greate seal a saulf-conduct graunted by the kinges majestie to the dowager of Scotlande, and to retayne with him for a record the originall thereof sent him signed by his highnes." The saulf-conduct itself is printed in Rymer's Collection, xv. 290 : it bears an earlier date, viz. 17 Sept. Some subsequent minutes of the Privy Council relating to preparations for this visit are given by Strype. There are many particulars of it in king Edward's Diary, and a narrative of the queen's reception is in MS. Harl. 290, art. 2.

P. 11. *Funeral of sir Michael Lyster.* The name of the lord chief justice of the king's bench was sir Richard Lyster, but that of his eldest son, here recorded, was sir Michael. See the memoir on the monument of sir Richard Lyster at St. Michael's church, Southampton, by Sir F. Madden, in the Winchester volume of the Archæological Institute. There is a portrait of a lady Lyster among the Holbein Heads: it may be doubtful to which lady of the name it belongs (see the pedigree given by Sir F. Madden); but Mr. Lodge, in his accompanying memoir, supposed it to be that of lady Mary, daughter of the earl of Southampton, wife of sir Richard, grandson of the chief justice. (See her funeral afterwards, p. 273.)

P. 12. *Funeral of lady Locke.* The imperfect funeral in this page probably belongs to the widow of sir William Locke, who has been noticed in p. 313. She was buried by his side on the 5th Dec. 1551. (Malcolm, ii. 156.) "Lady Elyzabeth Locke, latte wyf of sir William Locke knyght, decesyd on saynt Androwes daye at iij. of the cloke at after-none in good memory, the v. yere of the rayne of kyng Edward the vj. executors Rycharde Spreyngham and Thomas Nyoolles the elder: and buryed in the churche of our laydy of Bowe within the quyre. Cheffe morner, Mary Spryngened *(sic)*; [other mourners,] Elyzabeth Nyoolles, Elyzabeth Fyld, Ellen Meredyth, Jone Rawlyns." (MS. I. 3. in Coll. Arm. f. 846.)

Ibid. *Muster in Hyde Park.* This is described nearly in the same terms in the King's diary. Burnet has misprinted the date Dec. 4 instead of 7.

P. 13. *The Scot of St. Peter's in Cornhill.* This preacher has been before mentioned in p. 6 as "the Skott the curett" of St. Peter's. Whether he was the same as Richardson, whose popularity as a preacher is mentioned in p. 91, has not been ascertained.

P. 14. *The duke of Somerset's execution.* A narrative of this, with the last speech delivered by the duke, somewhat different from that in Stowe, has been printed from the Cottonian charters, by Sir Henry Ellis, in his Second Series of Original Letters, vol. ii. p. 215.

P. 15. *Execution of sir Thomas Arundell.* One of the "metrical visions" of George Cavendish, the gentleman usher of Cardinal Wolsey, furnishes some biographical particulars of sir Thomas Arundell: viz. that he was educated with Cardinal Wolsey, and was chancellor to queen Katharine Howard. He is also made to confess that "I was cheaf councellor in the first overthrowe of the duke of Somerset, which few men did know." (See Singer's edition of Cavendish's Life of Wolsey, 1825, vol. ii. p. 125.) A letter of the earl of Northumberland in 1527, directed "To his beloved cosyn Thomas Arundel, one of the gentleman of my lord legates prevy chambre," and at its foot "To my bedfellow Arundel," with which term he also commences, is printed from the duke of Northumberland's archives, ibid. p. 246. With regard to his fate there is a curious passage in a very rare book, bishop Ponet's "Short Treatise of Politic Power," which

Strype has quoted in his Memorials, vol. ii. 306 : but with an interpolation which, as it is made silently, is perfectly inexcusable. Writing of the earl of Warwick, Ponet states, ——" at th'erles sute Arundel hathe his head with the axe divided from the shoulders."

But Strype, imagining that the *earl of Arundel* (who was also involved in trouble at this period, having been fined 12,000*l.* in Jan. 1549-50,) was the suffering party named by the bishop, altered this passage thus :——

——" at the earl's suit, Arundel *escaped, otherwise had* his head with the axe *been* divided from his shoulders."

See the " Life of Henry Earl of Arundel, K.G." edited by J. G. Nichols, 1834, p. 7 ; or the Gentleman's Magazine for July 1833, p. 16, and for Feb. 1848.

P. 15. *Sir Michael Stanhope* also makes a poetical lament in Cavendish's Metrical Visions. He states that he had been dubbed knight by king Edward, and had been of his privy chamber. He was half-brother of the duchess of Somerset (as sir Thomas Arundell was half-brother of the countess of Arundel), and was great-grandfather of the first earl of Chesterfield. See a curious letter regarding his widow's funeral written by their son sir Thomas Stanhope in 1588, in the Archæologia, vol. xxxi. p. 212.

Ibid. *Funeral of the countess of Pembroke.* King Edward in his Diary records the death of the countess of Pembroke on the 20th Feb. 1551-2. As sister to queen Katharine Parr, she was a person of high consideration. A magnificent canopied monument to William Herbert, earl of Pembroke, and his countess Anne, with their recumbent effigies, and kneeling effigies of their three children, Henry earl of Pembroke, sir Edward Herbert knt. and Anne lady Talbot, was erected in St. Paul's cathedral, next the monument of John of Ghent, duke of Lancaster, and is represented in a plate of Dugdale's History of St. Paul's.

P. 16. *Funeral of sir Humphrey Style.* The name deficient in our MS. from the fire is supplied by the valuable MS. Harl. 897, f. 16 : " Sir Humfrey Style dysseased the 7th of Apryll 1552 in A°. R. E. vj^tl. vj^to. and beryed in the parish churche of Bekenham in the county of Kent." His monument with effigies on brass plate is remaining in that church : see Lysons's Environs of London, 1811, i. 412, and the epitaph printed in Thorpe's Registrum Roffense, p. 816.

P. 17. *Election of the earl of Westmerland of the garter.* In the privy council 10 May 1552. A warrante to the Exchequer to paye unto sir Gilberte Dethicke knighte, alias Garter principall kinge at armes, beinge presently to be sente by the kinges majestie to the earle of Westemerlande with the order of the Garter, the some of twentye poundes.

" A comissyon for the said sir Gylberte Dethicke to take upe v. poste horses for himselfe, his servantes, and guide." (MS. Harl. 352, f. 228 b.)

The following entry may here also be added :

" 22 Ap^l. 1553. A warrante to sir John Williames to pay unto sir Gilberte Dethicke knight, alias Garter principall kinge at armes, the some of xxj. poundes for schucheones by him sett upp in an°. 4° et 5° of the kinges [and queenes] majesties raigne at Grenewich, at the feaste of the order of the Garter, accordinge to a bill therof included in the same letter." (f. 250.)

Ibid. Line 20, *for* earl *read* duke.

Ibid. *Proclamations.* The two remaining blanks may perhaps be filled up, " un[der act of] parlementt," and " that [same d]ay."

Ibid. *Proclamation against fighting in churches or churchyards.* An undated proclamation to this purpose is transcribed in the Society of Antiquaries' collection, vol. ii. p. 104. It prohibits all persons from " henceforth to quarrell, fray or fight, shoote any hande-gonne, bring any horse or mule, into or through any cathedrall or other church, or by any other wales or meanes irreverently use the said churches or any of them."

P. 21. *Duke of Northumberland took horse towards Scotland.* He had been appointed lord warden of the Scotish Marches some months before : " 11th Oct. 1551. A letter to the lord chauncelor to make out for the duke of Northumberlande a pattente of the lord wardenshippe generall in the north partes foranempste Scotland, with asmuch fee, preheminence, and authoritie as any his predecessores in that offyce have had heretofore, with power also to substytute and make deputy wardenes under him, with such fees as any in that rowme heretofore have had, and further the allowance of C. lighte horsemen at x^d. by the daye." (Privy Council Book, MS. Harl. 852, f. 191.)

Ibid. *The king took horse on his progress.* King Edward's Diary, (May 23, 1551) gives the following enumeration of the bands of men of arms appointed at this time to accompany him on his progress :

Lord Treasurer	. 30	Earl of Rutland	. 15	Lord Cobham	. 20
Lord Great Master	. 25	Earl of Huntingdon	. 25	Lord Warden	. 20
Lord Privy Seal	. 30	Earl of Pembroke	. 50	Mr. Vice-chamberlain	15
Duke of Suffolk	. 25	Lord Admiral	. 15	Mr. Sadler	. 15
Earl of Warwick	. 25	Lord Darcy .	. 30	Mr. Sydney	. 15

Afterwards, on the 22d of June, it was agreed that the bands appointed to Mr. Sidney, Mr. Vice-chamberlain, Mr. Hobby, and Mr. Sadler, should not be furnished, but left off. Again, when the king was in Sussex, on the 24th July, "because the number of bands that went with me this progress made the train great, it was thought good they should be sent home, save only 150 which were picked out of all the bands. This was because the train was thought to be near 4000 horse, which were enough to eat up the country, for there was little meadow or hay all the way as I went."

P. 22. *Funeral of sir Robert Dormer.* Sir Robert Dormer, knighted in 1537, was grandfather of Robert first lord Dormer. His will is dated June 20, 1552, a few days before his death. " A° D^nl 1552 the ix^th of July sir Robert Dormer knight of Bokyngamshire dysseased at his manner howsse of Aston in the lordship of Wynge, and was buryed the xv[th] of the same mounth." (MS. Harl. 897. f. 12[b].) He is termed in our Diary "a great sheep-master in Oxfordshire;" the will of sir Edward Unton, in 1581, printed in the "Unton Inventories" (a publication of the Berkshire Ashmolean Society), is a remarkable illustration of that description of property in the same county.

P. 23. *Three great fishes.* "The viij. daye of August, there were taken about Quynborough three great fyshes called dolphins, or by some called rygges: and the weke folowyng, at Blackwall, were syxe more taken and brought to London, and there sold; the least of them was greater then any horse." Stowe's Summarie, 1566.

P. 24. *Master Maynard chosen sheriff.* John Maynard. Stowe relates this anecdote of his provision for serving the office: "whiche, about .ix. or .x. yeares before had geven out wares and jewelles, as it was thought, to the summe of .2000. markes, to be payde hym when he were sherife of London." Summarie, 1566.

Ibid. *Funeral of sir Anthony Wingfield, knight of the garter.* Biographical particulars of this distinguished person will be found in Lodge's Peerage of Ireland, 1789, vol. v. p. 262. The place of his burial is not there recorded; and if his body was left to rest at Stepney, the fact is now forgotten there, as no monument exists, and the register does not commence until 1568.

Ibid. *The vicar of Shoreditch, a Scot.* John Macbray, presented to the vicarage on the 15th May preceding (Ellis's Shoreditch, p. 21); deprived in 1554, and afterwards an exile. (Strype, Mem. ii. 341.)

Ibid. *Death of sir Clement Smith.* Sir Clement married Dorothy Seymour, sister of queen Jane, and of Edward duke of Somerset. King Edward, in his Diary, under the 24th March 1550-1, records his being "chidden" for having a year before heard mass.

Ibid. *Proclamation on the price of meat.* This was apparently a proclamation of the lord mayor, applicable to the city of London only: but similar regulations were made by the privy council, for the control of the markets in the country at large, or in such places as they chose to extend them to. A proclamation "set furthe by the kinges majestie, in the v. yere of his reigne," and referring to resolutions of the council made at Windsor on the 30th Aug. preceding, was printed by Grafton in the year 1551, (which would therefore be one year earlier than that noticed in the Diary,) and will be found in the collection in the possession of the Society of Antiquaries. It seems difficult to conceive how such regulations could be generally enforced: but no limitation of place is mentioned in the proclamation.

Ibid. *Sir John Jocelyn* is probably the person whose name is imperfect, of the family seated at Sawbridgeworth, near Hunsdon, in Hertfordshire (*not* Essex). See a John, stated to have died in 1553, in the pedigree in Clutterbuck, iii. 204.

P. 25. *Three great fishes.* Strype calls these "porpus's." In the third line of the passage read "m[orice-pikes.]"

Ibid. *Whalley the receiver of Yorkshire.* Richard Whalley of Screaton, co. Notts, esquire. The charges preferred against him are stated in the king's diary, under the 7th of June, and thence in Strype, Mem. ii. 381. Strype, p. (249), states that he had been politically active in endeavouring to procure the restoration of the duke of Somerset; he was, therefore, the same person who has been mentioned in p. 10 as among the protector's adherents then sent to the Tower. He died Nov. 23, 1583, aged 84; and further particulars respecting him will be found in Thoroton's Nottinghamshire, p. 130, together with an engraving of his monument and effigy.

Ibid. *Two sons of the king of Scots.* King James the Fifth had several natural sons, who are enumerated in Douglas's Peerage of Scotland, by Wood, i. 52. It does not appear which were the two who visited London in 1552; but James, afterwards the regent Murray, was at Paris in that year. (Ibid. ii. 255.) Another notice of their visit occurs in the form of "a passport for two of the late Scotch king's bastard sons, to transport out of the realm four dozen of bows, twenty dozen of arrows, and four gross of strings, and two geldings. Dated Oct. 1552." Strype, Mem. vol. ii. p. 517.

P. 26. *ij. great fishes.* These are also mentioned by Stowe, and with a very strange name: "The vii. daye of October were two great fishes taken at Gravesend, which were called *whirlepooles.* They wer afterward drawen up above the bridge." Summarie, 1566.

Ibid. *Seven serjeants of the coif.* The king's warrant to the lord chancellor to make out writs to these new serjeants, was dated in June preceding. Their names were, Robert Brook, James Dyer, John Caryll, Thomas Gawdy, Richard Catlyn, Ralph Rokeby, William Stamford, and William Dallison.—In line 6 of this paragraph fill up the blank with the word [council], that is, privy councillors.

P. 27. *Funeral of master Davenet.* This name was not Davenant, as might be imagined from our author's usual cacography. A later member of the family, John Davennet, was warden of the Merchant-taylors in 1592-3. Wilson's Merchant-taylors' School, p. 1151.

Ibid. *Funeral of master John Seymour.* His will, dated Dec. 7, 1552, and proved April 26, 1553, is recorded in the prerogative court of Canterbury, and briefly quoted in Collins's Peerage. He died unmarried, making his whole brother sir Edward Seymour, the ancestor of the present duke of Somerset, his heir.

P. 28. *The king's lord of misrule.* This important officer was "a gentleman, wise and learned, named George Ferrers." (Holinshed, 1st edit. p. 1709.) He was a member of Lincoln's Inn. (Stowe's Chronicle, p. 608.) Many curious documents respecting his revels in this and subsequent years are printed in Kempe's Loseley Manuscripts, 8vo. 1835, pp. 24, *et seq.* George Ferrers was probably the same person who, being member of Parliament for Plymouth in 1542, was arrested for debt in the city of London, and committed to the counter: whereupon he was reclaimed by the house of commons, and the sheriffs committed to the Tower: see a long narrative in the histories of London.

The procession of the lord of misrule, or " lord of merry disports " (as he was also called), into London, which occurs subsequently in this page, is also described in Stowe's Chronicle, p. 608: " hee was received by sergeant Vawce, lord of misrule to John Mainard one of the sheriffes of London."

Ibid. *Children of hospital.* This passage, when perfect, seems to have described the Christmas treatment of the children of Christ's Hospital, which, together with the two sister hospitals of St. Thomas and Bridewell, had just been founded by the city with the assistance of the crown. Its original object was to serve for all the fatherless children of London,—" to take the childe out of the strete, which was the seede and increase of beggary, by reason of ydle bringing-up, and to noryshe the same chylde in some good learning and exercise profitable to the common weale."—It was only on the 21st of the preceding month (Nov. 1552) that the children had been first taken into the hospital, "to the numbre of fower hundred." Stowe's Summarie, 1566.

Ibid. *Funeral of alderman Robinson.* Not " Robyn," as our diarist has the name. " Hereunder lyeth Master William Robinson, alderman of London, citizen and mercer, and merchant of the staple at Callis, and Elizabeth his wife. He deceased the thirtieth of December, 1552." Epitaph in Allhallows Barking.

P. 29. *Month's mind of sir Thomas Windsor.* Son and heir apparent of William second lord Windsor. He was made a knight of the Bath at the coronation of Edward VI.; and married Dorothy, daughter of William lord Dacre, of Gillesland ; but, as he had no issue male, the peerage went to a younger brother. Collins in his Peerage gives some extracts from his will, dated Nov. 8, 1552, and proved by his widow Jan. 16 following. His funeral probably took place at Bradenham in Buckinghamshire.

P. 30. *Kylling of a gentyllman [of] ser Edward North knyght in Charterhouse cheyr[chyard].* Sir Edward North occupied the Charterhouse at this time, and was made a baron about a year after this occurrence. Machyn must have omitted the word " of," and the party murdered would be a gentleman attached to the household of sir Edward North.

Ibid. *Fall of the great steeple at Waltham.* The tower stood in the centre of the cross. After the downfall recorded by our diarist, the nave was converted into the parish church, a wall being run up at its east end : and a new tower was built at the west end, which bears the date 1558. Morant's Essex, i. 45.

P. 31. *Funeral of sir William Sidney.* Sir William was father of sir Henry Sydney, K.G. and grandfather of the illustrious sir Philip. The ceremonial of his funeral occurs in I. 13. in Coll. Arm. f. 272. His epitaph at Penshurst is printed in Thorpe's Registrum Roffense, p. 918 : it describes him as "knight and banneret, sometyme chamberlen and after steward to the most mighté and famous prynce Kynge Edward the VIth, in the tyme of his being prynce." See also further of him in Collins's Memoirs of the Sidneys, &c. prefixed to the Sidney Papers, fol. 1746, p. 81.

P. 32. *Parson Whyt here wife of St. Alphe's.* John Veron the Frenchman was instituted to the rectory of Saint Alphage, Jan. 3, 1552. As elsewhere noticed, our author was prejudiced against him, and perhaps means him here by a nickname,—White-hair.

Ibid. *Commencement of the parliament.*—"Anno 7 Ed. sexti the first day of Marche the king kept his parliament within his pallace at Westminster. The(y) proceded from the gallery next into the closet, thorough the closett into the chapell to service, every man in their robes as at this day. Therle of Oxford bare the sword, and the marquis of Northampton as great chamberleyn went jointly with him on the right hand. The lord Darcy beinge lord chamberleyn bore the king's trayne, and was assisted by sir Andrew Dudley, chief gentleman of the privy chamber." (From a paper of precedents in MS. L. 15, in Coll. Arm. p. 130.)

Ibid. *Funeral of Henry Webbe esquire.*—"In the north-east of the chancell [of St. Katharine Coleman] an ancient tomb : Here lyeth the body of Henry Webbe esquire, Gentleman Usher to king Henry the Eighth. And here lyeth also Barbara his wife. She dyed the 5. day of Februarie, An. Dom. 1552. And he the last day [this date disagrees with our diary] of March 1553." Stowe's Survey, edit. 1633.

Ibid. *Funeral of Richard Cecil esquire.* This was the father of the great lord Burghley, whom our diarist on this occasion erroneously calls "sir Harry" instead of sir William Cecil. There is a monument to him, with kneeling effigies of himself, wife, and three daughters, (recently very carefully repaired,) in the church of Saint Martin at Stamford : an engraving of which is in Peck's History of that town, fol. 1727, p. 69, and in Peck's Desiderata Curiosa, vol. i. p. 4. In the inscription he is said to have died on 19th *May*, 1552. Lord Burghley in his Diary states the date on the 19th March 1553, with which Machyn's entry agrees.

P. 33. *The king removed from Westminster.* Strype, Memorials, ii. 397, has incorrectly placed this paragraph in a chapter dated 1552.

P. 35. *The proclamation of queen Jane* is printed in Nicolas's Lady Jane Grey, p. xl. from MS. Lansd. 198. An original printed copy exists in the collection of the Society of Antiquaries.

P. 36. *Drowning of Ninion Saunders.* Stowe has noticed more particularly the two incidents which happened to the young man and his master. "The 11. of July, Gilbert Pot, drawer to Ninion Saunders, vintner, dwelling at S. John's head within Ludgate, who was accused by the said Saunders his maister, was set on the pillory in Cheape with both his eares nailed and cleane cut off, for words-speaking at the tyme of the proclamation of ladie Jane ; at which execution was a trumpet blowne, and a herault in his coat of armes read his offence, in presence of William Garrard, one of the sheriffes of London. About 5. of the clocke the same day, in the afternoone, Ninion Saunders, master to the sayd Gilbert Pot, and John Owen, a gunmaker, both gunners of the Tower, comming from the Tower of London by water in a whirrie, and shooting London bridge towards the Blacke Fryers, were drowned at S. Mary Lock, and the whirrymen saved by their ores."

Ibid. *Political placard.* The paragraph now imperfect seems to have been that which furnished the following in Strype : "On the same 16th day, in the morning, some, to shew their good will to the lady Mary, ventured to fasten up upon Queenhithe church wall, a writing in way of a declaration, importing that the lady Mary was proclaimed in every country 'Queen of England, France, and Ireland,' (being an officious lye to do her service,) and likewise treating of divers matters relating to the present state of affairs."

Ibid. *Funeral of alderman sir Ralph Warren.* Son of Thomas Warren, fuller, son of William Warren of Fering in Essex ; sheriff in 1528, mayor in 1537, and again in 1544 (in the place of sir William Bowyer). On a fair marble tomb in the chancel of St. Osythe's, alias St. Benet Sherehog : "Here lyeth buried the right worshipfull sir Ralph Warren knight, alderman and twice lord mayor of London, mercer, merchant of the staple at Callis ; with his two wives, dame Christian and dame Joane, which said sir Ralph departed this life the 11. day of July, An. Dom. 1553." He was buried on the 16th. By his second wife Joan, daughter and coheir of John Lake, of London, sir Ralph left issue Richard Warren esquire, who married Elizabeth, dau. of sir Roland Lee knt. alderman and lord mayor, and Joan, married to sir Henry Williams alias Cromwell, by whom she had issue Oliver, Robert, Henry, Richard, and Johanna. "Lady Jone Waren, aforesaid, one of the doters and heyrs of John Lake, dysseassed at the howse of sir Henry Williams alias Cromwell knight, her son in lawe, called Hynchyngbroke, in the county of Huntyngton, on Wensday 8. of October, 1572, and the 14. yere of our most gracious soveraigne lady quene Elizabeth, and was beryed in the parish churche of St. Benedicke Sherehogge in London, on tewsday the . . . . vember, in the yere aforesaid." Her second husband was sir Thomas White, another lord mayor, and who is immortalized by his foundation of St. John's college, Oxford. Our diarist records their marriage, in p. 179.

A remarkable instance of the simplifying of arms is afforded by what was done in regard to sir Ralph Warren's monument at St. Osith's. It originally bore this crowded coat: Azure, on a chevron between three lozenges argent, three eagle's heads erased of the first, on a chief checky or and gules a greyhound courant ermine. "These armes were taken downe by his sonne Ric. Warren, and these sett upp in place thereof: Or, a chevron engrailed between three eagle's heads erased sable." Arms of the Lord Mayors, by William Smith, Rouge-dragon.

P. 36. *the iiij sqyre(s)* attendant at the same funeral were the four esquires of the Lord Mayor's house, namely, the swordbearer, the common hunt, the common crier, and the water-bailiff.

P. 37. *Proclamation of queen Mary.* A printed copy of the proclamation making known the title of queen Mary, is at the Society of Antiquaries.

Ibid. *Arrival of the lady Elizabeth.* In this passage read, " and odur [weapons,]" and add to it, " and cloth, according to their qualities." (Strype.) The " green garded with white " was then the royal livery.

P. 38. *The lord Montague.* The person intended by this designation was sir Edward Montague, who was lord chief justice of the common pleas, as sir Roger Cholmley was of the king's bench. The new queen appointed sir Richard Morgan and sir Thomas Bromley in their places.

Ibid. *Sir John Yorke* had been under-treasurer of the mint. Together with other officers of the same he had a pardon for all manner of trangressions, &c. July 21, 1552. (Strype.)

Ibid. *Rode through London my lady Elizabeth.* Stowe relates that the lady Elizabeth went to meet the queen on the 30th, the day after her arrival in London : he states that she was accompanied with a thousand horse, as says our diarist, but " Camden 500, and so I have heard my mother from her grandmother, who was one of them, relate, and that queen Mary then kissed every gentlewoeman [that] came with her sister." MS. note by the Rev. John Lynge, vicar of Yalding in Kent, in a copy of Stowe's Annals ; Retrospective Review, 2d Series, i. 341.

P. 39. *Funeral of lady Browne.* Lady Jane Ratcliffe, daughter of Robert earl of Sussex, the first wife of sir Anthony Browne, afterwards first viscount Montague, died at Cowdray on the 22d July, 1552, aged 20 : having had issue, Anthony father of the second viscount, and Mary afterwards countess of Southampton. There is a kneeling effigy of her on her husband's monument at Midhurst : see the inscriptions in Dallaway's Rape of Chichester, p. 291 (where for 1552 read 1553).

Ibid. *Funeral of king Edward the Sixth.* The ceremonial of this funeral is preserved in the College of Arms, I. 11, f. 117 b, and an abstract is given by Strype, Memorials, vol. ii. p. 431. The painters' charges are preserved in a paper bound in I. 10, in Coll. Arm. f. 117, of which Sandford has given the heads in his Genealogical History of the Kings of England, 1677, p. 472. Archbishop Cranmer and bishop Day were permitted to perform the service and a communion in English (see Burnet, vol. ii. p. 244). "The Funeralles of king Edward the Sixt," a poem, by William Baldwin, was reprinted by the Rev. J. W. Dodd, for the Roxburghe club, in 1817. Extracts had been given in the British Bibliographer.

P. 41. *Drowning of master Thomas a Bruges.* Sir John a Bruges, soon after created lord Chandos of Sudeley, had seven sons, who are enumerated in the Peerage, not including this Thomas.

Ibid. *Riot at the Paul's Cross sermon.* This incident is noticed in the public chronicles. Bourne, the preacher, offended the audience by speaking vehemently in the defence of bishop Bonner, and extremely against bishop Ridley. One of the populace threw a dagger at Bourne, which struck one of the sideposts of the pulpit. Maister Bradford, the celebrated Reformer, came forward to persuade the people to quietness, and by the help of that worthy man and of maister Rogers, (both of whom were afterwards sacrificed in cold blood by their religious adversaries,) Bourne was conveyed safely away into Paul's School. Grafton's Abridgement, 1566, and Stowe's Summarie of the same date.

The privy council, which was sitting at the Tower, took immediate alarm at this disturbance. The "order taken" on the same day, in concert with the lord mayor, will be found in their Register. (transcript in MS. Harl. 643, f. 1.) On the 16th Homfrey Palden was "committed to the counter for seditious wordes uttered by him againste the preacher Mr. Burne for his sermon at Paule's crosse on Sunday last ;" and the same day the celebrated Bradford and Veron, "two seditious preachers," were committed to the Tower, as was "Theodore Basill, alias Thomas Beacon, another seditious preacher." Ibid. pp. 2b, 3.

Ibid. *Sir John Gates and sir Thomas Palmer.* These two knights were beheaded with the duke of Northumberland on the 22d August. Stowe in his Summarie preserves a soubriquet of the latter : he was called, "buskin Palmer." See a note regarding him in the Life of Lord Grey of Wilton, p. 3. He had received a pardon for all treasons, &c. Feb. 1551-2.

Ibid. *Dr. Watson's sermon at Paul's cross.* "By a letter writtene in London August 22 by William Dalby is signified, on sondaye laste was a Sermone at Pole's crosse, made by one doctor Watsone ; theare was at his sermone the marques of Winchester, the earle of Bedforde, the earle of Penbrocke, the lord Wentworth, the lord Riche. They did sitte wheare my lord mayer and the aldermen wear wont to site, my lord maiore [marques?] sittinge uppermoste. Thear was also in the windowe over the mayor *(sic.)* the ould bushope of London, [Bonner the late bishop,] and divers othurs ; thear was 120 of the garde that stoode round aboute the crosse, wth their holberdes, to gard the preacher, and to apprehend them that would stirre. His sermon was no more eloquent than edifieinge ; I mean it was nether eloquent or edefieinge in my opinione, for he medled not withe the gospelle nor epistle, nor noe parte of scripture. After he had red his theame, he entred into a by mattere, and so spente his tyme ; 4 or 5 of the cheefe poynts of his sermone that I cane remember I will as breefly as I can reporte unto you, viz. : he requirede the people not to beleeve the preacheres, but that ther faithe should be firme and sure, because theare is suche vaneties amongeste them, and yf any mane doubte of his faithe, let him goe to the scriptures, and also to the interpreteres of the doctores, and interprit it not after thier owne brayne : he wished the people to have no newe faithe, nor to buld no newe temple, but to keepe the ould faythe, and edifye the ould temple againe. He blamed the people in a manner for that heartofore they would have nothing that was manes tradissyone, and nowe they be contented to have manes tradissyone, shewinge that in the firste yeare of the raigne of our soveraigne lorde king Edward the 6. theare was a lawe established that in the sacrament thear was the bodie and bloode of Christe not really but speritually ; and the nexte yeare after they established another lawe that thear was the body of Christe nether speritually nor really. Thes 2 in themselves are contraryes, thearfor they cannot be bothe trewe. He showed that we should ground o' faithe uppon God's word, wch is scripture, and scripture is the byble, wch wee have in Hebrue, Greeke, and Lattine, and nowe translated into Englishe ; but he doubtethe the translatyon was not true. Also he said theare hathe byne in his tyme that he hathe seene xx. catechesmes, and every one varinge from other in some points, and well he said they might be all false, but they could not be all true ; and thus perswading the people that they had followed menes tradissyones, and had gone astraye, wishing them to come home agayne and reedefy the ould temple. Thus, wth many other perswsiones, he spente the tyme tyll xi. of the clocke, and ended." (MS. Harl. 353, f. 141.)

P. 42. *The parson of St. Ethelburga*, whose sermon had offended, was John Dey, who was deprived in 1554.

Ibid. By "*sant Necolas Willyns*" or Wyllyms, (the MS. is uncertain) must be meant, it is presumed, the church of Saint Nicholas Olave's, on Bread-street-hill, destroyed at the great fire of 1666.

P. 43. *Burning of the Great Harry*. This famous ship had been built by Henry the Eighth upon the loss of the Regent in 1512 (some account of which calamity will be found in the Chronicle of Calais, p. 9.) The Great Harry was at Woolwich (where it was afterwards burnt), in the 1st year of Edward VI. and its equipment was then returned thus :

" The Henry Grace a Dieu, 1000 tons. Souldiers 349. Marryners 301. Gonners 50. Brass pieces 19. Iron pieces 102."

See the Archæologia, vol. vi. p. 218, and at p. 216 a fuller return of its "furniture" and ammunition. A view of this ship, made in 1546 by Anthony Anthony, one of the officers of ordnance, is preserved in the Pepysian library, and engraved in the Archæologia, vol. vi. pl. XXII. It is also one of the ships represented in the picture of the embarkation of Henry VIII. at Dover, May 31, 1520, now at Hampton Court, and engraved in a large size by the Society of Antiquaries in 1781. Another print, purporting to represent the Great Harry, published by T. Allen in 1756 from a supposed drawing by Hans Holbein, is pronounced by Mr. Topham, in Archæol. vi. 208, 209, to be the figure of a different ship, and supposed to be the Prince, built by James I. in 1610.

P. 43. *Funeral of sir John Harington.* Sheriff of Rutland the year before his death, and grandfather of John, created lord Harington of Exton in 1603. See Wright's History of Rutland, p. 148.

Ibid. *Funeral of John lord Dudley.* This nobleman sold the castle of Dudley to his cousin John duke of Northumberland, and was never summoned to Parliament. (Nicolas's Synopsis of the Peerage.) His pecuniary distresses are noticed by Dugdale, Baronage, ii. 216 ; and it is added that he " was commonly called the Lord *Quondam.*" [See this term used to bishop Latimer in p. 57 of this Diary.] His son and successor was restored to Dudley castle, which was forfeited by the duke's attainder.—See the funeral of the widowed baroness in p. 61.

P. 45. *The knights of the Bath* made at the coronation of queen Mary were, Edward earl of Devonshire, Thomas earl of Surrey, William lord Herbert of Cardiff, Henry lord Bergavenny, Henry lord Berkeley, John lord Lumley, James lord Mountjoy, sir Robert Rochester, controller of the queen's house, sir Henry Jerningham, sir William Powlett, sir Henry Clinton, sir Hugh Rich, sir Henry Paget, sir Henry Parker, and sir William Dormer. The arms of these knights are beautifully tricked in the Cottonian MS. Claudius C. III.

Ibid. *Coronation of queen Mary.* A document respecting the claims at this coronation has been printed in the Society's volume of RUTLAND PAPERS, p. 118 : and, as there mentioned, a formulary of the ceremonial is in the library of the Society of Antiquaries.

P. 46. *Knights made the morrow after the Coronation.* Their names were as follow, according to a list in the MS. Coll. Arm. I. 7. f. 74.

" The morowe after the day of Coronation, beinge the seconde day of October, at the palys of Wystmister, were dobyd the knightes of the carpet foloinge in the presence of the quenes majestie in her chamber of presens under the clothe of estate by therl of Arundell, lord stuarde of the quenes housse, who had of her highnes commission to execute the same :

The lord Garratte,	Sir Edward Walgrave,	Sir Christofer Allen,
The lord Borough,	Sir John Bourne, secretary,	Sir Richard Freston,
The lord Dudley,	Sir Raff Chamberlen,	Sir William Kelloway,
Sir Thomas Stanley,	Sir John Tyrell,	Sir Henry Garton,
Sir Edmond Wyndsor,	Sir John Hodlestone,	Sir John Tregonell,
Sir Henry Ratclyff,	Sir Robert Peckham,	Sir Ambrose Jermyn,
Sir Thomas Hastings,	Sir Harry Lea,	Sir Leonard Chamberlen,

Sir Thomas Gerarde,
The lord chef baron,*
The lord chef justyce,†
Sir George Gefforde,
Sir Thomas Packington,
Sir Thomas Lovell,
Sir John Spencer,
Sir William Fitzwilliam,
Sir Thomas Androus,
Sir William Courtney,
Sir William Gresley,
Sir Thomas Cave,
Sir Edward Lytelton,
Sir Philip Parreys,
Sir Thomas White,
Sir Thomas Metham,
Sir Rychard Lasen,
Sir Thomas Dawney,
Sir Robart Wyngfelde,
Sir Thomas Knyvett,
Sir Roger Woodhouse,
Sir Francis Stoner,
Sir John a Lye,

Sir Rychard Tate,
Sir Edmond Grene,
Sir Robart Lane,
Sir Rychard Stapleton,
Sir William Damsell,
Sir John Chichester,
Sir Harry Crypes,
Sir Thomas Palmer,
Sir Henry Ashley,
Sir Rychard Stranguishe,
Sir George Mathwe,
Sir John Cotton,
Sir John Pollarde,
Sir John Warburton,
Sir John Fermer,
Sir Thomas Berenger,
Sir John Constable,
Sir George Stanley,
Sir Rouland Stanley,
Sir Rauf Egerton,
Sir Rychard Molineux,
Sir Thomas Heskett,
Sir Thomas Wayman,

Sir John Croftes,
Sir Edmond Mauleverer,
Sir Rychard Bruges,
Sir James FytzJames,
Sir Thomas Verney,
Sir James Williams,
Sir William Meringe,
Sir Edward Pylson,
Sir Edward Fytton,
Sir William Warham,
Sir Thomas Whyte, lord mayor,
Sir Thomas Throgmerton,
Sir Edward Grevell,
Sir Henry Stafford,
Sir William Wygston,
Sir Harry Jones,
Sir John Bruse,
Sir Robart Whitney,
Sir Rychard Chudley,
Sir Thomas Baskerfelde,
Sir Thomas Tyndall,
Sir Rychard Wallwine.

The arms of these knights are beautifully tricked in the Cottonian MS. Claud. C. III. but they are differently arranged, and some made at other times are interspersed. On this authority some slight amendment of the orthography of the names has been made where it appeared necessary.

A commission dated 17 Oct. empowering the earl of Arundel " to make so many persons knightes, within the tyme of two daies next ensuinge the date hereof, as by us shall be named, or by hymselfe may be thoughte mete, so as he excede not in the hole the numbre of threescore," is printed in Rymer's Fœdera, vol. xv. p. 350: but qu. its date ?

P. 46. *Funeral of lady Bowes.* " The lady Anne Bowes, wyff to syr Martyn Bowes, departed this world the xix[th] of October in A°. 1553, and was beryed the xxij[th] of the same moneth at St. Mary Wollars churche in Lombart strete." (MS. Harl. 897, f. 13[b].) This was therefore the second of sir Martin's three wives, mentioned in the inscriptions on " A goodly marble close tombe under the communion table of St. Mary Wolnoth: Here

---

* Sir David Brooke, appointed chief baron on the 1st Sept. preceding.

† Sir Richard Morgan, of the common pleas. Sir Thomas Bromley was made chief justice of the queen's bench on the 4th Oct. which was two days later.

lyeth buried the body of sir Martin Bowes knight, alderman and lord maior of London, and also free of the Goldsmiths' company: with Cecilia, dame Anne, and dame Elizabeth, his wives. The which sir Martin Bowes deceased the 4. day of August, An. Dom. 1566." His will was also kept in the same church "in a faire table," *i. e.* there was an inscription recording his having given lands to discharge the ward of Langbourne "of all Fifteenes to bee granted to the king by parliament." Sir Martin Bowes was sub-treasurer of the mint under Henry VIII. and Edward VI. and resigned that office in Jan. 1550-1: see three grants made him on that occasion in Strype, Memorials, vol. ii. pp. (271), 494. The portrait of sir Martin Bowes, still preserved at Goldsmiths' Hall, is described by Malcolm, Londinium Redivivum, ii. 411.

P. 48. *Parson Chicken.* "Another priest called sir Tho. Snowdel, whom they nick-named Parson Chicken, was carted through Cheapside, for assoiling an old acquaintance of his in a ditch in Finsbury field; and was at that riding saluted with chamber-pots and rotten eggs." (Strype, Mem. iii. 113.) His real name, however, seems to have been Sowdley. Thomas Sowdley clerk was instituted to the rectory of St. Nicholas Coleabbey 25 July 1547, and to that of St. Mary Mounthaw 23 March following. He was deprived of both in 1554, but restored to the former after the return of the Protestant ministers, and died in 1564. (Newcourt, i. pp. 450, 507.)

P. 49. *Creation of heralds.* The office of York herald was vacant by the creation of Bartholomew Butler, esq. to be Ulster King of Arms (the first of that title) Feb. 2, 1552-3; that of Lancaster herald from the expulsion of Fulke ap Howell, esq. who had been convicted of counterfeiting Clarenceux's seal, and executed; Portcullis, Richard Withers, gent. had been degraded as an accomplice of Howell.* The new heralds and pursuivants were, 1. Martin Marruf, or Marlfe, made York herald; he died April 20 or 21, 1563. 2. Nicholas Tubman, made Lancaster; he died Jan. 8, 1558-9. (See p. 185.) 3. Hugh Cotgrave, made Rouge-Croix, afterwards Richmond herald, 1566. (see more of him in Noble's History of the College of Arms, p. 182.) 4. William Colborne, "my lord Cobham's servant," created Rouge-dragon; afterwards York Herald, Jan. 25, 1564; he died Sept. 13, 1567, and was buried at St. Dunstan's in the West. (See the Collectanea Topogr. et Geneal. vol. iv. pp. 99, 111.) 5. John Cockes, created Portcullis, was afterwards Lancaster, Jan. 18, 1558-9. (See p. 186.) His history is given in Noble, p. 183.

The writs of privy seal, dated the 22d and 24th Nov. for the creation of Lancaster and

---

* See Noble's College of Arms, p. 146, and in p. 155 "Lant says he was degraded." Yet in p. 147 that very blundering author has made Robert Fayery, the predecessor of Withers, to be the accomplice of Howell,—in 1551, although he goes on to say that he died in 3 Edward VI. *i. e.* 1549. Noble imagined that the cause of Withers's disgrace was his having attended on the duke of Northumberland to Cambridge; whilst it was also before his eyes (p. 183) that it was Cocke or Cocks the *new* Portcullis that had been the duke of Northumberland's servant.

York heralds, are printed in Rymer's Fœdera, vol. xv. p. 357 : and that for John Cooke (or Cookes) to be Portcullis, dated Jan. 3, in p. 359.

P. 50. *Funeral of [sir Henry Parker, son and heir of] lord Morley.* This funeral probably belongs to the son of lord Morley, who died in his father's lifetime. The funeral of lord Morley himself, who died in 1556, is noticed in p. 120.

Ibid. *The king of Spain's ambassadors.* These were ambassadors from the emperor Charles, father of Philip, to conclude a treaty for the queen's marriage—namely, the count d'Egmont, Charles count de Laing, Jehan de Montmorancy sieur de Corriers, Philip Negri, and Simon Renard : see Strype, Mem. iii. 58, and the marriage treaty in Rymer, vol. xv. p. 393. An extract from their Instructions may be seen in Burgon's Life of Gresham, i. 145.

P. 51. *Funeral of master Sturley esquire.* There seems to be no memorial of this gentleman remaining in connection with the history of Richmond. In August 1551, it was appointed that Mr. Sturley, captain of Berwick, should leave the Wardenship of the East Marches to the lord Evers ; but that person is again mentioned as a knight, sir Nicholas Sturley, in the following October. (King Edward's Diary.)

P. 52. *Sir Thomas Wyatt.* A copious narrative of Wyatt's rebellion, together with the letters written by the duke of Norfolk, lord Cobham, and others, to the Privy Council, on the occasion, (from the originals in the State Paper Office,) will be found in Cruden's History of Gravesend, 1842, 8vo. pp. 172 *et seq.*

Ibid. *Sir George Howard* was son of lord Edmund Howard, and one of the brothers of queen Katharine Howard. He was knighted by the duke of Somerset in Scotland in 1547 ; and in March 1550-1 had a warrant for office of Master of the Henchmen for one whole year. He was appointed to attend upon the young lords sent over the sea as hostages, whereof the earl of Hertford was one. Strype, Mem. ii. 539.

P. 54. *He lycted behind a gentleman into the court.* After his surrender sir Thomas Wyatt was taken to the court riding behind sir Maurice Berkeley on horseback. Stowe, p. 621.

P. 56. *Funeral of George Pargeter.* Sir Thomas Pargeter his father was lord mayor in the year 1531, and was buried at Allhallows, Bread-street. Catalogue of Lord Mayors, by W. Smith, Rouge-Dragon.

Ibid. *Execution of Mans.* No mention of this " rich man " occurs under Cranbrook in Hasted's History of Kent.

P. 57. *Funeral of sir William Goring.* The name here deficient is supplied by the

CAMD. SOC. 2 x

useful MS. Harl. 897, f. 8: " Sir William Goryng knight dyed at Westmynster the 4ᵗʰ
of Marche 1553, and was conveyd to his howse called Burton, and there buryed the xijᵗʰ of
Marche."   He was one of the gentlemen of the king's privy chamber, and his monument
at Bodecton alias Burton, is described in Dallaway's Rape of Arundel, p. 253 (with an
error of viij *for* iiij).   His funeral at length is in Coll. Arm. I. 3, f. 102.

P. 59.   *Cat hung on the gallows in Cheapside.*   The same outrage will be found noticed
in Stowe's Chronicle, p. 623, where the consecrated wafer is there termed " a singing-
cake," and in Foxe's Actes and Monuments, vol. iii. p. 99.

P. 60.   *Funeral ensigns of alderman Kyrton.*   Stephen Kirton, member of the Merchant-taylors in 1534.   He was never sheriff or lord mayor.   He bore four coats quarterly,
1. Argent, a fess and chevronel in chief gules ; 2. Argent, a crescent and bordure sable ;
3. Paly, argent and gules, a fess between three leopard's heads, all counterchanged ; 4.
Argent, a fesse between three butterflies gules.   (Lord Mayors, &c. by Wm. Smith,
Rouge-Dragon.)

P. 61.   *Funeral of the lady baroness Dudley,* widow of lord Dudley, noticed in
p. 334.   She was the lady Cecily Grey, second daughter of Thomas marquess of Dorset,
by Cecily, daughter and heir of William lord Bonville and Harington.

P. 62.   *Proclamation.*   This was probably the proclamation transcribed in the Society
of Antiquaries' collection, vol. ii. p. 124.   It is undated, but entitled " A proclamation
for suppressing of seditious rumours and libelles."

P. 63.   *Lord Garrett created earl of Kildare.*   Gerald Fitzgerald, reckoned as the
eleventh earl in succession of his family.   His father Thomas was executed at Tyburn,
together with his five uncles, on the 2d Feb. 1535 ; his grandfather Gerald the ninth earl
having died a prisoner in the Tower of London on the 12th Dec. preceding ; and was
subsequently pronounced attainted by an act of Parliament in Ireland passed in May
1536.   The young lord Garrett, or FitzGerald, having been educated abroad, is said to
have been introduced to the court of king Edward the Sixth, and knighted by him in
1552 (Lodge's Peerage of Ireland, by Archdall, vol. i. p. 94) ; but we have seen (p. 334)
that the latter statement is erroneous, and it is more probable that he did not return
before his kinsman and patron cardinal Pole and other eminent members of the old communion.   His patent of restoration was dated May 13, 1554, (Lodge,) and in the
following November he returned to Ireland.   He was now thirty years of age, and he
died in London, Nov. 16, 1585.

P. 64.   *A man that would have plucked the sacrament out of the priest's hand.*   Stowe
gives his name,—" a joyner that dwelt in Colman streete called John Strete ;" and adds
that in Newgate he " fayned him selfe madde : " but the latter statement is contradicted
by Foxe, who has commemorated Strete more at length.

P. 66. *Prince of Piedmont.* Though our diarist mentions this prince twice in this page, some mistake may be suspected. The prince really arrived in December, as afterwards mentioned in p. 79. Probably the person who came in June was his ambassador.

Ibid. *The maid that spake in the wall and whistled in Aldersgate-street.* This prototype of the Cock-lane ghost is noticed more fully by Stowe: her name was Elizabeth Croft, " a wenche about the age of eighteene yeares."

Ibid. *Proclamation for attendance of peers, &c. at the queen's marriage.* See this in the Soc. of Antiquaries' collection, vol. ii. p. 125.

P. 67. *Funeral of alderman John Lambard.* "Father to William Lambard esquire, well known by sundry learned bookes that he hath published." (Stowe.) He was sheriff in 1552 ; and was buried in St. Michael's, Wood-street. Arms, Gules, a chevron vaire between three lambs argent. (Wm. Smith, Rouge-Dragon.)

Ibid. *Funeral of alderman Austen Hynde.* Augustine Hynde, clothworker, sheriff in 1551. Arms, Gules, a chevron between three hinds or. (Wm. Smith, Rouge-dragon.) He was buried at St. Peter's in Cheap, and his epitaph will be found in Stowe: it states his death on the tenth of the month, and MS. Harl. 897, f. 25ᵇ. names the xij. whereas our diarist says the viij. His descendants will be found in MS. Harl. 897. His widow was remarried to alderman sir John Lyons, who is noticed in the next page.

P. 68. *Funeral of alderman sir Henry Amcotes.* Son of William Amcotes, of Astrop, Lincolnshire. He had been lord mayor in 1548, was buried in St. Michael's, Crooked-lane, where he had " a goodly ancient tombe within the south grated chappell: Hereunder lyeth the bodies of sir Henry Amcotes knight, alderman and lord maior of London, and dame Joane his wife. Which sir Henry Amcotes deceased the 5. day of September anno 1554. And the said dame Joane deceased the 4. day of September anno Dom. 1573." His arms were quarterly of eight, as blazoned and engraved in The Fishmongers' Pageant, fol. 1844, p. 14. A pedigree of his family will be found in the MS. Harl. 897, f. 52. They were afterwards of long continuance in Lincolnshire.

P. 69. *Proclamation* " for avoyding of vagabondes and idle persons from London, Westminster, and places adjoyning,"—this is transcribed in the Society of Antiquaries' collection, vol. ii. p. 126.

P. 70. *Funeral of the duke of Norfolk.* The MS. Harl. 897 says the duke died at Kenyng hall on Monday the 27. of August, and was buried at Fremyngham on Monday the last of September. His funeral is in Coll. Arm. I. 3, f. 103.

P. 71. *Funeral of lord de la Warr.* Thomas West, ninth lord de la Warr, succeeded his father 1525 ; K.G. 1549. He was buried at Broadwater, co. Sussex, where his tomb remains, and is described in Cartwright's Rape of Bramber, p. 38.

P. 72. Servant of sir George Gifford killed. Stowe says *Clifford,* but Gifford I believe is right. (See p. 335.)

Ibid. Imprisonment of Day the printer. John Day, whose great boast was that he had encouraged and supported Foxe in the construction of that gigantic work, the Actes and Monuments. See the memoir of Day by the present writer in the Gentleman's Magazine for Nov. 1832, vol. CII. ii. 417, where Day's monumental brass at Ampton, co. Suffolk, is engraved ; also further particulars communicated by the late Francis Douce, esq. and D. E. Davy, esq. in the same volume, pp. 597, 598 ; and a catalogue of the works printed by Day, and his portrait, in Ames's Typographical Antiquities, by Dibdin, vol. iv. pp. 41—177. One of the companions of Day's imprisonment was John Rogers, who suffered martyrdom soon after, (see p. 81,) and we may suppose that it was very much owing to his own sufferings at this time that he was instigated to "set a Fox to wright how Martyrs runne by death to lyfe." (Epitaph.)

Ibid. Death of the earl of Warwick. John Dudley earl of Warwick, the eldest son of the duke of Northumberland, was one of the knights of the Bath at the coronation of Edward VI. On the 29th April 1552, he was made master of the horse to the king (Pat. 6 Edw. VI. p. 5) ; but Collins, (Memoirs of the Sidneys, p. 31,) is wrong in saying he was afterwards chosen a Knight of the Garter. Strype, Mem. ii. 500, erroneously inserts the christian name of Ambrose to the patent of master of the horse. On receiving that office the earl of Warwick resigned that of master of the buck-hounds to his brother lord Robert Dudley. (Ibid. 501.)

P. 73. Sir John Lyons lord mayor. Son of Thomas Lyons of Perivale, co. Middlesex ; a member of the Grocers' company : and sheriff 1550. "He dwelled in Bucklersbury, and was buried in St. Syth's church, which toucheth on the south syde of his house." Arms, Azure, on a fess engrailed between three plates each charged with an eagle's head erased sable, a lion passant between two cinquefoils gules. (List of Lord Mayors, &c. by Wm. Smith, Rouge-Dragon.) Sir John Lyons bequeathed 100*l.* towards building a garner for corn at Queen Hithe, which was enlarged at the charges of the city in 1565. (Stowe.) See a notice of his widow hereafter, p. 346.

Ibid. Public penance at St. Paul's. Stowe, who varies in his account of the culprits, thus describes this ceremony : "The 4. of November, beeing Sunday, three preists that, beeing married, would not leave their wives, and two laymen that had two wives apeece, were punished alike, for they went in procession about Paules churche in white sheetes over them, and either of them a taper of waxe in the one hand and a rod in the other, and so they sate before the preacher at Paules crosse during the sermon, and then were displed on the heads with the same rods."

P. 75. Saint Erconwald's day. This passage may be completed (from Strype) thus— " should go to Paul's in procession in copes."

P. 75. *Cardinal Pole.* " The 24. of November cardinall Poole came oute of Brabant into England," &c. See Stowe's Chronicle, p. 625.

P. 76. *The cardinal's oration.* Cardinal Pole returned to England with legatine power to reconcile the kingdom to the church of Rome. He accomplished this mission as related in the Journals of the Commons, vol. i. p. 38 ; and in Foxe, iii. 110.

Ibid. *Thanks for the queen's quickening.* " The 28. of November the lord maior of London, with the aldermen in scarlet, and the commons in their liveries, assembled in Paul's church at nine of the clocke in the forenoone, where doctor Chadsey one of the prebends preached in the quire in the presence of the bishop of London and nine other bishops, and read a letter from the queen's councel, the tenor wherof was, that the bishop of London should cause *Te Deum* to bee sung in all the churches of his diocesse, with continual prayers for the queenes majestie, which was quickened with child. The letter being read, he began his sermon with this anthetime, *Ne timeas Maria, invenisti enim gratiam apud Deum.* His sermon being ended, *Te Deum* was sung; and solemne procession was made of *Salve festa dies* all the circuit of the church." (Stowe.) The letter of the privy council to the bishop here mentioned is printed in Fox, and in the Gentleman's Magazine for Dec. 1841, p. 596, taken from the broadside issued at the time by John Cawode the queen's printer. In the same article is also reprinted a ballad circulated on this occasion, accompanied by various other particulars of this disappointment of the unhappy queen. See also sir F. Madden's introduction to her Privy-Purse book.

P. 77. *The cardinal's coming to St. Paul's.* A fuller account of this solemnity will be found in Stowe, p. 625. Like his predecessor Wolsey, Pole went in procession " with a cross, two pillars, and two poleaxes of silver borne before him."

P. 78, *a sofferacan.* " Old Bird, I suppose (says Strype), formerly bishop of Chester, now bishop Bonner's suffragan."

P. 79. *Coming of the prince of Piedmont—*" by water, from—Gravesend " is the word deficient (as appears in Stowe.) He " landed at the duke of Suffolkes place." The following passage occurs in a letter dated the xij[th] of October: " It was told me this day the ambassador of Savoy was yesterday to see my lady Elizabethes house at Strand, and that there was order given for the putting of the same in areadines for the duke his master." Francis Yaxley to sir W. Cecill, in Ellis's Letters, iii. iii. 314.—Emanuel Philibert, prince of Piedmont and duke of Savoy, was at this time an exile from his dominions, which had been taken from his father Charles by Francis I. of France. Having greatly distinguished himself as an ally of king Philip at the battle of St. Quintin in 1557, he concluded a peace with France in 1559, and married Margaret daughter of Francis I. He died in 1580.

P. 80. *Funeral of lady Fitz Walter.* Lady Elizabeth Wriothesley, daughter of Thomas earl of Southampton. She was the first wife of Thomas Ratcliffe, (afterwards) third earl of Sussex, K.G. and had issue two sons, who both died young.

P. 81. *Knightes mayde by kinge Phillip* in his chambre upon Sunday the xxvij.ᵗʰ of January, in Anᵒ. 1554. (MS. Harl. 6064, f. 80ᵇ.)

Sir John Lyon, lorde maior of London.
Sir Robert Broke, lord chief justice of the comon place.
Sir Edward Saunders, judge.
Sir John Whiddon, judge.
Sir William Staimford [judge of the common pleas.]
Sir Clement Hygham [afterwards chief baron of the exchequer.]

The droughtes that is to be payde by them that be mayde knightes by the kinges Maᵈᵉ in his chambre under the degre of a baron : (Ibid. f. 79.)

Imprimis, to the office of armes for the enteringe of their armes in record					.	xxˢ.
Item, to the gentlemen ushers of the chambre	.	.	.	.	.	xxˢ.
Item, to the yeoman ushers	.	.	.	.	.	xˢ.
Item, to the gromes of the chambre	.	.	.	.	.	vˢ.
Item, to the pages of the chambre	.	.	.	.	.	vˢ.

Notwithstandinge these recordes afore rehersed, their was taken by them of the chambre of divers knightes that were made by kinge Phillip the xxvijᵗʰ of Januarie in Aᵒ. 1554, these summes followinge, the which was never had before :

Item, to the gentlemen of the privy chambre	.	.	.			xiijˢ. iiijᵈ.
Item, to the gentleman ushers of the chambre	.	.	.	.		xxˢ.
Item, to the yeoman ushers of the chambre	.	.	.	.		xˢ.
Item, to the gromes of the chambre	.	.	.	.		xˢ.
Item, to the pages	.	.	.	.	.	xˢ.

Ibid. *Funeral of the duchess of Northumberland.* Jane daughter and sole heir of sir Edward Guilford, lord warden of the Cinque Ports, and widow of John Dudley, duke of Northumberland. She gave birth to thirteen children, eight sons and five daughters. Her monument, decorated with coloured brass plates, still remains in Chelsea church, and is engraved in Faulkner's History of that parish. Her will, which is remarkable as having been written entirely with her own hand, though of considerable length, is printed in Collins's Memoirs of the Sidneys, &c. prefixed to the Sidney Papers, fol. 1746, p. 33.

P. 82. *Burning of bishop Hooper.* The letter from the queen to lord Chandos directing him to repair to Gloucester and assist at the execution of bishop Hooper, has been published in Miss Wood's Letters of Royal and Illustrious Ladies, iii. 284.

Ibid. *Marriage of lord Strange.* The date of this was Feb. 7th, not the 12th. "The vij. of February the lord Strange being maried at the court, the same day at night was a goodly pastime of *Juga cana* by cresset lyght ; there were lxx. cresset lightes." Stowe's Summarie, 1566.

P. 82. *The image of St. Thomas pulled down.* It had been erected only two days before. One Barnes a mercer, who lived opposite to the chapel, was suspected of being accessary to its destruction. He, therefore, was committed with some of his servants, and afterwards bound in recognizance to watch it, and make it good if defaced. The 2d of March it was restored at his charge ; but on the 14th (as Machyn records) again broken.

P. 83. *Funeral of the earl of Bedford.* John first earl of Bedford, K.G. created lord Russell 1539, and an earl in 1550. See a portrait with memoirs of him in Wiffen's House of Russell, vol. i. ; another in Lodge's Illustrious Portraits ; and his portrait is also in the collection by Houbraken, and in Chamberlain's Holbein Heads. The chapel at Chenies, which has ever since been the cemetery of the Russells, was built by his widow in 1556, in pursuance of his last will. His effigy at Chenies is described in Lipscomb's Buckinghamshire : but in the inscription, " Lord President of the Western *Portes* " is an error for Partes.

P. 86. *False report of the queen's delivery.* See the article before referred to in the Gentleman's Magazine for Dec. 1841, at p. 598. At St. Benedict Gracechurch the churchwardens paid to a prieste and six clerks for singing of *Te Deum* and playing upon the organs for the birth of our Prince (which was thought then to be), 1*l.* 8*s.* (Malcolm.)

Ibid. *Body of thief burned at Charing cross.* The name of the " pulter," or poulterer, the object of this posthumous vengeance, was Tooly. His case is related at large by Foxe. He had received pardon of some other crime July 5, 1553, the very day before king Edward's death. (Strype, Mem. ii. 509.)

P. 88. *The child supposed to speak.* " By a lettere dated in London, 11 May, 1555, it appeares that in Poules churche yearde, at the signe of the hedgehog, the goodwyfe of the house was brought to bedde of a mane child, beinge of the age of 6 dayes, and dienge the 7th daye followinge ; and halfe an houre before it departed spake these words followinge (rise and pray), and so continued halfe an howre in thes words, and then cryenge departed the worlde. Hereuppon the bushope of London examined the goodman of the house, and othur credible persones, who affirmed it to be true, and will dye uppon the same." (MS. Harl. 353, f. 145.)

Ibid. *Funeral of the countess of Westmerland.* Katharine, daughter of Edward Stafford, duke of Buckingham, K.G. and wife of Ralph earl of Westmerland. A letter from her to the earl of Shrewsbury, 25 Apr. 1544, has been published in Miss Wood's Letters of Ladies, iii. 182. She died at Holywell, the house of her son-in-law the earl of Rutland, in the parish of Shoreditch, on Tuesday, May 14, 1555. (MS. Harl. 897, fol. 78[b], 80.) In that church was erected a joint monument, with four kneeling effigies, representing Elinor (Paston) countess of Rutland, who died in 1551; this countess of Westmerland; her daughter Margaret countess of Rutland, who died 1560 (see Note hereafter to p. 215); and lady Katharine Constable, who died 1591, a granddaughter of the first; which see engraved in Ellis's Shoreditch, p. 56, or Nichols's Leicestershire, vol. ii. pl. xii.

P. 90. *Funeral of the queen of Spain at Saint Paul's.* The full ceremonial of this is preserved in the College of Arms, I. 14, ff. 111—114; and see a letter of the lord treasurer to the bishop of London respecting preparations for the solemnity in Strype, Memorials, iii. 220. The deceased was Jane, the grandmother of king Philip, and the aunt of queen Mary, being the elder sister of queen Katharine. She was the eldest daughter of Ferdinand the Catholic by Isabel queen of Castille; and having married Philip of Austria, they succeeded to the kingdom of Castille on the death of her mother in 1504. On the death of her father in 1516, her husband having previously died in 1506, she was from insanity unfit to reign, and her son Charles (afterwards emperor) was acknowledged sovereign of all Spain.

Ibid. *Proclamation for bringing in heretical books.* A printed copy of this, dated 13 June, is in the collection at the Society of Antiquaries: it is inserted in Foxe's Actes and Monuments, vol. iii. p. 271. Of its objects see also Strype, Mem. vol. iii. p. 250.

P. 91. *Funeral of alderman Thomas Lewen.* That the name which our MS. has here lost should be thus supplied is shown by the following inscription from the church of St. Nicholas Olave's: "Here lies the bodies of Thomas Lewen, ironmonger and some time alderman of the city of London, and Agnes his wife; which Thomas deceased the 29. day of June, Anno D'ni 1555, and the said Agnes deceased the 26. day of October, Anno D'ni 1562. This monument of Thomas Lewen and Agnes his wife was newly revived and beautified at the charge of the right worshipful company of the Ironmongers, of which he was free, the 29th May, Anno D'ni 1623." By his will dated in the year of his death (which is enrolled at Guildhall), Lewen left to the Ironmongers a messuage in Bread-street, and four other houses, for the observance of an obit, the support of four almspeople, and a scholarship at Oxford, and another at Cambridge of 50s. each: see the Report of the Commissioners of Public Charities, and abstract therefrom in Herbert's City Companies, p. 615. A portrait of alderman Lewen is still preserved at Ironmongers' hall. His arms were, Ar. on a chevron engrailed gules, between three crescents of the second, each charged with a bezant, as many estoiles or, and between them two lozenges of the field, each charged with a martlet sable, all within a bordure engrailed gu.—a somewhat remarkable example of a fully, but not unartistically, crowded coat. (MS. Harl. 6860.) He was sheriff 1537-8, but not lord mayor.—A few particulars remain to be given in a subsequent page on occasion of the death of Mrs. Lewen, the alderman's widow.

Ibid. *Master Eton.* George Eyton, master in 1557 (see p. 141.) William Heton was warden of the Merchant-taylors in 1566-7. Wilson's Merchant-taylors' School, p. 1150.

P. 91. *Master Rowe.* Sir Thomas Rowe was an alderman, sheriff in 1560, and lord mayor in 1568. By his will dated May 2, 1569, he was a munificent benefactor to the Merchant-taylors' company; as may be seen by the particulars given in Herbert's City Companies, p. 504. He died Sept. 2, 1570, and his monument at Hackney, having kneeling effigies of himself and wife, was engraved at the expense of his descendant Mr. Rowe-Mores in 1752, and inserted in Robinson's History of that parish, 1842, ii. p. 8. The very full and curious directions which he left for his funeral are printed in Lysons's Environs of London, 1811, vol. ii. p. 302. See memoirs of him also in Wilson's History of Merchant-taylors' school, pp. 5, *et seq.;* and a pedigree of his descendants in Rowe-Mores' History of Tunstall, 4to. 1780, p. xvii.

Ibid. *Master Hylle warden.* This was Richard Hills, the benefactor whom Stowe commemorates in his chapter on the "honour of citizens." He gave 500*l.* towards the purchase of the manor of the Rose, where Merchant-taylors' school was established; also (according to Stowe) fourteen almshouses for poor women on Tower-hill. The latter statement however is not confirmed by Herbert's account of the Merchant-taylors' almshouses; but it appears that by will dated June 28, 1586, he gave certain tenements in St. Botolph's, Aldgate, for the payment of 5*l.* yearly among six poor tailors, and that the Company still owns thirteen houses from this bequest. (Hist. of the City Companies, pp. 496, 506.) Strype mentions Richard Hills as having been resident at Strasburg in 1548, and commissioned by Cranmer to help Martin Bucer to his journey to England. He became master of the Merchant-taylors' company in 1561. (Wilson's Merchant-taylors' school, p. 10.)

Ibid. *Master God.* The Survay of Finsbury manor, dated 1567, mentions "a lodge and certain gardens and tenter grounds in the tenure of John God, merchant-taylor, inclosed on the north towards Chiswell-street by a brick wall." (Herbert's Twelve City Companies, ii. 389.) He was again warden of the company in 1563-4, and master in 1565-6.

Ibid. *All v. born in London, and taylors' sons all.* Herbert remarks, that, though "there are not at this time half a dozen tailor brothers of this dignified corporation," the case was quite the reverse formerly, (contrary to some affected aristocracy of the *Merchant-taylors,* absurdly advanced by the Rev. Dr. Wilson in his History of Merchant-taylors' School,) and the company itself continued a working one until the reign of James I. When it is recollected that the great city historian Stowe was a taylor of London, and his cotemporary Speed, the general historian, as well as Anthony Munday, Thomas Middleton, and others, besides a fair proportion of the distinguished civic senators and benefactors of former days, there can be no reason to despise the brethren of this very necessary craft, at any stage of its history, even if, besides "manufacturing pavilions for our kings, robes of state for our nobles, and tents, &c. for our soldiers," (Wilson, p. xix.) they also condescended to become "makers of ordinary garments" (ibid.) by stitching jerkins for our prentices, doublets for our shopmen, and trunk-hose for our cooks. It is true that trades were much more subdivided formerly than at present: thus we hear of bowyers and fletchers ; armourers and linen armourers (the latter were associated with the tailors) ; and there were cappers and hosiers, distinct trades, though the material they used, as well as the tailors, was cloth. But a tailor, or a "taylor," has remained much the same from generation to generation.

P. 93. *Departure of king Philip.* The king crossed to Calais on the 4th Sept. "and so foorth to Brusselles in Brabant to visite the emperour hys father." (Stowe's Summarie, 1566.) He went to assume the government of the Low Countries, and was received into Antwerp with great solemnity about the 18th January. (Ibid.)

P. 94. *Funeral of lady Lyons.* Alice wife of sir John Lyons then lord mayor, who has been noticed in p. 340. "A remembraunce for thenterament of my ladye Lyons" is in I. 3, in Coll. Arm. f. 94[b]. After the death of his first wife Alice, sir John Lyon married "Elsabeth doter of Lee and widow of Austen Hynde alderman and shreve of London. This Elsabeth dyed the xth of July in A° 1569. He dyed the 7th Sept. 1564 sans issue, wherefore he made his heyre . . . . . Lyon, his brother's son, of Acton, unto whose sons he gave all his landes." (MS. Harl. 874, f. 25[b].)

Ibid. *The Lollards' Tower.* When I wrote the note in this page, and another in p. 118, I was not aware that there had been any other "Lollards' Tower" than that still remaining at Lambeth. I have since noticed in Stowe's Survey that the southern bell-tower at the west end of St. Paul's cathedral was so called. The tower towards the north, next the Bishop's palace, was attached to " the use of the same palace ; the other, towards the south, is called the Lollards' Tower, and hath beene used as the bishop's prison, for such as were detected for opinions in religion, contrary to the faith of the church." The last prisoner Stowe had known confined there was in 1573. It is probable therefore that our Londoner meant the Lollards' Tower nearest at hand.

P. 95. *Funeral of master Barthelet.* Thomas Barthelet, made king's printer by patent dated 22 Feb. 21 Henry VIII. (1529-30). The place of his interment is not recorded. What is known respecting him, with a catalogue of his works, will be found in Ames's Typographical Antiquities, by Dibdin, vol. iii. pp. 271, *et seq.*

Ibid. *Burial of hereticks in Morefields.* This was the usual practice with those who by a natural death (if such a term can be applied to the result of imprisonment and privations) escaped the stake and the faggots. See in Foxe, vol. iii. p. 537, a graphic cut of such a burial, with archers from the neighbouring butts as spectators.

Ibid. *Funeral of doctor Wotton.* In St. Alban's Wood-street: " Here lieth Edward Wotton, doctor of phisick, ob. 5 Octobr. 1555, æt. 63, and Katharine his wife, who died 4 Decembr' 1558." (MS. Lansdowne 874.)

Ibid. *The serjeants' feast.* As many as eleven barristers had been recently called to be serjeants: see Dugdale's Chronica Series, p. 89. One of them, George Wood, had been excused. (Ibid.) Machyn, however, says, only seven were made. One of the new serjeants, Anthony Brown, was appointed the king and queen's serjeant by patent dated Oct. 16, the day of the feast. (Ibid. p. 91.)

P. 96. *The lord mayor's pageant.* The new mayor was "sir William Garrard, haberdasher, a grave, sober, wise, and discreet citizen, equall with the best and inferior to none of our time, deceased 1571, in the parish of St. Christopher, but was buried in this church of St. Magnus, as in the parish where he was borne. A faire monument is there raised on him. This monument is lately re-edified and new fenced by sir John Garrard, his sonne, and L. Maior 1602." (Stowe's Survay.) "He dwelled at the pissing conduit in St. Xp'ofer's parish." Arms, Argent, on a fess sable a lion passant of the first. (Wm. Smith, Rouge-dragon.)

P. 97. *Funeral of lord chancellor Gardiner.* The ceremonial of this is preserved in the Coll. Arm. I. 11. 121—124, and a second copy in pp. 127—133.—Machyn's extraordinary word "inowlle" is converted by Strype into "jewels:" and in my marginal note I have suggested "enamel." Both explanations are wrong: as no doubt our painter meant that the banners were painted with images of saints *in oil* and "with fine gold."

P. 98. *Committal of sir Anthony Kingston to the Tower.* This was for his "contemptuous behaviour and greate disorder by him lately comytted in the Parlemente house." He was discharged on the 24th Dec. See the minutes of the privy council, Dec. 10, 11, 18, 24. (MS. Harl. 353, ff. 146, 147.) He soon after again got into disgrace, and, being summoned to attend the privy council, died on his road to London. See Bayley's History of the Tower, pp. 449, 450.

P. 99. *Funeral of alderman Henry Heardson.* His widow Barbara was remarried to alderman Richard Champion; and she erected a monument in St. Dunstan's in the East, with kneeling effigies of herself and both the aldermen her husbands. See it described, with the poetical epitaphs, in Stowe's Survay. His arms were Argent, semée of fleurs-de-lis gules, a cross engrailed sable. He was never sheriff nor lord mayor. (List by Wm. Smith, Rouge-dragon.)

P. 100. *Funeral of alderman Christopher Allen.* This person also was not either sheriff or lord mayor, nor does his name even appear in Smith's lists.

Ibid. *Penance of Thomas Samson.* This could scarcely be Thomas Sampson, late rector of Allhallows, Bread-street, and afterwards successively dean of Chichester and Christchurch Oxford: for his enemies would scarcely have been satisfied with a mere penance. He was probably already fled abroad (see Wood's Athenæ Oxon.): his address to his late parishioners written at Strasburg is printed in Strype, Memorials, iii. Appx. No. xviii.

P. 100. *Funeral of master Leygett.* Thomas Legatt esquire of Havering, where probably he was buried. See Morant's Essex, vol. i. p. 62.

P. 101. *Execution of Fetherston.* Stowe gives the date of this as the 12th of March.

Ibid. *The blasyng star.* This is recorded by Stowe to have appeared on the 4th March, and continued for twelve days (Summarie 1566) ; but in his chronicle 1580 he limits its continuance to five nights from the 6th to the 10th of March.

Ibid. *Funeral of bishop Chambers.* "Anno 1555, the vij. daye of February, being fryday, died the reverend father in God Joh'n Chambre, late bishopp of Peterborough, betwene x and xj in the nyght, comitat. Northampt. in good and perfauct memory, levyng for his executors,

Sir Thomas Tresham knight, of Northamtonshire

Mr. Gryffyn the queenes attourney.

Mourners

Sir Thomas Tresham knyght, chief mourner

Sir William Fitzwilliam	Thomas Cotton esquier
Robert Wyngkfelde	John Fitzwilliam
Richard Wakerley	George Tresham

Banner berers

Thomas Hussey the baner of his armes

Joh'n Mountsteving the baner of the Trynytie

Joh'n Nauncycles the baner of our Lady

Robart Malorye the baner of St. Peter

Joh'n Mallorye the baner of St. John

" The saide bishopp was buryed in the mynster in a chapell in the high quyer on the ryghte hande on thursdaye the vj^th of Marche, according to the estate of a bishoppe." (MS. I. 3, in Coll. Arm. fol. 100^b.)

P. 102. *Gentlemen carried to the Tower.* The crime of these parties is thus given by Grafton : "A conspiracye was made by certayne meane persons in England, whose purpose was to have robbed the queenes exchequer, to thys intent as the talke was, that they myght be hable to mayntayne warre against the queene. This matter was uttered by one of the conspiracie, wherefore Udall, Frogmorton, Pecham, and one Staunton, were apprehended and put to death for the same. And certayne of the sayd conspiracy fled into Fraunce and other places." Abridgement, 1563.

Ibid. *Consecration of Cardinal Pole.* An account of this ceremony, at which the queen was present, will be found in Strype, Memorials, iii. 287.

P. 102. *Benett Smith hanged for the murder of master Rufford.* "An act of parliament passed in 1555 to take away the benefit of clergy from Benedict Smith of Edlesborough, yeoman, who had instigated Francis Coniers, of London, gent. and John Spencer, yeoman, by the promise of 40*l.* (in part of which 40*s.* and a gold ring was afterwards paid,) to murder Giles Rufford, esq. of Boteler's in Edlesborough, giving them two javelings and a dagge for that purpose. The murder was committed at Alconbury Weston, in the county of Huntingdon. This act, which is printed in Rastall's Statutes, was procured (the murderers being then not apprehended) by Margery, widow of Giles Rufford." (Lysons's Buckinghamshire, p. 691.) See also further particulars in Lipscomb's History of Buckinghamshire, vol. iii. p. 351 ; and the Journals of the House of Commons, vol. i. p. 45.

P. 105. *Funeral of sir John Gage, K.G.* The imperfect paragraph in this page probably relates to the funeral of sir John Gage, K.G. who died 18 April, 1556. He was buried at Firle in Sussex, where a monument with recumbent effigies of himself and his wife Philippa, daughter of sir Richard Guilford, K.G. still remains. See an engraving of it in Gage's History of Hengrave, 4to. 1822, and also a portrait and memoir of Sir John.

Ibid. *Conspiracy of Throgmorton, Udall, &c.* The intention was to rob the exchequer, as stated in the preceding page. The person called "Wodall" and "Waddall" by Machyn, is named Richard Udall by Holinshed (but once, p. 1766, l. 6, misprinted *Veale*). He was probably Richard, a younger son of sir William Uvedale of Wickham, Hants, by Dorothy, daughter and co-heir of Thomas Troyne (see the pedigree in Hutchins's Dorsetshire, 2nd edit. vol. ii. p. *503). A curious paper showing the interchanging of the names of Uvedale and Woddall will be found in the Collectanea Topogr. et Genealogica, 1838, v. 241.

P. 106. *Funeral of alderman sir Richard Dobbs.* Son of Robert Dobbs, of Batby in Yorkshire ; sheriff 1543, lord mayor 1551. Stowe mentions his monument in the church of St. Margaret Moyses, but gives no epitaph. Arms, Per pale argent and sable, a chevron engrailed between three unicorn's heads each charged with three gouts all counter-changed. (Wm. Smith, Rouge-dragon.) See the death and funeral of his widow in pp. 268, 269.

Ibid. *Funeral of sir Richard Morgan, chief justice of the common pleas.* The following anecdote is recorded with regard to the death of this person, after describing the execution of lady Jane Grey: "Judge Morgan, that gave the sentence against hir, shortly after fell mad, and in hys raving cryed continuallye to have the ladie Jane taken away from him, and so ended his life." Holinshed, first edit. 1577, p. 1733 ; and Foxe, vol. iii. p. 37.

P. 107. *Master West esquire slain by my lord Dacre's (Darcy's) son.* Our journalist here, and at p. 121, has miswritten Dacre for Darcy. The murdered man was Lewis West, of Wales near Doncaster, esquire, son and heir apparent of sir William West, of Aughton in the same county, whose death followed before the end of the year, and his funeral occurs at p. 161. The lord Darcy's son was George Darcy, whose name is not mentioned in the peerages, but has been traced in some other documents by Mr. Hunter, who, in his History of South Yorkshire, vol. ii. pp. 173—176, has printed a curious contemporary ballad relative to this event, accompanied by some other particulars connected with it. It arose from one of those family feuds which were still prevalent in the sixteenth century ; and the two sons of lord Darcy, John and George, were implicated in it, as well as the two sons of sir William West, Lewis and Edmund. The ballad is headed " The murder of the two brothers, Lewis and Edmund, by the sons of lord Darcy ;" but this is an error, for only Lewis was killed and one of his men, as the ballad itself states. The brothers West were returning from Rotherham fair, held on Whitmonday, to their cousin's house at Aughton, when they were assaulted by the Darcys, who were much more numerously attended, " with men three score," and after a desperate fight the result was as already stated. George Darcy, the younger brother, who appears to have been the actual murderer, took sanctuary at Westminster, and an account of the penance he performed is recorded by our chronicler, p. 121, as is his subsequent trial in p. 165.

P. 108. *The Grocers' feast.* In Kempe's Loseley Manuscripts, p. 160, is printed a warrant from the marquess of Winchester to the keeper of the great park of Nonesuch, transferring to the wardens of the company of Grocers, for their feast this year, the fee buck to which he was entitled by virtue of his office of high treasurer of England. There is some discrepancy, however, in the dates given.

Ibid. *Execution of lord Sands' son.* " The 18. of June one Sands, a younger son of the lord Sands, was hanged at Saint Thomas of Waterings, for a robbery that hee and other had committed on Witsunday last of 4000. pounds." Stowe's Chronicle.—He is not named in Dugdale's Baronage.

Ibid. *Funeral of sir Giles Capel.* Son and heir of the rich citizen sir William Capel, (historically known from the exactions he suffered from the ministers of Henry VII.) who died in 1515, and was buried in a chantry chapel which he had built at the church of St. Bartholomew the Little (recently removed to widen the approaches to the Royal Exchange). Sir Giles Capel was knighted in France in 1513, and his biography will be found in Collins's Peerage, 1779, vol. iii. p. 349 : being the lineal ancestor of the earls of Essex.—The funeral of his son and heir sir Henry occurs in p. 164.

P. 109. *Merchant-taylors' feast.* This is the subject of the first imperfect paragraph ; it was held on Saint Barnabas' day, the 11th of June.

Ibid. *Condemnation of lord La Warre*—" for high treason," says our diarist ; which statement has been adopted by Strype, Memorials, ii. p. 302, and thence by Bayley, History of the Tower of London, p. 452. But his crime was of a more private character, and one would rather suppose this was the date of his *pardon* than of his sentence. He had attempted to poison his uncle and predecessor, and was consequently by Act of Parliament, in 2 Edw. VI. disabled from succeeding him in title and estate. His uncle was now lately dead (see p. 339), and shortly after we find that the young lord joined the army in France, and distinguished himself at St. Quintin's. His claim to the dignity of a peer was not acknowledged until 1579 ; on that subject see Retrospective Review, 2d Ser. ii. 300. He died in 1595.

P. 109. *Execution of Peckham and Daniel.* "The 8. of July, Henry Peckham, son to sir Edmond Peckham, and John Daniel, were hanged and headed on Tower-hill, for being of counsell with them that should have robbed the queenes treasure of her exchequer, and their bodies buried in Barking church." Stowe's Chronicle.—Daniel's name remains cut on the wall of his prison, "JOHN DANIEL, 1556." See Bayley's History of the Tower of London, p. 207.

Ibid. *Funeral of lady Seymer.* Sir Thomas Seymer, mercer, was lord mayor in 1526, and died 11 Dec. 1532, leaving Mary his widow : see his epitaph in Ellis's Shoreditch, p. 54.

P. 110. *Funeral of lady Norwich.* Sir Robert Norwich was made chief justice of the common pleas in 1531, and died 1536. But, as the name does not appear in Morant's History of Essex, it is not ascertained where this funeral took place.

P. 111. *Death of alderman sir William Laxton.* Sir William Laxton, grocer, was son of John Laxton of Oundle in Northamptonshire ; sheriff in 1540, lord mayor 1544. He founded a school at Oundle ; see Bridges's Northamptonshire, ii. 410. He had a fair monument in Aldermary church, with a poetical inscription, which will be found in Stowe. He married Joan daughter of William Kyrby and widow of Harry Lodington, but had no issue by her. (MS. Harl. 897, f. 24.)

Ibid. *Pirates hung at Wapping at the low-water mark.* Other instances of this will be found at pp. 131, 231, 256, 281. Stowe mentions Wapping as "the usuall place of execution for hanging of pirats and sea-rovers, at the low-water marke, there to remaine till three tides had overflowed them :" adding, that in his time the gallows had been removed to a greater distance from the city, in consequence of the street which had grown up within the last fifty years, "almost to Radcliffe, a good mile from the Tower."

Ibid. *Death of bishop Day.* George Day, D.D. bishop of Chichester, consecrated in 1543. He was buried in his own cathedral. See a memoir of him in Dallaway's City of Chichester, 4to. 1815, p. 72. He refused to assent to the destruction of altars in 1550 (Archæologia, xviii. 149), and in 1553 was summoned to preach the sermon at queen Mary's coronation (ibid. 174).

P. 112. *Funeral of doctor John Bell, formerly bishop of Worcester.* His sepulchral brass, formerly in Clerkenwell church, is now in Parliament Street ; a small copy is engraved by Malcolm, Londinium Redivivum, iii. 212. See the epitaph in Stowe and the other Histories of London.

P. 113. *Funeral of Philip Dennis esquire,*—of London, died 3 Sept. 1556. (Epitaph.)

P. 114. *Funeral of [John] Lucas esquire.* " A faire plated stone on the ground in the chancell of St. Peter the poor. Here under this stone are buried the bodies of John Lucas of S. John's beside Colchester esquire, master of the requests to the most vertuous, noble, and worthy prince, king Edward the sixth. He departed this life the 28. day of October, An. Dom. 1556. And his daughter Margaret, late wife to Thomas Pennie doctor of physicke, here buried the 13. day of November 1587." (Stowe.) He was great-grandfather of the gallant cavalier who was created a peer by king Charles the First. (See Morant's Essex, iii. 227.)

P. 115. *William Harrys esquire* of Cricksea near Southminster, Essex, died 21 September 1555, says Morant, i. 366 ; which our Diary corrects to 1556. His pedigree will be found in MS. Harl. 874, f. 131ᵇ.

Ibid. *Funeral of sir John Champneys.* Son of Robert Champneys of Chew in Somersetshire ; he was a skinner, sheriff of London and Middlesex 1522, lord mayor 1534. Stowe notes in his Chronicle that he was blind. He bore for arms, Per pale argent and sable, a lion rampant gules, within a bordure counter-changed. (List by Wm. Smith, Rouge-dragon.) He was buried at Bexley in Kent, (see his epitaph in Thorpe's Registrum Roffense, p. 924.) His family long continued in that county (see Hasted, vol. i. p. 160, vol. iii. 326.)

Ibid. *Funeral of lord Vaux.* Thomas second lord Vaux of Harrowden, and K.B. succeeded his father 1523. Sir Harris Nicolas (Synopsis of the Peerage) was not certain of the date of his death.

Ibid. *Funeral of sir Richard Cotton.* King Edward visited sir Richard Cotton at Warblington on the 2—4 Aug. 1553 ; and he was made comptroller of the household on the 27th of the same month. (King Edward's Diary.) The queen dowager of Scotland had lodged at Warblington on the 28 Oct. 1552 (Ibid.)

Ibid. *Funeral of sir Henry Huberthorne.* Son of Christopher Huberthorne of Waddingworth in Lincolnshire ; sheriff 1542, lord mayor 1547. During his mayoralty he was knighted by king Edward VI. a few days after his accession, on the 6th Feb. 1546-7, immediately after the young sovereign had received the same degree from his uncle the Protector the earl of Hertford. There was a " fair marble stone under the communion table " at St. Peter's, Cornhill, recording his name and that of his wife Elizabeth, who died in 1551 (see p. 9.) " He dwelled in the very next house to Leadenhall, where sir William Bowyer [lord mayor in 1544] dwelled." Arms, Sable, a mascle within a bordure counterflory argent. (List by Wm. Smith, Rouge-dragon.)

P. 116. *Funeral of sir John Olyffe:* sometimes written Ayloffe ; sheriff in 1548-9, appointed the first alderman of Bridge ward Without, when the borough of Southwark was made one of the wards of the City, as detailed in Stowe's Survay, edit. 1633, p. 446. He was first a Barber-surgeon, and his portrait occurs in Holbein's picture of Henry VIII. delivering their charter to that company (see Gent. Mag. lix. 290) ; on becoming an alderman he was translated to the Grocers. He lived in Blackwell hall, and was buried in the adjoining church of St. Michael's Bassishaw ; where was a long epitaph in English verse, printed in Stowe, but with the erroneous date 1548 instead of 1554. Arms, Argent, on a chevron engrailed between three estoiles gules, three stag's heads caboshed argent, attired or. (List by Wm. Smith, Rouge-dragon.) His son John died July 17, 1579, and was buried in St. Stephen's, Coleman Street. See his wife and children in MS. Harl. 897, ff. 62ᵇ, 131ᵇ.

P. 116. *Burial of bishop Man at St. Andrew's Undershaft.* " Henry Man, doctor of divinity in the university of Oxenford, and sometime bishop of Man, which Henry departed this life the 19. day of October, An. Do. 1556, and lyeth buried under this stone."—" before the doore within the chancell." (Stowe.) The letters patent of his appointment by Henry VIII. dated 22 Jan. 1545-6 are printed in Rymer's Fœdera, xv. 85.

Ibid. *Funeral of alderman sir John Gresham.* Uncle to the celebrated sir Thomas. Biographical notices of him will be found in Burgon's Life of sir Thomas Gresham, vol. i. pp. 11, *et seq.* He was sheriff in 1537-8, and lord mayor in 1547-8. He was buried at St. Michael Bassishaw : and his epitaph is given by Stowe. Sir Rowland Hill and sir Andrew Judd were made overseers of his will. (Ibid. p. 19.) " He dwelled where sir Leonard Holiday now dwelleth." (Wm. Smith, Rouge-dragon.)

The death of so many old persons at this period is attributed by Stowe to " the hot burning fevers." Seven aldermen died within ten months,—Hardson, Dobbs, Laxton, Hobblethorne, Champneys, Ayloffe, and Gresham : they have all been noticed in these pages.

P. 117. *Master Offley sworn lord mayor.* Sir Thomas Offley, son of William Offley, of Chester, had been sheriff in 1553. He was knighted during his mayoralty on the 7th Feb. ; see p. 125. " He dwelled in Lyme strete, towards the north end of it, not farr from St. Andrew's Undershaft, where he is buried." Arms, Argent, on a cross flory-de-lis azure, between four choughs proper, a lion passant guardant or. (List by Wm. Smith, Rouge-dragon.) " The useful custom of the night-bellmen (preventing many fiers and more felonies) began in his mayoralty. He was the Zacheus of London, not for his low stature, but his high charity, bequeathing the half of his estate (computed, by a reverend divine, to amount to five thousand pounds) unto the poor. He died 1580, and was buried in St. Andrew Undershaft." Fuller's Worthies ; and, after noticing two other citizens of the name, Hugh and Robert, he adds, " I believe it was the first of these three Offleys on whom the rhythme was made,

> Offley three dishes had of daily rost,
> An egge, an apple, and (the third) a toast.

This I behold neither sin nor shame in him, feeding himself on plain and wholesome repast, that he might feed others by his bounty, and thereby deserving rather praise than a jear from posterity."

P. 118. *Funeral of alderman Goodyer.* Henry Goodyer (whose name does not occur in Smith's list of aldermen, and who was never sheriff,) became one of the trustees of the parish of St. Olave for Horseydown, in the 36th Hen. VIII. (See the account of St. Olave's grammar school in the Gentleman's Magazine for 1836, N. S. vol. v. p. 139.) On the 19 Jan. 1586 Hugh Gooder released and confirmed the said land to the governors. (Communication of G. R. Corner, esq. F.S.A.)

Ibid. *Funeral of lady Williams of Thame.* "The lady Elisabeth, late wyff to the right honorable sir John Williams knight, lord Williams baron of Thame, and lord chamberlen to king Phelype, doter of Bledloo, and afore wyff to Andru Edmondes of Essex, dyed on sonday the 25. of October 1556, and was beryed at Rycot in Bokynghamshire [Oxfordshire] the 4. of November next foloing." (MS. Harl. 897, f. 83.) The ceremony is recorded in Coll. Arm. I. 3, f. 101, and I. 9, f. 150^b. Christopher Edmundes esquire, her son by her first husband, bore the banner of her arms. See her husband's funeral in p. 217.

Ibid. *Man set in the pillory.* Stowe (1580) has a considerably longer account of this. The man was burnt on both cheeks, with the letters F and A for False Accusing one of the court of Common Pleas of treason. The like punishment the chronicler had once wished for one who had falsely accused his maister and eldest brother—apparently meaning himself.

P. 120. *Funeral of lord Morley.* "Sir Henry Parker lord Morley dyed on Wensday the 25. of November 1556, at his howsse of Hannyngbery Morley, and was beryed on Thursday the 3. of December next foloing." (MS. Harl. 897, f. 79^b.) In the church of Great Hallingbury: see Muilman's History of Essex, vol. iv. p. 143.

Ibid. *Funeral of Robert Downe master of the Ironmongers.* Of his benefactions to that company see Malcolm, ii. 40 ; and his will is enrolled at Guildhall.

Ibid. *Gregory a Spaniard.* Stowe calls this man " Gregory Carpenter, smith, and a Frenchman borne." His original crime was making counterfeit keys, wherewith to have opened the locks of Newgate.

P. 122. *Mistress Bowes, daughter of my lord Scrope.* Martin Bowes esquire, of Barking in Essex, second son of sir Martin Bowes, married to his first wife Frances, daughter of Richard Scrope, and heir of Elizabeth Amidas his wife, who was the daughter of Robert Amidas goldsmith of London by Margaret heiress of James Bryce ; see their issue in Vincent's Middlesex, Coll. Arm. 119 f. 484, Vincent's Essex 124, f. 105 ; or

MS. Harl. 897, f. 21. Our diarist was mistaken in supposing that this lady was " the do[ughter] of my lord Skrope," an error the more remarkable because Mary daughter of Henry lord Scrope married sir William Bowes (see Surtees's Durham, iv. 110.)

P. 125. *Lord Stourton's murder of the Hartgills.* Some account of this tragedy will be found in Holinshed, Stowe, Strype, and the other historians of the period : but Sir R. C. Hoare, in his History of Modern Wiltshire (Hundred of Mere, pp. 152—157) has collected at considerable length the particulars preserved of it—the first page and a half derived from various passages of our own diarist, but the narrative of the crime itself from an authentic MS. of the time. Some years before, lord Stourton's arbitrary violence had attracted the censure of the privy council : see its minutes under July 17, 21, 28, 1551. (MS. Harl. 353.)

Ibid. *Funeral of sir William Portman.* He had been made chief justice in 1554. His funeral insignia (made by our diarist) were remaining when St. Dunstan's was visited by Nich. Charles ; see Collectanea Topogr. et Geneal. 1837, vol. iv. p. 99 : see also his epitaph in Stowe, and the pedigree of Portman in Hutchins's Dorsetshire, vol. i. p. 154.

P. 127. *Funeral of the earl of Sussex.* " Sir Henry Ratclyff erl of Sussex and vyscount FitzWater, lord Egremont and Burnell, knight of the garter, lieutenaunte of the counties of Norffolk and Sussex, and late countrolor to the king and quenes majesties, dyed at sir Harry Sydney's howsse in Chanon Roo at Westmynster on Wensday the 15. [17] of February in the 3. and 4. yere of king Phelyp and queene Mary, 1556, and was beryed at St. Mary Poultney in London on Saterday the 27. of the same mounth." (MS. Harl. 897, f. 79.) The heralds' account of the ceremony is recorded in Coll. Arm. I. 15, f. 225, and printed in the appendix to Wilson's History of the parish of St. Laurence Pountney, 4to. 1831. That author states, (p. 10,) " In the north aisle of this church, originally parochial, then collegiate as well as parochial, and after the surrender again parochial only, were interred several members of the Radcliffe family, particularly Robert Radcliffe, earl of Sussex, who died 27th Nov. 1542, and Henry Radcliffe his son, who died 17th Feb. 1556-7. But at length the remains of these two earls were removed to Boreham in Essex." At Boreham was erected a sumptuous monument (now in ruins) with effigies of the three earls ; see Walpole's Anecdotes of Painting, &c. (1762, i. 160), and the epitaphs in Antiq. Repertory, or Wilson, *ubi supra.*

Ibid. *A Duke of Muscovea.* In preparation for his arrival, the Privy Council sent " A lettere to th' officers of the warderobe in the Tower, to deliver, or cause to be delivered, to Mr. Hussey, Governor of the Marchauntes-adventurers, or to three of that Company which he shall send for that purpose, a bed of estate with furniture and hangings for the chamber of the duke of Muscovia, to be by the said marchauntes redelivered when the said embassador shall be departed." Also another letter " to the officers of the Jewell-howse to deliver ij. pair of grete silver pottes to the said Governor to be used *ut supra.*" (Burgon's Life of Gresham, i. 372, from Minutes of the Privy Council, in the Council

Office, f. 511.) In p. 371 Mr. Burgon has by mistake called "master Dimmock's house" Denmark house. A full account of the reception of the ambassador, and a list of the presents he brought, will be found in Stowe's Chronicle, 1631, pp. 629, 630.

P. 127. last line. *For* Sturton *read* Salisbury, as in the next page.

P. 128. *Funeral of sir Edward Montagu.* The progenitor of the dukes of Montagu and Manchester, and earls of Halifax. He was buried at Weekley in Northamptonshire, where is his effigy, and the epitaph will be found in Bridges's History of that county, vol. ii. p. 347; also in Collins's Peerage, 1779, vol. ii. p. 83, together with his will and biographical notices; but his monument is there incorrectly placed at Hemington.

Ibid. *Funeral of sir Oliver Leader.* "Item, upon the seconde day of February in An⁰ 1554 sir Oliver Leader was made knight by kinge Phillip." (MS. Harl. 6064.) See in Thomas Mountain's narrative of his troubles, Strype's Memorials, vol. iii. p. 187, a picturesque account of his being received into the custody of sir Oliver Leader, then Sheriff of Huntingdonshire, "a man of much worship, and one that keepeth a good house," and of his courteous entertainment during his halt. Sir Oliver appears to have facilitated Mountain's escape at the sessions, by purposely forgetting to bring the writ with him. His funeral is recorded in Coll. Arm. I. 15, f. 272ᵇ.

P. 132. *Sir Thomas Chamber.* Some more of the pranks of this merry parson are related in p. 205: and see the note on that passage hereafter.

P. 133. *Funeral of lord Chandos.* "Sir John Bruges knight loord Chandos dyed at the castell of Sudley in Glostershire on monday the xijᵗʰ. of Apryll 1556, and was buryd the 3. of May in A⁰ predicto in the churche of Sudley." (MS. Harl. 897, f. 79ᵇ.) In Collins's Peerage his death is erroneously dated on the 4th of March.

Ibid. *Creations of Thomas Percy to the barony of Percy and earldom of Northumberland.* Our chronicler has given correctly the dates of these restorations. The patents are printed in Rymer's collection, xv. 461, 462. In the following August the Earl was made Warden of the Middle and East Marches towards Scotland. Ibid. pp. 468, 472, 475.

P. 135. *Scarborough castle.* Strype in his Memorials, vol. iii. Appen. lxxiii. has printed "the Names of the Prisoners taken in Scarborowe Castell the 28th of Apryll, An. 1557." Five were committed to the Tower of London, and twenty-seven remained in York Castle.

Pp. 135, 136. *Death and Funeral of sir Jaques Granado.* He was a native of Brabant: having distinguished himself in the campaign in Scotland in 1547 (Holinshed, 1st edit. p. 1620), he was one of the knights made at its close by the duke of Somerset at Berwick, Sept. 28. (Ibid. p. 1633). An annuity of 50l. was granted March 10, 1549-50, to sir Jaques Granado and Magdalen his wife, and to the longer liver: see the patent printed in Rymer, xv. 210. He appears to have filled the office of equerry or some similar post, as in Oct. 1551, he had a passport to conduct sixteen horses sent by Edward VI. to the French king. His widow "Mawdelyn" became the second wife of sir Robert Chester, and his daughter Katharine was married to Edward Chester, sir Robert's son and heir. (MS. Harl. 897, f. 55ᵇ.)

P. 137. *Three more hanged at Tyborne* (May 28), 1557. Stowe says these were Streightly or Stretchly (called William Stowe by our diarist in p. 142), Bradforde, and Proctor—three of Stafford's company from Scarborough castle.

P. 138. *Proclamation of war with France.* A transcript (from the printed copy) of this Proclamation may be found in Starkey's collections, MS. Harl. 353, f. 184. See also Holinshed, 1st edit. p. 1767; Stowe's Chronicle, 1631, p. 631.

Ibid. *Began a stage-play at the Gray freers of the Passyon of Cryst.* The word "began" seems to imply that the play lasted more than one day in its representation, or else that it was repeated. Mr. Collier has noticed its performance in his Annals of the Stage, vol. i. p. 167, and states it was first performed at the same place on Corpus Christi day 1556 (the previous year) before the lord mayor, the privy council, and many great estates of the realm; but he quotes no other authority but the present diary.

P. 140. *Burning of Store-house at Portsmouth.* The date was left incomplete in the MS. thus—"The x day of June." Strype has accordingly (Mem. iii. 377) attributed this event to the 10th of June. The real date is given by a contemporary account of the catastrophe under the hands of the mayor and burgesses of the town, which is printed in the Collectanea Topogr. et Genealogica, (1835,) ii. 251. In our diary, p. 140, the words supplied to the last deficiency, instead of "both were" should probably be "the beer-cellar."

P. 141. *Master Malory chosen sheriff.* Richard Mallory, mercer, son of Anthony Mallory, of Papworth, Cambridgeshire; sheriff 1557, lord mayor 1564-5. "He was a mercer, dwelled in Cheapsyde at Soper lane end, at the signe of the Golden Kay, and was buried in the Mercers' chapell." Arms, Or, a lion rampant and bordure gules. (List by Wm. Smith, Rouge-dragon.)

Ibid. *Christening of the duke of Norfolk's son.* Philip earl of Surrey, as he was called in his infancy, and afterwards the distinguished earl of Arundel of that name, was "borne at Arundell place in London 28. of July [June] 1557." (MS. Harl. 897, f. 79.) Stowe also has recorded his christening "in the queenes chapell at Westminster, in a font of gold." The king and lord chancellor stood godfathers "in proper person."

P. 143. *A great army.* In Starkey's collections, MS. Harl. 353, f. 188ᵇ. will be found " The Booke of the officers and Captaynes of horsmen and footmen of a Regiment of a Thousand horsmen, Four Thowsand footmen, and two thowsand Pyoners, wth. their Wages and entertainments, at the goinge to St. Quintens in the tyme of Queene Marye, primo July an°. 1557." (It is imperfect.) The word " Regiment " in this case appears equivalent to Army. A list of the captains will also be found in Holinshed, p. 1767.

P. 144. *Funeral of lady Roche.* It is difficult to ascertain whose widow this could be. There was a sir William Roche, lord mayor in 1541, but we have the funeral of his widow afterwards in p. 190. No other name resembling Roohe occurs in the list of mayors.

Ibid. *Funeral of master Latham.* Ralph Latham, esq. of Upminster, Essex, died July 19, 1556. (See Morant, i. 108.)

Ibid. *Funeral of mistress Draper, of Camberwell.* See genealogical notices of this family in the Collectanea Topogr. et Genealogica, vol. iii. p. 150.

Ibid. *Arrest of Waxham from the sanctuary at Westminster.* Abbat Feckenham was censured by the people for consenting to the surrender of this sanctuary man, and in his sermon at the funeral of the lady Anne of Cleves, he publicly defended his conduct, as may be seen in the Excerpta Historica, p. 312. The name of the culprit, which our diarist writes in three ways (see pp. 150, 151), is there spelt " Vawgh^a^m."

P. 145. *Inclosing of the nuns of Syon.* This royal foundation was one of the few that queen Mary was able to reinstate. Of this transaction see Aungier's History of Syon Monastery, 8vo. 1840, p. 96.

Ibid. *Funeral of the lady Anne of Cleves.* A very particular narrative of this solemnity, from MSS. in the College of Arms, will be found in the Excerpta Historica, 1831, together with the Will of the deceased. The body of the queen was buried, as Stowe says, " at the head of king Sebert," where " she lyeth in a tomb not yet finished." Engravings of what was erected of this tomb will be found in the Vetusta Monumenta, vol. ii. pl. 85, as well as in Dart and the other histories of Westminster Abbey. In p. 145, *for* sir Robert Freston *read* Richard ; and in p. 146, *for* William duke of Cleves *read* John.

Ibid. *Hearse for the king of [Portugal].* Machyn here made the error of naming the the king of Denmark, instead of the king of Portugal, John III. who succeeded his father Emanuel in 1521, and died 1557. He had married Jane aunt of king Philip, and hence arose the special observance of his obsequies in this country. They are briefly noticed by Holinshed, p. 1768 ; but are recorded at full in the College of Arms, I. 15, f. 246. At the beginning of this paragraph *for* xviiij *read* xviij.

P. 149. *Funeral of Hawley, Clarenceux.* " Thomas Hawley esquyer late Claren' kyng of armes dyed at his howsse in the parish of St. Gyles withowt Crepyllgate in London on sonday the 22. of August 1557, and was beryed in the churche there the 25. of August." (MS. Harl. 897, f. 17.) His funeral is recorded in Coll. Arm. I. 15, f. 254.

P. 149. *Death of the duchess of Norfolk.* She had not recovered from the birth of her first and only child. "This Mary duches of Norfolk, late wyff to the right highe and myghty prynce Thomas duke of Norffolk, erl of Surrey and Waren, lord Mowbray, Segrave and Brusse, and erl marshall of England, departed on Wensday the 25. of August at th'erl of Arundell her father's howsse, called Arundell place in St. Clementes parishe called the Danes withowt temple barre in London, 1557, in the 4. and 5. of kyng Phelyp and queen Mary, and was beryed the fyrst of Septembre next foloing in the parish churche of St. Clementes the Danes." (MS. Harl. 897, f. 79.) A long narrative of her funeral is in the College of Arms, I. 14, 95—99, and I. 15, 256—261.

P. 150. *Funeral of sir Harry Hussey.* "Sir Henry Hussy knight dyed at his howsse of Slynfold, co. Sussex, on saterday the xxviij of August, and was buryed in the parish church there on thursday next after, 1557. His wyef dyed in October next foloing, and buryed by her husband. His wyf was Brydget daughter of Spryng of Lanam in Suffolk: married first to William Erneley of Kacham in Sussex, by whom she had Richard, John, and Katharine; and secondly to sir Henry Hussey, by whom she had no issue." (MS. Harl. 897, f. 27b.) His month's mind is recorded in Coll. Arm. I. 15, f. 263.

Ibid. *Death of lord Harry Dudley.* Fourth son of John duke of Northumberland. He was condemned at the time of the ruin of his family, (see p. 48,) but pardoned by the queen. He married Margaret only daughter of lord chancellor Audley; and, leaving no issue, his widow became the second wife of Thomas fourth duke of Norfolk, and from this match descend the earls of Suffolk and Carlisle. The duke's former lady had expired just before the death of lord Henry Dudley, and their surviving partners intermarried before the end of the year. The duchess Margaret died at Norwich Jan. 9, 1563-4. (See lord Braybrooke's History of Audley End, 1836, 4to. pp. 27, 296.)

P. 151. *Death of sir John Cheke.* He was buried in London in St. Alban's, Wood-street; and his epitaph in Latin verse will be found in Stowe. His biography is well known from the Life by Strype; his "Gospel according to St. Matthew and Part of St. Mark, translated from the Original Greek, with Notes," was first published in 1843, with an Introduction by James Goodwin, B.D.

Ibid. *Monsieur Regamus.* Can this name mean Simon Renard, or Reynard? who had been in England shortly before (see p. 337).

P. 152. *Master Waters, serjeant at arms.* The name of "Edward Waters esquire, serjeant at armes, 1558," is among the burials at St. Dunstan's in the East recorded by Stowe.

P. 153. *Funeral of John Sackville esquire.* Of Chiddingleigh, Sussex, M.P. for Greenwich ; he married Margaret Boleyne, a great-aunt of queen Elizabeth, and was grandfather of the first earl of Dorset. He was buried at Withyham in the same county. See his will printed by Collins, Peerage 1779, vol. ii. p. 155.

P. 154. *Funeral of mistress Mildmay.* Agnes, daughter of —— Read and wife of Thomas Mildmay esquire, auditor of the court of augmentations, who shared so largely in the spoil of the monasteries that he greatly enriched his family, and (contrary to the view taken by Spelman " on Sacrilege," &c.) his descendants flourished so much, that in the reign of James I. there were nine families of Mildmay possessed of large estates in Essex. (See Morant, ii. 4). Sir Walter Mildmay of Apthorpe in Northamptonshire, chancellor of the exchequer to queen Elizabeth, founder of Emanuel college Cambridge, and ancestor of the earls of Westmoreland, was the auditor's fourth and youngest son. His eldest son, having married the heiress of the Ratcliffes earls of Sussex, brought the dignity of baron FitzWalter to his descendants, of whom the last in the male line was created earl Fitz-Walter in 1730, and died s. p. in 1756.

P. 155. *Funeral of the countess of Arundel.* A full account of this funeral is preserved in the College of Arms, I. 15, ff. 266 et seq. The lady was previously countess of Sussex, and a letter written under that signature in 1537 has been published in Miss Wood's Letters of Royal and Illustrious Ladies, vol. ii. p. 306. " This Mary, doter of sir John Arundell of the West [and widow of Robert earl of Sussex, who died in 1542,] departed this lyff on Wensday the 20. of October 1557, in the 4. and 5. yeres of king Phelyp and quene Mary in the said erl of Arundelles place in St. Clementes parishe called the Danes withowt temple barre in London, and was beryed the xxviij. of October next folowinge." (MS. Harl. 897, f. 79.) The same authority supplies the following record of the earl of Arundel's former wife: " The lady Kateren Maltravers, doter of the lord marquis Dorset, departed owt of this world the fyrst day of May in the xxiiij[th]. yere of H. 8. (1532,) and lyeth beryed at St. Bartylmewes the lyttell within sir Gyles Capell('s) chapell." (p. 13[b].)

P. 156. *Funeral of sir William Cavendish.* Treasurer of the chamber to king Henry VIII. king Edward VI. and queen Mary, and a member of the privy council. He had three wives, and the last was the memorable " Bess of Hardwick," afterwards countess of Shrewsbury; who gave birth by him to two sons, William afterwards the first earl of Devonshire, Charles father of the first duke of Newcastle, and three daughters, Frances wife of sir Henry Pierrepoint and ancestor of the dukes of Kingston, Elizabeth countess of Lennox and mother of the lady Arabella Stuart, and Mary countess of Shrewsbury. The life of Elizabeth countess of Shrewsbury has exercised the pen of several biographers ; but see particularly Miss Costello's Memoirs of Eminent English-women, 1844, vol. i.

P. 156. *Funeral of serjeant Walpole.* John Walpole, made a serjeant at law in 1554. Nothing but his coat and peneron remained in St. Dunstan's church, temp. Nich. Charles: (Collectanea Topogr. et Geneal. 1837, vol. iv. p. 102). Of this serjeant Walpole a full account will be found in Collins's Peerage, 1779, vol. v. p. 88.

Ibid. *Funeral of sir Nicholas Hare.* Having been a master of requests to Henry VIII. and Edward VI. he was constituted master of the rolls by patent 18 Sept. 1553. His wife Catharine survived him not quite a month. See their epitaph printed in Dugdale's Origines Juridiciales, fol. 1671, p. 178.

P. 157. *Funeral of sir John Hodylstone.* "Sir John Hodylston vyschamberlen to the kynge and one of the prevy counsell dyed at Sawson in Cambrydgeshire the 4. of November 1557, and was buryed the xjth of the same mounth in the parishe churche there. He maryed Brydget doter to sir Robert and syster to sir John Cotton, and had issue Edmond son and heyr, William, and Ales." (MS. Harl. 897, f. 25^b.) There is a full narrative of his funeral in the College of Arms, I. 15, f. 275.

Ibid. *Funeral of master .. anell.* Was this Pranell the rich vintner, father of the first husband of the celebrated duchess of Richmond?

P. 158. *Funeral of sir [John] Arundell.* "Sir John Arundell knight dyed at his manner of Southorne in the county of Oxford the 7th of November in A°. 1557, and was buryed the xiiijth of the same mounth in the parish churche there." (MS. Harl. 897, f.15^b.) He was the elder son of sir Thomas Arundell, who died in 1545, by lady Alianor Grey, daughter of Thomas marquess of Dorset; and brother to sir Thomas, who was beheaded in 1551-2 (see pp. 15, 323.) Sir John was also for some time confined in the Tower; as mentioned in the minutes of the privy council April 7, 1550, and 13 April 1551 (see MS. Harl. 352, ff. 76, 149^b.) By lady Anne Stanley, daughter of Edward earl of Derby, he was ancestor of the Arundells of Lanherne in Cornwall and Chideock in Dorsetshire.

Ibid. *Funeral of Tyrell captain of the galley.* "1557, Nov. 15, Mr. William Turrell sometime knight of Rhodes." Register of St. Martin's Ludgate; and his marriage at the same church, "1553, Nov. 9, sir William Tyrrell knt. and Mrs. Anne Freeman widow." Malcolm's Londinium, vol. iv. pp. 357, 358. He was brother to sir Henry Tyrell, of East Horndon, Essex: see Morant's History of that county, vol. i. p. 209.

Ibid. *Coronation of Norroy king of arms.* The instrument of the creation and coronation of Laurence Dalton to be Norroy king of arms, by letters patent dated 6 Sept. 1557, is printed in Rymer's Fœdera, vol. xv. p. 477; and that for William Harvey to be Clarenceux, dated the next day, in the following page.

Ibid. *Funeral of lord Bray.* "John lord Bray dyed in the late Black fryers in London on thursday the xixth of November 1557 and was beryed at Chelsey in the middest of the high chauncell with his father and grand-father the 23. of November." MS. Harl. 874, f. 79.—The full narrative of his funeral, which is recorded in the College of Arms, I. 15, f. 279, has been printed by Lysons in his Environs of London, and by Faulkner in his History of Chelsea.

P. 158. *Funeral of lady Clifford.* Widow of sir Thomas Clifford, knt. governor of Berwick, who had a gravestone in Westminster abbey, which was removed for the marble pavement. Dart, vol. ii. p. 23.

P. 160. *Funeral of lady Rowlett.* Dorothy, daughter of John Boles, of Wallington, co. Herts, and first wife of sir Ralph Rowlett, of whom see further in a subsequent note. There is a pedigree of Rowlett in Clutterbuck's Hertfordshire, vol. i. p. 217; but further information may be derived from that in the MS. Harl. 897, fol. 42.

P. 161. *Funeral of sir William West.* Strype, Mem. iii. 387, says "the same, I suppose, with him that went over lately in the expedition to St. Quintin's," but that was sir William West, the titular lord de la Warr (already noticed in p. 350). The present knight had served at an earlier date in the army of Henry VIII. He was of Amerdon hall in Essex, and Darley abbey, co. Derby, and the father of Lewis, whose untimely death has been noticed in p. 349. See the pedigree in Hunter's South Yorkshire, vol. ii. p. 173. "Sir William West knyght dyed at his howsse at Smythfeld in the suberbes of London the 8. day of December 1557, and buryed in St. Pulcres churche withowt Newgate of London the xiii^th of the same mounth. He had issue Edward, &c." (MS. Harl. 897, f. 19.)

P. 162. *Musters in London.* On the 6th Jan. the Privy Council sent " a letter to the maior of London that, albeite he was willed to send the v^c. men levied in London to Dover, forasmuche as it is sithence considered here that they may with beste speede be brought to the place of service by seas, he is willen to sende them with all speede by hoyes to Queenburgh, where order is given for the receavinge and placing of them in the shippes, to be transported with all speede possible." (MS. Harl. 643, p. 198.)

P. 163. *Funeral of lady Powis.* Anne widow of Edward lord Grey of Powis, whose death occurred in p. 7. She had remarried Randle Hanworth, esq.; and by the note of his will which Dugdale gives, Baronage, ii. 284, it appears that she desired to be buried either at St. Paul's or Westminster abbey. His interment was not at the parish church of St. Margaret's, Westminster, the register of which I have examined.

Ibid. *Funeral of sir Richard Freston.* He was interred at Mendham in Suffolk, where his monument remains. (See the Topographer, 1848, vol. ii. p. 239.) Dame Anne his wife, who died shortly before him (see p. 161), was a Coke.

Ibid. *Funeral of sir George Gyfford.* "Sir George Gyfford knight, son of Roger Gyfford esquyer [*who* maryed the doughter of Ansehalles, and had issue by her 13 sons and 7 doters, *and* dysseassed the xxiij^th of January 1522], dysseased on St. John's day in December 1557, and his mounthes mynde was kept the xx^th of January next foloinge. Sir George Gyfford maryed to his fyrst wyff the doter of Dyke of Sussex and wedoo of Goryng of Sussex; [*secondly ?*] one of the doters and heyres of John Bardfyld of Sheffeld in the county of Essex; [*thirdly ?*] doughter of Robert Trappes of London goldsmyth, late wyff to Shawe haberdasher of London, [*and had issue by the last*] Thomas, Prudence, and Lettyce." MS. Harl. 897, f. 23^b. where see trickings of the arms and alliances.

P. 164. *Funeral of sir Henry Capel.* Son and heir of sir Giles Capel, before noticed in p. 350. He had married a sister of the earl of Rutland, and had a numerous family; but, as they all died before him, he was succeeded by his brother Edward.

P. 165. *Funeral of Arthur Stourton esquire.* Ancestor of the Stourtons of Over Moigne, co. Dorset. See Collins's Peerage and Hutchins's Dorsetshire.

P. 166. *Funeral of alderman sir George Barnes.* Son of George Barnes, citizen and haberdasher of London; sheriff 1545-6, lord mayor 1552-3. He was buried at St. Bartholomew the Little, as was his widow (see p. 199). "He dwelled in Bartholomew lane, where sir William Capell once dwelled, and now [1605] Mr. Derham. His arms, Argent, on a chevron wavy azure, between three barnacles proper, three trefoils slipped of the first, were taken downe after his death by his sonne sir George Barnes, and these sett upp in stede thereof, Azure, three leopard's heads argent." The second sir George Barnes was also a haberdasher, and lord mayor in 1586-7. "He dwelled in Lombard strete, over-against the George, in the house which was sir William Chester's, and is buried in St. Edmund's church hard by." He bore the coat of leopard's heads quartered with, Argent, a chevron azure between three blackbirds.

P. 167. *Death of lady White.* Sir Thomas White, son of William White of Reading; sheriff 1546, lord mayor 1553. The founder of St. John's college, Oxford, and the principal benefactor of Merchant-taylors' school, as well as his native town and many other places. He died at Oxford Feb. 11, 1566, aged 72, and was buried in the chapel of his college. (See further particulars of him in Wilson's Merchant-taylors' School, p. 3.) The present paragraph relates to his first wife, whose parentage is not ascertained, but she was probably nearly related to lady Laxton the chief mourner at her funeral. Sir Thomas White's remarriage to lady Warren is noticed in p. 179, and the lady in a previous note (p. 330).

P. 168. *Funeral of lady Jenyns.* This daughter of sir John Gage, K.G. was the wife of sir John Jenyns, of Halnaker in Sussex, gentleman of the king's privy chamber, and in 1544 master of the ordnance at Boulogne, who died in 1547. See Gage's Hengrave, p. 235.

P. 168. *Loan from the city to the queen.* A loan was then called a " prest," which is probably the word our diarist could not remember. The amount of this prest was 20,000*l.* and it was to bear interest at 12 per cent. (Stowe.)

P. 169. *Earl of Sussex took his journey toward Ireland.* Where he had been for some time lord deputy.

Ibid. *Funeral of lady Rowlett.* Sir Ralph buried two wives within seven months (see before, p. 362). The second was one of the daughters of sir Anthony Cooke, and the circumstances of the marriage are thus mentioned in the Diary of sir Thomas Hoby: " Monday June 27, 1558, a mariage was made and solemnised between me and Elizabeth Cooke, daughter of sir Anthony Cooke knt. The same day was also her sister Margaret the queen's maid maried to sir Rauf Rowlet knt. who (*i. e.* the lady) shortly after departed out of this lief." (Communicated by the Right Hon. Lord Braybrooke.) " Sir Raff Rowlett had maryed ij. wyves, and dyed withowt issue of ether at his howsse of St. Albons the xixth of Apryll 1571, and was beryed in the parish church of St. Albons by his father the xxixth of May next foloinge." His father, also sir Ralph, had been one of the masters of the mint to Henry VIII.

P. 170. *Master Hawes chosen sheriff.* Alderman John Hawes; sheriff 1558-9, not lord mayor. Arms, Azure, on a chevron between three demi-lyons rampant or, three cinquefoils gules. (List by William Smith, Rouge-dragon.)

Ibid. *Master Champion,* the other sheriff, was a draper, afterwards sir Richard, " maior An°. 1566. He died without issue 1568. Buried at St. Dunstan's in the est, with these armes in the margent, Argent, on a fess gules between three trefoils slipped sable a spread eagle or, all within a bordure engrailed azure, charged with eight bezants: which were after taken downe, and these sett upp in the same place: Quarterly, 1 and 4 Argent, three trefoils slipped sable; 2 and 3 Argent, three human legs couped gules; on an inescucheon argent, a griffin segreant sable." (List by Wm. Smith, Rouge-dragon.) Sir Richard Champion's monument has been already noticed in p. 347.

Ibid. *Funeral of master Dodmer.* Son of sir Ralph Dodmer, lord mayor in 1530, who had been buried at St. Stephen's, Walbrook.

Ibid. *Funeral of doctor Huwys.* The letters patent appointing Thomas Huis or Huys, M.D. ordinary physician to the queen, with diets and allowances of wine, wax and bowge le courte, and an annual fee of 100*l.* were dated 2 Oct. 1553, and are printed in Rymer's Fœdera, vol. xv. p. 341.

Ibid. *Death of alderman Machell.* John Machell, sheriff in 1556. Arms, Per pale argent and sable, three grey-hounds courant counterchanged, collared gules. (Wm.

Smith, Rouge-dragon.) "He married Jone daughter of Harry Lodyngton, and she was remarried to sir Thomas Chamberlen knight, and she died 28. April 1565." (MS. Harl. 897, f. 24.)

P. 170. *The George in Lombard street.* "Next is a common osterie for travellers, called the George, of such a signe." Stowe: who adds that it had been the town mansion of the earls Ferrers, in which the brother of one of them was murdered, so early as 1175.

P. 171. *Funeral of master Morton.* Thomas Moreton, bachelor of law, was collated to the sinecure rectory of Fulham Sept. 23, 1554, and to the prebend of Bromesbury in the cathedral church of Saint Paul's Aug. 9, 1555. (Newcourt's Repertorium Londinense, vol. i. p. 118.) It appears, then, that those called the "grey amices" of St. Paul's were the prebendaries.

Ibid. *Funeral of doctor Peryn.* William Peryn prior of the Black Friars, whose name has before occurred as a preacher in pp. 100, 119, 131. A memoir of this person will be found in Wood's Athenæ Oxonienses (by Bliss), vol. i. p. 248. Our diary corrects that biographer's supposition that he survived queen Mary, and retired abroad.

P. 172. *Funeral of doctor William Cooke, dean of the Arches.* He died August 25, 1558, and his widow erected "a comely small monument" to him in St. Gregory's by St. Paul's; the Latin verses on which will be found in Stowe's Survay.

Ibid. *The brethren of Jhesus,* who attended the same funeral "in satin hoods and Ih♄ upon them," were the members of a guild which maintained a chapel in the crypt of St. Paul's, which is mentioned in p. 179 as "Jhesus chapell," and again in p. 221 as "Jhesus chapell under Powlles." It was afterwards called St. Faith's, and there is still a parish which retains vaults for interment in the same situation. The dean of St. Paul's was rector of the guild; and in Knight's Life of Colet, p. 84, will be found some account of its cartulary, beginning thus, "This booke bought and ordeigned by maister John Colett doctour of divinitie, dean of the cathedral churche of Paules, and rectour of the fraternitie and guild of Jhesus in the croudes of the said churche, William Cromwell and John Monk wardens of the same, recordeth," &c. The bells in the clochier or bell-tower which stood in St. Paul's churchyard were called Jhesus bells, and Stowe relates that sir Miles Partridge won them of Henry VIII. on a cast of dice against 100*l*.

Ibid. *Funeral of lord Windsor.* "William lord Wyndsor maryed to his first wyff doter and heyr of Samborne, and after the doter of Cowdrey of Hampshire: he dyed at his howsse of Brad[en]ham in Bokynghamshire on sonday the 14. of August in the 5. and 6. yeres of Phelyp and Mary, 1558, and was beryed on monday the 22. of the same mounth." (MS. Harl. 897, f. 80.) His son Edward lord Windsor, who died at Spa in Germany in 1573, desired in his will "his heart to be inclosed in lead and sent into England, to be buried in the chapel of Bradenham under the tombe of his lord and father, in token of a true Englishman," which was done accordingly (see Lipscomb's Buckinghamshire, vol. iii. p. 558) ; but there is now no other monument of the Windsor family in that church.

P. 172. *Funeral of sir William Stamford.* " Sir William Staunford knight, one of the kinges and the quenes ma^{ties} justyces of the common banke, dysseassed the xxviij^{th}. August An° D'ni 1558, about iiij. of the cloke in the afternone the same day in the 49 yere of his age, and iiij. dayes, and was buryed at Hadley j° die Septemb' in A° D'ni 1558. *He maried* Ales doughter of Joh'n Palmer esquyer, *and had issue* Robert Stamford son and heyr, 2. Thomas, 3. William, 4. Henry, 5. Raff, 6. Joh'n ; Frances wyff to Thomas Repington esquyer, Doraty, Kateren, Margaret." (MS. Harl. 897, f. 18.) His funeral insignia were remaining in Hadley church when visited by Nich. Charles, and will be found drawn in the Lansd. MS. 874, f. 60, with other memorials of his family. His personal biography will be found in Wood's Athenæ Oxonienses, (by Bliss,) vol. i. p. 262. He was the editor of the first edition of Ranulph de Glanville's treatise " De Legibus et Consuetudinibus Angliæ, printed by Tottel in 1554. (See Wright's Biographia Literaria, vol. ii. p. 279.)

Ibid. *Funeral of judge Morgan.* Francis Morgan, judge of the queen's bench, died on the 29th Aug. 1558. His burial was at Heyford, co. Northampton ; where a monument with effigies still remains. See it described, and the epitaph, in Baker's Northamptonshire, i. 188 ; Bridges's Northamptonshire, i. 523 : see also his pedigree in Baker, i. 184.

P. 173. *Funeral of master Dalbeney.* Arthur Dawbney, warden of the merchanttaylors 1566-7 and 1571-2, master 1574-5.

Ibid. *Funeral of sir Thomas Cave.* This funeral was not at Stamford, but at Stanford, co. Northampton, where there are still recumbent effigies of sir Thomas Cave and his wife ; see the epitaph in Bridges's Northamptonshire, vol. i. p. 582 ; and in Nichols's Leicestershire, vol. iv. pl. liii. fig. 1. is an engraving of the monument (Mr. Nichols having devoted two plates to the whole series of the Cave monuments, out of respect to the Rev. Sir Charles Cave, Bart. to whom he was indebted for an important portion of the materials of his work).

Ibid. *Funeral of sir Andrew Judd.* A name still well known as the founder of Tunbridge school. He also founded the Skinners' almshouses near Saint Helen's, Bishopsgate: see Herbert's City Companies, ii. 350. He had been sheriff in 1544, and lord mayor in 1551. His monument still remains in St. Helen's, Bishopsgate, and has kneeling effigies of himself, the first of his three wives, four sons, and one daughter : it is engraved in Wilkinson's Londina Illustrata, 1825, where also is a full memoir of him. Maitland, p. 1107, has printed the poetical epitaph *without his name*: it bears out our diarist's designation of him as a " merchant of Muscovy,"—

To Russia and Muscovea,
To Spayne, Gynny, withoute fable
Travaild he by land and sea
Both mayor of London and staple, &c.

" His only daughter Alice was maried to Tho. Smith customer, mother to sir John, sir Thomas, and sir Richard, now living." (1605). Arms, quarterly, 1 and 4, Gules, a fess reguléе between three boar's heads couped argent; 2 and 3, Azure, three lyons rampant argent. (List by Wm. Smith, Rouge-dragon.)

P. 174. *Funeral of sir Thomas Essex.* "In the north transept of Lambourn church is the monument of sir Thomas Essex, who died in 1558, with effigies of himself and Margaret his lady in alabaster." Lysons's Berkshire, p. 310.

Ibid. *Funeral of lady Southwell.* I have not ascertained who this was; but it may be as well to remark that Strype *assumed* she was the "wife to a privy councillor of that name;" and sir Henry Ellis, in his History of Shoreditch, p. 357, has quoted Strype apparently without having met with the lady's name in any other authority.

P. 175. *Funeral of lady Pecsall.* Eleanor fourth daughter of William first marquess of Winchester, K.G., and the first wife of sir Richard Pecsall: see pedigree in MS. Harl. 897, f. 54. There is a magnificent monument in Westminster abbey with kneeling effigies of sir Richard and both his wives, and of his four daughters by the first. See it engraved in Dart's History of that church, vol. i. p. 17.

Ibid. *Saint Martin's with the well and two bokettes.* This was the name by which the church of St. Martin Outwich was commonly known in the time of our diarist; and he mentions it again in pp. 211, 215, 302. Stowe says, after noticing *Three Needle* street (now Threadneedle street), "On the south side of which street, beginning at the east, by the Well with two buckets, now turned to a pumpe, is the parish church of S. Martin, called Oteswich, of Martin de Oteswich, Nicholas de Oteswich, William Oteswich, and John Oteswich, founders thereof," &c. The antiquities of this church have been excellently illustrated by engravings in a 4to volume of plates, published by Mr. Robert Wilkinson in 1797.

P. 176. *Funeral of Ralph Preston.* His name occurs as a member of the Skinners' company in a list made in 1537, and so do the same names as those of his mourners, namely, Thomas Percy, and three Banks', Rogier, Raynbone, and John.

Ibid. *Funeral of George lord Cobham.* The full ceremonial of this is preserved in the College of Arms, I. 15, f. 387. The monument of lord Cobham, with the effigies of himself and wife, remains in the church of Cobham near Gravesend, and was repaired in the year 1840 at the expense of Francis C. Brooke, esq. of Ufford Place, Suffolk, under the superintendence of the present writer and of Charles Spence, esq. of the Admiralty. (See

Gent. Mag. N. S. vol. xv. p. 306.) A portrait of lord Cobham by Holbein is engraved in the beautiful work by Chamberlain : it represents him in singular dishabille, with a bald head, surmounted by a flat cap.

P. 176. *Funeral of [Michael] Wentworth esquire.* Michael Wentworth esq. was the second son of Thomas Wentworth esq. of Wentworth Woodhouse, co. York. He is described in 1 Mar. 1554, as of Ottes in Essex esquire, and one of the masters of the queen's household. (Hunter's South Yorkshire, vol. ii. p. 388.) He afterwards became cofferer. He died October 13, 1558, and his name is entered in the parish register of St. Margaret's Westminster, as " Mr. Mychaell Wentworth." His son Thomas was seated at Mendham priory, Suffolk ; but his grandson Michael bought Wolley in Yorkshire, where the family has since continued (the representation passing in the last generation to a younger son of sir George Armytage, bart. who assumed the name). See Mr. Hunter's pedigree, *ubi supra.*

P. 177. *Funeral of doctor Owen.* George Owen, M.D. assisted at the birth of king Edward VI. and was afterwards his chief physician. An account of him will be found in Wood's Athenæ Oxonienses, (by Bliss,) vol. i. fol. 274.

P. 178. *A proclamation of queen Elizabeth,* dated 18 November, declaring the date of her accession to have been " from the beginning of the xvij[th]," will be found in The Egerton Papers, p. 28.

Ibid. *Death of cardinal Pole.* It seems to have been supposed by some persons at the time, that Pole died on the same day as queen Mary ; and it is so asserted by Hume and other writers. According to our diarist (who even mentions the hours) the cardinal survived the queen for two days.

P. 179. *The queen's coming to London.* See a note by Mr. Bruce on this subject in Hayward's Annals of Elizabeth, p. 9.

Ibid. *Funeral of master Skynner.* " Anthony Skynner esquyer, one of the 6 clarkes of the Chauncery, departed this world on monday the 21. of November, and beryed on fryday after, the 25. of the same mounth, in A. D'ni 1555. His wyff was the doter of Byllyng. He was buryed in Saint Brydes churche." (MS. Harl. 897, f. 22[b].)

Ibid. *Funeral of lady Cobham.* Anne eldest daughter of Edmund lord Bray, and sister and coheir of John lord Bray. The ceremonial of her funeral is in the College of Arms, I. 15, f. 293. Her effigy is on the monument already mentioned in p. 367.

P. 181. *Funeral of lady Cholmley.* The wife of sir Roger Cholmley, made serjeant at law 1532, king's serjeant 1545, chief baron of the exchequer 1546, chief justice of the king's bench 1552, and imprisoned for a time after queen Mary's accession (see before, pp. 38, 43).

Malcolm quotes from the register of St. Martin's Ludgate the burial of lady Cholmley as having taken place Dec. 8, 1558, and that of sir Roger Cholmley, July 2, 1565. Londinium Rediv. iv. 358. His daughter "my lady Beckwyth" was married at the same church to Christian Ken, esq. April 19, 1559. (Ibid. p. 357.) Sir Roger Cholmley and Christian his wife had a grant to purchase of the crown the manors of East and West Ham and Pleshey in Essex, March 24, 1552-3. (Strype.)

P. 181. *Funeral of sir Anthony Hungerford.* This was sir Anthony Hungerford, of Down Amney, in Gloucestershire, sheriff of that county 1552, and knight of the shire 1553. His body was carried to Great Bedwyn, Wilts, where " Anthony Hungerford knighte was buyried the xix^th day of November 1558." Collect. Topogr. et Geneal.v. 28.

Ibid. *Funeral of doctor Dunne.* Gabriel Dunne, M.A. was collated to the prebend of Mapesbury in the church of St. Paul's March 16, 1540, and admitted to the sinecure rectory of Stepney Oct. 25, 1544. He held both until his death. (Newcourt's Repertorium Londinense, vol. i. p. 175.) He had previously been a monk of Stratford abbey, near London, and the last abbat of Buckfastleigh in Devonshire: and was " the basest betrayer " of the reformer Tyndale. See Anderson's Annals of the English Bible, vol. i. pp. 534—537, and the Index.

Ibid. *Funeral of sir George Harper.* " Sir George Harper knight dysceased the 7. of December at his howsse within the late Blacke Fryers in London in the fyrst yere of quene Elizabeth 1558, and was buryed in the parishe churche of St. Marten's in Ludgate the xij^th of December. He had maryed Awdre doughter of sir John Gaynaford of Surrey, wyff before to George Tayler of Lyngfield in Surrey, and after to Caryngton of Sussex." (MS. Harl. 897, p. 26.) His widow was buried at the same church Jan. 27, 1559. Malcolm's Londinium Redivivum, iv. 358.

P. 182. *Funeral of queen Mary.* The ceremonial is in the College of Arms, I. 14, ff. 19—30, and again in ff. 202—214 ; and the painters' charges at f. 198.

P. 184. *Funeral of lady Rich.* Elizabeth, sister of Thomas Jenks of London, was the wife of the successful lawyer (himself of a London family) who founded the family of Rich, afterwards earls of Warwick and Holland. Richard first lord Rich survived until 1568, and was buried at Felstead, Essex. See Dugdale's Baronage, ii. 388.

Ibid. *Funeral of the bishop of Chichester.* John Christopherson, previously dean of Norwich, consecrated 21 Nov. 1557, deprived 1558.

Ibid. *Obsequies of the emperor.* The emperor's ambassador was present as chief mourner. The ceremonial is in the College of Arms, I. 14, f. 3, and I. 15, f. 284.

Ibid. *Funeral of sir Thomas Cheney, K.G.* Sir Thomas Cheney had been henchman to king Henry VII. He was honoured with the garter, made treasurer of the household to three successive sovereigns, and died warden of the cinque ports, Dec. 8, 1558. His liberality was great, his hospitality unbounded. He kept thirty horses in his stables, and two hundred and five servants in livery, for all of whom he more or less provided at his death. " Well," says Holinshed, " was that nobleman's son that happened to be preferred into his service." See his eulogy in Holinshed, vol. ii. p. 1171, and see Wiffen's Memoirs of the House of Russell, i. 396. " Sir Thomas Cheney knight, lord warden of the v. portes, knight of the garter and tresorer of the quenes howshold, dysceased at the Tower of London on thursday the xvth of December in A°. j°. Elizabeth, 1558, and after conveyed to his howsse called Sherland in the isle of Shepey, and there buryed on tewsday the 3. of January next foloinge." (MS. Harl. 897, f 17^b.) His epitaph is in Weever's Funerall Monuments, p. 284, and in Dugdale's Baronage, ii. 290. His second wife and widow Anne, daughter and heir of [sir John] Broughton, died at Toddington, co. Bedf. May 18, 1562, and was buried in the parish church there on the 27th. (Ibid.)

P. 185. *Funeral of sir John Baker.* Chancellor of the exchequer from the . . Hen. VIII. throughout the reigns of Edward and Mary.. He is said to have been the only privy councillor who refused to sign the letters patent popularly called the will of Edward VI. He was buried at Cranbrook in Kent, in which parish his mansion of Sizinghurst was situated. See Hasted's History of that county, vol. iii. p. 49.

Ibid. *Funeral of Edmund —Hapsam* is probably the name deficient, as he was one of the painters employed for queen Mary's funeral. (MS. I. 14, in Coll. Arm. f. 198.)

P. 186. *The Knights of the Bath* made at the Coronation of queen Elizabeth were in number eleven, viz. :—

John lord Darcy of the North,	Sir Robert Rich,	Sir John Berkeley,
John lord Sheffield,	Sir Roger North,	Sir Edward Unton,
John lord Darcy of Chiche,	Sir John Zouch,	Sir Henry Weston,
	Sir Nicholas Pointz,	Sir George Speke.

See Anstis's History of the Order of the Bath, App. lxx.; and Nicolas, Appx. p. xiv.

P. 187. *Funeral of Thomas Greenhill, waxchandler.* Our diarist, if he was not related to Greenhill, had much to do with him in the course of business, the wax-chandlers being greatly employed to provide lights for funerals. The Index will be found to refer to various particulars relating to him and his family.

Ibid. *Funeral of sir Oliver Laurence.* " Sir Olyver Larance knight dyed the fyrst of January 1559, and was buryed at Fernam, and after the seremony done, his hachementes were removed to the church of St. Mychell in Steple within th'yle of Purbek in the county of Dorset. Sir Olyver Larance knight maryed and had issue Edward his son and heir, who maryd doter of Trenchard." (MS. Harl. 897, f. 12ᵇ.) His wife was Anne Wriothesley, sister to the earl of Southampton. (Hutchins's Dorset, i. 325.)

P. 188. *Funeral of the marchioness of Winchester.* "Lady Elsabeth late wyff to the right noble and puissant prynce William marques of Wynchester erl of Wylshire knight of the garter and lord treasorer of England, dyed on Crystmas day the xxv. of December 1558, and was beryed at Basyng on Sonday the 5. of February next foloinge." (MS. Harl. 897, f. 80.) She was the daughter of sir William Capel.

Ibid. *Funeral of sir Thomas Pope.* This was the founder of Trinity college, Oxford. The original place of his interment is a matter of question (see the Biogr. Brit. 1760, p. 3404), which our diary does not determine. In his will he directed his executors to bury him in the church of that parish in which he should chance to die. This would be Clerkenwell. Stowe has preserved an inscription formerly in St. Stephen's, Walbrook: "Hic jacet Thomas Pope primus Thesaurarius Augmentationum, et Dᵃˢ Margaretta uxor ejus, quæ quidem Margaretta obiit 16 Jan. 1538." Margaret, who was his second wife, was no doubt interred there; but the remains of both, it seems, were afterwards removed to the college chapel, according to the inscription round the verge of the tomb—"corpora Thome Pope . . . et duarum Elizabethe et Margarete uxorum ejus." Elizabeth had been the name of his *first* as well as his third wife, but from the former he was divorced. It is to be presumed, therefore, the *third* was intended by the name Elizabeth; and she, after remarrying sir Hugh Poulet, of Hinton St. George, was brought to rest in the chapel in 1593. There is however only *one* female effigy lying by the founder's side: see an engraving in Skelton's Pietas Oxoniensis, 4to. 1830.

Ibid. *Fishmonger set in the pillory.* This man's punishment lasted three days, and is more fully described in Holinshed, 1st edit. p. 1778. It was a stroke of domestic policy, in order to acquire popularity for the queen, by the punishment of one of the hated royal purveyors. The victim was "one of maister Hunning's servants, that was also one of the takers of freshe fishe for the provision of the queenes house."

Ibid. *Funeral of the countess of Oxford.* Anne, daughter of Thomas Howard, second duke of Norfolk, K.G. and widow of John 14th earl of Oxford, who had died in 1526.

P. 190. *Funeral of lady Roche.* Sir William Roche was lord mayor in 1541, and buried in St. Peter's le Poor in Broad street (Smith's List), where the body of his wife was laid by his side.

P. 191. *Funeral of the old countess of Bedford.* Anne, sole daughter and heiress of sir Guy Sapcote, of Thornhaugh, co. Bedford, married first to sir John Broughton, of Toddington, co. Bedford; secondly, about 1518, to sir Richard Jerningham, who was one of the governors of Tournay, and afterwards employed in an embassy to Spain, who died in 1524; and, thirdly, in the spring of 1526, to sir John Russell, afterwards earl of Bedford (see note, p. 343). By her will, dated 19 Aug. 1557, she committed her burial to the discretion of the marques of Winchester lord treasurer, the abbat of Westminster, and the lord St. John. See further in Wiffen's Memoirs of the House of Russell, i. 391.

P. 191. *Funeral of sir John St. Loe.* This was the father of sir William St. Loe, captain of the guard to queen Elizabeth: see the memoirs of the latter, by the Rev. Joseph Hunter, F.S.A. in the Retrospective Review, Second Series, ii. 315. Stowe has enumerated in his list of persons buried at Great St. Helen's " Sir William Sanctlo, and sir William Sanctlo, father and sonne : " the former should (apparently) be sir John, and sir William would be buried there within a few years after.

P. 192. *Funerals of sir Anthony St. Leger, K.G. and lady St. Leger.* " Sir Anthony S⁺leger knight of the garter dyed at his howsse of Vuckham in Kent on thursday the 16. of Marche in A° j° Elizabeth, 1558, and buryed on wensday the 5. of Apryll next foloing in the parish church of Alhalows hard by the said howsse." (MS. Harl. 897, f. 17.)

" Lady Agnes S⁺leger late wyff to sir Antony S⁺leger knight of the garter, doter of Wadham of Hampshire, dyed at her howsse Vucham in Kent the 24. of Marche in A° j° Elizabeth, 1558, and was beryed ther in the parish churche on tewsday the 4. of Aprell next foloinge." (Ibid. f. 17ᵇ.) It is remarkable that the wife died eight days after the husband, but was buried one day before him. She was daughter of Hugh Warham of Croydon, and niece to archbishop Warham. Their seat and place of burial in Kent is properly written Ulcombe: see Hasted, ii. 423.

Ibid. *Funeral of sir Thomas Tresham.* The heralds' account of this is preserved in the College of Arms, I. 9, f. 158. His monument at Rushton Allhallows, Northamptonshire, is described in Bridges's History of that county, vol. ii. p. 72. It bears his effigy " in a gown, with his hands erected." See some anecdotes of sir Thomas Tresham and his thumb ring in Fuller's Church History.

Ibid. *At Powlles cross master Samson.* This it appears was the Rehearsal of the spital sermons just before mentioned. There had been no sermon at Paul's cross for many weeks, in consequence of the prohibition of unlicensed preaching. " Hereuppon no sermon was preached at Paules crosse untill the Rehearsall sermon was made upon the sunday after Easter : at which tyme, when the preacher was ready to mount into the pulpit, the keye could not be found : and when, by commandement of the lord mayor it was opened by a smyth, the place was very filthy and uncleane." Hayward's Annals of Elizabeth, p. 5.

Ibid. *Disputing between the Bishops and the new Preachers.* On this Conference see Hayward's Annals of Elizabeth, p. 19, and the references there given by Mr. Bruce ; also Zurich Letters, 1st series, letters iv. and v.

P. 193. *Funeral of lady Cary* (misnamed by the diarist *Gray*). Joyce, sister of sir Anthony Denny, knt. privy councillor to Henry VIII. was born 24 July, 21 Hen. VII. married first to William Walsingham, of Scadbury in Chiselhurst, Kent, by whom she had three sons, of whom the illustrious secretary was third and youngest; and secondly to sir John Cary of Plashey, co. . . . . made a knight of the carpet in 1 Edw. VI. by whom she was mother of sir Edward Cary, father of the first viscount Falkland and sir Adolphus Cary (see Clutterbuck's Hertfordshire, vol. i. p. 129, vol. ii. p. 107).

P. 193. *Peace with France.* See Hayward's Elizabeth, p. 36; Hayward dates the proclamation the 7th instead of the 8th April. The treaty, which was signed by Elizabeth at Westminster on the 20th Jan. and by Henry at Château-Cambray on the 2d April, is printed by Rymer, Fœdera, vol. xv. pp. 505—516.

P. 195. *The serjeants' feast.* This took place at the Inner Temple on the 19th of April. In the second line read, "and ix. [serjeants made]." Dugdale, indeed, gives the names of ten as having been called to the degree by writ tested by the queen on the 12th Dec. namely, Thomas Carus, Reginald Corbet, John Welsh, John Southcote, William Simmonds, George Wall, Richard Harper, Ranulph Cholmley, Nicholas Powtrell, and John Birch; and to these was added Richard Weston by writ dated 24 Jan. making in all eleven. Dugdale's Chronica Series.

P. 197. *Arrival of French ambassadors.* These were, Charles cardinal of Lorraine, Anne duc de Montmorenci, Jacques Marquis de Fronsac, Jehan de Morvillier bishop of Orleans, and the chevalier Claude de l'Aubespiere (see Rymer, xv. 503.)

P. 199. *Marriage of master Matthew Draper,* for so it should be read, not "master Mathew, draper." After this marriage with the Latin mass, it seems that the parties were remarried a fortnight after at Camberwell: as their wedding is recorded in the register of that parish under the 13th of June. See further of them and the family of Draper in Collectanea Topogr. et Geneal. iii. 199.

P. 201. *May Game.* The Ironmongers' company sent men in armour to "the May-game that went before the queenes magestie to Greenewich." Malcolm, ii. 48.

Ibid. *Funeral of Docwra.* This person was not "a doctor of the law," as our diarist terms him; but a proctor only, as shown by his epitaph in St. Faith's: "Here under this stone resteth, in the mercy of God, the body of M. Thomas Docwray, notary, late one of the proctors of the Arches, citizen and stationer of London, and Anne his wife. The which Thomas deceased the 23. day of June, An. Dom. 1559, &c." (Stowe.)

Ibid. *Bishops deprived.* Mr. Bruce has given a list of the deprived bishops, founded upon documents in Rymer's Fœdera, in Hayward's Annals of Q. Eliz. p. 27.

P. 202. *Muster before the queen in Greenwich park.* Stowe has described this muster at some length. The Grocers' company were, by a precept from the lord mayor, required to contribute to it "190 personnes, apte and picked men; whereof 60 to be with calyvers, flaskes, touche-boxes, morions, swordes, and daggers; 95 to be in corselettes, with halbertes, swordes, and daggers, for a shewe at Greenwich." Heath's Hist. of the Grocers' Company, p. 65.

P. 203. *Funeral of master Sadler*. No such " alderman " occurs in the list of Wm. Smith, Rouge-dragon.

P. 205. *Sir Thomas Chamber*. Thomas Chamber clerk was presented to the rectory of Trinity the Less near Queen Hithe July 10, 1555. His cession is not recorded. New-court identifies him with the incumbent of Horndon on the Hill in Essex 1544, Bradwell near Coggeshall 1551 to 1554, St. Mary Bothaw in London 1562 to 1563, Northampsted, Herts, 1563 to 1565 (where he was deprived), and Langford in Essex 1565 to 1585, where he died. If all or most of these belong to one person, and the dates are in a succession, which makes it possible, his frequent changes, and the deprivation in 1565, are in accordance with the scandalous character represented in our Diary : of which a former specimen was given in p. 132.

P. 206. *Master Sebastian, Phelips, and Haywood*. " Sebastian scolemaister of Powles " gave queen Mary on new-year's day 1557 " a book of ditties, written." (Nichols's Progresses, &c. of Q. Elizabeth, 1823, vol. i. p. xxxv.) Mr. Collier supposes his surname to have been Westcott (Annals of the Stage, i. 155).—Robert Phelipps was one of the thirty-two gentlemen of the chapel to king Edward VI. (Hawkins's History of Music, vol. iii. p. 481.—Of John Heywood as an author of interludes and master of a company of " children " players various notices will be found in Mr. Collier's work.

Ibid. *Nonsuch*. A memoir by the present writer on the royal palace of Nonesuch will be found in the Gentleman's Magazine for August 1837, New Series, vol. VIII. pp. 135—144. The earl of Arundel, as lord steward of the household, had obtained an interest in it, which seems almost to have amounted to an alienation, but it reverted to the Crown in 1591. His first dealings with it were resisted by sir Thomas Cawarden, (the subject of the following Note,) who had been the previous keeper.

P. 208. *Death and funeral of sir Thomas Cawarden*. Knighted by Henry VIII. at the siege of Boulogne in 1544, a gentleman of the king's privy chamber in 1546, and in his latter years master of the revels, tents, and pavilions. His altar-tomb remains in Bletchingley church, but without inscription. (Manning and Bray's Surrey, ii. 300.) Among other documents relating to sir Thomas Cawarden and his office, published in the Loseley Manuscripts, edited by A. J. Kempe, esq. F.S.A. 1835, 8vo. are (p. 175) his will dated St. Bartholomew's day 1559, and (p. 179) the charges of his obsequies, amounting to 96*l.* 15*s.* 1½*d.* and the funeral feast to 32*l.* 16*s.* 8*d.* The death of his wife shortly followed, and the charges of her funeral are also stated.

P. 209. *Thundering*. See this storm described also by Hayward, p. 29 ; also by Stowe, both in his Chronicle and in his Survay, when describing the church of Allhallows, the spire of which, he adds, though " but little damnified thereby, was shortly after taken downe, for sparing the charges of reparation."

P. 209. *Obsequy of the French king Henry II.* This took place at St. Paul's, and the ceremonial is preserved in the College of Arms, I. 13, f. 8, and I. 14, f. 7. There is a full abstract of it in Strype, Annals, i. 128—130, which is copied in Nichols's Progresses, &c. of Queen Elizabeth, i. 76—79.

P. 211. *Funeral of sir John Raynford.* Of Manningtree, Essex ; see Morant, i. 464.

P. 213. *Prince of Sweden.* John duke of Finland, second son of Gustavus king of Sweden. He came to negociate a marriage between his elder brother Eric and queen Elizabeth. See Hayward's Annals, p. 37. Notwithstanding the praise given him by Cecill in the passage which Mr. Bruce has there quoted, and the credit he gained by his princely living here (see our Diary, p. 230), his brother (then king of Sweden) imprisoned him on his return, in resentment for his ill success. (See Stowe's Chronicle, 1631, p. 640.)

Ibid. *Alderman Lodge sworn sheriff.* Son of William Lodge, of Cresset, in Shropshire: sheriff 1559-60, lord mayor 1563-4 : " in which year he gave up his cloak, but lived many yeares after, and was buried in Aldermary church with sir William Laxton, whose daughter he had married." Arms, Azure, a lion rampant argent, crusilly gules, within a bordure flory-de-lis of the second. (List by Wm. Smith, Rouge-dragon.) He was of the Grocers' company, and died, says Stowe, in 1583 ; but the inscription on his tomb in Aldermary church did not state the year of his death, but that of a more memorable mortality : " Here lyeth buried sir Thomas Lodge knight, and Dame Anne his wife. Hee was L. Maior in the yeere of our Lord God 1563, when God did visit this Citie with a great plague for our sinnes. For we are sure that our Redeemer liveth, and that we shall rise out of the earth in the latter day, &c. Job 19."

Ibid. *Alderman Martin sworn sheriff.* Afterwards mayor in 1567-8. Son of Lawrence Martin, of Melford in Suffolk. " He dwelled on the west side of Soper-lane, over against sir Stephen Soame." Arms, Argent, a chevron between three mascles within a bordure sable ; quartered with, Gules a fess engrailed between three swan's heads erased argent. (List by Wm. Smith, Rouge-dragon.) " A very good tombe " was erected in St. Antholin's, Budge-row, " Unto sir Roger Martin knight, a mercer and a marchant late," with verses, which may be seen in Stowe. He died Dec. 20, 1573, having had eight children, from Elizabeth " of Græcia soyle, and Castlynes race," the widow of Thomas Knowles, who died July 11, 1550, having had three children by him.

Ibid. *Master Huett chosen lord mayor.* Son of Edmund Hewitt, of Wales in Yorkshire. Sheriff 1553-4, lord mayor 1559-60. He was knighted during his mayoralty (see p. 224). This was sir William Hewitt, known as the ancestor of the duke of Leeds: Edward Osborne his apprentice, afterwards lord mayor in 1582, having married his only daughter and heir, whose life he had previously saved, when she fell from a window of her father's house on London bridge. Such is the tradition : but our old authority says that sir William " dwelled in Philpot-lane, nere Fenchurch-strete." Arms, Azure, on a

fees flory-de-lis or, between three lyons passant argent, three pewitts proper. (List by
Wm. Smith, Rouge-dragon.) He died in 1566-7, and was buried in the church of St.
Martin Orgar's, as his wife had previously been (see p. 266). Some extracts from his
will are given in Collins's Peerage.

P. 213. *Funeral of lady Cobham.* Dorothy, daughter of George lord Bergavenny, by
Mary, daughter of Edward duke of Buckingham. This funeral is recorded in the College
of Arms, I. 9, f. 161ᵇ, and I. 13, f. 14.

P. 215. *Alderman Rowe's daughter married.* The alderman had two daughters,
Mary married to Thomas Randall, and Elizabeth to sir William Garrard, of Dorney, Bucks.
(See Lipscomb's Buckinghamshire, iii. 274, 276.)

Ibid. *Did preach Crolley sometime a printer.* Strype has noted the first ordination of
Robert Crowley as a deacon, by bishop Ridley, Sept. 29, 1551. In the bishop's register
he is styled " stationer, of the parish of St. Andrew, Holborn." Of the productions of
his press Strype has given some particulars in Memorials, book 1, chap. 32 ; and of his
Thirty-one Epigrams, published in 1551, fifteen are reprinted in Strype's Appendix O O.
See also Ames's Typographical Antiquities, by Dibdin, vol. iv. pp. 325—335. In 1566
he was presented to the vicarage of St. Giles's without Cripplegate, where he died June
18, 1588. See further in Newcourt's Rep. Londin. i. 181, or Wood's Athenæ Oxon.

Ibid. *Funeral of sir William Fitzwilliam.* The name of the place (to be filled up) is
Windsor. " Sir Wm. Fitzwilliam, of the great park of Windsore, married Jane, d. to
Roberts." (MS. Lansd. 874, f. 53ᵇ. where his funeral atchievements are tricked.) His
epitaph, of eight Latin verses, on an altar-tomb in St. George's chapel, will be found in
Pote's History of Windsor, 1749, 4to. p. 372.

P. 216. *Funeral of the countess of Rutland.* Margaret daughter of Ralph earl of
Westmerland, wife of Henry second earl of Rutland, K.G. The conjoint monument of
this lady, her mother, and two other female relations, has been already noticed in p. 343.

Ibid. *Proclamation of Apparel.* This Proclamation was printed by Jugge and
Cawood. A copy is preserved in the library of the Society of Antiquaries. See Mr.
Collier's note on this subject in The Egerton Papers, p. 247 : also Strype, Annals, i. 186.

P. 217. *Funeral of Richard Knevett esquire.* One of the gentlemen pensioners to the
queen, died Nov. 1, 1559. Buried in the chapel of St. John the Evangelist, Westminster
abbey. Dart, ii. 60.

Ibid. *Funeral of sir Robert Southwell.* Constituted master of the rolls July 1, 1542 ;
resigned in 1550. He was brother to sir Richard Southwell, a member of the privy
council, and executor to Henry VIII. Sir Robert resided at Jotes Place in the parish of
Mereworth, Kent. (Hasted, iii. 269.)

P. 217. *Funeral of lord Williams of Thame.* Master of the jewel-house, temp. Edw. VI. He died on the 14th Oct. " within her majesties castell of Loudlowe in the conté of Sallop, wher he was late come, being lorde precydent ther appoincted of her grace's counsell in the said marches : " his body was brought to Thame, and a long account of his interment is preserved in I. 9, in Coll. Arm. f. 150ᵇ.

Ibid. *Funeral of Frances duchess of Suffolk.* Daughter of Charles Brandon, duke of Suffolk, and Mary queen dowager of France, daughter of king Henry VII. She was first married to Henry Grey, marquess of Dorset, who was created duke of Suffolk in 1551 (see p. 10) ; by whom she was mother of queen Jane : and afterwards accepted the hand of Adrian Stokes esquire, who erected her monument in Westminster abbey. Their portraits together are engraved by Vertue. Her style by our Diarist as " my lady Frances" did not arise either from ignorance or accident. The title " lady " was then equivalent to the modern title " princess ; " and the duchess usually bore it, as her daughter " the lady Jane " had done, as distinctive of her being a member of the Blood Royal.—The heralds' account of her funeral is preserved in the College of Arms, I. 9, f. 153-4, and I. 14, f.⁻154—157.

Ibid. *Funeral of alderman sir Thomas Curteis.* This person, who was M.P. for the city in 1547, sheriff 1546, and lord mayor in 1558, was the son of John Curteis, of Enfield, Middlesex. " He was first a pewterer, and dwelled at the upper end of Lombard-street," (list of mayors, by William Smith, Rouge-dragon): afterwards, on becoming an alderman, he joined one of the twelve great companies, choosing the Fishmongers. A marble tomb to his memory was erected in St. Dionis Back-church, with an inscription in Latin poetry, which may be seen in Stowe. It states that his sole heir was his granddaughter Anne, daughter of his son Thomas, and married to a gentleman named Stukeley. His arms were, Undée argent and sable, a chevron or between three bezants, on a chief of the third two dolphins addorsed between two anchors proper ; a crescent for difference.

P. 218. *Funeral of bishop Tunstall.* His epitaph, formerly on a brass plate under the communion table of Lambeth church, will be found in Ducarel's History of Lambeth, Appx. p. 40. It was written by Walter Haddon. He died on the 15 Nov. aged 85.

P. 219. *Funeral of sir Fulke Greville.* Grandfather of the celebrated sir Fulke Greville, K.B. the first lord Brooke. He died Nov. 10, 1559, and was buried at Alcester, co. Warw. where recumbent effigies of him and his wife were placed upon an altar-tomb an engraving of which will be found in Dugdale's History of Warwickshire.

P. 220. *Murder of master Wynborne.* " I have never met with Wynborne as the name of a family in Suffolk. John Whinburgh gent. of Whinburgh in Norfolk was also lord of Benacre in Suffolk, and it is possible the murdered man was of his family. Henry Whinburgh gent. by his will dated 31 Oct. 1544, left land in Whinburgh, Yaxham,

Rymerston, &c.   James was his son.   See Blomefield's Norfolk, x. 272."   (Communication of D. E. Davy, esq.)

P. 220. *New bishops made.* A tabular list of the new bishops will be found in Strype, Annals, i. 157.

P. 221. *Funeral of my lady Copley.* Elizabeth, widow of sir Roger Copley of Gatton, co. Surrey, who died in 1559, and daughter of sir William Shelley, justice of the common pleas. On an inquisition taken 29 April, 1560, she was found to have died seised of the manor of the Maze in Southwark (see the Collectanea Topogr. et Geneal. vol. viii. p. 255). See also the pedigree of Copley in the History of Surrey, by Manning and Bray, vol. ii. p. 231.

Ibid. *Funeral of lady Chandos widow.* Elizabeth, daughter of Edmund lord Grey of Wilton, married to John Brydges first lord Chandos: died 29 Dec. 1559. See her poetical epitaph in Jesus chapel, afterwards St. Faith's, printed by Stowe. Her will was proved on the 5th Jan.

Ibid. *Funeral of the late bishop of Carlisle.* Owen Oglethorpe, appointed 27 Oct. 1556, deprived June 1559.

Ibid. *Funeral of the late bishop of Lichfield and Coventry.* Ralph Baynes, elected 10 Nov. 1554; also deprived 1559. He died some weeks before Dr. Oglethorpe, when his burial at St. Dunstan's, Fleet Street, was thus entered in the parish register: "1559, Nov. 24. Mr. Doctor Banes." Collectanea Topogr. et Geneal. vol. iv. p. 116.

P. 222. *Play [at White]hall.* The conjecture made in the note is incorrect: for the play was at Whitehall. See the estimate of sir Thomas Cawarden for the court revels this Christmas, printed by Mr. Collier in his Annals of the Stage, vol. i. p. 174.

P. 223. *Funeral of Richard Chetwode esquire.* His pennon and surcoat were remaining at St. Dunstan's, temp. Nich. Charles, and their bearings are described in the Collectanea Topogr. et Geneal. 1837, vol. iv. p. 101.

P. 224. *Funeral of the late bishop of Winchester.* John White, warden of Winchester college, consecrated bishop of Lincoln 1554 (see p. 58), translated to Winchester 1556, deprived 1559. He was brother to alderman sir John White, to whose house he had been allowed to repair on coming out of the Tower (see p. 203), this being an instance (to which there are many parallels) of two brothers bearing the same Christian name. Sir Thomas White, of South Warnborough, Hampshire, was his brother-in-law, for, though not nearly related in paternal descent, there had been two marriages which connected the families, sir Thomas White having married Agnes sister to the bishop and sir John, and sir John having married for his first wife Sibell sister of sir Thomas White. See the Collectanea Topogr. et Geneal. vol. vii. p. 212.

P. 225. *Funeral of John Williams esquire.* Two members of this family were buried within a few days. The second (imperfect) paragraph relates to " John Williams esquyer, son and heyr to Renold Williams of Burfyld in Barkshire, maryd Cysely doter to Henry Poole of Wylshire, and dyed sans issu in Darby howsse near Powles the 16 of February 1559, and buryed at the parish churche of E(l)syng Spyttall." (MS. Harl. 879, f. 14.)

P. 228. *Veron admitted parson of St. Martin's at Ludgate.* John Veron, S.T.P. was instituted to this rectory 8 Mar. 1559, on the deprivation of John Morren, S.T.B. New-court (Repertorium, i. 415,) has misprinted the name Heron, and supposed this rector to be the same with John Heron, who was vicar of Little Canfield in Essex in 1544-5. Veron afterwards obtained the vicarage of St. Sepulchre, Oct. 21, 1560, and held both livings until his death in 1563, together with the prebend of Mora, to which he was collated Nov. 8, 1559. His first ordination as a deacon took place at Fulham Aug. 2, 1551, from the hands of bishop Ridley, his name being entered in the register as " Joh'es Veroneus, Senonens. dioc. in Gallia : " and he was made priest on the 24th of the same month. (Strype, Memor.) He previously translated into English from Latin the Short Pathway to Scripture of Zuinglius, which was printed at Worcester 24 May, 1550, and was dedicated to sir Arthur Darcy (see Strype, Memorials, Book I. chap. 34). On the 3d Jan. 1552 he was instituted to the rectory of St. Alphage in London, of which he was deprived in 1554. He is frequently noticed as a preacher by the writer of this Diary (see the Index).

P. 229. *Proclamation relative to the French king and Scotish queen.* See in Rymer, vol. xv. p. 569, the treaty with James duke of Chateau l'Herault, dated 27 Feb. 1559, the object of which was to prevent the union of Scotland to France.

P. 232. *Procession of knights of the garter.* This paragraph must not be passed without calling to remembrance a very curious print which exists representing queen Elizabeth accompanying the procession of the order of the garter, which was designed by Marcus Gerrard, and set forth by Thomas Dawes, Rouge-croix pursuivant, and of which there is a copy by Hollar in Ashmole's Order of the Garter, p. 515. It is, however, of a later date than the present Diary, namely the 20th year of the queen's reign, 1578.

Ibid. *Funeral of mistress Malory.* " April 26. Mrs. Anne Malory, wife of Richard Malory alderman, in the chapel of St. Thomas de Acre." Register of St. Pancras, Soper-lane. (Malcolm, ii. 177.) Our diarist seems to say that she died in childbed with her seventeenth child. The alderman was remarried on the 8th April following to Mrs. Lane at St. Benet Fink. (Ibid. p. 463.)

P. 235. *Funeral of mistress Allen.* At St. Leonard's Fish street hill was this inscription : " Here under this stone lieth Joane wife of William Allyn citizen and alderman, who died in childbed of her 9th child the 22. of May 1560." (MS. Lansd. 874, f. 10b.) Sir William Allen (for he was afterwards knighted) was the son of William Allen, citizen and poulterer of London ; was sheriff 1562-3, lord mayor 1571-2. "He was at first free of the Leathersellers, afterwards a Mercer. And dwelled when he was sheriff in Bow-lane; when he was maior, in Tower-strete. But buried at St. Botulphes without Bishopsgate, in which parish he was borne." Arms, Per fess sable and argent, a pale engrailed counterchanged, and three talbots passant of the second, collared gules. (List by Wm. Smith, Rouge-dragon.)

P. 235. *Funeral of Dr. Wendy.* Thomas Wendy, M.D. was one of the witnesses to the will of king Henry VIII. together with doctor George Owen and doctor Thomas Huicke, and they each received a legacy of 100*l.* (Rymer, xv. 117.) He was re-appointed physician to king Edward VI. March 3, 1546-7, with an annuity of 100*l.* (ibid. 143) ; and on the 22d Nov. 1548, was appointed one of the commissioners to visit the university of Cambridge (ibid. 178).

Pp. 236, 237. *Death and funeral of Anthony Hussey esquire.* From epitaphs in St. Martin's Ludgate, which will be found in Stowe, it appears that this person, a native of London, had been chief registrar of the archbishop of Canterbury and of the chapter of St. Paul's ; and had also for some years performed the functions of a judge in maritime causes, and a master in chancery. At length in his advanced years (having apparently resigned his office of registrar of the court of Canterbury to his son William, who died in the November before him, aged 28,) he became the governor of the company of merchants of Muscovy, which (it is stated in the same place) exercised their commerce among the Belgians as well as the Muscovites and Germans,—"lingua facundus, memoria tenax, ingenio, prudentia, doctrinaque pollens, morum comitate et probitate gratiosus." He died June 1560, æt. 63.

P. 238. *Secretary Boxall.* John Boxall, secretary of state to queen Mary : see notices of him in the Zurich Letters, 1st Series, p. 255.

Ibid. *The Merchant-taylors' feast.* As an old scholar of the grammar-school of this worshipful company, I cannot resist transcribing the memorandum made by the honest merchant-taylor John Stowe on the very memorable event of this year : "The xxj. of March, 1560, a notable grammar-schoole was founded by the mayster, wardens, and assistants of the worshipfull company of the Marchant-taylours of the citie of London, in the paryshe of S. Laurence Pounteney, the ryght worshypful Emanuell Lucar, Robert Rose, Wyllyam Merike, John Sparke, and Robert Duckyngton then being mayster and wardens of the same company." It will be seen that these names are the same as those given by our diarist in p. 239 ; but the Christian name of the master sorely puzzled him. Emanuell Lucar married the daughter of Paul Withypoll ; she died Oct. 29, 1537, and her husband erected a monument to her in St. Lawrence Poantney, with a very remarkable testimony to her varied accomplishments, written in English verse, which is preserved in Stowe's Survay.

P. 239. *Funeral of master Herenden.* This family is not noticed in Hasted's Kent, but some of their epitaphs, formerly in the parish church of "St. Anne's in the willowes," in the ward of Aldersgate, will be found in Stowe's Survay of London, 1633, p. 326. Richard Herenden of West Farleigh in Kent, esq. (probably the person whose funeral is here recorded) was father of Edward Herenden esquire, citizen and mercer of London, who died 1572.

Ibid. *Accident in Crooked lane.* This passage, so imperfect in our diary, is elucidated by one in Stowe's chronicle of 1560 : "The fifth of July, through shooting of a gunne which brake in the house of one Adrian Arten, a Dutchman in Crooked lane, and setting fire on a firken and barell of gunpowder, four houses were blown up, and divers other sore scattered."

Ibid. *Funeral of the earl of Huntingdon.* Francis second earl of Huntingdon, K.G. succeeded his father in 1554. He died at Ashby de la Zouche, June 22, 1560 (MS. Harl. 897, f. 80); and a full memoir of him will be found in Nichols's History of Leicestershire, vol. iii. pp. 580-583, and at p. 619 a description of his monument in the church of Ashby de la Zouche, of which a folio engraving is given, pl. lxxxiii. It bears recumbent effigies of the earl and of his countess, who was a niece of cardinal Pole, and acted in 1569 as administratrix of the cardinal's will.

P. 240. *Funeral of lady Chester.* Sir William Chester, draper, (son of John Chester, citizen and draper of London,) sheriff in 1554-5, lord mayor in 1560-1, was buried " with his wives," in the church of St. Edmund the King in Lombard-street. He was the son of sir John Chester, by Margaret, afterwards re-married to sir John Milborne, draper, lord mayor in 1522. Several memorials to these and other of his relatives were in the church above named ; but Stowe's account of them is confused. Sir William Chester " dwelled at the upper end of Lombard-street, over against the George, nere to St. Edmund's church, where he is buried." Arms, Per pale argent and sable, a chevron engrailed between three goat's heads counterchanged, horned or, within a bordure gules bezantée. (List by Wm. Smith, Rouge-dragon.)

P. 241. *Master Folkes proposed for sheriff.* Richard Folkes, clothworker, was an alderman, but never actually served sheriff. Arms, Sable, two bars argent charged with three cinquefoils azure ; a mullet for difference. (List by Wm. Smith, Rouge-dragon.)

Ibid. *Alderman Draper.* Christopher Draper, son of John Draper, of Melton Mowbray in Leicestershire; sheriff 1560-1, lord mayor 1566-7. Arms, Argent, on two chevronels between three escallops sable, six martlets or. (List by Wm. Smith, Rouge-dragon.) He was buried at St. Dunstan's in the East, and Stowe gives his epitaph, but with the incorrect date 1560. He died in 1580, aged 70. His daughters were married to Sir William Webbe, sir Wolstan Dixie, and sir Henry Billingsley, all subsequently lord mayors.

P. 241. *Funeral of lady Warner.* " Elizabeth, late wiff to sir Edward Warner knight, lieutenaunte of the tower of London; she was doter of Thomas Cobham, and dysceased the 8. of August 1560, and left issue a [son] whosse name is Edward." (MS. Harl. 897, f. 19.)

Ibid. *Funeral of master May, dean of Paul's.* William May, LL.D. He was the " *new* dean of Paul's," inasmuch as he had replaced Dr. Cole, but he had been previously dean from 1545 to the accession of Mary. At the time of his death he was designated to the archiepiscopal see of York : see in Dugdale's History of St. Paul's his epitaph, formerly in the choir of the old cathedral church.

P. 242. *Funeral of lady North.* Alice, daughter of Oliver Squyer, of Southby, near Portsmouth, widow of Edward Mirfyn of London (son of sir John Mirfyn, lord mayor in 1519,) and also widow of John Brigadine, of Northampton. After this, lord North married another lady who had had *three* husbands, and died himself before the end of 1565. The present lady was the mother of his children.

Ibid. *Funeral of lady Amy Dudley.* The name of " Amy Robsart " is invested with a prevailing interest as the heroine of poetry and romance. I have collected what is known of her, and endeavoured to sift the mysterious rumours of her assassination, in a memoir which appeared in the Gentleman's Magazine for December, 1845. I have now to append the following additional memorial : " Lady Amie Robsert, late wyff to the right noble the lord Robert Dudley, knight and companyon of the most noble order of the garter, and master of the horsse to the quenes moste excellent majestie, dyed on sonday the 8. of Septembre at a howsse of Mr. Foster, iij. myles from Oxford, in the 2. yere of quene Elizabeth, 1560, and was beryed on sonday the 22. of September next ensbewenge in our Lady churche of Oxford." (MS. Harl. 897, f. 80b.)

P. 243. *Funeral of sir (Nicholas) Pelham.* Sir Nicholas Pelham (to whom our diarist erroneously gave the Christian name John, which was that of his son and heir), was of Laughton in Sussex, and lineal ancestor of the earls of Chichester. He was M.P. for Arundel 1547, sheriff of Surrey and Sussex 1549, and knighted Nov. 17 in that year, and afterwards twice knight of the shire for Sussex. He died Dec. 15, 1560, æt. 44, and was buried in St. Michael's church, Lewes, where is his monument, with a kneeling effigy : of which see an engraving in Horsfield's History of Lewes, 4to. 1824, or the Gentleman's Magazine for Sept. 1825, p. 215.

Ibid. *Funeral of lord Monteagle.* Thomas Stanley succeeded his father 1523 ; made K.B. at the coronation of queen Anne Boleyne ; married first lady Mary Brandon, daughter of the duke of Suffolk, and secondly Helen daughter of Thomas Preston esquire of Levens in Westmerland, and widow of sir James Leybourne. He died at his castle of Hornby, co. Lancaster, Aug. 18, 1560, and was buried on the 16th Sept. at the parish church of Melling. His funeral is in the College of Arms, I. 13, f. 27; see also MS. Harl. 897, f. 83.

P. 243. *Reduction of the coinage.* On this subject see Ruding's Annals of the Coinage, vol. ii. pp. 135-142, Burgon's Life of Sir Thomas Gresham, vol. i. pp. 354-360, and the Zurich Letters, 1st Series, p. 93.

P. 244. *Funeral of Francis earl of Shrewsbury, K.G.* Misled by the diarist's spelling of the name Frances, the word " countess " was inadvertently inserted instead of " earl." He died at his manor of Sheffield 28 Sept. 1560, and the funeral took place at the same place on the 21st Oct. The ceremonial at full is printed in Peck's Desiderata Curiosa, lib. vii. pp. 17-21; and also in Hunter's Hallamshire, p. 56.

Ibid. *Burial of master Bulstrode ("Bulthered").* Thomas Bulstrode, of Hedgerley, Bucks, died 9 Nov. 2 Eliz. in the parish of St. Sepulchre. See the pedigree of Bulstrode in Aungier's History of Syon, Isleworth, and Hounslow, opposite p. 495.

Ibid. *Funeral of sir John Jermy.* Sir John Jermy was of Metfield and Brightwell in Suffolk, the latter of which is about five miles from Ipswich, and was therefore the residence to which our diarist alludes. He had been one of the knights of the Bath made at the coronation of quene Anne Boleyne.

P. 245. *Funeral of mistress Luson or Leveson.* This was the widow of " Nicholas Leveson, mercer, sheriff 1535. Buried at St. Andrew's Undershaft." Arms, Azure, a fess undy argent and sable, between three leaves or. (List by Wm. Smith, Rouge-dragon.)

P. 246. *Funeral of master Trapps, goldsmith.* This was one of a family of which several memorials were in the church of St. Leonard's, Foster-lane, which will be found printed in Weever's Funerall Monuments, and the several histories of London : particularly some curious English verses (A°. 1529), alluding to funeral ceremonies, which begin

> " When the bells be merrily roung,
> And the masse devoutly soung,
> And the meate [be] merrily eaten,
> Then shall Robart Trappis, his wyffs and his children be forgotten."

Another monument to Joyce Frankland, widow, daughter of Robert and Joane Trappes, was the erection of the principal and scholars of Brazenose college, Oxford.

Ibid. *Man slain in Saint Margaret's (Westminster) churchyard.* Buried, " Dec. the xxij day. John Harrys kylde." (Par. Reg.)

P. 247. *Installation of the duke of Vanholt at Windsor.* Adolphus duke of Holstein, elected 10 June, 1560, installed (by proxy) the 15th Dec. (Beltz.) He died Oct. 1, 1586.

P. 247. *Funeral of master Scott.* The registers of the family of Scott at Camberwell were printed in the Collectanea Topog. et Genealogica, vol. iii. p. 145, but the funeral described in this paragraph is not there recorded. He appears, however, to have been the Thomas Scott there mentioned in a note, whose name occurs in Cole's Escheats, i. 441.

P. 247. *Marriage at St. Pancras.* This was St. Pancras, Soper-lane, as appears from the register recording another event in the same family in the previous April (see p. 379).

P. 254. *Funeral of lady Jane Seymour.* Daughter of Edward duke of Somerset, and supposed to have been destined by him to become the consort of his nephew king Edward. A Latin letter written by her (of course under the dictation of her tutor) to the Reformers Bucer and Fagius, dated at Syon, June 12, 1549, is published in the Third Series of Zurich Letters, printed for the Parker Society. She was one of queen Elizabeth's maids of honour, and shortly before her death she had taken an active part in promoting the clandestine marriage of her brother the earl of Hertford with her companion the lady Katharine Grey, a line of conduct which would certainly have brought upon her the anger of her royal mistress, had she lived until it was discovered. (See Ellis's Orig. Letters, Second Series, vol. ii. p. 272.) Her age was only nineteen. See an engraving of her monumental tablet, with the inscription, erected by " her deare brother " the earl, in Dart's Westminster Abbey, vol. i. pl. 12. In the accounts of St. Margaret's parish, Westminster, is an entry of 10s. received at her funeral.

Ibid. *Death of sir Arthur Darcy.* Sir Arthur was the second son of Thomas lord Darcy, who suffered death for his share in the Pilgrimage of Grace. He had married Mary, daughter and co-heiress of Sir Nicholas Carew, K.G. whence his death at Bedding-ton, the mansion of that family. Lady Darcy's funeral has before occurred, in p. 222. Their epitaph in St. Botolph's, Billingsgate, will be found in Stowe's Survay.

P. 257. *Funeral of Bartholomew Compagni,* a Florentine. See a licence to him as the king's factor in Oct. 1550, in Strype, Mem. ii. 538, and his name occurs elsewhere Angli-cised to Compayne. Margaret, his daughter and heir, was mother of the maids to queen Elizabeth, and married to John Baptist Castillion, of Benham Valence, Berks. (Archæ-ologia, xxxii. 371.)

P. 259. *Funeral of lady Wharton.* " Lady Anne Ratclyff, daughter to Robert erl of Sussex and lady Margaret his wyff daughter of Thomas erl of Darby, late wyff to sir Thomas Wharton knight, son and heyr to Thomas lord Wharton, dyed the 7. of June, 1561, at the honner of Bewlew, otherwysse called Newhall, in Essex, and was beryed in the parishe churche of Boreham the xiiij[th] of the mounthe aforesaid : *leaving issue* Phelyp Wharton son and heyre, Thomas Wharton 2 son, Mary Wharton, Anne." (MS. Harl. 897, f. 18.)

P. 260. *Proclamation for slips and half slips.* This proclamation was dated 12 June 1561, and a MS. copy is in the library of the Society of Antiquaries. See its contents described in Ruding's Annals of the Coinage, *sub anno*. The name "slips" does not occur in the document, but it appears that the coins referred to were "base monies," one current for three half-pence, and the other for three farthings: and the same term was in use for many years after, as appears by the example from Shakspere's Romeo and Juliet, with others from Ben Jonson, &c. given in Nares's Glossary. From "Theeves falling out," by Robert Greene, we derive this exact definition: "Certain slips, which are counterfeit pieces of money, being brasse, and covered over with silver, which the common people call *slips*." (Harl. Misc. viii. 399.)

P. 262. *The king of Sweden.* In Haynes's Cecill Papers, p. 369, is the minute of a curious letter from the secretary to the lord mayor, dated 21 July, 1561, commencing with a statement that "The queenes majesty understandeth that sondry bookebynders and stationers do utter certen papers, *wherin be prynted the faces of hir majesty and the king of Sweden*. And, although her majesty is not miscontented that ether hir owne face or the sayd kyng's be prynted or portracted, yet, to be joyned in one paper with the sayd king, or with any other prynce that is knowne to have made any request for mariadg to hir majesty, is not to be allowed;" and the said portraits were therefore to be withdrawn from sale.

P. 264. *Burial of [William] Bill, dean of Westminster.* His sepulchral brass remains in the abbey, and has been engraved, as also a portrait derived from it, for the series of portraits of the deans of Westminster which accompany their lives in Neale and Brayley's History of Westminster Abbey. See also an engraving in Dart, i. 101.

Ibid. *Christening of Robert Dethick.* It was no unfrequent honour paid by queen Elizabeth to her subjects to stand godmother to their children. In a list of her presents of plate there are nine instances between the 21st April and the 24th Nov. 1561, and among them, "Item, given by her Majestie the 15th of July, to the chrystenyng of sir William Dethyk, alias Garter king at armes, his childe, oone guilte cup with a cover, per oz. 19¼ dim. oz. Bought of the Goldsmyth." Queen Elizabeth's Progresses, edit. 1823, vol. i. p. 129.

P. 265. *Master Avenon chosen sheriff.* Son of Robert Avenon, or Avenand, of King's Norton in Worcestershire; sheriff 1561-2; lord mayor 1569-70, and knighted. He was " buried at St. Peter's, at the Cross in Cheap." Arms, Ermine, on a pale gules a cross flory-de-lis argent, on a chief sable a mascle between two escallops of the third. (List by Wm. Smith, Rouge-dragon.) The epitaph of his widow "the lady Alice Avenon," at St. Laurence in the Jewry, will be seen in Stowe. She was the daughter and co-heir of Thomas Huchen, citizen and mercer, and married first Hugh Methwold mercer, and secondly John Blundell mercer, and had children by both, who are enumerated. The marriage took place in his mayoralty, as thus recorded in the register of Allhallows, Bread-street: "1570, Oct. 22, was married sir Alexander Avenon, lord mayor, and mistress Blunden, widow, by a license, within his own house." Malcolm, ii. 12.

P. 265. *Master Baskerville chosen sheriff.* Humphrey Baskerville, mercer, buried in the Mercers' chapel, 1563. Arms, Argent, on a chevron gules between three hurts a crescent or. (List by Wm. Smith, Rouge-dragon.)

Ibid. *Master Gilbert chosen alderman.* Edward Gilbert, goldsmith. Never sheriff or lord mayor. Arms, Azure, a chevron engrailed ermine between three spread eagles or. (List by Wm. Smith, Rouge-dragon.)

P. 266. *Funeral of auditor Swift.* He was auditor to the church of St. Paul's, and had this epitaph on a stone in the south aile of St. Botulph's without Bishopsgate: " Hic jacet Petrus Swift de London. generos. dum vixit auditor eccles. cathedrali D. Pauli London. Qui obiit 2. die Septemb. An. Dom. 1562. Cujus, &c." (Stowe.)

Ibid. *The young earl of Hertford brought to the Tower.* This was on account of his marriage with lady Katharine Grey, sister to the late queen Jane. Respecting this stolen alliance see several letters in Ellis's Second Series, vol. ii. pp. 272, *et seq.* and Bayley's History of the Tower of London, pp. 458-460.

Ibid. *Master Swift of Rotherham.* Robert Swift esquire, mercer, of Rotherham, where he "lyvyde many yeares in vertuous fame, grett wellthe, and good woorship," and had attained his 84th year. See his epitaph in Hunter's South Yorkshire, vol. ii. p. 18, and further particulars of him and his family in vol. i. of that work, p. 205. The name of his eldest son is of constant occurrence in Lodge's Illustrations, as one of the servants and most frequent correspondents of the earl of Shrewsbury.

Ibid. *Funeral of sir James Boleyne.* One of the uncles of queen Anne Boleyne. He was of Blickling, co. Norfolk, and was buried there on the 5th Dec. 1561; having died without issue. See the pedigree of Boleyne in Clutterbuck's Hertfordshire, vol. iii. p. 94; and see the History of Norfolk, by Blomefield and Parkin, fol. vol. iii. p. 627.

Ibid. *Great riches that myght have bene sene, and gyffyne to ....* The "great riches" burnt were church books and ornaments deemed superstitious. The MS. is as above; but it seems probable that the Diarist, repining against the act, with his Old Church bias, was thinking of the apostles' complaint against Mary Magdalene, and that the articles burnt "might have been *sold,* and given to the poor."

P. 267. *Funeral of master Cotgrave.* This may very probably have been the father of Hugh Cotgrave, who soon after became Richmond herald. His kinsman "master Tott, serjeant painter to Henry VIII." was an Italian, Antonio Toto, whose naturalisation occurs in Rymer, xiv. 595, and several notices of whom will be found in the Privy Purse Expenses of Henry VIII. edited by Sir Harris Nicolas, 8vo. 1827.

P. 268. *Christening of the earl of Hertford's son.* This was the first offspring of the stolen alliance noticed in the preceding page. The son was christened Edward, but died in infancy; and the second son, whose birth is afterwards mentioned in p. 300, received the same name.

P. 268. *Master Harper elected lord mayor.* Sir William Harper, son of William Harper, of the town of Bedford, sheriff 1556-7, lord mayor 1561-2. "He dwelled in Lombard-streete, where Mr. Butler now (1605) dwelleth. But was buried at Bedford, where he was borne." Arms, Azure, on a fess between three spread eagles or a fret between two martlets azure. (List by Wm. Smith, Rouge-dragon.) This was another of those worthy citizens, so many of whom have occurred in these pages, whose names are still remembered as the founders of our great educational establishments. The estates left by sir William Harper for the grammar-school of Bedford, lying in the vicinity of Bedford Row, the Foundling Hospital, and Lamb's Conduit-street, have of late years vastly increased in value, and proportionately benefited his foundation. He died Feb. 27, 1573, aged 77; and was buried in St. Paul's at Bedford, where is his effigy in brass plate, from which an engraving was published in Waller's Monumental Brasses, fol. 1841.

P. 269. *Master Gowth.* This preacher, who our Diarist informs us to have been son of John Gough the printer (see Ames's Typographical Antiquities, by Dibdin, vol. iii. pp. 202-416) is again mentioned in p. 285 as the parson of St. Peter's in Cornhill. He was John Gough clerk, presented to the vicarage of Braintree in Essex by John Gooday clothier, 3 Dec. 1554, deprived 1556; presented to St. Peter's Cornhill, by the mayor, aldermen, and commonalty of London 15 Nov. 1560, deprived 1567. (Newcourt, Repert. Lond. i. 526; ii. 89.)

P. 271. *Death and funeral of the good sir Rowland Hill.* This reverend senator has the highest character given him in his epitaph, which was placed "on a faire stone in the south aile of St. Stephen's Walbrook:"

> A friend to vertue, a lover of learning,
> A foe to vice, and vehement corrector,
> A prudent person, all truth supporting;
> A citizen sage, and worthy counsellor;
> A lover of wisdome, of justice a furtherer,
> Loe, here his corps lyeth, sir Rowland Hill by name,
> Of London late lord maier, and alderman of fame.

He was the son of Thomas Hill, of Hodnet in Shropshire; was sheriff 1541-2; lord mayor 1549-50. He founded a grammar school at Drayton in Shropshire, and performed other admirable acts of beneficence recorded by Stowe in his Survay, in his chapter "Honour of Citizens." "He dwelled in Walbrook, over against the said church of St. Stephen; and was buried at St. Stephen's in Walbrook 1561." Arms, Azure, two bars argent, on a canton sable a chevron between three pheons of the second, an eagle's head erased of the third, between two mullets gules. (List by Wm. Smith, Rouge-dragon.)

P. 272. *Proclamation on foreign coins.* This proclamation was dated the 15th of Nov. 1561, and is extant among the collection in the Society of Antiquaries' library. It is curious as representing in woodcuts the counterfeit angels of Tournay and Holland, in comparison with a genuine angel of Henry VIII. (See Ruding's Annals of the Coinage, *sub anno.*) The same proclamation is noticed in a Norwich Chronicle as follows:

" This year, upon sunday the 23d of November, there was sent from the Queen a Proclamation to be published, that pistoles and other foreign crowns of gold and silver, only French crowns excepted, should not pass from man to man as current money, but as bullion be brought into the Tower, there to have as much as they are worth." Papers of the Norwich and Norfolk Archæol. Soc. vol. i. p. 145.

P. 273. *Funeral of Laurence Dalton, Norroy king of arms.* See his epitaph in Stowe, and his funeral insignia described in the Collectanea Topogr. et Geneal. 1837, vol. iv. pp. 101-111. His funeral ceremony is recorded in the College of Arms. I. 13, f. 32, and his brass is drawn in the MS. Harl. 1099.

P. 274. *Christmas festivities in the Temple.* A long account of the celebration of these festivities will be found in Dugdale's Origines Juridiciales, pp. 150 *et seq.* and extracted in Nichols's Progresses, &c. of Queen Elizabeth, 1823, vol. i. p. 131.

Ibid. *The great O'Neill of Ireland.* This person, whom our Diarist in the next page takes the liberty to call " the wild Irishman," was John or Shane O'Neill, eldest son of Connac O'Neill, created earl of Tyrone by Henry VIII. in 1542. After a career the turbulence of which fully justifies Machyn's epithet, he was slain in the year 1567, by Alexander Oge MacConnell.

P. 275. *Funeral of the countess of Bath.* Margaret, only child of John Donnington, of Stoke Newington in Middlesex, married successively to sir Thomas Kytson, sir Richard Long, and John Bourchier earl of Bath. The last died in 1560. Her monument in Hengrave church, Suffolk, with recumbent effigies of herself and her three husbands, is engraved in Gage's History of that parish, 1822, 4to. p. 65; and in the same volume are several letters to and from her, an inventory of her property, her will, and an account of her funeral expenses, &c.

Ibid. *Play by the gentlemen of the Temple.* This play was the celebrated " Ferrex and Porrex," written by Sackville and Norton, the old editions of which bear in their title-page, that it was " shewed before the Queenes most excellent Majestie, in her Highnes court of Whitehall, the 18th Jan. 1561, by the gentlemen of the Inner Temple." Collier's Hist. of English Dramatic Poetry, i. 180.

Ibid. *Robert Cooke.* afterwards Clarenceux king of arms, was created Rose-Blanch pursuivant Jan. 25, and Chester herald Jan. 29, 1561; his patent for the latter office is printed in Rymer's Fœdera, &c. vol. xv. p. 620; followed by that advancing his predecessor, William Flower, to the office of Norroy (see the ceremony of creation mentioned in p. 276).

P. 275. *Funeral of Charles Wryothesley, Windsor herald.* He died "AT CAMDEN'S HOWSSE, in the parish of St. Pulcres in London." (MS. Harl. 897, f. 27ᵇ.) "Item. On Sounday the 25th of January, Anº. 1561, departed out of this world about sixe of the cloacke, Charles Wryotheley al's Windsour herauld, who was buryed at Saint Sepulcres churche w'hout Newgate, on Tuesday in the morning, at the which buriall the sayd corsse was covered with a pall of blacke velvett, and on the same was laid a rich coate of armes, and of each corner of the sayd corpes went a pursivant of armes in a mourning gowne and hood, and in their coates of armes. And after the corsse went Somersett herauld in his gowne and hood, and after him Mr. Garter and Mr. Clarencieux, and after them the rest of the office of armes not in blacke." From the Papers of Sir Edward Walker, Garter, "*Heralds, vol. I. p. 120, Coll. Arm.*" See also the MS. L. 13, f. 34.

P. 276. *Julyus Sesar "played."* I appended the editorial note to the word *played* in this passage, because it appeared to me very doubtful whether it was not added by a person who misunderstood what our Diarist meant to record. It is possible there was no play of Julius Cæsar performed on this occasion, beyond his personation among the men of arms, in the cavalcade, like one of the "men in armour" in my Lord Mayor's show. Mr. Collier, however, (Hist. of English Dramatic Poetry, i. 180; ii. 415,) has quoted this passage of our Diary as attesting the existence of an historical play, called Julius Cæsar, and which would have been the first English drama derived from Roman history.

P. 277. *Christening of master Cromwell's daughter.* The first supposition in the footnote is correct. The child's mother was the daughter of sir Ralph Warren, formerly lord mayor of London, and "my lady White" was grandmother as well as godmother, as will be seen by consulting the note already given in p. 330.

P. 279. *Funeral of Robert Mellish.* Died March, 1562. Epitaph in Stowe.

P. 280. *Marriage of master Bacon's daughter.* James Bacon, a brother of the lord keeper, was a fishmonger and alderman of London, and sheriff in 1569, but died in 1573, before arriving at the mayoralty. He was buried at St. Dunstan's in the East, and his epitaph will be found in Stowe's Survay, edit. 1633, p. 139.

P. 281. *Funeral of sir Giles Strangways.* This was the name of the knight our Diarist calls Strange. "Sir Gyles Strangwysh, of Melbury Sanford, in the county of Dorset, knight, dysceased the xjᵗʰ of Apryll, 1562, and is beryed in the churche of Melbury. He maryed Jone doter of John Wadham of Meryfelde in the county of Somerset, and by her had issue John Stranguysh son and heyr, George 2 son, Nycolas 3 son, Anne." (MS. Lansd. 897, f. 20ᵇ.)

P. 281. *Monstrous child.* The prodigious births of the year 1562 (see pp. 281, 282, 284) will be found duly chronicled by Stowe, and they are thus noticed in a letter of bishop Jewell to H. Bullinger: " Incredibilis fuit hoc anno toto apud nos cœli atque aeris intemperies.   Nec sol, nec luna, nec hyems, nec ver, nec æstas, nec autumnus, satisfecit officium suum.   Ita effatim et pene sine intermissione pluvit, quasi facere jam aliud cœlum non queat.   Ex hac contagione nata sunt monstra: infantes fœdum in modum deformatis corporibus, alii prorsus sine capitibus, alii capitibus alienis ; alii trunci sine brachiis, sine tibiis, sine cruribus; alii ossibus solis cohærentes, prorsus sine ullis carnibus, quales fere imagines mortis pingi solent.   Similia alia complura nata sunt e porcis, ex equabus, e vaccis, e gallinis.   Messis hoc tempore apud nos augustius quidem provenit, ita tamen ut non possimus multum conqueri.   Sarisberiæ, 14 Augusti, 1562."   Zurich Letters, 1st Series, epist. L.

P. 283.   *Funeral of master Godderyke.*   It seems not improbable, from the attendance at this funeral, that this was a brother or near relative of the late bishop of Ely and lord chancellor.   In the register of St. Andrew's he is styled sir Richard Goodricke.   (Malcolm.)

Ibid.   *Funeral of lady Cheney.*   See the note on sir Thomas Cheney in p. 369.   There is an effigy of the lady at Toddington; see the Topographer, 1846, vol. i. p. 156.

P. 284.   *The Ironmongers' Feast.*   At "A courte holden the xxvij. day of May, A° 1562," the following order was made, " Whereas the dyner hath hearetofore bene used to be kept upon the sondaye next after Trynitie sondaye, that the dyner shall from henceforthe be kepte upon the monday sevennight after Trynitie sonday, that is to saye, the mondaye next after the olde accustomed daye; and that the yeomondrye, as well househoulders as others, must be warned to be at the hall upon the sayd monday in their best arraye, as they have bene accustomed to be heretofore upon the sondaye, for to offer at the churche as aforetime ewsaid."   This was an alteration in accordance with the increased respect for the sabbath enjoined by the Reformation.   Mr. Christopher Draper, alderman, was master of the company on this occasion ; William Done and John Miston, wardens. (Communicated by John Nicholl, esq. F.S.A.)

P. 284.   *Helyas Hall.*   The real name of this prophet was Elizeus Hall : many particulars respecting him will be found in Strype, Annals, chap. 25.

P. 285.   *The monument of sir William Walworth.*   This memorable civic hero had founded a college for chantry priests attached to the church of St. Michael's, Crookedlane ; see his will printed in the Excerpta Historica, 1831. 8vo.   The college shared the fate of other religious foundations ; but the monument was now restored by the zeal of a member of the Fishmongers' Company, which afterwards kept it in repair, until it was destroyed in the great fire of 1665.   The poetical epitaph, which was added at one of the repairs, will be found in Weever's Funerall Monuments and the several Histories of London.   Stowe states the epitaph in his time bore the name of Jack Straw in lieu of that of Wat Tyler,—an historical error for which he severely censures the Fishmongers as " men ignorant of their antiquities ;" but our own Diarist has made a still graver error in naming Jack Cade, the rebel of the days of Henry VI.

P. 286. *Master Fuwilliam.* This probably records the burial of Thomas Fitz-William *alias* Fisher, who was a natural son of the Earl of Southampton, mentioned by Ralph Brooke in his Catalogue of Nobility. The Earl, who died at Newcastle when commanding the Van of the army sent against Scotland in 1542, left no legitimate issue.

P. 288. *Marriage of master Coke and master Nicholls's daughter.* " John Nicolls of London, gentleman, at this present (1568) comtroller of the workes at London bridge, and all other lands and revenues of the same, and in charge for provision of corne for the city of London," married for his first wife Christian Thompson, and had issue two daughters, Mary married to Francis Gerrard, and Elizabeth married to Edmond Cooke of Lizens in Kent gentleman—the marriage mentioned by Machyn. Mr. Nicholls married, secondly, Elen daughter of James Holt of Stubley, co. Lancaster. (Visitation of Middlesex, by Robt. Cooke, Clarencieux, 1568.) Machyn has afterwards (p. 305) noticed a christening at Mr. Nicholls's, probably of a daughter, by his second marriage. The descendants of his brother Thomas Nicholls (among whom was William Nicholls, dean of Chester,) are recorded in the Bedfordshire visitation of 1628. MS. Harl. 1531, f. 158.

Ibid. *My lord Giles's daughter.* Another daughter of lord Giles Pawlet was christened the next year at the same church : " lady Elizabeth Pawlett, 31 Aug. 1563 :" and on the 25th Julie, 1572, was buried at St. Botulph's " Lady Pallat, wife to the right hon. lord Gyles Pallat." Malcolm's Lond. Rediv. i. 344.

P. 289. *Alderman Chamberlain chosen sheriff.* " Rychard Chamberlen, ironmonger, alderman and late shreve of London, dyed on tuesday the xix[th] of November, 1566, in A° 9° Elizabeth' Regine, at his howsse in the parishe of St. Olyff in the Old Jury, and was beryed on Monday 25. of November, in the parishe churche there. *He married first* Anne, doughter of Robert Downe of London, ironmonger, *and had issue* Elizabeth wyff to Hugh Stewkley of London lawyar, Thomas Chamberlen, Rychard, Alexander, Robert, Margery, John, George; *secondly,* Margarat, wedo of Bristo groser of London, doter and one of th'eyrs of Nycolas Hurleton, of Cheshire, somtyme clerk of the grene cloth to king H. 8. She dyed sans issu." (MS. Harl. 897, f. 30.) Alderman Chamberlain's epitaph will be found in Stowe.

P. 290. *Funeral of the earl of Oxford.* " This John Vere, erl of Oxford, dysseased at his castell of Hemyngham in Essex on Monday the 3. of August, in the 4. yere of the quene our soveraigne lady Elizabeth, &c. 1562, and was beryed on tewsday the 25. of August next enshewing, at the parishe churche of Hemyngham. *He married first* Doraty, doughter of Raff erle of Westmerland, *and had issue* Kateren wyff to Edward lord Wyndesor ; *secondly,* Margery doughter of Golding, syster to sir Thomas Goldinge, *and had issue* Edward erl of Oxford, *and Mary.*" (MS. Harl. 897, f. 81.)

P. 291. *Master Hulsun master Heyword's deputy.* Sir Rowland Hayward died Dec. 5, 1593, having lived " an alderman the space of 30 yeares, and (at his death) the ancientest alderman of the said city." (Epitaph in St. Alphage, where his monument still remains, with effigies of two wives and sixteen children, and was repaired in 1777, when the church was rebuilt.) He was sheriff in 1563-4. It is therefore possible that sir Rowland may have been the "master Heyword" mentioned in this page; but then he appears to have been alderman of Cripplegate ward, and dwelt in Philip lane, by Cripplegate, in the house adjoining St. Alphage's church. (Arms of the Lord Mayors, by Wm. Smith, Rouge-dragon.) Master Hulsun may have been "deputy" alderman of the same ward; but buried at saint Bride's in Fleet-street on account of his connection with Bridewell hospital.

P. 291. *Funeral of the countess of Bedford.* Margaret daughter of sir John St. John of Bletsoe, and first wife of Francis second earl of Bedford. "Lady Margaret, countess of Bedford, dyed at Owborne the xxviij[th] of August, and was beryed the xth of September at Chenyes, in A° 1562." (MS. Harl. 897, f. 84.)

P. 292. *Funeral of lord* (not lady) *Mordaunt.* John first lord Mordaunt, summoned to parliament in 1558, died 28 Aug. 1562, at Turvey, co. Bedford, where he was buried, and a sumptuous monument erected with effigies of himself and lady, of which there is an engraving in Halstead's Genealogies, fol. 1785, p 593.

P. 293. *Funeral of sir Harry Grey, brother to the earl of Kent.* Richard earl of Kent, having much wasted his estate by gaming, died at the sign of the George in Lombard-street, in 15 Hen. VIII. and was buried at the White Friars in Fleet-street. Whereupon his brother and heir male, sir Henry Grey of Wrest, by reason of his slender estate, declined to take upon him the title of Earl. (Ralph Brooke's Catalogue of Nobilitie.) He died Sept. 24, 1562; and in his epitaph at St. Giles's, Cripplegate, was styled "Sir Henry Grey knight, sonne and heire to George lord Grey of Ruthen and earl of Kent." (Stowe's Survay.) The dignity was resumed by his grandson Reginald, in 1571. "Sir Harry Grey knight dyed at his howsse in London in Sant Gyles parishe the xvj[th] day of September, in the 4th yere of our soveraigne lady quene Elizabethe, and was buryed in the parishe churche there the xxij[th] of the same mounthe, and lyeth in the chapel of the south syde the quere. The said sir Henry maryd Anne doghter of John Blenerhasset, in the county of Suffolk." (MS. Harl. 897, f. 20 [b], where his issue is also stated.)

P. 294. *Cree-church.* The duke of Norfolk's town mansion (here written "Chrychyre") was near the church called St. Katharine's Cree-church or Christ's church, in the ward of Aldgate. It has been before mentioned in p. 186.

Ibid. *Funeral of mistress Chamley.* This paragraph is so imperfect that it is not certain that it relates to the wife of the Recorder. He, however, was buried at St. Dunstan's in the West in the following April (see p. 395), and his epitaph commenced—
"Ranulphus Cholmeley chara hic cum conjuge dormit."

Ibid. *Funeral of mistress Lewen.* See a former note (p. 344) on this lady's husband. At "a quarter court (of the Ironmongers' company) 19 Jan. 1562[-3] was brought into this house 2 salts with a cover, all gilt, weighing lxv. oz. which Mrs. Agnes Lewen lately gave at hir deceas to this company." Richard Chamberlain the sheriff, executor, and William Draper the overseer, of mistress Lewen's will, were both members of the same fraternity.

P. 296. *Master Hunton that married my lady of Warwick.* Sir Edward Unton, K.B. on the 29th April, 1555, married Anne, one of the daughters of the protector Somerset, and widow of John Dudley, earl of Warwick, the eldest son of John duke of Northumberland. See the memoirs prefixed to Unton Inventories, 1841, 4to. p. xxxvii.

Ibid. *Funeral of Arthur Dericote esquire.* Citizen and draper: see his poetical epitaph in Robinson's History of Hackney, vol. ii. p. 27, accompanied by some account of his funeral, derived from the present Diary. See also the MS. Lansdowne 874, f. 123b.

P. 297. *Funeral of sir Humphrey Browne.* This venerable judge of the common pleas had been first appointed in the 34 Hen. VIII. 1543, and had continued to sit on the bench through the reigns of Edward and Mary. Stowe records that he bequeathed "divers houses" to the parish of St. Martin Orgar's, but describes no other memorial of him.

Ibid. *Funeral of William lord Grey of Wilton, K.G.* The circumstancial account of this ceremonial, drawn up by one of the attendant heralds, is appended to the "Commentarie of the Services" of this nobleman, in the volume edited for the Camden Society by Sir Philip Grey Egerton, Bart. The church (left blank in p. 298,) was Cheshunt, co. Hertford; the preacher was Michael Reniger; and in line 17, *for* "master de[an's] plase," *read* "master De[nny's] plase."

P. 299. *Funeral of lady Dormer.* Sir Michael Dormer, who had been lord mayor in 1541, died in 1545, directing his body to be buried in the churchyard of St. Lawrence (not St. Olave's) in the Jury, London, where Elizabeth his wife lay; leaving issue by his wife Katharine (who was the lady here recorded) several children, whose names will be found in Collins's Peerage, *tit.* Dormer.

P. 300. *The double marriage of lord Talbot to lady Anne Herbert, and lord Herbert to lady Katharine Talbot.* Francis lord Talbot died before his father, and without issue, in 1582. The marriage here recorded of Lord Herbert, afterwards second earl of Pembroke, (who had been previously contracted to the lady Katharine Grey, and whose third wife was the celebrated Mary, sister to Sir Philip Sidney,) was also fruitless. On the occasion of Lady Katharine Talbot's marriage, her father inforced the ancient feudal right of receiving a benevolence from his tenants as *ayde pour fille marier.* See a letter of his on the subject, dated "From Coldharbar, the xxth of Marche, 1562[-3]," in Lodge's Illustrations of British History, i. 348; followed by an account of the sums collected in the counties of York, Nottingham, and Derby, which amounted to 321l. 7s. 6d.

P. 301. *Exposure of a termagant wife.* A custom somewhat similar still existed in parts of Berkshire towards the end of the last century, and about 1790 one of the members of the Camden Society witnessed a procession of villagers on their way to the house of a neighbouring farmer, in the parish of Hurst, who *was said to have beaten his wife.* The serenaders, consisting of persons of all ages and denominations, were well supplied with kettles, tin cans, cover-lids, hand-bells, pokers and tongs, and cows' horns, and, drawing up in front of the farm, commenced a most horrible din, showing at least that the ceremony was properly known by the name of "*rough music.*" After some time the party quietly dispersed, apparently quite satisfied with the measure of punishment inflicted by them on the delinquent.—For similar practices see Brand, ii. 151, and MS. Sloane 886.

P. 302. *Sir William FitzWilliam,* who died in the time of king Henry VIII. in the year 1534, was a merchant-taylor of London, and alderman of Bread-street ward. He was the first of his family at Milton, co. Northampton (now the seat of his descendant earl FitzWilliam), and was buried at Marham in that county : see Bridges's History thereof, vol. ii. p. 520.

Ibid. *Loss of the queen's ship the Greyhound.* A short account of this event will be found in Stowe's Chronicle. Sir Thomas Finch had been appointed to succeed sir Adrian Poynings as knight marshal of the army in France ; and, having previously sent over his brother sir Erasmus Finch to have charge of his band, and his kinsman Thomas Finch to be provost marshal, he at length embarqued in the Greyhound, " having there aboord with him, besides three score and sixe of his own retinue, foure and forty other gentlemen, two of them being brethren to the lord Wentworth, to wit, James Wentworth and John Wentworth, with divers others, who in the whole (accompting the marriners) amounted to the number of two hundred persons and upward." Having been driven back from Newhaven, they unwisely urged the captain " to thrust into the haven " of Rye "before the tide," and consequently the lives of all were lost, except four " of the meaner sort."

Ibid. *Sir Thomas Finch* was of Eastwell, co. Kent, by marriage with Katharine, elder daughter and co-heir of Sir Thomas Moyle, chancellor of the court of augmentations ; his eldest son, sir Moyle Finch, was created a baronet in 1611, and was direct ancestor of the earls of Winchelsea and Nottingham.

P. 303. *Funeral of lady Chester.* Katharine, daughter of Christopher Throckmorton esquire, of Coorse Court, co. Glouc. and the first wife of sir Robert Chester, receiver of the court of augmentations : see before, p. 316, and the pedigree of Chester in Clutterbuck's Hertfordshire, vol. iii. p. 363.

Ibid. *Funeral of lady Lane.* Sir Robert Lane was of Horton in Northamptonshire, being the son of sir Ralph Lane by Maud daughter of William lord Parr of Horton. By Katharine his first wife, daughter of sir Robert Copley of Bermondsey, (see before, p. 378) who is the lady here commemorated, he had three sons, all afterwards knighted, sir William Lane, sir Parr Lane, and sir Robert Lane. Bridges's Northamptonshire, vol. i. p. 368.

P. 303. *Funeral of alderman David Woodroffe.* Son of John Woodroffe, of Uscombe, Devonshire; sheriff 1554. In that capacity he was present at the executions of Bradford and Rogers the protestant martyrs, and John Foxe much abuses his cruel behaviour, contrasting it with the mildness of his colleague sir William Chester. " But what happened ? Hee was not come out of his office the space of a weeke, but he was stricken by the sudden hand of God, the one halfe of his bodie in such sort, that he lay benumned and bed-red, not able to move himself, but as he was lifted of other, and so continued in that infirmity the space of seven or eight years, till his dying day." He gave 20*l.* towards the conduit at Bishopsgate. (Stowe's Survay.) His son Stephen died Sept. 25, 1572, and was buried at St. Andrew Undershaft (Ibid.); and his grandson sir Nicholas Woodroffe, who lived at Leadenhall (in that parish), was lord mayor in 1579. A pedigree of the family, which was allied to others of eminence in the city, will be found in the History of Surrey, by Manning and Bray, vol. iii. pp. 176, 177.

P. 307. *Funeral of Ranulph Cholmley esquire, Recorder of London.* He had been elected Recorder in 1553. See his epitaph in Stowe's Survay, and his armorial insignia in the Collectanea Topogr. et Geneal. 1837, vol. iv. p. 102. His place in the pedigree of Cholmondeley will be seen in Ormerod's Cheshire, vol. ii. p. 356.

P. 308. *Funeral of sir James Stump.* This was the son and heir of a wealthy Wiltshire clothier, who made his fortune at Malmesbury, where he set up his looms in the abbey church and buildings immediately after the Dissolution, as related by Leland in his Itinerary. See the pedigree of this family, whose inheritance passed to the Knyvetts and so to the earls of Suffolk and Berkshire, in the Collectanea Topogr. et Genealogica, vol. vii. p. 81; also the funeral certificate of his daughter lady Knyvett and her husband in the Topographer, 1846, vol. i. p. 467. The churchwardens of St. Margaret's Westminster, received, " Item, of the overseers of the last will of sir James Stumpe knight, for a fyne of certen black clothe hanged up in our Lady chappelle the tyme of his buryall ij*s.* vj*d.* ; for his grave xiij*s.* iiij*d.*; for the belles iiij*s.* viij*d.*"

Ibid. *Funeral insignia of master Gyfford.* For " Northamptonshire " the Diarist should have written Southamptonshire : for this funeral gear was doubtless made for " John Gyfford esquire, heir apparent of syr William Gyfford knyght," who died 1 May, 1563, and was buried at Crondall, Hants. See his epitaph in Collectanea Topograph. et Genealogica, vol. vii. p. 223.

P. 309. *Funeral of lord Paget.* The first peer of that family, whose active part as a statesman is familiar from general history. " This William lord Paget dysseased at his howsse called Drayton, on wensday the ix^th of June, in the 5. yere of quene Elizabethe,

1563, and was beryed on Thursday the xviijth of July next enshewinge." (MS. Harl. 897, f. 81.) There is a monument with his effigies in Lichfield Cathedral, an engraving of which forms Pl. XVI. of Shaw's History of Staffordshire.

P. 310. *Ringing on the queen's removes.* The ringing of bells at these times was a constant observance : see particularly the extracts from the parochial accounts of Lambeth and St. Margaret's Westminster, published in Nichols's " Illustrations of the Manners and Expenses of Ancient Times," 1797, 4to. and continual entries throughout the Progresses of Queen Elizabeth and King James I. On the 20th of April, 1571, the ringers of Lambeth were paid 1s. " for rynging when the queenes majestie *rode about* St. George's fields." It might be supposed that Elizabeth was very fond of this noisy salutation; but the truth is, that her harbingers enforced their fines, as noticed in the present passage of the Diary, if the service was omitted. The same usage was customary at an earlier date, as shown by the following entry from the accounts of St. Margaret's for the years 1548 and 1549, " Also payd to the kyng's amner, when he would have sealyd up the church doors at the departure of the kyng's majestie the ij day of July, because the bells were not rung, ijs. iiijd."

Ibid. *A cross of blue set at every door.* These sad badges of the plague seem to have been made separately, probably painted on canvas. The churchwardens of St. Margaret's Westminster paid at this time, " Item, to the paynter of Totehill-street for payntinge of certeyne blewe crosses to be fyxed upon sondrie houses infected, vjd."

P. 311. *Proclamation.* On further consideration the sense of this paragraph seems to be that Englishmen were to be *allowed* privateering against the French : therefore, for the word " no," read " any " or " every." The proclamation next mentioned (p. 312) would be one relating to London only, where the French residents were to remain unmolested.

P. 312. *Taking of Newhaven.* The 28th of July was the day the town of Havre de Grace surrendered to the prince of Condé and his English allies. See Stowe's Chronicle under this date. On this subject see also the preface to the Chronicle of Calais, p. xvii.

Ibid. *Proclamation for killing dogs.* This was on account of their carrying the plague from house to house. The churchwardens of St. Margaret's Westminster paid this year, " Item, to John Welche for the killinge and carreinge awaye of dogges during the plague, and for the putting of theym into the ground and covering the same, iijs. ijd." The like measure was adopted on the recurrence of the plague in 1603, when, at seven payments from the 19th June to the 30th July, the churchwardens of St. Margaret's paid for the slaughter of no fewer than 327 dogs, at 1d. each.

P. 8. *Henry Williams* (Note in p. 320). " An epitaph of maister Henrie Williams, written by Thomas Norton (one of the versifiers of the Psalms), is extracted from The Songes and Sonnettes of lord Surrey, by Tottel, 1565, in Dr. Bliss's edition of Wood's Athenæ Oxon. i. 186.

P. 9. *The king wearing the order of St. Michael.* The robes of Saint Michael worn by king Edward the Sixth were preserved for fifty years after in the royal wardrobe,—Elizabeth, who never parted with any of her own gowns, nor with those of her sister that had come into her possession, retaining these also among her stores. They were thus described in the year 1600 : " Robes late king Edwarde the VIth's. Firste, one robe of clothe of silver, lyned with white satten, of th'order of St. Michale, with a brode border of embrodirie, with a wreathe of Venice gold and the scallop shell, and a frenge of the same golde, and a small border aboute that ; the grounde beinge blew vellat, embrodered with half-moones of silver; with a whoode and a tippet of crymsen vellat, with a like embroderie, *the tippet perished in one place with ratts ;* and a coate of clothe of silver, with demi-sleeves, with a frenge of Venice golde." Nichols's Progresses, &c. of Queen Eliz.— In the Addit. MS. (Brit. Mus.) 6297, art. 7 describes " How king Edward VI. received the order of St. Michael."

P. 27. *Funeral of sir Thomas Jermyn.* Sheriff of Norfolk and Suffolk in 33 Hen. VIII. 1541. His brave housekeeping and goodly chapel of singing-men were kept at Rushbrooke hall, near Bury St. Edmund's, where his family had been seated from a very early period. He was the lineal ancestor of Henry Jermyn, created lord Jermyn of Edmundsbury by king Charles I. and earl of St. Alban's by Charles II.

P. 35. *Proclamation of queen Jane.* In consequence of Grafton having printed this proclamation, he was declared to have forfeited the office of queen's printer; see the patent of John Cawoode's appointment in Rymer's Fœdera, vol. xv. p. 356, and Ames's Typographical Antiquities, by Dibdin, vol. iii. p. 482. The proclamation has been reprinted in the Harleian Miscellany, (Park's edition,) vol. i. p. 405.

P. 37. *The royal livery.* The passage relating to the princess Elizabeth's entry should conclude thus,—" all in green guarded with white, velvet, satin, taffety, and cloth, according to their qualities." Green and white formed the livery of the Tudors. At the marriage of Arthur prince of Wales the yeomen of the guard were in large jackets of damask, *white and green*, embroidered before and behind with garlands of vine leaves, and in the middle a red rose. In the great picture at Windsor castle of the embarkation at Dover in 1520, the Harry Grace à Dieu is surrounded with targets, bearing the various royal badges, each placed on a field party per pale *white and green*. The painting called king Arthur's round table at Winchester castle, supposed to have been repainted in the reign of Henry VII. is divided into compartments of *white and green*. The " queenes colours " are also alluded to in the following story of a rude jest passed on the new Rood in Saint Paul's :

" Not long after this (in 1554) a merry fellow came into Pauls, and spied the Rood with Mary and John new set up ; whereto, among a great sort of people, he made low curtesie, and said : Sir, your Mastership is welcome to towne. I had thought to have talked further with your Mastership, but that ye be here clothed in the Queenes colours. I hope ye be but a summer's bird, in that ye be dressed in white and greene." (Foxe, Actes and Monuments, iii. 114.)

Among the attendants on queen Mary in p. 38, three liveries are mentioned, green and white, red and white, and blue and green. The men in red and white were the servants of the lord treasurer (see p. 12, where several other liveries are described), and the blue and green would be those of the earl of Arundel or some other principal nobleman. Blue and white was perhaps king Philip's livery (p. 79).

In p. 59 we find that in 1554 even the naval uniform of England was white and green, both for officers and mariners. In note ᵈ in that page for "wearing" read "were in," which, without altering the sense, completes the grammar.

The city trained bands were, in 1557, ordered to have white coats welted with green, with red crosses (see p. 164).

The lady Elizabeth, however, did not give green and white to her own men. From two other passages (pp. 57, 120) we find her livery was scarlet or fine red, guarded with black velvet; and from the description of her coronation procession in p. 186, it seems that red or " crimson " was retained for her livery when queen.

P. 41. *Master Thomas a Bruges.* The person drowned is called by Stowe " Master T. Bridges sonne." He was therefore not a son, but a nephew, of the lieutenant of the Tower, sir *John* Brydges. In Foxe's Actes and Monuments, bishop Ridley relates a conversation which he had with doctor Feckenham and secretary Bourn, when in the Tower, which was commenced thus, " Master Thomas of Bridges said, at his brother master lieutenant's boord, I pray you, master doctors, tell me what a heretike is." (Foxe, vol. iii. p. 42.)

P. 44. *Funeral of John lord Dudley.* This is thus recorded in the register of St. Margaret's Westminster: " 1553, September 18. Sir John Sutton knyght, Lorde Baron of Dudley." And that of his widow (see p. 61, and Note in p. 338) occurs under her *maiden* name: " 1554, April 28. The Lady Cysslye Gray." The latter extraordinary circumstance is probably attributable only to the high rank of the Greys:—she was great-aunt to the Lady Jane. His son, " The right honorable sir Edwarde Dudley knighte, Baron of Dudleye, the lord Dudleye," was buried in the same church on the 12th August, 1586; and his great-grandson, " Sir Ferdinando Sutton knight, Baro: Dudley," [but really the son and heir apparent of Edward then lord Dudley,] Nov. 23, 1621. Also in 1600, Mary lady Dudley, widow of the former Edward, and sister to Charles lord Howard of Effingham, lord admiral. She died Aug. 21, 1600, and a monument with her recumbent effigy, and a kneeling effigy of her second husband Richard Mompesson esquire, now remains near the south-east door of the church. See the History of St. Margaret's Church by the Rev. Mackenzie E. C. Walcott, M.A. 1847, 8vo. p. 19.

P. 50. *No priest that has a wife shall not minister or say mass.* The numbers to whom this prohibition would apply may be imagined from the many marriages of priests which occur within a short period in the register of one parish, St. Margaret's Westminster :— .

1549. Feb. The fyrste day. Mʳ Doctoʳ Henry Egylsby, prieste, with Tamasyne Darke.

1551. April. The vjᵗʰ day. Mʳ John Reed, priest, with Isbelle Wyldon.

—— Oct. The vjᵗʰ day. Syr William Langborow, prieste, with Helen Olyver.

—— Dec. The xxxj day. Raffe Felde, prieste, with Helen Chesterfyld.

1551. April. The xxiijᵗⁱ day. Sir William Harvarde, prieste, with Alyce Kemyshe.

—— Dec. The xxvij day.. Sir Frauncis Constantyne, priest, with Alyce Warcoppe.

1552. Jan. The xxiijᵗⁱ day. Sir Marmaduce Pullen, priest, with Margaret Pen.

On the miseries and scandals which ensued on the forced dissolution of these marriages it is sufficient to refer to the works of Foxe, Strype, &c.

P. 50. *Every parish to make an altar, and to have a cross and staff.* Among many expenses incurred on the restoration of the Romish worship at St. Margaret's Westminster for rebuilding and adorning the altars, erecting a holy-water stock, making church furniture and vestments, and providing sacred utensils, occur the following entries, having special reference to the order mentioned in the text :

" Item, payde to a paynter for wasshyng owte of the scriptures of the highe altar table . . . . xij*d*.

" Item, payde for a crosse of copper and gylte, with Mary and John, with a foote of copper . . . . xxx*s*.

" Item, payde for a crosse-clothe of taffata, with a picture of the Trynytie, and for a table of waynskot, and for the payntyng of the Crucifix, Mary, and John, in the highe altar table . . . . xlij*s*. viij*d*.

" Item, payde for tenne pottelles of oyle . . . . . xj*s*. x*d*.

" Item, payde for the Roode, Mary and John . . . . x *li*.

And, next year, " Item, payde for payntyng the Roode, Mary and John . xl*s*.

In the first year of Elizabeth all was again destroyed—

" Payde to John Rialle, for his iij dayse work, to take down the Roode, Mary and John . . . . ij*s*. viij*d*.

" Item, payde to James Anderson for ij dayse work labouryng about the same, and for carieng of the stones and rubbishe abowt th' altars . . . xij*d*.

(Then follow several similar payments to other workmen).

" Item, to John Rialle, for taking down the tabille on the high altar, and takyng down the holly-water stock . . . . xij*d*.

" Item, to iij poore men for beryng of the alltar tabelle to Mr. Hodgis . iiij*d*.

" Item, for clevyng and sawyng of the Roode, Mary and John . . xij*d*.

Pp. 63, 139. *Corpus Christi day.* After the accession of Mary (says our Diarist, p. 63) this festival was kept with goodly processions, and torches garnished in the old fashion, and staff torches burning, and many canopies. All these particulars are confirmed by the parochial accounts of Saint Margaret's Westminster (still in perfect preservation at this and a still earlier period), from which the following extracts are made:

(In 1 Mariæ) Item, payde for breade, ale, and beere on Corpus Christie day   xix*d.*

Item, payde for a ffrynge of si[l]ke for the canypye, wayenge xviij ounces q°rter di. price the ownce xij*d.* summa . . . . . . xviij*s.* iiij*d.*

Item, payde to the brotherer for fasshonyng of the canopie and settyng on of the ffrynge . . . .   xiiij*d.*

Item, for iiij knoppes for the canopie staves, alle gilte . . . iiij*s.*

Item, payde for garnysshyng the iiij torches for Corpus Christye day, and the cariage of them from Londone . . . . .   ij*s.*

Item, flowres to the same torches . . . .   vj*d.*

Item, payde to iiij torche-bearers on Corpus Christye day .   viij*d.*

(In 2 Mariæ) Item, payde for flowres for the torches on Corpus Christie day   vij*d.*

Item, payde for v staf torches . . . . . x*s.* x*d.*

Item, payde for the garnyshyng of them . . . . xx*d.*

Item, payde to v men for beryng of the sayde torches . . . x*d.*

Item, payde for breade, ale, and beere . . . . xx*d.*

(In 3 Mariæ) Item, payde for iiij newe torchis wayeng lxxxxij*li. di.* at v*d.* the *li.* xxxviij*s.* viij*d.*

Item, payde for bote-hyre and for cariage of thame torchis . . vj*d.*

Item, payde for garnysshyng of the sayde iiij torchis . . xx*d.*

Item, payde to iiij men for beryng of the iiij great torchis . . viij*d.*

Item, payde to iiij children for bering the iiij staf torchis . . iiij*d.*

Item, payde to a man for beryng the great stremer . . . j*d.*

Item, payde hym that did beare the crosse . . . . ij*d.*

Item, payde for breade, wyne, ale, and beere . . . xxj*d.*

Item, payde for flowres the same day . . . . iiij*d.*

Pp. 64, 69, 74, 75. *Removes of king Philip and queen Mary.* These are thus recorded in the churchwardens' accounts of St. Margaret's Westminster:

"Allso payde to the ryngers the xij day of August (1553) when the queenes grace wente to Richmonde ; and the xxij day of September when she came from Richmonde to Westminster ; and the xix^th day of December, when her grace wente to Richemont, and the xxx day of December when her grace cam to Westminster . . . xvj*d.*

"Item, payde to the ryngers when the queenes majestie went from Westminster to Rychmond the xxix of May [1554; see p. 64] . . . iiij*d.*

"Item, payde the xvij. and xviij. day of August, when the kyng and the quene cam from Richemonde to Sowthwarke, and so from thens to Westmynster, for bread and drynk to the ryngers . . . . . . vj*d.*

"Item, the xxj. day when they came to the mynster, and allso the xxiij. day when they went to Hampton Coorte . . . . . viij*d.*

"Item, payde to the ryngers the xviij^tl [*read* 28th] day of September, when the kyng and the queenes majestie cam to Westmynster [see p. 69] . . iiij*d.*

" Item, payde to the ryngers of the belles the xij. day of November, when the kyng and the queenes majesties cam to the mynster to the masse of the holy gost [see p. 74]   iiijd.

" Item, payde to the ryngers on sayncte Andrewis day, when the kynges majestie came to the mynster   .   .   .   .   iiijd.

See this last mentioned in p. 77, but without noticing that it was the feast of Saint Andrew.

P. 67. *King and Queen's style.* The letters patent directing the lord chancellor to issue writs announcing the king and queen's style, dated at Winchester 27 July, 1554, are printed in Rymer's Fœdera, xv. 404.

Pp. 76, 82, 83. *Juego de cannas.* This sport, which the Spanish cavaliers brought with them from their native country, was long a favourite there. When Lord Berners was ambassador in Spain in 1518, " on midsummer daye in the morninge the king, with xxiij with him, well apparelled in cootes and clokes of goulde and gouldsmythe work, on horsback, in the said market-place (at Saragossa), ranne and caste canes after the countreye maner, whearas the kinge did very well (and was) much praysed ; a fresh sight for once or twise to behold, and afterward nothing. Assoone as the cane is caste, they flye; wherof the Frenche ambassador sayd, that it was a good game to teche men to flye. My lord Barners answered, that the Frenchmen learned it well besides Gingate, at the jurney of Spurres." (Letter from the ambassador in MS. Cotton. Vesp. C. i. 177.) It continued in practice when Charles prince of Wales visited Spain in 1623, and a pamphlet entitled, " A relation of the Royal Festivities and Juego de Canas, a turnament of darting with reedes after the manner of Spaine, made by the king of Spaine at Madrid, the 21st of August this present yeere 1623," is reprinted in Somers's Tracts and in Nichols's Progresses of King James I. vol. iv.—" The Juego de Cannas," remarks Sir Walter Scott, " was borrowed from the Moors, and is still practised by Eastern nations, under the name of El Djerid. It is a sort of rehearsal of the encounter of their light horsemen, armed with darts, as the Tourney represented the charge of the feudal cavaliers with their lances. In both cases, the differences between sport and reality only consisted in the weapons being sharp or pointless."

> " So had he seen in fair Castile
> The youth in glittering squadrons start,
> Sudden the flying jennet wheel,
> And hurl the unexpected dart."
>
> (Scott's Lay of the Last Minstrel.)

P. 79. *A Spanish lord buried at Saint Margaret's Westminster.* From the records of that church this is shown to have been " John de Mendoca, knyght." During the time that the servants of king Philip were about the court at Westminster, several other Spaniards occur in the same register : their names are here extracted :

1554. Sept. The xvij day.   Martyne, a spanyard.

—— Oct. The xjth day.   Martyne, a spanearde.

——   „   The xvijth day.   Sr Uther, a launce knyght.

——   „   The xviijth day.   Sr Henry, a launce knyght. .

—— Dec. The xxiij day.   Joh'n de mendoca, a knyght spaynearde.

—— March 2.   Joh'n de bevaunte [Debevaunco in the churchwardens' accounts].

——   „   The xth day.   Philippe, a spaynyshe childe.

——   „   The xiijth day.   Peter, a spaynearde, slayn w^t a horsse.

1555. May. The vjth day.   Francisco de espilla.

—— Auguste. The xxvij day.   Peter, a spaynearde.

—— September. The xjth day.   Agnes   , a spaynearde.

—— November. The firste day.   Fraunces, a spaynyshe childe.

——   „   The vjth day.   Margaret, uxor Ispanie.

—— January. The xvth day.   Corby, a portyngal.

1556. November. 6to die.   Marie spaniard.

1557. March 28.   Cornelius, spanyard.

—— May. primo die.   Peter Angle, spanyard.

—— June. 28 die.   Alberte, a spanyerd, off syknesse, of the house [*i. e.* a servant of the royal household.

The names of most of these are repeated in the churchwardens' accounts, indeed several times over, in this way :

Item, of Uther, a launceknyght, for iiij tapers	xvj*d.*
Item, of Uther, the launceknyght, for iiij torches . . .	viij*d.*
Item, of Uther, the launceknyght, for his grave . . .	vj*s.* viij*d.*
Item, of Uther, the launceknyght, for the clothe . . .	viij*d.*

Item, of Mr. Joh'n Demendoca, for knylle and peales . . .	xviij*d.*
Item, at the obsequy of Mr. Mendoca, kept the second and third day of January, for iij. tapers	xx*d.*
Item, at the obsequy of Mr. Joh'n Mendoca, for the belles . .	xviij*d.*

There is one Spanish marriage recorded in the register, but without names, merely thus : " 1555 Nov. the xth day a Spanyeard," and a similar difficulty was felt in christenings, as " 1558, Feb. the ixth day Mariana ispanica," and " March the xxj day Franciscus jspanicus." In Oct. that year occurs " The xxij^d day, Philippe Ruyz a spaynearde."

P. 90. *At the Grocers' feast my lord mayor did choose master Lee sheriff for the king.* The order observed " Upon Midsummer day, for the election of the Sheriffes of London, &c." will be found in Stowe's Survay, under the head of " Temporall Government." On that day (as still) the sheriffs were elected; but one had been previously " nominated by the Lord Maior according to his prerogative." This was done in the way intimated more than once in these pages, by drinking to him at a feast. A full and curious account of the mode in which this ceremony was performed at the Haberdashers' feast in the year

1583, is given in a letter of Mr. recorder Fleetwood to lord Burghley, printed in Ellis's Orig. Letters, 1st Series, ii. 290.

P. 101. *The blazing star* which is noticed in this page, and of which Stowe's account has been quoted in p. 348, was calculated by Halley to have been the same comet which had before appeared in the year 1264, and which, having completed its presumed revolution of two hundred and ninety-two years, may be expected to appear again in the present year, 1848. The learned Fabricius described the comet of 1556 as of a size equal to half that of the moon. Its beams were short and flickering, with a motion like that of the flame of a conflagration or of a torch waved by the wind. It alarmed the Emperor Charles the Fifth, who, believing his death at hand, is said to have exclaimed

His ergo indiciis me mea fata vocant.

This warning, it is asserted, contributed to the determination which the monarch formed, and executed a few months later, of resigning the imperial crown to his brother Ferdinand.

P. 111. *Funeral of (Robert) Heneage esquire.* Machyn was wrong in the christian name, giving, as in some other cases, the name of the son to the father. This was Robert Heneage esquire, auditor of the duchy of Lancaster, and surveyor of the queen's woods beyond Trent; and father of sir Thomas Heneage, afterwards chancellor of the duchy of Lancaster, and a privy councillor to queen Elizabeth. Though Stowe does not mention his monument at St. Katharine Creechurch, Collins (in Peerage, *tit.* Finch earl of Winchelsea) states that effigies in brass of Robert Heneage and his wife, who was Margaret sister to Thomas earl of Rutland, remained in that church, but the inscription was effaced.

P. 113. *Funeral of mistress Soda.* This singular name, which our Diarist alters to "Sawde," and which elsewhere occurs as Soday, was probably Spanish, the lady's husband having been a servant of queen Katharine. John Soda, the son, was apothecary to queen Mary, to which office he was appointed for life by letters patent dated 4 Jan. 1554, with a yearly fee of forty marks: see this document in Rymer, vol. xv. p. 359. His new-year's gift to the queen in 1556 was six boxes of marmalade and cordial. His daughter was the wife of alderman Greenway (see p. 405).

P. 114. *The Queen's return from Croydon.* "Item, payde for ryngyng of the belles at the cumyng of the queenes majestie from Croydyn to Westminster the xxjth of September iiij*d.*" This entry, from the accounts of St. Margaret's Westminster, differs two days from our Diarist.

Ibid. *Funeral of sir Humphrey Foster.* "Sir Humfray Foster knyght departed owt of this transytory worlde on fryday the xviijth daye of September, in the seconde and thyrde yers of our soveraynes kynge Philip and queen Marye, who left to his hole executor Mr. William Foster, son and hayre to the foresayde sir Humphery Foster; which was buryed the xxv[th] of September, in the parishe of Saint Nicolas besyde Charynge-crosse in the fylde, whose morners were these.

> Mr. William Foster, his sonne and heyre, chef morner.
> Mr. Wentworth.   Mr. Covertes.
> Sir Anthony Hungerford.   Mr. Myndes.
> Master Langley bare his standartt, and Mr. Shreve his pennon of armes.

Offycers for the oversyght of the same enterement, Chester herralde and Rugcrosse pursevant." (MS. Coll. Arm. I. 3. f. 101[b].)

P. 123. *Funeral of lady Chaloner.* This appears to have been the first wife of sir Thomas Chaloner, a distinguished statesman and author, who lived in his latter years "in a fair house of his own building in Clerkenwell close," built on part of the site of the dissolved nunnery. (See Biographia Britannica, &c.) Her first husband had been sir Thomas Leigh, of Hoxton, who died Nov. 25, 1545 ; and his poetical epitaph, formerly at Shoreditch, is printed in Ellis's History of that parish, p. 54. The lady has not been mentioned by her second husband's biographers, for sir Thomas afterwards married Ethelreda, daughter of Edward Frodsham, esq. of Elton in Cheshire, and she was the mother of sir Thomas Chaloner the younger, governor to Henry prince of Wales. This is shown by the epitaph of the latter at Chiswick, which states him to have died in 1615, aged 51. He was therefore born in 1564, the year before his father's death. Sir Thomas Chaloner the elder was born in 1515, and dying Oct. 14, 1565, was buried in St. Paul's cathedral. His widow Ethelreda was re-married to Edward Brockett, esq. of Wheathampsted, Herts, second son of sir John Brockett, which Edward lived until 1599. (See his epitaph in Clutterbuck's Herts, vol. i. p. 523.)

P. 137. *Celebration of Ascension day.* On this occasion in the preceding year (1556) the churchwardens of St. Margaret's Westminster made the following payments :

"Item, payde for breade, wyne, ale, and beere, upon th' Ascension evyn and day, agaynst my lord abbot and his covent cam in procession, and for strewyng erbes the same day, vij*s.* j*d.*"

Pp. 162, 163. *Soldiers sent to Calais.* The several parishes of the counties where musters took place were obliged to send their quota. Thus the churchwardens of St. Margaret's Westminster paid "for setting owt of soldyers the vij[th] day of January as apperethe by a bylle, iiij*li.* viij*s.* vij*d.* ob." "Item, for settyng forthe fyve soldyers to Portismothe the last yere of quene Mary xxxiij*s.* iiij*d.*"

P. 163. *Funeral of lady Powis.* Though the interment of this lady (as stated in p. 362) is not recorded in the parish register of Saint Margaret's Westminster, yet the following entries relative to her funeral occur in the churchwardens' accounts:

Item, of my lady Anne Pois for iiij tapers   .   .   .   . ij*s.* viij*d.*
Item, at the obsequy of my lady Anne Poys for the belles   .   . iij*s.* iiij*d.*
Item, of my lady Anne Pois for the clothe   .   .   .   . viij*d.*

P. 164. *So to the abbay to the masse.* " Item, payde for ryngyng when the Queenes Ma^d cam to the masse of the holy gost the xx^ti of January, vj*d*." (Accounts of St. Margaret's Westminster.)

P. 172. *Marriage of alderman John White.* This civic senator, whose name has frequently occurred in this volume, was the son of Robert White, of Farnham in Surrey. He was of the Grocers' company, served sheriff in 1556, and lord mayor in 1563. His first marriage has been mentioned in p. 378, in the note on the funeral of his brother the bishop of Winchester. The imperfect passage in p. 172 relates to his second marriage with the widow of alderman Ralph Greenway. She was Katharine, daughter of John Sodaye of London, apothecary to Queen Mary (see p. 403), and was again married to Jasper Allen, and buried at St. Dunstan's in the East, Oct. 9, 1576. In her will, dated the same year, she mentions her brother Richard Sodaye. Sir John White was buried at Aldershot in Hampshire in 1573 : see his epitaph, with some extracts from his will, in the Collectanea Topogr. et Genealogica, vol. vii. p. 212. See also his funeral atchievements engraved at the conclusion of the Introduction to the present Volume.

P. 185. *Funeral of mistress Matson.* Anne, daughter and heir of Richard Sackville, of Chepsted, Surrey, married first to Henry Shelley, of Worminghurst, Sussex, esquire, and had issue; and secondly to Thomas Matson, gent. (Visit. Sussex.) His funeral occurs in p. 208.

P. 206. *The Queen's grace stood at her standing in the further park.* "Shooting at deer with a cross-bow (remarks Mr. Hunter in his New Illustrations of Shakespeare) was a favourite amusement of ladies of rank; and buildings with flat roofs, called *stands* or *standings*, were erected in many parks, as in that of Sheffield, and in that of Pilkington near Manchester, expressly for the purpose of this diversion." They seem to have been usually concealed by bushes or trees, so that the deer would not perceive their enemy. In Shakspere's Love-Labours Lost, at the commencement of the fourth Act, the Princess repairs to a Stand—

> Then, Forester my friend, where is the bush
> That we must stand and play the murtherer in ?
> *Forester.* Here-by, upon the edge of yonder coppice,
> A Stand where you may make the fairest shoot.

Mr. Hunter further remarks that they were often made ornamental, as may be concluded from the following passage in Goldingham's poem called " The Garden Plot," where, speaking of a bower, he compares it with one of these stands—

> To term it Heaven I think were little sin,
> Or Paradise, for so it did appear ;
> So far it passed the bowers that men do banquet in,
> Or *standing made to shoot at stately deer.*

P. 216. *One West, a new doctor.* Probably this " railer " at roodlofts was the person commemorated in the following epitaph, who was not actually a doctor : " Here lyeth buried Mr. Reginald West, batchelor in divinity, and late parson of this parish, who deceased the second of October anno Domini 1563, for whose sincere, pure, and godly doctrine, as also his virtuous end, the Lord be praised for evermore." Under the Communion table at St. Margaret Pattens. Stowe.

Pp. 218, 228. *Sermons by bishop Jewell.* In the edition of bishop Jewell's Works now in the course of publication by the Parker Society, the editor, the Rev. John Ayre, M.A. remarks that the challenge which originated the bishop's important controversy with Dr. Cole was first given in his sermon at Paul's Cross, Nov. 26, 1559—the occasion noticed by Machyn in p. 218. " The sermon, with the challenge amplified, was preached at the court, March 17, 1560 [as mentioned in p. 228]; and repeated at Paul's Cross March 31, being the second sunday before Easter." This last date is from the contemporary title-page of the sermon itself: and therefore is not to be doubted. Our Diarist, however (p. 229) says that Crowley preached at Paul's Cross on that day.

P. 236. *Funeral of mistress Grafton,—*" the wife of master Grafton the chief master of the hospital, and of Bridewell." This was Richard Grafton the printer, who is known from his books to have resided at Christ's hospital, and from this passage it seems to have been in an official capacity. There are other items in the present volume which may be added to what Dr. Dibdin terms " the comparatively full account " of Grafton, in his edition of the Typographical Antiquities, vol. iii. He was evidently a man active in public business. He occurs twice as warden of the Grocers' company (pp. 90, 108), as a master of Bridewell (pp. 205), and as an overseer for the repairs of Saint Paul's cathedral (p. 262). He was also elected to Parliament for the city of London in 1554 and 1556, and in 1562 for Coventry.

P. 287. *The Skinners attend the Merchant-taylors' feast.* In the 1st Rich. III. a dispute for precedency between the Skinners and Merchant-taylors was determined by agreement that either should take precedence in alternate years, and that the master and wardens of each should dine with the other company on their respective feasts of Corpus Christi and the Nativity of St. John the Baptist. See the ordinance effecting this arrangement in Herbert's Twelve City Companies, vol. ii. p. 319; and see remarks by the present writer in Archæologia, vol. xxx. p. 500.

P. 292. *Saint Anthony's school.* This notice of Saint Anthony's school, so flourishing in 1562 as to have a hundred scholars, is remarkable, inasmuch as it seems to have shared the fate of the religious foundations. Stowe says in his Survay, " This schoole was commended in the reign of Henry the sixth, and sithense commended above others, but now decayed, and come to nothing by taking that from it which thereunto belonged," and he ascribes its " spoile " to one Johnson, the schoolmaster, who was " made prebend of Windsor." (Edmund Johnson, installed canon of Windsor 1560. Le Neve.)

P. 22. *Funeral of mistress Cowper, wife of the sheriff of London.* John Cowper, fish-monger, sheriff 1552, buried at St. Magnus. Arms, Azure, a saltire engrailed between four trefoils slipped or, on a chief of the second three dolphins embowed of the first. (List by Wm. Smith, Rouge-dragon.) "John Cooper, fishmonger, alderman, who was put by his turne of maioralty, [died] 1584." (Stowe.)

Ibid. *Funeral of mistress Basilia Cowper, late wife of master Huntley haberdasher, and after wife of master Towllys, alderman and sheriff.* This lady's first husband, Thomas Huntley, haberdasher, was sheriff 1540. His arms, Argent, on a chevron between three buck's heads erased sable three hunting-horns of the first. Her second husband was John Towles, sheriff 1554; buried at St. Michael's in Cornhill 1548. Arms, Party per pale and chevron ermine and sable, four cinquefoils counterchanged. (List by Wm. Smith, Rouge-dragon.) Stowe in his Survay calls him *Tolus*, and relates a story of a bequest he made to St. Michael's parish, which was "not performed but concealed." The name, it may be remarked, was derived from one of the churches dedicated to St. Olave; John atte Olave's would become John Toolys, and from the same abbreviation we have still Tooley Street in Southwark. The lady's third husband was probably John Cowper who occurs in the list of freemen of the mystery of the Fyshemongers in 1537 (Herbert's Twelve City Companies, ii. 7,) and who may have been father of the alderman mentioned in the preceding note.

P. 58. *Funeral of lady Ascough.* Sir Christopher Ascough, draper, who was the son of John Ascough of Edmonton in Middlesex, had been sheriff in 1525-6, lord mayor 1533-4, and was buried at St. John the Evangelist's in Watling-street. Arms, Gules, on a fesse argent, between three ass's heads couped or, as many estoiles azure. (List by Wm. Smith, Rouge-dragon.)

P. 76. *Funeral of sir Hugh Rich, K.B.* Having married Anne, daughter and sole heir of sir John Wentworth, of Gosfield in Essex, his body was buried in that church. His widow married secondly Henry lord Maltravers, only son of the earl of Arundel; he died at Brussels, June 30, 1556. She married thirdly William Deane esquire, her servant, nephew to Alexander Nowell, dean of Saint Paul's. Having had no issue, she died Dec. 5, 1580, and was buried with her first husband at Gosfield.

P. 90. *Master Lee chosen sheriff.* Son of Roger Leigh of Wellington in Shropshire, and apprentice of sir Rowland Hill, whose niece, Alice Barker, he married. He became "Sir Thomas Leigh, maior, the first yeare of Q. Elizabeth, 1559. He dwelled in the Old Jury, his house joyning on the north of Mercers Chapell, where he was buried. Arms, Gules, on a cross engrailed argent between four unicorn's heads erased or, (five hurts each charged with an ermine spot. His sonnes have since altred the armes to, Gules, a cross engrailed and in dexter chief a lozenge argent." (List by Wm. Smith, Rouge-dragon.) Sir Thomas Leigh died Nov. 17, 1571. His epitaph at the Mercers' Chapel will be found in Stowe's Survay and in Dugdale's Baronage, vol. ii. p. 464. By his second son William he was ancestor of the Lords Leigh of Stoneleigh, and by his third son William, grand-father of Francis Leigh, earl of Chichester.

P. 218. *Captain Grimston arraigned for the loss of Calais.* This was sir Edward Grimston, who had been appointed comptroller of Calais, Aug. 28, 1552 (King Edward's Diary.) See the pedigree of Grimston in Clutterbuck's Hertfordshire, i. 95.

P. 241. *This year (1560) were all the Roodlofts taken down in London.* Those parishes which had been backward in removing this relic of idolatry were now compelled to do so by authority. "Memorandum. At a vestry holden the 27th day of December in Anno 1560, there was showed unto the parishioners a letter sent from the lord of Canterbury's grace, directed to master alderman Draper, sheriff of London, and to the churchwardens with the rest of the parish, concerning the translating and pulling down of the rood-loft; whereupon it was agreed by the whole vestry, that the rood-loft should be taken down and translated by the discretion of the churchwardens. In witness whereof we the said parishioners have set-to our names the day and year above written." (Account of the church of St. Dunstan's in the East, by the Rev. T. B. Murray.)

So at St. Margaret's, Westminster, where the Rood itself had been removed in 1559 (see p. 399,) the Roodloft was left to the following year. It had been built at great expense in 1519, and its "new re-forming" was also a considerable charge to the pa-rishioners:—

"Item, paide to joyners and labowrers abowt the takyng downe and new reformyng of the Roode-loft, as by a particuler booke therof mad dothe and may appeare, xxxvij*li.* x*s.* ij*d.*

"Item, paide for boordes, glew, nayles, and other necessaries belonging to the saide loft   .   .   .   .   .   .·   .   . xiiij*li.* xiij*s.* ix*d.*

"Item, paide to a paynter for payntyng the same   .   .   . xij*d.*

(Then follow several other charges respecting the scaffolding.)

INDEX.

3 K

GLOSSARIAL INDEX.

about a man's body, to be hid or carried covertly." See its substance in Strype, Annals, ii. 603.

Death with a dart in his hand 125.

doer 46 ; qu. any office intended? or merely that the earl of Surrey was his grandfather's *deputy*, in doing or performing the duties of earl marshal?

dolle, a dole, or portion 197.

drousselars *rather* dronsselars 13 ; a kind of tabor or kettle-drum, usually written dronslade or dromslade.

dullo 33, duyllyll 47, dulle 73, duwylle 89, duwlle 96, dullvyll 125 ; a merry devil in the lord mayor's show, usually discharging squibs.

foist 270, fuyst 47, fuste 294 ; what is now called a barge ; *see* penoys.

gaune, or gang, week 236 ; Rogation week, when parochial perambulations were made.

genetes, gennets 124.

geton 13, gettene 38, gytton 19, 20 ; a guidon, the small flag for cavalry, &c.

giant 20, 45, 89, 186, 191.

godys man to the poor 170 ; probably meaning a bestower of goods.

"goodman of the house," and "goodwife " 34.

grandsire 164, grandfather.

green and white, the royal livery 37, 38, 59, 163, 164, 167. See note in p. 397.

hall, keeping of 28.

harness 33, 52, 79, 146, 155, 282, 293. The use of this word for body-armour is remarkably exemplified in a passage of Stowe's Chronicle relating to this very crisis : "On the fryday, which was Candlemasse daie (Feb. 2, 1553-4), the most parte of the householders of London, with the Maior and aldermen, were in harnesse ; yea this day and other daies the justices, sergeants at the law, and other lawyers in Westminsterhal, pleaded in harnesse."

herse of wax 43, 57, 180 ; a frame erected for candles at a funeral : also adorned with pennons, &c. (See introductory note on Funerals.) What we now call a hearse is described in p. 101 as " a wagon with iiij wheels, all covered with black."

hobby-horse 33, 89.

hokyll-bone 78.

holy-water stocks 45.

horse-litter, used to convey a corpse 43.

hott-howse, the residence of a bawd 104 ; commonly called a stew, *stupha* or bagnio, hot baths being there taken.

housekeeper, "the best housekeeper of a commoner in London " 293.

hoveles 8.

howslyng after the old fashion 42 ; joining in the mass.

hurly-burly, "herlé-borlé " 41.

in-gratt 17 ; this word is singular, and seems to be by way of a translation of engross, in which sense it here occurs. The common word was regrate, to buy wholesale and sell retail. See the Stat. 5 and 6 Edw. VI. against regrating, c. xiv. where the words are " regrators and *ingrossers*," which supplies the deficient word in the text. (Stat. of Realm, IV. part I. 148.)

ippocras 199, 216, 237.

Jack o' Lent 33 ; a puppet, thrown at in Lent, like Shrove-cocks. Brand's Antiquit. Ash Wednesday. Nares's Glossary.

jebett 54, jubett 60 ; gibbet.

kirtles, worn by the alms-knights of Windsor 258.

lacquey, "laké " 27.

laske 309, a flux. "Laske, a disease, flux de ventre." Palsgrave. "I have a laske, *sum cita alvo*." Horman.

lectorne 79 ; qu. a lecture?

licence to beg 292. Poor Stowe the chronicler, in his old age, had such a licence.

lodging scocheons 248.

lycted 54. Wyatt lighted, *i. e.* leaped up, behind another rider on horseback.

majesté, at a funeral 43, 160 ; canopy of the herse?

mantyll-frieze 67, *et passim*, probably frieze made purposely for mantles.

marbull-coats 12 ; made with wool or silk of various colours mixed together : see the Gentleman's Magazine, 1835, N. S. vi. 2, 114, 226.

march-paynes 171 ; from the Fr. *masse-pain*, a kind of sweet biscuit.
masket, a masquerade or show 276.
mastés 191, mastiffs. Fr. *mastin*. Palsg.
Milaner, " melener " 21, *now* milliner, a dealer in goods from Milan.
moketors 32, handkerchiefs. Fr. *mouchoir*. " Mockendar for a chyldre (*sic*), mouchoir. Mockedar," *id*. Palsgrave. Compare Cotgrave, v. Baverette, bavon, &c. " For eyen and nose the nedethe a mokadour." Lydgate's Minor Poems, p. 30, edit. Halliwell.
monumentt, qu. funeral or month's mind? 24.
mores-dance 20, 33, 89, 191.
mores-pikes 146, 230.
much-a-do, " myche a doo " 2.
murrey colour 195.
musters, a colour 195 ; for musterdevelers, or mustrevilers, probably cloth made at Montevillier, near Caudebec. " Mustredules colour, gris mealé." Palsgrave.
muscadell 199, 216.
musysyoners 125.

occupying her own gear, or bawdry, 295 (twice), 299.
" office taken away from him," a phrase for the misfortune afterwards termed being made a cuckold, 302.
oranges 196. A similar use of this fruit as a sportive missile occurs in a letter of lord Mountjoy written in 1516. A spy which he had sent to Lyons had seen the French king " many tymes uppon the water of Som with his young noblemen castyng oranges oute of one bote into another, and usyng many other pastymes with theym." Excerpta Historica, p. 288. *See* Porttyngales.
ouches, " owtchys " 130, set jewels, or brooches.

panchyd with his own sword, a man murdered, 170.
paper-ryall 291 ; marked with the crown ? Archæol. xii. pl. xv.
pastes, head-dresses for brides 240. " Paste for a lady or woman, unes paces." Palsgrave. Parishes kept " pastes " to let out at weddings, as they did the herse-cloths for funerals : and the customary charge made at St. Margaret's Westminster in the reigns of Edward VI. and Mary was

xij*d*. In the inventory of the church-goods of that parish in 1564, occurs, " Cerclet for brydes. Item, one past for brydes sett with perle and stone." But at this time its use seems to have been discontinued, as no such receipts occur as before.
peneston 91, a kind of coarse woollen cloth, mentioned in Stat. 43 Eliz. c. 10.
penoys 73, 96, a pinnace ; *see* fuyst.
porttyngales 237 ; oranges, called likewise in some parts of Italy *portogalli*.
preacher, " new preacher " 211, 214 ; applied to the Reformers.
prevermentt of perjury 104.
prick-song 106, 112, 171, 174.
progeny, for pedigree or genealogy, 14.
proper man 63, 177, 225. This was a term somewhat resembling " a tall man," but more commendatory.
prymse, *i. e.* mainprise 91.
pulter 86, *now* poulterer.
pyk-purs and cut-purse 18, 21.
pynion, the old orthography of penon, xxi.

quondam 57, 334 ; Fr. *ci-devant*.
qwarell 121. A quarry or quarrier was a candle containing ordinarily a quarter of a lb. of wax ; here " a great qwarell of half a lb." " *Doppiere*, a certain lyghte of waxe, as we call it a quarriere." W. Thomas, Ital. Dict. 1548.
qwest 15, a jury.
quick, alive, " a qwyck tree and a dead," 186.
qwyckenyng 76.

raylles 155, 157, 213, 245, 262, given to female mourners. A cloak, or loose gown ; see Nares.
recheuusly 40.
reculyd 202, recoiled.
the Reformation, whipping-post so called, 164.
regalls 45, 107, 180, 282.
regiment, equivalent to army 358.
rings, false, 109. See note in p. 408.
rochet 226, 229, 251. The rochet was " a linen vest, like a surplice, worn by bishops, under their satin robe. The word, it is true, is not obsolete, nor the thing disused, but it is little known, and therefore deserves explanation." (Nares.) Like " lawn sleeves " or the lately discarded wig, it seems to have

THE

CAMDEN SOCIETY,

FOR THE PUBLICATION OF

EARLY HISTORICAL AND LITERARY REMAINS.

AT a General Meeting of the Camden Society held at the Freemasons' Tavern, Great Queen Street, Lincoln's Inn Fields, on Tuesday the 2nd of May, 1848,

THE RIGHT HON. LORD BRAYBROOKE IN THE CHAIR,

HIS Lordship having opened the business of the Meeting,

The Secretary read the Report of the Council agreed upon at their meeting of the 19th April last, whereupon it was

Resolved, That the said Report be received and adopted, and that the Thanks of the Society be given to the Director and Council for their services.

The Thanks of the Society were also voted to the Editors of the Society's publications for the past year; and to the Local Secretaries.

The Secretary then read the Report of the Auditors agreed upon at their Meeting of the 29th April last, whereupon it was

Resolved, That the said Report be received and adopted, and that the Thanks of the Society be given to the Auditors for their trouble.

The Thanks of the Society having then been voted to the Treasurer,

a

The Meeting proceeded to the election of Officers, when

The Right Hon. Lord BRAYBROOKE, F.S.A.

was elected PRESIDENT of the Society; and

THOMAS AMYOT, Esq. F.R.S., F.S.A.
WILLIAM HENRY BLAAUW, Esq. M.A.
Ven. CHARLES PARR BURNEY, D.D., F.R.S., F.S.A.
JOHN PAYNE COLLIER, Esq. Treas. S.A.
CHARLES PURTON COOPER, Esq. Q.C., D.C.L., F.R.S., F.S.A.
WILLIAM DURRANT COOPER, Esq. F.S.A.
BOLTON CORNEY, Esq. M.R.S.L.
Sir HENRY ELLIS, K.H., F.R.S., Sec. S.A.
The Rev. JOSEPH HUNTER, F.S.A.
PETER LEVESQUE, Esq. F.S.A.
THOMAS JOSEPH PETTIGREW, Esq. F.R.S., F.S.A.
HENRY CRABB ROBINSON, Esq. F.S.A.
THOMAS STAPLETON, Esq. F.S.A.
WILLIAM JOHN THOMS, Esq. F.S.A. and
Sir HARRY VERNEY, Bart. M.P.

were elected as the COUNCIL; and

JOHN YONGE AKERMAN, Esq. Sec. S.A.
Rev. WILLIAM HARNESS, M.A. and
FREDERICK OUVRY, Esq. F.S.A.

were elected AUDITORS of the Society for the ensuing year.

Thanks were then voted to the Secretary; and to Lord BRAYBROOKE, for the interest he had always taken in the welfare of the Society, and for his able conduct in the Chair.

ELECTION OF OFFICERS, 1848.

AT a Meeting of the COUNCIL of the Camden Society held at No. 25, Parliament Street, Westminster, on Wednesday the 3rd May, 1848,

The Rt. Hon. Lord BRAYBROOKE, the President, in the Chair;

THOMAS AMYOT, Esq. was elected Director; JOHN PAYNE COLLIER, Esq. Treasurer; and WILLIAM J. THOMS, Esq. Secretary, for the Year next ensuing.

REPORT OF THE COUNCIL

OF

THE CAMDEN SOCIETY,

ELECTED 3rd MAY, 1847.

———

THE COUNCIL of the Camden Society, elected on the 3rd of May, 1847, have great pleasure in announcing to the Society that the investment standing in the name of the Trustees of the Society has, during the past year, been increased from £877 10s. 9d. to £900 14s. 9d. Three per cent. Consols. Like every similar institution, the Camden Society has suffered some diminution in its ranks, from the operation of public causes to which it is unnecessary to advert more particularly; but the number of members is still amply sufficient to maintain the Society in its course of usefulness, and to prove the wide interest still felt in the objects for which the Society was instituted.

The Council have added the following gentlemen to the List of Local Secretaries:—

The Rev. J. E. LEEFE, for Bishop Wearmouth;
WILLIAM TRAVIS, Esq., M.D., for Scarborough;
The Rev. J. W. BLAKESLEY, M.A., for Ware; and
RICHARD LEWIS REECE, Esq., for Cardiff, in the place of Richard Reece, Esq., F.S.A., who retires;

and again beg to impress upon the Members resident in the country and possessed of local influence, what important service they may render to the Society by taking upon themselves the office of Local Secretaries, by bringing its works under the immediate notice of friends who take an interest in the early literature and history of the country; or by disseminating through the usual provincial channels of information notices of the Books as they are published, and announcements of such as are forthcoming. The first success of the Camden Society may, in some measure, be attributed to the influence of such voluntary exertions on its behalf, and its continued prosperity cannot fail to be ensured by similar exertions.

The Council have to regret the deaths, during the past year, of—

The Right Hon. Sir JOHN BERNARD BOSANQUET, Knt., F.S.A.
His Grace the LORD ARCHBISHOP OF CANTERBURY.
Right Hon. the COUNTESS CORNWALLIS.
SAMUEL DUCKWORTH, Esq., M.A., Master in Chancery.
BALDWIN FULFORD, Esq.
JOHN BLACK GRACIE, ESQ., F.S.A. Sc.
Right Hon. the EARL OF HARROWBY, F.S.A.
Sir SAMUEL RUSH MEYRICK, K.H., F.S.A.
Right Hon. the EARL OF POWIS, K.G.
FRANCIS RIDDELL REYNOLDS, Esq.
J. W. SOUTHGATE, Esq.
GEORGE STOKES, Esq.
DANIEL WAKEFIELD, Esq., Q.C.
W. ARCHIBALD ARMSTRONG WHITE, Esq., F.R.S., F.S.A.

The Council have, during the past year, added the following works to the List of suggested Publications :

The Day-Book of John Dorne, a foreign bookseller residing in England in the year 1520, from a MS. in the Library of Corpus Christi College, Oxford. To be edited by the Venerable HENRY COTTON, D.C.L., Archdeacon of Cashel, and the Rev. JOHN WILSON, B.D., Fellow of Trinity College, Oxford.

Annales Cambriæ, an Early Chronicle of Wales, preserved among the Exchequer Records. To be edited by Sir HENRY ELLIS, from a transcript made by the late Mr. Petrie, and kindly placed at the disposal of the Camden Society by the Right Honourable Lord Langdale, Her Majesty's Keeper of Records.

The Request and Suite of a True-harted Englysheman wishing the welfare of his Native Contrey. From a MS. in the Library of Advocates, Edinburgh. To be edited by WILLIAM J. THOMS, Esq., F.S.A., Lond. and Sc.

Inedited Letters of Queen Elizabeth, addressed to King James VI. of Scotland, between the years 1581 and 1594. From the originals, in the possession of the Rev. Edward Ryder, of Oaksey, Wilts. To be edited by JOHN BRUCE, Esq., F.S.A.

It is to be remarked, that the materials for the last mentioned work, as also for the lately delivered Diary of Walter Yonge, Esq., are in the possession of a private gentleman. The Council have always felt it their especial duty not only to afford every facility for the printing historical documents deserving of publication found in private hands, and thereby render them available for general use, but to search out the possessors of such documents, and solicit them to permit their publication; and the Council, having reason to believe that such papers are scattered very widely throughout the country, and that they occasionally exist in the hands of persons who are neither aware of their importance nor of the means provided for making them available for historical purposes, during the past year issued a copy of their prospectus to every literary and scientific institution of the kingdom, requesting from the respective secretaries information as to the existence of any unpublished materials for the civil, ecclesiastical, or literary history of the United Kingdom which might be in the possession of any persons connected with such institutions.

The books issued during the past year have been

The Camden Miscellany, Vol. I.: containing, 1. The Register and Chronicle of the Abbey of Aberconway; 2. A Chronicle of the Lincolnshire Rebellion, in the year 1470; 3. The Papal Bull for the marriage of King Henry VII.; 4. A Journal of the Siege of Rouen in 1591, by Sir Thomas Coningsby, of Hampton Court, co. Hereford; 5. Letter of George Fleetwood, describing the Battle of Lutzen and the Death of Gustavus Adolphus, in 1632; 6. The Diary of Dr. Edward Lake, Chaplain and Tutor to the Princesses Mary and Anne, in 1677-78;

which belongs to the Subscription of the preceding year.

I. A Commentary of the Services and Charges of William Lord Grey of Wilton, K.G. by his son Arthur Lord Grey of Wilton, K.G. with Documents illustrating the Biography of those Noblemen. Edited by SIR PHILIP DE MALPAS GREY EGERTON, Bart. M.P., F.R.S., &c.

II. The Diary of Walter Yonge, Esquire, Justice of the Peace and M.P. for Honiton, from 1604 to 1628. Edited by GEORGE ROBERTS, Esq., from the original MS. in his possession.

and these will be followed by

III. The Diary of Henry Machyn, Citizen and Merchant-taylor of London, extending from the year 1550 to 1563, now the Cottonian MS. Vitellius F. v. Edited by JOHN GOUGH NICHOLS, Esq., F.S.A.

The Council have further to Report to the Society that they have recently taken a step calculated, as they hope, to promote in a very high degree the welfare of English Historical Literature. Circumstances having brought under their notice in a very striking manner the difficulties thrown in the way of gentlemen engaged in editing books for this Society, and indeed of all literary inquirers, by the peculiar constitution of the Prerogative Office, Doctors' Commons, under which the use of the ancient wills is precluded, except under embarrassing restrictions and upon payment of heavy fees, the Council unanimously agreed to address to His Grace the Archbishop of Canterbury the following Memorial:—

To the Most Rev. and the Right Hon. The LORD ARCHBISHOP OF CANTERBURY.

The humble Memorial of the President and Council of the Camden Society,
    Respectfully sheweth,

That the Camden Society was instituted in the year 1838, for the publication of early historical and literary remains.

It has the honour to be patronized by H. R. H. the Prince Albert; and was supported, from its institution, by the countenance and subscription of your Grace's predecessor in the See of Canterbury.

The Society has published forty volumes of works relating to English History, and continues to be actively engaged in researches connected with the same important branch of literature.

In the course of its proceedings, the Society has had brought under its notice the manner in which the regulations of the Prerogative Office in Doctors' Commons interfere with the accuracy and completeness of works in the preparation of which the Council is now engaged, and with the pursuits and labours of all other historical inquirers; and they beg leave respectfully to submit to your Grace the results of certain investigations which they have made upon the subject.

Besides the original wills deposited in the Office of the Prerogative Court, there is kept in the same repository a long series of register books, containing copies of wills entered chronologically from A.D. 1383 to the present time. These registers or books of entry fall practically into two different divisions or classes. The earlier and the latter books contain information suited to the wants of totally different kinds of persons, and applicable to entirely different purposes. Their custody is also of very different importance to the office. The class which is first both of number of books and in importance contains entries of modern wills. These are daily consulted by relatives of testators, by claimants and solicitors, principally for legal purposes, and yield a large revenue to the office in fees paid for searches, inspections, and copies. The second class, which comprises a comparatively small number of volumes, contains entries of ancient wills, dated before the period during which wills are now useful for legal purposes. These are never consulted by lawyers or claimants, nor do they yield any revenue to the office, save an occasional small receipt from the Camden Society, or from some similar body, or private literary inquirer.

With respect to the original wills, and the entries of modern wills, your memorialists beg to express clearly that this application is not designed to have any reference to them. Your memorialists confine their remarks exclusively to the books of entries of those ancient wills which have long and unquestionably ceased to be useful for legal purposes.

These entries of ancient wills are of the very highest importance to historical inquirers. They abound with illustrations of manners and customs; they exhibit in the most authentic way the state of religion, the condition of the various classes of the people, and of society in general; they are invaluable to the lexicographer, the genealogist, the topographer, the biographer,— to historical writers of every order and kind. They constitute the most important depository in existence of exact information relating to events and persons of the period to which they relate.

But all this information is unavailable in consequence of the regulations of the office in which the wills are kept. All the books of entry, both of ancient and modern wills, are kept together, and can only be consulted in the same department of the same office, in the same manner and subject to precisely the same restrictions and the same payments. No distinction is made between the fees to be paid by a literary person who wishes to make a few notes from wills, perhaps three or four hundred years old, in order to rectify a fact, a name, a date, or to establish the proper place of a descent in a pedigree, or the exact meaning of a doubtful word, and the fees to be paid by the person who wants a copy of a will proved yesterday as evidence of a right to property perhaps to be established in a court of justice. No extract is allowed to be made, not even of a word or a date, except the names of the executors and the date of the will. Printed statements in historical books, which refer to wills, may not be compared with the wills as entered; even ancient copies of wills handed down for many generations in the families of the testators, may not be examined with the registered wills without paying the office for making new and entire copies.

No such restrictions exclude literary inquirers from the British Museum, where there are papers equally valuable. The public Record offices are all open, either gratuitously or upon payment of easy fees. The Secretary of State for the Home Department grants permission of access to Her Majesty's State Paper Office. Your Grace's predecessor gave the Camden Society free access to the registers of wills at Lambeth—documents exactly similar to those at Doctors' Commons. The Prerogative Office is, probably, the only public office in the kingdom which is shut against literary inquirers.

The results of such regulations are obvious. The ancient wills at Doctors' Commons not being accessible to those to whom alone they are useful, yield scarcely any fees to the office; historical inquirers are discouraged; errors remain uncorrected; statements of facts in historical works are obliged to be left uncertain and incomplete; the researches of the Camden Society and other similar societies are thwarted; and all historical inquirers regard the condition of the Prerogative Office as a great literary grievance.

The President and Council of the Camden Society respectfully submit these circumstances to your Grace with a full persuasion that nothing which relates to the welfare of English historical literature can be uninteresting either to your Grace personally, or to the Church over which you preside; and they humbly pray your Grace that such changes may be made in the regulations of the Prerogative Office as may assimilate its practice to that of the Public Record Office, so far as regards the inspection of the books of entry of ancient wills, or that such other remedy may be applied to the inconveniences now stated as to your Grace may seem fit.

(Signed)   BRAYBROOKE, President.

THOMAS AMYOT, Director.	THOS. STAPLETON.
HENRY ELLIS.	WM. DURRANT COOPER.
J. PAYNE COLLIER, Treas^r.	PETER LEVESQUE.
HARRY VERNEY.	THOS. J. PETTIGREW.
H. H. MILMAN.	JOHN BRUCE.
JOSEPH HUNTER.	BERIAH BOTFIELD.
WILLIAM J. THOMS, Secretary.	BOLTON CORNEY.
CHS. PURTON COOPER.	

25, *Parliament Street, Westminster,*
       13 *April,* 1848.

Time for a reply has not yet elapsed: but the Council sincerely trust that on the next recurrence of the annual meeting they shall be able to report, that the memorial has been successful in procuring such a modification of the regulations of the Prerogative Office as will assimilate its practice to that of the public Record departments of the government; and by permitting the literary student to inspect, collate, and if necessary transcribe, the documents there deposited, further that which is the great object of the Camden Society, the dissemination of Historical Truth.

By Order of the Council,
                   THOMAS AMYOT, Director.
                   WILLIAM J. THOMS, Secretary.

REPORT OF THE AUDITORS,

DATED APRIL 29, 1848.

WE, the Auditors appointed to audit the Accounts of the Camden Society, report to the Society, that the Treasurer has exhibited to us an account of the Receipts and Expenditure of the Society, from the 1st of May, 1847, to the 29th of April, 1848, and that we have examined the said accounts, with the vouchers relating thereto, and find the same to be correct and satisfactory.

And we further report that the following is an Abstract of the Receipts and Expenditure of the Society during the period we have mentioned.

An ABSTRACT of the RECEIPTS and EXPENDITURE of THE CAMDEN SOCIETY,

from the 1st May, 1847, to the 29th April, 1848.

	£.	s.	d.		£.	s.	d.
Balance of last year's account	78	16	3	Paid for the purchase of £23 4s. 3 per Cent. Consols, invested for the benefit of the Society	20	0	0
Received on account of Members whose Subscriptions were in arrear at the last Audit	98	0	0	Paid for printing and paper of 1,250 copies of "Middleham Charters"	96	5	6
The like on account of Subscriptions due 1st May, 1847	730	0	0	The like of 1,250 copies of "Camden Miscellany," vol. I.	122	17	0
One year's dividend on £877 10s. 9d. 3 per Cent. Consols, invested in the names of the Trustees of the Society, deducting property-tax	25	17	10	The like of 1,250 copies of "Lord Grey of Wilton"..	76	5	0
				The like of 1,250 copies of "Walter Yonge's Diary"..	89	15	6
				Paid for binding 1,200 copies of "Middleham Charters"	43	4	0
Composition received from one Member ··················	10	0	0	The like for 1,200 copies of "Relations of England"	43	4	0
				The like for 1,200 copies of "Camden Miscellany," vol. I.	45	12	0
				The like for 1,200 copies of "Lord Grey of Wilton"	45	12	0
				Paid for delivery and transmission of 1,000 copies of "Middleham Charters," "Camden Miscellany," "Lord Grey of Wilton," and "Yonge's Diary," at 2d. per book, with paper for wrappers, &c.	47	16	2
				Paid for Miscellaneous Printing, Lists of Members, &c.	24	11	0
				Paid for Transcripts connected with works published or in progress	10	14	8
				Paid expenses connected with circulation of Prospectus	22	6	8
				One year's payment for keeping Accounts and General Correspondence of the Society	52	10	0
				Paid for postages, carriage of parcels, stationery, and other petty cash expenses	16	2	4
				Cash balance, viz. Sum remaining in hand for Composition £10 0 0			
				Balance of Subscriptions and other receipts 175 18 3			
					185	18	3
Total receipts for the year £942	14	1			£942	14	1

And we, the Auditors, further state, that the Treasurer has reported to us, that, over and above the present balance of £185 18*s*. 3*d*. there are outstanding various subscriptions of Foreign Members, of Members resident in places distant from London, and of Members recently elected, which the Treasurer sees no reason to doubt will shortly be received.

Given under our hands this 29th day of April, 1848,

GEO. GODWIN, JUN.   ROBT. LEMON.

As a postscript to this Report the Auditors take leave to refer to an arrangement, recently made by the Society of Antiquaries, which provides that one of the Auditors acting in the current year shall be re-appointed for the ensuing year; and, considering this a salutary provision, they venture to recommend its adoption by the Council of the Camden Society.

ROBT. LEMON.   GEO. GODWIN, JUN.

April 29, 1848.

MEMBERS OF THE CAMDEN SOCIETY,

FOR THE

TENTH YEAR, ENDING 1st MAY, 1848.

Those Members to whose names (c.) is prefixed have compounded for their Annual Subscriptions.

The Members whose names are printed in Small Capitals were on the Council of the year.

THE RIGHT HONOURABLE LORD BRAYBROOKE, F.S.A., *President.*

(c.) H. R. H. PRINCE ALBERT OF SAXE-COBURG GOTHA, K.G., F.R.S., F.S.A.

THE MOST REV. AND RIGHT HON. WILLIAM LORD ARCHBISHOP OF CANTERBURY. [Died Feb. 11, 1848.]

THE RIGHT HON. LORD COTTENHAM, LL.D., F.R.S., LORD HIGH CHANCELLOR.

THE MOST HON. THE MARQUESS OF NORTHAMPTON, D.C.L., PRES. R.S., F.S.A.

J. White Abbott, Esq. Exeter
Abraham Abell, Esq. Cork
Right Hon. the Earl of Aberdeen, F.R.S., F.S.A.
Joseph Ablett, Esq Llanbedr Hall
Rt. Hon. Lord Viscount Acheson
(c.) Sir Robert Shafto Adair
John Adamson, Esq. Sec. S. A. Newc. *Local Secretary at Newcastle*
(c.) Rev. James Adcock, M.A.
The Adelphi Reading Society, Basinghall-street
Professor Dr. Adrian, Hesse Darmstadt
Wm. Harrison Ainsworth, Esq.
Ralph Ainsworth, Esq. M.D.
John Yonge Akerman, Esq. Sec. S.A.
William Aldam, Esq.
(c) Edward Nelson Alexander, Esq. F.S.A. *Local Secretary at Halifax*
Robert Henry Allan, Esq. F.S.A.
George Edward Allen, Esq. Bath
Mr. William Allen
Franklin Allport, Esq.
Richard Almack, Esq. F.S.A.
Rev. Edward Constable Alston, M.A.
George Henry Ames, Esq. Bristol
Samuel Amory, Esq.
THOMAS AMYOT, Esq. F.R.S., F.S.A. *Director*
Alexander Annand, Esq. F.S.A.
Thomas Chisholme Anstey, Esq. M.P.
Samuel Appleby, Esq.
George Appleyard, Esq.
M. le Chevalier Artaud, Membre de l'Institut de France
Robert John Ashton, Esq. F.L.S.
Sydney Aspland, Esq.
The Athenæum Club

Fenton Robinson Atkinson, Esq.
Rev. William Atthill, M.A. Deanery, Middleham, Yorkshire. *Local Secretary at Middleham*
Benjamin Austen, Esq.
Australasian Public Library
W. Scrope Ayrton, Esq. F.S.A.
James Bacon, Esq.
Thomas Bacon, Esq. Redlands, Reading
Rt. Hon. Lord Bagot, LL.D., F.S.A.
James Evan Baillie, Esq.
George Baker, Esq. *Local Secretary at Northampton*
Rev. John Baldwin, M.A. Dalton
Rev. Bulkeley Bandinel, D.D. Bodley's Librarian, Oxford
Harwood W. Banner, Esq. Liverpool
W. G. J. Barker, Esq. Harmby, Leyburn, Yorkshire
(c.) George Barlow, Esq. Oldham
Benjamin Barnard, Esq.
E. C. Gee Barnard, Esq.
John Barnard, Esq.
Keith Barnes, Esq.
Ralph Barnes, Esq. Exeter
Charles Frederick Barnwell, Esq. M.A., F.R.S., F.S.A.
Rev. John Bartholomew, Morchard
Arthur Barr, Esq.
Mr. J. Bartlett, Blandford
J. R. Bartlett, Esq. New York
William Bateman, Esq. R.N.
R. R. Bayley, Esq.
Richard Bayley, Esq. Sheffield
Henry Ridley Beal, Esq.
John Beardmore, Esq. Uplands
His Grace the Duke of Bedford
John Thomas Bedford, Esq.

The Bedford Permanent Library
James Bell, Esq.
Robert Bell, Esq. Chiswick
Thomas Bell, Esq. F.R.S.
Charles Bellamy, Esq. D.C.L.
Samuel Belts, Esq.
Rev. Samuel Benson
Francis Benthall, Esq. F.S.A.
Henry Bentley, Esq.
John Bentley, Esq. Birch House
Michael Bentley, Esq.
Richard Bentley, Esq.
Peter S. Benwell, Esq. Henley
John Brodribb Bergne, Esq. F.S.A. *Auditor*
The Royal Library, Berlin
Charles William de Bernardy, Esq.
Samuel Berridge, Esq. Leicester
(c.) The Rev. John Bealy, D.C.L. Vicar of Benton, Northumberland
Sir William Betham, Ulster King of Arms, F.S.A., M.R.I.A. *Local Secretary at Dublin*
Richard Bethell, Esq. Rise, near Beverley
Edward Bevan, Esq.
La Bibliothèque du Roi, Paris
Robert Bickersteth, Esq. Liverpool
John Bidwell, Esq. F.S.A.
Leonard Shelford Bidwell, Esq. F.S.A.
Rev. George Augustus Biedermann, Rector of Dauntsey, Wilts.
Arthur Biggs, Esq. Bristol
(c.) John Billing, Esq. Reading
Henry Back, Esq. Trinity College Cambridge
Samuel H. Bindon, Esq.
William Bird, Esq. Rock Park

Thomas Birkbeck, Esq.
(c.) John Birkbeck, Esq. Anley House
The Birmingham Public Library
W. H. Blaauw, Esq. M.A. Beech-
    land. *Auditor*
John Blachford, Esq.
William Black, Esq.
John Burgoyne Blackett, Esq.
(c.) Rev. Joseph William Blakesley,
    M.A. *Local Secretary at Ware,*
    Herts.
Michael Bland, Esq. F.R.S., F.S.A.
Venble. George Bland, M.A., Arch-
    deacon of Lindisfarne
Charles Blandy, Esq. Reading
(c.) John Jackson Blandy, Esq. *Local*
    Secretary at Reading
William Blandy, Esq. Reading
Robert Willis Blencowe, Esq. M.A.
    The Hooke, near Lewes
Octavian Blewitt, Esq. Secretary to
    the Literary Fund Society
(c.) Rev. Philip Bliss, D.C.L., F.S.A.,
    Principal of New Inn Hall, Oxford.
    Local Secretary at Oxford
Bindon Blood, Esq. F.R.S.E., F.S.A.,
    Scot., M.R.I.A. Ennis, Ireland
Edward Blore, Esq. D.C.L., F.S.A.
B. Blundell, Esq. Temple
John Blunt, Esq.
Rev. Wm. Blunt, B.A. Under Master
    of Merchant-Taylors' School
Miss Bockett, Southcote Lodge, Berks
Henry G. Bohn, Esq.
Rev. J. A. Bolster, MA., M.R.I.A.
    Local Secretary at Cork
Mr. William Boone
B. W. Booth, Esq. Manchester
John Booth, Esq. Barton on Irwell
Mr. Lionel Booth
Rt. Hon. Sir John Bernard Bosanquet,
    Knt. M.A. [Died Sept. 26, 1847].
Rev. Joseph Bosworth, LL.D., F.R.S.,
    F.S.A. *Local Secretary at Derby*
(c.) BERJAH BOTFIELD, Esq. F.R.S.,
    F.S.A.
Lieut. Bowden, 22nd Foot
Miss Bower, Doncaster
Rev. Thomas Frere Bowerbank, M.A.
    Vicar of Chiswick
George Bowyer, Esq. D.C.L., F.S.A.
Mark Boyd, Esq.
David Bradberry, Esq.
The Subscription Library, Bradford,
    Yorkshire
Robert Greene Bradley, Esq. Bencher
    of Grey's Inn. *Local Secretary at*
    Lancaster
George Weare Braikenridge, Esq.
    F.S.A. Brislington House, Som.
Thomas W. Bramston, Esq. M.P.

Humphrey Brandreth, Esq. Houghton
    House, Beds.
Edward Wedlake Brayley, Esq. F.S.A.
George Brice, Esq. Queen's Coll. Oxf.
John Bright, Esq. M.D.
John Ruggles Brise, Esq. Spains
    Hall
Charles Bristed, Esq. Trin. Coll. Camb.
Thomas Broadwood, Esq.
William Brockedon, Esq. F.R.S.
William Bromet, M.D., F.S.A.
(c.) Right Hon. the Lord Brooke.
Francis Capper Brooke, Esq. Ufford,
    Place, Suffolk
Charles Bros, Esq.
The Right Hon. Lord Brougham and
    Vaux, F.R.S.
Rev. John Brown, M.A. Vice-Master
    of Trinity College, Cambridge
Robert Brown, Esq. Bishopwearmouth
Rev. Meredith Brown, Incumbent of
    Chiltre, Wilts
Samuel Cowper Brown, Esq. F.S.A.
    Shillingford Cross, near Exeter
Samuel Wm. Browne, Esq. Lewisham
William Henry Browne, Esq. Lewisham
Rt. Hon. Sir James L. Knight Bruce,
    Vice-Chancellor, F.R.S., P.S.A.
(c.) JOHN BRUCE, Esq. F.S.A. Hyde
    House, Minchinhampton. *Local*
    Secretary, and Auditor
The Royal Library, Brussels
Rev. Guy Bryan, M.A., F.S.A. Rec-
    tor of Woodham Walter, Essex.
    Local Secretary at Maldon
Mr. John Bryant
Henry T. Buckle, Esq.
George Buckton, Esq. Oakfield
Lieut.-Gen. Sir Henry Bunbury,
    K.C.B., F.S.A.
John Burder, Esq. F.S.A.
John William Burgon, Esq.
James Burn, Esq. W. S. Edinburgh
Ven. Chas. Parr Burney, D.D. F.R.S.,
    F.S.A. Archdeacon of St. Alban's
John Burrell, Esq. Durham
Robert Burrell, Esq. Durham
Edmund Burrow, Esq.
Decimus Burton, Esq. F.R.S., F.S.A.
John M. Burton, Esq. Greenwich
Johnson Atkinson Busfield, Esq. Brad-
    ford, Yorkshire
Rev. Thomas Byrth, D.D., F.S.A.,
    Rector of Wallasey, Cheshire
Benjamin Bond Cabbell, Esq. M.P.,
    F.R.S., F.S.A.
Frederick Caldwell, Esq.
Rt. Hon. Lord Campbell
Union Society, Cambridge
J. S. Cardale, Esq. Leicester
The Cardiff Institution

(c.) The Rev. Edward Cardwell, D.D.
    CAMDEN'S Professor of Ancient
    History, Oxford
W. Henry Pole Carew, Esq. Anthony
(c.) Peter Stafford Carey, Esq. M.A.
Rt. Hon. the Earl of Carlisle, F.R.S.
Edward John Carlos, Esq.
Rev. John Carr, M.A. Fellow of Bal-
    liol college, Oxford
William Thomas Carr, Esq.
John Carter, Esq. Coventry
George Alfred Carthew, Esq. East
    Dereham, Norfolk
(c.) Cornelius Cartwright, Esq. Dudley
W. C. Cartwright, Esq.
Rev. W. Carus, M.A. Fellow of Trin.
    Coll. Camb.
The Rt. Hon. Earl Cawdor, F.R.S.
Edward P. Cearns, Esq. Liverpool
Mr. James Chaffin, Islington
Thomas Chapman, Esq. F.R.S. F.S.A.
William Chapman, Esq. Richmond
(c.) William Chappell, Esq. F.S.A.
Sir William Chatterton, Bart.
J. M. G. Cheek, Esq. Evesham. *Local*
    Secretary at Evesham
Rt. Rev. the Lord Bishop of Chichester
(c.) John Walbanke Childers, Esq.
    M.P.
Francis Cholmeley, Esq. F.S.A.
Rev. Henry Christmas, M.A., F.R.S.,
    F.S.A., Sec. N.S., Librarian of Sion
    College, &c., &c.
Henry Christy, Esq.
F. Churchill, Esq.
Charles Clark, Esq. Middle Temple
Rev. Francis Foreman Clark, B.A.,
    Townfield House, Staffordshire
William Clark, M.D. Professor of
    Anatomy, Cambridge
Joseph Clarke, Esq.
Thomas Clarke, Esq. F.R.S., F.S.A.
Rev. Patrick Clason, D.D. Edinb. For
    the Library of the Free Church of
    Scotland
Rev. Jacob Clements, M.A. Upton St.
    Leonard's, near Gloucester
(c.) Rev. Alfred Butler Clough, B.D.,
    F.S.A. Jesus College, Oxford
Charles Thornton Coathupe, Esq.
    Wraxhall, near Bristol
James Cobb, Esq. Yarmouth
J. Ingram Cobbin, Esq.
Sir Wm. S. R. Cockburn, Bart.
    M.A.
William Colbourne, Esq. Chippenham
Francis George Coleridge, Esq. Ottery
    St. Mary, Devon
The Hon. Sir John Taylor Coleridge,
    one of the Judges of the Queen's
    Bench, M.A.

JOHN PAYNE COLLIER, Esq. Treas. S.A. Director of the Shakespeare Society. *Treasurer*

Mr. Edwin Collings, Bath

Edward Collins, Esq.

Thomas Combe, Esq. Oxford

Rev. C. Comberbach, Stonor

John Comport, Esq. F.S.A. Strood. *Local Secretary for Rochester*

The Library of Congress, Washington

(c.) Rev. John Connop, M.A. Bradfield Hall, Berkshire

Edward Conroy, Esq. M.A., M.R.I.A.

William Conway, Esq. Rathmines

Lord Albert Conyngham, F.S.A.

William Henry Cooke, Esq. Barrister-at-Law, Temple

Charles Henry Cooper, Esq. Coroner for Cambridge

CHARLES PURTON COOPER, Esq. Q.C., D.C.L., F.R.S., F.S.A.

Rev. James Cooper, M.A. St. Paul's School

Thomas Henry Cooper, Esq. F.L.S.

WILLIAM DURRANT COOPER, Esq. F.S.A.

The Royal Library of Copenhagen

The Lord Bishop of Cork, Cloyne and Ross

George Richard Corner, Esq. F.S.A.

(c.) BOLTON CORNEY, Esq. M.R.S.L.

Rev. Tho. Corser, Stand, Manchester

Rev. G. E. Corrie, B.D. Fellow of Cath. Hall, and Norrisian Prof. of Divin. in the Univ. of Cambridge

Right Hon. Countess Cornwallis [Died Nov. 4, 1847].

Andrew Coventry, Esq. Advocate

Rev. M. Cowie, M.A. St. John's Coll. Cambridge

William Crafter, Esq. Gravesend

(c.) James T. Gibson Craig, Esq.

George L. Craik, Esq.

Very Rev. John Anthony Cramer, D.D. Dean of Carlisle

Rev. Richard Crawley, M.A. Steeple Ashton, Wiltshire

Charles Crawley, Esq.

Sir Archer Denman Croft, Bart.

Rev. Richard Croft, Vicar of Hartburn, Northumberland

Anthony Crofton, Esq. Barrister

John Crofts, Esq. Bradford, York

The Rt. Hon. John Wilson Croker, LL.D., F.R.S.

THOMAS CROFTON CROKER, Esq. F.S.A., M.R.I.A.

James Crosby, Esq.

Crosby Hall Literary and Scientific Institution

John Cross, Esq. Barrister-at-Law

James Crossley, Esq. *Local Secretary at Manchester*

James Dodsley Cuff, Esq.

Rev. Samuel Cumming, B.A. Old Romney

George Godfrey Cunningham, Esq. Redcol, East Lothian

Peter Cunningham, Esq. Treasurer of the Shakespeare Society

Miss Richardson Currer, Eshton Hall

Henry Curwen, Esq. Workington Hall, Cumberland

The Rev. Henry Curwen, Rector of Workington

The Hon. Edward Cecil Curzon

Edward Dalton, Esq. LL.D., F.S.A.

John Dalton, Esq. West Belney, near Lynn

Thomas Dalton, Esq. Cardiff

George Daniel, Esq.

George Webb Dasent, Esq. M.A.

William Davie, Esq. Town Clerk of Glasgow

Francis Robert Davies, Esq. Dublin

Robert Davies, Esq. F.S.A. Town Clerk of York

Richard Davies, jun. Esq. Llangefni

Thomas Stephens Davies, Esq. F.R.S. L. and Ed. F.S.A.

David Elisha Davy, Esq. Ufford, Suffolk. *Local Secretary*

Matthew Dawes, Esq. F.G.S.

Vesey Thomas Dawson, Esq.

Rev. Arthur Dayman, M.A. Shillingstone Rectory, Blandford

Charles Deane, Esq.

Rev. J. Bathurst Deane, M.A., F.S.A.

George Kenyon Dearden, Esq. Bury, Lanc.

James Dearden, Esq. F.S.A. Rochdale

Right Hon. Earl de Grey, Pres of R. Inst. Br. Architects, F.S.A.

Rev. D. C. Delafosse, M.A.

Philip Chilwell De la Garde, Esq.

Mons. Jules Desnoyers, Sec. de la Soc. de l'Histoire de France

His Grace the Duke of Devonshire, K.G., D.C.L.

F. H. Dickinson, Esq.

William Dike, Esq.

Charles Wentworth Dilke, Esq. LL.B.

Joseph C. Dimsdale, Esq.

(c.) John Disney, Esq. The Hyde, Ingatestone

(c.) George Dodd, Esq. M.P., F.S.A.

Charles Cooper Doggett, Esq.

Mr. Dolman, Bond street

Charles Dorrien, Esq. Sennicots, Chichester

John Edward Dowdeswell, Esq. Pull Court, Worcestershire

(c.) Charles Downes, Esq.

Thomas D'Oyly, Esq. D.C.L. Serjeant-at-Law

Samuel Duckworth, Esq., M.A. Master in Chancery [Died Dec. 3, 1847].

Thomas Farmer Dukes, Esq. F.S.A.

Philip Bury Duncan, Esq., M.A., Keeper of the Ashmolean Museum

David Dundas, Esq., M.A., Temple

William Pitt Dundas, Esq. Deputy Clerk Register of Scotland

John Dunn, Esq. Paisley

Enoch Durant, Esq. F.S.A.

Right Rev. the Lord Bishop of Durham, F.R.S., F.S.A.

Rev. Alexander Dyce, B.A.

Rev. Thomas Dyer, M.A. Abbot's Roding, Ongar, Essex

J. Compton Dyke, Esq. Rochester

Mr. Thomas Eaton, Worcester

Thomas Edgworth, Esq.

Sir Philip de Malpas Grey Egerton, Bart. M.P., F.R.S., V.P.G.S.

Benjamin Elam, Esq.

Rev. H. T. Ellacombe, M.A., F.S.A. Bitton, near Bristol

J. Bardoe Elliott, Esq.

George Percy Elliott, Esq. Barrister-at-law, Temple

Sir HENRY ELLIS, K.H., LL.B., F.R.S., Sec. S.A., Principal Librarian of the British Museum

(c.) G. Stevenson Ellis, Esq.

Rev. John Joseph Ellis, M.A., F.S.A.

Joseph Ellis, jun. Esq. Richmond

Rt. Hon. the Earl of Ellesmere

John Fullerton Elphinstone, Esq.

Charles Norton Elvin, Esq. East Dereham, Norfolk

Hastings Elwin, Esq.

William Empson, Esq. M.A.

C. Engledew, Esq. Haddington, N.B.

The Erechtheium Club

The Rt. Hon. Thomas Erskine

George Essell, Esq. Rochester

Thomas Grimston Bucknall Estcourt, Esq. M.P. for the Univ. of Oxford

Rev. Henry Herbert Evans, M.A.

Herbert Norman Evans, Esq.

Thomas Evans, Esq. Cardiff

C. W. Evors, Esq.

(c.) John Leman Ewen, Esq. Valewood, Haslemere, Sussex

(c.) Joseph Walter King Eyton, Esq. F.S.A. Lond. & Scot.

George Lockton Faithfull, Esq. Tring

The Right Hon. Lord Farnham

(c.) Sir Walter Farquhar, Bart.

James William Farrer, Esq. Master in Chancery, F.S.A.

Mr. Thomas Faulkner, Chelsea

Tarver R. Fearnside, Esq.
Dr. Feder, Head Librarian to the Court of Hesse Darmstadt
Rev. George O. Fenwicke, F.S.A.
Copley Fielding, Esq. Brighton
Rev. Henry Fielding, M.A. Salmonby Rectory, near Horncastle
William Figg,. Esq. Lewes
Charles Filica, Esq.
John Joseph Ashby Fillinham, Esq.
(c.) Sir Edmund Filmer, Bart. M.P. East Sutton Place, Kent
John Goate Fisher, Esq. Yarmouth
Paul Hawkins Fisher, Esq. The Castle, Stroud
Wm. Stevenson Fitch, Esq. *Local Secretary at Ipswich*
Robert Fitch, Esq. Norwich
The Right Hon. Earl FitzWilliam
Rev. Henry Fletcher, Ulceby, Linc.
John W. Fletcher, Esq. Brazenose College, Oxford
(c.) Thomas W. Fletcher, Esq. F.R.S., F.S.A. *Local Secretary at Dudley*
(c.) Rev. William Fletcher, M.A. *Local Secretary at Southwell*
Sir William J. H. Browne Folkes, Bart. F.R.S., F.S.A.
(c.) George Folliott, Esq.
Rev. Josiah Forshall, M.A., F.R.S., F.S.A. Sec. to the British Museum
John Forster, Esq.
John Forster, Esq. Newton-in-the Willows
Matthew Forster, Esq. Belsize
W.E. Forster, Esq. Bradford, Yorkshire
Hon. George M. Fortescue
Edward Foss, Esq. F.S.A.
W. F. Foster, Esq. Stamford-hill
Lieut. Colonel Charles Richard Fox
Charles B. Fox, Esq.
Charles Larkin Francis, Esq.
Henry Ralph Francis, Esq. M.A. late Fellow of St. John's Coll. Camb.
Miss Francis, Hampstead
Richard Frankum, Esq.
William French, Esq.
Thomas Frewen, Esq. Brickwall House
Charles Frost, Esq. F.S.A. Pres. of the Lit. and Philos. Soc. of Hull. *Local Secretary*
The Ven. R. Hurrell Froude, M.A. Archdeacon of Totness
Right Hon. Sir Herbert Jenner Fust, LL.D. Dean of the Arches
(c.) John Lewis Ffytche, Esq. Linc. Coll. Oxf. Thorp Hall, Louth
Charles Gambier, Esq. Harley-street
Rev. Richard Garnet, F.S.A. British Museum
Thomas Garrard, Esq. F.S.A. Bristol

Thomas Gaspey, Esq.
Herr Von Gévay, Vienna
Professor Aug. Fred. Gfroeroer, Director of the Royal Library, Stuttgard
John Gidley, Esq. Exeter
Edward Gifford, Esq. Admiralty
Richard James Gilman, Esq.
William Anthony Gilman, Esq.
Thomas Ward Gleadow, Esq. Hull
The Literary and Scientific Association of Gloucester
(c.) John Hulbert Glover, Esq. F.S.A. Librarian to Her Majesty
Sir Stephen R. Glynne, Bart. F.S.A.
George Godwin, jun. Esq. F.R.S., F.S.A. Hon. Sec. Art. Union. *Auditor*
Henry Godwin, Esq. F.S.A. Newbury
Gabriel Goldney, Esq.
Aaron Asher Goldsmid, Esq.
Sir Isaac Lyon Goldsmid, Bart. F.R.S. F.S.A.
Rev. William Goode, M.A. F.S.A. Rector of St. Antholine, London
James Gooden, Esq. F.S.A.
Jonathan Gooding, Esq. *Local Secretary of Southwold*
Alexander Gordon, jun. Esq.
W. Ormsby Gore, Esq. M.P.
Richard Gosling, Esq.
The Gottingen University Library
James Robert Gowen, Esq. F.G.S.
John Black Gracie, Esq. F.S.A. Sc. [Died 1847.]
Charles Graham, Esq. F.S.A.
The Rev. James Graves, Borris in Ossory
Francis Graves, Esq.
The Library of the Hon. Society of Gray's Inn
Henry Green, Esq. Spalding
John Green, Esq.
John Greenall, Esq. Warrington
Benjamin Wyatt Greenfield, Esq. Barrister-at-Law, Shirley, Southampton
Greenwich Society for the Diffusion of Useful Knowledge
Hon. and Very Rev. George Neville Grenville, M.A. Dean of Windsor
Charles Cavendish Greville, Esq.
Charles Griffin, Esq. Glasgow
Philip Griffith, Esq.
Rev. Robert H. Groome, M.A.
John Grundy, Esq. Hampton Court Palace
The Lady Charlotte E. Guest
Edwin Guest, Esq. M.A. Fellow of Caius Coll. Camb.
Sir John Guise, Bart. Rendcomb
Daniel Gurney, Esq. F.S.A.

(c.) Hudson Gurney, Esq. V.P.S.A. F.R.S.
Russell Gurney, Esq. Barrister-at-law
John Matthew Gutch, Esq. F.S.A. *Local Secretary at Worcester*
Frederick Gwatkin, Esq.
Mr. Henry Gwyn
Miss Hackett, Clapham, Surrey
William D. Haggard, Esq. F.S.A., F.R.A.S., M.N.S.
Mr. David Haig, Advocates' Library, Edinburgh
Edward Hailstone, Esq. F.S.A. London and Edinb. Horton Hall. *Local Secretary at Bradford, Yorkshire.*
Mr. Charles Hall, Blandford.
Mrs. Hall.
John Hall, Esq.
(c.) Thomas Henry Hall, F.R.S.
Henry Hallam, Esq. M.A., F.R.S., V.P.S.A.
Charles William Hallett, Esq.
William R. Hallett, Esq. Cliff Lodge, Leyburn, Yorks.
James Orchard Halliwell, Esq. F.R.S., F.S.A.
William Richard Hamilton, Esq. F.R.S., V.P.S.A.
John Hampden, Esq. Leamington.
Robert Handyside, Esq. Advocate, Sheriff of Stirlingshire.
Philip Augustus Hanrott, Esq. F.S.A.
(c.) J. A. Hardcastle, Esq. Hatcham House, New Cross.
John Stockdale Hardy, Esq. F.S.A. *Local Secretary at Leicester.*
(c.) Ven. Julius Charles Hare, M.A., Archdeacon of Lewes.
James Hargraves, Esq. Manchester.
Rev. William Harness, M.A.
Edward M. Harrison, Esq.
William Henry Harrison, Esq.
Henry Harrod, Esq. Hon. Sec. of the Norfolk and Norwich Archæological Society, Norwich
Right Hon. the Earl of Harrowby, F.S.A. [Died Dec. 26, 1847].
Leonard L. Hartley, Esq. Middleton Lodge, Darlington.
Rev. Edward Hawkins, D.D. Provost of Oriel College, Oxford.
Edward Hawkins, Esq. F.R.S., F.S.A.
Rev. Edward Craven Hawtrey, D.D., F.S.A., Head Master of Eton
Rev. J. M. Heath, M.A. Fellow of Trinity Coll. Camb.
Henry Heffil, Esq. Diss, Norfolk
Frederick Heisch, Esq.
Alexander Henderson, M.D., F.S.A.
E. T. Henry, Esq. Caius Coll. Camb.
James Henwood, Esq. Hull

Hon. Algernon Herbert, M.A.
Samuel R. Heselton, Esq.
R. W. Heslop, Esq. *Local Secretary at Ripon*
Thomas Hewitt, Esq. M.A. Cork
Henry William Hewlett, Esq.
James Heywood, Esq. F.R.S., F.S.A.
Thomas Heywood, Esq. F.S.A.
T. Heywood, Esq. Manchester
George Hickman, Esq. Marlow
Rev. W. Hildyard, Market Deeping.
Henry Hill, Esq. Barrister-at-Law
(c.) Rev. Herbert Hill, M.A. *Local Secretary at Warwick*
Jere Hill, Esq. Bristol
Matthew D. Hill, Esq. Q.C.
John Hill, Esq. M.A.
John Hodgson Hinde, Esq.
Charles H. Hingeston, Esq.
J. H. Hippisley, Esq.
Sampson Hodgkinson, Esq.
W. B. Hodgson, Esq. Liverpool
James Maitland Hog, Esq. of Newliston
(c.) James Holding, Esq. Basingstoke
(c.) Robert Hollond, Esq. M.A., M.P.
Richard Hollier, Esq. F.S.A.
Bryan Holme, Esq. New Inn
Edward Holme, M.D. Manchester
Robert Home, Esq.
Mr. William Hood
John Hooper, Esq. Reading
A. J. Beresford Hope, Esq. M.A., M.P.
James R. Hope, Esq.
The Right Hon. John Hope, Lord Justice Clerk, Edinburgh
Charles Hopkinson, Esq. M.A.
Edmund Hopkinson, Esq. Edgeworth House, Cirencester
William Hopkinson, Esq. *Local Secretary at Stamford*
Alfred John Horwood, Esq
Abraham Howard, Esq.
W. Waters Howard, Esq.
Edward Howes, Esq. M.A.
John Hubback, Esq. Barrister-at-Law
William H. Huffam, Esq. Hull
Rev. John William Hughes, M.A.
The Hull Subscription Library
Rev. Abraham Hume, D.D. *Local Secretary at Liverpool*
William Powell Hunt, Esq. Ipswich
John Hunter, Esq. jun. W.S. Edinb.
Rev. JOSEPH HUNTER, F.S.A.
(c.) Richard Charles Hussey, Esq. F.S.A. Birmingham
(c.) Rev. Robert Hussey, B.D. Student of Christ Church, Oxford
William Hutchison, Esq.
Sir Robert Harry Inglis, Bart. LL.D., F.R.S., F.S.A., M.P. for the University of Oxford

(c.) Rev. James Ingram, D.D., F.S.A. President of Trin. Coll. Oxford
(c.) Cosmo Innes, Esq. Advocate, Sheriff of Morayshire, Edinburgh
The Royal Irish Academy
David Irving, Esq. LL.D. Edinburgh
Library of King William's College, Isle of Man
The Islington Literary and Scientific Society
The Hon. James Ivory, one of the Lords of Session in Scotland
Henry Jackson, Esq. *Local Secretary at Sheffield*
Rev. Stephen Jackson, M.A. Ipswich
Rev. Thomas Jackson, M.A. Incumbent of St. Peter's, Mile End
B. Jacob, Esq. Dorchester
Rev. William Jacobson, M.A. Vice-Principal of Magdalen Hall, Oxford
G. P. R. James, Esq. Walmer
(c.) Rev. L. W. Jeffray, Preston
Rev. Richard Jenkyns, D.D. Master of Balliol Coll. Oxford
William Jerdan, Esq. M.R.S.L.
Rt. Hon. the Earl Jermyn, F.S.A.
James Jermyn, Esq. Reydon, Suffolk
Theophilus Fairfax Johnson, Esq.
George Jones, Esq. R.A.
Mr. Jones, Organist, Middleham
(c.) Joseph Jones, jun. Esq. *Local Secretary at Oldham*
Rev. H. Longueville Jones, M.A.
Pitman Jones, Esq. *Local Sec. Exeter*
Richard Jones, Esq.
William Samuel Jones, Esq.
Dr. Keller, Chief Librarian of the University Library, Tubingen
Sir Fitzroy Kelly, M.P., Q.C.
John M. Kemble, Esq. M.A.
Robert Palmer Kemp, Esq. Yarmouth
Rev. George Kennard
The Kensington Book Society
John Kenyon, Esq.
James Kerr, Esq. Coventry
Philip Kernan, Esq.
John Kerr, Esq. *Local Sec. at Glasgow*
Edward Key, Esq. Holbeach
John M. Kibbey, Esq. Collegiate School, Peckham
Richard T. Kindersley, Esq. Master in Chancery
Thomas King, Esq.
Thomas W. King, Esq. F.S.A. Rouge Dragon Pursuivant of Arms
The King's Inns Library, Dublin
George Ritchie Kinloch, Esq. Edinb.
Charles Knight, Esq.
Charles König, Esq. K.H., F.R.S.
Rt. Hon. Henry Labouchere, M.P.
David Laing, Esq. F.S.A. L. and Sc.

Henry Eyres Landor, Esq. Warwick
John Newton Lane, Esq. King's Bromley Manor, Lichfield
William Lang, Esq. Bristol
Right Hon. Lord Langdale, Master of the Rolls
J. B. Langhorne, Esq. Richmond, Yorkshire
Rev. Lambert B. Larking, M.A.
(c.) Dr. J. M. Lappenberg, For. Memb. Soc. Ant. *Local Sec. at Hamburgh*
Rev. John Latham, Derby
John Laurie, Esq.
Mr. W. Law
Andrew Lawson, Esq. Boroughbridge
Sir William Lawson, Bart. F.S.A.
Robert Leadbitter, Esq. Newcastle
Edmund L. H. Lechmere, Esq. Hon. Sec. of Oxford Architectural Society, Christ Church, Oxford
Thomas Lee, Esq.
Rev. John E. Leefe. *Local Secretary at Bishop Wearmouth*
Leicester Literary and Philosophical Society
Henry Leigh, Esq. Moorfield Cottage, Swinton, Manchester
Sir T. Pemberton Leigh, Q.C., M.P.
Robert Lemon, Esq. F.S.A. *Auditor*
Popham Lethbridge, Esq. Greenwich Hospital.
Charles Lever, Esq.
PETER LEVESQUE, Esq. F.S.A.
The Lewes Library Society
Rev. T. T. Lewis, M.A. Bridstow, near Ross. *Local Secretary*
Mr. Lewis A. Lewis
William Wrixon Leycester, Esq.
Rt. Rev. Lord Bishop of Lichfield
Henry Liddell, Esq. Bombay
William Liddiard, Esq.
Alfred Lillingston, Esq. Southwold
The Lincoln Permanent Library
Mons. De Roux de Lincy. *Local Secretary at Paris*
John Lindsay, Esq. Barrister-at-Law, Maryville, Cork
Rev. John Lingard, D.D. Hornby, Lanc.
The Hon. Society of Lincoln's Inn
Right Rev. the Lord Bishop of Llandaff, Dean of St. Paul's, F.S.A.
William Horton Lloyd, Esq. F.S.A.
Henry F. Lockwood, Esq. F.S.A. Hull
Rev. John Lodge, M.A.
The Right Hon. and Rt. Rev. the Lord Bishop of London
City of London Library, Guildhall
The London Library
The London Institution
The City of London Literary and Scientific Institution

Gwalter B. Lonsdale, Esq.
C. W. Loscombe, Esq. Clifton
Henry Albert Loscombe, Esq. Andover
Rev. Richard H. Low, Ahascragh, Galway
Very Rev. Thomas Hill Lowe, M.A. Dean of Exeter
(c.) James Lucas, Esq. Stirling
Ebenezer Ludlow, Esq. M.A. Serjeant-at-law
Robert Wheatley Lumley, Esq.
The Right Hon. Lord Lyndhurst, LL.D., F.R.S.
Colin Campbell Macaulay, Esq.
John David Macbride, Esq. D.C.L. Principal of Magdalen Hall, Oxf.
William M'Clure, Esq. Eccles
J. Whitefoord Mackenzie, Esq. W.S.
Miss Macleod
Alexander Maconochie, Esq. of Meadowbank, Edinburgh
Allan A. Maconochie, Esq. Advocate, Professor of Laws, Glasgow
Robert Maconochie, Esq.
John MacPhail, Esq. Edinburgh
(c.) Sir Frederick Madden, K.H., F.R.S., F.S.A. Keeper of the MSS. in the British Museum
James Maidment, Esq. F.S.A. Scot.
Rev. Samuel Roffy Maitland, F.R.S., F.S.A.
Thomas John Manchee, Esq. Bristol
The Manchester Athenæum
The Portico Library, Manchester
Exchange Street Library, Manchester
W. S. Mare, Esq. Magdalen College, Cambridge
James Heywood Markland, Esq. F.R.S, F.S.A. Treas. of the Roxb. Club. *Local Secretary at Bath*
Hon. George P. Marsh, M.C. Washington, U. S.
Rev. Herbert C. Marsh, M.A. Prebendary of Peterborough
Rev. B. R. Marsham, D.C.L., Warden of Merton College, Oxford
George Martin, Esq. M.A. Cork
Rev. Robert Martin, M.A. Anstey Pastures, near Leicester
Studley Martin, Esq. Liverpool
Theodore Martin, Esq. Edinburgh
Henry Wenman Martin, Esq.
Philip Martineau, Esq.
Thomas Mason, Esq. F.S.A. Copt Hewick, near Ripon
William Matchett, Esq. Bracondale
John Mee Mathew, Esq. F.S.A.
Daniel Charles Meadows, Esq. Great Bealing, Suffolk
(c.) David Melville, Esq. B.A.

The Very Rev. John Merewether, D.D. Dean of Hereford, F.S.A.
Samuel Merriman, M.D.
Rev. W. H. R. Merriman. *Local Secretary at Frome*
Francis Mewburn. Esq. Darlington
A. G. F. Meyer, Counsellor of Justice, Hanover
Sir Sam. Rush Meyrick, K.H., F.S.A. [Died April, 1848].
Mons. Michelet, Memb. de l'Institut, Professeur d'Histoire au Collége Royal de France
John Miland, Esq.
Andrew Miller, Esq. Cardiff
(c.) Wm. Henry Miller, Esq. F.S.A.
Samuel Mills, jun. Esq.
Rev. Thomas Mills, Rector of Stutton
Rev. HENRY HART MILMAN, M.A. Prebendary of Westminster
James Milner, Esq.
Rev. John Mitford, M.A., Rector of Benhall, Suffolk
Nathaniel Cranch Moginie, Esq.
Cyril John Monkhouse, Esq.
Mons. Monmerqué, Membre de l'Institut de France
Mr. John Moore, Tewkesbury
Maurice Peter Moore, Esq. Sleaford
Thomas Moore, Esq. Sloperton Cottage, Devizes
Rev. W. Moore, D.D. Spalding
Edward Raleigh Moran, Esq.
John Shank More, Esq., Professor of the Law of Scotland, Edinburgh
William Bowyer Morgan, Esq.
Mr. John Morris, Bath
Rev. James Morton, B.D. Preb. of Lincoln. *Local Sec. at Hulbeach*
Joseph Morton, Esq.
Thomas Moule, Esq.
J. D. Moxon, Esq. Bristol
James Patrick Muirhead, Esq. M.A.
Baron Eligius von Münch-Bellinghausen, Kh. Hof-Secretär, Vienna
Rev. Jerom Murch, Bath
Charles Robert Scott Murray, Esq.
Rt. Hon. Sir John Archibald Murray, one of the Lords of Session
(c.) Sir Francis W. Myers, K.C.S. Pentlow Hall, near Sudbury, Suffolk
Peter Rickards Mynors, Esq.
T. H. Naylor, Esq. M.A.
(c.) T. C. Neale, Esq. Chelmsford
Richard Neave, jun. Esq.
John Nedham, Esq. Leicester
Joseph Neeld, Esq. M.P., F.S.A.
G. W. Newell, Esq. Holyport, Berks
Charles Thomas Newton, Esq. B.A. British Museum
Iltid Nicholl, Esq. Usk

J. Bowyer Nichols, Esq. F.S.A.
John Gough Nichols, Esq. F.S.A., Treasurer of the Surtees Society
(c.) Rev. William L. Nichols, M.A.
John Noble, Esq. F.S.A.
George Stewart Nicholson, Esq.
James Nightingale, Esq. Wilton
Rev. George Barons Northcote, Somerset Court, Bridgwater
George Offor, Esq.
The Public Library, Oldenburg
J. Walker Ord, Esq. M.D., Guisborough, Yorkshire
George Ormerod, Esq. D.C.L., F.R.S. F.S.A. *Local Secretary at Chepstow*
Sir Frederick A. Gore Ouseley, Bart.
Frederick Ouvry, Esq F.S.A..
The Oxford and Cambridge Club
Samuel Alexander Pagan, M.D.
Peter Page, Esq. Sheen
William Dunkley Paine, Esq.
Sir Francis Palgrave, K.H., F.R.S. Deputy Keeper of Records
Alfred Zouch Palmer, Esq. Sonning
Arthur Palmer, Esq. Bristol
Arthur Hare Palmer, Esq. Bristol
Charles John Palmer, Esq. F.S.A. *Local Secretary at Yarmouth*
Henry Andrewes Palmer, Esq. Bristol
John Palmer, Esq. Dorney Court
The Hon. Sir James Parke, Knt. one of the Barons of the Exchequer
William Parke, Esq. Wolverhampton
Charles Parker, Esq.
John W. Parker, Esq. West Strand
Kenyon S. Parker, Esq.
Joseph Parkes, Esq.
Anthony Parkin, Esq. Cheltenham
Charles Frederick Parkinson, Esq. Capt. H.M. 73d Foot
Rev. Richard Parkinson, B.D., F.S.A. Principal of St. Bees' College
Rev. Dr. Parkinson, Ravendale, Great Grimsby
John Parsons, Esq. Oxford
The Hon. Sir John Patteson, one of the Judges of the Court of Queen's Bench, M.A.
Jacob Howell Pattisson, Esq. LL.B. Witham, Essex
Mr. J. G. Payne, Wallingford
John Thomas Payne, Esq.
Anthony Peacock, Esq.
Reginald Peacock, Esq. 'Downhill House, near Sunderland
Rev. James R. Pears, Bath
George Peel, Esq. Brookfield House Cheadle, Cheshire
Rt. Hon. Sir Robert Peel, M.P., F.R.S., F.S.A.
Henry Perkins, Esq.

Very Rev. the Dean of Peterborough
Mr. John Petheram
Louis Hayes Petit, Esq. F.R.S., F.S.A.
THOMAS JOSEPH PETTIGREW, Esq.
F.R.S., F.S.A.
William Vesalius Pettigrew, Esq. M.D.
Mr. William Pickering
Rev. John Piccope, Manchester
Simon Fraser Piggot, Esq.
Rev. John Hearne Pinckney, D.D.
John Pitcairn, Esq.
(c.) Robert Pitcairn, Esq. F.S.A. Sc.
Thomas Joshua Platt, Esq. Q.C.
Charles Innes Pocock, Esq. Bristol
Lewis Pocock, Esq. F.S.A.
(c.) John Innes Pococke, Esq.
The Rev. Nicholas Pococke, M.A.
James Prince Pollard, Esq.
Thomas Ponton, Esq. M.A., F.S.A.
Rev. Thomas B. Pooley, M.A. Vicar of
Thornton in Lonsdale, Yorkshire
Henry Pope, Esq.
Robert Porrett, Esq. F.S.A.
Rev. Edw. A. Powell, M.A. Ampthill
John Powell Powell, Esq. Quex Park
(c.) Right Hon. the Earl of Powis,
President of the Roxburghe Club.
[Died Jan. 17, 1848].
Rev. Richard Cowley Powles, Fellow
of Exeter College, Oxford
Charles Poynder, Esq. Henley
Samuel P. Pratt, Esq. Bath
(c.) Osmond de Beauvoir Priaulx, Esq.
Rev. Thomas Price, D.D. Hackney
Richard Price, Esq. M.P.
Rev. George Proctor, D.D.
Robert Proctor, Esq.
Edward Protheroe, Esq. M.P., F.S.A.
Marlborough Pryor, Esq.
G. P. Putnam, Esq. New York
Hamilton Pyper, Esq. Advocate
Madame la Maréchale Duchesse de
Raguse
J. M. Rainbow, Esq.
Rev. James Raine, M.A., F.S.A.
Newc., Secretary of the Surtees
Society. *Local Secretary at Durham*
Chas. Ranken, Esq. B.A. Gray's Inn
Wm. Rayner, Esq. M.D. Stockport
John Read, Esq. Derwent Hall
Rev. Joseph Bancroft Reade, M.A.,
F.R.S. Stone vicarage, Bucks
Mr. William Reader
Richard Lewis Reece, Esq. *Local
Secretary at Cardiff*
Frederick John Reed, Esq. Dulwich
Henry Reeve, Esq.
S. H. Remson, Esq. New York
Thomas Charles Renshaw, Esq.
John Airey Repton, Esq. F.S.A.

Francis Riddell Reynolds, Esq. [Died
Dec. 28, 1847].
The Hon. S. E. Spring Rice
(c.) Edward Priest Richards, Esq.
(c.) Charles G. Richardson, Esq.
Cha. Jas. Richardson, Esq. F.S.A.
Lawford Richardson, Esq. Blackheath
(c.) Ralph Richardson, Esq. M.D.
Greenfield Hall, Holywell
Rev. Richard Richardson, Canterbury
Charles Rickards, Esq.
Samuel Rickards, Esq.
Edward Widdrington Riddell, Esq.
Charles Julius Roberts, Esq. M.D.
J. E. P. Robertson, D.C.L.
Henry Robinson, Esq.
Henry Crabb Robinson, Esq. F.S.A.
Wm. Robinson, Esq. LL.D., F.S.A.
John Roby, Esq. M.R.S.L.
Rev. Daniel Rock, D.D.
Rev. Henry Rogers, Birmingham
Rev. John Rogers, M.A. Canon of Exeter
Mr. Rohrmann, Vienna
The Hon. Sir Robert Monsey Rolfe,
one of the Barons of the Exchequer
Wm. Henry Rolfe, Esq. Sandwich
John Romilly, Esq. M.A.
Sir George Rose, F.R.S.
Rev. Henry John Rose, B.D. Rector
of Houghton Conquest, Beds.
Robert P. Roupell, Esq. Q.C., M.A.
Rev. Martin Joseph Routh, D.D.
President of Magdalen Coll. Oxf.
James Yeeles Row, Esq.
Daniel Rowland, Esq. F.S.A.
Richard Roy, Esq.
Edward Rudge, Esq. F.R.S., F.S.A.
Charles Edmund Rumbold, Esq.
The Russell Institution
James Russell, Esq. Barrister-at-Law
Rt. Hon. Andrew Rutherfurd, M.P.
His Grace the Duke of Rutland, K.G.,
D.C.L., V.P.R.S.L.
William B. Rye, Esq. British Museum
The University of St. Andrew's
Rev. Richard J. St. Aubyn, M.A.
The Most Hon. the Marquess of Salis-
bury, D.C.L.
Rt. Rev. the Lord Bishop of Salisbury,
D.D., F.R.S., F.S.A.
Frederick Salmon, Esq.
Charles Sanderson, Esq. Sheffield
William Salt, Esq. F.S.A.
Anthony Salvin, Esq. F.S.A.
Thomas Sanders, Esq. M.A. Fellow of
King's College, Cambridge
William Sandys, Esq. F.S.A.
Wm. Devonshire Saull, Esq. F.S.A.
Mrs. Daniel E. Saunders, Gloucester
Thomas Bush Saunders, Esq. M.A.
Thomas Saunders, Esq. F.S.A.

Thomas Field Savory, Esq. F.S.A.
Edward Scholfield, M.D. Doncaster
James John Scott, Esq. Barrister
(c.) Rev. Robert Scott, M.A. Fellow
of Balliol Coll. Oxford
Edward Cator Seaton, M.D.
William Selwyn, Esq. Q.C.
Rev. William Sewell, M.A. Professor
of Moral Philosophy, Oxford
William Shackell, Esq. M.R.S.L.
(c.) Rt. Hon. Sir Lancelot Shadwell,
Vice-Chancellor of England, M.A.
Sir Cuthbert Sharp, Knt.
Rev. Lancelot Sharpe, M.A., F.S.A.
George Shaw, Esq. M.D. Leicester
Daniel Shears, Esq. jun.
Robert Shelley, Esq.
Samuel Shepperd, Esq. F.S.A.
Evelyn Philip Shirley, Esq. M.A.
Rev. Thomas Short, B.D. Fellow of
Trinity Coll. Oxford
Right Hon. Earl of Shrewsbury, F.S.A.
G. Nicholls Simmons, Esq. Truro
Sir John Augustus Francis Simpkin-
son, M.A., Q.C., F.S.A.
J. B. Simpson, Esq. Derby
Samuel Weller Singer, Esq. F.S.A.
Edward Skegg, Esq.
Mr. R. Slocombe, Leeds
Alex. A. Smets, Esq. Savanna, Georgia
Edward Smirke, Esq. M.A.
Sir Robert Smirke, R.A., F.S.A.
Sydney Smirke, Esq. F.S.A.
Benwell Smith, Esq.
Charles Roach Smith, Esq. F.S.A.,
Hon. Sec. of Brit. Archæol. Asso-
ciation, Hon. Mem. of Soc. of Antiq.
of Spain, Normandy, &c.
George Frederick Smith, Esq.
H. Porter Smith, Esq.
Henry Stone Smith, Esq.
John Abel Smith, Esq. M.P.
Rev. J. J. Smith, M.A. Fellow of
Caius Coll. Cambridge
Newman Smith, Esq. Croydon Lodge
George Smurthwaite, Esq. Richmond,
Yorks.
Clement Taylor Smythe, Esq.
William Smythe, Esq. Advocate
Frederick Snaith, M.D. Holbeach
Mr. John Snare, Reading
Rev. W. Sneyd, M.A. Ch. Ch. Oxf.
Rev. George D'Oyly Snow
His Grace the Duke of Somerset,
K.G., D.C.L., F.R.S.
S. Leigh Sotheby, Esq. M.N.S.
William Spalding, Esq. Advocate, Pro-
fessor of Rhetoric, Edinburgh
Charles Spence, Esq. Admiralty. *Local
Secretary at Plymouth*
Andrew Spottiswoode, Esq.

(c.) John Spottiswoode, Esq. of Spottiswoode

Thomas Henry Spurrier, Esq. Douglas

George James Squibb, Esq.

Rev. Thomas Stacey, M.A. Cardiff

THOMAS STAPLETON, Esq. V.P.S.A.

Sir George Thomas Staunton, Bart. D.C.L., F.R.S., F.S.A.

(c.) Rev. William Staunton, M.A.

G. Steinman Steinman, Esq. F.S.A.

Mr. Thomas G. Stevenson, Edinburgh

Seth William Stevenson, Esq. F.S.A. *Local Secretary at Norwich*

John Stirling, Esq. Edinburgh

(c.) Rev. Charles William Stocker, D.D. St. John's Coll. Oxford

The Royal Library, Stockholm

George Stokes, Esq. *Local Secretary at Cheltenham.* [Died 1847.]

Henry Sewell Stokes, Esq. *Local Secretary at Truro*

Rev. Thomas Streatfeild, F.S.A.

Miss Agnes Strickland, Reydon Hall

(c.) Rev. Joseph Stroud, M.A.

John Stuart, Esq. Q.C.

John Stuart, Esq. Secretary to the Spalding Club, Aberdeen

Lord P. James Crichton Stuart, M.P.

John J. J. Sudlow, Esq.

Edward Swaine, Esq. F.S.S.

Clement Tudway Swanston, Esq. Q.C., F.S.A.

(c.) Sir John Edw. Swinburne, Bart. F.R.S., F.S.A., Pr. S. Ant. Newc.

Thomas Noon Talfourd, Esq. Serjeant-at-Law

Mrs. Tattershall, Liverpool

Edward Taylor, Esq. Gresham Professor of Music

Richard Taylor, Esq. F.S.A.

Mr. John Taylor, Gower-street

John Godfrey Teed, Esq. Bencher of Gray's Inn

Joseph Francis Tempest, Esq. F.S.A.

Christopher Temple, Esq. Q.C.

Rt. Temple, Esq. The Lache, Chester

The Hon. Society of the Inner Temple

Mons. Alexandre Teulet, Employé aux Archives, Paris

Robert Tewart, Esq.

Robert Thackthwaite, Esq.

Sir Fred. Thesiger, M.P.

Mr. Benj. Thomas, Cheltenham

WILLIAM J. THOMS, Esq. F.S.A. Corresponding Member of the Soc. of Ant. of Scotland. *Secretary*

Jon. Thompson, Esq. Stubbing Court

Rev. W. H. Thompson, M.A. Fellow of Trinity College, Cambridge

Mark B. Thornhill, Esq. Patna, E.I.

Mrs. Thornhill, Ryde, Isle of Wight.

Ven. Thomas Thorpe, D.D. Archdeacon of Bristol

Benjamin Thorpe, Esq. F.S.A.

Joseph Win Thrupp, Esq.

Rev. Mark Aloysius Tierney, F.R.S., F.S.A. Arundel

Rev. Nicholas C. Tindal

(c.) William Tite, Esq. F.R.S., F.S.A.

(c.) Rev. James Henthorn Todd, D.D. M.R.I.A. Fellow of Trinity Coll. Dublin, Sec. Irish Archæol. Soc.

William Tooke, Esq. F.R.S., M.R.S.L. V.-P. Soc. of Arts, Treas. of Roy. Soc. Lit. and the Lit. Fund Soc.

Charles Towneley. Esq. F.S.A.

John Towneley, Esq.

Rev. George Tyler Townsend, M.A., Trin. Coll. Cambridge

(c.) Rev. J. Montgomery Traherne, M.A., F.R.S., F.S.A.

Wm. Travis, Esq. M.D., F.S.A. *Local Secretary at Scarborough*

Sir Walter Calverley Trevelyan, Bart. F.S.A. Newc.

Rev. H. B. Tristram, Exeter

W. J. A. Tucker, Esq.

Gladwin Turbutt, Esq. Ogston Hall

William B. D. D. Turnbull, Esq. F.S.A. Sc. *Local Sec. at Edinburgh*

Alfred Turner, Esq.

Dawson Turner, Esq. F.R.S., F.S.A.

Francis Turner, Esq. Barrister-at-law

Robert S. Turner, Esq.

Rev. Samuel Blois Turner, M.A., F.S.A. Halesworth, Suffolk

Rev. Charles Turnor, B.A., F.S.A., F.R.A.S.

John Tyas, Esq.

Samuel Tymms, Esq. *Local Secretary at Bury St. Edmund's*

(c.) Edward Tyrrell, Esq. City Remembrancer, Guildhall

William Tyson, Esq. F.S.A. Bristol

(c.) J. R. D. Tyssen, Esq. F.S.A.

William E. Underwood, Esq.

Adam Urquhart, Esq. Sheriff of Wigtonshire, Advocate

George Vacher, Esq.

Frederick Vallé, Esq.

Harris Valpy, Esq. Reading

A. A. Vansittart, Esq. Bisham Abbey

Edward Vernon Utterson, Esq. F.S.A.

M. Aart Veder, Rotterdam

(c.) Sir HARRY VERNEY, Bart. M.P. Claydon House, Bucks

The Right Hon. Lord Vernon

William Vines, Esq. F.S.A.

Gabriel Vrignon, Esq.

Henry Waite, Esq. Stoke Newington

Daniel Wakefield, Esq. Q.C. [Died .]

Arthur Walford, Esq.

Thomas Walford, Esq.

D. M. Walker, Esq. Gloucester

John Walker, Esq. Prestwich Lodge

Lionel A. B. Waller, Esq.

William Elyard Walmisley, Esq.

Charles Walton, Esq.

William Wansey, Esq. F.S.A.

John Ward, Esq. Durham

Mr. Charles Warne, Blandford

Patrick Warner, Esq. Ardeer, N.B.

William A. Warwick, Esq. Chesterton

Warwickshire Natural History and Archæological Society

Albert Way, Esq. M.A., F.S.A.

Rev. Thomas William Weare, M.A.

Rev. John Webb, M.A., F.S.A., M.R.S.L., Tretire, Herefordshire

Rev. Montagu Webster, Bridgenorth

John Weld, Esq.

Charles Welford, Esq. New York

Rev. Charles Wellbeloved. *Local Secretary at York*

Sir Richard Westmacott, R.A., F.S.A.

(c.) The Most Noble the Marquess of Westminster

His Excellency M. Van de Weyer, Belgian Minister

John Welchman Whateley, Esq.

William Whateley, Esq. Q.C.

James Whatman, Esq. M.A., F.R.S., F.S.A., Vinters, near Maidstone

Richard Charles Wheeler, Esq.

Rev. William Whewell, D.D., F.R.S., F.S.A. Master of Trinity College, Cambridge.

Gordon Whitbread, Esq., M.A.

Anthony White, Esq.

Rev. Robert Meadows White, B.D.

Wm. Archibald Armstrong White, Esq., F.R.S., F.S.A. [Died Dec. 7, 1847.]

Mr. H. A. Whitehead, Gloucester

Charles Shapland Whitmore, Esq.

Mr. Henry Whitmore, Manchester

Right Hon. Sir James Wigram, Vice-Chancellor, M.A., F.R.S., F.S.A.

Thomas Willement, Esq. F.S.A.

Charles M. Willich, Esq.

Horace Hayman Wilson, Esq. M.A. Professor of Sanscrit. Ox. and rector of the Asiatic Soc.

(c.) Rev. John Wilson, B.D. Fellow of Trin. Coll. Oxford

Sir Giffin Wilson, F.R.S. Mast. Chancery

Joshua Wilson, Esq.

(c.) Lea Wilson, Esq. F.S.A.

(c.) Lestock Peach Wilson, Esq.

John Wimbridge, Esq., F.S.A.

Benjamin Godfrey Windus, Esq.

Thomas Windus, Esq. F.S.A.

William Wingfield, Esq. Master in Chancery

Charles Winn, Esq. Nostel Priory

Rev. Robert Wintle, B.D. Culham

Rev. Thomas Wintle, B.D., Fellow of St. John's College, Oxford

David Williams Wire, Esq.

Mr. John Wodderspoon, Ipswich

The Ducal Library, Wolfenbuttel

Henry Annesley Woodham, M.A. Jesus College, Cambridge. *Local Secretary at Cambridge*

William Woodman, Esq. Morpeth, Northumberland

Frederick Woodward, Esq. Brazenose College, Oxford

Edward Woolley, Esq.

William Wordsworth, Esq.

Francis Worship, Esq.

Rev. Thomas Worsley, M.A. Master of Downing College, Camb.

Rev. John Reynell Wreford, F.S.A. *Local Secretary at Bristol*

John Francis Wright, Esq.

Rev. Godfrey Wright, Bilham House

Rev. J. Wright, M.A., F.R.S.,F.S.A.

Thomas Wright, Esq. M.A., F.S.A. Corr. Memb. of Inst. of France

Wm. Battie Wrightson, Esq. M.P.

The Library of the Writers to the Signet, Edinburgh

Rt.·Hon. Charles Watkin Williams Wynn, F.R.S., F.S.A.

Rev. Philip Wynter, D.D. President of St. John's College, Oxford

Francis Wm. Moseley Wyvill, Esq. Fingall, near Bedale

Joseph Brooks Yates, Esq. F.S.A. West Dingle, near Liverpool

Rev. Samuel Wildman Yates, M.A.

London, J. B. Nichols and Son, Printers, 25, Parliament Street.

LaVergne, TN USA
20 May 2010

183422LV00004B/15/P